THE LETTERS OF

EDWARD FITZGERALD

VOLUME I

1830-1850

The Letters of Edward FitzGerald

Edited by

Alfred McKinley Terhune

and

Annabelle Burdick Terhune

VOLUME I 1830-1850

Princeton University Press

Princeton, New Jersey

Published by Princeton University Press, Princeton, New Jersey
In the United Kingdom: Princeton University Press, Guildford, Surrey

Library of Congress Cataloging in Publication Data will
be found on the last printed page of this book

The calligraphy of the Persian for the letters
was executed by Mohammed Mikail.

This book has been composed in Linotype Caledonia
Designed by Bruce D. Campbell
Printed in the United States of America
by Princeton University Press, Princeton, New Jersey

TO

TWO STAUNCH FRIENDS

HARRY RICHARDSON CRESWICK

AND

WILLIAM PEARSON TOLLEY,

BOTH MEMBERS OF THE FITZGERALD FELLOWSHIP

AND TO THE MEMORY OF ANOTHER,

FRANK LAWRENCE LUCAS

Contents

List of Illustrations

Chart of Letters 1830-1850

Date (1830)	*From*	*To*	*First Publ.*	*Location*
[Jan. 29]*	[Geldestone]	Allen	Unpubl.	Trinity College
[Jan. 31]	[Geldestone]	Allen	Unpubl.	Trinity College
[April 21]	[Paris]	Allen	Bit in WAW,I,4	Trinity College
[April 24]	[Paris]	Allen	Unpubl.	Trinity College
[May 16]	[Paris]	Allen	Unpubl.	Trinity College
[May 21]	[Paris]	Allen	Unpubl.	Trinity College
[July 26]	Southampton	Allen	Unpubl.	Trinity College
[Nov. 10]	Naseby	Allen	Bit in WAW,I,5	Trinity College
[1830's]	[Cambridge]	George Hilton	Unpubl.	Trinity College
1831				
[March 15]	[London]	Allen	Unpubl.	Trinity College
[c. April 15]	[London]	Allen	One line in WAW,I,10	Trinity College
[April]	[London]	Ed., *Hone's Year Book*	*Hone's*, April 30	
N.D.		Ed., *Athenaeum*	*Athenaeum*, July 9	
[Oct. 10]	[Geldestone]	Thackeray	Ray, *Thackeray Letters*,I,164	Mrs. Dickinson
[Nov. 12]	[London]	Allen	Unpubl.	Trinity College
1832				
[May 31]	[London]	Allen	Unpubl.	Trinity College
[July 31]	[Southampton]	Allen	In part in WAW,I,10	Trinity College

* Brackets around dates or places from which letters were written mean they have been supplied. Blanks under "Location" indicate the original letters have not been found and they have been taken from other sources.

Chart of Letters

Date (1832)	*From*	*To*	*First Publ.*	*Location*
[Late Aug.]	Tenby	Allen	Unpubl.	Trinity College
Nov. 21	London	Allen	In part in WAW,I,12	Trinity College
Nov. [27]	London	Allen	In part in WAW,I,14	Trinity College
[Dec. 7]	[London]	Allen	In part in WAW,I,18	Trinity College
1833				
[Feb. 4]	[Cambridge]	Allen	Unpubl.	Trinity College
Feb. 24	Manchester	Allen	Extract in WAW,I,22	Trinity College
[March 14]	Cambridge	Allen	Unpubl.	Trinity College
[Mid-May]	Cambridge	Allen	Unpubl.	Trinity College
Sept. 27	Geldestone	W. B. Donne	In part in WAW,I,23	Mary Barham Johnson
[Oct. 25]	London	W. B. Donne	In part in WAW,I,24	Mary Barham Johnson
[Nov. 8]	London	Allen	Unpubl.	Trinity College
Nov. 19	London	W. B. Donne	In part in WAW,I,27	Mary Barham Johnson
1834				
May 25	Cambridge	Allen	Unpubl.	Trinity College
June 31	Wherstead	Allen	Extract in WAW,I,30	Trinity College
[Aug. 28]	Geldestone	Allen	Unpubl.	Trinity College
Sept. 9	Geldestone	Allen	In part in WAW,I,31	Trinity College
Oct. 6	Geldestone	W. B. Donne	Hannay,p. 1 and Johnson	Mary Barham Johnson
[Dec. 6]	Wherstead	Allen	Unpubl.	Trinity College
1835				
[Feb. 5 or 12]	London	W. B. Donne	In part in WAW,I,32	Mary Barham Johnson
May 23	Manchester	Allen	In part in WAW,I,34	Trinity College
June 11	Warwick	Allen	Unpubl.	Trinity College

The Tennyson letters given the editors by Sir Charles Tennyson credited to "Tennyson Estate" are now in the Tennyson Research Center.

Date (1835)	From	To	First Publ.	Location
July 2	[London]	A. Tennyson	In part in *Tennyson Memoir*,I,155	Yale
July 4	Wherstead	Allen	In part in WAW,I,37	Trinity College
[July 8]	Somersby	A. Tennyson to FitzGerald	Unpubl.	Tennyson Estate
July [29]	Wherstead	Thackeray	In part in WAW,I,40	Mrs. Dickinson
Oct. 31	Boulge	Allen	In part in WAW,I,42	Trinity College
1836				
[Feb. 4]	Boulge	Allen	Unpubl.	Trinity College
March [21]	London	W. B. Donne	In part in WAW,I,43	Mary Barham Johnson
Oct. 7	Paris	Thackeray to FitzGerald	Shorter,p. 7	Mrs. Dickinson
Oct. 23	London	W. B. Donne	Hannay,p. 4 and Johnson, p. 4	Mary Barham Johnson
1837				
Jan. 1	[Geldestone]	Allen	Extract in WAW,I,46	Trinity College
Jan. 10	[Boulge]	Allen	In part in WAW,I,47	Trinity College
[Feb. 12]	Boulge	Allen	In part in WAW,I,49	Trinity College
[Late March]	[London]	A. Tennyson to FitzGerald	Unpubl.	Cambridge Univ.
March 29	Boulge	W. B. Donne	*Donne and Friends*,p. 29	
[April 5]	Boulge	Thackeray	Ray, *Thackeray Letters*,I,330	Mrs. Dickinson
[April 21]	[Boulge]	Allen	In part in WAW,I,50	Trinity College
[Sept. 1]	[Lowestoft]	Thackeray	Ray, *Thackeray Letters*,I,345	Mrs. Dickinson
1838				
April	London	B. Barton	WAW,I,52	
[May 10]		A. Tennyson to FitzGerald	Unpubl.	Morgan Lib.
[June 8]	[London]	B. Barton	WAW,I,55	
Aug. 28	Lowestoft	Allen	In part in WAW,I,58	Trinity College
Sept. 10	Boulge	Laurence	Glyde, *Life*, p. 36	
Nov. 29	[Boulge]	Thackeray	Ritchie, Biographical Introduction, IV,xiv	Mrs. Dickinson

Chart of Letters

Date (1839)	From	To	First Publ.	Location
[April 10]	Geldestone	F. Tennyson	WAW,I,60	
[April 28]	Geldestone	Allen	In part in WAW,I,62	Trinity College
[Spring]	Geldestone	B. Barton (Fragment)	Unpubl.	Transcript, Trinity College
[July 20]	[Boulge]	Pollock	In part in WAW,I,64	Cambridge Univ.
July 24	Bedford	B. Barton (Fragment)	WAW,I,67	
Aug. 14	Boulge	Pollock	In part in WAW,I,69	Cambridge Univ.
Aug. 22	Boulge	W. B. Donne	*Donne and Friends*, p. 49	
Oct. 20	Halverstown	B. Barton	WAW,I,72	
[Nov. 23]	London	B. Barton	Barton, *New Letters*, p. 11	Univ. of Virginia
[Dec. 30]	[Geldestone]	W. B. Donne	In part in WAW,I,117	Mary Barham Johnson
1840				
[Jan.]	[Geldestone]	B. Barton	WAW,I,118	
Feb. 3	Hastings	Pollock	In part in WAW,I,75	Cambridge Univ.
[Feb.]	London	J. Kerrich	*19th Century*, March, 1909, p. 466	
[Feb. 17]	[London]	B. Barton	Barton, *New Letters*, p. 18	Univ. of Virginia
[April 4]	Boulge	Allen	Extract in WAW,I,77	Trinity College
[May 1]	Geldestone	Pollock	Extract omitted in WAW,I,77	Cambridge Univ.
June 7	Bedford	F. Tennyson	In part in WAW,I,80	Cambridge Univ.
July 12	Boulge	Allen	Bit omitted in WAW,I,82	Trinity College
July 25	Boulge	Allen	WAW,I,85	Trinity College
Aug. 31	Bedford	B. Barton	WAW,I,87	
Sept. 4	Bedford	Thompson	Unpubl.	Trinity College
[Oct.]	Holbrook	B. Barton	In part in Barton, *New Letters*, p. 23	Univ. of Virginia
Nov. 9	Boulge	Laurence	WAW,I,89	
[Nov.]	[Geldestone]	B. Barton	Barton, *New Letters*, p. 16	Univ. of Virginia
[Nov. 30]	[Geldestone]	B. Barton	Unpubl.	Transcript, Trinity College

Date (1841)	*From*	*To*	*First Publ.*	*Location*
Feb. 10	Boulge	Pollock	WAW,I,92	Cambridge Univ.
[c. Feb. 15]	[Boulge]	Pollock	Bit omitted in WAW,I,94	Cambridge Univ.
[Feb. 18]	Boulge	Thompson	Bit omitted in WAW,I,96	Trinity College
[Feb.]	Boulge	Mrs. John Charlesworth	Unpubl.	Cambridge Univ.
[Feb.]	[Mablethorpe]	A. Tennyson to FitzGerald	Extracts omitted in *Tennyson Memoir*,I,178	Tennyson Estate
March 21	Boulge	F. Tennyson	In part in WAW,I,98	Cambridge Univ.
March 26	Boulge	Thompson	In part in WAW,I,102	Trinity College
[April 24]	London	B. Barton	Barton, *New Letters*, p. 32	Univ. of Virginia
May 29	Geldestone	Pollock	WAW,I,103	Cambridge Univ.
[June 17]	[Lowestoft]	B. Barton	Barton, *New Letters*, p. 38	Univ. of Virginia
July 26	Ireland	F. Tennyson	In part in WAW,I,105	Cambridge Univ.
Aug. 8	Bray	B. Barton	Barton, *New Letters*, p. 40	Univ. of Virginia
Sept. 2	Edgeworths-town	B. Barton	WAW,I,107	
[c. Sept. 15]	Naseby	F. Tennyson	In part in WAW,I,110	Cambridge Univ.
Sept. 28	Naseby	Laurence (Fragment)	WAW,I,109	
[Nov. 20]	London	B. Barton	Barton, *New Letters*, p. 27	Univ. of Virginia
Nov. 27	London	B. Barton	WAW,I,113	
Dec. 24	London	B. Barton	Barton, *New Letters*, p. 44	Univ. of Virginia
Dec. 29	Brighton	B. Barton	WAW,I,116	
1842				
Jan. 16	London	F. Tennyson	In part in WAW,I,90	Cambridge Univ.
Jan. [16]	London	B. Barton	Barton, *New Letters*, p. 45	Univ. of Virginia
Jan. 20	London	B. Barton	Barton, *New Letters*, p. 24	Univ. of Virginia
Jan. 24	[London]	B. Barton	WAW,I,119	
Feb. 6	London	F. Tennyson	In part in WAW,I,121	Cambridge Univ.

Date (1842)	*From*	*To*	*First Publ.*	*Location*
Feb. 19	[London]	B. Barton	Barton, *New Letters*, p. 49	Univ. of Virginia
Feb. 21	London	B. Barton	WAW,I,124	
Feb. 25	London	B. Barton	WAW,I,127	
[March 2]	[London]	B. Barton	Barton, *New Letters*, p. 52	Univ. of Virginia
March 5	London	B. Barton	WAW,I,130	
[March 12]	London	B. Barton	Barton, *New Letters*, p. 54	Univ. of Virginia
[March 17]	[London]	B. Barton	Barton, *New Letters*, p. 55	Univ. of Virginia
March 26	London	B. Barton	Barton, *New Letters*, p. 57	Univ. of Virginia
[March 31]	[London]	F. Tennyson	In part in WAW,I,131	Cambridge Univ.
[May 1-3]	[Boulge]	Pollock	In part in WAW,I,134	Cambridge Univ.
May 11	Boulge	Pollock	In part in WAW,I,136	Cambridge Univ.
[May 22]	[Geldestone]	Pollock	In part in WAW,I,137	Cambridge Univ.
May 22	Geldestone	Laurence (Fragment)	WAW,I,138	
[June]	[Geldestone]	Pollock	In part in WAW,I,139	Cambridge Univ.
June 19	Boulge	Laurence (Fragment)	WAW,I,141	
June 24	Geldestone	Pollock	Extract deleted in WAW,I,142	Cambridge Univ.
[June]		A. Tennyson to FitzGerald	Bit in Charles Tennyson, p. 192	Tennyson Estate
Aug. 16	Bedford	F. Tennyson	In part in WAW,I,144	Cambridge Univ.
[Aug.]	Bedford	Laurence (Fragment)	WAW,I,147	
[Aug., latter half]	[Keysoe]	Allen	Extract in WAW,I,148	Trinity College
Aug. 29	Bedford	Allen	In part in WAW,I,149	Trinity College
Sept. 17 [16]	London	Pollock	Extract in WAW,I,151	Cambridge Univ.
Sept. [16]	London	B. Barton	WAW,I,158	
[Sept. 16]	London	Carlyle	Unpubl.	Cambridge Univ.
Sept. 18	London	Carlyle to FitzGerald	WAW,I,154	Trinity College
Sept. 20	Naseby	Pollock	In part in WAW,I,159	Cambridge Univ.
Sept. 22	[Naseby]	B. Barton	WAW,I,161	
Sept. 23	Naseby	Carlyle	Unpubl.	Cambridge Univ.

Date (1842)	From	To	First Publ.	Location
Sept. 25 [24]	London	Carlyle to FitzGerald	WAW,I,157	Trinity College
Sept. 27	Naseby	Carlyle	Unpubl.	Cambridge Univ.
Sept. 28	Naseby	Laurence (Fragment)	WAW,I,164	
Sept. 29	Chelsea	Carlyle to FitzGerald	Unpubl.	Trinity College
[Sept. 30]	[Naseby]	Carlyle	Unpubl.	Cambridge Univ.
Oct. 1	Chelsea	Carlyle to FitzGerald	Unpubl.	Trinity College
Sept. [Oct.] 2	Naseby	Carlyle	Unpubl.	Cambridge Univ.
Oct. 3	Chelsea	Carlyle to FitzGerald	Unpubl.	Trinity College
Oct. 7	Naseby	Carlyle	Unpubl.	Cambridge Univ.
Oct. 9	Naseby	Carlyle	Unpubl.	Cambridge Univ.
Oct. 10	Chelsea	Carlyle to FitzGerald	In part in Carlyle *New Letters*, I, 272	Trinity College
[c. Oct. 15]	[London]	B. Barton	Barton, *New Letters*, p. 64	Univ. of Virginia
Oct. 22	Boulge	Rev. John Charlesworth	Unpubl.	Cambridge Univ.
Nov. 18	[Boulge]	Allen	In part in WAW,I,165	Trinity College
1843				
[Jan.]	Geldestone	F. Tennyson	In part in WAW,I,166	Cambridge Univ.
[Mid-Feb.]	London	B. Barton	Barton, *New Letters*, p. 77	Univ. of Virginia
[March]	[London]	B. Barton	Unpubl.	Univ. of Virginia
[March]	London	Mrs. Stephen Spring Rice	Unpubl.	Cambridge Univ.
[March]	London	F. Tennyson	Unpubl.	Cambridge Univ.
[April]	[London]	B. Barton	Barton, *New Letters*, p. 67	Univ. of Virginia
[April]	[London]	W. K. Browne (Fragment)	T. Wright, *Life*, I, 171	
[June]	London	Milnes	Unpubl.	Trinity College
July 11	Dublin	Laurence (Fragment)	WAW,I,167	
[July]	Halverstown	F. Tennyson	In part in WAW,I,168	Cambridge Univ.

Date (1843)	*From*	*To*	*First Publ.*	*Location*
[c. July 16]	Halverstown	Carlyle	Unpubl.	Library of Scotland
Aug. 9	Ballysax	Milnes	Unpubl.	Trinity College
Aug. 16	Scotsbrig	Carlyle to FitzGerald	Carlyle *New Letters*,I,299	Trinity College
Aug. 17	Ballysax	B. Barton	WAW,I,169	
Aug. 31	Ireland	F. Tennyson	In part in WAW,I,170	Cambridge Univ.
[Sept. 2]	on board the L'Urgent	Carlyle	Unpubl.	Cambridge Univ.
Sept. 9	Naseby	Carlyle	Unpubl.	Cambridge Univ.
[Sept. 12]	Naseby	B. Barton	Barton, *New Letters*, p. 68	Univ. of Virginia
Sept. 12	Naseby	F. Tennyson	Unpubl.	Cambridge Univ.
Sept. 28	Bedford	Mrs. Spring Rice	Unpubl.	Cambridge Univ.
[Oct.]	[Geldestone]	Laurence (Fragment)	Glyde, *Life*, p. 40	
Oct. 15	Geldestone	F. Tennyson	Unpubl.	Cambridge Univ.
Oct. 21	Geldestone	B. Barton	Barton, *New Letters*, p. 75	Univ. of Virginia
[Nov.]	London	B. Barton	Unpubl.	Transcript, Trinity College
Dec. 10	Boulge	F. Tennyson	In part in WAW,I,171	Cambridge Univ.
Dec. 21	Boulge	Laurence (Fragment)	WAW,I,173	
1844				
Jan. 9	London	Carlyle to FitzGerald	Carlyle *New Letters*, I, 303	Trinity College
[Jan. 30]	Boulge	B. Barton	Unpubl.	Univ. of Virginia
[Feb. 2]	[Cheltenham]	A. Tennyson to FitzGerald	Unpubl.	Tennyson Estate
[Feb. 4]	Holbrook	Allen (Fragment)	Unpubl.	Trinity College
Feb. 17	London	Carlyle to FitzGerald	Carlyle *New Letters*, I, 306	Trinity College
Feb. 24	Boulge	F. Tennyson	Extract omitted in WAW,I,177	Cambridge Univ.
March [c. the 1st]	[Boulge]	Mrs. John Charlesworth (Fragment)	WAW,I,181	Trinity College
[March 3]	Chelsea	Carlyle to FitzGerald	Barton, *New Letters*, p. 66	
March 5	Boulge	Mrs. John Charlesworth	WAW,I,184	Trinity College

Date (1844)	From	To	First Publ.	Location
[c. March 10]	Boulge	Mrs. John Charlesworth	WAW,I,182	Trinity College
[March 15]	Boulge	Mrs. John Charlesworth	WAW,I,183	Trinity College
March 20	Boulge	Carlyle	Unpubl.	Cambridge Univ.
[April 7]	London	B. Barton	WAW,I,196	
April 11	London	B. Barton	WAW,I,186	
April 11	[London]	Mrs. John Charlesworth	WAW,I,185	Trinity College
[April 20]	London	Mrs. John Charlesworth	WAW,I,188	Trinity College
April [24]	London	B. Barton	Barton, *New Letters*, p. 80	Univ. of Virginia
[April 26]	[London]	B. Barton	Barton, *New Letters*, p. 83	Univ. of Virginia
[April 27]	London	B. Barton	Barton, *New Letters*, p. 85	Univ. of Virginia
[May]	[Boulge]	B. Barton	Barton, *New Letters*, p. 79	Univ. of Virginia
May	[Boulge]	Laurence	WAW,I,194	
May 7	Boulge	Mrs. John Charlesworth	WAW,I,190	Trinity College
May 24	Boulge	F. Tennyson	In part in WAW,I,190	Cambridge Univ.
June 7	[Boulge Cottage]	J. B. Alexander	Unpubl.	Univ. of Virginia
[June 13]	London	B. Barton	WAW,I,197	
[Latter half, June]	Boulge	W. B. Donne	Hannay and Johnson, p. 12	Mary Barham Johnson
July 4	Boulge	Laurence	WAW,I,198	
[c. July 16]	[Boulge Cottage]	Allen	In part in WAW,I,200	Trinity College
July 29	London	Carlyle to FitzGerald	Carlyle *New Letters*, I, 315	Trinity College
August 22	Geldestone	B. Barton	WAW,I,201	
Sept. 17	London	B. Barton	Barton, *New Letters*, p. 88	Univ. of Virginia
Sept. 17	London	John Barton	Barton, *New Letters*, p. 89	Syracuse Univ.
Sept. 28	Leamington	B. Barton (Fragment)	WAW,I,203	
Oct. 10	Boulge	W. B. Donne	Hannay and Johnson, p. 8	Mary Barham Johnson
Oct. 10	Boulge	F. Tennyson	Extract omitted in WAW,I,204	Cambridge Univ.
Oct. 26	Chelsea	Carlyle to FitzGerald	Carlyle *New Letters*, I, 320	Trinity College
[Late Oct.]	[Boulge]	Mrs. John Charlesworth	Unpubl.	Cambridge Univ.
[Late Oct.]	[Boulge]	Mrs. John Charlesworth	Unpubl.	Trinity College

Date (1844)	*From*	*To*	*First Publ.*	*Location*
Nov. 20	Geldestone	B. Barton	Barton, *New Letters*, p. 90	Univ. of Virginia
[Nov. 27]	[Geldestone]	B. Barton	WAW,I,207	
Dec. 8	Boulge	F. Tennyson	In part in WAW,I,208	Cambridge Univ.
Dec. 29	Brighton	B. Barton	Barton, *New Letters*, p. 92	Univ. of Virginia
1845				
Jan. 4	London	B. Barton	WAW,I,214	
[Jan. 11]	London	B. Barton	Barton, *New Letters*, p. 94	Univ. of Virginia
Jan. 14	Cheltenham	A. Tennyson to FitzGerald	*Tennyson Memoir*, I, 223	Tennyson Estate
[Jan. 17]	London	B. Barton	Barton, *New Letters*, p. 97	Univ. of Virginia
Jan. 28	Boulge	Cowell	Unpubl.	Cambridge Univ.
Jan. 29	Boulge	W. B. Donne	Extract in WAW,I,216	Mary Barham Johnson
Feb. 6	Boulge	F. Tennyson	In part in WAW,I,216	Cambridge Univ.
Feb. 8	London	Carlyle to FitzGerald	In part in Carlyle *New Letters*, I, 324	Trinity College
[c. Feb. 8]	[Boulge]	B. Barton	Bit omitted in Barton, *New Letters*, p. 77	Univ. of Virginia
[Feb. 27]	[Boulge]	W. B. Donne	Hannay, p. 10	Mary Barham Johnson
April 3	Geldestone	B. Barton (Fragment)	WAW,I,218	
April 4	Chelsea	Carlyle to FitzGerald	*Blackwood's Edinburgh Magazine*, Oct., 1903, p. 446	
[c. May 1]	[Boulge]	Cowell (Fragment)	Unpubl.	Cambridge Univ.
[May 14]	London	B. Barton (Fragment)	WAW,I,219	
[May 18]	[London]	B. Barton	WAW,I,220	
[May 28]	[London]	B. Barton	Barton, *New Letters*, p. 86	Univ. of Virginia
[c. June 1]	London	B. Barton	Barton, *New Letters*, p. 36	Univ. of Virginia
June 12	Boulge	F. Tennyson	WAW,I,221	
[c. June 12]	[Boulge]	Cowell	Unpubl.	Cambridge Univ.
[June 15]	[Boulge]	Cowell	Unpubl.	Cambridge Univ.
June 27	London	Carlyle to FitzGerald	Unpubl.	Trinity College

Date (1845)	From	To	First Publ.	Location
July 4	Boulge	Allen	Unpubl.	Trinity College
[July 28]	Halverstown	Allen	Unpubl.	Trinity College
Aug. 2	Halverstown	B. Barton	Barton, *New Letters*, p. 98	Univ. of Virginia
Aug. 15	Ireland	B. Barton	Barton, *New Letters*, p. 100	Univ. of Virginia
Aug. 18	Chelsea	Carlyle to FitzGerald	Unpubl.	Trinity College
Aug. 23	Chelsea	Carlyle to FitzGerald	In part in Carlyle *New Letters*,II,I	Trinity College
Aug. 27	Bedford	Allen	In part in WAW,I,225	Trinity College
Sept. 8	Bedford	B. Barton (Fragment)	WAW,I,226	
Sept. 23	Geldestone	W. B. Donne	In part in WAW,I,227	Mary Barham Johnson
[Sept. 25]	Boulge	F. Tennyson	Unpubl.	Cambridge Univ.
[Oct. 4]	Boulge	Cowell	Unpubl.	Cambridge Univ.
[Oct.]	Boulge	F. Tennyson	In part in WAW,I,229	Cambridge Univ.
[c. Nov. 1]	[Boulge]	B. Barton	Barton, *New Letters*, p. 102	Univ. of Virginia
[Nov. 22]	London	B. Barton	Barton, *New Letters*, p. 74	Univ. of Virginia
[Dec. 29]	Geldestone	B. Barton	Barton, *New Letters*, p. 103	Univ. of Virginia
1846				
[Jan.]	[Boulge]	Carlyle	Unpubl.	Cambridge Univ.
Jan. 19	London	Carlyle to FitzGerald	Unpubl.	Trinity College
[Jan. 22]	Boulge	Carlyle to FitzGerald	Unpubl.	Cambridge Univ.
[Jan. 29]	Boulge	W. B. Donne	Hannay and Johnson, p. 14	Mary Barham Johnson
[Late Jan.]	[Boulge]	B. Barton	Unpubl.	Univ. of Virginia
[Feb. 2]	Boulge	B. Barton	Unpubl.	Univ. of Virginia
[Feb. 8]	Geldestone	B. Barton	Unpubl.	Univ. of Virginia
[Feb. 14]	Geldestone	B. Barton	Barton, *New Letters*, p. 104	Univ. of Virginia
[March]	[Boulge]	B. Barton	Unpubl.	Univ. of Virginia

Date (1846)	*From*	*To*	*First Publ.*	*Location*
March 8	Boulge	W. B. Donne	WAW,I,233	Mary Barham Johnson
[March]	Boulge	F. Tennyson	Extracts deleted in WAW,I,230	Cambridge Univ.
April 8	London	Carlyle to FitzGerald	Extract in WAW,I,235	Trinity College
[April]	London	B. Barton	Barton, *New Letters*, p. 121	Univ. of Virginia
[April]	London	W. Pickering	Unpubl.	Norman Scarfe
[May 5]	London	B. Barton	Barton, *New Letters*, p. 123	Univ. of Virginia
[June 5]	[Boulge]	Carlyle	Unpubl.	Trinity College
[c. June 8]	Boulge	W. B. Donne	WAW,I,236	Mary Barham Johnson
July 26	Liverpool	Carlyle to FitzGerald	Unpubl.	Trinity College
[Summer]	[Boulge]	Cowell (Fragment)	WAW,I,234	
July 28	Boulge	Cowell	Unpubl.	Cambridge Univ.
Sept. 15	Bedford	Cowell	WAW,I,238	Trinity College
Sept. 19	Bedford	B. Barton	Barton, *New Letters*, p. 125	Univ. of Virginia
Sept. 22	Chelsea	Carlyle to FitzGerald	Barton, *New Letters*, p. 131	
[Sept. 24]	Bedford	B. Barton	Barton, *New Letters*, p. 128	Univ. of Virginia
[Oct. 18]	[Cambridge]	B. Barton (Fragment)	WAW,I,239	
Oct. 29	Bury St. Edmunds	Cowell	Unpubl.	Cambridge Univ.
[Oct. 31]	Boulge	W. B. Donne	Extract in WAW,I,240	Mary Barham Johnson
Nov. 12	Cheltenham	A. Tennyson to FitzGerald	Extract in *Tennyson Memoir*, I, 233	Tennyson Estate
[Nov. 18]	Boulge	Pollock	WAW,I,241	Cambridge Univ.
[Nov.]	[Boulge]	Cowell	WAW,I,243	Trinity College
[Nov.]	Boulge	Cowell	Unpubl.	Trinity College
1847				
[Early Jan.]	London	B. Barton	Barton, *New Letters*, p. 133	Univ. of Virginia
[Jan. 13]	[Woodbridge]	Cowell	WAW,I,244	Trinity College
[Jan.]	[Boulge]	Thackeray	Ray, *Thackeray Letters*, II, 265	Berg Coll.

Date (1847)	From	To	First Publ.	Location
[c. Feb. 8]	[Boulge]	Carlyle	WAW,I,246	
[March 31]	[Geldestone]	B. Barton	Barton, *New Letters*, p. 135	Univ. of Virginia
[May 7]	London	Cowell	Unpubl.	Cambridge Univ.
[May 7]	[London]	B. Barton	Barton, *New Letters*, p. 136	Univ. of Virginia
[June 15]	Boulge	Cowell	Unpubl.	Cambridge Univ.
[June 20]	Geldestone	Laurence	WAW,I,247	
June 29	Boulge	Carlyle	WAW,I,249	
[July 24]	Boulge	Cowell	In part in WAW,I,261	Trinity College
[July 26]	[Boulge]	Cowell	Unpubl.	Trinity College
[Late July]	[Boulge]	Lucy Barton	Unpubl.	Univ. of Virginia
[July 30]	[Boulge]	Cowell	Unpubl.	Cambridge Univ.
[c. Aug. 9]	[London]	Laurence (Fragment)	WAW,I,258	
Aug. 16	Exeter	B. Barton (Fragment)	WAW,I,253	
Aug. 22	Somersetshire	W. B. Donne	In part in Hannay, p. 16	Mary Barham Johnson
Aug. 29	Gloucester	B. Barton (Fragment)	WAW,I,254	
[Sept. 4]	[Leamington]	F. Tennyson	WAW,I,256	
[Sept. 8]	Leamington	B. Barton	Barton, *New Letters*, p. 138	Univ. of Virginia
Sept. 14	Scotsbrig	Carlyle to FitzGerald	Unpubl.	Trinity College
[Sept. 20]	[Bedford]	B. Barton	Deletion in Barton, *New Letters*, p. 140	Univ. of Virginia
[Sept. 20]	Bedford	Carlyle	WAW,I,259	FitzWilliam Museum
Oct. 1	Bedford	Allen	Unpubl.	Trinity College
Oct. 5	Bedford	B. Barton	Barton, *New Letters*, p. 142	Univ. of Virginia
[Oct. 15]	Boulge	Cowell	Unpubl.	Cambridge Univ.
[Oct. 19]	Boulge	Allen	Unpubl.	Trinity College
[Nov. 5]	[Woodbridge]	W. B. Donne	Hannay and Johnson, p. 19	Mary Barham Johnson
[Dec.]		Lucy Barton	Unpubl.	Univ. of Virginia
[Dec. 13]	Holbrook	B. Barton	Unpubl.	Univ. of Virginia
[Late Dec.]		A. Tennyson to FitzGerald	*Tennyson Memoir*, I, 260	Tennyson Estate

Chart of Letters

Date (1848)	*From*	*To*	*First Publ.*	*Location*
Jan. 1	Boulge	Allen	Unpubl.	Trinity College
[Jan. 5]	Geldestone	B. Barton	Barton, *New Letters*, p. 143	Univ. of Virginia
Jan. 8	Geldestone	B. Barton	Barton, *New Letters*, p. 145	Univ. of Virginia
Jan. 13	Geldestone	Cowell	Extract in WAW,I,264	Trinity College
[Jan. 13]	Beccles	B. Barton	Barton, *New Letters*, p. 151	Univ. of Virginia
[Jan. 18]	Geldestone	B. Barton	Barton, *New Letters*, p. 152	Univ. of Virginia
[Jan. 25]	Boulge	Cowell	WAW,I,265	Trinity College
[Jan. 30]	Boulge	Laurence	WAW,I,266	
March 2	Boulge	Allen	In part in WAW,I,268	Trinity College
[March]	Boulge	Cowell	WAW,I,285	Trinity College
[March]	Boulge	Allen	Extract in WAW,I,268	Trinity College
[April 8]	Geldestone	B. Barton	Barton, *New Letters*, p. 157	Univ. of Virginia
[April 16]	Cambridge	B. Barton	Barton, *New Letters*, p. 158	Univ. of Virginia
April 24	Boulge	Cowell	Unpubl.	Cambridge Univ.
[c. May 1]	[Boulge]	Cowell	Unpubl.	Cambridge Univ.
May 4, July 2	Boulge	F. Tennyson	WAW,I,269	
[May 18]	London	B. Barton	Barton, *New Letters*, p. 159	Univ. of Virginia
[May 20]	[London]	B. Barton	Barton, *New Letters*, p. 160	Univ. of Virginia
June 5	Boulge	Cowell	Unpubl.	Cambridge Univ.
June 5	Boulge	Allen	Unpubl.	Trinity College
[Mid-June]	[Boulge]	W. B. Donne	Hannay, p. 22	Mary Barham Johnson
[June 30]	Boulge	Cowell	Unpubl.	Cambridge Univ.
[July 11]	Boulge	Cowell	Unpubl.	Cambridge Univ.
Aug. 15	Boulge	Cowell	Unpubl.	Cambridge Univ.
[Late Aug.]	[Boulge]	Cowell	In part in WAW,I,273	Trinity College
[Sept. 9]	London	B. Barton	Barton, *New Letters*, p. 162	Univ. of Virginia
Aug. [Sept.] 13	Bedford	B. Barton	Barton, *New Letters*, p. 160	Univ. of Virginia
Sept. 20	London	W. B. Donne	Hannay and Johnson, p. 24	Mary Barham Johnson

Date (1848)	*From*	*To*	*First Publ.*	*Location*
[Sept. 22]	[London]	Cowell (Fragment)	Unpubl.	Cambridge Univ.
[Sept. 27]	Boulge	Cowell	Unpubl.	Cambridge Univ.
[Oct. 1]	Boulge	Mrs. Cowell	Unpubl.	Cambridge Univ.
[Oct. 3]	[Boulge]	B. Barton	Barton, *New Letters*, p. 58	Univ. of Virginia
Sept. 23	Mirehouse	Spedding to FitzGerald	Unpubl.	Univ. of Virginia
[Oct. 28]	London	B. Barton	Barton, *New Letters*, p. 163	Univ. of Virginia
[Nov. 4]	[London]	B. Barton	Extract omitted in Barton, *New Letters*, p. 164	Univ. of Virginia
[Nov. 11]	[London]	B. Barton	Barton, *New Letters*, p. 166	Univ. of Virginia
[Late Nov.]	London	Cowell	WAW,I,274	Trinity College
[Nov. 29]	London	Cowell	Unpubl.	Trinity College
[Dec. 2]	[London]	B. Barton	Barton, *New Letters*, p. 167	Univ. of Virginia
[Dec. 11]	London	Cowell	Unpubl.	Cambridge Univ.
[c. Dec. 23]	[Boulge]	Cowell	Unpubl.	Cambridge Univ.
Dec. 27	Boulge	W. B. Donne	WAW,I,276	
[Dec.]	[London]	Allen (Fragment)	In part in WAW,I,279	Trinity College
1849				
[Jan. 21]	Boulge	Cowell	Unpubl.	Cambridge Univ.
Jan. 21	Boulge	W. B. Donne	Hannay and Johnson, p. 26	Mary Barham Johnson
Feb. 9	Boulge	Laurence (Fragment)	WAW,I,278	
[c. Mar. 1]	[Woodbridge]	Cowell	WAW,I,280	
March 9	Boulge	W. B. Donne	*Donne and Friends*, p. 176	
[c. March 15]	[Woodbridge]	W. B. Donne	Hannay and Johnson, p. 28	Mary Barham Johnson
April 4	Geldestone	W. B. Donne (Fragment)	Hannay and Johnson, p. 30	Mary Barham Johnson
April 25	Geldestone	Allen	Unpubl.	Trinity College
May 14	Bury St. Edmunds	Cowell	Unpubl.	Cambridge Univ.
[c. May 15]		Milnes	Unpubl.	Charles E. Merrill
[May 25]	Boulge	Cowell	Unpubl.	Cambridge Univ.

Date (1849)	*From*	*To*	*First Publ.*	*Location*
June 3	Boulge	Cowell	Unpubl.	Cambridge Univ.
[June 11]	London	Cowell	Unpubl.	Cambridge Univ.
June 19	Boulge	F. Tennyson	WAW,I,281	
June 22	Chelsea	Carlyle to FitzGerald	Unpubl.	Cambridge Univ.
June 23	Boulge	Cowell	Unpubl.	Cambridge Univ.
[June, last week]		Carlyle	Unpubl.	Library of Scotland
July 10	Halverstown	Carlyle to FitzGerald	Unpubl.	Trinity College
[July 16]	[Woodbridge]	Cowell	Unpubl.	Cambridge Univ.
Aug. 1	Boulge	Cowell	Unpubl.	Cambridge Univ.
Aug. 15	Boulge	Allen	Unpubl.	Trinity College
Oct. 22	Richmond	G. Crabbe of Merton	In part in WAW,I,284	Trinity College
Nov. 2	Richmond	W. B. Donne	Hannay and Johnson, p. 32	Mary Barham Johnson
Nov. 4	Richmond	Cowell	Unpubl.	Cambridge Univ.
Nov. 9	Richmond	G. Crabbe of Bredfield		Clippings from de Soyres family
Nov. 9	Richmond	Cowell	Unpubl.	Cambridge Univ.
Nov. 20	Bedford	G. Crabbe of Bredfield (Fragment)	Unpubl.	Univ. of Virginia
Dec. 7	Bedford	F. Tennyson	In part in WAW,I,286	Cambridge Univ.
Dec. 13	Bedford	Allen	Extract in WAW,I,289	Trinity College
Dec. 26	Richmond	Cowell	Unpubl.	Cambridge Univ.
1850				
[Jan. 17]	London	W. B. Donne	In part in WAW,I,290	Mary Barham Johnson
Feb. 16	Boulge	W. B. Donne	Hannay, p. 35	Mary Barham Johnson
Mar. 4	Boulge	Allen	In part in WAW,I,293	Trinity College
March 7	[Bramford]	F. Tennyson (Fragment)	WAW,I,291	
[March 12]	[Woodbridge]	Cowell	Unpubl.	Cambridge Univ.
April 9	Boulge	Cowell	Unpubl.	Cambridge Univ.

Date (1850)	*From*	*To*	*First Publ.*	*Location*
April 17	London	F. Tennyson	In part in WAW,I,294	Cambridge Univ.
May 7	Boulge	Spedding	Unpubl.	Tennyson Estate
[May 10]	Boulge	Cowell	Unpubl.	Cambridge Univ.
May 29	Boulge	Allen	Unpubl.	Trinity College
[June 1]	[Monk Soham]	Cowell	Unpubl.	Cambridge Univ.
July 19	Boulge	Cowell	Unpubl.	Cambridge Univ.
Aug. 1	Boulge	Cowell	Unpubl.	Cambridge Univ.
[Aug. 3]	Boulge	Cowell	Unpubl.	Cambridge Univ.
[Aug. 8]	[Boulge]	Cowell	Unpubl.	Cambridge Univ.
[Aug. 12]	Boulge	Cowell	Unpubl.	Cambridge Univ.
Aug. 15	Boulge	F. Tennyson	Extract omitted in WAW,I,297	Cambridge Univ.
[Aug. 22]	[Boulge]	Cowell	Unpubl.	Cambridge Univ.
[Sept. 25]	Holbrook	Cowell	Unpubl.	Cambridge Univ.
Sept. 29	[Holbrook]	The Cowells	Unpubl.	Cambridge Univ.
Sept. 29	Boulge	Cowell	Unpubl.	Cambridge Univ.
[Oct. 4]	Boulge	W. B. Donne	In part in WAW,I,300	Mary Barham Johnson
[Oct. 28]	Boulge	Cowell	Unpubl.	Cambridge Univ.
[Oct. 30]	Boulge	Mrs. Cowell	Unpubl.	Cambridge Univ.
Nov. 2	Boulge	Allen	Unpubl.	Trinity College
[Nov. 8]	Bury St. Edmunds	Cowell	Unpubl.	Cambridge Univ.
[Nov. 10]	[Bury St. Edmunds]	Mrs. Cowell (Fragment)	Unpubl.	Cambridge Univ.
[Nov. 16]	Boulge	W. B. Donne	Hannay and Johnson, p. 36	Mary Barham Johnson
Nov. 22	Boulge	Cowell	Unpubl.	Cambridge Univ.
[Dec. 11]	[Woodbridge]	Cowell	Unpubl.	Cambridge Univ.
Dec. 17	Chelsea	Carlyle to FitzGerald	Unpubl.	Trinity College
[Late 1850]		Lord John Russell	Barton, *New Letters*, p. 148	

Chart of Letters

Date (1850)	*From*	*To*	*First Publ.*	*Location*
[Dec. 20]	Lawford	Cowell	Unpubl.	Cambridge Univ.
[Dec. 31]	Boulge	Cowell	Unpubl.	Cambridge Univ.
Dec. 31	[Boulge]	F. Tennyson	In part in WAW,I,302	Cambridge Univ.

Foreword

More than a thousand unpublished FitzGerald letters and all the widely scattered published ones are brought together in these volumes, which represent the first attempt at a complete edition of FitzGerald's correspondence. Many of the unpublished letters contain significant new material: the hundreds to Edward Byles Cowell, who introduced FitzGerald to Persian, reveal his views on translation and the course of his studies; the "Naseby" letters to Carlyle not only give a full account of his successful efforts to locate exactly the battlefield of Naseby on the FitzGerald estate, Naseby-Wooleys, for Carlyle's *Cromwell*, but also demonstrate FitzGerald's capability for meticulous research; other letters show his interest and deep concern, sometimes anguish, over the religious, political, and social controversies of the time. His developing skepticism after his university years and his outspoken dislike for "the Ritualism and Romish tendencies" of the Church as a result of the Oxford movement were shared by some, but by no means all, of FitzGerald's friends. The letters point up his concern for the poor and his contempt for the affluent who refused to meet their obligations to mitigate poverty and injustice. It is interesting that each letter was written with the interests of the friend to whom he was writing in mind. He often used quotations from foreign languages in his letters—Greek, Latin, French, German, Italian, Spanish, or Persian—but *never* unless the recipient knew the language as well as or better than FitzGerald did. He had a good reading knowledge of a number of foreign languages, but it did not embarrass him, on the rare occasions when he wrote in French, that his grammar was sometimes faulty. The French letters were written "just for fun," mostly to George Crabbe and Sir Frederick Pollock. He took greater pains when he wrote to Garcin de Tassy or other French literary figures, but these letters seem not to have survived.

FitzGerald corresponded with friends from many walks of life. His friendships with Tennyson, Thackeray, and Carlyle were intimate and were based on mutual respect and admiration. "I had no truer friend," the Poet Laureate wrote when FitzGerald died. "He was one of the kindliest of men." On the eve of his departure for America in 1852 Thackeray wrote to FitzGerald, "I should like my daughters to remember that you are the best and oldest friend their Father ever had, and that you would act as such." Shortly before the novelist's death his daughter Anne asked him, "Which, of your friends, have you cared for most?" "There was Old Fitz," he replied, "and I was very fond of Brookfield once." FitzGerald gave freely of his ample means when both poet and novelist sorely needed funds during their apprentice years. Carlyle reported, "He [Tennyson] said of you that you were a man from whom one could accept money: which was a proud saying; which you ought to bless heaven for." From Paris, where he had taken his wife to be treated for mental illness, Thackeray wrote in 1841, "A couple of months hence I shall ask you to pay my wife's pension for a month, a heavy sum of £20." Carlyle wrote at the age of seventy-three, "Your letter has really entertained me: I could willingly accept twelve of that kind in a year—twelve, I say, or even fifty-two. . . . Why not call when you come to Town? I again assure you it will give me pleasure and be a welcome and wholesome solace to me."

Readers are introduced to an engaging company of lesser lights of the last century through FitzGerald's letters: James Spedding, "the Wise," editor of Francis Bacon; Frederick Tennyson, Alfred's eldest brother, poet in his own right, and man of many humors; Frederick Pollock, barrister and Queen's Remembrancer, who, like Richard Monckton Milnes, knew everyone "worth knowing"; Fanny Kemble, occasionally identified by her married name, Mrs. Pierce Butler, the dynamic sister of mercurial "Jacky" Kemble; William Bodham Donne, miscellaneous writer, second Librarian of the London Library, Examiner of Plays for the Queen, a man of lambent humor; E. B. Cowell, the scholar who tutored FitzGerald in Persian; Samuel Laurence, the portrait painter; and others. Beside these are arrayed a gallery of East Anglian personalities, from Bernard Barton, the genial Quaker bank-clerk poet of Woodbridge, and Herman Biddell, the yeoman-farmer of Playford, to Posh Fletcher, Lowestoft fisherman and, in FitzGerald's eyes, a Carlylean hero.

It is not possible adequately to express gratitude to the hundreds of people who have helped with this work. Members of FitzGerald's family (all who knew him personally now gone) were more than kind: Mary Eleanor and Olivia Kerrich, Madeleine de Soyres, all grand-nieces, and Gerald FitzGerald, a grandnephew. They began giving us valuable assistance and frequent hospitality before the Terhune biography of Edward FitzGerald was published and they continued as long as they lived. The original water-color painting of FitzGerald by Thackeray, reproduced in this work, was their gift to the editors; it had belonged to the Cowells, who gave it to the grandnieces. Other grandnieces and grandnephews who were helpful included Adeline Wybrow, Gladys Funajoli, the Reverend Edmund FitzGerald Kerrich, and John Dalzell Kerrich. Later generations of the FitzGerald family who have been valued friends include Brigadier Walter Kerrich, John Kerrich of Johannesburg, South Africa, John de Soyres, and their children.

Without the approval and cooperation of the Council of Trinity College, Cambridge, and the Syndics of Cambridge University Library, who own hundreds of the FitzGerald letters, this work would not have been possible. They have our gratitude as do H. R. Creswick, FitzGerald scholar and the only man who has ever been, successively, Librarian of the Bodleian Library and of Cambridge University Library, and H. M. Adams, former Librarian of Trinity College Library. Unforgettable holidays were spent with the Creswicks at their home, Conington Hall, near Cambridge. Mr. Adams was responsible for many kindnesses but none more appreciated than the "office" he gave us in the basement of Trinity College Library where we could type directly from manuscripts. Hot-water pipes ran through our "office," making it snugly warm throughout the winter months. Mr. Adams' aide, Arthur Halcrow, who later became Mayor of Cambridge, eased many of our labors at Trinity College Library. Some of the men at Cambridge who gave unstintingly of their help and support, and whose friendships we cherished, are gone: F. L. Lucas, brilliant Fellow of King's College; the Reverend H. F. Stewart, the noble religious Dean of Trinity College who knew both Edward Cowell and Aldis Wright and who gave us Cowell's account to him of the genesis of FitzGerald's Persian studies as well as explanations and background information given him by Aldis Wright for some of the FitzGerald letters at Trinity; A. H. Hollond, academic Dean of Trinity College and Professor of Law; A. J. Arberry, Professor of Oriental Studies; Sir Arthur Quiller-Couch; and others. Many of these scholars wanted the edition to include all extant letters *to* FitzGerald as well as from him, but we have restricted letters to FitzGerald to those which show the nature of the friendships or clarify matters under discussion in his letters.

Another friend who has our deep affection and gratitude for his generosity and hospitality is Sir Charles Tennyson, grandson of Alfred Lord Tennyson. When he first gave us the FitzGerald-Tennyson letters, they were in the vault of his bank in London, where we copied them by hand. Later, he entrusted them to us to have them microfilmed at Cambridge. His gracious wife was also invariably helpful and kind to us. Sir Charles represented the trustees of his grandfather's estate, and to them also we express our appreciation.

At this point acknowledgment must be made of signal indebtedness to a group of distinguished scholars and authorities in their fields who have helped with the manuscript. Two Iranian friends, Mostafa Elm, Ambassador from Iran to the Sudan, and Fazlollah Reza, Ambassador from Iran to Canada, have taken great pains and devoted many hours to deciphering, identifying, and translating the many Persian passages in the correspondence. FitzGerald's transcription of Persian script often posed problems which baffled all but those with intimate knowledge of Persian literature and culture. Among Dr. Elm's publications is a translation into Persian of *The Heritage of Persia* published by the Oxford University Press. Dr. Reza, an authority on Háfiz, is former Chancellor of the University of Teheran and former Ambassador from Iran to Unesco in Paris. Malcolm Maclaren, Fred H. Jackson, and Herbert Woodbury have given invaluable assistance in the fields in which they are authorities. In matters relating to FitzGerald's sailing, we were fortunate to be able to call upon another friend, Frank Hussey, yachtsman, authority on East Coast sailing, and author of *"Old Fitz," Edward FitzGerald and East Coast Sailing*. The willingness with which these busy men have given of their time and knowledge is typical of the response the editors received without exception throughout the progress of the work.

Although a complete list of all those to whom appreciation is due is too long to include here, some additional friends must be named: from FitzGerald's Suffolk, Norman Scarfe, W. G. Arnott, Dr. A. Daly Briscoe, who lived in FitzGerald's Little Grange, Harry Wilton, Harry Goodwin, Miss Violet Loder, and all the owners of FitzGerald homes. By a curious coincidence, during our early visits, three of them were occupied by Whites—Sir Robert Eaton White at Boulge Hall; H. H. Lachlan White at Bredfield House; and Mrs. Janet White at Geldestone Hall. A special salute is due the memory of other FitzGerald admirers who helped in numerous ways: Catharine B. Johnson, granddaughter of William Bodham Donne, and Mrs. Ritchard B. Fuller, granddaughter of William Makepeace Thackeray, both of whom furnished valuable manuscripts and material and charming hospitality; members of the families of Thomas Carlyle and James Spedding, who were unforgettably helpful as the work was launched; David Low, beloved cartoonist and former president of the Omar Khayyám Club of London, which made the editor an honorary member, an honor he prized as it "fittingly perpetuated the memories of Edward FitzGerald and Omar Khayyám through its rare good fellowship"; John Henderson, secretary of the Omar Khayyám Club, who took a deep interest in the progress of the work; Mrs. Eugene Meyer, knowledgeable and loyal friend; Rudolf Bultmann, theologian; Vincent Redstone, friend and adviser to many American scholars, and his daughters; and Bliss Perry, whose magic fostered the deep interest of the editors in FitzGerald at the outset.

Owners of the letters in this edition (identified in the Chart of Letters) have without exception given wholehearted consent to their publication. Gordon Ray and other scholars whose names appear frequently in footnotes have been more than cooperative. Countless libraries in this country and abroad, through their dedicated staffs, have had a part in preparing material for the manuscript. Many are named in the Chart of Letters. Among those who have contributed are Robert Haynes of Harvard College Library; Herbert Cahoon, of the Pierpont Morgan Library; members of the reference department and staff of the Bird Library at Syracuse University over a long period of time; and the same groups at the Olin Library at Cornell University.

My last words of gratitude must go to the capable and sympathetic members of Princeton University Press who gave extraordinary assistance and counsel at a time when they were deeply appreciated. Jerry Sherwood, Editor, with infinite patience, has given great care to every stage of the long process of getting the manuscript through the press; Miriam Brokaw, Associate Director and Editor, and Bruce Campbell, Designer, have been equally kind and generous with their skills. Their contributions and the meticulous care the editors took in preparing the manuscript will, we hope, reduce to a minimum the errors that are inevitable in any work of this size.

ANNABELLE B. TERHUNE

Little Grange
Skaneateles, N.Y.
1977

PUBLISHER'S NOTE

Alfred McKinley Terhune died in December of 1975, when the preponderance of the work on these letters was nearing completion. His widow, Annabelle Burdick Terhune, has gallantly and with dedication carried this vast project through, relying on her years of close collaboration with him, her intimate knowledge of the material, and his extensive and careful notes and records.

History of Previous Publication

The standard edition of Edward FitzGerald's correspondence thus far has been the selection made by W. Aldis Wright for *The Letters and Literary Remains*. Correspondence formed one of the three volumes in the first edition, 1889. The letters were published separately, with some forty additions, in two volumes in 1894. The following year Wright produced *Letters of Edward FitzGerald to Fanny Kemble*, part of which had already been published. *More Letters of Edward FitzGerald* was added to the sequence in 1901. The contents of all these were combined for the first four volumes of the 1902-03 seven-volume, and final, edition of the *Literary Remains*. Wright passed over hundreds of letters available to him and freely deleted portions of the majority of those selected. "It seemed better," he stated, "to create the desire for more than to incur the reproach of having given more than enough."

Wright succeeded in creating a desire for more FitzGerald letters, and other editors responded to the demand. Francis Hindes Groome, son of FitzGerald's friend Archdeacon Robert Hindes Groome, was the first to add to the correspondence. In *Two Suffolk Friends*, a brief memoir of his father and FitzGerald, he included letters of FitzGerald to his merchant friend Frederick Spalding. The book was published in 1895.[1] *Edward FitzGerald and "Posh"* by James Blyth, recounting FitzGerald's experience as a partner of Joseph Fletcher of Lowestoft in the ownership of a herring lugger, is made up essentially of letters to Fletcher; it appeared in 1908. In 1923 Captain F. R. Barton published *Some New Letters of Edward FitzGerald*, written to Bernard Barton. The volume was issued in New York the following year as *Edward FitzGerald and Bernard Barton*. FitzGerald's correspondence with his publisher, *Letters from Edward FitzGerald to Bernard Quaritch*, edited by C. Quaritch Wrentmore, was published in 1926. The latest selection, *A FitzGerald Friendship*, 1932, is a portion of the corre-

[1] An editorial error names R. H. Groome as the recipient of letters to Frederick Spalding, transcribed from *Two Suffolk Friends*, in a book of selections from FitzGerald's works published by Rupert Harte-Davis in 1962.

spondence with William Bodham Donne, edited by Donne's granddaughter Mrs. Catharine B. Johnson and Professor Neilson C. Hannay.

Numerous letters have appeared in biographies and memoirs of FitzGerald's friends: *Life and Letters of Edward Byles Cowell*, 1904; *William Bodham Donne and His Friends*, 1905; *Alfred Lord Tennyson, A Memoir*, 1897; and *Tennyson and His Friends*, 1911. Mrs. Hester Thackeray Fuller, Thackeray's granddaughter, permitted the editors of his papers to include FitzGerald's manuscript letters to him, parts of which are included in Lady Ritchie's Biographical Edition of her father's works. These have subsequently been printed in Gordon Ray's *Letters and Private Papers of William Makepeace Thackeray*. Fragments of FitzGerald's correspondence have been published in other books and periodicals too numerous to mention. Letters previously published have required thorough editing. FitzGerald's handwriting at its best is easily read; at its worst it is almost indecipherable, and errors of transcription are common. Many published letters have been misdated.

The present editors have obtained microfilm copies of virtually every major segment of FitzGerald's extant correspondence. Where such reproduction could not be made, typescript copies were taken and carefully checked. Only one important collection and portions of three other major collections have evaded discovery: the originals of the letters to Samuel Laurence have not been found; those portions of the correspondence to Frederick Tennyson and Bernard Barton which Wright published in the *Literary Remains* have disappeared; and the originals of almost all the letters in *William Bodham Donne and His Friends*, left on a Norwich tramcar after publication, were never recovered. These four segments, therefore, are reprinted as previously published.

The present work almost triples the number of letters published in the *Letters and Literary Remains*. About a thousand unpublished letters have been added, and those printed elsewhere have been combined with Wright's. Many letters which the editors have identified as previously published could have been classified as unpublished, for complete texts replace many fragments.

FitzGerald Chronology

1809	March 31	Born Edward Purcell at the White House, near Bredfield, Suffolk, son of John and Mary Frances FitzGerald Purcell
	May 7	Baptized at parish church, Bredfield
1816-18		Family lives in France, first year at Saint-Germain-en-Laye, second at Paris in house once occupied by Robespierre in Rue d'Angoulême
1818		John Purcell takes FitzGerald name and arms on death of his wife's father, September 6, 1818
	Autumn	Attends King Edward VI Grammar School, Bury St. Edmunds, Suffolk, with his brothers, John and Peter
1826		Family moves to Wherstead, near Ipswich
	February 7	Admitted as pensioner, Trinity College, Cambridge
	October	Goes into residence at Cambridge in rooms at 19 King's Parade where he lodged until he took his degree. Building now marked by a plaque to commemorate FitzGerald's residence
1829	October	First meets Thackeray, then in first year at Cambridge
1830	January 15-21	Takes final examinations
	February 23	Receives degree as one of the poll
	Spring	Goes to Paris after visiting his sister Eleanor and her family at Geldestone, Norfolk
	Mid-April	Joined in Paris by Thackeray, a truant from Cambridge
	End of May	Returns to England and spends several months at Southampton
	November	Goes to Naseby Wooleys in Northamptonshire, where he begins assisting his father in management of family properties. Writes "Meadows in Spring" at Naseby
	November 15	W. B. Donne marries Catharine Hewitt
1831	March-July	In London as escort for his mother

	April 30	"Meadows in Spring" published in *Hone's Year Book*
	July 9	Same poem appears in the *Athenaeum*
	Summer and autumn	Chiefly at Geldestone
	November	Takes his former lodgings in Cambridge for the term. Spends three weeks in London with Thackeray, end of October, first two weeks of November
1832	May 29	His sister Jane marries the Rev. John B. Wilkinson
	July 24	Goes to Southampton
	Late August	Leaves for Tenby where he is joined by John Allen
	November	In London
1833	Lent and May terms	At Cambridge, except for a fortnight in February at Castle Irwell, Manchester, one of his parents' homes
	September 31	In London lodgings, 7 Southampton Row, Bloomsbury
	End, October	Visits Allen at Tenby
1834	May term	At Cambridge
	End of May	Visits W. K. Browne at Bedford
	June	Returns to family home, Wherstead Lodge
	Summer	At Geldestone
	July 31	Allen marries Harriett Higgins
	October 14	Returns to Wherstead
	December 14	Takes lodgings at 17 Gloucester Street, Queen Square, London
1835	April	With Alfred Tennyson, visits James Spedding for three weeks at his home, Mirehouse, near Keswick, Cumberland
	May 1	Spends week at Ambleside with Tennyson. Spedding joins them. Meets Hartley Coleridge
	May	Fortnight at Castle Irwell; thence to Warwick
	July 3	Returns to Wherstead Lodge
	August	Family occupies Boulge Hall near Woodbridge
	Autumn and winter	At Boulge Hall. George Crabbe, son of the poet, appointed to living at nearby Bredfield. Friendship follows
1836	Summer	With relatives in Ireland
	August 20	Thackeray marries Isabella Shawe in Paris
	Autumn	At Naseby. Goes to London for two weeks
	Christmas	At Geldestone
1837	January and February	At Boulge

	March	In London
	Spring	Furnishes cottage outside gates of Boulge Hall park. Spends May in London
	Summer	At Lowestoft
	Winter	At Boulge Hall
1838	Summer	Chiefly at Bedfordshire and in London
	Late August	At Lowestoft with Browne
	Mid-September	Returns to Boulge
	October 30	Leaves for Geldestone. Visits Donne
1839	January	In London as escort for his mother
	Spring	At Geldestone
	Summer	Boulge and Bedford
	September and October	In Ireland
	Christmas	With the Kerriches at Geldestone
1840	February 11	Goes to London
	April and May	At Geldestone. Visits Donne at Mattishall
	Early June	At Leamington where he meets A. Tennyson by chance; they visit Warwick, Kenilworth, and Stratford together
	June	In Bedford
	July	At Boulge Cottage
	August	At Bedford with Browne. Visits school and college friend, William Airy, at nearby Keysoe
	September	Supervises harvest at Naseby
	October and November	In Suffolk
	December	Holidays at Geldestone
1841		His "Chronomoros" published in *Fulcher's Sudbury Pocketbook* for 1841
	January	At Geldestone
	February and March	Supervises labor on the Boulge estate
	July and August	In Ireland. Visits family of Maria Edgeworth at Edgeworthstown
	September	Supervises harvest at Naseby
	November and December	In London at 19 Charlotte Street. A. Tennyson in lodgings nearby at 9 Charlotte Street
	Christmas	With his mother at Brighton

1842	January and February	In London. Buys pictures
	March	In London with A. Tennyson. FitzGerald traps the poet into arranging publication of *Poems*, with Edward Moxon. Aids Tennyson in preparing volume
	April	At Boulge
	Summer	Visits Geldestone, Mattishall, Cambridge, and Bedford
	September 15	Taken by Samuel Laurence to meet Thomas Carlyle at Chelsea and agrees to aid Carlyle in research for Carlyle's *Cromwell*
	September 17-October 11	At Naseby. Locates mass grave identifying "center" of battlefield on family estate. Makes sketches of the field of battle for Carlyle
1843	April	Visits Mrs. William Frere at Cambridge and Dr. George Peacock, Dean of Ely
		Stays with Thackeray in London at 13 Great Coram Street for three weeks
	June	In London with Frederick Tennyson who has returned from Italy for a visit
	July 11-September 1	In Ireland. Visits his brother Peter in Ballysax, Kilcullen, and the Edgeworths
	September and October	In Bedford, Geldestone, Norwich, and Woodbridge
	November	Goes to London to stay ten days with Thackeray
	December	At Boulge
1844	January and February	Continues gathering data for Carlyle's *Cromwell*
	Easter	With Browne at Bedford
	March 30	Pollock marries Juliet Creed
	April	In London
		The diary of George Crabbe of Merton records that FitzGerald spent 130 evenings between 1844 and 1851 at Bredfield with the Crabbes, often dining and sometimes staying overnight
	August	At Geldestone
	August 28	Goes to Leamington for the wedding on September 2 of his sister Andalusia to the Rev. Francis de Soyres
	Autumn	London, Winchester, Bedford, Naseby, and Boulge
	November	Geldestone

	Christmas	At Brighton with his mother
1845	January	At 19 Charlotte Street, London, for three weeks
	January 20	Returns to Boulge Cottage
	January 28	Writes the first of more than 300 extant letters to E. B. Cowell
	April	At Geldestone
	May 1	Leaves Boulge to spend three days at Cambridge and to visit Bedford before going to London
	May 9	Arrives in London; takes lodgings at 39 Norton Street, Fitzroy Square on May 13
	May 28	His father in Ireland, where Peter Purcell, Fitz-Gerald's uncle, is gravely ill
	June 8	Returns to Boulge
	July 27-August 16	Visits his uncle at Halverstown, Kilcullen, Ireland
	August 20	Arrives at Bedford to visit Browne, and Airy at Keysoe
	September	Chiefly in Norfolk
	October 4	Learns of Cowell's engagement to Elizabeth Charlesworth
	November 22	Goes to London. Lodges at 18 Charlotte Street
	Christmas	At Geldestone
1846	January	Returns to Boulge
	April	Visits Cambridge en route to London for two months
	July	W. B. Donne moves to Bury St. Edmonds
	Summer	At Boulge, Beccles, and Lowestoft
	October	Two weeks at his old rooms in King's Parade. Prompted to write *Euphranor, a Dialogue on Youth*, not published until 1851
	October 12	Francis B. Edgeworth dies in Ireland
	December	Christmas at Boulge Cottage with Barton
1847	May	Ten days in London with friends
	June	At Boulge. Frequent meetings of "The Woodbridge Wits"
	June 22	At Carlyle's request interviews William Squire of Yarmouth about Cromwell letters, later declared spurious
	July	At Boulge
	August 8	Begins summer wanderings—this year in the West Country

	September 4	At Leamington with his parents
	September 9	To Bedford to visit Browne and Airy
	October 19	John Allen appointed Archdeacon of Salop
	October 23	Elizabeth Charlesworth and E. B. Cowell are married
	November and December	At Boulge. Visited by John Allen
1848	February 26	Major Moor dies
		Concerned over High Church ritualism and defections to Rome, drafts petition to Lord John Russell
	March and April	Visits Monk Soham, Geldestone, Bury St. Edmunds, and Cambridge
	May and June	His father's mining venture at Manchester ends in failure and bankruptcy. FitzGerald in London involved in his father's tangled business affairs
	September	Further bankruptcy proceedings. FitzGerald stays in Spedding's rooms, 60 Lincoln's Inn Fields
	End of September	Furnishings at Boulge Hall sold at auction. The estate, part of Mrs. FitzGerald's inheritance, not involved
	October	Goes into his old lodgings at 19 Charlotte Street
	November 28	His brother Peter comes from Ireland and stays with him
	December 2-6	With Peter visits his mother at Brighton
	Christmas	With Bernard Barton in Woodbridge
1849	January	Donne visits him at Boulge Cottage
	February 19	Bernard Barton dies
	March	Begins preparing a selection from Barton's letters and poems at request of Barton's daughter Lucy
	April	At Geldestone
	May	FitzGerald's parents separate
	June 4	Goes to London until June 13
	July and August	Corrects proof for Barton volume. Beginning of friendship with John Childs and his son Charles, printers of Bungay
	October	Barton volume published
	October 22-November 10	Visits his mother in Richmond
	November 12	Goes to London
	November 17	Goes to Bedford

	Christmas	With his mother at Richmond
1850	January	At 19 Charlotte Street
	February 9	Returns to Boulge
	April 17	Goes to London for ten days "to haggle with lawyers"
	June	Visits R. H. Groome at Monk Soham
	June 13	Alfred Tennyson and Emily Sellwood are married
	June 20	Visits Charles Merivale at Lawford, Essex
	July 2	Merivale marries Juditha Mary Sophia Frere
	August 6-8	With Spedding visits the Cowells at Bramford
		Has begun to "nibble at Spanish"
	November 6	Tennyson accepts appointment as Poet Laureate
	November 14	Urged by his wife, Cowell matriculates at Oxford
		Visits Donne at Bury St. Edmunds and goes to Cambridge
	November 25	Arranges with Childs of Bungay to print *Euphranor*
	December 20	With W. H. Thompson visits the Merivales at Lawford
1851	January	*Euphranor* published by Pickering
	January 16-February 28	At Spedding's, 60 Lincoln's Inn Fields. Visits his mother at Ham
	February 28-March 5	Stays with Thackeray at 13 Young Street, Kensington
		Returns to Boulge
	April	Attends concerts by Charles Childs' chorus at Bungay
	August 11	Arranges music of Purcell's *King Arthur* for Childs
	August 25	Teaches children of Boulge and Debach to sing. Devises simple method, "Singing in One Clef," for the purpose
	October	Cowells leave Bramford for Oxford
		First visit to George Crabbe at Merton
	December 1	At 19 Charlotte Street
	December 6	Visits Peter at Richmond
1852	January 12	Returns to Boulge
	February 12	Writes that *Polonius* has been published by Pickering
	March	Visits John Allen at Prees, Shropshire
	March 18	His father dies

	Mid-May	Goes to his mother's at Ham for a fortnight
	June 3	Leaves Ham for Bedford
	June 12	Donne appointed Librarian of London Library
	June 28	Begins five-day trip to Lincoln, York, Hull, and Yarmouth
	July 20	Squire Jenny of Hasketon buried
	August	Reads Calderón's *El Mágico prodigioso* and *La Vida es sueño* with Cowell
	October 1	Savile Morton is stabbed and dies in Paris
	October 11	Has read eleven Calderón plays. Is translating *El Pintor de su deshonra*
	October 20	At Bury St. Edmunds with Donne
	October 22	Returns to Boulge to arrange a reading of *Richard III* by Fanny Kemble at Woodbridge
	October 23	Translation of *El Pintor* completed
		Anna Smith of Farlingay marries William Ling of Otley
	October 30	Thackeray sails for lecture tour in United States. Before departure, asks FitzGerald to act as his literary executor
	November 9	Asks Donne to submit *El Pintor* to Charles Kean for London production. Kean rejects the plan
	December	Visits Spedding in London
	December 10	Goes to Oxford to see the Cowells. Begins study of Persian with Cowell during this visit
	December 24	Family Christmas party at his mother's at Brighton
	December	Visits his brother John and the A. Tennysons at Seaford
	December 29	First appearance of Persian script in FitzGerald's correspondence—his signature in a letter to Mrs. Cowell
1853	February	Visits Robert Phelps, Master of Sidney Sussex College, Cambridge
	February and March	At Geldestone
	March 21	Returns to Boulge
	May 30	His *Six Dramas of Calderon* "committed to type"
	August 27-September 6	Entertains F. Tennyson at Boulge
	October 6	Finishes examination of Sir William Jones's Persian Grammar

	October 12	Visits A. Tennyson at Twickenham. Frederick there, about to return to Italy
	November	Vacates Boulge Cottage and takes up residence at Farlingay, Job Smith's farm near Woodbridge
	November 21	At Geldestone
		Translates his first Persian poem, "The Gardener and the Nightingale," an apologue from Sádí's *Gulistán*
	Christmas	With Crabbe at Bredfield
1854	January	Crabbe of Merton's wife dies
	February 13	Leaves Bredfield to visit Donne at the London Library, 12 St. James Square
	March, second week	Begins five-week visit at Oxford. Lodges at 1 Long Wall Street
	April 15	Goes to Bath to visit the de Soyres. Lodges at 15 Beaufort, East
	April	Works on *Euphranor*
	May	Reading Jámí's *Salámán and Absál*
		Calls on Walter Savage Landor
	May 17	Leaves Bath
	June 1	Arrives at A. Tennyson's, Farringford, Freshwater, Isle of Wight
	June 14	Leaves Isle of Wight for London
	June 20	To Crabbe's at Bredfield
	July	Visits Cambridge, Thompson at Ely, and Merton
		Begins teaching himself German
	August	At Boulge Hall
	September-October 11	With Crabbe at Bredfield
	October 11-November 18	Chiefly at Farlingay
	November 18-December 26	At Geldestone
	December 26	To Ipswich
1855	January 10	To Bredfield Rectory
		Compressing *Salámán and Absál* into "a very readable form"
	January 30	His mother dies
	February	In London settling his mother's estate
	February 9	Sends "metrical abstract" of *Salámán* to Cowell
	March	London

	April	Submits *Salámán and Absál* to *Fraser's Magazine*
		Visits the Cowells at Oxford
	April 16	Returns to London
	May 2	*Fraser's* returns *Salámán* MS; too long for their use
	May 19- End of June	At Bredfield
	June	*Euphranor*, second edition, published. Sends copy to Cowell, June 19
	July 23	At Spedding's in London
	July 28	Reports mother's estate cleared in Chancery
	July 31	At Bredfield
	August 8-18	Carlyle visits FitzGerald in Suffolk
	September 5	To London to see F. Tennyson and his wife
		Cruises with Spring Rice on government cutter. Touches at Boulogne and Brighton
	October	Visits with George Borrow at Yarmouth
	November	Goes on walking expedition along the coast
	November 5	Returns to Geldestone
	December 19	Goes to London
	Christmas	With Peter at 3 Park Villas, Richmond
1856	January 1	At 31 Portland Street, Portland Place
	January 3	Sends text of *Salámán* to Childs for printing
	February	Cowell appointed Professor of Modern History and Political Economy in the Presidency College, Calcutta
	March	Goes to Oxford
	April 4	Gives copy of *Salámán and Absál* to Cowells who are preparing to leave for India. Includes dedicatory letter to Cowell
	April	Cowell transcribes and sends to FitzGerald portions of the Ouseley MS of Omar Khayyám's *Rubáiyát*, recently discovered by Cowell in the Bodleian
	June 12	Reaches Paris with W. K. Browne and George Crabbe of Merton on a visit to the Continent
	June 15-20	To Strasbourg, Heidelberg, Frankfurt, Rhine trip to Cologne, to Aix-la-Chapelle, Brussels, Antwerp
	June 20	Ostend to London
	June 27- July 14	With the Cowells at Rushmere near Ipswich. His last meeting with them before their departure for India

		Cowell gives FitzGerald complete transcript of the Ouseley MS of the *Rubáiyát* of Omar Khayyám
	July 14	To Bredfield Rectory
	August 1	The Cowells sail for India
	October	At Geldestone
	October	Reluctantly preparing for marriage to Lucy Barton
	November 4	Married at Chichester
	December 15-January 1	Living alone at 31 Great Portland Street. His wife in Norfolk
1857	January	The FitzGeralds take lodgings for two months at 24 Portland Terrace, Regent's Park
		Begins study of Attár's *Mantic Uttair*. Plans a metrical abstract
	February 25	Corresponds with Garcin de Tassy about Attár's *Mantic*
		Donne resigns post at London Library
	March 26	J. M. Kemble dies in Dublin
	March-May 19	London
		Translating the *Agamemnon* of Aeschylus. Printed privately in 1869; published 1876
	April	Donne succeeds Kemble as Licenser of Plays
	May 3	Lucy goes to Gorlestone to search for summer lodgings
	May 19	Goes to Bedford
		Translating Omar into "Monkish Latin"
	June 5	Joins his wife at Gorlestone
	June 15	Receives transcript of Calcutta MS of the *Rubáiyát* of Omar Khayyám sent by Cowell from India
	July 1	Goes to Geldestone
	July 14	Completes his first study of the Calcutta MS on first anniversary of the day he and Cowell finished their reading of the Ouseley MS at Rushmere
	July, last week	Walking tour. Visits Lowestoft, Aldeburgh, Oxford
	August 1	Geldestone
	August	The FitzGeralds conclude that their marriage is a failure and decide to separate
	September	Bedford
	September 16	Crabbe of Bredfield dies. FitzGerald attends the funeral, September 22

	October 4	Returns to Bedford
	November 3-December 1	At Brighton
	December 1	Returns to London, 31 Great Portland Street
	Christmas	With Donne
1858	January-May	In London
		Submits translation of *Omar* to Parker, at his request, for *Fraser's Magazine*
	May 1	About to leave London for Teignmouth to visit Andalusia
	June 25	At Geldestone
	July	Visits John at Boulge
	August	In Warwickshire
	September	At Merton with Crabbe
	October	At Geldestone
	December 9	Lodges at 88 (formerly 31) Great Portland Street, London
	Christmas	With Peter at Twickenham
1859	January	Retrieves *Omar* from *Fraser's Magazine*. Intends to publish privately
	February	W. K. Browne critically injured, crushed by his horse
	March	Visits his wife in Kent for a few days
	March 23	Goes to Browne's
	March 28	Leaves Bedford for Geldestone
	Late March	Publishes first edition of *Rubáiyát of Omar Khayyám*
	March 30	British Museum receives its copy of the *Rubáiyát*
	March 30	W. K. Browne dies
	April	Learns that Cowell has sent a lithograph edition of Omar's quatrains
	June	At Geldestone and Lowestoft
	September	Visits Francis Duncan, in Dorset
	October 3	At Lowestoft
	November	Fortnight at Geldestone
	November 24	At 10 Marine Terrace, Lowestoft, until May, 1860
1860	April	"Play-Stalls," first of FitzGerald's contributions to *East Anglian Notes and Queries* appears. Signed "F" or "E.F.G." Occasional communications through 1870
	Mid-May	Leaves Lowestoft for a fortnight in London

	June-December	At Farlingay Hall
	July 12	Witnesses launching of a boat for use on Deben
	August 18	First of his contributions to *Notes and Queries* appears. All in 1860 and 1861. Signed "Parathina"
	December	Moves from Farlingay Hall to lodgings on Market Hill, Woodbridge
	December 7	Searches for a house
1861	January 30	Orders sailboat for the Deben to be built at Beccles
	April 22 or 23	Boat arrives at the Deben. FitzGerald names it the *Waveney*
	April	Visits Aldeburgh
	May	Hears that F. Tennyson has settled in Jersey
	June	Supports Third Suffolk Volunteer Rifles at Woodbridge
	c. July 10	Whitley Stokes discovers FitzGerald's *Rubáiyát* in Quaritch's penny-box
	October	Visited by Donne for three days
	November	W. H. Thompson discovers FitzGerald's *Rubáiyát* at Quaritch's shop
1862	March	Buys yacht. Proves a "shabby concern"
	May	Rents *Criterion*, yacht of ten tons
	June 20	The Rev. John Wilkinson dies
	Summer	Sails on North Sea and River Deben
		Pirated edition of FitzGerald's *Rubáiyát* printed in Madras, India
1863	April	His sister Eleanor dies at Geldestone
	May 26	Visits Crabbe at Merton for a week
	June 3	Visits Thompson at Ely
	June	*Scandal*, his fourteen-ton schooner, launched at Wivenhoe, Essex
	July 28	Sails to Holland in *Scandal*
		Visits Rotterdam, Amsterdam, and the Hague
	August	W. Airy visits him for a week
	September 2	Ruskin reads the *Rubáiyát* and leaves note addressed "To the translator of Omar Khayyám" with Edward Burne Jones
	October	F. Tennyson visits FitzGerald in Woodbridge for three days
	December 24	Thackeray dies

1864	January	Commissions Samuel Laurence to paint a sketch in oils of his last portrait of Thackeray
		Goes to Geldestone
	April	Visits Caroline and Mary Crabbe in Wiltshire
	May	Cowells have returned from India
	May	Buys cottage and six acres of land on Pytches Road, Woodbridge. First called Grange Farm, subsequently named Little Grange. ("Grange Farm" ignored in the Chronology to avoid possible confusion)
	June	Visits Kerriches at Geldestone
	July	Ten-day cruise along south coast
	Mid-November	Sends translation of *El Mágico prodigioso* (*The Mighty Magician*) to Childs at Bungay to be printed
1865	February	Sends copies of *The Mighty Magician* to friends
	March	Two rooms being added to Little Grange
	April	Prints translation of *La Vida es Sueño* (*Such Stuff as Dreams are Made of*)
	May 9	Spring Rice dies
	August	Churchyard dies
	August 21	Begins cruise with Peter and his wife to Ramsgate, Dover, Calais, etc.
1866	February	Revising the *Rubáiyát*
	March 1	Mentions Joseph (Posh) Fletcher for first time
	March	Thompson elected Master of Trinity
	April 21	Mrs. Carlyle dies
	June	Peter's wife dies
	June 5	Francis Duncan visits him
	June 5-26	Becomes member of Royal Western Yacht Club of Ireland
	June 26	Sails to Cowes, Isle of Wight, and the South Coast in *Scandal*
	July 7	Little Grange ready for occupancy, but FitzGerald continues to occupy Market Hill lodgings
	July-September	East Coast sailing; Peter and Kerriches at Lowestoft
	October	Relays Thompson's suggestion that Cowell apply for appointment to the Chair of Sanskrit to be established at Cambridge
	November	Peter remarries
1867	January 5	Arranges to build a herring-lugger at Lowestoft. Posh Fletcher to be captain

	May	Campaigns among friends for Cowell's election
	June 7	Cowell elected Professor of Sanskrit at Cambridge
	August	Agrees to prepare second edition of *Rubáiyát* for Quaritch
	August 20	*Meum and Tuum*, the herring-lugger, leaves for North Sea fishing
	September	With Cowell at Felixstowe
	October 24	Receives French translation of *Rubáiyát* by J. B. Nicolas
	December 11	First letter to W. A. Wright
	December 26	At Lowestoft to wind up lugger's accounts—a poor season
1868	February 25	*Rubáiyát*, second edition, ready; 200 copies sent to Quaritch
	March 29	Difficulties with Posh, who neglects bookkeeping
	July 11	The Thompsons at Lowestoft with FitzGerald
	October 28	Sends Cowell manuscript of *Agamemnon*, written ten years before
	December	Has sent *Agamemnon* to printer
	December	Christmas issue of Samuel Tymms's *East Anglian . . . Notes and Queries* contains first of FitzGerald's "Sea Words and Phrases Along the Suffolk Coast"
1869	Mid-March	Consults Londan oculist about impaired eyesight
	April	R. H. Groome made Archdeacon of Suffolk
		Preparing edition of Crabbe's *Tales of the Hall*
	April 25	Sends Cowell a copy of *Agamemnon*
	September	Donne spends three days with him on *Scandal*
	October	C. E. Norton reviews *Rubáiyát* in *North American Review*
	November	*Meum and Tuum* shows a profit for first time
		Further concern over Posh's financial irresponsibility
		Merivale made Dean of Ely
		"Sea Words and Phrases Along the Suffolk Coast" in Christmas issue of *East Anglian*
1870	June 28	Dissolves partnership with Posh
	August	Cowells in Lowestoft for two months. FitzGerald living on *Scandal*
	Summer	Second edition of *Rubáiyát* "pirated" by Colonel James Watson and friends in Columbus, Ohio

	December 28-January 23	Edwin Edwards, London artist, and his wife at Little Grange as FitzGerald's guests; their first visit
		"A Capfull of Sea-Slang for Christmas" in *East Anglian*
1871	March 6	John Kerrich of Geldestone dies
	May	Sells *Scandal*
	July 1	First mention of Tichborne trial
	July 4	Earliest extant letter to Fanny Kemble
		Kerrich nieces, as usual, spend summer at Little Grange
	October 17	Mr. and Mrs. Edwards return to Little Grange for six weeks
	October 22	Donne and daughter Valentia visit FitzGerald at Woodbridge
	December	Adding two more rooms to Little Grange
		During this year, printed privately second edition of *Salámán and Absál.* Small printing by Cowell Steam Printing Works, Ipswich
1872	March	Working on translation of Sophocles' Oedipus plays
	March 25	Receives request from Quaritch to reprint *Rubáiyát.* Second edition sold out
	March 31	Agrees to third edition
	May 10	Pollock visits FitzGerald at Woodbridge
	July 12	Visits Peter at Sydenham
	August 1-5	F. Tennyson visits FitzGerald
	August 23	Receives copy of third edition of *Rubáiyát*
	Mid-September	To Lowestoft for a month
1873	January	FitzGerald has his picture taken by Cade, photographer of Ipswich
	April	Carlyle identifies FitzGerald as translator of *Rubáiyát* for C. E. Norton
	April 13	Norton sends Ruskin note of September 2, 1863, about *Rubáiyát* to Carlyle
	April 14	Carlyle forwards Ruskin note to FitzGerald
	April 17	Writes Norton acknowledging Ruskin note. Origin of correspondence with Norton
	August 18-25	At Aldeburgh
	August 29	Asked to vacate Market Hill lodgings

	December 5	FitzGerald given a month's notice to vacate rooms
	December 17-January 11	At Lowestoft. More financial trouble with Posh
1874	January	Loder of Woodbridge prints "The Two Generals"
	Late January	Occupies Grange Farm in Pytches Road
	February-April	At Lowestoft and Grange Farm alternately
	Mid-April	Anna Biddell renames Grange Farm, Little Grange
	Mid-July	Goes to Edinburgh by sea; thence to Abbotsford, Lochs Lomond and Katrine
		Visits Peter and Donne in London
	August 19	William Airy dies
	August 25	Donne retires as Licenser of Plays
	September 13	Goes to Lowestoft, the Cowells to be there a month
	Christmas-April 25	With nieces at Lowestoft
1875	February	FitzEdward Hall writes on FitzGerald's works in *Lippincott's Magazine.* Except for *Six Dramas of Calderon*, first published identification of FitzGerald as author
	February 13	Peter dies at Bournemouth
	April 19	First mention of Sévigné correspondence
	October 30-November 4	Mowbray Donne and wife visit FitzGerald at Little Grange
	November	Joins in commemorating Carlyle's eightieth birthday
1876	January 21	Sends revision of privately printed *Agamemnon* to Quaritch for publication
	July 30	Receives copy of Quaritch's edition of *Agamemnon*
	September 14	A. Tennyson and son Hallam surprise FitzGerald with a visit in Woodbridge
	September 15	Tennysons and FitzGerald drive to Ipswich and take steamer to Harwich and back
	September 16	Tennysons leave. FitzGerald goes to Dunwich
	December 9-13	At Lowestoft
	December 23-25	Entertains Irish cousins at Little Grange
	December 25-January 2	At Lowestoft with nieces and nephews
1877	February 4-April 18	At Lowestoft

	c. February 15	Colonel James Watson writes FitzGerald about pirated edition of *Rubáiyát* printed in Columbus, Ohio, in 1870
	March	Francis Hindes Groome, Archdeacon Groome's son, begins editing "Suffolk Notes and Queries" in *Ipswich Journal.* FitzGerald a contributor during 1877 and 1878
	May 8-22	Edmund Kerrich and family at Little Grange
	May 24	Valentia Donne marries the Rev. R. F. Smith
	June	T. S. Perry reviews FitzGerald's works in the *Atlantic Monthly*
	July	James Russell Lowell, en route to Spain as Ambassador, proposes to visit FitzGerald at Woodbridge
	August 7	Charles Donne, Rector of Faversham, Kent, marries Augusta Rigden
	August 31-September 10	At Dunwich. Makes acquaintance of Charles Keene, *Punch* artist
	August 31	Quaritch proposes publishing the *Rubáiyát* and *Salámán and Absál* in one volume. FitzGerald delays giving consent
	September 10-15	Entertains Crabbe at Little Grange
1878	January 5	Sends his *Readings in Crabbe* to Wright for criticism
	January 25	Hears that James Osgood of Boston has published *Rubáiyát*
	March	Calendar of Lamb's life printed by Loder
	June	Norton invites FitzGerald to visit him in America
	July 13	To Dunwich for a week
	August 19	Quaritch again offers to reprint the *Rubáiyát* and *Salámán* together
	September	At Lowestoft
	October	Resolves to print *Readings in "Crabbe's Tales of the Hall"*
	December 9	Quaritch offers £25 to publish one thousand copies of *Rubáiyát-Salámán* volume
	December 15	Norton asks for FitzGerald's *Oedipus*
	December 23-27	At Lowestoft with Kerrich nieces
1879	January 21	Agrees to Quaritch's terms for the *Rubáiyát-Salámán* volume
	March 17-19	In London

	May 4	His brother John dies
	May	Sends *Crabbe* to Wright and Fanny Kemble
	May	Jessie Cadell publishes article on *Rubáiyát* in *Fraser's Magazine*
	May 28-31	Visits Crabbe at Merton
	July 10	Sends volume of *Crabbe* to Norton, with one for Longfellow
	August 2	Receives *Rubáiyát-Salámán* volume
	August 11-September 27	At Lowestoft where Cowells are spending a month
	September 15	Edwin Edwards dies
	October 1-6	To London to see Mrs. Edwards and Fanny Kemble
	December 11	His sister Andalusia dies
1880	January	FitzGerald's "Percival Stockdale and Baldock Black Horse" published in *Temple Bar*
	January 23-30	At Lowestoft with Edmund Kerrich
	February	"Oedipus in Thebes," Part I of *The Downfall and Death of King Oedipus* printed
	February	In London two days to see friends
	March 4	Sends "Oedipus in Thebes" to Norton
	April 2	At Lowestoft with Cowell and Wright
	June 9-12	Visits Crabbe and his sisters at Merton
	July 6-14	At Aldeburgh
	August 2-October 11	At Lowestoft with nieces
	August 30-September 2	FitzGerald and Wright visit Crabbe at Merton
	September 4	Lowell again proposes to visit FitzGerald
	November 22	In London. Sees Fanny Kemble, Mrs. Edwards, Donne, the Nurseys, and Keene
	December 15	Reports "pains and heaviness about the heart"
	December 31	Wright visits FitzGerald at Little Grange for three days
1881	January	Sends "Oedipus at Athens" to Wright for criticism Eyes troubling him again
	February 5	Carlyle dies
	February	Sends copy of "Oedipus at Athens" to Fanny Kemble
	March 1	Spedding struck by a cab in London
	March 9	Spedding dies

	March 13	Sends "Oedipus at Athens" to Norton with a preliminary letter to serve as preface to *The Downfall and Death of King Oedipus*
	April 14-21	Wright at Little Grange for Easter holidays
	May 27-30	Charles Keene visits FitzGerald
	Mid-July	Visits Cambridge for two days
		Continues to Merton. Caroline and Mary Crabbe there. Stays until July 21
	July 30	Borrow dies
	August	Revises *Euphranor* again
	August 10-13	At King's Head Inn, Beccles. Visits Geldestone and Lowestoft
	Late August	Visited by Donne and Groome
	August 27-September 14	His sister, Jane Wilkinson, on visit from Italy
	September 17	Keene comes to Little Grange
	September 19	Goes with Keene to visit Crabbe at Merton, meeting Wright there
	September 22	Keene and FitzGerald return to Little Grange
	September 26	Keene leaves Little Grange
		FitzGerald goes to Aldeburgh for a week
	December	E. H. Whinfield sends FitzGerald his *Quatrains of Omar Khayyám* (dated 1882)
	December 7	Receives profile medal of Calderón from the Spanish Royal Academy in recognition of his translations
	Christmas	Wright at Little Grange
1882	February 17-20	In London; sees Donne, the Nurseys, Mrs. Edwards, Fanny Kemble, and Keene
	April	"Virgil's Garden" published in *Temple Bar*
	May 2	To Lowestoft
	May	Final edition of *Euphranor* printed
	May 25-June 2	Keene at Little Grange
	June	FitzGerald declines an invitation to visit the A. Tennysons
	June 16-21	With Crabbe at Merton Rectory
	June 20	Donne dies
	August-September 11	At Clare Cottage, Aldeburgh
	September 23-30	At Lowestoft

	November	Brief visits to Aldeburgh
1883	February 22	Sends copy of *Crabbe* to Ruskin
	March	Revises Introduction to his *Readings in Crabbe* and arranges for 200 copies to be printed. Pages not ready until after FitzGerald's death. Later bound with text printed in 1879 for Quaritch's 1883 edition
	March 22	Wright spends Easter holidays at Little Grange
	April 3	Draws up his last will
	May 1	Composes letter to Wright, entrusting to him copies of his works, "corrected in the way that I would have them appear, if any of them ever should be resuscitated." A box containing the works and the letter were found after FitzGerald's death
	May 2	In London on business. To Chelsea with Keene to see Carlyle's house and his statue on the Embankment
	May 18-28	Keene at Little Grange. Joined by Groome
	May 31	FitzGerald very well, he reports to Pollock
	June 13	Goes to George Crabbe's at Merton for his annual visit
	June 14	FitzGerald dies
	June 19	Is buried in Boulge churchyard

Editorial Practices

Readers may be assured that the editors have held emendations of the letters to a minimum. Periods, or end-stops, have been substituted for the dashes FitzGerald frequently placed at the ends of sentences. He often doubled his punctuation. One finds a colon followed by a dash and underscoring of words in quotation marks in his manuscripts. The duplication has been eliminated. A common peculiarity is his practice of writing "it's" for "its," and "your's" for "yours," etc. These apostrophes have been ignored. On the other hand one stylistic feature prominent in all of FitzGerald's writing—his use of capital letters—has been retained. For their presence he offered a simple and straightforward explanation: "I love the old Capitals for Nouns." It will be observed, however, that his fondness for capitals sometimes bestows upper-case dignity upon other parts of speech.

At times FitzGerald became infected with italics. The editors have reduced but not eliminated his underscoring. Occasionally punctuation has been revised for the sake of clarity, but the need for such changes was rare. Accents have been preserved as far as possible, following FitzGerald's not very consistent usage. A mere dozen or so misspelled words were found in the entire correspondence. Numerals in the manuscript have usually been spelled out; abbreviations, other than those which are standard and formal, have for the most part been expanded; *etc.* has been substituted for *&c.*

Readers should not be confused by noting that letters written in one locale sometimes bear an "alien" address. Fitzgerald was simply providing a convenient address for a reply. Some letters, usually those written to friends abroad, were composed over a period of weeks. The dates when these were begun have been selected in fixing their places in the sequence.

Practices for which FitzGerald is in no wise responsible remain to be mentioned. For the sake of uniformity and convenience to the reader, the few date-lines that FitzGerald placed at the close of letters have been transferred to the customary place in the heading. Usually, where a signature is missing, the manuscript or a portion of it has been lost.

The Persian passages posed many problems. Minor emendations have been made. Transposition of characters and occasional obvious confusion of characters have been corrected. For the most part, however, the Persian appears as FitzGerald wrote it; errors are present. Some originate in the manuscripts or texts from which FitzGerald translated. His transcript of the Calcutta manuscript of Omar Khayyám's *Rubáiyát* was particularly faulty. "The script is indeed inferior, and in many places hard to decipher; yet FitzGerald evidently persevered courageously in his task of reading it, acquitting himself of this self-imposed labour in a manner not unworthy of a professional scholar," states A. J. Arberry, Professor of Arabic at the University of Cambridge, in the introduction to his *Romance of the Rubáiyát*, the definitive edition of FitzGerald's masterpiece. Other errors result from limitations in FitzGerald's command of Persian and from problems posed by complex imagery communicated by a language of simple syntax. This is always an obstacle to penetrating to exact meanings of ideas expressed. The Persian in the letters has been literally translated. Gratitude is due and warmly extended to Professor Jerome W. Clinton of the Department of Near Eastern Studies for his work with the calligrapher throughout the preparation of the Persian for publication, and his many hours of checking and rechecking it for accuracy.

One editorial innovation has been adopted. When the postmark is the sole clue to the date of a letter, that date has been selected and is identified by "Pmk." In bibliographical references the place of publication is London unless otherwise identified.

Greek, Latin, and Persian passages have been translated in footnotes. Modern European languages have not been.

The editors have been able to check a large proportion of the letters with original manuscripts. When the text was taken from a printed source that could not be collated, the forms of the printed sources have been retained.

Biographical Profiles

Following the accounts of "Old Fitz" and the FitzGerald family, profiles of FitzGerald's principal correspondents and friends are arranged in alphabetical order.

"Old Fitz"

The bald record of Edward FitzGerald's life may be found in the Chronology. The letters themselves expose his personality with a clarity, thoroughness, and honesty beyond reach of biographers. Readers, nevertheless, will be aided by a sketch of his life which avoids the skeletal quality of the chronology on the one hand and the profuse detail of correspondence on the other.

"Old Fitz," as he was known by most of his friends for most of his life, was born at Bredfield White House, near Woodbridge, Suffolk, March 31, 1809. By one day, he said, he avoided becoming an April Fool. His name, at birth, was Edward Purcell. "A clever, lively lad" and droll as well, he probably first attended a dame's school in Woodbridge; in France private tutors instructed the children at home from 1816 until 1818. Upon the return to England the three boys, John, Peter, and Edward, were enrolled at the King Edward VI Grammar School at Bury St. Edmunds. There FitzGerald formed the first of many lifelong friendships—those with W. B. Donne, James Spedding, John M. Kemble, and William Airy. In October, 1826, he matriculated at Trinity College, Cambridge. After having been an erratic scholar at Bury, he proved to be an indifferent student at Cambridge. The "set books" required by the rigid course of study failed to interest him, and he substituted a wide range of reading of his own selection. Nevertheless, Connop Thirlwall, Fellow and Tutor at Trinity, FitzGerald wrote later, "took a little fancy to me I think." Although he more than half expected to be plucked, FitzGerald obtained a pass degree in February, 1830.

Thackeray described FitzGerald at Cambridge as "a very good fellow but of very retired habits." His love of music and his skill as a pianist, however, moved him to join Camus, a musical society; but he cared not at all for the Union or other popular undergraduate groups. In fact, while at the University he revealed the independence of spirit and opinion characteristic of him through life. A year after taking his degree he described the typical Cambridge undergraduate as being "made up of scraps" and endowed with a "Farrago of College information." However, at Trinity he widened his circle of lifelong friends. It was there that he first met John Allen, to whom many of his early letters were written, W. H. Thompson, later Master of the College, Charles Merivale, Robert Hindes Groome, William Makepeace Thackeray, and others. The three Tennysons, Frederick, Charles, and Alfred, were his contemporaries at Cambridge; but he did not make their acquaintance while there.

A liberal allowance of £300, rented lodgings in Soho and its environs, the home of his parents to resort to whenever he wished, a second home at Geldestone Hall, Norfolk, where his favorite sister, Eleanor Kerrich, lived encircled by ten children who provided "the best company in the world," made it possible for FitzGerald to enter upon the life of a genteel gypsy after taking his degree. A few duties were expected of him. For a number of years he supervised, not very methodically or professionally, labor on the family estates. His mother required his attendance at Portland Place during the season. He accompanied her willingly to theater and opera but reluctantly to formal dinners. He served willingly, also, as escort for sisters when occasion demanded. For the rest, he led a carefree bachelor life, wandering about Britain or settling down in Charlotte Street lodgings to enjoy pleasures London provided and the companionship of Cambridge friends as they gravitated to the metropolis.

In 1837, two years after his father took possession of Boulge Hall as his country residence, FitzGerald set up as an independent householder in a thatch-roofed cottage outside the park gates. The dwelling was sheltered by Scotch firs and oaks, and casement windows opened upon beds bright with anemones of "Tyrian dyes, and Irises of a newer and more brilliant prism than Noah saw in the clouds." Boulge Cottage was his home for sixteen years. While there, he acquired a new circle of friends: genial Bernard Barton, the Quaker poet, and Thomas Churchyard, solicitor and amateur artist, both of Woodbridge; and George Crabbe, son of the poet and Vicar at Bredfield, a mile across the fields from Boulge. "We are the chief Wits of Woodbridge," Fitz-

Gerald wrote. W. K. Browne of Bedford, a youth when FitzGerald first met him in 1832, became one of his most intimate friends, and for a number of years Bedford provided virtually a third home for him. Accepting Browne's hospitality was a concession on FitzGerald's part, for usually, when visiting friends, he took lodgings near his "host" and spent part of each day in his company. During the Christmas season of 1844 he made the acquaintance of Edward Byles Cowell of Ipswich, a youth of eighteen whose scholarship and insatiable hunger for a knowledge of languages eventually drew FitzGerald into the study of Spanish and Persian. It was Cowell who, at Oxford, discovered the manuscript of the *Rubáiyát* of Omar Khayyám which was to provide the foundation for FitzGerald's fame. A dramatic touch was added to their friendship when, in 1847, Cowell married Elizabeth Charlesworth of Bramford, near Ipswich, a woman with whom FitzGerald had fancied himself in love a decade before.

As his older comrades married, formed new ties, and became more and more involved in their vocations, London lost most of its attraction for him. He sickened of formal dress—"velvet waistcoats and ever-lustrous pumps." The metropolis, he protested, "melts away all individuality into a common lump of cleverness." Recalling his London life at a later date, he wrote, "What bothered me in London was—all the Clever People going wrong with such clever Reasons for so doing which I couldn't confute."

Gradually the rural peace and rustic beauty of his cottage home triumphed over the blandishments of the city. "The reign of primroses and cowslips is over, and the oak now begins to take over the empire of the year and wear a budding garland about his brows," he reported from Boulge in 1845. "Over all this settles the white cloud in the West, and the Morning and Evening draw toward Summer." He spent his mornings reading—and writing, though he did not tell his friends so —walked with his dog in the afternoon, and at evening foregathered with his neighbors or sat "with open windows, up to which China roses climb, with my pipe, while the blackbirds begin to rustle bedwards in the garden, and the nightingale to have the neighborhood to herself. . . . And such verdure! white clouds moving over the new fledged tops of oak trees, and acres of grass striving with buttercups. How old to tell of, how new to see!"

London's "modern wits" suffered by contrast with his unsophisticated country neighbors. "I am amazed at the humour and worth and noble feeling in the country," he told Frederick Tennyson. "I can still find the heart of England beating healthily down here," where every one, he added later, "with whatever natural stock of intellect endowed, at least grows up his own way, and flings his branches about him, not stretched on the espalier of London dinner-table company."

But FitzGerald's Arden was not devoid of storms and tempests of one kind or another. His father's bankruptcy in 1848 involved all the children as creditors, but FitzGerald accepted his own loss philosophically, despite the fact that he was compelled to curtail expenditures considerably for a time. On the other hand it was impossible for him to muster comparable equanimity to cope with his quixotic marriage to Lucy Barton, an account of which is given in Lucy's Biographical Profile.

Although the failure of his marriage caused him to be diffident about meeting some old friends, FitzGerald never dropped any, nor did he ever become the recluse that writers have striven to make him. This is a topic to be touched upon later. His marriage and his father's bankruptcy were two in a series of experiences from 1848 to 1859 that changed the manner but not the essence of his life.

For three years after his father's failure FitzGerald was involved in litigation arising from the bankruptcy; but court hearings and business trips made it possible, despite diminished income, to enjoy frequently the companionship of London friends. Other results from the misfortune were the separation of his parents in 1849 and his father's death three years later. The bankruptcy was partly responsible, also, for FitzGerald's abandoning his beloved cottage at Boulge in November, 1853; and for the next seven years he lodged, while in Suffolk, with Job Smith, a farmer, at Farlingay Hall on the outskirts of Woodbridge. Cowell had left Bramford to matriculate at Oxford in 1851, and FitzGerald thereby lost another bond with his old life.

The departure of the Cowells for India five years later was a greater loss, for the young scholar had provided intellectual stimulus which lent zest to FitzGerald's sedentary life. Separation from the Cowells had been preceded by the death of his mother the previous year and was followed by his marriage in November. Deaths of two friends shattered what remained of the pattern of his past life. George Crabbe of Bredfield died in September, 1857; and in February, 1859, Kenworthy Browne was fatally injured in an accident while returning to Bedford after a day's riding to the hounds and died the following month. It was Browne's death that finally made London intolerable to FitzGerald. The two had visited the city together frequently and the memory of his friend so haunted FitzGerald in streets and taverns as to "fling a sad shadow over all."

Despite the trials, sorrows, and vexations which beset him at the time, FitzGerald produced his major works during the decade of the fifties. It is obvious that he had always aspired to write. His early letters to Allen and Thackeray contain a number of original poems; and in 1831 his "Meadows in Spring" was published, a poem so fresh in sentiment and original in form and style that Lamb envied the unknown author. Unfortunately, perhaps, FitzGerald was neither prodded by need nor spurred by ambition to strive for public recognition or acclaim. While at Boulge, conforming to lifelong practice, he read voraciously, filled commonplace books with gleanings from his reading, translated from the classics and from European literature passages that particularly impressed him, wrote poetry, as his letters attest; but published nothing until he was forty years of age. At that point in his life writing for publication was thrust upon him when he consented in 1849 to prepare a volume of selections from Barton's poems to be sold by subscription. The "Memoir of Bernard Barton" he provided for the book disclosed the lucid, rhythmic prose he had been perfecting *in camera*. Having, as it were, taken the plunge by this venture, FitzGerald published *Euphranor, A Dialogue on Youth* in 1851; *Polonius, a Collection of Wise Saws*, extracted mainly from his reading, in 1852; and a second edition of *Euphranor* in 1855. Meanwhile he had been studying Spanish and Persian with Cowell. This avocation produced *Six Dramas from Calderon* in 1853, the only book ever to bear his name as author; and *Sálamán and Absál*, translated from the Persian of Jámí, in 1856. All were printed at FitzGerald's expense, but each bore the imprint of the London publisher who placed the book on sale. FitzGerald wrote freely to friends about these works and sent copies to them. Not one of the books, however, realized anything beyond a modest sale.

At the Bodleian Library, in 1856, Cowell discovered the Omar Khayyám manuscript and made a copy for FitzGerald. The "curious Infidel and Epicurean Tetrastychs" provided diversion during the doleful months of his life with Lucy. For two and a half years he labored over manuscripts which Cowell provided. In March, 1859, the *Rubáiyát of Omar Khayyám* was placed on sale in the shop of Bernard Quaritch, Castle Street, London. The British Museum received its copy March 30, the day Kenworthy Browne died. The poem suffered the fate of FitzGerald's other works. For two years the paper-covered booklets lay virtually ignored on Quaritch's shelves until, in the spring of 1861, most of them were tumbled ignominiously into the penny box outside the door. From this lowly nook the poem emerged to be acclaimed for the beauty of melody, rhythm, phrase, and allusion in which its haunting speculations are expressed, and to win a place among the masterpieces of English poetry. The first edition achieved a fame of its own by becoming one of the most highly prized of modern rare books.

While at work on the *Rubáiyát*, FitzGerald was also translating the *Mántik-ut-Tair* or *Parliament of Birds* by the Persian poet Attár. After publication of his masterpiece, FitzGerald concentrated on the *Mántik*, intending to condense or, as he phrased it, give "a Bird's-eye view of Attár's Bird-Parliament." However, the poem, an entertaining and ingeniously contrived allegory, did not appear in print until the publication of his *Literary Remains*.

As Browne's death spoiled London for FitzGerald, the deaths of other old friends spoiled the Suffolk countryside. "Somehow," he wrote from Farlingay, "all the Country round is become a Cemetery to me: so many I loved there dead." He was angered, moreover, by the *Suffolk Landowners, New Style* who, he complained, "only use the Earth for an *Investment*," defacing its beauty in their zeal. He turned his back on groves of oaks, on fields where grass battled with buttercups, and in December, 1860, took lodgings in two rooms that looked out upon bustling Market Hill in Woodbridge. Before the town broadened the placid River Deben, flowing between low-lying banks to join the sea at Woodbridge Haven, some nine miles below. For the next sixteen years sailing was his principal recreation from June until November. On the river he sailed his sixteen-foot half-decked *Waveney*, with a "captain" as navigator; on the sea he cruised in the fourteen-ton schooner yacht, the *Scandal*, with a crew of two. His skiff was named the *Whisper*. Lowestoft, rather than Woodbridge, was, essentially, his home port at the height of each sailing season. Impaired eyesight, which made reading difficult while aboard, compelled him to part with the yacht in 1871; but he continued to sail the *Waveney* for a number of years and never entirely abandoned the sport. He also ventured into commercial sailing by building a herring lugger in 1867 and entering into partnership with Joseph (Posh) Fletcher, a Lowestoft fisherman whose simplicity and sturdy independence took FitzGerald's fancy. Posh, however, proved to be an irresponsible businessman; and in 1870 the partnership was dissolved.

For twenty years or more FitzGerald had searched for a house, rather than lodgings or a cottage, in which to establish his home, and had weighed the merits of this town and that in turn without reaching any decision. Upon moving to Market Hill he intensified his search, restricting it to Woodbridge; but he found nothing to satisfy his exacting taste. "All the better homes are occupied by Dowagers like Myself," he complained. "At last," said his attorney, "he said he had made up his mind; and, as he had not been able to find anything that did suit him, he had fully decided to buy one that did not suit." The unsuitable property was a cottage and six acres of land on Pytches Road in the northern fringe of the town. The attractive dwelling which FitzGerald fashioned by adding two rooms to the original structure was not ready for occupancy until July, 1866, two years after he had made the purchase. But, at last having acquired a home, FitzGerald felt no desire to become its tenant. Little Grange, as the house came to be called, provided a summer refuge for Kerrich nieces; but its owner remained in his Market Hill lodgings until 1874, when he was compelled by the landlord to vacate the rooms. He then reluctantly moved into his "chateau," which in the meantime had been further enlarged by the addition of two more rooms. FitzGerald grew to love Little Grange and there lived out his remaining years.

Although vitally interested in the life and welfare of Woodbridge and its environs, FitzGerald admitted few of his neighbors to friendship. He had found the gentry "a Circle . . . quite unendurable to walk in." The "stupid dullness" of their formal dinners, he said, had driven him "out of the Society hereabout as much as anything else." He preferred the company of "unaffected and (best of all) unconventional People." Herman Biddell, gentleman farmer of nearby Playford, who devoted much of his spare time to painting, was such a person; George Manby, grain merchant and church warden of Woodbridge, was another, "a John Bull: with Sense, Veracity, Experience, and Decision; better to me than all the colourless Squires, who know nothing that I don't know better: and that's not much." Others whom FitzGerald accepted were John Loder, printer and bookseller; Frederick Spalding, unsuccessful businessman but master of miscellaneous information; William Martin, writer of popular books, one of the many Peter Parleys —all of Woodbridge; Stephen Jackson, owner and publisher of the Ipswich *Journal*; and a handful of others.

With most of his fellow citizens FitzGerald was frostily and punctiliously formal. Though a gentle man, he refused to play the role of Gentleman, for which he was qualified by birth and means. The distinction was one few townspeople could understand, and his bohemian nonconformity confused and offended them. They considered him an "oddity"—and with cause, by their lights. Glaring evidence was offered by his persistence in occupying lodgings while owning a pleasant home. And any normal man, any Gentleman, to be sure, would prefer transportation in a passenger coach in the Ipswich train over the "Horse-box" in which FitzGerald once reached Woodbridge "with John Grout, his Man, half-a-dozen Horses, two Dogs, and a Cat." There were many worthy townsfolk, moreover, who never forgave him his cavalier treatment of Lucy Barton.

The years FitzGerald spent at Market Hill and Little Grange formed no vacuum, either intellectual or social, in his life. Reading continued to be his most constant diversion as it had been since childhood. When weakened eyesight compelled him to do so, he employed schoolboys to read to him each evening; it interfered with writing also, but failed to stem the stream of letters. His script often approached the illegible, as the editors know all too well, but the quality of the content never declined. He continued to work on manuscripts, and the labor of his Woodbridge years produced three versions of the *Rubáiyát*, two revisions of *Salámán and Absál*; a third edition of *Euphranor*; adaptations of two more Calderón plays, *The Mighty Magician* and *Such Stuff as Dreams are Made of*; a version of the *Agamemnon* by Aeschylus; another drama from the Greek, *The Downfall and Death of King Oedipus*, "taken from" *Oedipus Tyrannus* and *Oedipus Coloneus* by Sophocles; a condensation of Crabbe's *Tales of the Hall*; and minor pieces. Only three of the books were trade publications: *Agamemnon*, a volume containing the third version of *Sálamán and Absál* and the fourth of the *Rubáiyát*, and an edition of *Readings from Crabbe.*

The routine of Woodbridge life was enlivened by visits of old friends who sought him out: Archdeacon Groome, with his wealth of Suffolk lore, songs, and anecdotes, W. B. Donne, William Airy, Francis Duncan, W. H. Thompson, Frederick Pollock, who had become Sir Frederick, Samuel Laurence, Frederick Tennyson, and, in 1876, the Poet Laureate, who spent three days as FitzGerald's guest. These two "fell at once into the old Humour as if we had only been parted twenty Days instead of so many Years."

Advancing years, distance, and deaths, however, reduced the frequency of meetings with old companions; but the void was filled by nephews, nieces, and younger friends; among these, George Crabbe, son of Crabbe of Bredfield, and Donne's sons, Mowbray and Charles. Newly formed friendships also included those with Edwin Edwards, a London artist, and his wife; Aldis Wright, Trinity bursar, scholar, and librarian; Wright's antithesis, unconventional, whimsical Charles Keene, artist for *Punch*, who found FitzGerald to be "quite one of our kidney." All were welcome and frequent guests at Little Grange. Keene would arrive bearing long-neglected books and a viol or his favorite musical instrument, bagpipes. He played the latter while pacing FitzGerald's "Quarter Deck," a path that ran the length of the Little Grange property behind the house. "Keene has a theory that we open our mouths too much," FitzGerald told Groome, "but whether he bottles up his wind to play the bagpipes, or whether he plays the bagpipes to get rid of his bottled-up wind, I do not know."

As years crept by, FitzGerald's letter-writing increased, for new correspondents were added to the old. Through letters he resumed a friendship with Fanny Kemble after a lapse of thirty years or more. The part played by Charles Eliot Norton of Harvard in identifying FitzGerald as the translator of the *Rubáiyát* opened a spirited correspondence between the two. This in turn led to an "epistolary friendship" with Eliot's friend, James Russell Lowell, the American poet. While serving as Ambassador to Spain and later to the Court of St. James, Lowell proposed several times to spend a day at Woodbridge; but, as was his practice, FitzGerald discouraged so brief a visit. Unless friends, and especially new friends, were able to spend three days or so, FitzGerald protested that the journey was not worth their while; and he urged them to wait until time could be spared for the longer stay. Lowell's official and contingent social responsibilities made such a holiday impossible.

Relinquishing the *Scandal* in 1871 had not checked FitzGerald's love for his "old Doctor," the sea. He paid protracted visits to Lowestoft—in winter as well as summer—virtually every year until his death, and Cowell often arranged vacation holidays to coincide with his sojourns there. Dunwich and Aldeburgh were other coastal haunts. He sometimes made flying trips to these villages for "a toss" or "splash" on the sea in a hired boat. As a child he had caught his first glimpse of the ocean at Aldeburgh, where his family had spent vacations, and he formed a love for the place that never waned. "There is no sea like the Aldeburgh sea. It talks to me," FitzGerald once said. Occasionally he traveled farther afield. He once reached Scotland—a trip that gave rise to a FitzGerald myth—and at another time spent four days there. After the decade of the sixties, during which he avoided London, he resumed visits to attend opera and art exhibitions and to meet a few of his old friends. He was in London, it so happened, only a month before his death. After Crabbe of Bredfield died, FitzGerald rarely permitted a year to pass without paying at least one visit to the younger George

Crabbe at Merton, Norfolk. Now and again the Rector's sisters, Caroline and Mary, were guests at the same time. Such occasions, FitzGerald wrote, "were like old times at Bredfield."

Crabbe arranged one of these reunions for mid-June, 1883. On the thirteenth FitzGerald made the journey from Woodbridge—seventy-five to a hundred miles in those days, for the trip involved five changes of trains. Crabbe noted during the evening that his guest was not as animated as usual. The following morning, when FitzGerald failed to appear for breakfast, Crabbe went to his room and found him "as if sleeping peacefully, but quite dead."

Five days later FitzGerald was buried in the churchyard at Boulge. A horizontal stone which marks the grave bears a Biblical verse of his own choosing—

It is He that hath made us and not we ourselves.

With the passage of time the reputations of many who achieve fame become burdened with biographical barnacles—legends and fables, distortions and exaggerations—which seem to possess greater vitality than truth. FitzGerald has been the victim of a generous share of them, and two require comment here.

Over and over again we read that he turned his back on London and friends there, retired to Suffolk, and became a recluse. "FitzGerald, the recluse," in fact, has become a cliché; but the fallacy in the epithet is easily exposed. The sketch of his life discloses a clear and decidedly normal pattern.

During his twenties, the decade after he left Cambridge, his letters testify to a natural youthful zest for London with its stimulation provided by theaters, concerts, art exhibitions, and companionship. Although he often went to the city during his thirties, its enticements began to pall; and his native soil lured him with rural charms. He centered his life in Suffolk. It is hardly unusual for a man entering middle age to prefer Suffolk to London, but few are so fortunate as FitzGerald in being free to indulge their preferences. As he approached the age of forty, he was beset by financial reverses; and stringency curtailed freedom of choice and movement. Trips to the city, for the most part, were restricted to those required by business. Upon coming into his inheritance at the age of forty-six, he again went to London more frequently. Nevertheless, were it not for friends there, he said, he would rarely go to London. As he approached fifty, when the deaths of friends blighted both London and inland Suffolk for him, his only exceptional deviation from the common pattern of lives took place, and he cultivated new interests. Summer months, formerly devoted to traveling about and visiting friends, were spent sailing. He entertained friends aboard ship while he owned the *Scandal* or sailed with them on the Deben. He acquired new friends. The stream of guests, old friends and new, who visited Little Grange could hardly be termed a trickle.

Such was the pattern of FitzGerald's life. We may wonder how sociable a man may be and still qualify as a recluse.

The second barnacle to be noted is the charge that at some point in his life—the point is never specifically fixed—FitzGerald sacrificed the intimacy of many old friendships as a result of his "ascetic bent" and through his criticism of the later works of literary friends. Thackeray and Tennyson are customarily cited when such statements are made.

We need merely to glance at the "Chronology" to learn that FitzGerald and Thackeray met with normal frequency during years of supposed estrangement, despite the pressures imposed on the novelist by writing, editing, and lecturing. In March, 1851, FitzGerald spent three days at Thackeray's Young Street home; and FitzGerald's letters mention meetings on an average of once a year between 1851 and 1858—among the busiest years of Thackeray's life. It is likely that not all their meetings were recorded. The depth and warmth of their later friendship is clearly attested by letters exchanged in 1852. Their last meeting took place in 1858, five years before Thackeray's death.

FitzGerald's criticism of Tennyson's work after 1842 is presumed to have chilled the poet's regard for "Old Fitz." In the letters readers will find many adverse judgments of Tennyson's later poetry expressed with frankness befitting a brother, because FitzGerald criticized with the freedom granted an old, intimate, and trusted friend. Despite his normal sensitiveness under critical fire, Tennyson granted the freedom and bore with the frankness, and numerous letters exchanged until FitzGerald's death affirm the genuine affection which the poet sustained for his old friend. Although frequently urged, FitzGerald could not be persuaded to repeat a visit paid to the Tennysons at Farringford in 1854; but, it should be recalled, when the poet visited Woodbridge, the two fell into their old ways as though they had been separated only a score of days rather than so many years.

When writers are tempted to state that FitzGerald lost touch with old companions, they would do well to compare the number of friendships they have retained over half a century with the number FitzGerald kept vital over that span of time.

FitzGerald's Music

FitzGerald's letters reveal his love for music and his highly personal preferences in musical composers and their works, but they contain very few references to FitzGerald's own musical compositions. His music for Thackeray's "Ho, Pretty Page," his ballad-opera of Scott's *Pirate*, done at Charles Keene's request for Joseph Crawhall, and a few others are mentioned. Some of his compositions were printed, but many more were in manuscript when he died; some of them have survived.

FitzGerald was composing music as early as 1834. In 1853 he wrote Spring Rice, "Your talk of the old Cambridge days has made me send you the enclosed piece of music which I found in a Music Book dated 'Cambridge, 1834'—when I was in the top room at Bacon's, the Tobacconist's, and we often looked down on the market. That was a time of some musical impulse; and I remember this directly I saw it: the whole room and place rose up before me. As it is connected with a place and time in which you figure, and has really some beauty in it I think, I send it to you. It is in the old style, which you will not think obsolete for such words: and must be sung by a Tenor. I have really a sort of love for it—very much from association, I think, with old times." In 1834 FitzGerald had taken his degree but was still very much a part of the musical life he had known as an undergraduate when he was a pianist for Camus, the Cambridge Musical Society.

Drafts of a group of FitzGerald's musical compositions survive in Trinity College Library. In them he set to music poems by Tennyson, Byron, Samuel Rogers, Isaak Walton, Ebenezer Elliott, Sir J. Van Brugh, James Hogg, Shakespeare, and others, as well as some by himself. In his 1949 BBC broadcast of some of the Trinity compositions, Alec Robertson said, "Their charm lies in the melodic line, which the piano parts faithfully follow, and in their simplicity." In 1977, the thirtieth Aldeburgh Festival of Music and the Arts devoted its last night to "Old Fitz and his Music."

Others have set FitzGerald's poetry to music. A critic has commented that FitzGerald would have liked the simple setting of Lehmann's *In a Persian Garden*, which she had based on his *Rubáiyát*, and which had first been performed in 1896. A few years later, George Bantok's elaborate work based on his *Rubáiyát* was staged as a "Festival Performance" by the London Symphony Orchestra and the London Choral Society.

Another facet of FitzGerald's musical activity is clarified by material at Trinity College Library—his attempts to teach underprivileged and untrained groups in Suffolk to sing. He wrote Frederick Tennyson in 1851, "I am trying to teach the bumpkins of the united parishes of Boulge and Debach to sing a second to such melodies as the women sing by way of Hymns in our Church: and I have invented (as I think) a most simple and easy way of teaching them the little they need to learn. How would you like to see me, with a bit a chalk in my hand, before a black board, scoring up semibreves on a staff for half a dozen Rustics to vocalize? Laugh at me in Imagination." At Trinity is his carefully worked-out plan which he heads "Singing in One Clef." In it he uses analogies familiar to his pupils to explain musical terms. The octave is compared to days of the week, Sunday to Sunday, "the 8th being the *same* as the *first*, only higher up or lower down."

An interesting item at Trinity College is a letter from Archdeacon Robert H. Groome, also a good amateur musician, evaluating FitzGerald as a musician and composer. "He was a true musician . . . he truly appreciated all that was good and beautiful in music. . . . He was a good performer on the piano and could get such full harmonies out of the organ that stood in one corner of his entrance room at Little Grange as did good to the listener. . . . And then at times he would fill up the harmonies with his voice, true and resonant to the last. . . . He was not a great but he was a good composer." It must be said, however, that he will always be best known in the field of music in all probability for "his comments on music in the letters, put down casually enough, but often with rare perception and with his great gift of splendid phrase making." To these words, Alec Robertson added, "Some of FitzGerald's phrases alone are worth pages of professional criticism."

The FitzGerald Family

Edward FitzGerald's name at birth was Edward Purcell. He was the son of John Purcell, who in 1801 married his first cousin Mary Frances FitzGerald. The union was one of several which united the two Anglo-Irish families. On the death of his father-in-law in 1818, Mr. Purcell assumed the FitzGerald name and arms.

John Purcell (1775-1852), a descendant of the Barons of Loughmoe, was the eldest son of a wealthy surgeon of Richmond Hill, Dublin. He enrolled at the Inner Temple, London, after taking his degree at the University of Dublin in 1794, but never practiced law. Possessing ample means, he settled at Bredfield, Suffolk, after his marriage and devoted himself to politics, his duties as a squire, and the sports of a country gentleman. He served as High Sheriff in both Suffolk and County Waterford, held a commission as Lieutenant-Colonel in the Volunteers, and represented Seaford, Sussex, in Parliament from 1826 until the borough was abolished by the reform of 1832.

Mr. FitzGerald, as he should be called, was a prosperous, benevolent landlord and a jovial host. "Draw closer, gentlemen," he would urge his guests, "and I will give you a glass of wine that never paid one farthing to his Majesty's customs—the King, God bless him!" Though a successful squire, he was a luckless businessman. At least two of his agents absconded with large sums of money, and a coal-mining venture on his wife's estate at Pendleton, near Manchester, brought ruin to him, to relatives, and to friends who had invested in the speculation. His Pendleton Colliery Company failed in 1848 and Mr. FitzGerald was declared bankrupt before the year was out. Mrs. FitzGerald's fortune, not involved in the bankruptcy, later provided ample inheritances for the children. In 1849 the parents separated, and three years later Mr. FitzGerald died at the age of seventy-six. The failure of his mining venture still preyed on his mind. "That engine works well," he murmured as he lay in the stupor of death.

Mr. FitzGerald was overshadowed by his wife, Mary Frances (1779-1855), a woman of striking beauty and imperious bearing, descended from the fiery Earls of Kildare. On the death of her father, also named John FitzGerald, in 1818, she was reputed to be the wealthiest commoner in England. Her properties included Little Island, the FitzGerald Irish seat near Waterford; Boulge, Suffolk; Castle Irwell, the Manchester estate; Naseby Wooleys, Northamptonshire, which embraced most of Naseby Battlefield; and Gayton in Staffordshire. The FitzGerald town house was at 39 Portland Place, an impressive London address. There Mrs. FitzGerald spent the season, entertaining and indulging her passion for theater and opera, Edward often in attendance. FitzGerald's friend Frederick Pollock recalled seeing Mrs. FitzGerald "in black velvet and diamonds" at the Haymarket Opera, where she had a box in the third tier. She frequented fashionable Brighton and sometimes visited Leamington Spa. To Edward, chiefly, fell the responsibility of serving as her escort when her husband was unable to do so.

Mrs. FitzGerald proved to be more accomplished as a *grande dame* than as a mother. "My dear," Edward once overheard his grandmother tell her daughter, "you are a very fine woman, but *a bad Mother*." When his mother joined the children in the nursery, said FitzGerald, "we . . . were not much comforted." One of his sisters described their life as "one of extreme discipline and entire obedience."

After separating from her husband, Mrs. FitzGerald established her home at Richmond, Surrey, where Edward visited her periodically. She died there in January, 1855. Like her husband, she had reached the age of seventy-six.

Edward was the sixth of eight children born to John and Mary Frances FitzGerald. His brothers, John and Peter, were both older than he. Three sisters, Mary Frances, Mary Eleanor, and Jane, were also his seniors; Isabella and Andalusia his juniors. Mary Frances, the eldest child, died in 1820 at the age of eighteen. Perhaps the influence of Mrs. FitzGerald's personality was responsible for an almost complete absence of "clannishness" in the family relations. Each member selected an orbit in which he moved independently of the rest. "As a general rule," FitzGerald once wrote, "no one of my Family is ever to be heard of from a Kinsman." When John died at Boulge Hall, Edward, who lived only three miles distant, had not been within his gates "these dozen years"; nor did he surmount his aversion to funerals to attend his brother's rites. "We were very good friends of very different ways of thinking," he said. Although the independence which members of the family maintained seemed often to resemble indifference, most of them were tied to each other by strong bonds of affection.

John (1803-79) took his degree at Cambridge with the intention of entering the Church. Illness, which impaired his vision, prevented him from taking orders; and he compromised by becoming an extremely zealous, sincere, but eccentric evangelical lay preacher. He would hold services in a chapel, on the shore of Naseby reservoir, on street corners in Ipswich—wherever and whenever he could attract a congregation. When a High Church rector was named to Boulge parish in 1867, John was so indignant that he built a chapel nearby and served as pastor. Many anecdotes testify to his eccentricity, and equally numerous are the stories which attest to his deep sincerity and generous benevolence. His many and liberal benefactions included the founding of an almshouse at Seaford in 1858.

John married twice. His first wife, by whom he had two sons, Maurice and Gerald, died in 1837, five years after their marriage. He remarried in 1844. On the death of his mother in 1855 he inherited the family estates and maintained Boulge, which he had occupied for some years, as his seat until his death in May, 1879.

Peter FitzGerald (1807-75) was an indifferent student at Bury St. Edmund's School. After a short term spent in the army, he married in 1832 and joined Purcell relatives in County Kildare, Ireland. He farmed first at Halverstown, later at Ballysax. After his mother's death in 1855, he lived for a few years at Richmond, then at Twickenham. His first wife died in 1866, and within a year he married his housekeeper, a union of which Edward approved.

The two men were thoroughly congenial. Edward visited his brother both in Ireland and in England; and Peter and his wife would spend vacations at Lowestoft when Edward was there, cruising with him in the *Scandal.*

While wintering at Bournemouth in 1874, after having spent the previous ten winters at Cannes, Peter contracted bronchitis; he died in February, 1875. "A more amiable Gentleman did not live," Edward wrote, "with something *helpless* about him—what the Irish call an 'Innocent man'—which mixed up Compassion with Regard, and made it perhaps stronger." Peter's last words were Edward's name, thrice repeated.

FitzGerald's favorites among his sisters were Mary Eleanor and Andalusia, but his deepest love was reserved for Mary Eleanor (1805-63). In 1826, she married John Kerrich of Geldestone Hall, Norfolk, near Beccles, where the Waveney River forms the border between Suffolk and Norfolk. When FitzGerald took his degree in 1830, he went immediately to Geldestone and, until his sister's death, was a constant and welcome guest there. A room was always kept ready for him because his visits were often made without warning. He would sometimes enter the music room through French windows and announce his arrival by playing a favorite selection on the piano.

His correspondence contains many passages describing the idyllic tenor of life at Geldestone. "Here I am like the Father of a delightful family, without the responsibilities attached," he wrote. The family was large as well as delightful. There were twelve children: Walter, Edmund, Charles, John, Eleanor Frances, Elizabeth, Amelia Jane, Mary, Andalusia, Anna Maria Theresa, Adeline, and Eleanor. (Eleanor Frances appears to have died young.) During one visit he wrote, "The day passes in eating, drinking, riding, driving, talking and doing nonsense: the intervals being filled with idleness." Unfortunately, the Arcadian aspect of Geldestone evaporated with the failure of the Pendleton Colliery Company. Kerrich, one of the directors, had invested heavily in the project; when the company failed, stringent sacrifices became mandatory, and his losses embittered Kerrich for the remainder of his life. Mary Eleanor died in 1863. When her husband died in 1871, the family left Geldestone.

FitzGerald assumed the responsibility of watching over his nieces. He joined them frequently at Lowestoft and rebuilt his home, Little Grange, mainly for their summer use. His favorite among the girls was Anna Maria, called Annie and described by FitzGerald as "Capital Annie." Ten of the family survived their uncle, who provided generously for them by making them his residuary legatees.

FitzGerald's sister Jane (b. 1806) was one of the two sisters for whom he manifested only moderate affection. The second was Isabella. In 1832 Jane married the Reverend John B. Wilkinson, Rector of Holbrook near Wherstead, the FitzGerald home at the time, and, said FitzGerald, "made him very Evangelical—and tiresome." Despite his description of the clergyman as "tiresome," FitzGerald admired Wilkinson. After an acquaintance of twenty years FitzGerald stated that he had "never known Wilkinson to do anything, or say anything, he believed to be wrong." The clergyman died in 1862 and Jane went to Florence to live. In the autumn of 1881, eighteen months before Edward's death, she returned to Boulge for a visit and called several times at Little Grange. Age and the deaths of brothers and sisters had mellowed FitzGerald. As the lone survivors of the once large family sat in the garden, talking of old days, he rested his hand on hers. "We seemed as if we could not part," wrote Jane, "but he would not be persuaded to return to Italy with me."

Isabella (1810-64) contrasted sharply with her sisters and brothers. She "is pretty generally in a whirl of plans, which the common race of mortals cannot keep pace with," FitzGerald once reported. In 1843 she married Gaetano Vignati—"a desperate match," said FitzGerald three days before the wedding. He was not concerned that the groom was "without a decent coat on his back, and without a penny in the coat he had." His apprehension stemmed from misgivings that Vignati would be unable "to manage" Isabella "and, knowing my sister as I do, I have every reason to fear the issue on all accounts." Despite its imminence, FitzGerald was not sure the wedding would take place. "She may kick over the traces, and say 'No' at the foot of the altar," he told Frederick Tennyson. The wedding, however, was held on October 18 without untoward incident, and the couple left for the Continent the following day.

Vignati, it appears, proved capable of managing his volatile wife. The two are rarely mentioned in the correspondence, but the references which appear contain no evidence that the marriage was not a success. FitzGerald, moreover, found Vignati to be a worthy brother-in-law.

During the decade of the thirties FitzGerald frequently expressed concern for the health of Lusia, as his youngest sister, Andalusia (1813-79), was usually called. Although his references to her affliction are obscure, they contain implications of mental disturbance; but evidence indicates that he was unduly alarmed. Her complaint was not grave enough to deter John Allen's brother Bird from becoming engaged to her. Moreover, when Bird, a Commander in the Royal Navy, lost his life on the Niger Expedition in 1841, Lusia bore the shock with fortitude. Three years later she married the Reverend Francis de Soyres, Curate at Geldestone, and led a normal life as wife and mother. She spent most of her life after marriage in the West Country—Teignmouth, Bath, and Exeter—where FitzGerald often paid long visits. "He sent us little ones into fits of laughter by his stories," his nephew John reported, "one, of the culprit who receives sentence from a pompous magistrate at Woodbridge and retorts with a rude gesture (executed by E.F.G. in pantomime solemnly.)" Lusia died at Exeter in December, 1879, seven months after the death of her brother John.

William Airy

"William Airy . . . came to see me here: and then we went together to Bury to ramble over our old School Haunts. This also was really a pleasant thing to me," FitzGerald wrote in 1861. The two had also been fellow students at Trinity College. Airy (1807-74) was a brother of Sir George Airy, Astronomer Royal, and a cousin of FitzGerald's friends, the Biddells of Playford, near Woodbridge.

Airy may have possessed intellectual powers not recognized by his companions at school and college. When Jacky Kemble won first prize for declamation at Cambridge in 1829, he wrote to W. B. Donne that their former Bury schoolmate had placed second to him. "Who in the name of wonder would have thought of seeing Airy in possession of a prize for English composition?" he asked.

From 1836 until his death Airy was Vicar of Keysoe, Bedfordshire, and after 1845 Rector of nearby Swineshead as well. He also served as Domestic Chaplain to the Duke of Manchester at Kimbolton Park, near Keysoe. FitzGerald visited him on trips to Bedford, and Airy was one of his most frequent guests at Woodbridge. In the course of a stroll on the banks of the Deben one evening, Airy asked another guest if he knew which horse had won the St. Leger that day. "You are a pretty elderly divine to be so interested in turf transactions," observed FitzGerald.

Airy wrote on archeological subjects and published a digest of those portions of the Domesday Book which relate to Bedfordshire.

John Allen

Simplicity and sincerity were traits FitzGerald valued highly, and he found both in John Allen (1810-86), to whom many of his early letters were written. The two met as undergraduates at Trinity College where Allen, devout and humble, prepared to enter the Church. His remarkable naïveté proved to be one of his greatest assets. He was a thoroughly honest man: many would charge that he carried honesty to extremes. Fearless and frank in criticism, he made it a principle to report to the targets of his censure any criticism he uttered beyond their hearing. On one occasion he was told that a bishop, accustomed to writing while riding on trains, insured privacy by saying, "Occupied," when fellow passengers appeared at the door of his compartment. "Then," said Allen, "he lied." Integrity compelled him to repeat the remark in a letter to the prelate. In due time Allen's own bishop advised him to apologize. Allen wrote, "Bishop Lonsdale bids me to apologize to your Lordship, and I therefore hereby apologize. Your Lordship's faithful servant John Allen." Cardinal Manning, who knew Allen as a young man, described him as "simple, upright, fearless."

The son of a Pembrokeshire clergyman, Allen matriculated at Cambridge in 1828, two years after FitzGerald entered the University. Allen's college diary, now in the library at Trinity, reflects the simplicity and humility of the writer and bears a striking resemblance to the diary kept by Ralph Waldo Emerson as a young man. After taking his degree in 1832, Allen taught school in London but within a year was appointed lecturer in mathematics and, later, chaplain at King's College, then recently established in the Strand. In 1834 he married Harriet Higgins of Hertfordshire. He won the favor of William Otter and John Lonsdale, principals under whom he served at King's. Both men were elevated to bishoprics, and through their patronage Allen advanced in his career. In 1839 he was named one of the first three Inspectors of Schools, a post he filled until 1846, when he was appointed to the living of Prees, Shropshire, fourteen miles north of Shrewsbury. He was made Archdeacon of Salop the following year. Older clergymen accepted the appointment with scant enthusiasm, but Allen's fearlessness and his capable and conscientious administration of the district, sorely in need of sound and courageous leadership, silenced malcontents. One of his first acts as Vicar at Prees was to remove the padlock from a pew reserved by a squire who rarely attended church. While archdeacon he increased the salaries of his clergy and is said to have built or restored churches in every parish under his jurisdiction. He was tolerant in matters involving nonconformists, and when he resigned from his living in 1883 dissenters in the area formally expressed their regret at his action. Although outspoken, Allen was a kindly, indefatigable pastor. He bowed neither to rank nor to wealth. Evidence bears out the statement by his biographer that "his manners were the same to a washerwoman as to a duchess."

Until he went to Prees, Allen was one of FitzGerald's most intimate friends, sought out always on FitzGerald's visits to London. In 1832 and again in 1833 FitzGerald joined Allen at Tenby while "Johnny" was vacationing in his native Pembrokeshire. Only once, however, did FitzGerald visit Prees. In March, 1852, he spent a fortnight with the Allens and their ten children at the vicarage. Called upon to play the harmonium at a church service, he suggested an announcement, to be made by one of the boys, that the congregation would be privileged that day to hear a performance by "a distinguished foreigner, Signor Geraldino." After his visit, FitzGerald wrote that he had found "dear old Allen . . . as much of a boy . . . (almost) as he used to be twenty-four years ago." The two men never met again.

When FitzGerald died, Allen wrote to F. H. Groome, Archdeacon of Suffolk, "I owe very much to our dear friend. I daily strive to act on lessons that were brought to my conscience by what I saw in him—a most true friend" (Trinity College MS).

Bernard Barton

Of Bernard Barton, cheerful, kindly, amiable, and ingenuous, FitzGerald wrote, "Few, high or low, but were glad to see him at his customary place in the bank. . . . Few, high or low, but were glad to have him at their tables . . . he was equally pleasant and equally pleased, whether with the fine folks at the Hall, or with the homely company at the Farm. . . ."

"The Quaker Poet," as Barton (1784-1849) is often called, a widower with an only daughter, Lucy, settled in Woodbridge in 1810. He conscientiously performed his duties as clerk in Alexander's bank in the Thoroughfare; but his heart was in his home, his books, his pictures, and his poetry. After two early ventures into print, he published five volumes of verse between 1822 and 1828. Three later volumes completed his works. At times he considered abandoning stool and ledger for a literary career, but from this rash step he was dissuaded by warnings from Lamb, Southey, and Byron. That he wrote verse rather than poetry, Barton himself freely admitted. His poems reveal skill in turning a felicitous phrase but little originality in thought or form. The books, FitzGerald stated, "contained many pretty poems; but many that were hasty, and written more as task-work."

Barton twice visited Charles Lamb, who addressed some of his sprightliest letters and soundest advice to him. In 1846 Barton sent Sir Robert Peel two sonnets, FitzGerald wrote, "begging him to retire to Tamworth and not alter the Corn Laws." The Prime Minister responded by inviting the poet to dinner at Whitehall, and Barton accepted. Peel, as a man, cordial though quiet and unobtrusive, impressed Barton profoundly; but "not one word of politics" did he speak or hear spoken in the course of the evening; and he departed still skeptical of the soundness and wisdom of his host's legislative policies. Barton was granted a Civil List pension of £100 a few months later. Only rarely could Barton be induced to leave Woodbridge, but through correspondence he created a wide circle of friends. Among writers with whom he corresponded—besides Lamb, Southey, and Byron—were John Mitford, Felicia Hemans, William and Mary Howitt, John Bowring, and John Lockhart. FitzGerald introduced Barton to W. B. Donne, and for a decade these two exchanged letters notable for their banter and wit.

FitzGerald may have known Barton a dozen or fifteen years before they became friends, for Wherstead Lodge near Ipswich, the FitzGerald home for a time, was among the halls where the poet was an occasional guest. It was not until after the FitzGeralds took possession of Boulge in 1835 that an intimate friendship developed between the two men. Despite the forty-three-year difference in their ages, Barton became a frequent guest at FitzGerald's cottage; and the door of his modest home in Woodbridge swung open readily and often to admit the younger man for a supper of toasted cheese and ale, followed by a reading from a Scott novel or animated talk of pictures, poetry, and friends.

After spending Christmas Day with Barton in 1848, FitzGerald wrote to Donne, "He seems only pretty well: is altered during the last year: less spirits, less strength; but quite amiable still." The poet was fully aware of the symptoms of failing health noted by his friend, but the knowledge failed to dampen his humor. For forty years, he said, he had "taken almost as little exercise as a milestone and far less fresh air." Only five days before his death, he wrote that although he suffered little acute pain "the trouble about [his] breathing" makes a man think "how long he may be able to breathe at all. But if the hairs of one's head are numbered, so, by a parity of reasoning, are the puffs of one's bellows."

Barton died February 19, 1849. FitzGerald sent an obituary and a funeral notice to the *Ipswich Journal* and immediately, at Miss Barton's request, set about preparing a volume of his friend's poems and letters to be sold by subscription. The purpose was to supplement Miss Barton's limited resources. From many of the selections he deleted portions and revised much of the remainder—"mending BB's dropped stitches," as he put it—to give the poems "logic and fluency"; and, he could have added, to provide polish which Barton's lines lacked when first published. The volume, which appeared before the year was out, had a satisfactory sale, thanks largely to FitzGerald's zeal in obtaining subscribers. It was well received, and a second printing was required in 1850, followed three years later by a trade edition. Most modern readers will find the chief merit of the book in FitzGerald's "Memoir of Bernard Barton," which serves as an introduction to the volume. The essay, a biographical gem, is noteworthy for its dispassionate judgment, narrative ease, and beauty of style.

Lucy Barton

Bernard Barton's wife died in giving birth to their only child, Lucy, and the infant was cared for by a grandmother in whose home she spent her youth. When mature enough to take charge of her father's household, she joined him in Woodbridge and proved to be a young woman of more than average intellectual vigor. Having adopted the

Anglican rather than the Quaker faith, perhaps at the boarding-school in which she had been educated, she took an active part in church affairs. She formed and taught a Sunday school class which met in her home. *Bible Letters for Children*, published in 1831, was the first of a number of religious books which she wrote for juveniles. One of these, *Bible Stories for Children*, which FitzGerald helped her to prepare, sold for one shilling sixpence and went through six editions between 1849 and 1857.

Lucy lacked physical charm. She was tall and large of frame; her stride was mannish, her voice deep, her features heavy. Relatives, and others qualified to write about her, invariably allude to her strong will and determination. This is the woman to whom FitzGerald quixotically became engaged and reluctantly married.

Although the two were about the same age—Lucy a few months the senior—the engagement could in no wise be attributed to romantic attachment, at least on his part. FitzGerald mentions Lucy only occasionally in letters to Barton, and the references are decidedly impersonal. The explanations of the engagement offered by the Barton and FitzGerald families differ at points but agree that FitzGerald unwittingly became involved in a promise or proposal of some kind at the time of Barton's death. Crabbe of Merton's manuscript notes in Trinity College Library support this. "In 1849 Bernard B. died," Crabbe wrote, ". . . and it was then that E.F.G. seemed more unhappy. I suppose on account of his promise." The Barton theory is that FitzGerald, having recognized that Lucy's meagre property would not provide sufficient means for her support, "impetuously offered to make up the deficiency from his income." It is thought that Lucy's refusal of the plan and FitzGerald's self-censure for making what Lucy may have construed as an indelicate proposal eventually engendered an engagement. Whatever the means, the fact remains that FitzGerald's rigid sense of propriety and adamantine integrity made it impossible for him to free himself unless Lucy consented. This she refused to do.

FitzGerald was involved in the financial entanglements attendant upon his father's bankruptcy in the years immediately following Barton's death and lacked means to establish a home. Lucy became a companion to the grandnieces of her father's wealthy friend and benefactor, Hudson Gurney of Norfolk. There is no record of any meeting of the couple during a seven-year engagement, nor has any correspondence between them come to light. While living with the Gurneys, FitzGerald stated, Lucy forgot "the plainness and simplicity of a Quakeress" and was transformed into a "Lady." Through an intermediary, FitzGerald made at least one effort to break the unwelcome betrothal; but Lucy replied that "*she* had no fears for the future." On the death of his mother in 1855, FitzGerald inherited a fortune. Further postponement could no longer be justified.

The ill-matched pair were married November 4, 1856. Both had reached the age of forty-seven. Both were strong-willed. Antagonistic tastes and temperaments doomed the marriage from the outset. FitzGerald wished to live with as little change as possible in his life and habits. Lucy wished to convert her Bohemian husband into a model of Victorian propriety. Never before had FitzGerald been bound by routine and conformity. He rebelled; and, after eight bitter months, the unhappy couple separated. FitzGerald settled the income from an investment of £10,000 on Lucy, which provided an income of £300 annually until her death at the age of ninety. FitzGerald rarely mentioned his marriage to friends; but, when he did, he placed blame for the failure upon himself for not "bearing and forbearing after carrying out his engagement and contract." One friend reported that he absolved Lucy "of any *design* in the matter." She, at least after his death, did not blame FitzGerald. In a letter written September 4, 1883, to George Crabbe to accompany forty letters from FitzGerald to her father which she wanted Crabbe to read before sending them on to Aldis Wright (as usual she was not mentioned in any of them), she said, "I can have no greater satisfaction than to send you any scraps that may help to show him as he really was—so good so kindly and so true—for there never was anybody like him!"

The woeful interlude had a profound effect on FitzGerald's career. Shortly before his marriage he had obtained the first transcript of Omar Khayyám's *Rubáiyát.* He found diversion and refuge in translation, for the Persian poet, he wrote, "breathes a sort of Consolation to me!" The marriage altered his life, also. It made him averse to seeking out most of his old friends and to meeting socially the Suffolk gentry with whom his status allied him. He always welcomed friends from either group when they came to him, but he refused to enter any homes except those of a very few intimates.

George Borrow

"I remember first seeing you at Oulton, some twenty-five years ago," FitzGerald wrote to George Borrow in 1875. The statement assigns the meeting to the time when Borrow was laboring to complete *Lavengro.* W. B. Donne, who had then known the novelist personally for at least two years, was probably instrumental in bringing the pair together.

Borrow's thorny temperament rarely educed friendship. "Whom should I send them to?" he asked John Murray, the publisher, on receipt of a half dozen copies of his book *The Zincali.* "Do you think I have six friends in the world?" FitzGerald was probably drawn to him by those traits which repelled others: a rugged, aggressive independence and a contempt for "genteel humbug," the "gentility nonsense of the times." A common interest in languages was another bond. Their relations were always amiable, even cordial. For a decade after becoming acquainted, they met with relative frequency at Oulton, Borrow's home near Lowestoft, Gorleston, Yarmouth, and London.

Their first meeting coincided with the beginnings of FitzGerald's study of Spanish. Borrow had published *The Zincali; or, An Account of the Gypsies of Spain* in 1841 and *The Bible in Spain* the following year. When *Six Dramas of Calderon* was published in 1853, FitzGerald sent him a copy and received "a very handsome letter" in response. Borrow reciprocated with a copy of *Romany Rye* when it appeared in 1857. The work, FitzGerald told E. B. Cowell, contained "some excellent things and some very bad (as I have made bold to write to him—how shall I face him!)." He faced him boldly. Frederick Spalding recorded in his diary that FitzGerald told the author, "part of it he didn't believe—and never could have happened, quite expecting to be knocked down while telling him so."

FitzGerald appears to have sought Borrow's companionship during the cheerless months of his married life. Their third and fourth meetings, he once recalled to Borrow ironically, were "at my own happy home in Regent's Park; then ditto at Gorleston." In 1856 and 1857, while FitzGerald was first translating the *Rubáiyát,* the two met more frequently, drawn together by their interest in Persian. FitzGerald lent Borrow some of his Persian texts, including the transcript of the Ouseley manuscript of Omar Khayyám's verses.

After the failure of his marriage, FitzGerald restricted visiting to the homes of a very few friends. And so, in 1875, he declined "a very kind invitation" from Borrow, explaining, "For the last fifteen years I have not visited any of my very oldest friends, except the daughters of my old friends George Crabbe, and Donne—once only. . . . I could not go to you, after refusing all this while to go to older—if not better—friends."

William Kenworthy Browne

FitzGerald devoted his life, essentially, to books and letters. But, to modify Matthew Arnold slightly, "an inextinguishable sense haunted him that he had not made what he should." Time and again he expressed discontent with himself for his mode of life and admiration for the man who balanced thought and action. He pointed to Chaucer and Shakespeare as successful men of business as well as poets, and noted that "neither Yeomanry Drill—nor daily Plough—drove the Muse out of Burns." FitzGerald came to believe that the weaknesses he found in himself and his peers were engendered in school and college. He agreed with Newman that "polite and elegant education . . . teaches us to think, speak, and be affected aright, without forcing us to *do* what is right."

In William Kenworthy Browne (1816-59) of Bedford, FitzGerald found the qualities which he admired, balanced as he thought they should be. Browne was a youth of sixteen, seven years FitzGerald's junior, in 1832 when they became acquainted on a steam packet to Wales. They later lodged at the same boarding house in Tenby. Despite the difference in their ages, a rare friendship developed between them. FitzGerald watched the lad merge into the young man of eighteen, "quick to love and quick to fight—full of confidence, generosity, and the glorious spirit of Youth," and become the man of forty, "Farmer, Magistrate, Militia Officer—Father of a Family—of more use in a week than I in my Life long."

FitzGerald paid frequent and prolonged visits to Browne's home, and they often visited London together. Both benefited. FitzGerald's love of books and art rubbed off on the younger man, and Browne's round of activities drew FitzGerald out of his study and broke the sedentary mold of his life. For a time FitzGerald kept a horse at Bedford, and occasionally was persuaded to do a little shooting. Browne was an ardent angler, and the pair frequently roamed the banks of the Ouse together. In place of rod and creel, however, FitzGerald was inclined to carry sketchbook and color-box, "poking about" making "horrible sketches." His abuse of his painting was misplaced, for he had considerable skill with brush and pencil. Reading tended to be neglected in Bedford. "While I have Browne at my side I do not read much," FitzGerald wrote in 1838, "he being very much better than books in my opinion."

On his journeys between Suffolk and Bedford, FitzGerald frequently passed through Cambridge, where "the hard-reading, pale, dwindled students looked as if they were only fit to have their necks wrung." They suffered by comparison with Browne, who had not attended a university, and FitzGerald came to attribute the difference between friend and students to their educations. He determined, he said, "to do something as far as I could against a training system of which I had seen so many bad effects." The result was *Euphranor*, his "Dialogue on Youth," published in 1851, in which he criticized the curriculum of English schools and recommended reforms.

Browne married Elizabeth Elliott of Goldington, near Bedford, in 1844. The couple first lived at Goldington Hall; but in September, 1858, they moved to a larger house, Goldington Bury. The following January Browne was returning from a day's hunt with the Elstow Harriers when his horse reared, slipped on the turf, and fell back on its rider, fatally crushing him. He clung to life until March 30. FitzGerald was summoned from London a week before his friend's death; while wandering about the house one day, he picked up the copy of *Euphranor* he had given the stricken man. In it he wrote, "This little book would never have been written, had I not known my dear friend William Browne, who, unconsciously, supplied the moral."

Thomas Carlyle

After achieving modest success as reviewer, essayist, and translator of German literature, Thomas Carlyle (1795-1881) in 1834, at the age of thirty-eight, left Scotland to begin his career in London as the writer of strange books for bewildered and not always friendly British readers. FitzGerald's reactions to his works varied during the 1830's. He condemned the "raving book about Heroes" as "perfectly insane," but defended the *Miscellanies* against the abuse of his London companions. Carlyle's review of Varnhagen von Ense's memoir of his wife touched him, FitzGerald wrote, "as all his writings do. . . . All this time I think Carlyle is a one-sided man; but I like him because he pulls one the opposite side to which all the world is pulling one."

Samuel Laurence, who had painted Carlyle's portrait, took FitzGerald to Cheyne Row to meet him on September 15, 1842. The historian, engaged in research for his work on Cromwell at the time, remarked that he had visited Naseby battlefield the previous May and had verified accounts of the movements of Loyalist and Puritan troops.

Questioning by FitzGerald, whose family owned most of the site, revealed that Carlyle had walked over "what was not the field of Battle." He was reluctant to believe that he could have erred; FitzGerald, who had just come from Naseby and was about to return, consented to engage in research on Carlyle's behalf. FitzGerald's account of the "bone-rummaging" into which his offer led him is related with verve and humor in letters of September and October, 1842.

One can hardly conceive of two men whose personalities and temperaments contrast more sharply than do those of Carlyle and FitzGerald. However, the help FitzGerald lent while *Cromwell* was being written led to a friendship which held firm until Carlyle's death. FitzGerald became a frequent guest at Cheyne Row, although it was not until 1849 that Mrs. Carlyle decided that their visitor from Suffolk was "very good and rational" and "got to like him." FitzGerald was adept in dealing with the sometimes genial, sometimes fractious, and always strong-willed Sage of Chelsea. The younger man was neither awed by his friend's reputation nor overwhelmed by his tirades on men and affairs. He endeavored "not to antagonize with him," FitzGerald reported; but he never hesitated to assert his own honest opinions. He told Carlyle that the more he read of *Cromwell*, "the more I was forced to agree with the verdict of the world about him. Carlyle only grunted and sent forth a prodigious blast of tobacco smoke." He described FitzGerald as "an excellent, modest, and affectionate character. . . ."

Carlyle's popularity waned with the publication of *Latter-Day Pamphlets* in 1849 and 1850. Readers had been entertained and remained tolerant as long as he denounced mankind and social ills in the abstract, but they resented direct attacks on their statesmen as "Stump Orators" and on the parliamentary system as "government of Jackasserie." The *Pamphlets*, FitzGerald wrote, "make the world laugh, and his friends rather sorry for him. But . . . there is a bottom of truth in Carlyle's wildest rhapsodies."

After a number of invitations which came to naught, Carlyle, in August, 1855, consented to endure the "shrieking mad . . . rail operations" and visit his friend in Suffolk. FitzGerald erred in predicting that the celebrated insomniac would be able to "sleep composedly" during his rustication; Carlyle, nevertheless, spent ten days as his guest and was confident, he wrote from Chelsea, "I *have* got good by my Suffolk visit."

FitzGerald appears to have called on the Carlyles for the last time in June, 1859. He fell into the practice thereafter, as he did with many old friends, of writing to them twice yearly. While in London in the autumn of 1880, FitzGerald was "all but tempted" to call once more at Cheyne Row where he had spent "many pleasant evenings . . . all kind and pleasant at all times." He let the opportunity slip. Carlyle died at the age of eighty-six the following February.

Thomas Churchyard

"On Saturday I give supper to Bernard Barton and Churchyard," FitzGerald wrote in 1843. "We are the chief wits of Woodbridge. And one man has said that he envies our conversations! So we flatter each other in the country." The "wits" usually numbered four, George Crabbe, Vicar of Bredfield, who lived only a mile from FitzGerald's cottage, completing the quartet.

Thomas Churchyard (1798-1865), attorney and amateur artist, was a member of the Woodbridge firm of Meadows, Churchyard, and Brooke. FitzGerald probably made his acquaintance through Bernard Barton. Although Churchyard was indifferent toward his legal practice and considerably more enthusiastic about painting, he was an able and respected lawyer. Guy Maynard, former Curator of the Ipswich and Christchurch Mansion Museums, related that one client seeking legal advice was informed by a clerk that the lawyer was engaged but would see him shortly. Churchyard *was* busy in his office, engrossed in the pleasant task of painting a picture. Considerable time passed. The client asked the clerk to remind Churchyard that he was still waiting. The same answer came back. "Mr. Churchyard will see you shortly." After another irksome delay, the client directed, "Will you ask Mr. Churchyard whether he will see me now or whether I should consult another attorney?" After a brief consultation in the inner office the clerk returned with the message, "Mr. Churchyard says to go to Hell —you'll find lots of attorneys there."

"I am just such a poet as my neighbour Tom Churchyard is an artist," Barton once wrote. "He will dash you off slight and careless sketches by the dozen, or score, but for touching, re-touching, or finishing, that is quite another affair, and has to wait, if it ever be done at all. Of course we are a couple of lazy slovenly artistes, for our want of pains, but as the old proverb has it, 'There is no making a silken Purse out of a Sow's ear.'" Churchyard, nevertheless, was indignant when children's handkerchiefs bearing some of Barton's verses were sold in shops at a penny each. He condemned the articles as "an indignity, an insult," and said that he "would cuff any urchin whom he caught blowing his nose on one of his sketches!"

FitzGerald states that Churchyard was an able judge of pictures by Gainsborough, Constable, and Crome, the Norwich artist, whose works he collected. Since he had a wife and nine children to support, Churchyard's devotion to art at the expense of his vocation was the source of concern to his friends. From Lowestoft FitzGerald once wrote that the artist-attorney was there also, "sketching when he ought, I suppose, to be at his Law Stool." His seven daughters and younger son also painted.

After his death Churchyard's pictures sold locally for ten shillings or so each, but just a century later he won recognition and endorsement from a larger public. At a show held in Woodbridge in 1965 the entire exhibit was sold. The demand for his pictures persists, and £200 have been paid for some. His work is exhibited in the British Museum and the Victoria and Albert as well as in Christchurch Mansion, Ipswich, and Castle Museum, Norwich. Representative oils, water-colors, and ink sketches have been reproduced by Denis Thomas in *Thomas Churchyard of Woodbridge*, published in 1966.

The Cowells

Two years after he made the acquaintance of Edward Byles Cowell (1826-1903), who was to become his tutor in Persian, FitzGerald wrote of him, "He ought to do something in the world; for, as far as I see, his delicacy of discrimination is as great as his capacity for amassing—a rare combination." A few years later FitzGerald urged George Borrow to call on his young friend in Ipswich, asserting that Cowell was "a great Scholar, if I may judge: such as I have not hitherto seen anything at all like from the Universities, etc." That Cowell did not make a greater mark in the world may be attributed to extreme shyness, a zealous dedication to teaching, and a resolution to spend as many hours as he could in the seclusion of his study.

While a boy at Ipswich Grammar School, Cowell manifested a hunger for languages that Latin, Greek, and French failed to satisfy. He attempted to master Sanskrit by himself but, finding that too difficult, contented himself temporarily with a study of Persian. Before he left school at the age of sixteen, he had begun to contribute translations from the odes of Háfiz to the *Asiatic Journal.* Cowell's father, a merchant and maltster of Ipswich, died in 1842, and Edward was compelled to abandon his formal education and enter his grandfather's counting house, applying himself to "figures all the day and at Persian and Greek in the mornings and evenings."

FitzGerald evidently first met Cowell during the Christmas season of 1844, probably at the home of the Reverend John Charlesworth, who lived at Bramford, near Ipswich, but was Rector of Flowton, only a mile or two distant. Elizabeth, one of his two daughters, was a friend of FitzGerald's sisters and sometimes visited them. Her poems, displaying extremely modest creative talents, appeared rather frequently in the almanacs and "Ladies Memorandum" books of George W. Fulcher of Sudbury, Suffolk. In 1839 Fulcher published a volume of her verses bearing the title *Historical Reveries*, which was republished in London, with additions, in 1891 under the title, *Leaves of Memory*.

In the autumn of 1845 Elizabeth announced her engagement to Cowell, her junior by fourteen years. A Cowell family legend relates that when FitzGerald heard the news, he exclaimed, "The deuce you are! Why, you have taken my Lady!" The story distorts the facts, because FitzGerald first learned of the engagement from separate letters sent to him by the couple. It is true, however, that as early as 1835 he had been, or had fancied himself as being, in love with Elizabeth. A year later he contemplated proposing to her, but never did. The Cowells were married in October, 1847. FitzGerald's affection, revived with Elizabeth's removal beyond his reach, became intensified as an overtone to his despair arising from the promise that eventually resulted in marriage to Lucy Barton. In his biography of FitzGerald, Thomas Wright names Caroline Crabbe, daughter of the Vicar of Bredfield, as FitzGerald's inamorata, an identification flatly contradicted by numerous letters, particularly those to Frederick Tennyson in 1850.

After their marriage the Cowells took possession of the Bramford house which the Charlesworth family had vacated after Elizabeth's father was appointed to a London parish. FitzGerald was a frequent visitor at the cottage, voraciously reading Greek and Latin classics in the original with Cowell, stimulated by the light which the younger man's learning threw on the works. The easy companionship he maintained with his friends, and his code of propriety, testify that he never openly revealed his old attachment, even though hints of it crept into letters to Elizabeth.

It was clear to Cowell's wife that the volumes over which he pored out of his own interest, rather than those over which he labored in his vocation, were the books for which he was intended. She urged him to enter a university. Cowell, however, mistrusted his preparation as well as his capacity for formal scholarship. After a struggle in which FitzGerald played the part of the devil's advocate—almost literally, in Elizabeth's eyes—Cowell was persuaded to matriculate at Magdalen College, Oxford, in November, 1850. FitzGerald went frequently to Oxford while Cowell was in residence there.

Before leaving Bramford, Cowell had tutored FitzGerald in Spanish and had directed his attention to the plays of Calderón. On a rainy Sunday at Oxford in December, 1852, when FitzGerald seems to have been idle, restive, and peevish, Cowell suggested that he study Persian, "and guaranteed to teach the grammar in a day." Thus the origin of FitzGerald's career as a translator of Persian poetry. Cowell took his degree in 1854 and in June, 1856, was appointed Professor of History and Political Economy at the Presidency College in Calcutta. Only a month before, while working in the Bodleian Library, he had discovered a hitherto unknown manuscript of *rubáiyát* by the Persian mathematician and astronomer, Omar Khayyám. He transcribed the verses for FitzGerald and a few weeks later, on August 1, departed for India, where he remained until 1864, when ill-health forced him to return home.

When the University of Cambridge established a chair of Sanskrit in 1867, W. H. Thompson, Master of Trinity College, serving that year as Vice-Chancellor, wrote to ask FitzGerald if Cowell would stand for the appointment. Cowell became a candidate and FitzGerald solicited votes among his university friends in his support. Cowell was successful, and he spent the remainder of his life in Cambridge. He established an international reputation as an Orientalist. At a special meeting in 1898, Cowell was given the first gold medal of the Royal Asiatic Society, an award granted every three years to a leading scholar.

FitzGerald rarely visited the Cowells after their return from India, but they frequently arranged to spend parts of their vacations with him at Lowestoft. Both outlived their friend. Elizabeth died in 1899; her husband, four years later.

The Crabbe Family

George Crabbe of Bredfield

FitzGerald never met George Crabbe, the Suffolk poet; but he became well-acquainted with him, as it were, through his works and through his son, also George, to be identified, for convenience, as Crabbe of Bredfield. The younger Crabbe, a widower with a large family, was appointed Vicar at Bredfield in 1834, the year before the FitzGeralds occupied Boulge Hall, about a mile distant. Crabbe, fifty years old in 1835, was almost twice FitzGerald's age; but the two became firm friends; and the "Rectory," as the Bredfield vicarage was popularly called, became a second home to the bachelor of Boulge Cottage. During the forties the Vicar's son, George Crabbe of Merton, stated, "FitzGerald was a great deal at Bredfield, generally dropping in about seven o'clock, singing glees with us, and then joining my Father over his cigar, and staying late and often sleeping. He very often arranged concerted pieces for us to sing in four parts, he being tenor." Portions of the youngest Crabbe's diary in Trinity College Library show that FitzGerald often lunched and dined at Bredfield. After vacating Boulge Cottage for Farlingay Hall in 1853, he stayed at the vicarage frequently, and he lodged Carlyle at both places when the latter visited him in Suffolk. The Vicar was equally at home at the cottage. Returning one evening from Aldeburgh, FitzGerald was surprised to find the clergyman "smoking in my room, with a bottle of Port (which he had brought with him!)." A neighbor had called at the vicarage, and Crabbe, fearing that his guest would tarry all evening, declared that he had business with FitzGerald, "and so decamped."

Crabbe, one of the Woodbridge Wits, was sincere and guileless, impulsive and sensitive. FitzGerald never knew when an innocent difference of opinion would offend his tetchy companion; and Bernard Barton, intimate friend of both, frequently found it necessary to serve as peacemaker between the two. "I am glad of thy frank admission that thou hast been a thought too captious toward that Cottager," Barton wrote to Crabbe on one occasion. "You are both a little eccentric, but despite your eccentricities, capable of cordially appreciating each other, and do so, bating brief moods. . . . I always feel certain you will jumble together again. I would not have a serious quarrel between you for a good deal." They always did "jumble together" again, and when Crabbe died in 1857, FitzGerald wrote, "To manhood's energy of mind, and great bodily strength, he united the boy's heart: as much a boy at seventy as boys need be at seventeen; as chivalrously hopeful, trustful, ardent, and courageous; as careless of riches, as intolerant of injustice and oppression, as incapable of all that is base, little, and mean."

Although Crabbe denied his father by condemning poetry as "a useless art," he wrote a life of the poet for the first collected edition of his poems, published in 1832. The biography was highly praised at the time, and FitzGerald declared it to be "one of the most delightful memoirs in the language." In 1840 Crabbe published another work, *An Outline of a System of Natural Theology*, "a sad mistake," said FitzGerald, for his friend lacked the training in logic that the subject required.

When Crabbe died, September 17, 1857, FitzGerald wrote to his son, "I can't say . . . what a heap of unrepaid obligations I feel always on my Shoulders for the kindness and all the happy peaceful Times I have experienced at Bredfield for the past ten years." At Crabbe of Merton's request, FitzGerald contributed an obituary of his friend to the November issue of the *Gentleman's Magazine*, which is published in the *Letters and Literary Remains.*

George Crabbe of Merton

Only a few of the Crabbe letters in FitzGerald's correspondence are to the Vicar of Bredfield; many are to his son. A portion of the Merton letters was destroyed, but a generous share was preserved, including about two dozen in elementary French.

Despite the fact that FitzGerald sang glees with the children at Bredfield vicarage, he first "seemed a proud and punctilious man" to young Crabbe. After taking his degree at Cambridge in 1842, however, the younger man discovered his neighbor to be extremely companionable. He visited at Boulge Cottage, sometimes drove FitzGerald to Ipswich, Geldestone, and other points, and occasionally spent a few days in London with him.

After serving for five years as Curate at Copdock, near Ipswich, Crabbe, in 1851, was appointed Rector of Merton, Norfolk, by Lord Walsingham, the patron. The same year he married his cousin Emily Louisa Crabbe, who died three years later leaving him with two daughters.

FitzGerald described young Crabbe as "one of the most modest, intelligent, and agreeable men I know." The first year of Crabbe's incumbency at Merton FitzGerald visited him there and continued to do so virtually every year for the remainder of his life. Crabbe's two surviving sisters, for whom FitzGerald felt a paternal regard, were sometimes guests at the same time. After a week with the three in 1880, FitzGerald wrote of it as "the only visit of the sort I now make." It was "very pleasant," he continued, "the people all so sensible, and friendly, talking of old days." Crabbe's visits to Woodbridge were equally gratifying, and in 1856 he and W. K. Browne spent a fortnight with FitzGerald in Paris, the Rhine country, and Belgium.

In one respect the letters to Crabbe are exceptional, for in them FitzGerald discusses personal subjects more freely than in letters to any other of his peers—financial matters, for example. He placed unreserved confidence in his friend's judgment.

On June 13, 1883, FitzGerald arrived at Merton for his annual visit. The following morning he was found dead in his bed. Crabbe was one of the three executors named in FitzGerald's will. Crabbe died a year later. His malady, consumption, had compelled him to spend the winter seasons since 1866 in the Mediterranean area or on the south coast of England.

The Crabbe Sisters

FitzGerald felt a deep concern for Crabbe's unmarried sisters, Caroline and Mary, who had been "but slenderly provided for." After their father's death they lived first with a brother-in-law, a widower with an infant daughter, at Southam, near Leamington in Warwickshire. In 1863 they settled at Bradford-on-Avon in Wiltshire. FitzGerald visited them at both places as well as at Merton. At his death he bequeathed generous sums to the daughters of six of his friends. His bequest to the Crabbe sisters was £1,000.

It is to be hoped that, once and for all, the tale can be scotched that FitzGerald fell in love with and proposed to Caroline Crabbe. The fable originated with Thomas Wright and has been repeated by subsequent writers. The woman who served as ladies' maid at Bredfield vicarage flatly denied the story when questioned by John Loder at Aldis Wright's request. Loder's letter to Wright is now among the FitzGerald papers at Trinity College. Thomas Wright's statement probably resulted from his attempt to account for rumors that FitzGerald had been in love during his years at Boulge. It is true that he had been in love: letters here published clearly identify Elizabeth Charlesworth, later Mrs. E. B. Cowell, as the object of his affections, but his guarded devotion to her predated, and persisted beyond, his residence at Boulge Cottage.

George Crabbe, the Poet

We have said that FitzGerald's ties with Crabbe the poet were through his family and works. Indirect influences as well probably contributed to his becoming defender of the poet's reputation. His mother, FitzGerald stated, was the only woman he knew who read Crabbe with pleasure. Crabbe, moreover, was the favorite author of Benjamin Heath Malkin, the headmaster at Bury School. Crabbe associations, too, hovered about FitzGerald's beloved Aldeburgh, the poet's birthplace on the coast where he lived several years in penury while struggling for recognition.

As early as 1865 FitzGerald suggested to John Murray, Crabbe's publisher, a volume of selections which he, FitzGerald, proposed to edit. Murray, however, would "not meddle." Nevertheless, FitzGerald began to prepare the work by means of scissors and paste, his "Harp and Lute," as he called them. His method was to compress the narratives by providing brief prose passages "to bridge over pages of stupid Verse." In time he concentrated on *Tales of the Hall.* Friends in America offered his work to publishers there, but they proved to be as wary as Murray had been. In 1879, therefore, FitzGerald printed privately three hundred fifty copies of *Readings from Crabbe's "Tales of the Hall"* and sent copies to selected friends, asking their advice about publication. Quaritch placed fifty copies on sale at his shop. Although reception of the volume, even by friends, was lukewarm, FitzGerald persisted in his effort to revive interest in "Nature's sternest painter." In 1883 he arranged with Quaritch to take over the sale of the entire printing. A revised preface was being printed when FitzGerald died in June, and the book was published the following month.

William Bodham Donne

"I shall spend my time here wholly with my dear Donne: who shares with Spedding my oldest and deepest love," FitzGerald once wrote from Bury St. Edmunds.

William Bodham Donne (1807-82) was a native of Norfolk. His great-aunt, Mrs. Anne Donne Bodham, in whose home at Mattishall the Donnes lived, was the cousin who sent the poet Cowper his "Mother's picture out of Norfolk." The Donnes, moreover, were related to John Johnson, Cowper's "Johnny of Norfolk"; and W. B. Donne's son Charles married a daughter of Jacky Kemble.

FitzGerald and Donne were schoolmates at Bury St. Edmunds. In 1826 Donne matriculated at Gonville and Caius, Cambridge; but, holding conscientious objections to signing the Thirty-nine Articles, he left the university without taking a degree. Some years later he considered returning to complete his terms of residence, willing to sign the Articles, he said, "even if they were forty." Family responsibilities, however, forced him to abandon the plan.

Upon leaving Cambridge he returned to Mattishall to pursue independent studies, chiefly in classical literature and history. In 1830 he married his cousin Catharine Hewitt. Within eight years their children numbered five. "Pray how soon may Papas begin to calculate the number of their offspring?" he wrote to a friend on the birth of his fourth child. ". . . I had my doubts and felt (did you?) a sort of wryness and constriction at the ends of my mouth when it amounted to a Holy Alliance! Moreover our friends make their congratulations in a lower key, and do not keep up one's spirits as well as at first." Donne's civic responsibilities while living at Mattishall included service as a local magistrate. He supported his family by writing on classical literature and history and contributing miscellaneous essays and reviews to the *Gentleman's Magazine*, to *Edinburgh Review*, and other leading periodicals.

"Many men are *liked*, but Donne is *loved*," one of his friends wrote. Donne's charm lay in his gentle manner, genial humor, and genuine modesty. FitzGerald, who thoroughly enjoyed the companionship which awaited him at Mattishall, always found a hearty welcome there. "His life and conversation are the most perfectly philosophic of any I know," Donne once declared. "He is Diogenes without his dirt." The children—the "Goths and Vandals," as FitzGerald called them—loved their father's friend. "He is a most agreeable person," wrote Mrs. Donne, "laughter-loving and ever suited to make holiday. The children . . . spare him not."

Mrs. Donne, whose state of health had caused her husband anxiety for years, died in 1843. In 1846 his great-aunt, Mrs. Bodham, died in her ninety-seventh year. During the summer Donne left Mattishall for Bury St. Edmunds and entered his sons in the school which he and FitzGerald had attended. Appointed Librarian of the London Library in 1852, he left his mother in charge of the Bury home and occupied rooms provided for him at 12 St. James Square. Soon after he settled in London, he also assumed the duties of Examiner of Plays, serving as deputy for Jacky Kemble, who was in Germany but who returned to England and his post in 1855. On Kemble's death in 1857, Donne was named his successor and held the office until 1874. After leaving the library Donne lived for brief periods at Walton-on-Thames and at Blackheath, but in 1859 moved to Weymouth Street, Portland Place, where he spent the remainder of his life. He published a number of books on general as well as classical subjects and continued to contribute to periodicals until a few years before his death.

The understanding, depth, and warmth of the friendship between the two men are manifest. Donne was "delighted at the glory" FitzGerald achieved by his translation of the *Rubáiyát*. "It is full time," he wrote, "that Fitz should be disinterred, and exhibited to the world as one of the most gifted of Britons." FitzGerald kept in personal touch with Donne long after he had ceased to seek out his other old friends, calling on him three times during the months before Donne's death, June 20, 1882.

Through FitzGerald, Donne made the acquaintance of Bernard Barton, with whom he carried on an active correspondence in which FitzGerald is frequently mentioned. It was through Donne that FitzGerald first met George Borrow. Chief among the many correspondents the two men had in common was Fanny Kemble. FitzGerald corresponded, also, with Donne's children after they reached maturity, and entertained two of the sons, Charles and Mowbray, from time to time at Little Grange. Both had taken degrees at Cambridge. Charles Edward (1832-1907) entered the church in 1858 and from 1866 to 1900 was domestic chaplain to the Marquess Townshend and Vicar of Faversham, Kent. William Mowbray (1833-1908) entered the Inland Revenue Office in 1858 and rose to the position of Secretary. He retired in 1894. A third son, Major Frederick Clench Donne (1834-75), served in India, where he was severely wounded in 1858 during the Mutiny. After an extended leave of absence he returned to duty but was invalided home in 1867.

Robert Hindes Groome

The amiable "homespun" country parson, Robert Hindes Groome (1810-89), was one of many of FitzGerald's friends marked by a sturdy sense of humor. Groome, Rector of Monk Soham, near Woodbridge, entertained companions and guests by drawing upon an inexhaustible store of stories, anecdotes, and reminiscences recounted in the Suffolk dialect of which he was master. One recollection was of a neighboring farmer preparing to emigrate to America. "How are you going, Wilding?" Groome asked. "I don't fare to know rightly," was the reply, "but we're goin' to sleep the fust night at Debenham, and that'll kinder break the jarney." Debenham was four miles from his home. A woman in the parish received a letter from her son, postmarked Hull. "That did give me a tarn at fust," she told the Rector, "for I thought that come from the hot place." Groome was well read in the plays of Elizabethan dramatists other than Shakespeare. In one of his charges he quoted from *'Tis Pity She's a Whore.* The passage impressed a canon who was present. "What play is it from?" he asked afterward. "Ford's," replied Groome, " 'Tis a Pity She's—no better than she should be."

FitzGerald and Groome probably first became acquainted at meetings of Camus, the music society at Cambridge. FitzGerald was one of the pianists; Groome, a cellist. Groome, a student at Gonville and Caius, took his degree in 1832 and, after serving as curate in two parishes, in 1845 succeeded his father at Monk Soham. When he became Archdeacon of Suffolk in 1869, FitzGerald wrote, "Surely he will never dare come here again to sing over old Cambridge Songs with me."

From 1861 to 1866 Groome was editor of the *Christian Advocate and Review.* His son Francis, author of *Two Suffolk Friends*, biographical sketches of his father and FitzGerald, edited a series of "Suffolk Notes and Queries" for the *Ipswich Journal* in 1877 and 1878. Father and son wrote "two-thirds of the whole" under a number of aliases, Francis recorded. One of the Archdeacon's contributions, "The Only Darter," written in dialect, has won a place in Suflolk folklore. FitzGerald, who also provided a few items for the column, printed Groome's story and sent copies to friends.

The preface to the *Letters and Literary Remains* concludes with Groome's recollections of FitzGerald's love for music. "He was a good performer on the piano," Groome wrote, "and could get such full harmonies out of the organ that stood in one corner of his entrance room at Little Grange as did good to the listener. Sometimes it would be a bit from one of Mozart's Masses, or from one of the finales of some one of his or Beethoven's Operas. And then at times he would fill up the harmonies with his voice, true and resonant almost to the last."

Four yew trees at the gate of the Monk Soham churchyard were a gift from FitzGerald to Groome.

FitzEdward Hall

FitzEdward Hall was the first to call FitzGerald to the attention of the reading public. To "Our Literary Gossip" in the February, 1875, issue of *Lippincott's Magazine*, published in Philadelphia, Hall contributed an item in which he praised the *Rubáiyát*, identified the translator by name, and noted FitzGerald's other works, including the *Bird Parliament* which existed only in manuscript. "Everything that he has produced," Hall wrote in closing, "is uniformly distingushed by marked ability; and, such being the case, his indifference to fame, in this age of ambition for literary celebrity, is a phenomenon which deserved to be emphasized."

Hall, philologist and student of Eastern languages and literatures, was and remains a brilliant unknown. Of American birth, he left Harvard without a degree in 1846 at the age of nineteen to pursue a runaway brother who had gone to Calcutta. He remained in India for sixteen years and there became acquainted with E. B. Cowell, his source of information about FitzGerald's works. He mastered Sanskrit, Hindi, Persian, and other languages and in 1853 became Professor of Sanskrit and English at the government college at Benares. He went to England in 1862 and became Professor of Sanskrit, Hindustani, and Indian jurisprudence at King's College, London. The impressive list of Indian manuscripts he either translated or edited and his works on Indian philosophies won for him the degree of Doctor of Civil Law from Oxford in 1860 and Doctor of Letters from Harvard in 1895.

In 1869 Hall retired to the Suffolk village of Marlesford, near Woodbridge, where he continued work in Sanskrit but applied himself chiefly to philology. For years he devoted four hours daily to voluntary assistance in the compilation of the *Oxford English Dictionary*, and he played a major part in producing Joseph Wright's *English Dialect Dictionary*.

FitzGerald and Hall corresponded but, though living only six or seven mile apart, never met. To Aldis Wright, Hall described himself as "a social leper." The aspersion is probably explained, in part at least, by Cowell, who wrote, after Hall's death in 1901, "He was a little hasty in temper, but he was thoroughly kind at heart . . . though one could not help wishing that his language had been sometimes gentler in controversy."

Charles Keene

The last of FitzGerald's most congenial friendships was formed in 1877 with Charles Keene (1823-91), illustrator of *Punch*. He had the marked sense of humor that characterized most of FitzGerald's friends, and the two had, Keene said, "kindred tastes—artistic, social, musical—all round." FitzGerald described his friend as "a man who can wonder and revere, and read such Folios as I cannot more than look at. Fond of old English Music as of Ditto Books; and playing on the Bagpipes." He commented, "Little must the readers of *Punch* know what a queer spirit lurks behind those woodcuts of his."

Their friendship started at Dunwich, where Keene was visiting the Edwardses. When he returned to London, he wrote, "At Dunwich there was an old literate who had the only lodging in the place, a great friend of Tennyson's and of Poor Thackeray's, and quite a character—an Irishman, an author, and bookworm. . . . We met every evening and talked belles lettres, 'Shakespeare and the musical glasses' till midnight." Later he said, "I hear he has just bought some land on the skirts of the town, to save a windmill thereon, that otherwise would have been pulled down. Doesn't that show him to be the right sort?"

Keene was a native of Suffolk and had gone to the Ipswich School with E. B. Cowell and his younger brother whom he called, according to his custom of giving names to all of his friends, "Big Badger" and "Little Badger." FitzGerald was "The Literate," Edwards, "The Master," etc. Although he had already shown his artistic bent, Keene left Ipswich at the age of sixteen to study law in London. The work was not congenial to him and he was happier when he was apprenticed for five years to Whympers, wood engravers. When he left them, he worked for the *Illustrated London News* and other periodicals. In 1851 he joined *Punch*, the publication with which he was identified for the rest of his life. He made designs for many stories, among them *The Cloister and the Hearth, Evan Harrington, Brother Jacob, Mrs. Caudle's Curtain Lectures*, and *Robinson Crusoe.* In 1879 eight of his plates and ten of his initial letters for the *Roundabout Papers* appeared in the *édition de luxe* of Thackeray. The following year he sent the original drawings for his Thackeray woodcuts to FitzGerald.

In his own profession, Keene was known as an artists' artist, a master in black and white; to *Punch* readers he was regarded as an amusing illustrator; in France he was honored as one of the foremost etchers of the day.

Keene was a frequent visitor at Little Grange. "We talked art and the belles lettres all day in his garden," he reported on one occasion, "and smoked long churchwarden pipes in the evening." Music was always on the agenda, for both were fine musicians. Keene had an exceptional voice; he was one of the original Moray ministrels and a member of Leslie's and other famous choirs. "I am expecting my grave Friend

Charles Keene, of *Punch,* to come here for a week—bringing with him his Bagpipes, and an ancient Viol and a Book of Strathspeys and Madrigals; and our Archdeacon will come to . . . talk over ancient Music and Books; and we shall all three drive out past the green hedges, and heaths with their furze in blossom," FitzGerald announced. From London Keene sent to Little Grange "one or two musical gems to play in the dark on your organ and I'll sing them." It was Keene who later persuaded FitzGerald to adapt Sir Walter Scott's *Pirate* for a ballad opera Joseph Crawhall, Keene's good friend, wanted written.

On one of Keene's visits to Little Grange, FitzGerald took him to Merton and he recorded, "On Monday we went to visit his friend Crabbe, a parson, grandson of the poet. His parish is in an out-of-yr-way part of Norfolk. We had to change five times in getting there by rail, and had to wait four hours in Norwich. . . . Another visitor joined us on the road, Aldis Wright. . . . Crabbe is very nice fellow, about fifty, a widower, living with his daughter. . . . The parson and Wright used to retire about 10 P.M. but FitzGerald and I sat and smoked in the greenhouse for a couple of hours more. He is a capital companion . . . a great scholar; a slashing critic about pictures."

Keene's arthritis and other infirmities had already begun to bother him during these years. However, a few months after FitzGerald's death, perhaps to fill the void created by the cessation of his visits to Little Grange and to Dunwich, Keene, a non-golfer, joined the Felixtowe Golf Club to get away from London to "the beautiful links." He never married. When he died on January 4, 1891, the leader in the *Times* declared that Charles Keene's "honest, innocent, and kindly gaiety humiliated nobody and wounded nobody" and that he was "irresistibly humourous and never unmannerly."

The Kemble Family

Fanny Kemble

The Kembles, John, Charles, and Sarah—Mrs. Siddons—were long the pride of British theatergoers; peers and aristocrats freely opened their doors to them. Mrs. FitzGerald formed a warm friendship with Charles Kemble's wife, who also acted, and described her as "the most witty, sensible, and agreeable" woman she knew. The Kembles were entertained at Portland Place, and there FitzGerald became acquainted with the two daughters, Frances Anne and Adelaide. Both were lifelong friends; and Frances, better known as Fanny, became one of his principal correspondents.

FitzGerald was not impressed by Fanny's acting when, at the age of nineteen, she captivated London playgoers in her debut as Juliet at Covent Garden, where her father was actor-manager. Charles Kemble lost control of the theater in 1832 and embarked for America to fill his empty purse. Fanny accompanied him as his leading lady; but when he returned to England two years later, she remained behind as wife of Pierce Butler of Philadelphia. The chief properties of the Butler family were plantations and slaves in Georgia.

Within a year it was evident that Fanny and her husband were unsuited to each other. Pierce wanted a puppet for a wife, and Fanny was no puppet. She described herself and her brother John, FitzGerald's Bury St. Edmunds schoolmate, as being "endowed with such robust self-esteem and elastic conceit as . . . could never be effectually snubbed." Her social and professional life had combined to foster independence, pride, and strength of will. A prime cause of friction was her "unequivocal condemnation" of slavery. In Pierce's code, the Butler domestic economy was none of Fanny's business. Fanny bore her husband two daughters, but conjugal incompatibility reached an intensity she could not brook. In 1845 she returned to England and fifteen months later resumed her career in the theater. In 1849 Pierce was granted a divorce on grounds of desertion and gained custody of the children.

Fanny's second venture as an actress was brief. Within a year she left the stage in favor of giving readings of Shakespeare plays. FitzGerald underwrote an engagement at Woodbridge in 1852. Twenty-seven years passed before the two met again, but from time to time each received reports of the other through letters from William Bodham Donne. FitzGerald sent Fanny copies of his two late Calderón plays when they were printed in 1865, and two years later began the correspondence which was maintained until his death. Fanny called FitzGerald's letters his "Lunacies," for he took the full of the moon as a signal to write. On her part, Fanny strictly observed what he called her "Law of the Medes and Persians." She never wrote to anyone unless she received a letter; she always responded; she returned the same quantity of paper received.

John Mitchell Kemble

"Very clever, very confident, very wayward . . . few . . . had so much the making of a great man in him," one of his friends wrote of John

M. Kemble (1807-57). The mercurial "Jacky," as he was commonly called, was indeed a bundle of brains, energy, industry, eloquence, and, as a young man, flippancy. He matriculated at Trinity in 1825, threw himself zealously into a variety of extracurricular activities, and became a member of the Apostles. During his third year he spoke seventeen times at the Union and served as president during the Lent term. To the dismay of his sister Fanny, he espoused any and all liberal causes. Set books were neglected for political essays and newspapers. Jacky preferred James Mill to Paley, and Coleridge to Locke; and he emerged from a tripos examination boasting gleefully that he had seized the occasion "to crumple up that sciolist Paley," a university "favorite son" theologian. Perhaps he had, but at the cost of having his degree withheld for one year.

Kemble, a pupil at Bury St. Edmunds when FitzGerald entered the school, possessed the histrionic powers of his family. "I never heard such capital declamation as *his* Hotspur and Alexander's Feast, when we were at Bury together," FitzGerald once wrote, and later said that "one of the finest pieces of acting he ever saw" was Jacky's Hotspur in *Henry IV*, given at the school.

After failing to take a degree in 1829, Kemble spent several months in Germany but was summoned home the following spring, no doubt because of his father's financial reverses at Covent Garden Theater. Jacky was compelled to abandon his original plan to read law and returned to Cambridge to receive his degree and prepare to enter the Church. His heart was not in his new role and summer found him with other Apostles in Spain engaged in the Torrijos Expedition, the nineteenth-century version of the twentieth-century Lincoln Brigade action. The following year he returned to Cambridge, ostensibly to prepare for the Church but actually to qualify for a living which would provide time and means to pursue the study of philology, a subject to which he had been attracted while in Germany. At Cambridge he laid the foundation of a brilliant career as an Anglo-Saxon scholar. Jacob Grimm, with whom he corresponded and whom he visited at Göttingen in 1834 and 1835, described the young scholar as "very learned."

In 1836 Kemble became editor of the *British and Foreign Review; or European Quarterly Journal.* Shortly afterward, in September, he married Natalie Wendt, daughter of a professor of philosophy at Göttingen. The "British and Foreign" ceased publication in 1844! but, in 1840, Jacky had succeeded his father as Examiner of Plays. As late as 1844 Fanny described her brother's marriage as happy, but Kemble and his wife subsequently became estranged. In 1847 he was living with his son and two daughters in a small cottage near Cassiobury, Herts. The following year he established residence in Hannover for the purpose of obtaining a divorce through German courts. During his absence Donne served in his place as Examiner of Plays. Kemble published two books in 1849, one of them his meritorious *Saxons in England*; his next major work was not published until 1857, the year of his death.

Kemble returned to England in May, 1855, and for a year his prospects were bright. He was promised support for three projected major studies and, FitzGerald reported, thought that "the World was beginning to comprehend him." Too late. While in Dublin to deliver a lecture before the Royal Irish Academy in 1857, he was stricken with pneumonia and died March 26. One daughter, Mildred, married W. B. Donne's son, Charles Edward; the other, Gertrude, became the wife of Charles Santley, concert and opera baritone.

FitzGerald was also acquainted with Kemble's younger brother Henry, who had attended Bury while FitzGerald was at school and later entered the army. For notes on a portion of his career, refer to the letter to John Allen of May 21, 1830, n.5.

Samuel Laurence

FitzGerald appears to have made the acquaintance of Samuel Laurence (1812-84), the Victorian portrait painter, in 1838. They may have been introduced by James Spedding, who studied art in London after taking his degree and possibly became acquainted with Laurence at that time. At any rate, Spedding was one of Laurence's most intimate friends. "He is one of the men of whom you feel certain that they will never tire you, and never do anything which you will wish they had not done," Spedding wrote. He concluded his description of the artist by quoting Peacock's *Headlong Hall*:

> Nature had but little clay
> Like that of which she moulded him.

Laurence, a native of Guildford, Surrey, exhibited his first portraits at the Society of British Artists, Suffolk Street, in 1834. Two years later he sent three portraits to the Royal Academy. FitzGerald, attracted to Laurence as a man from their first meeting, appears to have recognized in him an artist of promise. He commissioned Laurence to paint an oil portrait of John Allen, which was completed in September,

1838. The Laurence portrait of Alfred Tennyson, original of the frontispiece in Hallam Tennyson's memoir of his father, was another early commission from FitzGerald. As a result of FitzGerald's zeal in advancing his friend's career, others of his friends and several members of his family sat for the artist.

Thomas Carlyle was among the many prominent Victorians whose portraits Laurence painted. Others were Dickens, Browning, Lord Ashburton, Sir Henry Taylor, F. D. Maurice, Trollope, J. A. Froude, and George Grote. In 1854 Laurence visited the United States, where James Russell Lowell was one of his subjects. While in Cambridge the artist was the guest of Longfellow. The Americans preferred Laurence's crayon portraits to his oils. FitzGerald also preferred his work in crayon and frequently questioned the merit of Laurence's theories of color, formulated after a study of the Old Masters during a visit to Italy early in his career. "He can draw," FitzGerald once wrote, "but he never could, never can, and never will colour." Advice and frank criticism, never heeded, appear frequently in FitzGerald's letters to the artist. Suggestions were not restricted to technique. Once, when Laurence was about to leave for the Lake Country, FitzGerald cautioned him that if he painted Hartley Coleridge, he should "put him not only in a good light, but to leeward of you in a strong current of air."

Laurence did not exhibit at Suffolk Street after 1853 but continued to enter his work at the exhibition of the Royal Academy until 1882. In the National Portrait Gallery at present are nine of his oil paintings, including the early Tennyson and an unfinished head of Thackeray, and nine of his chalk drawings. The National Gallery in Edinburgh has a head of Carlyle in crayon.

Posterity is deeply indebted to Laurence. It was he, not Thackeray as FitzGerald later mistakenly recalled, who introduced Old Fitz to Carlyle in 1842 while the historian was preparing to write his work on Oliver Cromwell. The results of the meeting form a fascinating and amusing chapter in the FitzGerald correspondence.

James Russell Lowell

It was not the fault of James Russell Lowell that he and FitzGerald never met. He tried. So did FitzGerald. Repeated attempts, however, produced only repeated failures.

FitzGerald esteemed Lowell as a literary critic and, it may be said, communicated with him indirectly for a year by discussing his essays in letters to Charles Eliot Norton. Lowell "responded" in January, 1877, by sending a copy of his *Three Memorial Poems*, just published, a gift promptly acknowledged. The following June Lowell was appointed American Minister to Spain in recognition of the years he had devoted to poetry, to social and political criticism in prose and verse, and to active participation in politics. Tenure as Professor of Belles Lettres at Harvard had provided him with marked if not rare qualifications for a diplomatic appointee—a knowledge of the language and literature of the nation to which he was accredited. Before his departure for Madrid, via England, he wrote to propose a day's visit with FitzGerald at Woodbridge. Lowell spent less than a week in London; and FitzGerald's reply, delayed in delivery, did not reach him until he was about to leave for the Continent. "I shall still hope to see you . . . some day when I am passing through England," wrote Lowell before his departure. Two years later, while planning his itinerary for a leave of absence to be spent in America, he again proposed to "run down" to Woodbridge, but his wife was taken with a severe attack of typhus and he was compelled to forego the trip.

In January, 1880, Lowell was named Minister to Great Britain. In September and again in the summer of 1881 he repeated his offer to make the seventy-five-mile journey to Woodbridge. To all the proposals FitzGerald responded in the same vein: "Let it not be for the 'few hours' only which you speak of but a few days rather." When Lowell wrote in 1881, FitzGerald was entertaining Kerrich nieces at Little Grange. "Oh, my dear Sir," he replied, "come if you will some future day when, if you care to see my ancient Self at all, you can see somewhat more of it than in that hurried Handshake of Welcome and Adieu! It would really weigh upon me—the idea of your coming all this way, with so little time as you have to spare."

Time for a longer visit was beyond Lowell's control. "It is one of my great regrets that I never saw him, one of my most poignant that he may have thought me neglectful," Lowell wrote later. "I was so overwhelmed with bothers, Irish and other, so bewilderingly busy with duties official and social, that I could never find time to visit him at Woodbridge, and the state of Mrs. Lowell's health was such that I could not, most of the time, ask him to make his home with me, if by some rare chance he came to London."

Charles Merivale

"C. Merivale, Dean of Ely, Roman Historian; a man of infinite dry humour, and quaint fancy. . . . I have known him from College days, fifty years ago; but have never read his History," wrote FitzGerald of Charles Merivale (1808-93) to James Russell Lowell in 1878. In his brief account FitzGerald omitted one of his friend's claims to fame. He was a pioneer in the infant sport of rowing at Cambridge and helped to organize, and rowed in, the first Oxford-Cambridge boat race held at Henley in 1829. Of the match, "The less I say about it, the better," Merivale wrote. He was a member of the Apostles and was described by "Jacky" Kemble as "the kindest hearted and one of the mildest of scoffers." On the genealogical table which Merivale drew up for his autobiography he noted:

> Of all our Elders here assorted,
> Not one was hanged nor one transported.

Merivale matriculated at St. John's College in 1826 after spending eighteen months at the East India College at Haileybury in preparation for civil service in India. As that course of study drew to a close, he decided that he preferred the life of a scholar to that of a government official. His place at Haileybury was taken by John Lawrence, who, according to Merivale, "became the main instrument in defending the Empire" at the time of the Sepoy Mutiny. "And," Merivale recorded, "thus it was that I saved India."

Merivale's ambition at Cambridge was to become a Fellow of his college to justify his transfer from Haileybury. He held a fellowship at St. John's from 1833 to 1849. His long residence at Cambridge was terminated when he was appointed to a living in 1848. "I am not destined to rot at Great Snoring [Norfolk]," he wrote to W. B. Donne. "On the contrary, I have had the offer of, and accepted, Lawford, a parish near Manningtree, in Essex, on the railway between Ipswich and Colchester." There FitzGerald visited him a number of times. In 1850 Merivale married Judith Frere, youngest sister of his close friend John Frere and a niece of Serjeant William Frere, Master of Downing College.

"A better book . . . never blessed a generation of schoolmasters and schoolboys," one literary historian wrote of Merivale's *Fall of the Roman Republic*. Merivale's chief work, however, is *The History of the Romans Under the Empire*, published in seven volumes between 1850 and 1864. In 1869 Gladstone offered him the Professorship of Modern History at Cambridge, which Merivale refused. The chair was offered to James Spedding the same year; he, too, declined the appointment. In November Gladstone notified Merivale that he had been selected as Dean of Ely, a post he readily accepted. There is a tradition that, for his first sermon at the Cathedral, Merivale took as his text, "From henceforth let no man trouble me."

After Merivale's marriage in 1850 the two friends did not meet until a chance encounter at Lowestoft brought them together again in 1871. They met a number of times subsequently during Merivale's vacation visits there.

Richard Monckton Milnes, First Baron Houghton

One despairs of doing justice to the enigma that was Richard Monckton Milnes (1809-85), whose personality is aptly described by James Pope-Hennessy as "sparkling" and "fitful." His contemporaries devised many epithets to describe him. To the Carlyles he was "a Robin Redbreast," and to another friend, "the Bird of Paradox." Sydney Smith called him "The Cool of the Evening," because, Emerson wrote, "he is so entirely at Home everywhere, and takes life so quietly"; but Fanny Kemble declared that his "serene self-satisfaction and smiling self-sufficiency" during his heyday suggested the phrase. Milnes appears as Mr. Vavasour in Disraeli's *Tancred*, a characterization which, for its acid quality, may appropriately be called an etching. The portrait, though distorted, is not unlike. Vavasour is a man of "catholic sympathies and eclectic turn of mind," qualities that prevented Milnes, despite genuine gifts, from attaining greatness in his chosen fields, literature and politics. Disraeli also focused on the breakfasts for which Milnes was famous. "Whatever your creed, class or country, one might almost say your character, you were a welcome guest at his matutinal meal, provided you were celebrated. . . . He liked to know everybody who was known. . . . He was also of the opinion that everyone who was known ought to know him. . . . His life was a gyration of energetic curiosity. . . ."

Milnes, however, was a worthier man in life than in Disraeli's fiction. He could laugh at himself, and did so when friends twitted him with the fact that the benches in the House of Commons quickly emptied when he rose to speak. He sat in the House from 1837 until he was raised to the peerage in 1863, first as a Conservative, then as a Whig, but liberal always. After the publication of one of his volumes of poems, Carlyle advised him to "try prose"; to which Milnes responded, "Poetry is so convenient for veiling the commonplace!" Emerson described him as "the most good-natured man in England . . . fat, easy, affable, and obliging."

As the first editor of Keats, Milnes in 1848 brought that poet out of limbo; but the aid he freely gave to living authors was even more praiseworthy. Francis Espinasse asserts that he "was among the first to recognize and proclaim Carlyle's genius." In 1839, the year before the first English edition of Emerson's *Essays* appeared, he wrote the first review of the American's work to be published in England. He was always ready to help young and struggling authors. "Milnes made it his business to be kind," wrote Henry Adams. With all this, he was also a lover of gossip and a raconteur of coarse and ribald stories. Moreover, "his erotic collection of books, engravings, etc.," according to Swinburne, was "unrivalled upon earth."

Although FitzGerald was a contemporary of Milnes at Cambridge, he told James Russell Lowell that he "never indeed was very intimate with him; but always found him a good-natured, unaffected man." Between 1833 and 1844 he published seven volumes of poetry. In these FitzGerald found little to praise. Their interest in literature and the many friends they had in common linked the two men. Milnes was one of the correspondents to whom FitzGerald, in the closing years of his life, sent an annual letter.

Major Edward Moor

FitzGerald had a boyhood hero in the person of Major Edward Moor (1771-1848), a family friend who had served in the army in India. Upon retiring in 1806, the major settled at Bealings House, Great Bealings, about two miles west of Woodbridge and the same distance from FitzGerald's early home at Bredfield. While living at Bredfield the FitzGeralds took Christmas dinner each year at Bealings House and entertained the Moors each New Year's Day. FitzGerald formed a deep and lasting affection for the kindly Moor. "When you see my dear Major, give him my love," is a characteristic message in the letters. When Moor died in 1848, FitzGerald wrote, "He has not left a better man behind him."

In 1782, when only eleven years of age, Edward Moor went out to Madras as a cadet. He mastered the native tongue and served with such distinction that he was commissioned lieutenant at the age of seventeen. Wounded in action in 1790, he was cited for gallantry and ordered home on sick leave. He married Elizabeth Lynn, daughter of a Woodbridge surgeon, in 1794 and returned to India with the rank of captain two years later.

After his retirement and return to Suffolk in 1806, he established a reputation as an Orientalist by publication of *The Hindu Pantheon*, *Oriental Fragments*, and other books on Eastern subjects. For half a century *The Hindu Pantheon* was recognized as the only authoritative work in English on ancient Hindu deities.

Major Moor should not be credited with stimulating FitzGerald's interest in Persian, as he has been by some. His field was principally Indian culture and languages. Moreover, FitzGerald was not persuaded to study Persian until after his old friend's death. FitzGerald took a keen interest in one of the major's books, *Suffolk Words and Phrases*, a five-hundred-page dictionary of provincialisms published in 1823. For a time FitzGerald considered combining that work with *The Vocabulary of East Anglia* published in 1830 by the Reverend Robert Forby of Hincham, Norfolk, "taking the more accurate Forby for groundwork, to be illustrated with Major Moor's delightful Suffolk Humour, and adding the Sea Phrases in which both are wanting." FitzGerald's glossary was anticipated by one published in 1866 by John G. Nall in *Great Yarmouth and Lowestoft*. As a result, FitzGerald's venture shrank to a series of vocabularies, "Sea Words and Phrases Along the Suffolk Coast," published in December issues of the *East Anglian Notes and Queries* between 1868 and 1870.

Major Moor's daughter Charlotte married William Page Wood, Lord Hatherley, who became Lord Chancellor and with whom FitzGerald was also acquainted. The major died in the Wood house in Westminster, February 26, 1848. FitzGerald wrote a few years later, ". . . somehow all of us in our corner of Suffolk knew something of him; and so again loved something of him. For there was nothing at all about him not to be beloved."

Savile Morton

"My wild Irishman," FitzGerald's epithet for Savile Morton (1811-52), accurately described the man. Brilliant, charming, unstable, improvident, and amatory, Morton was the delight and the despair of his friends, many of whom were FitzGerald's intimates. Morton and four brothers, members of a wealthy family of County Cavan, had all attended Cambridge. Savile matriculated at Trinity, became an Apostle, and in 1834 took his degree as twenty-second Wrangler.

His father died soon afterward, and it was discovered that the estate was heavily encumbered, leaving the family in straitened circumstances. Morton nevertheless traveled frequently in Italy, often in the company of Frederick Tennyson; his economy appears to have been involved and precarious. "My receipts all have been from Feb. 42, out of my own Estate Fifty-five Pounds, Thirty-seven from Frederick [Tennyson], Ten from my Mother and Thirty from you," Savile wrote to FitzGerald in September, 1842. "From that time to the present all the money I have finger'd is Forty Pounds sent me by Pierce [his oldest brother] about six months ago." It would seem that, with reasonable care, Morton should have managed to live comfortably on his £172: two years later Frederick, Arthur, and Septimus Tennyson supported themselves satisfactorily in Italy on eight shillings a day.

While in Italy in 1841 Morton decided to take up painting "in good earnest" but, FitzGerald wrote, "as elsewhere he was unable to settle down to any regular or continuous Practice of Study; and becoming weary of the Pencil that exacted it, he returned to England to see what might be done with the Pen." Morton became foreign correspondent for the *Daily News* when it was founded in January, 1846, and represented the paper at Constantinople, Athens, Madrid, Vienna, and Berlin.

Savile's "quite conscientious habit" of considering every woman fair game was a matter of deep concern to his friends. Thackeray wrote that Morton was "*shocking* about women," and that when he was attracted to one, "He lusts after her and leaves her." When FitzGerald censured him, Morton "really felt *hurt*" at his harshness. Remonstrance failed to produce reform. "Poor Elizabeth's story is sad," FitzGerald once told Frederick Tennyson. "Morton found her innocent and religious. What can he do to make her amends?" There is no evidence that he did anything to make amends. Retribution caught up with him in 1852 while he was serving in Paris as correspondent for the *Morning Advertiser*. He engaged in an intrigue with the wife of Harold Elyott Bower, representative of the *Morning Post*, whom Morton had known while at Cambridge. Mrs. Bower suspected her husband of infidelity, and, after a child was born to her in September, 1852, taunted him with the avowal that Morton was the father of the infant. Morton, who had been welcomed in the home by husband as well as wife, was in an adjoining room at the time. Bower, snatching up a knife, sought him out, and, when Morton tried to flee, stabbed him in the neck, killing him. Bower escaped to England but returned voluntarily to stand trial. The jury acquitted him after deliberating "about three minutes." Mrs. Bower returned to England and went into mourning for her dead lover. "Didn't he die in character?" FitzGerald asked Spring Rice.

"Morton often writes to me; and very good his letters are all of them," FitzGerald wrote. When Savile was in need of funds in 1844, FitzGerald transcribed portions of his correspondence into an article, hoping to place them in *Fraser's Magazine* "and bring the writer £10." More than two years later, through Thackeray, the article was submitted successively to *Fraser's* and *Blackwood's Magazine* to raise money for "poor Elizabeth." *Fraser's* rejected the manuscript and *Blackwood's* lost it. So convinced was FitzGerald of the merit of Morton's letters that, thirty years later, he tried to induce Frederick Pollock, W. B. Donne, and Charles Eliot Norton in turn to find a market for a second article made up from the remainder. He again met with failure. The manuscript is among FitzGerald's papers at Trinity College Library and bears the title, "Fragments of some Letters from an ill-starred Man of Genius."

Writers on Morton have commonly misspelled his name "Saville," and Thomas Wright in his *Life of FitzGerald* confuses him with his brother Pierce. Wright also includes a description of Morton among the "Pen Portraits" he erroneously attributes to FitzGerald.

Charles Eliot Norton

Charles Eliot Norton's acumen coupled with warmth of personality kindled spontaneous companionship upon acquaintance. During a decade spent abroad at intervals between 1849, three years after his graduation from Harvard, and 1873, he came to know many of Britain's intellectual elite. One of his first British friends was John Ruskin; one of the last was Thomas Carlyle. These two, with Edward Burne-Jones and Norton formed the cast in a dramatic sequence of events that brought about the identification of FitzGerald as the anonymous translator of the *Rubáiyát* thirteen years after the poem was published.

The ensuing friendship between FitzGerald and Norton was initiated and sustained solely through correspondence.

Burne-Jones, an intimate friend of both Ruskin's and Norton's, in 1863 lent Ruskin one of the copies of the *Rubáiyát* that Swinburne had bought at Quaritch's penny box in 1861. Ruskin was so impressed that he left with the artist a note of praise to be sent to the translator if and when he was identified. In the autumn of 1868, Norton also first read the poem at the home of Burne-Jones. He spent the next three years on the Continent, during which period Burne-Jones heard that the translator was a "Reverend Edward FitzGerald" who lived "somewhere in Norfolk and was fond of boating." This he reported to Norton on his return to England in 1872, and Norton repeated the rumor to Carlyle while discussing the poem with him shortly afterward. Although FitzGerald had never told Carlyle of the work, Carlyle immediately fixed upon him as the translator. Norton relayed the information to Burne-Jones, and, through Norton and Carlyle in turn, the note left in his care reached FitzGerald.

On his return to America in 1857, Norton had entered upon a literary career, contributing essays and reviews to the *Atlantic Monthly*, recently established with his friend James Russell Lowell as editor. In 1864 the two became editors of the *North American Review*, to which, in October, 1869, Norton contributed the first thorough critique of the *Rubáiyát*. He never told FitzGerald of the essay, despite the fact that his part in identifying the translator resulted in an "epistolary friendship," as Norton described it. Their active exchange of letters did not begin until December, 1875, when, through Carlyle, Norton requested a copy of *Agamemnon*. Norton was directly responsible for FitzGerald's polishing and printing in 1880 and 1881 *The Downfall and Death of King Oedipus*, his adaptation of Sophocles' *Oedipus Tyrannus* and *Oedipus Coloneus*, kept in manuscript since the printing of *Agamemnon* in 1869.

Norton was appointed Professor of the History of Fine Arts at Harvard in 1875. His invitations to visit Shady Hill, his home in Cambridge, elicited from FitzGerald a characteristic reply: "It is all too late for that." Norton urged Lowell to seek out FitzGerald while in England in 1887 en route to Madrid as United States Minister to Spain. Lowell failed in the attempt, but his efforts to arrange a meeting opened a new correspondence. FitzGerald's letters to the two Americans contain sustained passages of his best literary criticism garnished with entertaining reminiscence and literary gossip.

Perry Nursey

Fame ignored Perry Nursey (1771-1840), a man of varied talents who, during FitzGerald's youth, lived at Little Bealings, not far from Bredfield. Marriage to a woman with considerable means enabled him to abandon his profession, surgery, settle in Bealings, and devote himself to painting. Under his care the gardens at The Grove were noted for their beauty, and Nursey is sometimes identified as a landscape architect or landscape "gardener." It is also recorded that he was an accomplished violinist.

Evidence that Nursey held artists in high esteem is found in names given five of his children: Poussin Hazard, Claude Lorraine, Richard Wilson, Fontaine Lavinia, Rosalba Violante, and Marietta Syrani. Among his friends was Sir David Wilkie, R.A., who sometimes visited at The Grove. Robert, Nursey's eldest son, became engaged to Wilkie's sister but died shortly before the marriage was to take place. Two of Nursey's sons became artists, though one, Perry, after a promising start turned his back on art and entered the Church. The youngest son, Claude Lorraine, studied at the Royal Academy and, later, under Wilkie in his studio. He subsequently became headmaster of an art school. Lithographs of some of his pictures have become collectors' items.

Nursey sold The Grove about 1824 and, in 1833 was declared bankrupt, which may account for FitzGerald's frequent reference to him as "poor Nursey." He was not, however, reduced to indigence. After living for a number of years near Ipswich, he moved to 3 Broadley Terrace, London, where he died in January, 1840.

FitzGerald, who owned a few of Nursey's pictures and a great number of his sketches, was convinced that he had genuine talent. From London he once wrote to Bernard Barton, "There is as genuine a feeling of Nature in one of Nursey's sketches as in the Rubenses and Claudes here; and if that is evident, and serves to cherish and rekindle one's own sympathy with the world about one, the great end is accomplished." There is evidence that FitzGerald's admiration was justified. "That man could paint," declared a Bond Street art dealer to whom FitzGerald showed some of Nursey's pictures. It is unfortunate that FitzGerald merely entertained, but did not carry out, a proposal to enter one of Nursey's paintings, "The Wave," in exhibitions of works of Old Masters held in London in 1872.

FitzGerald's regard for the Nursey family never diminished. In a letter to Marietta, written in 1867, he declared, "Indeed, if Perry had stuck to Painting, he would have made a Fortune by the finished style of Painting which is so much admired in England." At his death FitzGerald left Marietta an annuity of £30.

William Frederick Pollock

Personal Remembrances, published by Sir William Frederick Pollock (1815-88), suggests that Frederick, the name by which he was generally known, was unduly impressed by rank and fame. However, his attachment to FitzGerald, who lacked both, was deep and genuine. Pollock was one of the few friends busily engaged in careers who wrote to FitzGerald freely and without prompting. The earliest extant letter to him is dated July 20, 1839; the last May 31, 1883, only a fortnight before FitzGerald's death. In the course of his extremely active social life, he constantly encountered FitzGerald's friends "of the old days" and passed on news about them. Meetings with Spedding, Thompson, Alfred Tennyson, Donne, Venables, Milnes, Merivale, Garden, the Proctors, Laurence, and others are frequently noted in Pollock's diary. In May, 1872, he spent two days with FitzGerald in Woodbridge.

Pollock entered Trinity in 1832 and became intimate with Spring Rice, who probably introduced him to FitzGerald on one of the latter's visits to Cambridge. After taking his degree in 1836, Pollock read law at the Inner Temple and was admitted to the bar in 1838. In 1846 he became a Master of the Court of Exchequer, in which his father was Chief Baron, and in 1874, Queen's Remembrancer. Pollock senior was created baronet on his retirement in 1866, and Frederick succeeded to the title in 1870.

A man of wide cultural interests, Pollock numbered among his friends many of the leaders in literature, art, and the theater. He was an intimate friend of William Macready, served as one of his executors, and edited his *Reminiscences*, with selections from his diaries and letters. In 1854 Pollock published a blank verse translation of Dante's *Divine Comedy*.

When FitzGerald died, Pollock wrote to George Crabbe of Merton, "It was indeed, as you say—a noble character combined with a singularly delicate humour—and an extraordinary fine feeling in all that belongs to literature and art—courteous and thoroughly unselfish."

Pollock's grandfather, saddler to George III, produced remarkable progeny. Jonathan, Frederick's father, was not only an eminent jurist but also an active member of The Royal Society. Jonathan's brother David became Chief Justice of the Supreme Court of Bombay and was knighted in 1846. Another brother, George, entered the service of the East India Company and, after a distinguished military career, was created Field Marshal in 1870; he became a baronet two years later. Pollock's son Frederick also became a famous jurist. His correspondence with Justice Oliver Wendell Holmes of the Supreme Court of the United States was one of the major publications of 1941.

Bernard Quaritch

"I am delighted at the glory E.F.G. has gained by his translation of the Rubáiyát of Omar Khayyám," wrote W. B. Donne in 1876. ". . . and Bernard Quaritch deserves a piece of plate or a statue for the way he has thrust the Rubáiyát to the front."

There is no doubt that Donne made a valid point. Quaritch (1819-99) was helpful to FitzGerald during their long association, first as book dealer, later as publisher. It is equally true, of course, that Quaritch did not lose on their transactions, although his profits were probably modest.

In 1842, at the age of twenty-three, Quaritch, a native of Saxony, settled in London after spending eight years as a clerk in bookshops in Nordhausen and Berlin. He obtained employment with Henry Bohn, London's leading dealer in second-hand books at the time and later publisher of the famous Bohn Libraries series. Quaritch recorded that he once told his employer, "Mr. Bohn, you are the first bookseller in England, I mean to become the first bookseller in Europe." The young man's words were no idle boast, for he achieved and his firm has maintained front rank among book dealers of the world. In 1847 he founded his own business at 16 Castle Street, Leicester Square, and in 1860 moved his shop to 15 Piccadilly.

FitzGerald first traded with Quaritch as a book dealer about the year 1853. When the *Rubáiyát* was printed early in 1859, Quaritch agreed to be identified on the title page as the publisher and to place the booklet on sale at his shop. Two hundred and fifty copies were printed at FitzGerald's expense. The story, often repeated, that the translator kept forty copies, carried the remainder to 16 Castle Street, and "dropped" them on the counter as a "present" to the book dealer is refuted by letters to Quaritch dated March 31 and April 5, 1859.

Quaritch's imprint appears in six of FitzGerald's publications, but only four of them were actually published by him: the *Rubáiyát*, third edition; *Rubáiyát*, fourth edition, combined with *Salámán and Absál*, third edition; *Agamemnon*; and *Readings in Crabbe*. Quaritch suggested publication of the third edition of the *Rubáiyát*, and from February to December, 1868, repeatedly petitioned FitzGerald for permission to publish the fourth. The translator consented to the last only on condition that *Salámán and Absál* be included in the volume. Quaritch also initiated publication of *Agamemnon*, previously issued privately. A brisk trade with American buyers was chiefly responsible for his zeal for publication.

Although vexed at times by what he considered Quaritch's questionable taste in "puffing" his books by various means and, on occasion, identifying him as the author, FitzGerald regarded Quaritch more as a friend than as a businessman to be dealt with impersonally. In 1876 he invited him to Woodbridge "to sail in my Great Ship." Quaritch, too, urged FitzGerald to visit him at his home in Hampstead. Neither accepted the other's invitation.

After FitzGerald's death Quaritch and Aldis Wright contended for the right to publish FitzGerald's collected works. A compromise was reached, though not to Quaritch's advantage. With Houghton, Mifflin and Company, he published an edition in America in 1887. The two volumes were dedicated "To the American People, whose early Appreciation of the Genius of Edward FitzGerald was the chief Stimulant of that Curiosity by which his Name was drawn from its anonymous Concealment and advanced to the Position of Honour which it now holds." Wright's first edition of the *Letters and Literary Remains*, in three volumes, appeared in 1889.

Frederick Spalding

When the Third Suffolk Rifle Corps of the militia was formed at Woodbridge in 1860, FitzGerald abandoned his customary indifference to civic matters. From the outset he was one of the company's most loyal supporters and benefactors. Participation as a patron of the unit led to acquaintance with Frederick Spalding, one of the first recruits, who gained the rank of ensign and served as secretary of the corps. Spalding, twenty-five years old when the two men met, was employed as a clerk on one of the quays at nearby Melton. His extra-mercantile interests included books, coins, pictures, birds, and Celts—a range of avocations and knowledge that made him a welcome guest at Market Hill and Little Grange. In exchange for entertainment and the companionship of a social superior, Spalding willingly relieved FitzGerald of a burden of routine chores and took over the role of companion-factotum. Each man was grateful for what the other contributed to the alliance.

It is evident that Spalding was an excellent clerk although it is difficult to discover among his talents any promise of business ability. In such matters FitzGerald was prone to be uncritical when friendship was involved. In 1862 he lent Spalding £500 to set up as a coal, grain, and building-supply merchant at Melton. In March, 1868, FitzGerald burned the note for the loan and a month later, Spalding recorded in his diary, told him that he need pay no further interest on the indebtedness because "£7.10. half-yearly made no difference to him, but might to me in my little business."

Spalding required more than money to succeed, and in 1876 the venture ended in bankruptcy. "I cannot learn that his Future is yet provided for," FitzGerald wrote to one of Spalding's acquaintances. "If he could muster sufficient Capital, he would do best in a Curiosity Shop; or (without Capital) as an assistant, if not Chief, at some Museum. He has really accurate knowledge, as well as Taste and Liking, in such matters."

"My dear old Fitz is always right about men," Thackeray had declared many years before. In 1885, after employment at Hadleigh, Suffolk, and at Cambridge, Spalding was appointed curator of the Castle Museum at Colchester, Essex, the site of one of the earliest and most important Roman settlements in Britain. The museum is noted for its collection of Roman antiquities. Spalding held the post until 1901, the year before his death.

James Spedding

"He was the wisest man I have ever known: not the less so for plenty of the Boy in him: a great sense of Humour, a Socrates in Life and in Death," FitzGerald said of James Spedding (1808-81), who shared with W. B. Donne FitzGerald's "oldest and deepest love." Caryle called Spedding "one of the best of men."

FitzGerald and Spedding met at the Grammar School at Bury St.

Edmunds, where both prepared for Cambridge. Spedding's father, a retired army officer of means whose home was Mirehouse on Bassenthwaite Lake, Cumberland, changed his residence to Bury while John, James, and Edward, three of his four sons, were enrolled at the school. James, or "Jem," as FitzGerald frequently called him, was at the head of his class the last three years he spent at Bury, 1825-27.

At Trinity College Spedding became one of the Apostles and was beloved by members and non-members as well for qualities which set him apart through life—a keen and open mind, tolerance, wisdom, and a genuine appreciation of his fellows, whatever their talents. He seems to have impressed all with whom he came in contact by his poise and singular maturity of manner. When William Wordsworth visited Cambridge in December, 1830, Spedding was on sufficiently intimate terms with his "fellow Laker" to entertain him in his rooms at Trinity. There can be no doubt that the poet was a willing guest, for he talked freely and did not leave his host and the five undergraduate guests until almost two in the morning. During these years Spedding was also acquainted with Robert Southey and was on terms of easy companionship with Hartley Coleridge.

After he took his degree in 1831, Spedding spent most of the next four years in Cambridge, hoping to be appointed Fellow of Trinity. He attended an art school in London for several months in 1833, and a portrait sketch of FitzGerald, which he drew in May of that year, is now in the Fitzwilliam Museum. He failed to receive the fellowship he sought; however, he held an honorary fellowship from 1872 until his death. He refused a professorship of modern history at Cambridge in 1869 (also offered to and refused by Charles Merivale) and an honorary degree in 1874. From 1835 to 1841 he served in the Colonial Office as assistant to Henry (later Sir Henry) Taylor at a salary of £150 a year. Thanks to independent means, Spedding was not compelled to live in penury. Until 1867 he occupied rooms in Lincoln's Inn Fields. When he entered the Colonial Office, he expected, in time, to be assigned to some recognized post. However, the experience of his postgraduate years at Cambridge was repeated: no permanent appointment was offered him, so he resigned in 1841. The following year he went to the United States as Secretary of the historic commission headed by Lord Ashburton. In 1847, the office of Under Secretary of State, commanding a salary of £2,000, was offered to him by Lord Grey, but Spedding rejected the appointment. His ambition and activity had been diverted into other channels.

Spedding's interest in the personality and career of Francis Bacon, originating during his undergraduate years, had increased during the intervening period, and the research he pursued in leisure time revealed to him the inadequacies of published collections of Bacon's correspondence. He determined to prepare a new edition. His original plan expanded, with the result that he devoted thirty-three years of his life to editing the letters and works and writing the biography of the Elizabethan jurist. The first volumes were published in 1857; the last in 1874.

Despite the fact that Spedding produced the standard edition of Bacon's works, FitzGerald deeply regretted that his friend had devoted his life to re-editing that "which did not need such re-edition, and to vindicate his Character which could not be cleared." Time and again FitzGerald urged "Jem" to apply his time and talents to the plays of Shakespeare. "I never heard him read a page but he threw new light on it," FitzGerald wrote. Spedding did, in fact, play an active part in the nineteenth-century interpretation and correction of Shakespeare's plays.

Spedding was an excellent scholar, a gracious host, a thoroughly agreeable companion, a gentle man, and a gentleman. When he was fatally injured by a cab in March, 1881, FitzGerald wrote of him, "*My dear* old Spedding . . . lives—his old Self—in my heart of hearts . . . he is but the same that he was from a Boy—all that is best in Head and Heart—a man that would be incredible had one not known him."

Stephen Spring Rice

Among friendships FitzGerald formed on visits to Cambridge in years immediately after taking his degree was that with Stephen Spring Rice (1814-65), son of Thomas Spring Rice of Mt. Trenchard, County Limerick, at the time M.P. for the town of Cambridge and Under-Secretary for Home Affairs. Stephen matriculated at Trinity in 1832 but appears to have left the University without a degree to become private secretary to his father, who, from 1835 to 1839 served as Chancellor of the Exchequer. In the latter year Spring Rice, senior, retired from public life and was created Baron Monteagle. One of his last official acts was to submit the Penny Postage Bill to the House of Commons.

In recollections of their early friendship, FitzGerald recalled evenings spent in Spring Rice's rooms over Bacon's tobacco shop on Market Hill. Both were frequent guests at "musical evenings" arranged by Mrs. William Frere, wife of the Master of Downing, and held in the Lodge of that college. Mrs. Frere, who had studied voice under John Sale, himself a pupil of Handel, was "the most perfect private singer" FitzGerald ever heard. Her daughter Ellen Mary and Spring Rice were married in 1839. The Spring Rices were among the friends whose hospitality FitzGerald freely accepted. He often visited them at their home, Hither Green, Lewisham, before his marriage.

Stephen was appointed Commissioner of Customs in 1838, Deputy Chairman of the Board of Customs in 1856. During these years he often entertained friends, FitzGerald among them, on Channel cruises on a government cutter, the *Vigilante.* "I shall not forget the gallant Cutter and her merry Crew nor the delight of once more bowling before a Breeze unpolluted with Smoke, Grease, and Smut," FitzGerald told his host after a cruise in September, 1855, when they touched at Boulogne and Brighton. Through Spring Rice's influence FitzGerald succeeded in having a buoy placed to mark the shifting sandbar at the mouth of the Deben. "But really my Boy—('at last I *have* got one,' is the saying here)—is a good Boy, not only to his Parent, but to other wayfarers over the Bar," FitzGerald wrote.

Spring Rice's constitution was not robust, and ill health forced him to retire from government service in 1859. He spent the remainder of his life at Mt. Trenchard, avoiding the rigors of British winters by trips to Madeira or other southern points. He died at sea May 9, 1865, while returning from one such visit to the Mediterranean. His son Thomas succeeded to the title of Baron Monteagle on the death of Stephen's father in 1866.

FitzGerald's friend is always referred to as "Spring Rice"—Spring being the name of his mother's family. The name is frequently given as "Spring-Rice," a form that appears to have been adopted by Stephen's son.

The Tennyson Family

Alfred Tennyson

To be sure, the Alfred Tennyson (1809-92) whom FitzGerald knew was dark of complexion, often moody of manner, the "tetchy" poet sensitive to criticism, who has been limned in biographical sketches without number. However, the Tennyson who was FitzGerald's friend actually bore little resemblance to the portraits which writers, both sympathetic and hostile, have handed down to posterity. FitzGerald's Tennyson was "gipsy-like" in features and "black-blooded," a "six-footer" powerful of frame—a poet who, as a young man, hurled a heavy iron bar over a haystack at Somersby, Lincolnshire, where he was born and reared. Two "bumpkins" who stood by said that no other man in the two parishes could perform the feat. Until tamed by marriage and the Laureateship in 1850, FitzGerald's Tennyson was a thorough bohemian, utterly indifferent to the dictates of convention. To the dismay of his more decorous friends, he smoked, whenever and wherever he pleased, "the strongest and most stinking tobacco out of a small blackened old pipe on an average of nine hours every day." FitzGerald said that he smoked twelve hours out of twenty-four, and Mrs. Carlyle predicted that he would never marry, for "no woman could live in the atmosphere of tobacco-smoke which he makes from morn to night." Mrs. Carlyle was no prude on the subject of tobacco, for "Tom" was a "powerful" smoker and Jane herself smoked cigarettes.

FitzGerald's Tennyson was the Tennyson of the Cock Tavern in Fleet Street where, Spedding related, the poet's dinner one evening consisted of "two chops, one pickle, two cheeses, one pint of stout, one pot of port, and three cigars." After the meal Spedding had to take his companion's regrets to the Kembles: "he could not go because he had the influenza." For years FitzGerald's Tennyson was an aspiring poet who, having fallen afoul of hostile criticism and having suffered financial losses through an unhappy investment, became a hypochondriac. He resorted again and again to hydropathy but each time returned from his water cures to fall again into "general mismanagement," as FitzGerald termed it, smoking as before and drinking his usual bottle of port a day. FitzGerald's Tennyson was a man of humors. "Alfred Tennyson has reappeared," Spedding once wrote John Allen from London, "and is going today or tomorrow to Florence, or to Killarney, or to Madeira, or to some place where some ship is going—he does not know where." However, FitzGerald's Tennyson was a man who, throughout his life, impressed people by his independence of opinion, deep sincerity, and remarkable ingenuousness.

The friendship between "Old Alfred" and "Old Fitz," as they commonly called one another, became firmly established in 1835 when they were guests at Spedding's home in Cumberland; but evidence points to a meeting as early as 1833. After leaving Spedding's, Fitz-

Gerald wrote to offer Alfred money when he was in need of funds. In 1844 Carlyle wrote to FitzGerald that Tennyson had recently spent a day with him. "He said of you that you were a man from whom one could accept money; which was a proud saying; which you ought to thank heaven for." FitzGerald was serving as benefactor of Thackeray and the artist Samuel Laurence during the same years. One of his commissions to Laurence about 1840 was to paint the oil portrait of the poet which is now in the National Portrait Gallery.

Rebuffed by antagonistic criticism after the publication of a volume of his poems in 1832, Tennyson refused to venture again into print, despite the constant pleading of friends, FitzGerald among them. His silence was not broken until 1842 when FitzGerald "carried him off . . . with violence to Moxon." The two volumes, *Poems*, published in May, FitzGerald frequently asserted, contained "the last of Old Alfred's best." Except for an occasional poem and isolated passages, he found little to admire in Tennyson's later work and was extremely frank in criticism. "He is the same magnanimous, kindly, delightful fellow as ever; uttering by far the finest prose sayings of anyone," FitzGerald wrote Alfred's brother Frederick after the publication of *In Memoriam* in 1850. The success of the elegy to Arthur Hallam, however, proved eventful in Tennyson's career. It firmly established him as a leading poet, led to his being named Poet Laureate, and made it possible for him to marry.

FitzGerald's lack of enthusiasm for the poet's later work produced no alteration in their friendship. He spent ten days with the Tennysons at their home, Farringford, Isle of Wight, in June, 1854, and was often urged to repeat the visit. He made two efforts to comply in 1856 but was unable to fix a date when his friends were free. He refused subsequent invitations because the poet lived "on a somewhat large scale, with perpetual Visitors." On September 14, 1876, FitzGerald's housekeeper at Little Grange handed him Tennyson's calling card on which was written, "Dear Old Fitz—I am passing thro' and will call again." The last three words were crossed out and "am here" was written above. Tennyson, accompanied by his son Hallam, remained two days in Woodbridge. "We fell at once into the old Humour," said FitzGerald, "as if we had only been parted twenty Days instead of so many Years."

While preparing his volume *Tiresias, and Other Poems* for the press in 1883, Tennyson wrote a Prologue to the title poem, in which he recalled his visit of seven years before and paid tribute to the *Rubáiyát.*

FitzGerald died before the book was published. In an Epilogue, added to the selection, the poet wrote:

> The tolling of his funeral bell
> Broke on my Pagan Paradise
> . . . .
> . . . and made the rhymes,
> That miss'd his living welcome seem
> Like would-be guests an hour too late
> Who down the highway moving on
> With easy laughter find the gate
> Is bolted, and the master gone.

To Frederick Pollock, Tennyson wrote, "I had no truer friend: he was one of the kindliest of men, and I have never known one of so fine and delicate a wit."

Frederick Tennyson

Even the nooks and crannies of Somersby Rectory must have been taxed by the Tennyson menage. Besides the parents and their eleven children, the household included a staff which, at times, numbered ten. The environment and the incongruent influences of a father, "amazing sharp," and a gentle, over-indulgent mother produced boys who matured as eccentric men. Frederick (1807-98), the eldest of seven sons, was the most eccentric of all.

From Eton, where his career had been brilliant but "erratic," he proceeded to Cambridge, where he proved to be not only brilliant and erratic, but truculent as well. His neglect of attendance at chapel evoked the penalty of impositions, which he also neglected. When called before the Dean, he coolly asked why Charles Wordsworth, son of the Master of his College, Trinity, had received a lighter punishment for the same offense. His curiosity resulted in his being threatened with rustication by the Convention of the College, but Frederick is reported to have stated that there was no need to discuss the matter "as he intended to take his name off the books." Expulsion for three terms was imposed, nevertheless, and his degree was not granted until 1832.

Under pressure from his patriarchal grandfather, Frederick for a time considered entering the Church; but, "a pretty Parson I shall make, I'm thinking," he wrote. His grandfather died in 1835, however, and Frederick inherited property at Grimsby, on the Lincolnshire coast, which increased in value with the growth of the railroads and made him independent for life. He went to Italy, where he traveled frequently in the company of Savile Morton and where he made his home for almost twenty-five years. In 1839 he married Maria Giuliotti, daughter of the Chief Magistrate of Siena, and settled at Florence. A family legend has it that one of his diversions was to sit in his great hall, designed by Michael Angelo, being entertained by "his forty fiddlers." In 1859 he moved to the island of Jersey, where he lived until two years before his death in London in 1898.

There is no clue to when FitzGerald and Frederick became acquainted, but by 1839 their friendship was well established. The two had much in common. Both loved literature, music, and painting; both had independent means; and both were indifferent to the dictates of propriety. Whenever Frederick returned to England the two friends tried to meet; and FitzGerald often recalled one of their outings to Gravesend in 1843. "Really," he wrote the following year, "if these little excursions in the company of one's friends leave such a pleasant taste behind in the memory, one should court them oftener." To be sure, they always quarreled, FitzGerald noted, but "I mean quarrel in the sense of a good strenuous difference of opinion supported on either side by occasional outbursts of spleen."

FitzGerald often chaffed Frederick on his preoccupation with the occult and esoteric. "Have you settled yet whether spirit can exist separately from matter?" he asked as early as 1839. Frederick's interests included table-rapping, "spirit writing," and spiritualism. He was in turn a Swedenborgian, an Anglo-Israelite, and a member of the Church of the New Jerusalem; but before his death he returned to the Anglican faith.

Frederick visited FitzGerald a number of times in Suffolk—more often, in fact, than any other of FitzGerald's old London friends. Their final meeting took place in 1872 in Woodbridge when Frederick crossed to England from Jersey with a neighbor, a "Spiritual Medium, who has discovered the original Mystery of the Free Masons." Tennyson's friend threatened to publish an exposé, to the Masons' "total Discomforture," if they refused to buy the information. "All this old Frederic is as earnest about as a Man, or a Child, can be," FitzGerald reported.

"Tennyson, the poet," instantly identifies Alfred, but during their Somersby years six of the Tennyson boys and three of the girls busily wrote poetry. The modest reputations later established by Frederick and the second son, Charles, were overshadowed by Alfred's success.

Frederick, in 1854, published *Days and Hours*, which he had already had privately printed in Italy. Thirty-six years passed before his next volume appeared. In 1890, at the age of eighty-three, he published *The Isles of Greece*, followed in 1891 by *Daphne* and in 1895 by *Poems of the Day and Year*.

FitzGerald's esteem for the Tennysons was not restricted to Frederick and Alfred. Writing once to Frederick about a younger brother, Septimus, he said, "I have a tacit regard of the true sort for him, as I think I must have for all of the Tennyson build. I see so many little natures about that I must draw to the large, even if their faults be on the same scale as their virtues."

FitzGerald sometimes spells Frederick's name with a *k*, sometimes without; Aldis Wright drops the *k* in *Letters and Literary Remains*; the Tennysons use the *k*.

William Makepeace Thackeray

On his return to Cambridge for the Michaelmas term of 1829, FitzGerald engaged William Williams, a recent Senior Optime, to coach him in preparation for degree examinations in February. Williams had just returned from Paris where he had spent the summer as companion and tutor to another Trinity undergraduate, William Makepeace Thackeray (1811-63). Thackeray, beginning his third term at Cambridge, continued to read under Williams' guidance. The tutor introduced his two charges to each other when they met in his rooms one day early in the term.

The encounter was like contact of flint and steel. The spark of acquaintance quickly took on the glow of warm and hearty friendship. Unfortunately for FitzGerald's immediate needs, both found talking, walking, sketching, and singing rollicking songs more to their taste than poring over the books set by their course of study. Thanks partly to his own indolence, partly to Thackeray's companionship, FitzGerald obtained his degree in February by the narrowest of margins. He went to Paris and, when the Easter vacation arrived, was joined there by Thackeray, who had told Williams that he intended to spend the holiday in Huntingdonshire. The two visited museums, roamed the avenues, dined at boulevard restaurants, and talked "nonsense of all kinds." One may "listen in" on the talk in which they engaged through the medium of FitzGerald's letter of October 10, 1831. Thackeray remained at Cambridge only one term after his return. He left, his daughter Lady Ritchie recorded in the Biographical Edition, because he believed he was "wasting time upon studies which, without more success than was possible to him, would be of no use in later life." There is ample evidence that he was wasting his time; there is no evidence that he was wasting it in studying. His extracurricular activities, innocent enough in the main, included losing £1,500 to professional gamblers. In the following decade he sorely needed the friend FitzGerald proved to be.

After leaving the university Thackeray spent almost a year in Germany, and on his return to England read law for a time at the Middle Temple. In July, 1832, he came into an inheritance estimated at about £20,000. Partly through misfortune but chiefly through unfortunate speculations, he contrived to lose almost the entire patrimony in little more than a year. After a brief venture in business, he bought *The National Standard*, a weekly journal which failed thirteen months later. A large portion of his funds evaporated with the failure of a bank in India; other sums were lost at gaming tables. In December, 1833, he wrote his mother that he "ought to thank heaven for making him a poor man." His reason: "it has made me much happier than I should have been with money." Mrs. Thackeray's reply is not on record.

The young man next turned to Paris to study art, for he possessed skill at illustration and caricature. While there, he served also as correspondent for *The Constitutional and Public Ledger*, a liberal daily paper established in 1836 on whose board of directors Thackeray's stepfather, Major Henry Carmichael-Smyth, one of the founders, served as chairman. On the prospect of steady income, Thackeray married Isabella Shawe in Paris in August, 1836. *The Constitutional* failed within a year, and its Paris correspondent returned to England to begin a literary career.

FitzGerald watched the trials and reverses of his friend with anxious eyes. He wrote encouraging letters. He commissioned the apprentice artist to copy pictures for him, and, later, to illustrate his copy of Fouqué's *Undine*, which both greatly admired. He urged friends to buy Thackeray's earliest books. For a time he considered publishing a volume of Sir Roger de Coverley essays illustrated by Thackeray. Nor was all his financial aid indirect. A few weeks after marriage, Thackeray wrote from Paris, "Your two letters arrived. . . . As for the money, you have made me so used to those kinds of obligations that I don't say a word more. . . . I intend with your money to buy chairs and tables to decorate this chamber, for as yet I have only hired them." Four years later Thackeray wrote his mother from London ". . . and was it not fine of Fitz: on whom I had been obliged to spunge—yesterday I sent him some of the money back: and received a letter in return as follows 'What the devil do you mean?'—my 10£ note was enclosed in the letter."

After the birth of their third child in May, 1840, Thackeray's wife failed to recover her strength and fell into so deep a depression that she attempted suicide. For five years her husband placed her under medical care in a number of mental hospitals, hoping that she would be sufficiently restored to resume her place at home. She never recovered. "I don't care to write to my friends and pour out lamentations which are all the news I have to tell," wrote Thackeray during this period; but he unburdened his tormented mind freely in letters to FitzGerald.

By 1846 Thackeray had published two full-length novels, three books of travel, many tales, and numerous reviews and sketches. Except for the three travel books, his work had appeared in periodicals, and all had been published anonymously or under a variety of pseudonyms. Although he was known to and was accepted by the literati, he was virtually unknown to the public. With the publication of *Vanity Fair*, in numbers, during 1847 and 1848, Thackeray's literary powers were first widely recognized, and his reputation as a novelist was firmly established.

Popularity followed success. He was courted by the *beau monde* and became a social lion, rewards which afforded him supreme satisfaction. "He is become a great man I am told": FitzGerald wrote to Frederick Tennyson, "goes to Holland House and Devonshire House: and for some reason or other will not write a word to me." Within a few days FitzGerald received a long, chatty letter Thackeray had begun three months previously. "I am always yours," wrote Thackeray in closing, "and like you almost as much as I did 20 years ago. God bless you my dear old fellow."

Such passages are found in virtually every letter exchanged by the two friends—sufficient evidence to contradict the belief, widely held, that their affection for each other cooled after the novelist achieved fame. Readers who harbor that misconception should turn to the letters both wrote when Thackeray left for America in 1852. Naturally, their paths in life diverged as Thackeray became involved in his career and the whirl of life open to a successful writer, a role he loved to play. FitzGerald, on the other hand, was being more and more attracted by the quietude of Suffolk. Nevertheless, FitzGerald continued to visit the novelist on trips to London. His letters record seven separate meetings in six different years during the decade of the fifties. One evening as he sat in London lodgings in January, 1857, Thackeray "came in looking gray, grand, and good-humoured." Their final meeting took place in London a year later.

"He was a very fine Fellow. His books are wonderful," FitzGerald wrote after Thackeray's death in December, 1863. As he reread *The Newcomes*, he seemed to hear Thackeray "saying so much in it; and it seems to me as if he might be coming up my Stairs, and about to come (singing) into my Room, as in old Charlotte Street, etc., thirty years ago."

William Hepworth Thompson

One of FitzGerald's friends at Cambridge was William Hepworth Thompson (1810-86), who succeeded William Whewell as Master of Trinity. The names of the two appear often together in entries in John Allen's diary. Like FitzGerald, Thompson was shy and reserved, and perhaps each responded positively to the reticence of the other.

In contrast to FitzGerald, Thompson was ambitious for university honors and became an excellent scholar of the classics. When he took his degree in 1832, he was ranked tenth Senior Optime in mathematics and fourth in the first class in the classical tripos. Except for the year 1836, when he served as headmaster of the Collegiate School at Leicester, Thompson spent his entire professional life at Trinity. He was named Fellow in 1834 and Tutor ten years later. In 1853 he became Regius Professor of Greek, a post which carried with it, at that time, appointment as Canon of Ely. In 1866 he became Master of Trinity.

Thompson impressed many as being cold and haughty, a manner which should be attributed to his intense shyness. He was ill at ease in company. True, he was merciless when he met with vulgarity, viciousness, or pretension. "We are none of us infallible," he once observed to a Junior Fellow, "not even the youngest of us." Remarks of this kind led those who did not know him well to conclude that Thompson was temperamentally sardonic. All who needed help and sympathy, however, discovered him to be extremely kind, just, and understanding. His students revered him. "He has done himself great injustice by his singular reserve and shrinking from public show," an old friend stated when Thompson died. "It is sad to see such a character fall into the hands of those who have nothing to say of him but to repeat his jokes under the solemn name of sarcasms."

Thompson was a meticulous scholar. He published editions of Plato's *Phaedrus* in 1868 and of the *Gorgias* in 1871. Both were long accepted as standard texts of the two dialogues. His intention to publish either a complete edition or a translation of Plato came to naught, for his painstaking method of writing and editing made the project impossible. As Master of Trinity he supported many reforms in the university as well as in the college.

Richard Chenevix Trench

Every age produces men of singular merit whom indifferent posterity unjustly consigns to limbo. Richard Chenevix Trench (1807-86) is one of these. To him, as Archbishop of Dublin, fell the difficult task of reconstituting the Anglican Church in Ireland after disestablishment in 1869. When he retired, clergy and laity alike praised him for the skill, tact, and understanding he brought to bear on the problems of adjustment. He advocated a revision of the Bible as early as 1858 and was appointed to the group to revise the New Testament when the commission was established in 1870. A paper entitled "On Some Deficiencies in Our English Dictionaries," which Trench read before the Philological Society in 1857, initiated the proposal to compile the Oxford *New English Dictionary*.

Although FitzGerald and Trench were contemporaries at Trinity, they did not become acquainted until after 1836. During a tour on the Continent after taking his degree in 1829, Trench visited Spain and was one of the Apostles who joined the Torrijos expedition the following year. Ordained priest in 1833, he served in several curacies, among them that of Alverstoke, where Samuel Wilberforce was Rector. When Wilberforce became Bishop of Oxford in 1845, he appointed Trench his examining chaplain. On June 21, 1856, the *Times* prematurely announced that Trench had been offered the Bishopric of Gloucester and Bristol. "The Queen waxed wroth thereat," Donne reported, "and said, 'The *Times* should not make *her* Bishops.'" The following October Trench was appointed Dean of Westminster. "I am very glad Trench was not made a Bishop," FitzGerald wrote, "and am rather sorry he is a Dean . . . [we want] Trench to keep in his study and write us good Books. He is a fine fellow." Trench was made Archbishop of Dublin in 1864 and served there until his retirement in 1884, two years before his death.

He published five volumes of poems as a young man but after 1842 directed his attention chiefly to theology and philology. His *Study of Words*, published in 1851, was described by FitzGerald as "a delightful, good, book, not at all dry." Similar volumes followed in 1855 and 1859. In 1856, three years after the publication of FitzGerald's *Six Dramas of Calderón*, Trench published a translation of two plays by the Spanish dramatist, a project which had attracted him as early as 1839. In his introductory essay, Trench praised FitzGerald's translations, calling them "far the most important and worthiest contribution to the knowledge of the Spanish poet which we have yet received . . . written as they are in English of an exquisite purity and vigour, and dealing with poetry in a poet's spirit . . . how little likely Calderón is to obtain a more gifted translator. . . ."

FitzGerald and Trench met infrequently even as young men, and their correspondence was desultory; nevertheless it was maintained at least until 1880, three years before FitzGerald's death.

Henry Schütz Wilson

First in England publicly to identify FitzGerald as the translator of the *Rubáiyát of Omar Khayyám* was Henry Schütz Wilson (1824-1902), minor writer and critic. Wilson wrote Quaritch in 1876 asking permission to use FitzGerald's name and "any particulars" Quaritch could give him about "so masterly a translator" for a review he was writing. Quaritch sent the letter to FitzGerald who replied that "Mr. Wilson will do as he finds most convenient to himself in naming one . . . as the understood translator, or simply saying 'The Translator'." FitzEdward Hall had identified FitzGerald as the author in America the previous February in *Lippincott's Magazine* but the word had not reached English critics. "I am much obliged to Mr. Wilson for his Good Word, and Good Deed, 're' Omar and myself," FitzGerald acknowledged. Their subsequent correspondence reveals a mutual respect and a deep admiration for FitzGerald's work on the part of Wilson.

After finishing his formal education at a private school in Highgate, Wilson spent ten years in a commercial house in London where he mastered German, French, and Italian. He later became assistant secretary of the electric company, retiring on a pension at the age of forty-six when the business was taken over by the post office. He was then free to devote all his time to travel, study, writing, and mountain climbing. He had already produced two novels and had written on Goethe, whom he admired. After his retirement he wrote essays, reviews, and criticism for many London magazines, books on mountaineering, and another novel. All of his novels were translated into German.

A member of the Alpine Club for many years, he reached the top of the Matterhorn in August, 1875, ten years after the first successful ascent, and repeated the feat in August, 1876. He wrote up his exploits in magazines and books and sent copies to FitzGerald, who responded, "The Mountain came to Mahomet—as near as he wishes such a Mountain to come," and "I must say I like them best at a considerable distance, when they look more or less Cloud-like, do not shut out Sun, Moon, and Stars, and—are not to be ascended." He expressed wonder that a man who spent so much time with books and writing could keep in condition for mountain-climbing. However, Wilson was an accomplished fencer and a hard-working "volunteer," a Captain in the artists' corps.

FitzGerald's regard for him was evident when he arranged a meeting for Wilson with Fanny Kemble, but theirs was not the close relationship he had with many of his friends. Wilson was deeply interested in the German and English stage and was sought after in literary and artistic circles. FitzGerald credits him with sparking the interest that resulted in the next edition of the *Rubáiyát.*

William Aldis Wright

"I have struck up an Acquaintance, by Letter only, with Aldis Wright of Trinity," FitzGerald reported to a friend in March, 1869. "We are both East Anglians; his Father a very respectable, and even a venerable, old Dissenting Minister at Beccles, near which I used to be a good deal at my Brother in law's house. So Wright and I exchange a little gossip about Suffolk words."

The senior Wright was minister of a Baptist congregation. His son, born in 1831, prepared for Cambridge in local schools and was admitted to Trinity in 1849. He was eighteenth wrangler when he completed his terms in 1854, but his status as a Dissenter barred him from receiving a degree. When religious tests for eligibility were removed in 1856, he returned to the university and was awarded an A.B. in 1858. He spent the remainder of his life at Cambridge, becoming in turn Librarian, Senior Bursar, Fellow, and Vice Master of Trinity. He did not lecture, and never married. "Few undergraduates ventured to speak to him," one of his friends recorded, "and even the younger Fellows of his college were kept at a distance by the austere precision of his manner. His old-fashioned courtesy made him a genial host, but his circle of chosen friends was small."

Wright's reputation is based chiefly on his Cambridge, Globe, and Clarendon editions of Shakespeare; but his range of scholarship was wide. In 1870 he was appointed to the committee selected to revise the Authorized Version of the Bible, a labor for which he was exceptionally qualified. His knowledge of sixteenth-century English was a valuable adjunct to his command of Hebrew. Assigned to the Old Testament segment or "Company" of the committee, he served as its secretary and missed only one of the group's 794 meetings, all held in London.

His "little Gossip" with FitzGerald about Suffolk words led to discussion of Elizabethan diction and problem passages in Shakespeare's plays. FitzGerald read and commented on many of the texts as Wright prepared his manuscripts for publication. Wright became a frequent guest at Woodbridge, at first while on trips required by bursary duties. After FitzGerald occupied Little Grange, he often spent Easter and Christmas holidays at the "Chateau."

FitzGerald granted himself the luxury of revising his own works in print or, as he once expressed it, "in another Glass than one's own MS." He did not restrict the practice to radical alteration of proof; he subjected his books to constant revision as well. Six weeks before his death he packed a number of his works in a tin box and enclosed a letter addressed to Wright. "I do not suppose it likely that any of my works should be reprinted after my Death. . . . However this may be, I venture to commit to you this Box containing Copies of all that I have corrected in the way that I would have them appear if any of them ever should be resuscitated." FitzGerald's family and executors accepted the letter as designation of Wright as literary executor; Wright interpreted the statement as FitzGerald's "last wishes" in regard to his writings, and he set about to fulfill them. He added works other than those in the box and included a volume of letters for his first edition of the *Letters and Literary Remains* published in 1889.

Wright died in May, 1914. Three months later the first World War drew the curtain across the stage on which FitzGerald, his correspondents, and his editor had played their parts.

THE LETTERS OF

EDWARD FITZGERALD

VOLUME I

1830-1850

To John Allen

[Geldestone, Beccles]
Pmk., January 29, [1830][1]

Dear Allen,

I write to entrust you with one or two commissions for me.

First, will you go to my rooms, and look for two Quarto Volumes of "Heber's" Journal.[2] These, bid Mrs. Perry[3] to pack in paper: and send them by the Ipswich Coach to "John FitzGerald, Jun[r],[4] Esq: Wherstead Lodge, Ipswich."

Will you also ask her to send *me* a pair of pumps I left there, my hairbrush, my cigars. Also will you order at Feaks's[5] for me a pair of shoes of the same size and thickness as my last pair: to be made as quickly as possible, so that they may come in the same parcel as my cigars, brush, etc. My direction is "E. FitzGerald: Geldestone Hall, Beccles."[6] I had a tedious journey here: I do not know how long I may remain here. I have of course decided nothing of what I shall do: though my Father has decided something for me in reducing my allowance from £300 to £200. This wretched policy to induce me to succumb to my Mother defeats its own end: for it shows to what a stretch he is put to. I must certainly betake myself to France and live there on what I have.[7]

I have no time for more now. A large and fine piano constitutes my happiness here. Pray write and make Thackeray[8] Postscriptive and send a drawing, as his are very much admired here.

Believe me your very affectionate friend,

Ed. FitzGerald

[1] FitzGerald had remained at Cambridge for a week after taking his final examinations, and left for Geldestone on the 27th.

[2] Reginald Heber (1783-1826), Bishop of Calcutta and writer of famous hymns. EFG refers to his *Narrative of a Journey through the Upper Provinces of India from Calcutta to Bombay, 1824-25*, 2 vols., 1828.

[3] Mrs. Jane Perry, hosier and glover of 19 and 20 King's Parade, with whom EFG had lodged at Cambridge. The site of his rooms at No. 19, opposite King's College Chapel, is marked by a plaque.

[4] John FitzGerald, Jr., Edward's elder brother. Wherstead Lodge, overlooking the River Orwell, two miles south of Ipswich, was the FitzGerald Suffolk home at this time.

[5] John Feaks, maker of boots and shoes in St. John's Street.

[6] Norfolk residence of John Kerrich, husband of EFG's favorite sister, Mary

Eleanor. The village, now spelled Geldeston, is two and a half miles west of Beccles, Suffolk.

[7] The cause of this friction has not been determined.

[8] William Makepeace Thackeray matriculated at Trinity College in February, 1829, but left in June, 1830, without taking a degree. EFG made his acquaintance during the Michaelmas term, 1829.

To John Allen

[Geldestone Hall]
[January 31, 1830]

Dear Allen,

I am obliged to you for transacting my business so well. £3 is a capital sum for the Cicero's, etc. I perceive that you have not received the letter which I wrote a day or two ago: giving you more business for me to do. However, you have got it by this time.

I write on this Sunday because I have nothing else to do, and besides have something about myself to tell you—which is merely this, that I have been induced (*very*, *very* much in consequence of your opinion) to write to my Mother. My mind was made up by my Brother-in-law's advice. I always felt that my letter was written more from a hope of utility, than from a sense of duty: therefore, all the good that can be done has been done, and it is only left to apologize for the manner of doing it. This, you will say, is rather a Paley-like doctrine: and rather betokening that I committed the crime with a view to repent of it. But this is not the case: for I thought not of the duty at the time, but only of the advantage. Enough of this subject.

I have not got on with Jeremy Taylor,[1] as I don't like it much. I do not like subdivisions of virtue, making a separate article of each particular virtue or crime: I much more like the general, and artless, commands of our Saviour. Who can say anything new after him? It seems to me absurd to attempt it, except as far as concerns stepping into a bishoprick.

Is Thackeray back? I suppose Cambridge is beginning to fill. I am almost sorry I am not coming up again.

I have received an answer this morning from home: and we are all as before.

It now begins to strike me that I may have put my first letter to you into the post without directing it: which is *a boar*. In it I told you my direction. E.FG. Geldestone Hall: Beccles.

I have now decided to go abroad: and shall probably not return to Cambridge: but shall see about this. The money which I have from Deighton[2] will you keep till I write to you again? It is almost likely that letters may be delayed very much from the snow.

[FitzGerald here sketched a view of Beccles from Geldestone. The drawing is too heavy in execution for reproduction.]

I have just looked at the *Quarterly Review*: it has *adopted Cobbett's views* on the Subject of England,[3] and is obliged to confess that "*Something must be done.*" Will people now believe that there is some danger?—And now that I have got my degree, and the Quarterly speaks the truth, believe in nothing except in my

remaining your very sincere friend
Ed[d] FitzGerald

P.S. I hope you did not forget to stick my exeat[4] on the books. If you can find any channel to dispose of my clock, do, and give the amount to any beggar. Seriously speaking, do what you please with it. And now (I dared not mention it when present lest it should offend your Welsh blood) I have left a lamp which cannot be sold, or only for so little as to be ridiculous, which I beg you to take, as it will very well light up your panelled room. Now don't be absurd, as it is of no earthly use to me.

P.S. the P.S. Give Mrs. Perry the Clock. Tell Thackeray I shall write to him soon.

[1] EFG spent his last evening as a student in Cambridge, January 26, 1830, with friends in Allen's rooms. Allen recorded in his diary that night, ". . . talked when alone with FitzGerald on serious subjects & begged him to think about religion, promised me he would—gave him . . . Jeremy Taylor's holy living and dying—pray God that it might be of service to him" (Trinity College MS).

Jeremy Taylor (1613-67), English divine, published *The Rule and Exercise of Holy Living* (1650) and *The Rule and Exercise of Holy Dying* (1651).

[2] J. Deighton, bookseller in Trinity Street, to whom Allen had sold EFG's books. The firm, now Deighton, Bell and Co., Ltd., is still in business at No. 13.

[3] EFG refers to "Internal Policy," a long article in the January *Quarterly Review* which examined government policies. It described the Commons as a "sort of overgrown club" in which "all real business is drowned in debates and reports." The writer guardedly recommended reform to counter the "signs of revolution" which "are upon us" (*Quarterly Review*, Article IX, Jan., 1830, pp. 228-77).

William Cobbett (1762-1835), radical journalist, politician, and Member of Parliament from 1832 until his death, one of the most controversial figures of the time. In Parliament and in the *Political Register*, which he published, he fought for reforms, being especially zealous on behalf of the Reform Bill and efforts to improve the lot of farmers and laborers. The *Quarterly* article urged that aid be given to agriculture.

[4] *Exeat*, a certificate issued at the end of term stating that a student has "kept" the required number of days in residence.

To John Allen

[Paris]
[April 21, 1830]

Dear Allen,

Thackeray came unexpectedly to Paris, and is unexpectedly gone.[1] I meant to have written you a long letter but his return is so very sudden that I have no time. This letter is written in the fumes of a dinner of two francs a head in the Palais Royal.

You are not to think I am angry with you. On the contrary I love you better than ever for your earnest talking, and count very much on seeing you again. I had half written a very long and whining letter to you in very bad spirits, in which I had determined to come back to England directly. But Thackeray came: and turned all my sorrow to joy: for I was really delighted to see him. He is now off for London. I very much feel the loss of you, my dear Allen, at many times, particularly in my religious wanderings and despondencies: which are very frequent and very distressing. I am tost about very much, but think I am coming very quick *round to a rooted belief in Christianity.* I shall say thus much and no more about myself, because it is a piece of egotism which is alone excusable because I know you take some interest in my welfare: not to mention my everlasting welfare. I have sometimes thought of coming and living at Milford Haven where I shall have my dear preacher near me. Paris is an unprofitable place. I have not been to a church etc. So much for myself.

We hear to day that Thackeray is in the second class of the Little Go.[2] What does this matter? I suppose you are in the First. My dear Allen, you gave me no account of any friends: of Walford, Wilson,[3] of whom I was anxious to hear whether the first was well, and the second got through his degree. How did all this go on? Write me a long letter, dear Allen. I am anxious to hear of you. Your last note was a paltry thing: and a very idle thing.

Paris is very gay: very full: but it will empty at the first of May. Shall I go to Italy, or England? I know some persons going to Italy who offer me to go. I have an Aunt residing here who is very kind to me.

This scrappy letter is written in the hurry of question and answer about packets, and hotels, and Little Goes from Thackeray, and Waiters, and myself: so you must excuse me. Tomorrow we are to get you your seal before he starts: which we shall try to get a handsome one. I was wishing to send you something from Paris, but there is nothing peculiar here. Again I tell you to forgive this scrawl, which is written in company and disturbance. I think next term will be a very pleasant one at Cambridge, as it always is. I remember many pleasant walks with you last year: the fruit of which was generally a fit of ague each time. If you see Roe (the Engraver, not the Haberdasher) give him my remembrance and tell him I often wish for him in the Louvre: as I do for you, my dear Allen: for I would think you would like it very much. There are delightful portraits (which you love most) and statues so beautiful that you would for ever prefer statues to pictures. There are as fine pictures in England: but not one statue so fine as any here. There is a lovely and very modest Venus: and the Gladiator: and a very majestic Demosthenes, sitting in a chair, with a roll of writing in his hands, and seemingly meditating just before rising to speak. It is quite awful. I can no more. Write a long letter to me on thin paper to save the postage: and believe me your very sincere friend

E.FG.

P.S. I hear that you put my money to *my account* at Mortlock's: I asked you to put it to *my brother's at Coutts.*[4] However, as it is, take it out of Mortlock's: and pay bills at Edward's the cook: Mason the printseller: for I think (am not sure) that I left without paying them. I ordered Mrs. Perry to send my books and prints to Wherstead Lodge: Ipswich.

P.P.S. Smith[5] in the Crescent will do up the prints: pay him from the money.[6]

1 Amid the confusions of the Palais Royal of which he speaks, EFG apparently wrote "unexpectedly gone" in place of "unexpectedly *going*." Thackeray was still with him as he wrote, and delivered the letter to Allen in Cambridge on April 23.

In 1862, while writing his essay "Dessein's" for the *Cornhill Magazine* (*Roundabout Papers*), Thackeray recalled this excursion "about which my benighted parents never knew anything. . . . How did I come to think of this escapade, which occurred in the Easter vacation of the year 1830? . . . I met my college tutor only yesterday. We were travelling, and stopped at the same hotel. . . . I felt inclined to knock at his door and say, 'Doctor Bentley, I beg your pardon, but do you remember, when I was going down at the Easter vacation in 1830, you asked me where I was going to spend my vacation? And I said, With my friend Slingsby, in Huntingdonshire. Well, sir, I grieve to have to confess that I told you a fib. I had got £20 and was going for a lark to Paris, where my friend Edwards was staying.'" Thackeray's tutor was William Whewell, Master of Trinity, 1841-66. "Edwards," of course, was EFG.

[2] "Little Go," a university examination taken by undergraduates during the Lent term of the second year.

[3] Henry Walford and Thomas Wilson, both of Trinity, took degrees with EFG and entered the Church. Wilson served as Vicar of Farnley, Leeds, 1836-73. Walford was at Bury with EFG. Data on his career are lacking.

[4] The firm of Mortlock and Sons was absorbed by Barclay's Bank in 1896. Coutts was the famous banking house, Coutts and Co.

[5] William H. Smith, book- and print-dealer.

[6] This letter was addressed, facetiously, to "Joshua Allen, Knight, Esqre." Allen had a brother, Joshua, but EFG did not know him at the time.

To John Allen

[Paris]
[April 24, 1830]

Dear Allen,

Sansum[1] is returning: so I send you a few more lines. I have no more to say new of myself or anything else since my last. My last fortnight has been spent in talking nonsense of all kinds: this is nothing very new: but it is against my real wish, and (I think) inclination: and I shall have no more of it, for I have no one to talk it to. I think of going into the country this week, and, if I like it, shall stay.[2] . . . I have been reading at nights your Jeremy Taylor,[3] which is a [bea]utifully written book: but I want something more elementary, and fundamental. However, it is always a great strengthening of belief to see great minds believing: to be sure, a great many have not believed: but many have. When once belief is made, the way is plain, and the rest remains with oneself to do: but one has it not in one's power always to believe. I am very anxious to hear from you.

Thackeray is to me a little gayer than when I saw him last: but as kind as ever. He tells me he had not seen so much of you last term.[4]

I am obliged suddenly to conclude: and it must be in a business like way. I sent a letter to you by Thackeray telling you what you were to do with the money, of which I have never heard anything. Thackeray tells me that he does not know whether he paid you £5 or not for me: . . . £5 may be sent in a letter to me, as a bank is. . . . Pray let there be no more mistakes about banks etc., as I shall come off the worse by them. In my letter by Thackeray I directed you to pay two bills with the rest of the money.[5]

Ever yours sincerely,
E. FitzGerald

[1] John Sansum (1811-88), of Trinity, took his B.A. in 1832. J. A. Venn (*Alumni Cantabrigienses*) describes him as "a landowner in Mecklenburg." He died at Gries, Austria.

[2] Ellipses in this letter indicate that a segment of the page is torn off.

[3] See letters to Allen, Jan. 31, 1830, and May 23, 1835.

[4] Allen's diary hardly bears this out. He recorded at least 38 meetings with Thackeray between January 31 and March 30, the eve of Thackeray's departure for Paris.

[5] On April 28, Allen drew £3 9s. from Mortlock's and paid Edwards, the cook, £2 17s. and Mason, the printseller, 12s. (Allen Diary).

To John Allen

[Paris]
[May 16, 1830]

Dear Allen,

How is it that I have heard nothing from you? Pray do not be so idle, but write: I think I have sent you two letters and you have not written a word. I have expected to hear from [you] concerning my money, whether my bills were paid, and to receive the £5 I asked you to send in a letter.[1] If you have not done [so], the man who carries this letter to you, will carry one back to me: his name is Eaton.[2]

I was on the point of setting out for England with him, meaning to live in Devonshire or Wales for the Summer: but my Aunt,[3] who has just recovered from a long illness, fell down in the street and injured some bone in her back: this, though not dangerous, will keep her ill some time, and therefore, as she is very poor, I think I shall stay here, and do what I can. I hope to get to England in the Summer.

Now pray do write, on every account, as I wish to hear from you: tell me all the Cambridge news that is. Has Thackeray got the commission in the Registrar's Office? Tell me all. I envy you at Cambridge this delicious weather: and am very anxious to live in England, while it is liveable in, for I think it is fast waning away:[4] and then one may go to Switzerland, or Spitzbergen or wherever one can.

Farewell, dear Allen: you do not deserve a longer letter.

Yrs. sincerely
E.FG.

P.S. Eaton will give you this letter and come for the answer. Now, manage to settle all my affairs by that time. Were my books and prints sent to my home?

Tell Thackeray I have no time to write: but wish I had. Ask Sansum if he sent the musical snuffbox to my sister.[5] I hope he has. Remember me kindly to him, especially if he has done this. Farewell.

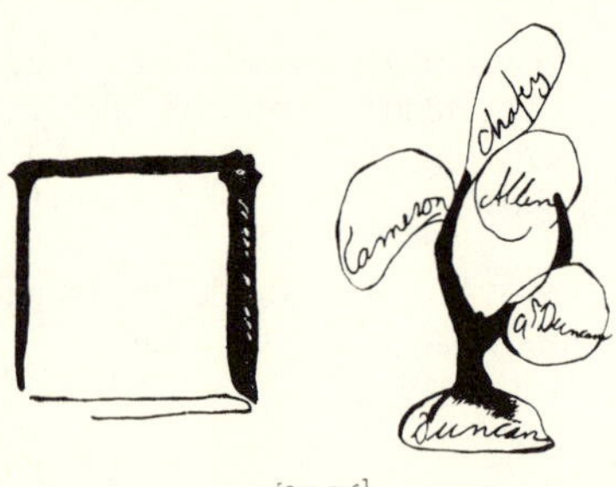

[See n.6]

Tell me all the trivial things at Camb. I don't care a penny for the big ones: tell me about my friends Tom Wilson, Heath, etc.[7]

[1] Allen may have encountered some difficulty in collecting EFG's money. On April 28, after receiving the letter delivered by Sansum, Allen recorded in his diary that he "called on Thackeray about FitzGerald's money." It was not until May 13, however, that he wrote, "Got Thackeray's £5 but could not get Sansum's then . . . in the evening Sansum produced a check for the money and took tea with me." Four days later Allen "sent off FitzGerald's [letter] containing the halves of Sansum's and Thackeray's £5 notes, No's. 12256 & Nos. 33678." On May 18 Allen received the letter above and the following day sent the remaining halves of the two notes.

[2] Eaton appears to be a courier.

[3] Either Anne or Isabella, the two sisters of EFG's father, both of whom died unmarried.

[4] This is the first appearance of a sentiment EFG repeats again and again in his correspondence. Another characteristic remark closes the letter.

[5] Probably a gift for Mrs. Kerrich.

[6] Francis Duncan (b. 1807), the "root" of the Friendship Tree, matriculated with EFG at Trinity in 1826. Duncan took his degree in 1830 and married within a few months. He entered the Church in 1831 and, after holding a succession of curacies, became Rector of West Chelborough, Dorset, near Dorchester, which living he held until 1872. EFG visited him there in 1847 and again in 1859. In June, 1866, Duncan, then described by EFG as "a Hypochondriac Man, nervous, and restless, with a vast deal of uncouth Humour," was "seized with a Passion" to see his friend once more and visited EFG in Woodbridge. (See letter to W. H. Thompson, [June, 1866].)

Alexander Duncan (b. 1809) took his degree in 1834. William L. Chafy (1807-78), of Sidney Sussex, took his degree in 1829 and entered the Church the following year. He was a Fellow of Dulwich College from 1836 to 1857, when he retired and spent the remainder of his life at Bath. Jonathan Henry L. Cameron

(1807-88), of Trinity, took his degree in 1831 and entered the Church in 1836. He successively held a number of livings, the last as Rector of Shoreham, Kent, from 1860 to 1888. The two Duncans, Allen, and Chafy all attended Westminster School. For Allen, see Biographical Profile.

[7] Douglas Heath (1811-97), of Trinity, was Senior Wrangler (leader of the first class in the mathematical examinations list) and winner of first-class honors in the classics in 1832. Called to the bar in 1835, he was Judge of the Court of Requests from 1838 to 1847 and of the Bloomsbury County Court from 1847 to 1865. He contributed to philosophical and philological periodicals and edited the legal portions of James Spedding's edition of the works of Francis Bacon.

EFG, Spedding, and Frederick Pollock were Heath's guests in Surrey on June 28, 1838, the day of Queen Victoria's coronation. Pollock recorded, ". . . in the early afternoon, a beautiful warm day, we four were assembled on the edges of a long open bath . . . surrounded by thick bushes—a most tempting spot for the purpose. As the hour of the placing of the crown on the Queen's head in Westminster Abbey approached, we made ready for the plunge, and when the sound of the distant salutes of cannon reached us we all took headers into the water, and swam about singing 'God save the Queen'" (*Personal Remembrances of Sir Frederick Pollock*, 2 vols., 1887, I, 114).

FitzGerald seems to have considered illustrating his letter with a picture which failed to progress beyond the frame. He was then inspired to draw what could be called "A Tree of Friendship," designating those Cambridge friends whom he met through Francis Duncan. Allen recorded in his diary on September 22, 1830: "My intimacy with FitzGerald . . . arose from being almost dragged by Young Duncan to a breakfast party on a Sunday at his brother's which I had refused to go to." FitzGerald inserted an unwarranted e *in the name of William Chafy.*

To John Allen

[Paris]
Friday [May 21, 1830]

Dear Allen,

I received your letter this morning and in it halves of the £5 notes. I did not expect the other £5 but am glad it is come for I am poor. I start for England in a week, as I purpose now: I shall go by Havre de Grace and Southampton and stay for a month or two perhaps at Dartmouth a place on the Devonshire coast. Tell Thackeray that he is never to invite me to his house,[1] as I intend never to go: not that I would not go out there rather than any place perhaps, but I cannot stand seeing new faces in the polite circles. You must know I am going to become a great bear: and have got all sorts of Utopian ideas into my head about society: these may all be very absurd, but I try the experiment on myself, so I can do no great hurt. Where I shall go in the summer I know not.

If I had any right to bless you, my dear Allen, I would do so: for all your kindnesses to me: which, believe me, do not fall on barren ground, but will some day or other bring forth a crop of something better than weeds. I may truly say that I improve every day in works, if not in belief and words. I still vacillate like a fool between belief and disbelief, sometimes one, sometimes the other for I have no strength of mind, and very little perception. When I get to England I mean to study the Bible incessantly.

I earnestly hope that you and I may see each other to live together for a little time: whenever you like: I am in want of a companion. No one can live cheaper than I do.

Walford in the Church![2] I beg his pardon, but he is a most miserable, sordid, contemptible little being. What news of Duncan? In writing back, which you must do by return of post else I shall be gone, tell me what your direction will be, and what Williams' is.[3] Poor Williams: I do think he was a very amiable fellow. So Thackeray is to be an Apostle.[4] You did not tell me if he had got his Registrar's Office. Kemble is a poor vapid creature, I think: think of a man fiddling away his life in spouting at the Union! I see a good deal of his brother here who is a fine, generous, fellow.[5] I hope Tom[6] will get through: except that he will then be in the Church.

Tell me in your answer if there is any book I can get you here: any sets of sermons of Massillon[7] etc., for all books are so very cheap here. Nor don't scruple to tell me any: for however large the sets, they cost absolutely nothing.

Good bye dear Allen: I shall think often of you: and hope you will write in England to me. In the mean time as you pray for me, I will not forget you in my silent prayers "Τῳ αγνῳ[σ]τῳ Θεῳ"[8]

Yr's
E.FG.

Your answer must be by return of post.
Direct this time
A Monsieur E FitzGerald
Chez Mlle Purcell
28 Rue de la Ferme des Mathurins
Paris
Can you read it? "Rue de la Ferme des Mathurins."

P.S. You must have incurred expense by all the trouble you have had: do pray tell me what it is: or ask for something to cover it.

[1] Major and Mrs. Henry Carmichael-Smyth, Thackeray's stepfather and mother, lived at Larkbeare House, near Ottery St. Mary, in Devon, where Thackeray urged EFG to visit him.

[2] See letter to Allen, [Apr. 21, 1830], n.3.

[3] William Williams (1804-69), of Corpus Christi College, took his B.A. degree as seventh Senior Optime in 1829. (Senior Optime, one who receives second-class honors in the university mathematical examinations.) He entered the Church the following year and served as Curate at West Tisted, Alresford, Hampshire, from 1831-33; Vicar of St. Bartholomew's, Hyde, Hants, 1833-68; and was Master of St. Mary Magdalene Hospital, 1846-68. Williams had accompanied Thackeray to Paris as his tutor in the summer of 1829, and it was in Williams' rooms in Cambridge that EFG first met Thackeray in the fall term of that year.

During his Cambridge days, at least, Williams seems to have been something of a humorist. EFG credits him with being editor of the *Snob*, a student humorous magazine to which Thackeray contributed. The *Snob* was succeeded by the *Gownsman*, also edited by Williams.

[4] Thackeray never became a member of "The Apostles." For *Apostles*, the Cambridge Conversazione Society, see letter to Allen, [Mar. 15, 1831], n.8.

[5] EFG's strictures on "Jacky," though severe, were not unwarranted. Dean Merivale reported that Kemble at Cambridge "was bitten with politics, devoted himself to the Union and the cultivation of oratory, gave up all his time to newspapers and political essayists." (*Autobiography of Dean Merivale*, ed. J. A. Merivale, 1899, p. 59). EFG later came to esteem Kemble and his "fiery energy."

EFG's subsequent opinion of Henry, the younger Kemble, is not known; but in Paris he appears to have been captivated, as many others were to be, by the young man's good looks and charming manners. Fanny Kemble described her brother to Henry James as "very handsome . . . but very luxurious and selfish, and without a penny to his name." His gambit to win the hand of the heiress daughter of Martin Thackeray, former Vice-Provost of King's College, Cambridge, was checked by that gentleman with the threat of disinheriting his daughter. Miss Thackeray, according to Fanny, "a dull, plain . . . girl . . . very much in love with H.K.," determined to disobey her father and accept the consequences, a prospect the young man did not at all relish. "Then," said Fanny, "all his effort was to disentangle himself. He went off, shook himself free of his engagement, let the girl go." Ten years later, after the death of Mr. Thackeray, he again proposed. This time the young lady refused him. Fanny's account of the affair in a conversation with Henry James provided the substance of the novelist's *Washington Square* (F. O. Matthiessen and K. B. Murdock, *Notebooks of Henry James*, New York, 1947, pp. 12-13).

[6] "Tom" Wilson. See letter to Allen, [Apr. 21, 1830], n.3.

[7] Jean Baptiste Massillon (1663-1742), created Bishop of Clermont in 1717 and in 1719 elected to the French Academy. His sermons, dealing with morality rather than dogma, are noted for their excellence and their gentle but effective persuasiveness.

[8] "To the unknown God" (Acts 17:23).

To John Allen

Southampton
July the Something
I forget what.
[Pmk., July 26, 1830]

Dear Allen,

Are you yet at Pourtsmouth? I have been staying at this place since my return from France which is near two months back. I have been very long in not writing to you. I have just returned from a visit to Williams,[1] and saw him installed in his parsonage, and eat of his meat and drank of his beer, and tasted all the produce of his glebe. It is a nice parish: and Williams ought to be a happy man. He seems conscientious in his view of his situation, and sets himself busily to work with his own conduct and thoughts: he is naturally active-minded, and will altogether do good to others as well as to himself, as I hope. I hope one day to see you, my dear Allen, in the same situation: you have long ago prepared your mind for it, and few can be fitter than you are.

When shall I see you? I do not know how long I shall stay at Southampton. I would come to Portsmouth to see you but I have such an arrant dislike to Portsmouth. Pray do not take this as neglectful: perhaps I may come after all.

The first person I met on landing in England was Frederic[2] Duncan *Esq.* in a white hat and nankeens: very pale, with his fingers out of his glove's ends, sketching down the street. After felicitations etc., Duncan asked me to go into his lodging: up I went and found a pretty woman at work who was introduced to me as *Mrs. Duncan*! She is a pleasant good humoured person who seems to obey all his whims which are not a few. He is now gone to Jersey with her: he was here nearly three weeks with me. He says he is not happy and quite wretched at marriage: he seems to have no reason to be unhappy. He is a kind generous person at heart.[3]

What news of any of my friends? What is become of Thackeray? Are you going to see Williams in his parsonage he is very anxious to see you.[4] He has a nice little church: the country is pretty about him. Write to me concerning your movements and abodes. Williams has written a letter directed to Mr. Mason's: mine goes to the Post Office: so that each is to give notice to you of the other that you may get both our letters. Believe me your very affectionate friend

Edward FitzGerald

The King[5] is coming down to you. My dear fellow, you will be stunned by those horrid cannons. I live here at a boarding house for two guineas a week. Good bed, good board, and amusing company. My address is the Anspach Hotel.

Anspach Hotel.

[1] At West Tisted.

[2] Thoughtlessly written for *Francis*.

[3] Duncan's marriage seems to have turned out very well. See letters of Aug. 29 and [Sept. 4], 1847.

[4] Allen visited Williams in mid-August and on the 19th walked to Southampton by way of Winchester, a distance of thirty miles. The next morning, "though very stiff," he sought out EFG and they walked to Netley Abbey, "talked of Old Duncan's marriage and tried to make him [EFG] steady in his views on religion. . . . returned home . . . pleasant chat about Apostles, Cambridge men &c." On the 21st they crossed to Cowes in the Isle of Wight to attend the regatta. There they saw the expatriate French royal family, "save unhappy Charles X," who had been forced to abdicate on August 2 (Allen Diary).

[5] William IV had succeeded his brother, George IV, June 26, 1830. *The Hampshire Telegraph and Sussex Chronicle* (Portsmouth) announced on July 12 and again on July 26 that the king proposed visiting Portsmouth in August. On September 13, however, the paper stated that the visit, "we are sorry to say, has been relinquished" (*Hampshire Telegraph and Sussex Chronicle*, Sept. 13, 1830, p. 4).

To John Allen

Naseby, Northampton
[November 10, 1830]

My dear Allen,

I know you have got Percy's Reliques. Will you send me written out the Ballad of the "King and the Miller of Mansfield" or at all events see, either in the ballad or the notes, what the Miller's name was, what King it was, and what pension and rank he bestowed on the Miller when the Miller came to court to see him.[1] Please do this last, which is best and less trouble. And write directly.

I am come to Naseby and find my brother not here,[2] but he will be here soon, I believe. This place is solitary enough, but I am well off in a nice farm house. I wish you could come and see the primitive inhabitants, and the fine field of Naseby. There are grand views on every side: and all is interesting.

I do not yet know how long I shall be here. Are you hard at work now? Tell Sansum I hope he was not licked by Snobs on the 6th[3] of which day I heard a very dire Prophecy and Lamentation from some people in the Coach from Cambridge. If any dreadful bloodshed occurs send me a list of the Killed and Wounded. I hope to find poor Sansum only among the latter, poor fellow. Make him add a *Rescript* to your letter to enliven me among the Aborigines of Naseby.

Do you know, Allen, that this is a very curious place with odd fossils: and mixed with bones and bullets of the fight at Naseby; and the identical spot where King Charles stood to see the battle, whereon my dad has erected a *pillow*[4] to commemorate it. All this is true though said in fun: and the people are really curious. In talking of my dad, his agent has just decamped with something above £5000 of my dad in his pocket. Pleasant this, to hear of a November morning . . .[5] the first frosts!

How I have come to write so long a letter as this I cannot tell. I do wish you and Sansum were here to see the curiosities. Can't you come? I am quite the King here I promise you.

Yrs. very sincerely
E.FG.

I am going to-day to dine with the Carpenter, a Mr. Ringrose, and to hear his daughter play on the piano-forte. Fact.

My blue Surtout daily does wonders. At Church its effect is truly delightful.

[1] *Reliques of Ancient English Poetry*, published in 1765 by Thomas Percy (1729-1811), later Bishop of Dromore. "The King and the Miller of Mansfield" appears in the Second Book of the Third Series in the volume.

The king is Henry II, who, given shelter for the night by a miller, is served venison pie for supper. The miller's son explains, "Now and then we make bold with our king's deer . . . Never are wee without two or three in the roof." Henry takes all in good grace. In the morning courtiers join the king, and the miller is dismayed to learn the identity of his guest. The king, however, "Gave him great living, and dubb'd him a knight."

The miller is nameless until the king summons him and his family to a feast at Westminster on St. George's Day. At the close of the banquet

Then Sir John Cockle the king call'd unto him,
And of merry Sherwood made him o'er seer;
And gave him out of hand three hundred pound yearlye:
Take heed now you steale no more of my deer.

[2] EFG wrote from Naseby Wooleys, a property inherited by his mother in 1810. The estate included much of the battlefield on which Cromwell and Sir Thomas Fairfax defeated Charles I on June 14, 1645. Fire destroyed a portion of the hall at Naseby Wooleys on February 12, 1948, but it was immediately rebuilt. The Naseby village inn is still called The FitzGerald Arms. The brother whom EFG expected was probably John.

[3] "SNOBS. A term applied indiscriminately to all who have not the honour of being Members of the University; but in a more particular manner to the '*profanum Vulgus*,' the Tag-rag, and Bobtail, who vegetate on the sedgy banks of Camus; and who appear to have a natural antipathy to the '*Gens Togata*' " (*Gradus ad Cantabrigiam* by a Brace of Cantabs, 1824, p. 101).

EFG seems carelessly to have written "6th" instead of "5th." The evening of Guy Fawkes' Day is the occasion of a rally of students and townspeople which packs Market Hill, the town center. Spirits run high; innocent fun is often succeeded by malicious mischief; and, in the past, at least, town and gown clashes were common. In EFG's day undergraduate "bloods" often terminated evening parties by venturing into the streets to engage in free-for-alls with "townies" or with "bargees," as the river bargemen were called.

[4] As young men both EFG and Thackeray amused themselves by distorting words, especially names, in this way. To Carlyle, the pillar became "that ass of a column." The monument, an obelisk, stands on a hilltop, overlooking the battlefield, about a quarter of a mile from Naseby on the road to Clipston. In 1842, while writing his work on Cromwell, Carlyle visited the field and assumed that the shaft marked the center of the battlefield. As a result he misread his contemporary sources describing the action of the battle. "So much for guesses at history," observed EFG. See letters of Sept. and Oct., 1842.

[5] Mr. FitzGerald was the victim of at least one other dishonest agent. His manager of a coal mine at Pendleton, near Manchester, in 1833 absconded with further sums (Stephenson Letters, British Museum Add. 38,781 f. 59). Sealing wax covers one word at this point.

To John Allen

[London]
[March 15, 1831]

My dear Allen,

As you are such a bad correspondent, I have written chiefly to Sansum, principally to blow him up for stealing leaden lions from harmless lamps: a species of cruelty, which though it does not come under Mr. Martin's act,[1] is one of those outrages of humanity which society should take much notice of. Ask Sansum if the Lion in any way offended him, by grinning or other wise. Oh Lord! I can fancy Sansum tumbling home, and with that perverse face of his that he can sometimes put on, first concocting the plan, and then up the lampost in a second! Your letter was a very dull one in every way: you were as lazy as possible while writing it: sometimes cocking your legs upon over the fire place, and only writing scrap by scrap. You must write me a better one soon. If you don't take care, Allen, you'll go out in the Poll[2] just as Sansum will. Things are going on well here. New converts are daily made to support the new Bill.[3] My Father set out against it at first, but is coming over, I think.[4] The question with him is, not whether the Bill is a good one, for he thinks it is: but whether he ought to vote for the disfranchisement of his own borough: wherein he certainly would not be its representative, because no borough would ever wish to be disfranchised. It is the general opinion now that it will be carried. At first bets were 3 to 1 against it: but on Friday or Thursday they were even. Nothing can equal the anxiety of the Members. I wish they had proposed universal suffrage:[5] but I know that you wouldn't listen to my wherefore. If you write, will you send Old Duncan's direction? Is he in the Church?[6]

You are now such a heterogeneous sort of animal that I scarcely know how to talk to you. When you first came to College you were wrapped up in old books and Theology: but now you are a little bitten with Unions, and Quinquagints,[7] and Tennysons, and Tennants,[8] and aren't half so much "*a whole*" as you used to be. I suppose after leaving College you will settle down: but I think your principles which were formerly strong enough, ooze away through your fingers' ends. To me you look like a Quaker turned into an Opera Dancer in a Pantomime. Is all this ill-natured? No, I swear it is not: but first impressions are the strongest: and as my first impression of you was a very pleasant one, I am angry that you are altered. For, before, you were very set apart from Cambridge men: and had a single object in view: but now you are more made up [of] scraps, like them, and get more of the Farrago of College information: so that you are no longer John Allen: *but* I will not say but it is necessary that this must take place at College: but do keep a look to yourself that you mayn't get of the common Cambridge run. I will say that you are not half so bad as I have made you out to be: but still, I think you will be so, unless you look sharp. And all this I say because I love Johnny Allen—

Believe me your very affectionate
E. FitzGerald

I forgot that one of your likings is pictures: which is a good one, and quite set apart from what I have been talking of. Well then, the British Gallery is pretty good: and I have been to Wilkie's house[9] to see his new pictures which are fine. Will you come up to London? I have lodgings apart from my home where I breakfast, etc. Herein can you be well lodged and boarded. I should be glad to get your acquaintance for my family, but we are different from other people, and I never have introduced any of my friends to my Father or Mother, as it is quite out of their way. We have absolutely no society whatever.[10] Perhaps Sansum will be coming up at Easter. I believe I shall go to Seaford somewhere about then.

1 Richard Martin (1754-1824), M.P. for Galway, a pioneer in the campaign for humane treatment of animals and one of the founders of the Royal Society for the Prevention of Cruelty to Animals (1824). He was ridiculed by press and public and dubbed "Cruelty Martin" for his pains. His bill to prevent ill-treatment of horses and cattle, popularly known as "Martin's Act," was passed by Parliament in

1822. Martin's solicitude for beasts was curiously balanced by a zest for duelling.

[2] The Poll: from οἱ πολλοί, hoi polloi. The Poll was made up of students who read for ordinary or pass degrees, not for honors. Allen was eighteenth Senior Optime in 1832. Sansum did, indeed, "go out in the Poll," as EFG had predicted.

[3] A reference to the first of two attempts to reform Parliament which preceded passage of the Great Reform Bill of 1832. The bill had been introduced on March 1 and was first read on the 9th. It was defeated in the Commons on April 19, 299 to 291. A second bill, debated through the summer of 1831, was approved by the Commons by a majority of 109 on September 21 but was defeated by the Lords on October 3. Although EFG writes of "the new Bill" there can be no doubt that he refers to that introduced in March, 1831. An entry in Allen's diary for March 16 alludes to the closing portion of the letter proper. "A letter of most kind reproof from dear FitzGerald which I fully deserved." Easter, referred to in the postscript, fell on April 3 in 1831.

[4] EFG's father owned considerable property at Seaford, Sussex, and, as Baron of Seaford, represented that borough in Parliament, 1830-32. The borough was one of the 56 abolished by the Reform Bill. "Baron," ancient title of M.P.s from the Cinque Ports.

[5] Later, in the Commons' debate on the second bill, enfranchisement of all rate-payers was proposed but was defeated, 123 to one.

[6] Francis Duncan was ordained deacon in 1831 and priest in 1835.

[7] By "Unions" EFG referred to the Cambridge Union Society, the famous debating club, which at that time met in a rear room of the Red Lion Inn.

The "Quinquagint" (The Fifty) evolved from the Union. Henry Alford (1810-71; B. A. Trinity, 1832; later Dean of Canterbury) recorded in his diary October 12, 1830, "After, went to the first meeting of the 'Fifty,' a society for true practice in speaking culled from the Union." Alford was elected secretary of the group. J. W. Blakesley was president; James Spedding, J. H. Cameron, and Arthur Hallam were "committee men" (*Life of Henry Alford*, ed. Mrs. Alford, 1874, p. 61). Sir Frederick Pollock stated that in 1832 "the debates at the Union were, however, much damaged by the institution of a smaller debating society, called The Fifty, to which most of the best speakers betook themselves" (*Personal Remembrances*, I, 48).

[8] EFG and Tennyson, kindred spirits in their sturdy independence and resistance to conformity, had been contemporaries at Trinity for two years but had never become acquainted. EFG knew the poet by sight, however, and had been present "at some Cambridge gathering" when he recited folk ballads. EFG evidently did not know that Tennyson had left Cambridge the previous month without taking a degree.

Both Tennyson and Robert J. Tennant, also of Trinity, who took his degree in 1831, were members of the Cambridge Conversazione Society, commonly known as The Apostles, a group of undergraduates, for the most part keen-witted and talented. At each weekly meeting one member read a paper, which was then discussed. The papers covered a wide range of subjects, philosophical, aesthetic, social. EFG probably had The Apostles in mind when he wrote "the common Cambridge run" with their "Farrago of College information." But Spedding, Donne, and Kemble, schoolboy and lifelong friends, were Apostles; and within two or three years EFG made the acquaintance of both Tennyson and Tennant.

[9] David Wilkie (1785-1841), first noted for canvases portraying common scenes from daily life, at this time lived at 24 Lower Philmore St., Kensington. While

visiting the Continent, 1825-28, he came under the influence of Italian and Spanish masters. As a result he changed his style and choice of subject, for which he was severely criticized. EFG obviously approved his "second manner." Throughout his correspondence EFG's evaluations of the arts are thoroughly individual and unswayed by professional or popular opinions.

[10] EFG means *no society in common with his parents.* His rented London lodgings were usually in Charlotte Street, not far from his parents' residence in fashionable Portland Place. There, at No. 39, Mrs. FitzGerald entertained lavishly and Edward conscientiously paid his *devoirs.* No. 39 now houses the British College of Nurses.

To John Allen

[London]
[c. April 15, 1831]

My dear Allen,

I forget whether I wrote to you after I had been to Williams:[1] I think not, however. Williams is well, and good, and happy. Did you see Hadon when you were at Alton?[2] He is a very nice man.

I have been ever wishing to get into the country, but find that I am very useful to my Mother: and as I wish to do all that may be good, I do not leave town: nor shall, till July. I do hope to see you in London when you leave Cambridge: and beg you will come and call upon me.[3] My Father leaves London on the 2nd. of June. I hope you will write directly to me to let me know. You are now I believe in the midst of a college Examination— or about to be so. This is your last— is that a pleasant or an awful thought?[4]

I spent my time (a fortnight) delightfully at Williams's— rambling about. He and several clergymen round about him are getting Saints— which I hail as good. In fact, the clergy begin to see that the old Parson of fifty years ago is not worthy his pay, and, by his remissness and poor example, cause the people to grumble, and get bad. Here is the Bishop of London[5] now bringing in a bill that private parsons may not have private Chapels— as if only those who were paid were to be religious or to administer religion. Pay is only meant to ensure a certain competent number of teachers— the more we get without pay, *besides,* the better. But perhaps those who are paid are afraid lest, if others do it for nothing, people may look rather hard at their gains. I suppose you don't agree in this. I have it very much to heart, and fancy I can trace all the present spirit of Revolt and Infidelity to the laxity of the Old Clergy. They certainly, in general, did not act up to what even every Christian is told in the Bible— much less up to the energy and purity of teachers of Christianity.[6]

Deuce take it all my paper's up before I have asked you about any thing or told you anything. The Reform Bill is to be carried by 150 majority, they say.[7]

Yrs everlastingly
Edw[d] FitzGerald

P.S. If you write within this week, write enclosed to my Dad— but not after— for he leaves town. ∴ write directly.[8]
P.S. I have bought A. Tennyson's poems. How good "Mariana" is.[9]

[1] This visit to Williams was probably made on the Easter trip to Seaford, mentioned in the previous letter.

[2] Alton, Hampshire, where John Allen's future wife, Harriet Higgins, lived.

[3] Allen spent several days in London after the close of term. He called without success at 39 Portland Place on June 4 but found EFG at home the following day. On June 6 the two visited the National Gallery and the exhibition of the Royal Academy, then held in Somerset House. Allen, for one, ended the tour "very tired of pictures" (Allen Diary). Thackeray was in town at the time and sometimes met with his two friends.

[4] Trinity examinations taken at the close of the May term. Allen was to take university honors examinations the following January.

[5] See n.6.

[6] Since the Revolution of 1688, which terminated the reign of the Stuarts, the English clergy had become, as G. M. Trevelyan puts it, "the least clerical of priesthoods." Many clergymen were more concerned with hunting, dining, and wining with the gentry than with their clerical responsibilities. Appointments to livings and ecclesiastical offices were won through preferment rather than through ability and merit. The abuses of plural holdings of livings and non-residence were viewed with indifference. A relatively small proportion of the clergy enjoyed the "plums," while many lived in poverty. EFG's comments are a manifestation of the pressure which produced sweeping church reforms between 1836 and 1840.

Charles James Blomfield (1786-1857), Bishop of London, 1826-56, was a leader in the reform movement.

[7] See letter of [Mar. 15, 1831], n.3.

[8] By this means EFG could take advantage of the franking privilege enjoyed by his father as a Member of Parliament. Until the adoption of Rowland Hill's recommendation for uniform postage and the use of stamps, mail fees were collected upon delivery. The bill which established penny postage in January, 1840, canceled the M.P.s' franking privilege.

[9] This is EFG's first enthusiastic praise of Tennyson's poetry. In June, 1830, had appeared *Poems, Chiefly Lyrical,* the poet's second venture into print but the first to come to the attention of critics. "Mariana" is one of the most successful poems of his long career.

To William Hone
Editor, *The Year Book*[1]

[April, 1831]

The Meadows in Spring

These verses are in the old style; rather homely in expression; but I honestly profess to stick more to the simplicity of the old poets than the moderns, and to love the philosophical good humor of our old writers more than the sickly melancholy of the Byronian wits. If my verses be not good, they are good humored, and that is something

'Tis a sad sight[2]
 To see the year dying;
When autumn's last wind
 Sets the yellow wood sighing
  Sighing, oh sighing!

When such a time cometh,
 I do retire
Into an old room,
 Beside a bright fire;
  Oh! pile a bright fire!

And there I sit
 Reading old things
Of knights and ladies,
 While the wind sings:
  Oh! drearily sings!

I never look out,
 Nor attend to the blast;
For, all to be seen,
  Is the leaves falling fast:
  Falling, falling!

But, close at the hearth,
 Like a cricket, sit I;
Reading of summer
 And chivalry:
  Gallant chivalry!

Then, with an old friend,
 I talk of our youth;
How 'twas gladsome, but often
 Foolish, forsooth
  But gladsome, gladsome.

Or, to get merry,
 We sing an old rhyme
That made the wood ring again
 In summer time:
  Sweet summer time!

Then take we to smoking,
 Silent and snug:
Nought passes between us,
 Save a brown jug;
  Sometimes! sometimes!

And sometimes a tear
 Will rise in each eye,
Seeing the two old friends,
 So merrily;
  So merrily!

And ere to bed
 Go we, go we,
Down by the ashes
 We kneel on the knee;
  Praying, praying!

Thus then live I,
Till, breaking the gloom
Of winter, the bold sun
Is with me in the room!
Shining, shining!

Then the clouds part,
Swallows soaring between:
The spring is awake,
And the meadows are green,—

I jump up like mad;
Break the old pipe in twain;
And away to the meadows,
The meadows again!

Epsilon.[3]

1 William Hone (1780-1842), a valiant fighter in early nineteenth-century battles for freedom of the press, began his public career as a political satirist and religious skeptic; he ended it as a hack writer and devout dissenting lay preacher. The *Year Book* was the last of three miscellanies edited by him: *Every-Day Book*, 1825-26; *Table Book*, 1827; *Year Book*, 1831. All were issued in weekly numbers at 3d., monthly parts at 1s., and published as 14s.-volumes at the end of the year. Compiled as "Perpetual Calendars . . . Relating Popular Amusements, Sports, Ceremonies, Customs, and Events" and including "Biography, Natural History, Art, Science, and General Literature," the works achieved a popularity which they held throughout the century. Hone, a wretched businessman, by 1835 had lost all rights in the publications through bankruptcy.

2 Misprinted as "sighe" in the *Year Book*.

3 *Year Book*, Apr. 30, 1831, columns 510-11. The pages of Hone's miscellanies were printed in double columns, each bearing a number.

"The Meadows in Spring," FitzGerald's first published poetry thus far identified, has a curious history. The version given here appeared in Hone's Year Book, *April 30, 1831.*[1] *On July 9 the poem was also published in the* Athenaeum. *The dual appearance is probably accounted for by a note, which the* Athenaeum *editor appended to the poem, in which an apology is offered for delay in publishing the verses.*[2] *It would appear that FitzGerald first sent his lyric to the* Athenaeum, *superior in reputation and dignity to Hone's miscellany. When the poem failed to appear in the literary weekly, FitzGerald apparently reasoned that it had been rejected. He then sent his lines to Hone, who found them admirably suited for his use. Poems appropriate to the seasons frequently appeared in his "calendar" publications.*

Internal evidence supports this theory. The two versions differ somewhat in text. Alterations in the Year Book *are distinct improvements on the* Athenaeum *text. The cliché, "lorn damsels," in the* Athenaeum *is changed to "ladies" in the* Year Book. *"Down on the ashes / We kneel . . ." is altered to "Down by the ashes. . . ." Punctuation, faulty in the* Athenaeum, *is improved in the* Year Book.

A third version of the poem (again with variants) appears in a com-

monplace book, compiled by John Allen, now in the library of Trinity College. Allen's copy bears the heading, "E.F.G., Naseby, Spring, 1831." This dating has been accepted, thus far, as fixing the date of composition. Other evidence, however, indicates that the poem was probably written while FitzGerald was at Naseby in November, 1830. His movements during the spring of 1831 are rather fully accounted for in his letters of that season, and no visit to Naseby is mentioned. Neither the Athenaeum *version nor that copied by Allen bears a title. It appears that Hone supplied "The Meadows in Spring" to his version to add appropriateness for April publication. His choice of title was not unhappy.*

FitzGerald's letter to the Athenaeum *follows, although, as has been noted, it was probably written before that to Hone.*

[1] *Athenaeum,* July 9, 1831, p. 442.
[2] See Appendix three.

To the Editor of the Athenaeum

[N.D.]

Sir,

These verses are something in the old style, but not the worse for that: not that I mean to call them good: but I am sure they would not have been better, if dressed up in the newest Montgomery fashion, for which I cannot say I have much love. If they are fitted for your paper, you are welcome to them. I send them to you, because I find only in your paper a love of our old literature, which is almost monstrous in the eyes of modern ladies and gentlemen. My verses are certainly not in the present fashion; but, I must own, though there may not be the same merit in the thoughts, I think the style much better: and this with no credit to myself, but to the merry old writers of more manly times.

Your humble servant,
Epsilon

'Tis a dull sight
To see the year dying,
When winter winds
Set the yellow wood sighing:
Sighing, oh! sighing.

When such a time cometh,
I do retire
Into an old room
Beside a bright fire:
Oh, pile a bright fire!

And there I sit
  Reading old things,
Of knights and lorn damsels,
  While the wind sings—
    Oh, drearily sings!

I never look out
  Nor attend to the blast;
For all to be seen
  Is the leaves falling fast:
    Falling, falling!

But close at the hearth,
  Like a cricket, sit I,
Reading of summer
  And chivalry—
    Gallant chivalry!

Then with an old friend
  I talk of our youth—
How 'twas gladsome, but often
  Foolish, forsooth:
    But gladsome, gladsome!

Or to get merry
  We sing some old rhyme,
That made the wood ring again
  In summer time—
    Sweet summer time!

Then go we to smoking,
  Silent and snug:
Nought passes between us,
  Save a brown jug—
    Sometimes!

And sometimes a tear
  Will rise in each eye,
Seeing the two old friends
  So merrily—
    So merrily!

And ere to bed
  Go we, go we,
Down on the ashes,
  We kneel on the knee,
    Praying together!

Thus, then, live I,
  Till, 'mid all the gloom,
By heaven! the bold sun
  Is with me in the room,
    Shining, shining!

Then the clouds part,
  Swallows soaring between;
The spring is alive,
  And the meadows are green!

I jump up, like mad,
  Break the old pipe in twain,
And away to the meadows,
  The meadows again!

The Athenaeum *version calls for further comment. The allusion to "the newest Montgomery fashion" in FitzGerald's note to the editor could refer to either of two poets, James Montgomery (1771-1854) or Robert Montgomery—originally Gomery (1807-55). The poetry of both, though lacking aesthetic appeal, was extremely popular at the time. Robert produced didactic pseudo-epics, condemned by Macaulay as "detestable verses on religious subjects." James, a shade or two superior to Robert as a poet, also wrote long religious poems but also a good number of short pieces. He achieved greatest success as a writer of hymns. Robert was the more active of the two in the early thirties.*

To FitzGerald's offer, "If they are fitted for your paper, you are welcome to them," the editor responded: "They are fitted for any paper, and most welcome to us. The writer must not imagine that the delay in their appearance was occasioned by any doubt; but the pressure of temporary matters—and poetry itself is sometimes temporary, and contributors touchy. His verses are not, indeed, in the Montgomery style, or the latest fashion—they are not all glare and glitter, patch and paint, and meretricious ornament—they are deep in feeling, and sweet in harmony; but we must not write commendations even on contributors. We have a suspicion that we could name the writer—if so, we are sure his name would grace our pages as much as his verses."

FitzGerald revealed in 1873 that the editor suspected the anonymous contributor to be Charles Lamb. Lamb, one of Hone's staunchest friends,[1] *frequently contributed to the miscellanies; and it was he who first disclosed the dual appearance of the poem. "The* Athenaeum *has been hoaxed with some exquisite poetry, that was, two or three months ago, in Hone's Book," he wrote about August 1 to Edward Moxon, only recently established as a London publisher. In a note of August 5, Lamb added, "That* is *the poem I mean. I do not know who wrote it, but [it] is in Hone's book as far back as April. 'Tis a poem I envy—* that *and Montgomery's Last Man (nothing else of his). I envy the writers, because I feel I could have done something like it."*[2] *See Appendix Three.*

[1] To the *London Magazine* of May, 1825, Lamb contributed "Quatrains," a poem of six stanzas beginning, "I like you, and your book, ingenuous Hone! . . . By every sort of taste your work is graced." Hone acknowledged the friendship by dedicating the first volume of the *Every-Day Book* to Lamb and his sister Mary.

[2] The text of these letters, as given here, is from E. V. Lucas' *Letters of Charles and Mary Lamb*, 3 vols. (New Haven, 1935), III, 319-20. Earlier editors, including Alfred Ainger in *The Letters of Charles Lamb*, 2 vols. (New York, 1888), II, 273, quote both passages as though taken from a single undated letter.

The following letter to Thackeray is the only one which has survived in toto *from what FitzGerald later described as an "immortal summer of foolscap." The handwriting crams almost every square inch of four foolscap pages. Both correspondents began such letters each week, leaving them on their desks and adding to them, as will be noted, whenever inclination prompted. The letters were closed on Sunday, and a new one would be started for posting the following week. EFG completed this letter Sunday, October 9, but misdated it at the end "October 11, 1831." The letter is clearly postmarked October 10, which was a Monday.*

To W. M. Thackeray

[Geldestone Hall]
Pmk., Beccles
October 10, 1831

My dear Thackeray,

I have just come home from a walk of two hours or so, and put my letter to you in the post. It rained so hard in the morning that I could not get my early walk—so I lay in bed; for I think there is no difference, in the matter of wholesomeness, between lying in bed, or sitting up, provided one does not sleep, or have too much blanket. I gave you plenty of advice about health in my last, I think. I shall come to London, with some of my sisters, about the 20th of October—will you be there then? Do, if you can.[1] I had got over all doubts as to Chirstianity (that is to say thoroughly disbelieved in it) except the Miracles—but I think the evidence of them is to be doubted. But Paley is very clever about them—it is a case made out as by a lawyer, and he thoroughly answers Hume on the point of there being any likeness between Christ's miracles, and the Abbé Paris.[2] Religious people are very angry with one for doubting: and say "You come to the question determined to doubt, not to be convinced." Certainly we do: having seen how many follow and have followed false religions, and having our reason utterly against many of the principal points of the Bible, we require the most perfect evidence of facts, before we can believe. If you can prove to me that one miracle took place, I will believe that he is a just God who damned us all because a woman eat an apple; and you can't expect greater complaisance [than] that, to be sure. You are wrong, my dear Thackeray, in fancying that Christ does not call himself God—every page of the Bible will shew you he did. There is one thing that goes some way with me: if Christ was not really God, he was either a fanatic, or an imposter: now his morals and advice are too consistent, and too simple and mild, for a fanatic: and an imposter, one fancies, would not have persevered in such a blameless life, nor held in his heart at once the blasphemous design of calling himself the Son of God and a code of principles which the best and wisest of men never preached before. What do you say to this point? Think of it. I am in a quandary of doubts.

You are a genuine lover of the theater. When we are in London we must go to the pit. Now, Thackeray, I lay you ten thousand pounds that you will be thoroughly disappointed when we come together—our letters have been so warm, that we shall expect each minute to contain a sentence like those in our letters. But in letters we are not always together: there are no blue devilish moments: one of us isn't kept waiting for the other: and above all in letters there is Expectation! I am thus foreboding because I have felt it—and put you on your guard very seriously about it, for the disappointment of such hopes has caused a flatness, then a disgust, and then a coldness betwixt many friends, I'll be bound. So think of meeting me not as I am in my letters (for they being written when in a good humour, and read when you have nothing better to do, make all seem alert and agreeable) but as you used to see me in London, Cambridge, etc. If you come to think, you will see there is a great difference. Do not think I speak thus in a light hearted way about the tenacity of our friendship, but with a very serious heart anxious lest we should disappoint each other, and so lessen our love a little. I hate this subject and to the devil with it./ 7 at night. I always come up to my room after dinner, at which we are not more than an hour: my sisters go into the drawing room, and I, as I drink no wine, come up here, and generally "spin a yarn" with you. Swift, Bolingbroke, and Pope were three very clever men—Pope I admire more and more for his sense. As to his poetry, I don't know of much. But still it is prose more beautifully and tastefully dressed than any one has ever made it—and he has given even epigrams the appearance of poetry.[3] I am angry with Hume for admiring the French so: and standing up so for polite manners to the ladies—a practice which turns Nature topsy turvy. I have got the character of being rather a brute in society—can't help it; I am worth more, I believe, than any young lady that ever was made, so I am more inclined to tell them to open the door for me, than for me to get up and do it for them. This is a most horrid sentence, on second thoughts—for millions of girls have existed a million times more virtuous than I am; and I am ashamed of having said it. I ought to scratch out the sentence—but why should you not see that I can say a silly thing? (i.e. because I so often say wise ones—N.B. sic cogitat vanitas) I never do write poetry now: and am sure you will make a much better hymn to God save the Emperor[4] than I could. T'is a noble air. I am elevated by my glass of port, and am looking round the table to see what I can be at. There is Byron—Hume—Helvetius—Diderot—Shakespeare. I have not read Shakespeare for a long time. I will tell you why. I found that *his manner* stuck so in my head that I was always trying to think in his way; I mean with his quaint words, etc.—this I don't wish. I don't think I've read him for a year. I expect a rich treat when I begin the old dear again. Your caricature of Death[5] is a very good one indeed—don't exaggerate the faces, pray, but get them near to Nature—which will make it impressive—but excessive caricature will spoil it. I did not know that I had been so foreboding of Death in my last letter: I want to live long, and see everything. I am glad you have taken to Cowper: some of his little poems are affecting far beyond anything in the English language: not heroic, but they make me cry. The Poplar field, is one of the best: and Alexander Selkirk. Good Night—I am going to Hume—his Essays are the most clear I ever read./ Thursday morn. "Greece, for her wisdom famed for ages, and always quoted in our schools, could only boast of seven sages—think of the number of her fools!" This is a translation of a French epigram, a very tolerable one I think./ ½ past one. What have I been doing the last hour? Behold these verses, they are the fruits, for they never came into my head before: but the wind was blowing hard at the windows and I somehow began to think of Will Thackeray: so the cockles of my heart were warmed, and up spouted the following: I have drunk a glass of port, and so sit down to transcribe them.

1

I cared not for life: for true friend I had none
I had heard 'twas a blessing not under the sun:
Some figures called friends, hollow, proud, or cold-hearted
Came to me like shadows—like shadows departed:
But a day came that turned all my sorrow to glee
When first I saw Willy, and Willy saw me!

2

The thought of my Willy is always a cheerer;
My wine has new flavour—the fire burns clearer:
The sun ever shines—I am pleased with all things—
And this crazy old world seems to go with new springs;—
And when we're together, (Oh! soon may it be!)
The world may go kissing of comets for me!

3

The chair that Will sat in, I sit in the best;
The tobacco is sweetest which Willy hath blest;
And I never found out that my wine tasted ill
When a tear would drop in it, for thinking of Will.

4

And now on my windows October blows chilly,
I laugh at blue devils, and think of my Willy:
I think, that our friendship will not drop away
Like the leaves from the trees, or our locks when they're grey:
I think that old age shall not freeze us, until
He creeps with Death's warrant to me and my Will.

5

If I get to fifty—may Willy get too:
And we'll laugh, Will, at all that grim sixty can do;
Old age?—let him do of what poets complain,
We'll thank him for making us children again;
Let him make us grey, gouty, blind, toothless, or silly,
Still old Ned shall be Ned—and old Willy be Willy!

6

We may both get so old that our senses expire
And leave us to doze half-alive by the fire:
Age may chill the warm heart which I think so divine,
But what warmth it has, Willy, shall ever be thine!
And if our speech goes, we must pass the long hours
When the Earth is laid bare with a Winter like our's,
Till Death finds us waiting him patiently still,
Willy looking at me, and I looking at Will!

There are my verses—I have polished them a little more, which has not done them any good. Take them, however, and may they tell no lies—I must go and get a walk—I am half blind with writing out these things./ 5 o'clock. I have had a long walk, and have such a composing vein to day that my head is in a swim of different thoughts. The metre of these verses has made me drunk; there is a rolling in it: or else this intoxication is a proof that I feel what I have said. I could do anything now—would you were here; I am just in the humour for a pipe. I desire you to make some lines to me as your Neddy. Wait your opportunity when a fit comes on you. Never mind about their goodness: I dare say I shall think these bad tomorrow when I am cool./ 7 at night. pp. (i.e. past port) My one glass is down—that descended upon a bed of boiled pork, which I had gorged before. Boiled leg of pork, parmesan cheese, and a glass of port, maketh a dinner for a prince. What shall I be at? I think I could versify enormously. I have more verses in my head about Willy: but you have enough, I think. Ye Gods! I am in a fit state of mind to sit with Willy in the Cigar Divan,[6] or the Sultan's Divan! I believe I am mad today. What hath made me mad? A great October wind which whistles at my window when I am indoors and blows me along when out of doors. I think I could drive four-in-hand just now. Lord Edward's death I have read—I think it dull very. I think he is a poor creature as to mind—he had the valour of a brute. He gave in to Revolutionary principles without thought, but through Irish impulse.[7] I have a wondrous inclination for to sing. A glass or two more of Port would make me rate myself above 20 Lord Edwards. No Hume, no nothing reasonable have I read for I wish now that all morality was impulse, and all the system of the world too. I keep hurrying on my spirits, not letting them stop—hurra—hurra—the dead can ride—i.e. those who are dead in heart. I don't pretend to have, like Mrs. Norton, a heart like a "withered nut that rattles in its shell"[8] but I see few people I care about, and so, oh Willy, be constant to me. Don't suppose I am drunk—only my one poor glass of port—but like the hares in March, I have my seasons. Perhaps tomorrow I shall be like a fellow after a debauch. In my walk to day I drew an old house near Beccles which I send. What a glorious tune the British Grenadiers is—nothing goes so near to make me cry as that song. There is great feeling in it. "When e'er they come to quarters in any country town, the lasses cry 'Huzza, lads, the Grenadiers are come: The Grenadiers are come, my boys, their lovers' hearts to cheer—then hip, hurra, hurra boys, for the British Grenadiers!'" Capital stanza that is, isn't it? And the tune is noble.[9] On Christianity, are you true, and, if you are, must we give up liking the British Grenadiers! Come to London—oh come, my dearest boy, and we'll yet have a good meeting. My feeling of security is now so great that I believe the great comet will not touch us, but hit the colure: which, in its turn, will fix on the comet so as to freeze it to death in 24 hours!!!![10] All we have to hope, in that case, is that the earth won't be the Comet's for his freezings are assuredly fire. Good Night—I shall be in London on the 20th or probably before. Come you up then, and we will hunt for lodgings for thee and be merry. Hurra! hurra! hurra! God bless you, my dear Boy: may we never part!

Here is a flight of crows to the right of the wish—a good omen.

Friday/ I think I made a fool of myself last night in my letter—there is no affectation however for I was in tip top spirits. Today I am also very well. Do you know anything of a Court of Love which formerly was in Provence? It is mentioned in Hume's Essays.[11] I should like to know something of it: my head is already at work cooking up some dramatic materials out of it. I am planning a play on it—I wonder where there is any account of it. However, I suppose it was a court where lovers pleaded their causes and their proposals and differences were judged. These are good materials for a play, and quite new./ 7 at night. I have been thinking of this plot all day.[12] Saturd: Morning. Did not write much to you yesterday, certainly. Last night I was seized all of a sudden with a tune I had heard Fanny Kemble[13] sing to—the fit remained on me all the evening, and on coming up to bed I made some verses to it. I send you them and the tune, which you may get your Mammy to play for you. It is a pretty tune—the words tol de rol. To day, there is a most extraordinary heat in the atmosphere—quite unseasonable—something seems brewing. We are all stupid. I will write out the words to the tune.

1

Farewell to merry summertime—I hear the wintry gale
That bids me fill my pipe again, and tap the foaming ale.
The trees are dying fast without, and cheerless is the scene,
But tobacco leaves are sprouting, boys, and friendship's evergreen!

2

In summer, Friendship wanders out along the sunny plain,
But she swears she never feels so strong as o'er the fire again:
I hear the winds cry piping by:—let's tackle to our cheer,
And drink a merry stirrup-cup to the departing year.

3

Old year full lusty hath thy youth, and summer manhood been,
Stretched out at ease beneath the sun, or in the forest green.
But now your pipe is cracked with age, and peevish you are grown,
While you chatter in the wood that you have starved to skin and bone!

4

No matter, friends—kind Nature blows some good with ev'ry gale:
And if October kills the year, he brews our nutbrown ale;
Then let's fill our glasses up, and drink his health with hearty minds
In ale as yellow as his leaves, and stronger than his winds!

There you be—all done, no more fun. You can sing them an you please. They are rather of the Williams[14] order on a reperusal./ 8 at night. Shall be glad to see you, my boy. This letter shall go to post tomorrow. "Tomorrow to fresh Church and parsons new!"[15] T'will be Sunday. Good Night./ Sunday, I shall seal my letter. Shall I have one from you to morrow?

October 11, 1831[16]

[1] Thackeray had taken chambers at 5 Essex Court, Middle Temple, and was reading law under William Taprell, a special pleader. EFG spent three weeks in London with Thackeray and left for Cambridge about November 15. (See letter to Allen, Nov. 12, 1831, n.4.)

[2] William Paley (1743-1805), Cambridge theologian and lecturer on Moral Philosophy at the University, in 1794 published his *View of the Evidences of Christianity*, one of the "set books" EFG had studied as an undergraduate. Paley defends the credibility of Biblical miracles and follows with an attack on "any other similar miracles," frequently directing his argument toward the essay "Of Miracles" by David Hume (1711-76). Hume cited miracles claimed to have been effected at the tomb of the Abbé Paris (1690-1727), French theologian and Jansenist, and other reported miracles to demonstrate the unreliability of testimony offered in their support. Paley, in Part I, Proposition II, of his *Evidences* likewise discredits the Abbé Paris miracles, refusing to accept them as comparable with those recorded in the Bible. No controversy between the two writers is involved. They differ only in their reasons for disbelieving reports.

[3] This evaluation of Pope was commonly held by the Romantic critics. EFG's judgment on Pope's "prose" parallels a passage in William Hazlitt's *Lectures on the English Poets* (1818): "The question whether Pope was a poet, has hardly yet been settled, and is hardly worth settling; for if he was not a great poet, he must have been a great prose-writer" ("On Dryden and Pope," *Complete Works*, ed. P. P. Howe, 1930, V, 69).

[4] Probably Nicholas I of Russia. A revolt the Poles had successfully maintained for a year had ended with the reoccupation of Warsaw by Russian forces in September, 1831. One of the objectives of the revolutionists was the deposition of Nicholas as King of Poland, a title he claimed.

In the caption of a grimly humorous cartoon of Death in a letter of October 2, to which EFG subsequently refers, Thackeray had alluded to the revolt. Evidently he had suggested that EFG write a hymn, "God Save the Emperor." Only portions of Thackeray's letter are extant in a volume made up by EFG from fragments of the correspondence, now in the Berg Collection of the New York Public Library.

[5] The drawing is reproduced in the Thackeray *Biographical Edition*, IX, xxxiii, and in *The Letters and Private Papers of William Makepeace Thackeray*, ed. Gordon N. Ray, 4 vols., 1945-46, I, opposite p. 163.

[6] Cigar divans were smoking parlors in early 19-century London. "The best cup of coffee to be had in London is at the Cigar Divan, No. 102, Strand. You pay 1s. to enter the Divan, which will entitle you to a cup of coffee and cigar, and the privileges of the room, the newspapers, chess, etc." A list of taverns "that cook joints every quarter or half an hour from 5 P.M. to 7 P.M., (charge 2s. a head)" includes "Simpson's at the Cigar Divan, No. 102 Strand" (Peter Cunningham, *A Handbook for London*, 2 vols., 1849, I, xxiii-xxiv).

Gentlemen never smoked in the presence of ladies, and smoking in the streets was frowned upon until well past mid-century. Thomas Hughes, author of *Tom Brown's School Days,* "made himself conspicuous by smoking on the way home from the Temple about 1848." (Mrs. C. S. Peel, "Homes and Habits," *Early Victorian England,* G. M. Young, ed. 2 vols., 1934, I, 99). EFG was brazen enough to walk up Regent Street with a cigar in his mouth in 1843.

[7] Lord Edward Fitzgerald (1763-98), one of the leaders of the Society of the United Irishmen in its struggle for Irish independence during the last decade of the eighteenth century. *The Life and Death of Lord Edward Fitzgerald* had been published the previous July by Thomas Moore, the Irish poet. Most historians have agreed with EFG's characterization of the patriot. They acknowledge his charm, generosity, and wit, but describe him as hot-headed and deficient in qualities of leadership.

[8] Mrs. Caroline Norton (1808-77), granddaughter of Richard Brinsley Sheridan. EFG misquotes the opening lines of a poem (which fails to rise above the lyric pitch of the quotation) published in *The Undying One, and Other Poems* (1830):

> My heart is like a withered nut,
> Rattling within its hollow shell;
> You cannot ope my breast, and put
> Anything fresh with it to dwell.

There are three stanzas in the piece, each beginning with the initial line.

[9] "The British Grenadiers," a popular jingoistic song which appears to have circulated in a number of versions. The air is the same for all and was identified by Granville Bantock as "Sir Nowell's Delight (1634)" (*One Hundred Songs of England,* ed. Granville Bantock, Boston, 1914, p. 24). Bantock further states that the Grenadier Guards adopted the song as their regimental march. EFG's source appears to have been an obscure version, for his stanza is found in none of those examined in a number of song collections.

[10] The approach of Biela's Comet to within 20,000 miles of the earth had been predicted for November 27, 1832. When it became generally known that its orbit was so near the earth's, the information "produced a panic among many persons who feared that the two bodies actually would meet" (Charles P. Olivier, *Meteors,* Baltimore, 1925, p. 65). Before its expected return in 1866, Sir John Herschel wrote, "The orbit of this comet very nearly intersects that of the earth at the place which the earth occupies on or about November 30. If ever the earth is to be swallowed up by a comet, it will be on that day of the year. In the year 1832 we missed it by a month" (Mary Proctor and A.C.D. Crommelin, *Comets,* 1937, p. 91).

Biela's Comet no longer exists. Upon its appearance in 1845, it was observed to have split into two fragments. In 1866 observers noted a shower of meteors, which was repeated in 1872. The comet had disintegrated. Curious theories about it are expounded in *Ragnorak* by Ignatius Donnelly (New York, 1883).

The term "colure," used by EFG, applies to either of two great circles of the celestial sphere, intercepting at the celestial poles, which would, indeed, be an area of extreme cold. This fact validates the reading of "freeze" and "his freezings are assuredly fire" in EFG's rather weak badinage. The point is mentioned because FitzGerald's handwriting is often difficult to decipher and there has been considerable discussion among scholars about words in this letter. EFG spells colure, "cholure."

[11] In his essay, "Of Political Society," Hume wrote, "Among nations, where an

immoral gallantry, if covered with a thin veil of mystery, is, in some degree, authorized by custom, there immediately arise a set of rules, calculated for the conveniency of that attachment. The famous court or parliament of love in Provence formerly decided all difficult cases of this nature" (*Essays, Moral, Political, and Literary*, 2 vols., eds. T. H. Green and T. H. Grose, 1898, II, 201).

[12] Although the manuscript seems not to have survived, EFG may actually have written a play on the subject. Thackeray, his memory failing him, recorded in his diary, June 10, 1832, "J. Kemble told me of a play of F.G.'s of wh. I had never heard & wh. he must have been writing during our correspondence last year, this is not open of him. Kemble says it possesses very great beauties. I should like to judge for myself" (*Thackeray Letters and Papers*, I, 208).

[13] Frances Ann (Fanny) Kemble (1809-93), daughter of the actor, Charles Kemble, and sister of EFG's school and college friend, John M. Kemble. See Biographical Profile.

[14] William Williams. See letter to Allen, May 21, 1830, n.3.

[15] EFG parodies the last line of Milton's "Lycidas": "Tomorrow to fresh Woods and Pastures new."

[16] EFG's error for October 9.

To John Allen

[London]
Pmk., November 12, 1831

My dear Allen,

I had taken Mrs. Perry's lodgings[1] for all this term, but my Mother wants a gentleman at Brighton[2]—so I shall be forced to give up my projected stay at Cambridge, I am afraid. I am coming down to you on Monday or Tuesday. Now, as you are reading,[3] I shall never come and see you, but you can come to me when you are tired of reading. I have plenty to talk to you about. I wanted to write to you in the vacation but did not know where to direct to. Thackeray and I kept up a red-hot correspondence all the summer. I have now been three weeks in town with him.[4] He is well, I am well. All these things we will talk over when we are together. Is Sansum alive? Tell him I am so.

Now all I have to say is that you are not to care a hang for me when I come [to][5] Cambridge, but go on reading, reading—only coming to see me when you have nothing else to do.

Yrs
E. FitzGerald.

Saturday
15 Jermyn Street.

P.S. Prepare your eyes to see me in a new black surtout.

[1] The rooms in King's Parade which he had occupied as an undergraduate.

[2] Brighton, Sussex, in 1831 six hours from London by coach, had been a fashionable seaside resort since the mid-eighteenth century. Mrs. FitzGerald was a frequent visitor. To Edward it came to be "that hatefullest of all places" with "the roaring unsophisticated ocean at one side, and four miles length of idle, useless, ornamental, population on the other."

[3] "Reading," that is, preparing for the tripos, the university honors examinations. The preparation was called "cramming" in that day as it is today.

[4] In a letter received by EFG at Cambridge on which he noted, "First Letter after my dep: fro: London: in Novr 1831," Thackeray wrote, "I dont think my room will ever appear comfortable again—here are your things lying in the exact place you left them—God bless you dear dear FitzGerald . . . the Kembles have called J. yesterday Henry to day—[Friday] he is a dear fellow & we talk about nothing but you and the theatres—the two things I like best in the world." Thackeray began his letter on Wednesday, November 16, and concluded it on Monday, the 21st, with, "I am *coming* to you tomorrow." Thackeray spent four days at Cambridge at this time, but he appears to have delayed his departure from London, for the letter was postmarked there on November 23 (*Thackeray Letters and Papers*, I, 172, where the letter is dated "16-23 November 1831.").

[5] A corner of the page is torn off.

To John Allen

[London] Thursday
May 31st alas [1832]

Dear Allen,

I can make no plan of our co-residence yet:[1] for I leave London tomorrow, rather suddenly, and on no very pleasant commission: but so it is. It is of no use to tell you what this is: I don't think I ought.[2] I do not know however that I shall be long away: send me a letter and tell me what your direction will be when you leave Cambridge. I got in [in] time to see my sister married on Tuesday morning:[3] the ceremony is impressive: especially to the bride and bridegroom, as one might imagine would be the case. Thackeray is here and well: Mazzinghi also.[4] I did not find the Machiavelli you spoke of: but have got another. I go to Seaford, Sussex, where you may write to me: that is all the direction necessary. Remember me to all I know, to whom a remembrance from me is becoming, and so farewell, with many feelings of love to yourself. London is miserable enough with its wet: but that is neither here nor there.

I forgot to tell you that when I came up on the mail, and fell a-dozing in the morning, the sights of the pages in crimson and the funerals which the Lady of Shalott saw and wove, floated before me: really, the poem has taken lodging in my poor head.[5]

Ever yours most affectionately
E. FitzGerald

[1] EFG had gone to London on May 16 or 17 after a visit to Cambridge. He and Allen had proposed spending a portion of the summer together.

[2] See letter of Nov. 21, 1832, and Biographical Profile of his sister Andalusia.

[3] Jane Theresa FitzGerald married the Reverend John Brewster Wilkinson, Rector of Holbrook, Suffolk, May 29, 1832. EFG wrote to Allen in January, 1848, "You have doubtless seen many good men in your wanderings: but I have seen no other Wilkinson. . . . in twenty years I have never known Wilkinson do anything, or say anything, he believed to be wrong—I verily believe!" EFG could probably have made the same statement about Allen.

[4] Thomas John Mazzinghi (1810-93), Trinity College, Cambridge; B.A. 1832; M.A. 1835. He attended Charterhouse School with Thackeray, through whom EFG made his acquaintance. Admitted to the Inner Temple in 1829 and called to the Bar in 1842, Mazzinghi served with the Indian Law Commission, 1865-69. From 1873 until his death he was librarian of the William Salt Library, Stafford. After EFG's death Mazzinghi sent Aldis Wright contradictory accounts of their first meeting; but through his information, Thackeray's correspondence, and Allen's diary it is evident that the two were introduced during Thackeray's four-day visit to Cambridge in November, 1831. The two men corresponded, but members of the Mazzinghi family stated that EFG's letters had been destroyed.

[5] EFG refers to "The Lady of Shalott," published in Tennyson's *Poems* the following December although dated 1833. Manuscript copies of the poet's early works circulated freely among his friends; and EFG had read one in Allen's possession.

To John Allen

[Southampton]
Tuesday
[July 31, 1832]

My dear Allen,

I have been at Southampton a week. I have been waiting for letters from Thackeray for some time, and lo I this morning received one stating that he had been in this neighbourhood for a fortnight or more and was gone to Havre de Grace, by a packet that starts from here. And thus have we played at bopeep together.[1]

If it were possible for you to live with me, I would come down into Wales by a Coach tomorrow—but I am but a bad walker. I shall not return to Seaford,[2] so I have the summer before me. Write by return of post else I shall have left this place, for Havre perhaps to join Thackeray; and if you think you can be with me any time, I would give a good deal to bring it about. Notwithstanding, you will not of course hurt the feelings of your relations. Do write by return of post, for on Monday the packet sails for Havre, and I may be off.[3]

And now I will tell you of a pilgrimage I made that put me in mind of you much. I went to Salisbury to see the Cathedral, but more to walk to Bemerton, George Herbert's village.[4] It is about a mile and half from Salisbury alongside a pleasant stream with old-fashioned watermills beside: through fields very fertile. When I got to Bemerton I scarcely knew what to do with myself. It is a very pretty village with the Church and Parsonage much as Herbert must have left it. But there was no memorial of him either in or outside the walls of the church: though there have been Bishops and Deans and I know not what all so close at hand at Salisbury. This is a great shame indeed. I would gladly put up a plain stone if I could get the Rector's leave. I was very sorry to see no tablet of any kind.[5] The people in the Cottages had heard of a very pious man named Herbert, and had read his books—but they don't know where he lies.[6] I have drawn the church and village: the little woodcut of it in Walton's Lives is very like. I thought I must have passed along the spot in the road where he assisted the man with the fallen horse:[7] and to shew the benefit of good examples, I was serviceable that very evening in the town to some people coming in a cart: for the driver was drunk and driving furiously home from the races, and I believe would have fallen out, but that some folks, amongst whom I was one, stopped the cart. This long history is now at an end. I wanted John Allen much to be with me. I noticed the little window into which Herbert's friend looked, and saw him kneeling so long before the altar, when he was first ordained.[8] Farewell. Pray write. I am at my old friend Weeks's Hotel, *Above Bar*, Southampton. Do not write unless your letter can reach me by Sunday. The case is, if [we] can reside together, let it be: but I am too poor a walker to go over S. Wales.

Yours E.FG.

P.S. Tell me whereabout in Pembrokeshire Bosherston is—near Milford Haven, or where?[9]

[1] Thackeray had reached his majority July 18 and came into a patrimony of about £20,000, a portion of which had already evaporated. Since 1829 he had been spending freely and gambling foolishly. Anticipating imminent independence, he had written to EFG from Devon the first week in July, "My dear Teddikin will you come with me to Paris—in a month? We will first take a walk in Nor-

mandy, and then go for a fortnight or so to Paris. I have a strange idea that I shall be in Italy before the autumn is over, and if my dear dear old Teddibus wd but come with me we will be happy in a Paradise of pictures—what say you o my Teddibus—"(Thackeray Letters and Papers, I, 247). Thackeray sailed from Plymouth July 19 and spent a week on the Isle of Wight and three days at Fareham, Hants, a mere ten miles from EFG at Southampton. He embarked for Havre July 31, the day EFG received the letter proposing the trip.

[2] See letter to Allen, [Mar. 15, 1831], n.4.

[3] EFG went to Wales, not to France, as the letters which follow reveal.

[4] George Herbert (1593-1633), divine and poet.

[5] EFG did not carry out his proposal; but in 1896 just such a "plain stone" as he had considered was placed in the north wall of St. Andrews. Into the stone is cut a Greek cross and the briefest of legends, "G. H. 1632." A stained-glass memorial window was placed in the west wall in 1934, the cost being met by contributions from Herbert's admirers throughout the world (Data supplied by the Reverend M. Hurst-Bannister of Bemerton Rectory).

[6] Herbert is buried beneath the altar in Bemerton Church.

[7] Walton records that once, while walking to Salisbury to meet with some friends, Herbert "saw a poor man with a poorer horse, that was fallen under his load: they were both in distress, and needed present help; which Mr. Herbert perceiving, put off his canonical coat, and helped the poor man to unload, and after to load, his horse. The poor man blessed him for it, and he blessed the poor man; and was so like the good Samaritan, that he gave him money to refresh both himself and his horse; and told him, 'That if he loved himself he should be merciful to his beast'" (Izaak Walton, "The Life of George Herbert," *The Complete Angler and the Lives of Donne, Wotten, Hooker, Herbert and Sanderson*, 1906, p. 409).

[8] "When at his induction he was shut into Bemerton Church, being left there alone to toll the bell,—as the law requires him," says Walton, "he stayed so much longer than an ordinary time . . . that his friend Mr. Woodnot looked in at the church window, and saw him lie prostrate on the ground before the altar; at which time and place—as he after told Mr. Woodnot—he set some rules to himself, for the future manage of his life; and then and there made a vow to keep them" (ibid., 395).

[9] Bosherston, in southwest Pembrokeshire, about six miles southwest of Pembroke and a mile or so from St. Govan's Head. Allen's brother William was Rector of Bosherston and of St. Brides.

To John Allen

Tenby, Tuesday
[Late August, 1832]

My dear Allen,

I have taken a very nice lodging, looking out on the sea with two bedrooms—I cannot have less. Pray come then and fill one of them, for a week, and live with me.[1] I have arranged all matters. I think I heard you say you were going to Bosherston at the end of this week: why not come here? I have not the conscience to ask you to leave Freestone,[2] but I think one's brother can always spare one better than one's cousins can. Pray do come my dear fellow.

Also pray tell your cousin, whom I know by no other name than what you call him, Tom, that I shall be very glad if he will come for as long as he can and will at any time—in his excursions to Balls, etc. I shall be very glad to give him bed and bachelor's fare, for as long as he will.

Now do, *do*, come—as little children say.

Yours ever
E.FG.

My compliments to Mr. and Mrs. Allen, and your cousins.

Come at the end of the week, and we will go and hear Hare[3] preach, which he will do: or go to Penally.[4] God bless you.

[1] At Tenby, an attractive seaside town on Carmarthen Bay, EFG took lodgings at Rees's boarding house, later named Tenby House, in High Street opposite a flight of steps descending to an area of fishermen's dwellings at water level. At the time of EFG's visit, Rees's stood in Back Street, a thoroughfare separated from High Street by a row of houses extending from Tudor Square. These dwellings were subsequently removed and the two streets became one (Letter of George Bentley, London publisher, to Aldis Wright, Jan. 22, 1894, Trinity College Library). "Tenby—I don't remember a pleasanter place," EFG wrote in October, 1859. Another lodger at Rees's at the time was W. Kenworthy Browne of Bedford, a lad of sixteen whose acquaintance EFG had made on the steam packet from Bristol to Tenby. See Biographical Profile.

[2] At Freestone Hall, near Milton, six miles north of Tenby, lived John Allen's cousin, James Allen. Besides the parents, the family included a son, Thomas (subsequently referred to in the letter), and three daughters, Fanny, Mary, and Anne. Fanny married Allen's brother William. Upon arriving in Wales, EFG may have first joined Allen at Bosherston. They then visited at Freestone Hall, after which EFG went to Tenby where he remained for some weeks, possibly through September. He returned to Freestone and Tenby for a brief visit the following autumn. Vivid memories of these visits appear in his letters for many years. Part of Freestone Hall was demolished later in the century and the remainder was converted into a farmhouse (Thomas Wright, *The Life of Edward FitzGerald*, 2 vols., 1904, I, 103, n.2).

[3] Augustus William Hare (1792-1834), the rector of Alton Barnes, Wiltshire, brother of the more famous liberal theologian, Julius Hare (1795-1855), with whom, in 1827, he had published *Guesses at Truth.* Augustus had married Maria Leycester, daughter of the rector of Stoke-upon-Terne, Shropshire. During August and September, 1832, while visiting Mrs. Hare's father and stepmother at Tenby,

Hare preached frequently in Tenby Church (Augustus J. C. Hare, *Memorials of a Quiet Life*, 2 vols., 1872, I, 445-46).

[4] Penally, a village about a mile southwest of Tenby.

To John Allen

London[1]
Nov. 21, 1832

My dear Allen,

I suppose it must seem strange to you that I should like writing letters: and indeed I don't know that I do like it in general. However, here I see no companions, so I am pleased to talk to my old friend John Allen: which indeed keeps alive my humanity very much. I find my sister,[2] to appearance, much better than when I came. I think my society has done her a great deal of good. I am with her a good deal. I have been about to divers Bookshops and have bought several books—a Bacon's Essays, Evelyn's Sylva, Browne's Religio Medici, Hazlitt's Poets,[3] etc. The latter I bought to add to my Paradise,[4] which however has stood still of late. I mean to write out Carew's verses in this letter for you, and your Paradise. As to the Religio, I have read it again: and keep my opinion of it: except admiring the eloquence, and beauty of the notions, more. But the arguments are not more convincing. Nevertheless, it is a very fine piece of English: which is, I believe, all that you contend for. Hazlitt's Poets is the best selection I have ever seen. I have read some Chaucer too, which I like. In short I have been reading a good deal since I have been here: but not much in the way of knowledge.

I saw Mazzinghi[5] on Sunday. He was at the lakes in the summer: where he was laid up of Asthma—an uncommon complaint for a young man. I suspect he weakens himself by Morison[6] whose pills he persists in taking. He maintains his old theories: Owen of Lanark,[7] Morison etc. There is something very grand in Mazzinghi's notions I think: they are all extravagant and wild, but so consistent with each other: neither does he like any thing by halves. I went to the theater last week to see Jonson's Every Man in his Humour.[8] It is a good but over rated play. It was tolerably well done: but does not tempt me to the theater a second time.

You must remember to give my best remembrances to all your relations at Freestone: and to assure them very truly that I do not forget them. As I lay in bed this morning, half dozing, I walked in imagination all the way from Tenby to Freestone by the road I know so well: by the watermill, by Gumfreston, Ivy tower, and through the gates, and the long road that leads to Carew.[9] Now for the poet Carew:[10]

1

Ask me no more where Jove bestows,
When June is past, the fading rose:
For in your beauty's orient deep,
The flowers, as in their causes, sleep.

2

Ask me no more whither do stray
The golden atoms of the day:
For in pure love did Heav'n prepare
Those powders to enrich your hair.

3

Ask me no more whither doth haste
The nightingale when June is past:
For in your sweet dividing throat
She winters, and keeps warm her note.

4

Ask me no more where those stars light
That downward fall at dead of night:
For in your eyes they sit, and there
Fixed become, as in their sphere.

5

Ask me no more if east or west
The phoenix builds her spicy nest:
For unto you at last she flies,
And in your fragrant bosom dies.

These lines are exaggerated, as all in Charles's time, but very beautiful. Of music I have little: only at night after my sister has gone to bed. She has no pleasure in it, and that sort of thing soon dwindles, without an edge being given now and then.

Think of my idleness in not sending your Purple Island.[11] There has it been lying all ready packed up for more than a fortnight. It shall go today or tomorrow, I swear it. I have bought a new edition of Wordsworth in four volumes very nice.[12]

Last week I was unhappy and in low spirits on account of the same turmoil in my head that I had once at Seaford. For that I had the satisfaction of finding a cause, smoking: but for this I have none, except the notion that it may be a defect in my reason or head, which is what annoys me. Living close by my sister who has this malady pronounced exaggerates my fears: which I hope are groundless. I find that if I do not employ my thought much, I keep my head light and clear: but, otherwise, not. I am always fresh and clear headed of a morning: but become more rambling of an evening: which seems to shew that my brain *wears* by use: the idleness of sleep repairs it. This may be fancy. The other night when I lay in bed feeling my head get warmer and warmer I felt that if I should pray to some protector for relief, I should be relieved: but I have not yet learned the certainty of there being any. It is a melancholy thing, that the want of happiness and security caused by scepticism is no proof of the truth of religion: for if a man is miserable because he has not a guinea it may make him happy to believe he has a guinea, but still he has it not. So if one can delude oneself into a belief, it is a happiness: but some cannot help feeling all the time that it is a delusion. But all this is useless talk: and I must ask you to excuse it.

Good bye, my dear fellow: I hope you and all yours are as well as possible. Perhaps I shall soon laugh at my fancies if fancies they are: in the meantime I shall stand strict centinel over my head: for all is well if one *is conscious* there is something wrong, or may be something wrong. It is from my want of a Father above that I thus confess myself, for consolation's sake, to my very best friend: and I truly believe that had I been with you I should never have had a tittle of this uneasiness.

Yours most affectionately

E.

[1] EFG at this time was staying in the family town house, 39 Portland Place.

[2] Andalusia. See Biographical Profile. EFG refers to Lusia's health again later in the letter and comments on an ailment of his own which he describes as his "hot head." He keeps Allen informed about the complaint for some years before the topic disappears from his letters. Physicians find EFG's reports of his symptoms too obscure and meager to identify a specific disorder. In 1864 his affliction returned and he consulted a doctor in London. Frederick Tennyson reported to the Poet Laureate that EFG "has been ill with his old complaint, blood to the head" (Hallam Tennyson, *Alfred Lord Tennyson, A Memoir*, 2 vols., 1897, I, 494). "Blood to the head" was, perhaps, a physician's diagnosis.

[3] *Sylva, or a Discourse on Forest Trees and the Propagation of Timber* (1664), by John Evelyn (1620-1706), Royalist, diarist, and miscellaneous writer. *Sylva*, a

plea for reforestation, was written to support an appeal by the Commissioners of the Navy. The work is said to have induced landowners to plant "millions" of oak trees which provided timber needed for warships a century later. Some poet might still write of Evelyn as Wordsworth wrote of his Puritan contemporary—

> Milton! thou should'st be living at this hour:
> England hath need of thee:

for, included in his works, is *Fumifugium,* a protest against the pollution of London's air by smoke.

Religio Medici, published in 1643 by Sir Thomas Browne (1605-82), a collection of opinions on a wide variety of subjects relating to religion, produced by a man at times skeptical, at times credulous.

In 1824 William Hazlitt (1778-1830) published *Select British Poets,* "or new elegant extracts from Chaucer to the present time, with critical remarks." His zeal in bringing his anthology up to date seems to have involved him in copyright difficulties. The listing for the volume in the *British Museum Catalogue* includes the note: "This edition contains extracts from the works of poets living at the time of its publication. It was suppressed and re-issued the next year with these extracts omitted." The 1825 edition bore a new title, *Select Poets of Great Britain.* It is possible that EFG's copy had come from Hazlitt's private library. "I post you Hazlitt's own copy of his English Poets, with a few of his marks for another Edition in it," EFG wrote to C. E. Norton on February 7, 1876. "If you like to keep it, pray do: if you like better to give it to Hazlitt's successor, Mr. Lowell, do that from yourself." *The British Museum Catalogue* gives the title of the 1824 anthology only; the *English Catalogue of Books,* 1801-36, gives the title only of the 1825 issue. The implication of both entries is that a single title (though they do not agree on *one*) was used for both editions. P. P. Howe, in his *Life of William Hazlitt,* errs in stating, "*Select Poets of Great Britain* . . . made its appearance in this summer [1824]" (New York, 1922, p. 368).

4 Paradise Book, the title of commonplace books into which the two copied favorite poems.

5 See letter of May 31, [1832], n.4.

6 James Morison, who called himself "the Hygiest." Originally a merchant, in 1825 he began "peddling" his nostrum after, states the DNB, he had cured himself of an illness. "Morison's Pills" have gained fame through Carlyle's use of the term in *Past and Present* to brand proposed legislative panaceas for the social ills of the time. (Carlyle spelled the name *Morrison.*) "The Hygiest" advertised extensively and, apparently, successfully. Reporting on the health of his stepfather, Major Henry Carmichael-Smyth, in the autumn of 1841, Thackeray wrote to EFG, "In the last twenty years he has been successively a convert to Abernethy's blue-pills, of which he has swallowed pounds—to Morison's ditto—which he flung in by spoonfuls" (*Thackeray Letters and Papers,* II, 37).

7 Robert Owen (1771-1858), English industrial and social reformer, noted for the enlightened labor-management policies developed at the cotton mills at New Lanarck, near Glasgow, of which he was part owner. Improved housing, stores in which wares of the best quality were sold at cost, day schools for children to the age of ten, and separate evening schools for youths and adults were among the benefits Owen provided for his laborers. His proposals to guide the evolution of rural villages into industrial towns by establishing "communistic" societies in

garden cities were too radical for acceptance. As a result of misguided zeal and heterodox views, particularly on religion and marriage, Owen lost popularity and support. "Owenism," the foundation of modern British socialism, came to represent in the popular mind a combination of trade unionism, heresy, and sexual license.

[8] The London *Times*, Nov. 10, 1832, records, "Theatre Royal, Drury Lane. This evening (1st time these 15 years) Ben Jonson's *Every Man in His Humour.*" The cast included William Macready as Kitely; William Farren as Brainworm; and J. P. Harley as Master Stephen.

[9] Carew Castle, five or six miles east of Tenby, near Milton. Gumfreston was a village, and Ivy Tower, a manor house en route.

[10] Thomas Carew (1595-1640).

[11] *The Purple Island, or the Isle of Man* by Phineas Fletcher (1582-1650), a poem in twelve cantos published in 1633. The work is an elaborate allegorical description of the human body and mind.

[12] Published in July by Longman, Price, 24s (*English Catalogue*, 1801-36).

To John Allen

London
Nov. [27, 1832][1]

My dear Allen,

The first thing I do in answering your letter is to tell you that I am angry at your saying that your conscience pricks you for not having written to me before. I am of that superior race of men, that are quite content to hear themselves talk, and read their own writing. But, in seriousness, I have such love of you, and of myself, that once every week, at least, I feel spurred on by a sort of gathering up of feelings, to vent myself in a letter upon you: but if once I hear you say that it makes your conscience thus uneasy till you answer, I shall give it up. Upon my word I tell you, that I do not in the least require it. You, who do not love writing, cannot think that any one else does: but I am sorry to say that I have a very young-lady-like partiality to writing to those that I love: but I find it hard work to those I care not for. Your letter is a very delightful one: yes I do say so: though you will think I jest: for I see it was written not without many pauses as to what you should say: especially on the third side, which is natural. I shall do as you say about reading for Christianity: and read Barrow, Hooker, and Jeremy Taylor.[2] I assure you, a slender pretence will make me throw myself upon Christianity. I have always told you that I knew a religion to be necessary for men. I am surprised to read in Bacon that "Atheism did never perturb states" and he instances that the times of Augustus, which were inclined to Atheism, were quiet and well ordered times.[3] They were dissolute times, however, in private manners, I fancy: but one would fancy that dissolute men would always make unquiet subjects. But certainly, I may judge that belief is a comfort to an unquiet mind.

The Purple Island is the identical edition you speak of. I have got Castra[4] which is *not* worth the money: though it is full of fine ideas. Every time I write I shall send you something for your Paradise: each of which pieces will be worth the Postage, as you will confess. I have been reading Shakespeare's Sonnets: and I believe I am unprejudiced when I say, I had but half an idea of him, Demigod as he seemed before, till I read them carefully. How can Hazlitt call Warton's the finest sonnets?[5] There is the air of pedantry and labour in his. But Shakespeare's are perfectly simple, and have the very essence of tenderness that is only to be found in the best parts of his Romeo and Juliet besides. I have truly been lapped in these Sonnets for some time: they seem all stuck about my heart, like the ballads that used to be on the walls of London. I have put a great many into my Paradise, giving each a fair white sheet for himself: there being nothing worthy to be in the same page. I could talk for an hour about them: but it is not fit in a letter. Pickering is publishing a new Edition of Walton's Angler, which will cost £5.[6] This is a little too much, methinks: but they say it will pay excellently. I had a letter from Thackeray saying he was coming over here: but I know not if 'twill hold.

I shall tell you of myself, that I have been better since I wrote to you. Mazzinghi tells me that November weather breeds Blue Devils —so that there is a French proverb, "In October, de Englishman shoot de pheasant: in November he shoot himself." This I suppose is the case with me: so away with November, as soon as may be. "Canst thou my Clora" is being put in proper musical trim:[7] and I will write it out for you when all is right. I am sorry you are getting so musical: and if I take your advice about so big a thing as Christianity, take you mine about music. I am sure that this pleasure of music grows so on people, that many of the hours that you would have devoted to Jeremy Taylor, etc., will be melted down into tunes, and the idle train of thought that music puts us into. I fancy I have discovered the true philosophy of this: but I think you must have heard me enlarge. Therefore "satis."

I have gabbled on so long that there is scarce room for my quotation. But it shall come though in a shapeless manner,[8] for the sake of room. Have you got in your Christian Poet,[9] a poem by Sir H. Wotton—"How happy is he born or taught, that serveth not another's will"? It is very beautiful, and fit for a Paradise of any kind. Here are some lines from old Lily, which your ear will put in the proper metre. It gives a fine description of a fellow walking in Spring, and looking here and there, and pricking up his ears, as different birds sing. "What bird so sings, but doth so wail? Oh! 'tis the ravished nightingale: 'Jug, jug, jug, jug, terue,' she cries, and still her woes at midnight rise. Brave prick-song! who is't now we hear? It is the lark so shrill and clear: against heaven's gate he claps his wings, the morn not waking till he sings. Hark, too, with what a pretty note poor Robin Redbreast tunes his throat: Hark how the jolly cuckoos sing 'Cuckoo' to welcome in the Spring: 'Cuckoo' to welcome in the Spring."[10] This is very English, and pleasant, I think: and so I hope you will. I could have sent you many a more sentimental thing, but nothing better. I admit nothing into my Paradise, but such as breathe content, and virtue: I count "Back and syde" to breathe both of these, with a little good drink over.[11]

Wednesday [November 28, 1832]

P.S. I sealed up my letter yesterday, forgetting to finish. I write thus soon becase I gets a frank." You shall benefit by another bit of poetry. I do not admit it into my Paradise, being too gloomy: but it will please both of us. It is the prototype of the Pensieroso.

Hence all you vain delights!
As short as are the nights
Wherein you spend your folly!
There's nought in this life sweet,
If man were wise to see 't,
But only melancholy;
Oh sweetest melancholy!
Welcome folded arms, and fixed eyes,
A sigh, that piercing mortifies,
A look that 's fastened to the ground,
A tongue chain'd up without a sound!

Fountain heads, and pathless groves,
Places which pale passion loves!
Moonlight walks, when all the fowls
Are warmly hous'd, save bats and owls!
A midnight dell, a passing groan!
These are the sounds we feed upon;
Then stretch our bones in a still gloomy valley;
Nothing's so dainty sweet as [lovely] melancholy.

(From the *Nice Valour, or the Passionate Madman*, by Fletcher.)[12]

I think these lines are quite of the finest order, and have a more headlong melancholy than Milton's, which are distinctly copied from these, as you must confess. And now this is a very long letter, and the best thing you can do when you get to the end, is to Da Capo, and read what I ordered you about answering. My dear fellow, it is a great pleasure to me to write to you; and to write out these dear poems.

The principal body of this letter, or as Mathews[13] has said, "The guts of it," was written yesterday. Last night was another of my blue Devil nights: no God, no sleep. I hope these fancies may go: and that they are but fancies.

In the Spring I am going to live at the cottage I told you of[14]—can you not come? You will do me good, indeed you will. My remembrance to all at Freestone. I am now going to walk round the Park with my sister.

Believe me that I am your very loving friend,

E.FG.

[1] This letter, begun on November 27 and finished the following day, was franked by EFG's father, exercising his privilege as an M.P. The letter is addressed to Allen at "Llamphey, Pembroke." Above the address, doubtless in FitzGerald senior's hand, is written, "London November twenty eight 1832." Below, appears the signature "Jh° FitzGerald." The letter is cancelled with a crowned stamp which reads

28 No 28
1832

[2] Isaac Barrow (1630-77), theologian, mathematician, divine, and, for the last eight years of his life, Master of Trinity College, Cambridge, where he had been student and Fellow. Barrow's sermons were noted for content and, one might add, for length. At a service attended by the Lord Mayor and Aldermen of London, Barrow's sermon, biographers record, required three and one half hours for delivery. Puritans, it is evident, did not hold a monopoly on homiletic prolixity. By his contemporaries, Barrow was ranked as a mathematician second only to his pupil, Isaac Newton.

Richard Hooker (1553-1600) and Jeremy Taylor (1613-67), also theologians. The readings in works of the old English divines which Allen recommended produced little alteration in EFG's religious views, but they were responsible, probably, for the hearty admiration he frequently expressed for their style.

[3] In his essay, "On Superstitions," Bacon states, "*Atheisme* leaves a Man to Sense; to Philosophy; to Naturall Piety; to Lawes; to Reputation; All which may be Guides to an outward Morall vertue, though *Religion* were not; But *Superstition* dismounts all these, and erecteth an absolute Monarchy, in the Mindes of Men. Therefore *Atheisme* did never perturbe *States*; For it makes Men wary of themselves, as looking no further: And we see the times enclined to *Atheisme* (as the Time of *Augustus Caesar*) were civil Times" (*Essays*, ed. W. Aldis Wright, Golden Treasury Series, 1863, pp. 68-69). Allen, turning to the essay, could

hardly miss the significance of the passage as a defense of EFG's position in their running debate.

[4] One can only guess at EFG's reference here. Perhaps he alludes to *Vie de Catherine II*, by Jean Henri Castra, Paris, 1797.

[5] Thomas Warton (1728-90), clergyman, *bon vivant*, professor of poetry at Oxford, 1757-67, and Poet Laureate, 1785 until his death. Warton was a pioneer in the Romantic revolt against the "correct" 18th-century poetry after the manner of Pope. His *Poems* (1777) were notable for their revival of the sonnet.

[6] Upon publication the edition sold for 6 guineas, not £5 as EFG had heard. "The Complete Angler, with original notes and Memoir by Sir H. Nicolas, 2 vol's imp., Pickering, 1833-36" (*English Catalogue*, 1801-36). A large paper edition was offered at 10 guineas.

[7] See letter of Dec. 7.

[8] EFG refers to the lines written as prose below.

[9] The title, probably, of one of Allen's commonplace books. EFG quotes the opening lines of Sir Henry Wotton's "The Character of a Happy Life." Sir Henry (1568-1639), poet and diplomat, was Provost of Eton from 1624 until his death.

[10] Lyric by John Lyly (1544-1606), poet and dramatist. Songs he wove into his plays are among the most delightful of Elizabethan lyrics. EFG quotes one sung by Trico in *Campaspe* (V, 1).

[11] Another song from an early play. This, one of the oldest and best of English drinking songs, is sung to open Act II of *Gammer Gurton's Needle* (c. 1562). The refrain runs:

Back and side go bare, go bare,
  Both foot and hand go cold;
But Belly, God send thee good ale enough,
  Whether it be new or old!

This rollicking farce, our first true English comedy, is credited to William Stevenson, Fellow of Christ's College, Cambridge.

[12] John Fletcher (1579-1625) of Beaumont and Fletcher fame. The lines quoted, Fletcher's best-known lyric sometimes given the title "Melancholy" are sung by "the Passionate Lord, the Duke's distracted Kinsman" (III, 3). Fletcher, as often, wrote *The Nice Valor* with a collaborator, possibly Thomas Middleton.

[13] Probably Charles Mathews (1776-1835), popular comedian. For the last 16 years of his life he toured successfully with a series of sketches, "Mathews at Home," in which he was the sole actor. His son Charles (1803-78) was also a comedian.

[14] The FitzGerald Suffolk home at this time was attractive Wherstead Lodge overlooking the River Orwell two miles south of Ipswich. The property, owned by Sir Robert Harland, was leased from about 1825 to 1835. If EFG considered occupying a cottage at Wherstead, he did not carry out the plan. Five years later, on the FitzGerald estate at Boulge, he found a cottage to meet his needs; and there he lived for 16 years.

To John Allen

[London]
Pmk. Dec. 7, 1832

My dear Allen,

You can hardly have got through my last letter by this time. I hope you liked the verses I sent you. The news of this week is that Thackeray has come to London, but is going to leave it again for Devonshire directly. He came very opportunely to divert my Blue Devils: notwithstanding, we do not see very much of each other: and he has now so many friends (especially the Bullers)[1] that he has no such wish for my society. He is as full of good humour and kindness as ever. The next news is that a new volume of Tennyson is out:[2] containing nothing more than you have in MS. except one or two things not worth having. I will give you a specimen—it is to Christopher North, and you will judge if it will do much good. Turn up the sheet.[3]

To Christopher North[4]

You did late review my lays,
  Crusty Christopher;
You did mingle blame and praise,
  Rusty Christopher.
When I learn't from whom it came
I forgave you all the blame,
  Musty Christopher:
I could *not* forgive the praise,
  Fusty Christopher.

Thursday Evening. Thackeray is going tomorrow: he was to have spent this day with me: but promises are not iron. There is a very nice selection of Wordsworth come out,[5] published by Moxon in Bond Street who has brought out Tennyson's book. He has also published a very beautiful little volume of Shakespeare's and Milton's Sonnets.[6] Either of these I will get you on your wishing it.

When you write back (of which there is no hurry) send me an account that you and your Brother were once telling me at Bosherston, of three Generals condemned to die after the siege of Pembroke in Cromwell's time: and of the lot being brought by a little child.[7] Give me their names, etc. (if you can) pretty circumstantially: or else, tell me where I can find some notice of it.

Friday. This letter has been written by scraps; and not unpleasantly:

for by this means I have you in my thoughts every day. This is a regular London fog: so that I can hardly see to write.

I have been poring over Wordsworth lately: which has had much effect in bettering my Blue Devils: for his philosophy does not abjure melancholy, but puts a pleasant countenance upon it, and connects it with humanity. It is very well, if the sensibility that makes us fearful of ourselves is diverted to become a cause of sympathy and interest with Nature and mankind: and this I think Wordsworth tends to do. I think I told you of Shakespeare's sonnets before: I cannot tell you what sweetness I find in them.

So by Shakespeare's Sonnets roasted, and Wordsworth's poems basted,
My heart will be well toasted, and excellently tasted.

This beautiful couplet must delight you, I think. I will also give you the two last verses about Clora: though it is more complete and better without them; strange to say. You must have the goodness to repeat those you know over first, and then fall upon these: for there is a sort of reasoning in them, which requires proper order, as much as a proposition of Euclid. The first of them is not to my liking, but it is too much trouble about a little thing to work it into a better. You have the two first stanzas[8]—"ergo"

3

Nothing can utterly die:
Music aloft upspringing
Turns to pure atoms of sky
Each golden note of thy singing:
And that to which morning did listen
At eve in a rainbow may glisten.

4

Beauty, when laid in the grave,
Feedeth the lily beside her:
Therefore the soul cannot have
Station or honour denied her:
She will not better her essence,
But wear a crown in God's presence.

Q.E.D.

And I think there is quite enough of Clora and her music. I am hunting about the town for an ancient drinking cup, which I may use when I am in my house, in quality of housekeeper. Have the goodness to make my remembrances to all at that most pleasant house Freestone: I am quite serious in telling you how it is by far the pleasantest family I ever was among.

My sister is far better. We walk very much and see such sights as the town affords. This day I have bought a little terrier to keep me company. You will think this is from my reading of Wordsworth: but if that were my cue, I should go no further than keeping a primrose in a pot for society. Farewell, dear Allen. I am astonished to find myself writing a very long letter once a week to you: but it is next to talking to you: and after having seen you so much this summer, I cannot break off suddenly.

I am your most affectionate friend,

E.FG.

Have you got this beginning to your MS. of the Dream of Fair Women?[9] It is very splendid.

1

As when a man that sails in a balloon
Down looking sees the solid shining ground
Stream from beneath him in the broad blue noon,—
Tilth, hamlet, mead and mound:

2

And takes his flags, and waves them to the mob
That shout below, all faces turn'd to where
Glows rubylike the far-up crimson globe
Filled with a finer air:

3

So, lifted high, the Poet at his will
Lets the great world flit from him, seeing all,
Higher through secret splendours mounting still
Self-poised, nor fears to fall,

4

Hearing apart the echoes of his fame—

This is in his best style: no fretful epithet, nor a word too much.

[1] The Bullers, Charles and Arthur, of Morval, Cornwall, who had taken degrees at Cambridge. Charles, Liberal M.P. for Liskeard, was "the genialist radical I ever met," wrote Carlyle, who had tutored the brothers.

[2] *Poems*, published in December, post-dated 1833.

[3] EFG turned his page sideways to write the lines "To Christopher North."

[4] Tennyson's 1830 volume, *Poems, Chiefly Lyrical*, had been extravagantly lauded by a number of London critics. Arthur Hallam, permitting friendship to master judgment, had lavished praise to the point of absurdity in a review in the *Englishman's Magazine*. Eighteen months after the poems appeared, John Wilson, better known by his pen name, Christopher North, in *Blackwood's Magazine*, accused Tennyson of "affectation" but admitted that the young poet had genius and imagination. North then appears to have read Hallam's review and, in May, 1832, published a second article in which he bequeathed to posterity illuminating, representative morsels of early 19th-century criticism. He described a critique in the *Westminster Review* as "the purest mere matter of moonshine ever mouthed by an idiot-lunatic, shivering in palsied dotage." Hallam's review was a "narcotic dose administered by a crazy charlatan." He dismissed seventeen of Tennyson's poems as "miserable" or "mere drivel"; praised others; and closed with the remark that in spite of his "not infrequent silliness . . . Alfred Tennyson is a poet."

[5] *Selections from the Poems of William Wordsworth*, published in May, 1831.

[6] *Sonnets of Shakespeare and Milton*, 1830.

[7] EFG may have considered basing a story on an incident in The Great Rebellion, later treated with considerable freedom by Mark Twain in "The Death Disk." For a year following the capture of Charles I in June, 1647, sporadic revolts against Parliament flared up throughout Britain. One of the most stubborn broke out in Pembrokeshire where John Poyer, a colonel commanding Pembroke Castle for Parliament, declared for the king and was joined by two fellow officers, one of them commander-in-chief of the forces in the county. After a month's siege by Cromwell, the castle surrendered and the leaders were captured. The three officers, found guilty of treason, were subject to the death penalty. It was decided, however, that only one, to be selected by lot, should die. "The Prisoners were not willing to draw their own destiny; but a child drew the lots, and gave them: and the lot fell to Colonel Poyer. He was shot in Covent Garden" (Bulstrode Whitlocke, *Memorials of the English Affairs* . . . , quoted by Thomas Carlyle, *Oliver Cromwell's Letters and Speeches*, 1845, I, 418).

[8] The missing stanzas read:

To A Lady Singing

1

Canst thou, my Clora, declare
  After thy sweet song dieth
Into the wild summer air,
  Whither it faileth or flieth?
Soon would my answer be noted,
Wert thou but sage as sweet throated.

2

Melody, dying away,
  Into the dark sky closes
Like the good soul from her clay,
  Like the fair odor of roses:
Therefore thou now art behind it,
But thou shalt follow, and find it.

The poem, with the title "To a Lady Singing," is published in the *Letters and Literary Remains*, VII, 333-34.

[9] The lines quoted were the beginning of Tennyson's "Dream of Fair Women" in *Poems*, 1833. They were dropped in all subsequent printings.

To John Allen

[Cambridge]
[February 4, 1833]

My dear Allen,

I got your letter by chance, when going into Trinity Chapel on Sunday Night. I do not scold you for not writing a common answer to a common letter: but for not telling me when such an event happens to you, as this situation at the college:[1] if it was only that you are one hundred and fifty miles nearer me than before, it is a thing good to be told me.

You will see by the top of my paper that I am got to my old love, Cambridge:[2] I am not to be long here just now, but I hope to come back. You talk of leaving town for a week at Easter—shall it not be to come and see me in the country? I suppose however you will go to Portsmouth.

I shall write you no more sad letters, if indeed they make you sad: but the great reason is that I am less sad myself: it is always so when I get among strangers: or rather those unconnected with some of my dark views. This makes me like Cambridge, though there are many things I dislike. I dined at Thompson's[3] last week, with a very pleasant party: Kemble[4] is up here, and very pleasant. We all cry out for you to be here: but I know it is not to be expected. I hope you will see Mazzinghi in town, who has a mind of a very noble build, in my opinion. I suppose you have seen Thompson who was going to town, and vowed to find you out.

I do not like to touch on a subject, which makes both of us sad, but which fills your letter: yet I cannot but hope that, though I am afraid there will ever be a great gulph between us, you will not think it right to distance yourself from me. You do not seem to think of it yet: but I do not know how far your religious opinions may carry you hereafter. It is useless wading again into the subject: I do not wish to convince you, nor any one else: and I am afraid I cannot be convinced. I wish that the not being happy without the prospect of Heaven were a proof of Religion: but alas! 'tis no more so, than a beggar's not being happy without a penny in his pocket is a proof that there soon will be a penny in his pocket: it will make him happy to believe so, but the penny is as far off as ever. But I am sorry to have said thus much about it. I shall never renew the subject without your wish: but I will hear all you have to say, very candidly: why not, since it would make me happy to be of your persuasion?

I should have enjoyed being in London with you, and very likely may go thither for some time by and bye. You have a good deal of leisure, have you not? You know of course that Tennant is engaged at the other University:[5] have you seen Spedding?[6]

Do not write yet, for I don't know where my direction will be.

P.S. Tuesday. I am able to tell you that you may write when you please to me at "Castle Irwell, Manchester."[7] This sounds grand: but 'tis a funny little castle, like a needle box this is the scale of it, truly. I go thither on Thursday: and this is another duty visit: but I hope not to lose my newly recovered spirits, tho' it is a desolate place. Today I give wine to some of your friends, Heath, Thompson, Kemble etc. Would you were here, my dearest fellow. Macpherson[8] is here, and comes also to day. Your name is often spoken by all. You told me nothing of your relations and my friends at Freestone: and I assure I never write to you without thinking of them, and wishing them happiness.

So farewell, Master John Allen: I will drink your health this day. I had a very characteristic letter from Mazzinghi two days ago. Last night I smoked for the first time: and came home merry, and played the Harmonious Blacksmith[9] out of pure remembrance of you. Remember the direction "Castle Irwell Manchester". I am your most affectionate Friend

E.FG.

1 Allen had been appointed lecturer in mathematics at King's College, London, established in 1831. He was later named chaplain and held both posts until 1839.

2 During the first four years after taking his degree, EFG often returned to Cambridge to visit friends who were still in residence. He occupied his old rooms at Mrs. Perry's in King's Parade when they were available.

3 William Hepworth Thompson, made Fellow of Trinity in 1834; Regius Professor of Greek, 1853; and Master of Trinity, 1866. See Biographical Profile.

4 Volatile "Jacky" Kemble had at last settled down to his career as scholar after an erratic and unpromising preparation. See Biographical Profile. He had returned to Cambridge in October, 1832, to study Anglo-Saxon and philology.

[5] University College, London, the "secular" college established in 1828.

[6] James Spedding, one of EFG's sturdiest friends. See Biographical Profile.

[7] Castle Irwell, Manchester, one of the estates inherited by EFG's mother. It was located opposite Higher Broughton on a tract of land formed by a loop in the River Irwell. The Castle Irwell race track is located on a portion of the estate.

[8] William Macpherson (1812-93), legal writer, took his degree at Cambridge in 1834 and was called to the Bar in 1837. He served as Master of Equity in the Supreme Court, Calcutta, 1848-59. After his return to England, he edited the *Quarterly Review*, 1860-67. He was a leading authority on the application of international laws and customs to medical services in war.

[9] The familiar title of the air on which Handel wrote variations of his "Suite in E Major." No source has been identified, though it is believed to be based on a French song (*Grove's Dictionary of Music and Musicians*). While an undergraduate, EFG had been a pianist in *Camus*, a musical society composed of senior members of the colleges as well as students, all of whom took part in the programs. Concerts were given five times each term, each program opening with an overture by Handel. EFG's lifelong love for "the Master," fostered at this time, never extended to his oratorios, not even *The Messiah*.

To John Allen

Manchester
February 24, 1833

Dear Allen,

You see by the top of my paper that I am at Manchester. I shall be very glad to get back to Cambridge, where I spent a very pleasant week. I do not see that I can leave this before a fortnight however, when I shall return to Cambridge, and stay there for some time. I think I have done duty enough in the family way this year, and I shall go and let my soul loose in the way I like best for some weeks to come after this. I should like to hear from you how you get on in your new vocation: and how you like it. But your pen is not to be commanded. Here I have been reading nothing to do me good: for Manchester is a horridly illiterate place, and there are no books to be got. I beg you to go some day to King's Street, leading from Holborn into Bloomsbury Square: there is a bookseller there, who had a little blackletter Stowe's Chronicles,[1] very dirty and burnt bound in vellum: a 32mo. I think. If he has it now pray get it for me, if it only costs three shillings or so as I believe it does: but not else. I know not what possessed me not to buy it when I saw it. The bookseller is a very nice man, and gives catalogues. I have several books I want to get: but I shall come to London to provide for myself. If you get this little Stowe, you shall send it to me at Cambridge when I get thither: which God hasten.

I am fearful to boast, lest I should lose what I boast of: but I think I have achieved a victory over my evil spirits here: for they have full opportunity to come, and I often observe their approaches, but hitherto I have managed to keep them off. Lord Bacon's Essay on Friendship is wonderful for its truth: and I often feel its truth. He says that with a Friend "a man *tosseth* his thoughts," an admirable saying,[2] which one can understand, but not express otherwise. But I feel that, being alone, one's thoughts and feelings, from want of communication, become heaped up and clotted together, as it were: and so lie like undigested food heavy upon the mind: but with a friend one *tosseth* them about, so that the air gets between them, and keeps them fresh and sweet. I know not from what metaphor Bacon took his "tosseth," but it seems to me as if it was from the way haymakers toss hay, so that it does not press into a heavy lump, but is tossed about in the air, and separated, and thus kept sweet. But enough of this to you who can expound Bacon or any one else "better nor I can" as Sansum[3] would say. Do you want a Tillottson's Works in Folio?[4] I can get it for you here, a very good copy. Say if you do, and I will go to that pitch of Friendship which it is not recorded that Pylades did for Orestes, viz, to carry four folio volumes in a stage coach all the way from Manchester to London for you.

And now is not this a merrier letter than all my former ones? Have you seen Thackeray? He lives at No 5 Essex Court, Middle Temple: Mazzinghi also you should see. You have never told me anything about your and my friends at Freestone: I know not why my mind recurs so often to them, but I suppose because they were so kind and agreeable. And therefore, upon my honour, I wish to know if they are well, and happy: this is a common question of form, but I do wish to know. I should like mightily to "toss" a few thoughts with you about our goings on in Pembrokeshire, which is next dear to Suffolk to my mind: but a time will come.

Farewell, my dear fellow: all good things be with you, is my prayer.

Your most affectionate friend
E. FitzGerald.

[1] *A Summarie of English Chronicles*, first published in 1561 by John Stow (1525?-1605).

[2] "On Friendship" contains the passage, "whosoever hath his Minde fraught, with many Thoughts, his Wits and Understanding doe clarifie and breake up, in the Communicating and discoursing with Another: He tosseth his Thoughts, more

easily; He marshalleth them more orderly; He seeth how they looke when they are turned into Words; Finally, He waxeth wiser then Himselfe; And that more by an Houres discourse, then by a Dayes Meditation" (*Bacon's Essays*, ed., W. A. Wright, 1863, p. 111).

[3] John Sansum, one of their Trinity friends.

[4] John Tillotson (1630-94), latitudinarian and popular preacher who became Archbishop of Canterbury in 1694. EFG misspelled the name.

To John Allen

Cambridge—Thursday
[March 14, 1833]

You most unprincipled man,

I being filled with great kindness just now, turn again to you: who are a good subject to vent one's kindness upon: notwithstanding your never writing to me. I am filled with this kindness just now by having read Undine[1] at Breakfast. I think I must be a very great fool, and it must look like vile affectation to talk of being moved by books, and childish books, in this manner: but I swear it is so (as to me). Nor is there any thing to affect in it, because it shews that one has a mind which lies ready to be swayed either way by good or bad: which is truly the case with me. So it happens that whenever I open Undine, I become very tender and loving: and in such a humour, I do not like to think that perhaps if I were to read a page of Voltaire I should feel inclined to scoff. When I am in these humours I cannot believe that I should so soon change again into their opposites. It is great vanity to tell other folks of one's feelings, as if one were a great man: but I speak of them because I suppose you feel the same kind of thing. After having read Herbert or Jeremy Taylor, and become suffused with their spirit, do you not wonder that you ever go back again to coldness and worldliness? Our good feelings are so entrancing while they last: but that is the reason they last so short a time: but our more paltry propensities are cold and rational, and so stay by us, and become part of our natures. When I came from Leicester the other day on the Coach, I am sure I felt like an Angel: it was a fine morning, the country richly tilled and full of promise, and here and there spires of churches, and little villages, over the face of the country. I felt tears in my eyes often, I could not tell why. Now I was not ashamed of feeling this: but I am ashamed now I tell you of it: it looks like foolish romance but it is not: however it requires an indulgent friend to confide it to. Indeed I don't know that I could pay a higher compliment to your kindness than running on in this way to you. I do so half involuntarily, and [am] ashamed of myself: and always ready to cry "Damnation" as Mazzinghi does when he gets up and rams his foot through the panel of a door.

I hear Spedding is coming here on Saturday[2]—why not send me a letter by him? Here I get on very pleasantly. Thackeray talks of coming here. Did he tell you that I should be overjoyed if you came down, but that I had not asked you, as I thought your duties would not let you? I could give you bed, and board as long as you would: and here are all your friends for company: but I suppose it is useless asking. I am in a sort of Shakespeare Club,[3] where they read Shakespeare: it is good so far as that men may meet together pleasantly once a week, under his noble name. We are also to have a dinner on his birthday, I believe, which I shall like well.

I have looked over this letter, and really it is almost venturing too much confidence in your good nature to send such a thing—no news—nothing worth hearing, much less paying for. But I have got to the end and it shall go. Good bye my dear Johnny Allen.

Did you buy my Stowe's Chronicles?

Your most affectionate friend
E.FG.

P.S. Observe, as an instance of what I have said in Pages 1 and 2, the little worldly demand in the last paragraph of my letter, "Did you buy my Stowe's Chronicles?" coming after those etherial feelings I talk of. Tarnation!

[1] *Undine,* a fairy romance published in 1811 by Baron Friedrich de la Motte Fouqué (1777-1843), German poet, dramatist, and prose writer. EFG was charmed by the story and frequently refers to it. In 1834 he commissioned Thackeray to illustrate his copy with watercolors. See letter to Allen, June 31, 1834, n.3.

[2] "Spedding has returned to Cambridge, and will remain there until October," R. C. Trench wrote to J. W. Blakesley on April 1, 1833 (*Richard Chenevix Trench, Letters and Memorials*, 2 vols., 1888, I, 136-37).

[3] The Shakespeare Club was an informal reading group.

To John Allen

Cambridge Tuesday
[Mid-May, 1833]

My dear Johnny,

I send thee an Essay by Spedding,[1] as I promised. I hope it may come in time. They were talking here yesterday of there being two small livings in the gift of Trinity vacant just now, and that it was thought that the fellows would not want to take them. Would it not be well to enquire something about them for you? I shall enquire and send you such particulars as I can.[2] But perhaps you should learn yourself from Peacock,[3] or some other sure source. Here I have been very merry and idle—doing nearly nothing. All your and my friends are well, and talk of you every day. If you see the vile Thackeray, ask him wherefore he hath not sent me his Paper.[4]

I expect to come up to London in a fortnight or so. Spedding will be in town also for about a week, somewhere at that time: and I hope we then shall go and see one or two things together. I have very great love indeed for him. He has drawn a set of drawings of all the circle here which are capital: and we talk of having them lithographed if possible. I have been sitting to him this morning, and my phiz is impaled on Paper for ever.[5]

I could wish you were here to talk a turn with me in the walks. The Chestnut trees are in their usual glory at this season, crowned over and over with blossom:[6] and I never saw the fields so rich. I have been laughing out of measure of late: by which learn that I am in good case. Bless thee my boy and farewell—

Your most affectionate friend
EFG

[1] Spedding's essay was a pamphlet described by EFG at the time of Spedding's death 50 years later as "his own printed Report of a Speech he made in what was called the 'Quinquaginta Club' Debating Society . . . at Cambridge about the year 1831." Urged by his father, Spedding published the speech anonymously the following year with the title *Substance of a Speech Against Political Unions, delivered in a Debating Society in the University of Cambridge.* Henry Taylor, later Spedding's colleague in the Foreign Office, quoted portions of the essay in the notes to his historical drama, *Philip van Artevelde,* introducing the passages with, "Our own political unions, and the effects which they are calculated to produce, have never been described in a more philosophic spirit and temper, or more forcibly, than in the speech from which the following extract is taken." At the close of his quotations from Spedding, Taylor added, "It is a singular trait of the times, that a speech containing so much of sagacity and mature reflection . . . should have been delivered in an academical debating club, and should have passed away in a pamphlet, which, as far as I am aware, attracted no notice . . . a brilliant Parliamentary reputation might be built upon a tithe of the merit" (*Philip van Artevelde,* 5th edit., 1849, pp. 286-88).

[2] Allen did not leave King's College at this time.

[3] George Peacock (1791-1858), mathematician and astronomer; Trinity, B.A., 1813; Fellow, 1814; tutor, 1823-39; and Dean of Ely, 1839-58.

[4] Thackeray had invested in a tottering weekly newspaper impressively named the *National Standard and Journal of Literature, Science, Music, Theatricals, and*

the Fine Arts, and the change of control was announced in the issue of May 11. For a year he was a very busy young man, assuming a large share of editorial responsibilities and, once at least, running over to Paris because, as he wrote to his mother, "It looks well . . . to have a Parisian correspondent" (*Thackeray Letters*, I, 262). The *National Standard* fluttered weakly for almost a year before ceasing publication. Thackeray obviously recalled the experience when Mr. Batchelor likens *his* venture with the *Museum* to Moses Primrose's investment in green spectacles (*Lovell the Widower*, Biographical Edition, XII, 67). Despite the unhappy fate of the *National Standard*, Thackeray was to try his hand once more, and no more successfully, at journalism. With his stepfather, Major Henry Carmichael-Smyth, in April, 1836, he founded the *Constitutional and Public Ledger*, the last issue of which appeared on July 1, 1837.

[5] Spedding's drawing was made as EFG sat reading. The lower part of the sketch is roughly drawn but the artist took considerable pains with head and features. The drawing may be seen in the Fitzwilliam Museum at Cambridge, Exhibit 674.

[6] EFG probably refers to the "flowering Chestnuts of Jesus" College which he mentions in the closing words of his dialogue, *Euphranor*, and which are vividly remembered by all who have visited Cambridge in the spring.

To W. B. Donne[1]

Geldestone
Sept. 27, [1833]

Dear Donne,

I got your very kind letter this morning. I was on the point of going to London on Tuesday: but I cannot resist coming over to see you: and I shall come on Monday. I hear there is an excellent Coach from Norwich to London Daily. I write, contrary to your order, because I wish you to know beforehand that your drive to Norwich will not be in vain —at least if I can help it.

As to my history since I have seen you, there is little to tell. Divinity is not outraged by your not addressing me as a Reverend—I not being one.[2] I am a very lazy fellow, who do nothing: and this I have been doing in different places ever since I saw you last. I have not been well for the last week: for I am at present rather liable to be overset by any weariness (and where is any to be found that can match the effect of two Oratorios?),[3] since for the last three months I have lived on vegetables—that is, I have given up meat.[4] When I was talking of this to Vipan,[5] he told me that you had once tried it, and given it up. I shall hear your account of its effect on you. The truth is, that mine is the wrong time of life to begin a change of that kind: it is either too early, or too late. But I have no doubt at all of the advantage of giving up meat: I find already much good from it, in lightness and airiness of head, whereas I was always before clouded and more or less morbid after meat. The loss of strength is to be expected: I shall keep on and see if that also will turn, and change into strength. I have almost Utopian notions about *vegetable diet,* begging pardon for making use of such a vile, *Cheltenhamic,* phrase. Why do you not bring up your children to it? To be sure, the chances are, that, after guarding their vegetable morals for years, they would be seduced by some roast partridge with bread sauce, and become ungodly. This actually happened to the son of a Dr. Newton[6] who wrote a book about it and bred up his children to it—but all such things I will tell you when I meet you. Gods! it is a pleasant notion that one is about to meet an old acquaintance in a day or two.

Believe me then your most sincere friend,
E. FitzGerald.

Pipes—are their names ever heard with you? I have given them up, except at Cambridge. But the word has something sweet in it—Do you ever smoke?

[1] See Biographical Profile.

[2] It is unlikely that Donne had been serious in writing the remark that elicited this response.

[3] EFG appears to have attended the 1833 choral festival at Norwich. Elaborate choral recitals, for which singers and instrumentalists were imported from London, had developed in the provinces, usually in cathedral cities. Oratorios were popular features of the programs. The Norwich festival, one of the best known, began in 1824 and was held triennially.

[4] Vegetarianism interested EFG for a number of years, as this and others of his letters reveal. Throughout his life he normally restricted his diet at home to vegetables, milk, and fruit, but he was not averse to partaking of meat, poultry, and seafoods, and he always provided them for his guests.

[5] David Jennings Vipan of Thetford, Norfolk, friend of William Bodham Donne and John Kemble. He was at Trinity in 1831, but EFG does not appear to have known him there. Vipan traveled extensively in Germany and Hungary and was one of the first to champion Hungary in the revolt against Austria in 1848. He died the following year at the age of 44 (Aldis Wright papers, Trinity College Library).

[6] In 1811 John Frank Newton published privately, in London, *Return to Nature, or a Defense of the Vegetable Regimen; with some account of an experiment made during the last 3 or 4 yrs. in the author's family.* The book was reprinted in *The Pamphlet,* vols. 19 and 20, in 1822 (Library of Congress Catalogue).

To W. B. Donne

7 Southampton Row
Bloomsbury
Pmk., Oct. 25, 1833

Dear Donne,

I got your very kind letter this morning. You must not blame me for writing even a long letter, considering how it is your own Kindness that has called me out once again. It is indeed very well that I did not come to you: not to mention that I have the pleasure of looking forward to coming in the future. I should first of all have given you joy on the birth of *another* son:[1] which I do: and hope you may ever have joy in him. As to myself, and my diet, about which you give such excellent advice: I am still determined to give the diet I have proposed a good trial: a year's trial. I agree with you about vegetables, and soups: but my diet is chiefly *bread*: which is only a little less nourishing than flesh: and, being compact, and baked, and dry, has none of the washy, diluent effects of green vegetables. I scarcely ever touch the latter: but only pears, apples, etc. I have found no benefit yet; except, as I think, in more lightness of spirits: which is a great good. But I shall see in time.

I am living in London in the quarter of the town which I have noticed above: in a very happy bachelor-like way. Would you would come up here for a few days. I can give you bed, board, etc. Do have some business in town, please. Spedding is here: taking lessons of drawing,[2] before he goes for good into Cumberland: whither, for my sake and that of all his friends, I wish he never would go: for there are few such men, as far [as] I know. He and I have been theatricalizing lately. We saw an awful Hamlet the other night—a Mr. Serle—and a very good Wolsey, in Macready: and a very bad Queen Catherine, in Mrs. Sloman, whom you must remember.[3] I am going to-night to see Macready in Macbeth: I have seen him before in it: and I go for the sake of his two last acts, which are amazingly fine, I think. Come and give us and the great world a look. Arthur Malkin[4] is also in town, and many men whom you do, or would, know. I am sure you want to see your lawyer here: (though I suppose you don't meddle much with them). Or you want books—so cheap here that it is worth the journey here and back to get them. Have you seen all Milton's Prose Works in one very handsome Volume for twenty-two shillings?[5] It is in a fine clear type: and for those who want those works, is a fine prize. I am close to the British Museum, in which I take great pleasure in reading in my rambling way.[6] I hear of Kemble lately that he has been making some discoveries in Anglo-Saxon MSS. at Cambridge that, they say, are important to the interests of the church: and there is talk of publishing them, I believe.[7] He is a strange fellow for that fiery industry of his: and, I am sure, deserves some steady recompense.

Tennyson has been in town for some time: he has been making fresh poems, which are finer, they say, than any he has done. But I believe he is chiefly meditating on the purging and subliming of what he has already done: and repents that he has published at all yet.[8] It is fine to see how in each succeeding poem the smaller ornaments and fancies drop away, and leave the grand ideas single. I don't know if you understand what I mean: nor does it much matter.

I have lately bought a little pamphlet which is very difficult to be got, called The Songs of Innocence, written and adorned with drawings by W. Blake[9] (if you know his name) who was quite mad, but of a madness that was really the elements of great genius ill-sorted: in fact, a genius *with a screw loose*, as we used to say. I shall shew you this book when I see you: to me there is particular interest in this man's writing and drawing, from the strangeness of the constitution of his mind. He was a man that used to see visions: and make drawings and paintings of Alexander the Great, Caesar, etc., who, he declared, stood before him while he drew.

This is a long and tiresome letter, I fear: and full of all sorts of things. All I shall say more is to wish again, and again that you would come up here. Why, it is but a day's journey: and now the weather is fine. I need not tell you how very glad I am always to see your handwriting: but you are a man who reads and so I only ask you to write when you are inclined at any spare hour. And so believe me to be your very affectionate friend

E. FitzGerald

1 Donne's second child, William Mowbray.

2 In classes conducted by Henry Sass (W. H. Thompson papers, Trinity College Library). Sass (1788-1844), having won small recognition as an artist, "devoted himself to elementary art teaching preparatory to the Academy Schools, in which he was very successful" (Samuel Redgrave, *A Dictionary of Artists of the English School*, 1874).

3 Thomas J. Serle had opened a week's engagement at the Royal Victoria Theatre, Monday, October 7, with *Hamlet*. William Macready (1793-1873) played Wolsey in Shakespeare's *Henry VIII* at Drury Lane October 21 and 22. He appeared in *Macbeth* on the 25th when Mrs. Sloman played Lady Macbeth for the first time. The Royal Victoria management may have had some doubts

about Mr. Serle's drawing power as Hamlet for it announced that the play would be followed by "an Hungarian National Pas de Deux by Herr Eckner and Monsieur Carelle. After which, a ballet pantomime, called *The Miller*; or *The Lover's Rendezvous.* To which will be added *Intrigue.* To conclude with a *Grand Masquerade*, in which will be introduced a Grotesque Pas de Trois, by Herr Eckner, Mademoiselle Rosier, and Mrs. Chickini." In contrast to this offering, the "second feature" for Macready's *Henry VIII* at Drury Lane was merely *Timour the Tartar*, and that for *Macbeth, One O'clock*; or, the *Knight of the Wood Daemon* (London *Times*, Oct. 7, pp. 21-22).

[4] Arthur Malkin (1803-88), son of EFG's headmaster at Bury St. Edmund's Grammar School. He took a first class in the Classical Tripos at Cambridge in 1825. Fanny Kemble, in her *Records of a Girlhood*, says that he would "undoubtedly have risen to distinction but for . . . the hesitation of speech which closed almost all public careers" to him. He bought an estate, Corrybrough, at Tomatin, Invernessshire, where the "shooting" was excellent, and lead the life of a country gentleman. Fanny Kemble calls him "one of the earliest of Alpine explorers" and credits him with having "furnished a great part of John Murray's first 'Handbook' for Switzerland" (Frances Ann Kemble, *Records of a Girlhood*, 1 vol. edn., New York, 1879, p. 84).

[5] "The Prose Works of Milton, with introductory review by Robert Fletcher, 25s., Sept., 1833" (*English Catalogue*).

[6] Throughout his life EFG filled commonplace books with extracts culled from his reading. On the first page of one of these, he wrote:

E. FitzGerald
October 15, 1833
Museum Book
1833

Below the second date was drawn a jug labeled "Sack 1661." Beside it is a wineglass. Many of the passages are from old English writers to whom EFG refers in his letters. Some of the pages contain pen-and-ink sketches; a few, in water colors, are of men and women clad in the dress of the 16th and 17th centuries. Pages from the *Museum Book* are reproduced in T. Wright's *Life*, II, 247-93.

[7] Professor Bruce Dickins, of Cambridge University, says of Kemble at this time that he worked in the university and college libraries "acquiring a more intimate knowledge of the manuscript sources for Old English literature and history than any scholar had had since [Humfrey] Wanley" (Dickins, *J. M. Kemble*, p. 11). The chief product of his "fiery industry" this year was an edition of *Beowulf* (1833).

[8] There is no evidence that EFG had yet made Tennyson's acquaintance. Their first recorded meeting took place in the spring of 1835 when both were guests of Spedding's at Mirehouse (See A. McK. Terhune, *The Life of Edward FitzGerald*, 1947, pp. 78-81). After his skirmish with reviewers following the appearance of *Poems* in 1832, Tennyson did not again publish until 1842. A total of 86 poems had been included in the 1830 and 1832 volumes, and only 40 of these were retained in 1842 (Charles Tennyson, *Alfred Tennyson*, 1949, p. 193). Tennyson radically revised most of the reprinted poems during his "ten years' silence."

[9] William Blake (1757-1827), *Songs of Innocence* (1789). The text and designs were engraved on copper by Blake, and binding was done by the poet's wife.

To John Allen

London, Saturday[1]
Pmk., Nov. 8, 1833

My dear Allen,

I said I would write to you soon after my reaching London:[2] and it is no trouble nor task, but a pleasure to do so. You need not alarm yourself with the prospect of having to answer: for I by no means require it. I got into Bristol at 12 on Wednesday Night after starting from Tenby at half past 9: and setting out from Bristol at 6 the next morning, reached London at 8. This was very well, I thought—nor was I tired. I found my sister much as I had left her. Today I have been into Holborn, and to Cornish's in the Little Turnstile, but he knew nothing of a reprint of the Purple Island:[3] nor any other bookseller, that I could find, knew of any reprint. Notwithstanding, I found a very good secondhand octavo copy, with notes (which are necessary enough, Heaven knows) which I bought and will send to you as I best can. It is quite modern and has not the old spelling which is a fault. The Purple Island does not mean the Heart alone, but the whole Body: and two cantos are taken up in describing it allegorically and anatomically. I always find either of these, alone, difficult enough to understand: but now they are mixed, very particularly so. Therefore are the notes very useful to explain when the liver, the bowels, etc. are meant. But all this you will see.

My Paradise[4] has not got on. I subscribed to a library, and after paying my money found the man had not a poet in his library except, I believe, Milton and Thompson. So I must go to another. I have seen no Cambridge men yet save "Walker a non walkendo".[5] I see the Kembles' house is to be let.[6] Pray make my best remembrances to all your cousins at Freestone.[7] It is useless to thank you and them for all your kindness: but I beg you to believe that I feel it much. As to you, my dear Allen, even truth itself in the shape of praise to yourself, is offensive—but this a thing I have often to keep myself in mind of, when I want to give you a dish of love and praise.

The windows are full of prints of Scott and a new print of Byron is come out with a great dog. They are printing Shakespeare, poems and all, in fifteen volumes to correspond with Murray's Byron:[8] a company I don't approve of either as regards the type, or the taste of associating the two authors. There is no want of new books as you may fancy—Gomery's[9] books are to be had for two shillings apiece at all shops. I cannot make a successful picture of Miss Hoskins for the mouth as I would fain wish to do for you.[10]

London is empty and cold. I send you a *cut out* of Erasmus from the Penny Magazine—done in my best style.

Farewell my dear Boy—this letter is indeed not worth paying for: but you asked to hear from me. The sight of your handwriting will always be delightful to me: but never trouble yourself to write. Yours most affectionately

E.FG.

39 P.P.[11]

1 "Saturday" written in error. The postmark is Nov. 8, which was Friday.

2 From his second and last trip to Pembrokeshire.

3 *Purple Island.* See letter of Nov. 21, 1832, n.11.

4 His commonplace book of lyric poetry.

5 Possibly Joseph Walker (1807-99), who was at Trinity with EFG. He was later Rector of Billing, Northants. This is the only mention of him in the correspondence.

6 Charles Kemble's "ruinous mismanagement" had led to the bankruptcy of Covent Garden in 1829. When he lost control of the theater in the autumn of 1832, he left with his daughter Fanny for an American tour. The Kemble home was at the intersection of Great Russell and Montague Streets, property later taken over for the expansion of the British Museum. In her *Records of a Girlhood*, Fanny Kemble places the dwelling at the corner of Great Russell Street and Montague Place (p. 546). Montague Place runs parallel to Great Russell Street.

7 Although EFG addressed his letter to Allen at Freestone, he had not yet heard of the death of Anne Allen on November 4. He later referred to her "light hair and China-rose complexion—too delicate!" At some later date he wrote the poem beginning:

> The wind blew keenly from the Western sea,
> And drove the dead leaves slanting from the tree—
>   Vanity of vanities, the Preacher saith—
> Heaping them up before her Father's door
> When I saw her whom I shall see no more—
>   We cannot bribe thee, Death.

([On Anne Allen], *Letters and Literary Remains*, VII, 334-36)

8 *Plays and Poems of Shakespeare*, with life, notes and plates from Boydell's edition. 15 vols., Valpy, 1832-33. *The Works of Lord Byron*, with his letters and journals, and life, by T. Moore. 17 vols., Murray, 1832.

9 Robert Montgomery, whose name originally had been Gomery.

10 At this point in his letter EFG had sketched the head of a woman. This sentence was written over it. Miss Hoskins, probably someone in Pembrokeshire, has not been identified.

11 39 Portland Place, the FitzGerald town residence.

To W. B. Donne

7 Southampton Row
Nov. 19, 1833

Dear Donne,

Your book I got, and read through all that seemed to concern me the first day. I have doubted whether it would be most considerate to return you thanks for it, making you pay for a letter: or to leave you thankless, with a shilling more in your pocket. You see I have taken the latter [? former], and God forgive me for it. The book is a good one, I think, as any book is, that notes down *facts alone*, especially about health. I wish we had diaries of the lives of half the unknown men that have lived. Like all other men who have got a theory into their heads, I can only see things in the light of that theory; and whatever is brought to me to convince me to the contrary is only wrought and tortured to my view of the question. This lasts till a reaction is brought about by some of the usual means: as time, and love of novelty, etc. I am still very obstinate and persist in my practices. I do not think Stark[1] is an instance of vegetable diet: consider how many things he tried grossly animal: lard, and butter, and fat: besides thwarting Nature in every way by eating when he wanted not to eat, and the contrary. Besides the editor says in the preface that he thinks his death was brought about as much by vexation as by the course of his diet: but I suppose the truth is that vexation could not have had so strong hold except upon a weakened body. However, altogether I do not at all admit Stark to be any instance: to be set up like a scarecrow to frighten us from the corn, etc. Last night I went to hear a man lecture at Owen of Lanark's establishment[2] (where I had never been before), and the subject happened to be about Vegetable Diet: but it was only the termination of a former lecture, so that I suppose all the good arguments (if there were any) were gone before. Do you know anything of a book by a Doctor Lamb[3] upon this subject? I do not feel it to be disgusting to talk of myself upon this subject, because I think there is great interest in the subject itself. So I shall say that I am just now very well: in fine spirits. I have only eaten meat once for many weeks: and that was at a party where I did not like to be singled out. Neither have I tasted wine, except two or three times. If I fail at last I shall think it a very great bore: but assuredly the first cut of a leg of mutton will be some consolation for my wounded judgement: that first cut is a fine thing. So much for this.

Spedding is still in town: and I hope is to be so for some time more. We (that is London in general) are just now revelling in the golden fogs of the season. By the way I think he (that is Spedding) told me he wrote to you a few days ago. Kemble is about to give Lectures,[4] I believe—have you heard from him lately?

Dear Donne, I am always very pleased to get a letter from you: so there is never any apology to be made for them. Rain letters, if you please: I will bear. It is seldom one finds a man who is willing to write: I count myself a good correspondent: but then I am an idle man: and I never expect any studious man to force himself from his books and better meditations to keep pace with me. Have you heard that Arthur Malkin is to be married? to a Miss Carr,[5] with what Addison might call a pleasing fortune: or perhaps Nicholas Rowe. "Sweet, pleasing friendship, etc. etc." Mrs. Malkin is in high spirits about it, I hear: and I am very glad indeed. God send that you have not heard this before: for a man likes to be the first teller of a pretty piece of news. Spedding and I went to see Macready in Hamlet the other night:[6] with which he was pretty well content, but not wholly. For my part, I have given up deciding on how Hamlet should be played: or rather have decided it shouldn't be played at all. I take pleasure in reading things I don't wholly understand; just as the old women like sermons: I think it is of a piece with an admiration of all Nature around us. I think there is a greater charm in the half meanings and glimpses of meaning that come in through Blake's wilder visions: though his difficulties arose from a very different source from Shakespeare's. But somewhat too much of this. I suspect I have found out this as an useful solution, when I am asked the meaning of any thing that I am admiring, and don't know it.

Believe me, dear Donne, to be ever your affectionate friend,

E. FitzGerald.

[1] William Stark (1740-70), medical writer and physician. In June, 1769, he began a series of experiments on diet which eventually ruined his health. *The Works of the late William Stark* was edited by James Carmichael-Smyth (1788).

[2] After the failure of his "Village of Co-operation" at New Harmony, Indiana, in 1828, Robert Owen returned to England and became active in promoting "Trading Associations," the forerunners of modern cooperatives, and in the trade union movement. In 1833 he moved his National Equitable Labour Exchange, a cooperative establishment, from Gray's Inn Road, where it had been opened the previous September, to a location in Charlotte Street, which, G.D.H. Cole states, was "long to be the centre of Owenite activities in London" (*Robert Owen*, Boston, 1925, chap. XV, passim).

[3] EFG's memory slipped. He refers to the book on vegetarianism by Dr. John

Newton, about which he had written Donne on September 27. The book was dedicated to Dr. William Lambe (not Lamb).

[4] Kemble lectured at Cambridge in 1834 on the *History of the English Language, First, or Anglo-Saxon, Period.* When congratulated on the size and distinction of his audience at the first lecture, which according to Donne was well attended, he said, "I'll soon thin them" (Dickins, *J. M. Kemble*, p. 11). The following August he wrote to Trench, "I have carried the point of getting people to take an interest in the history of their language . . . and, even more, have created a school which will take up my work when I cease from labour" (*Trench, Letters and Memorials*, I, 163). According to Dickins, a second course was announced but never given.

[5] Arthur Malkin married Mary Anne, daughter of the Reverend J. A. Carr, Rector of Hadstock, Essex, in 1833. For Malkin, see letter to Donne, Oct. 25, n.4.

[6] Macready played *Hamlet* at Drury Lane on November 11 and again on November 15 in 1833. *Blue Beard* concluded the evening's program.

To John Allen

Cambridge
May 25, 1834

Dear my Johnny boy,

Heath[1] is going up to town tomorrow: so I will send thee a salutation. Perhaps I should have written before: and I am sure I don't know what has kept me from so doing: except, I suppose, that no subject protruded itself up from my brains which called for a transmission to you. I expect to be in town before long. And then we will make the most of the last evenings perhaps that we shall ever have together, both bachelors. We have been rejoicing much here in the sunshine of James Spedding's presence: he looked for you in town, but you were flown off for the Whitsuntide Holydays. He will be in town very shortly, however, and I hope that we may all be there at the same time. I have been trying to arrange a plan that he and I might voyage for a few days in Suffolk, and see our pictures at home, and one or two other small sights: but I know not if I can manage it. He is willing to go: but I have previously pledged myself to go and spend a week near Bedford with a young man whom I formed an acquaintance with in the steam packet to Tenby.[2] I think I must go there as I have promised very deeply: and he has put off other engagements to serve me.

How are you, and how are all the kind party at Cheltenham? At least, I suppose them to be still there. I hope your Cousin Mary is better both in health and spirits. For myself, I have been very well indeed since I have been here: having only had a kind of Influenza which I soon got rid of. I persist in my diet as before. I also now walk better, and am altogether much stronger: but a great deal of this is perhaps owing to dry, warm, weather. We have not had a regular Pic nic this term. One was contemplated to Grantchester: but was given up from one cause and another: so, in the place of it, five or six of us went forth through the fields to Clayhithe, a village down the river: and there eat Pike, and drank porter. Pray do you take interest in this engrossing question about Dissenters? We hear of nothing else here: and now that Thirlwall has stept forth in a pamphlet, which speaks out more decidedly than anything has done hitherto, every tongue is set wagging: and the talk is of plenty of replies etc.[3] That I may not be wholly out of tune for controversy, and unfit for the world I live in, I have begun polemics (if that is the name) with Swift's Tale of a Tub: which I try myself in much. Have you ever read it? Of course you have, though. Pray have you [he][4]ard from Sansum?[5] He never ans[wered] my last.

Farewell, my dear fellow—I long to see you again. Do you know that I am improved in my principles? I am, I assure you, as you will see by and bye. Believe me to be ever your most affectionate friend,

E.FG.

Unless you write directly, you had [best] not write at all: as I shall be off to Bedford by the end of the week.

1 Douglas Heath. See letter to Allen, May 16, 1830, n.7.

2 W. Kenworthy Browne. See Biographical Profile.

3 Membership in the Church of England and subscription to the Thirty-nine Articles were ancient requirements for admission to degrees at the old English universities. After passage of the Reform Bill in 1832, Nonconformists demanded that "all religious tests be abolished, and the Universities be thrown open for the education and graduation of men of all creeds." Controversy became rife and heated. A bill to abolish the religious test, passed by the Commons in 1834, was defeated in the House of Lords where the Duke of Wellington warned that the bill "would inflict a mortal wound between Church and State." Connop Thirlwall, an assistant tutor who favored reform, published a pamphlet, *Letter on the Admission of Dissenters to Academic Degrees*, and was forced to resign his post at Trinity. In 1871, 37 years after this storm, the Universities Test Act abolished the controversial requirements (principal source, L. C. Campbell, *On the Nationalization of the Old English Universities*, 1901, pp. 41-49).

4 MS is damaged.

5 John Sansum; see letter to Allen, Apr. 24, 1830, n.1.

To John Allen

Wherstead Lodge, Ipswich
June 31, 1834 [sic]

Dear my Johnny,

I am put to writing to you upon a subject of which I have but very slender hopes of realizing as much as I wish. But there is no harm in trying. My brother in law, Mr. Wilkinson, and my sister want to leave their Rectory[1] for about six or seven months this winter, for the sake of her health: and they can no where find any man, with his wife, who will live in their house, and carry on the business of the parish till they return. I suppose now that it is useless to expect that you would do this? He has heard of you by report, and is much in love with you thereupon: the only chance would be, if you were perchance to hear of some permanent living, which would make you give up your appointment at King's College, but which yet could not, or need not, be entered upon for some little time. I suppose that I talk like an ignoramus upon this matter. But ifaith it would be very good an you were to come here: there is a very capital house in the midst of the parish: large garden: school house attached: the parish in admirable order: nothing to have to set on foot, but only to carry on: in fact, all complete, only wanting a good man like yourself, and a good woman, as I dare say your wife will be, to preside. I would live quite close all the time: and seem as good as the best. This is a very nice neighbourhood. N.B. The house has a good library attached: full of divines: so that you would need no bother about books. I suppose this is talking to the wind, however: but I desire much that you would write to me, even to refuse. I wish that you would write sometimes: I know that you will have a great deal to do: but still I am very anxious to hear from you sometimes. Do you know that I have rather a melancholy retrospect of my last stay in town: it seems to me that I saw little of you: and that we are diverging into different ways of life, and thinking. But I hope not.[2]

I have been reading the Spectator since I have been here: and I like it very much. Don't you think it would make a nice book to publish all the papers about Sir Roger de Coverley alone, with illustrations by Thackeray?[3] It is a thing that is wanted: to bring that standard of the old English Gentleman forward out of the mass of little topics, and fashions, that occupy the greater part of the Spectator. Thackeray has illustrated my Undine in about fourteen little coloured drawings—very nicely.

I forgot to tell you about my brother in law's curacies here, that he has already engaged a man for them. I asked him directly I got here, remembering your brother:[4] but all was settled.

My dear fellow, I mean on your marriage[5] to give you a nice set of China: which will be more useful to you than a Silver Teapot. I revolved it in my mind for some time. I shall leave them in London under your Mother's care, so that you shall have them when you come to town. Come, I don't believe that your marriage shall make any great difference in you, after all: and when I meet you, I shall not be able to offend you by many loose and foolish things that I am accustomed to scatter about heedlessly when I meet you with others: I always repent me of having done so: but the joy of meeting you puts me into that tip top merriment that makes me sin: if I only loved you half as well, my conversation would be blameless to you. But you forgive me: and it is almost sad to me to think that I shall never be able to sin, and repent, again, in that fashion. And now farewell, my best boy: if you see the kind people of Freestone, tell them that I do not forget them. Do you know that it is not impossible that I may have to carry a sister of mine upon a visit to Miss Malkin at Cowbridge[6] this summer: and then I will certainly go and see them. But this is very doubtful.

I am here in the country in brave health: rising at six withal: and pruning of rose trees in the garden. Why don't you get up early?[7] in the summer at least. The next time we meet in town I mean to get an artist to make me your portrait:[8] for I often wish for it. It must be looking at me. Now write very soon: else I shall be gone: and know that I am your very true friend,

E.FG.

Listen. Here doth lie interr'd
One that scarcely ever err'd.
A Virgin modest, free from folly:
A Virgin knowing, patient, lowly:
A Virgin blest with beauty here:
A Virgin crown'd with glory there.
Holy Virgins, read, and say
We shall thither all one day.
Live well. We must
All come to dust.

In Enfield Churchyard.[9]

Is not this pretty!

[1] At Holbrook, about five miles south of Ipswich. The FitzGerald home at Wherstead was three miles north of Holbrook; hence EFG's subsequent remark about living "quite close." Allen did not accept EFG's proposal.

[2] This letter was published by Aldis Wright as though it began with the following paragraph. No deletion is indicated.

[3] Although Thackeray had come into an inheritance estimated at £20,000 in 1832, he had already lost most of it. Concerned about his friend's reverses, EFG attempted to find means to aid him, and the commission to illustrate *Undine* was one of the results. On the flyleaf of the book EFG wrote, "The drawings in this volume were made by W. M. Thackeray, as we sat talking together two mornings in the spring of 1835 or 1836 at the house of his step-father, Carmichael-Smyth, in Albion Street, Hyde Park, London." This letter reveals that EFG erred in attempting to fix the date. Thackeray's daughter, Anne Thackeray Ritchie, wrote in her preface to the *Christmas Books* in her Biographical Edition of Thackeray's works, "Mr. FitzGerald gave him orders for drawings to distract him, and also to bring money into his empty purse" (IX, xliii). EFG's copy of *Undine* is now in the Berg Collection at the New York Public Library. EFG's volume of "Sir Roger" never materialized.

[4] Apparently James Allen (1802-97), an older brother who had attended Trinity and took his degree in 1825. He was not ordained deacon until December, 1834; priest, a year later. He became Dean of St. David's in 1878 (Venn, *Alumni Cantabrigiensis*).

[5] Allen met Miss Harriet Higgins of Alton, Hants, during the Long Vacation of 1831 while studying at Portsmouth, and they "came to an understanding."

[6] No doubt a member of Benjamin Heath Malkin's family. EFG's schoolmaster had married Charlotte, daughter of the Reverend I. Williams of Cowbridge, Glamorgan.

[7] Time after time in a diary which Allen kept while at Trinity, he recorded his determination to rise early. "Oh," reads one entry, "if I could get up in the morning and amend my life!" And two days later, "Through God's help I was enabled to get up to Chapel this morning." Earlier in the year he had "swapped" an umbrella with Thackeray for an alarm clock, but it had proved no more efficacious than his prayers (Allen Diary, Feb. 23, Nov. 7, 9, 1830).

[8] No portrait was painted at this time, but some years later EFG commissioned his friend, Samuel Laurence, to paint Allen's portrait in oils.

[9] EFG wrote his "Enfield epitaph" on the outside of the letter.

To John Allen

Geldestone Hall
Pmk., August 28, 1834

My dear Allen,

Why don't you write to let me know at least if you are married or not?[1] or alive or not? For I know one as little as the other. I wrote some four weeks ago to you, directing to Llamphey.[2] Did you ever get my letter? I don't scold you however, my dear boy: for since you never were a good boy at your letters, what must you be now when you have three sermons a week to write, and are married to boot? I tremble to think of it. Therefore as I am an idle man I think it is as well to send another letter in search of you: and if both are fruitless, why there's no great harm done. I have been here now a month, enjoying myself well: but for the last week the weather has changed from the former great heat to cold and wet: and I am not so well. I am afraid that I am become a downright pensioner of the sun. I solace myself with reading the Spectator which I like very much: and some of Scott's Novels of an Evening: this with rowing, music, and, till this last cold fit of weather, strolling about all day, has made my days pass on very smoothly. I'll tell you what I have it in my head to do: which perhaps I told you before: and that is to publish all the Sir Roger de Coverley papers in the Spectator by themselves in one Volume: so making the life of a Country Gentleman of that time. I should like Thackeray to illustrate it, which he would do beautifully:[3] but perhaps it would be too expensive making engravings of all the Dezigns. Don't you think this is a good plan? For Sir Roger is very fine: and a character worthy of all acceptation among Englishmen. When I go to London I will see about this. The Volume would not be much more than 120 Duodecimo pages: I should like to have it in a very small old Quarto. When I shall be in London I do not know: but I suppose some time in the winter. I heard from Thackeray a few days ago: he is just about to set off to Paris with his Grandmother: and to set to studying of painting seriously.[4] I suppose it is certain that you will return to town by the beginning of October. I have not heard from any of our acquaintance except Thackeray. I shall miss him in London very much indeed.

My brother in law and my sister are so kind to me that I am almost spoiled. Their children are growing up very nicely: and are great friends of mine.

Sometimes I ponder upon what change your marriage will make in you: I suppose I shall miss some things, and gain others. I hope, and ask again, that you will remember what I told you about your Sermons: that you are to bring them all to London for me to see. I should like very much to hear how all my kind friends at Freestone are: and I think you should write if only to satisfy me upon this point. So do. I shall be here for a fortnight more at least. I don't know where I shall go after that: but I think very likely to the sea side somewhere. I have been swimming lately in the river here: till this cold weather came I went every day to bathe. I [don't][5] think it does me any good: but I wished to know how to swim: and I was getting on famously. It is a very nice river here: it is called the Waveney. I have bought Blair's Grave with Blake's drawings.[6] I got it for 15s. which is cheap. The print of the Warrior, the Counsellor, the King, the Lady, and the Infant in front is worth the money, I think. Farewell, my dear fellow: I really wish much to hear that you and yours are well. Believe me to be your very affectionate friend

E. FitzGerald

Geldestone Hall, Beccles, Norfolk.

The golden laws of love shall be
  Upon these pillars hung:
A simple heart; a simple eye;
  A true and constant tongue;
Let no man for more love pretend
  Than he has hearts in store;
True love begun will never end;
  Love one and love no more.

Marquis of Montrose[7]

[1] Allen had married Harriet Higgins August 2.

[2] Allen had been substituting during the summer for the clergyman at Lamphey (so spelled in the *Post Office Directory*) near Tenby.

[3] See preceding letter, n.3.

[4] Thackeray went to Paris in September and studied art, indolently, until in 1836 he ventured into journalism for the second time.

[5] The MS is torn.

[6] Robert Blair's poem, *The Grave*, with twelve plates designed by William Blake, had been published in 1808.

[7] From "An Excellent New Ballad" by James Graham, first Marquis and fifth Earl of Montrose (1612-50). The stanza is the ninth in Part II of the poem, as given by Mark Napier in the *Memoirs of the Marquis of Montrose* (2 vols., Edinburgh, 1856, Appendix, p. xxxviii).

To John Allen

Geldestone Hall
Sept. 9 [1834]

Dear Allen,

I have really nothing to say, and I am ashamed to be sending this third letter all the way from here to Pembrokeshire for no earthly purpose: but I have just received yours: and you will know how very welcome all your letters are to me when you see how the perusal of this one has excited me to such an instant reply. It has indeed been a long time coming: but it is all the more delicious. Perhaps you can't imagine how wistfully I have looked for it: how, after a walk, my eyes have turned to the table, on coming into the room, to see it. Sometimes I have been tempted to be angry with you: but then I thought that I was sure you would come a hundred miles to serve me, though you were too lazy to sit down to a letter. I suppose that people who are engaged in serious ways of life, and are of well filled minds, don't think much about the interchange of letters with any anxiety: but I am an idle fellow, of a very ladylike turn of sentiment: and my friendships are more like loves, I think. Your letter found me reading the Merry Wives of Windsor too: I had been laughing aloud to myself: think of what another coat of happiness came over my former good mood. You are a dear good fellow, and I love you with all my heart and soul. The truth is I was anxious about this letter, as I really didn't know whether you were married or not—or ill—I fancied you might be anything, or anywhere. But all's right. God bless you. I have not been so well lately, as the weather has turned to cold and rain: but I must push through the winter gallantly. Do you know that I think I have improved myself very much this summer: I mean in conduct and thoughts: especially in one thing, which I shall leave you to guess at. I have even made one or two very pleasant acquaintances in the neighbourhood.

As to reading I have not done much. I am going through the Spectator: which people nowadays think a poor book: but I honour it much. What a noble kind of Journal it was! There is certainly a good deal of what may be called "pill," but there is a great deal of wisdom, I believe, only it is couched so simply that people can't believe it to be real absolute wisdom. The little book you speak of I will order and buy. I heard from Thackeray, who is just upon the point of going to France; indeed he may be there by this time. I shall miss him much.

I suppose this is the last letter I shall send you during your stay at Llamphey. When I shall be in town, I cannot say: nor do I know whither I shall go when I leave this place: which will be in a fortnight. It seems an absurd thing that a man who has all the world before him doesn't know where to go: but this is really the case with me.

After having got so far with this letter, I have still some compunctions as to sending it to you: but I suppose it will end in my sending it. I have nothing to say, when all is said, but that I love you more and more. How glad I am that you are happy in your wife. By my faith, the good humour your letter has put me into has smoothed down a great lump of indigestion, which even Shallow and Silence had not done: they had tickled my fancy with laughter: but your letter has spread a bit of [gladness][1] about the heart, which is nearer the digestion than the head, I suppose: and though I cannot partake of the early dinner that is just about to be, I look round about me with a more complacent eye. I must ask you again to give my best remembrances to the Freestone party. A Bazaar at Tenby! How well can I imagine it. It is the sort of thing I could dream of: and see you and your Wife walking up the street towards me: then Mr. Richards, perhaps, with his bag of gold, black in the face: and other quaint things.

Farewell, my dearest fellow: you have made me very happy to hear from you: and to know that all is so well with you. Believe me to be your ever affectionate friend,

E. FitzGerald

[1] A portion of the page is torn away.

To W. B. Donne

Geldestone
October 6 [1834][1]

Dear Donne,

I have been intending to write to you for some days past: and now I am vexed that I have not, seeing that the days slip away so, and that I am so soon about to leave this place. For I wanted to ask you to come over here and see me for a day or two: and I do heartily ask you to do so now. We don't leave here till the 14th of this month: surely you can come for a day. I should be sorry to leave the country without seeing you again, as I don't know when I may be back. Present my compliments to Mrs. Donne and beg her in my name, and I hope with your own desire to back it, to spare you for a very little time. I know you are somewhat shy of strangers: but you need be in no fear here: for we are homely people; and don't put ourselves out of the way: and so if you can put up with dining off a joint of meat at half past one with us and the Children, and can stand an occasional din of the same Children romping in the passage, I think you have no excuse at all. I don't speak of entertaining you, or shewing you sights, which

I think is a poor compliment to a man: here are books, and you may do as you please. There are however one or two things that I wish very much to shew you, and to talk to you about. I want to go to Norwich; and will meet you on any day there and bring you here:[2] there is a Coach every day, that starts from Norwich at about four in the Afternoon. I have not, you see, hinted at any chance of my coming over to you, because you are distracted with carpenters, bricklayers, etc., and I beg that you will not think of it. But please do come here, if it is only for a day: as much more as you can: my sister heartily begs that you will.

I should have been gone some time before, but that my sister wished me to remain till she herself was going away. It is chiefly this that has kept me from writing to you about this: I was not aware that I was going to be here so long. I have enjoyed myself much this summer, and the weather is now most beautiful. Your letter was most welcome to me, as your letters always are: this latter hint I hope you will attend to. I have not heard of Spedding: but I have written to him. Pray do you happen to know who are the new fellows of Trinity? I think the Election is about this time: I am interested for one or two: especially for a man that you have heard Spedding talk of, named Thompson.[3] I believe, however, that he is pretty certain of one.

After leaving this place, I believe I shall be in Suffol[k] for a month: and then probably in London. You mus[t] come up to London this winter, Donne: we will get abroad in that sinful place, and be very profane indeed. But it is the first part of my letter which you are now to think of: and yet I wish you would think but once, and slap your thigh, and say "Damme, if I wont".

And so I remain your affectionate friend

E. FitzGerald

[1] In *A FitzGerald Friendship* (Catharine B. Johnson and N. C. Hannay, eds., New York, 1932) the letter is dated [1830?]. Reference to the candidacy of W. H. Thompson for a fellowship at Trinity definitely fixes the 1834 date.

[2] Donne's home, South Green House, at Mattishall (pronounced Mattshal), near East Dereham, Norfolk, lies about 35 miles northeast of Geldestone by road; Norwich is about halfway between the two villages.

[3] Henry Alford gives the result of the 1834 election in his *Journal* under entry of Oct. 1, "The fellowships have just announced themselves; the list is as follows: —1. [Edmund] Lushington; 2. [Henry] Alford; 3. [William Hepworth] Thompson; 4. [Edward W.] Hamilton; 5. [William] Dobson; 6. [Thomas R.] Birks" (*Life of Alford*, p. 99).

To John Allen

Wherstead
Pmk., December 6, 1834

Dear Allen,

Your last letter was very delightful to me, as your letters always are. I am not now writing to ask for a reply, but to let you know that I shall be in London, I believe, at the end of next week. You are only to write to me in case you are going to leave London: for in that case I should probably delay my going thither. If I do not hear from you to that effect, I shall take it for granted that you are to remain in town during the Vacation, and I shall come up forthwith. Do you know of any nice lodgings in the neighbourhood of my old ones?[1] I would take Franklin's gladly if they were vacant: for I found the people to be always quiet and civil. I long much to see you, and to pay my compliments to Mrs. Allen. I had a letter from Spedding three weeks ago in which he was good enough to ask me to go and stay with him in Cumberland:[2] I should go, but for my ridiculous laziness. I am going on Monday to carry my sisters into Norfolk: when I shall pay a visit of a day or two to my friend Donne; and then hey for London! I hope that I shall come in for some of your sermons: and if you are on Duty, I shall be a very constant churchgoer.[3] I hope also that you have brought up with [you] your Llamphey sermons. My dear Fellow, if I have any very prominent wish in my heart, it is that I had a living of a thousand a year for you in a pleasant country. I wish much that you were in the Country, as I suppose that you do yourself. As I came home through a wood the other day, I began to think if I should marry, and have a small house and garden here in Suffolk; and so forth. I am sadly in want of a home in the Country, and have often thoughts of advertising for room in some family, where there was cheerful society.

Thackeray is still in Paris, I believe: but his last letter to me did not give much hope of his having set seriously to work. I wish he would with all my heart. Did you ever chance to read Tremaine?[4] I have done so lately, and I think that it is very well worth reading indeed: though it is not exactly a book after my fashion, nor one that I wish to have. But it is a manly and noble book, I think: and of a different order from the novels of the day. I have just finished reading Hall's Chronicles, which is a book *without a single merit*, I think: but I wanted to read over the ground which had supplied Shakespeare with matter: though I believe indeed that Shakespeare got at Hall's matter through Holinshed.[5] You will think that I am going to set up for a scholar, in thus getting through a big book: but it is no such thing indeed. I have a theory that it is good for people in these days, who are liable to be attracted and carried about by so many winds of letters, to read very stupid books with nothing new: so as to deaden that craving for novelty that we have. This I dare say you will think to be one of my humbugs.

Good bye, dear Allen. Make my compliments to Mrs. Allen, and believe me ever your affectionate friend

E. FitzGerald

I go to Norfolk on Monday.

[1] In November, 1833, EFG had lodged at 7 Southampton Row. The letter which follows is dated from 17 Gloucester Street, Queen Square.

[2] At Mirehouse on Bassenthwaite Lake, near Keswick.

[3] Allen was chaplain of King's College as well as lecturer in mathematics.

[4] *Tremaine, or the Man of Refinement*, published in 1825 by Robert Plumer Ward (1765-1846), barrister, statesman, and miscellaneous writer. The novel, described as "a metaphysical and religious romance," ran through four editions in a year.

[5] *The Union of the . . . Families of Lancaster and York* by Edward Hall (d. 1547). Raphael Holinshed (d.1580?); *Chronicles of England, Scotland, and Ireland.*

To W. B. Donne

17 Gloucester Street
Queen Square, London
[February 5 or 12, 1835]

Leisure—by C. Lamb

They talk of Time, and of Time's galling yoke,
That like a mill stone on man's mind doth press,
Which only works and business can redress:
Of divine Leisure such foul lies are spoke,
Wounding her fair gifts with calumnious stroke.
But might I, fed with silent Meditation,
Assoiled live from that fiend Occupation,
Improbus Labor which my Spirit hath broke:
I'd drink of Time's rich cup, and never surfeit:

Fling in more days than went to make the gem,
That crowned the white top of Methusalem:
Yea, on my weak neck take, and never forfeit,
Like Atlas bearing up the dainty sky,
The heaven-sweet burthen of eternity.[1]

Dear Donne,

Here I have sent you the Plutarch, and here is my letter. Your letter was most welcome. There was no need at all for you to write till you were inclined: and glad as I am to hear from men I love, I would rather they never wrote at all, than bored themselves: for I know what a task it is. I think that I am more addicted to the work than most men. I suppose from being so much an idle man. I hope you will like the book, which is I think a very handsome one: and, if the matter is good, is well worth the money as any I ever saw.

I have been buying two Shakespeares—a second and third Folio—the second Folio pleases me much: and I can read him with a greater zest now. One had need of a big book to remember him by: for he is lost to the theatre: I saw Mr. Vandenhoff play Macbeth in a sad way a few nights ago: and such a set of dirty ragamuffins as the rest were could not disgrace any country barn.[2] Manfred I have missed by some chance:[3] and I believe "it was all for the best" as pious people say. The Theatre is bare beyond anything I ever saw: and one begins to hope that it has touched the bottom of its badness, and will rise again.[4] I was looking the other day at Sir W. Davenant's alteration of Macbeth:[5] who dies, saying, "Farewell, vain World: and that which is vainest in't, Ambition!"

Edgeworth,[6] whom I think you remember at Cambridge, is come to live in town: and I see him often at the Museum. The want of books chiefly drove him from Italy: besides that he tells me he likes a constant change of scenes and ideas, and would be always about if he could. He is a very original man I think, and throws out much to be chewed and digested: but he is deficient in some elements that must combine to govern my love and admiration. He has much imagination of head, but none of heart: perhaps these are absurd distinctions: but I am no hand at these definitions. His great study is metaphysics: and Kant is his idol. He is rather without company in London, and I wish much to introduce him to such men as I know: but most of your Apostolic party[7] who could best exchange ideas with him are not in town. He is full of his subjects, and only wants opponents to tilt at. You once spoke to me of writing to him: if you wish to do so, his address is—8 Portland Terrace, Regents Park. By the way, this puts me in mind of my sins: that I actually kept your packet nearly three weeks before I delivered it at Mr. Harvey's house.[8] Did this matter? I hope not. A kind of fatality kept me from going there: it is some way off, and I didn't know the way: no excuse this, however.

The life of Coleridge[9] is indeed an unsatisfactory thing: I believe that everybody thinks so. You seem to think that it is purposely unsatisfactory, or rather dissatisfactory: but it seems to me to proceed from a kind of enervation in De Quincey. However, I don't know how he supports himself in other writings.

It is useless, I know, to ask you here: and yet sometimes an empty bedroom belonging to me makes me think that you would become it very properly. Douglas Heath[10] is very anxious to see you: as are many of his clique. He is a very nice fellow, and I like him more every day. My friend Johnny is happier and better than ever: he is coming to me this evening: I wish much you were here. I don't know how much longer I shall be in town, but I suppose nearly a month more.

I am in lodgings at No. 17 Gloucester Street, Queen Square; but when you are minded to write, 39 Portland Place is the safest direction.

To fill up my letter I send you a sonnet of C. Lamb's—out of his Album Verses—please to like it—"Leisure."

[FitzGerald wrote the title, the first and half of the third lines, then continued:]

I have begun it wrong, so I shall write it out on the first page. Farewell, dear Donne: I am much pleased to hear that Mrs. Donne and your boy are better: pray give my Compliments to both in the proper degree: and believe me to be yours ever most affectionately

E. FitzGerald.

[1] From *Album Verses.*

[2] John Vandenhoff played Macbeth at Covent Garden on February 2 and 9, 1835. EFG's "ragamuffins" included John Cooper, Macduff; G. Bennett, Banquo; Mrs. Sloman, Lady Macbeth. Perhaps EFG intended to write, "could not but disgrace."

[3] Byron's *Manfred* was a dramatic success during the 1834-35 season.

[4] EFG's hopes for the theater were unfulfilled for many years. Melodrama, comic burlesques, adaptations of French and German plays, and "spectaculars" of various kinds were the normal theater fare.

[5] Sir William D'Avenant (1606-68), dramatist and producer who "improved" Shakespeare to meet Restoration taste. His *Macbeth*, described as a tragedy with "Alterations, Amendments, Additions, and new Songs" was likened by John Downes, D'Avenant's prompter, to "an opera with singing and dancing in it."

[6] Francis Beaufort Edgeworth (1809-46), half-brother of the novelist Maria. He entered Trinity with EFG in 1826, and the two may have sat side by side

as they waited to matriculate, for his signature immediately precedes EFG's in the matriculation book. Edgeworth attempted without success to set up a school at Eltham in 1836; a year or two later he returned to his home, Edgeworthstown, County Longford, Ireland, to manage his brother's estate.

[7] Alluding to the Cambridge Apostles. Donne was a member.

[8] Doubtless William Harvey (1796-1866), wood engraver and designer, mentioned occasionally in W. B. Donne's correspondence. His work included illustrations for Edward W. Lane's *Thousand and One Nights*.

[9] Coleridge had died July 25, 1834; and four articles, "Samuel Taylor Coleridge: by the English Opium-Eater," had been published in *Tait's Magazine*, September-November, 1834, and January, 1835. Coleridge and De Quincey had been intimate friends. Written with extreme frankness, the essay had offended surviving members of Coleridge's family and many of his friends, among them Wordsworth and Southey who were included in the reminiscences.

[10] See letter to Allen, May 16, 1830, n.7.

In the spring Spedding repeated his invitation to FitzGerald to visit him in Cumberland. He also invited Tennyson who thought at first that he would have to refuse. However, he raised £15 by selling his gold Chancellor's Medal, awarded at Cambridge in 1829 for his poem, "Timbuctoo," and wrote that he would make the journey.[1] *Passages in FitzGerald's letters suggest that he and Tennyson had met previously, but their first recorded meeting took place at this time.*

The two guests spent the last three weeks of April[2] *at Mirehouse, Spedding's home on Bassenthwaite Lake, three miles north of Keswick. Although the trio managed to climb Dod Fell, one of the lesser peaks, rain kept them within doors much of the time. They amused themselves by sketching, and one of FitzGerald's drawings of Tennyson appears as an illustration in the* Tennyson Memoir.[3] *FitzGerald's spirits were brightened by the sight of daffodils growing in profusion in the field before the house, but these provided no consolation for Tennyson, who grew restive under enforced confinement and tended to be "grumpy."*

Tennyson entertained his companions reading poetry by Wordsworth, Keats, and Milton, and poems of his own, some as yet unpublished. He read dramatically, "mouthing out his hollow oes and aes . . . his voice very deep and deep-chested, but rather murmuring than mouthing, like the sound of a far sea or of a pine wood," FitzGerald recorded. "There was no declamatory showing off in A.T.'s recitation of his own verse, sometimes broken with a laugh, or a burlesque twist of voice, when something struck him as quaint or grim."[4]

Upon leaving Mirehouse about May 1, FitzGerald and Tennyson went to Ambleside, some fifteen miles south of Keswick, and took lodgings for a week at an inn. "Resting on our oars one calm day on Windermere," he recorded, Tennyson "quoted from the lines he had lately read us from the MS of 'Morte d'Arthur' about the lonely Lady of the Lake and Excalibur—

> *Nine days she wrought it, sitting all alone*
> *Upon the hidden bases of the Hills.*

'Not bad that, Fitz, is it?'" Tennyson remarked. At another time FitzGerald mentioned his brother-in-law, saying, "A Mr. Wilkinson, a clergyman." Tennyson's quick ear caught the meter. "Why, Fitz," he exclaimed, "that's a verse, and a very bad one, too." The poet later maintained that he had composed the line, a claim which FitzGerald staunchly disputed.

Spedding joined his friends for their last two days at Ambleside and introduced them to Hartley Coleridge, son of Samuel Taylor Coleridge, who lived nearby in a cottage at the foot of Nab Scar. Coleridge took dinner with them one day at the inn, and FitzGerald noted that he "did not sit still three minutes in his chair without getting up to walk about while he talked." At the end of the week Spedding and Tennyson returned to Mirehouse, and FitzGerald went to Castle Irwell. Spedding later sent an account of his guests to William Bodham Donne:

"E.F.G. was here for about a month, and left us some three weeks ago. He is the Prince of Quietists. I reckon myself a quiet man, but that is nature; in him it is principle. Half the self-sacrifice, the self-denial, the moral resolution, which he exercises to keep himself easy, would amply furnish forth a martyr or a missionary. His tranquillity is like a pirated copy of the peace of God. Truly he is a most comfortable companion. He would have everybody about him as tranquil as himself.

"Do you know that Deville, the phrenologist, predicted of him that he would be given to theology and 'Religion in the supernatural parts'? Was there ever so felicitous a mistake? Was there ever a stronger instance of the organs of marvellousness and veneration predominant, though driven so effectually out of their ordinary, if not their natural channel? I take this to be the secret of all that is strange and wayward in his judgments on matters of art: for very strange and wayward they appear to me, though so original and often so profound and luminous.

"There tarried with us at the same time a man who is in many points his opposite . . . to wit, Alfred Tennyson . . . he is a man always discontented with the Present till it has become the Past . . . but is dis-

contented because it is past. But though this habit makes him gruff and dyspeptic enough at times, you must understand that he is a man of a noble spirit and a tender heart."[5]

Nostalgic reminiscences of his Mirehouse visit appear in FitzGerald's letters at the time of Spedding's death in 1881.

[1] C. Tennyson, *Tennyson*, p. 155.

[2] In later years EFG repeatedly spoke of the visit as having been made in May. The letter which follows and other sources definitely fix the April dating.

[3] I, 153.

[4] *Tennyson Memoir*, I, 194.

[5] Frances M. Brookfield, *The Cambridge "Apostles,"* New York, 1907, pp. 267-68.

To John Allen

Manchester
May 23, 1835

Dear Allen,

I think that the fatal two months have elapsed, by which a letter shall become due to me from you. Ask Mrs. Allen if this is not so. Mind, I don't speak this upbraidingly, because I know that you didn't know where I was. I will tell you all about this by degrees. In the first place, I staid at Mirehouse till the beginning of May, and then, going homeward, spent a week at Ambleside, which, perhaps you don't know, is on the shores of Winandermere. It was very pleasant there: though it was to be wished that the weather had been a little better. I have scarce done anything since I saw you but abuse the weather: but these four last days have made amends for all: and are, I hope, the beginning of summer at last. Alfred Tennyson staid with me at Ambleside: Spedding was forced to go home, till the last two days of my stay there. I will say no more of Tennyson than that the more I have seen of him, the more cause I have to think him great. His little humours and grumpinesses were so droll, that I was always laughing: and was often put in mind (strange to say) of my little unknown friend, Undine—I must however say, further, that I felt what Charles Lamb describes, a sense of depression at times from the overshadowing of a so much more lofty intellect than my own: this (though it may seem vain to say so) I never experienced before, though I have often been with much greater intellects: but I could not be mistaken in the universality of his mind; and perhaps I have received some benefit in the now more distinct consciousness of my dwarfishness. I think that you should keep all this to yourself, my dear Allen: I mean, that it is only to you that I would write so freely about myself. You know most of my secrets, and I am not afraid of entrusting even my vanities to so true a man. It would be disgusting to talk so much about oneself to anyone but to such as you, whom I always have, and always shall consider, a kind of Father Confessor to me: don't laugh, or blush—for I am very serious—I hope you will tell me very fully about yourself, and your goings on. Perhaps you and yours are in just the same way as when I left you: but one is always wishful to have a full account after a silence of two months, thinking how many things may happen in a much shorter interval. Pray, do not forget to say how the Freestone party are. My heart jumped to them, when I read in a guide book at Ambleside, that from Scawfell (a mountain in Westmoreland) you could see Snowdon.[1] Perhaps you will not see the chain of ideas: but I suppose there was one, else I don't know how it was that I tumbled, as it were, from the very summit of Scawfell, upon the threshold of Freestone. The mind soon traverses Wales. I have not been reading very much—(as if you ever expected that I did!)—but I mean, not very much for me—some Dante, by the aid of a Dictionary: and some Milton—and some Wordsworth—and some Selections from Jeremy Taylor, Barrow, etc., compiled by Basil Montagu[2]—of course you know the book: it is published by Pickering. I do not think that it is very well done: but it has served to delight, and, I think, to instruct me much. Do you know South?[3] He must be very great, I think. It seems to me that our old Divines will hereafter be considered our Classics—(in Prose, I mean)—I am not aware that any other nations have such books. A single selection from Jeremy Taylor is fine: but it requires a skilful hand to put many detached bits from him together: for a common editor only picks out the flowery, metaphorical, morsels: and so rather cloys: and gives quite a wrong estimate of the Author, to those who had no previous acquaintance with him: for, rich as Taylor's illustrations, and grotesque as his images, are, no one keeps a grander proportion: he never huddles illustration upon the matter so as to overlay it, nor crowds images too thick together: which these Selections might make one unacquainted with him to suppose. This is always the fault of Selections: but Taylor is particularly liable to injury on this score. What a man he is! He has such a knowledge of the nature of man, and such powers of expressing its properties, that I sometimes feel as if he had had some exact counterpart of my own individual character under his eye, when he lays open the depths of the heart, or traces some sin to its root. The eye of his portrait expresses this keen intuition: and I think that I should less like to have stood with a lie on my tongue before him, than before any other I know of.

I wrote to Mazzinghi some time ago, telling him that I would let him know through you where a letter would find me. However, he need not write unless he pleases: but I think that you must, if you please: directing to me at the Post Office, Leamington, Warwickshire: that is, if you write within a fortnight's time: which please to do.

I beg you to give my best remembrances to your lady, who may be always sure that in all I wish of well for you, she is included: so that I take less care to make mention of her separately. But you must take care to let me know how she is. So farewell, my dear fellow, for the present. This is a long and very ill-written letter: so that I fear you will be tired of decyphering it. Tell me what books you have [been] reading and buying. I dare say you have a much longer list than I have given you: mine was soon exhausted, good lack! I leave this place very soon, and go into Warwickshire by Liverpool.

I am ever yours most affectionately,

E.FG.

P.S. I have read over my letter, and, as you see, have inserted a line where I tell you about the comparative altitude of my intellect—a pretty subject to treat a friend with! It seemed to me that you would misunderstand me, and suppose that I meant to insinuate that I had never been in company with any person superior to myself except Tennyson. Perhaps this very feverishness that I should be misunderstood is a far worse vanity than the other would have been—more unmanly, I think. How Jeremy would have dissected me, and set the case so clear before me that I should have blushed with shame.

[1] Scawfell Pike (usually spelled Scafell), highest peak in England; Snowdon, highest in North Wales, a hundred miles south across the Irish Sea in Caernarvon. FitzGerald's imagination nimbly carries him another hundred miles south to the home of Allen's cousins at Freestone in Pembrokeshire.

[2] *Thoughts of Divines and Philosophers* (1833), edited by Basil Montagu (1770-1851), legal and miscellaneous writer who published a number of such anthologies. EFG's remarks which follow show how closely he had read Jeremy Taylor's *Holy Living and Dying*, which had been Allen's parting gift on his friend's departure from Cambridge in 1830. Taylor, it will be noted, had risen considerably in EFG's opinion since that time. See letter to Allen [Jan. 31, 1830].

[3] Robert South (1633-1716), a somewhat disputatious divine with strong Royalist leanings. His forceful sermons were notable for their homely, humorous appeal.

To John Allen

Warwick
June 11, [1835]

My dear Allen,

I can't think what's become of you. I wrote a letter to you from Manchester,[1] asking you to write to me while I was in this part of the world: but I have sent to the Leamington Post Office[2] (whither I desired you to direct) but no letter. I should not have written now, but that I think it possible that you may have written: for they have a malpractice at that Post Office to send letters to the chief Inn of the Place, supposing that all passers-through will stop there. So I think your letter may have been lost. If not, unless you have been in sickness or sorrow, I shall be very glad to hear from you: for as it is, I don't know but that you may have been in both. Indeed, I should not have written now, but that I heard from Farish[3] that he had seen you: but when this was, he didn't say. I shall be here ten days more—please to write. My direction is, at Mr. Standish's, High Street, Warwick.

So farewell—

Yours ever
E.FG.

[1] The letter of May 23, immediately preceding.

[2] Leamington, or Leamington Spa, two miles east of Warwick.

[3] George Farish (1809-36), a student at Queen's while EFG was at Cambridge. Farish had been an Apostle; upon taking his degree in 1832, he was admitted to the Inner Temple. He died at Madeira in November, 1836 (*Alumni Cantab.*).

To Alfred Tennyson[1]

[London]
July 2, [1835]

Dear Tennyson,

. . . I suppose you have heard of the death of James Spedding's Sister in law—for my part, I only came to know of it a day or two ago: having till then lived out of communication with any one who was likely to know of such things. After leaving you at Ambleside, I stayed a fortnight at Manchester, and then went to Warwick, where I lived like a King for a month. Warwickshire is a noble shire: and, the Spring being so late, I had the benefit of it through most of the month of June. I sometimes wished for you, for I think you would have liked it well. I never lived among finer fields and . . . Dear Tennyson, . . . [I have] heard you sometimes say you are bored by the want of such a sum: and I vow to the Lord that I could not have a greater pleasure than transferring it to you on such occasions. I should not dare to say such a thing to a small man: but you are not a small man, assuredly: and even if you do not make use of my offer, you will not be offended, but put it to the right account. It is very difficult to persuade people in this world that one can part with a Banknote without a pang. It is one of the most simple things I have ever done to talk thus to you, I believe: but here is an end: and be charitable to me.[2] . . . Edgeworth . . . a wonderful man, but I shall be very serious lest he should wean you away from indulging in quaint and wonderful imaginations, and screw you up too tightly to moral purpose.[3] If this sentence is unintelligible to you, I will console you with one that is as clear as daylight. Your name has penetrated into France: there has been a review of your Poems in a paper called the "Voleur," in which you are called—guess what—"jeune enthousiaste de l'école gracieuse de Thomas Moore." This I think will make you laugh: and is worth postage.[4]

Now I have told you all that I have in my head: it is fortunate that the sheet of paper is just spacious enough for my outpourings. The "Morte d'Arthur" has been much in my mouth . . . inwardly [and] audibly: . . . and miles round Warwick.

I am yours ever truly,
E. FitzG[d.]

P.S. When I was at Manchester, I bought a small Dante for myself: and, liking it well, the same for you: for I had never seen the edition before, and I dare say you have not. It is small but very clearly printed: with little explanations at the foot of each page—very welcome to me. The proper price was ten shillings—but I only gave three.

[1] The letter is written on quarter-sections of a single large sheet, twice folded. Unfortunately, some substance (ink, it appears) blots out four large segments of the MS.

[2] At the close of his college career EFG's parents granted him an annual allowance of £300, sufficiently liberal to provide for his simple wants and extravagant whims. He was already helping Thackeray financially. That Tennyson later availed himself of the offer is established by Carlyle, who wrote to EFG in October, 1844, after Tennyson had spent a day at Cheyne Row, "He said of you

that you were a man from whom one could accept money; which is a proud saying; which you ought to bless heaven for."

[3] Tennyson did not lack for advice during the years of his novitiate. His Apostle friends, "dedicated" and "serious," strove to persuade him to give "significance" and "direction" to his poems. Francis Edgeworth, not an Apostle, appears to represent additional counsellors with similar advice. On the other hand there were those like EFG who urged the poet to give full rein to his fancy and creative talent. (For Edgeworth, see letter to Donne [Feb. 5 or 12, 1835].)

[4] Thackeray had written to EFG from Paris in May, "I read the other day a review of Tennyson's poems in the 'Voleur'—I was glad to see that his name had penetrated so far; and he will be pleased to know that they call him, Jeune enthousiaste de l'ecole gracieuse de Thomas Moore" (*Thackeray Letters and Papers*, I, 288). EFG's remark about the *Voleur* quotation's being "worth postage" was probably motivated by a complaint made by Tennyson that one review had followed him from place to place until it had accumulated postage fees totaling £1 8s.

To John Allen

Wherstead
July 4, 1835

Dear Allen,

I did not get the letter which you wrote to me at Warwick—till yesterday, when I arrived here from London. The letter went from place to place after me: perhaps I cherish it the more from its coming at last. I am sorry you make many excuses for not writing: for, however long you are silent, I always know that you are true, and remembering of me: besides your uneasiness about your wife has been enough to damp a stronger resolution than yours. This seems to me to have been a sad year for delicate persons. My brother John's wife,[1] always delicate, has had an attack this year, which she can never get over: and while we are all living in this house cheerfully, she lives in separate rooms, can scarcely speak to us, or see us: and bears upon her cheek the marks of death. She has shewn great Christian dignity all through her sickness: was the only cheerful person when they supposed she could not live: and is now very composed and happy. You say sometimes how like things are to dreams: or, as I think, to the shifting scenes of a play. So does this place seem to me. All our family, except my mother, are collected here: all my brothers and sisters, with their wives, husbands, and children: sitting at different occupations, or wandering about the grounds and gardens, discoursing each their separate concerns, but all united into one whole. The weather is delightful: and when I see them passing to and fro, and hear their voices, it is like scenes of a play. I came here only yesterday. I have much to tell you of: I mean, much in my small way: I will keep all till I see you, for I don't know with what to begin in a letter.

I hope most fervently that your wife is better, and will be better. A long cough is never to be neglected: nor a short one, neither. When you see her again pray give her my best remembrances. I suppose that you will not get this letter till after your return from Cambridge: it is not much matter when. I was very disappointed not to find you in London: whither I went for four days: I assure you, that to see you was the reason of my going.

Edgeworth introduced me to his wife[2] and sister-in-law, who are very handsome Spanish ladies, seemingly of excellent sense. The wife is the gentler, and more feminine: and the sister more regularly handsome, and vivacious. I think that he is a very remarkable man: and I like him more the more I see of him.

What you say of Tennyson and Wordsworth is not, I think, wholly just. I don't think that a man can turn himself so directly to the service of morality, unless naturally inclined: I think Wordsworth's is a natural bias that way. Besides, one must have labourers of different kinds in the vineyard of morality, which I certainly look up to as the chief object of our cultivation: Wordsworth is first in the craft: but Tennyson does no little by raising and filling the brain with noble images and thoughts, which, if they do not direct us to our duty, purify and cleanse us from mean and vicious objects, and so prepare and fit us for the reception of the higher philosophy. A man might forsake a drunken party to read Byron's Corsair: and Byron's Corsair for Shelley's Alastor: and the Alastor for the Dream of Fair Women or the Palace of Art: and then I won't say that he would forsake these two last for anything of Wordsworth's, but his mind would be sufficiently refined and spiritualised to admit Wordsworth, and profit by him: and he might keep all the former imaginations as so many pictures, or pieces of music, in his mind. But I think that you will see Tennyson acquire all that at present you miss: when he has *felt* life, he will not die fruitless of instruction to man as he is. But I dislike this kind of criticism, especially in a letter. I don't know any one who has thought out any thing so little as I have. I don't see to any end, and should keep silent till I have got a little more, and that little better arranged.

I am sorry that all this page is filled with this botheration, when I have a thousand truer and better things that I want to talk to you about. I will write to you again soon. If you please to write (but consider it no call upon you, for the letter I have just got from you is a stock that will last me in comfort this long while) I shall be at Wherstead all July—after that I know not where, but probably in Suffolk. Farewell, my best of fellows: there is no use saying how much I wish that all your sorrow will be turned to hope, and all your hope to joy. As far as we men can judge, you are worthy of all earthly happiness.

I am your most affectionate friend,

E.FG.

[1] EFG's brother John had married Augusta Jane Lisle, daughter of Charles March Phillips of Clarendon Park, Leicestershire, November 18, 1832. Four months before her death in August, 1837, EFG wrote to Allen, "We shall lose a perfect Lady, in the complete sense of the word, when she dies."

[2] In 1831, Francis Edgeworth had married Rosa Florentina, daughter of Don Antonio Eroles, of Catalonia, Spain.

A. Tennyson to FitzGerald[1]

Somersby, Wednesday
[July 8, 1835]

Many, many times, my dear Fitz, have I both thought of you and spoken of you, and quoted your sayings and doings, as those who live with me and know me can testify and long ere this had I written to you and exprest my sincere repentance for not having answered on the instant your last kind letter—truly kind it was, and if I did not dislike warm cockles, which warm or cold are a bad fish, I would say that it warmed the cockles of my heart—but unfortunately I mislaid your letter, and your direction escaped my memory. I am not such a beast, my dear fellow, as you take me for. Grumpy at receiving a warmhearted brief from an honest man! I may have been sometimes grumpy in the North, for I was out of health, and the climate Arctic, and Spedding had a trick of quiet banter that sometimes deranged one's equilibrium but grumpy to *you*—never, as I hope to be saved, and on that I take my master of keys as Brookfield[2] used to say.

I have not forgotten our quiet sojourn at the end of Windermere, nor our rows on the lake, nor the crabs that I caught therein, nor your over-fastidiousness about the fine arts—how can I forget all these or thee

as just a man
As e'er my conversation coped withal[3]—

and the sooner I see thee again the better.

I heard of you or somebody very like you the other day, from a little pursy gentleman, master of Caistor School, who told me he met a freshlooking Mr. FitzGerald, a graminivorous animal, in some coach,[4] and that you were going to Canwick, which I take it is near Lincoln—and so, near me. Why didn't you either come on to me or write me word that I might come and see you at Lincoln? It would have been no small refreshment to me in this land of sheep and squires to have lookt upon your sonsie face once more.

However, I will see you once again ere I die. I am going to live in or near London—the equal dearth at once of books and men in this county, cooperating with petty miseries ten times worse to bear than good hard knocks of Providence, have long rendered this part of the world distasteful to me—in the metropolis, methinks, I must light upon you, now and then—and we will have a hermit's root-dinner together and talk over old things.

But do not let me live for so long a time again without hearing from you—you see I answer this letter of yours immediately, for I only got it last night—tho' I will not say as Oliver Goldsmith does to his brother Maurice—"if you have a mind to oblige me, write often whether I answer or no."[5] Yet I assure you, no man can oblige me more by writing and I promise to do my best in answering you. If you knew how warm a glow of gratitude pervaded me, when I saw your name at the bottom of the sheet, you would let your accusation of "grumpy" and grumbler sleep for ever and a day.

In hope to see thee sooner or later
believe me, always thine
A. Tennyson

[1] This letter, the content reveals, was written after Tennyson had received a second letter from EFG following the visit to Cumberland. Somersby was Tennyson's birthplace and home in Lincolnshire.

[2] William Henry Brookfield (1809-74), Trinity, B.A., 1833; ordained priest, 1836; became, during the 40's, an extremely popular preacher in London. W. H. Thompson wrote of Brookfield, "He was far the most amusing man I ever met, or shall meet. At my age it is not likely that I shall ever again see a whole party lying on the floor for purposes of unrestrained laughter, while one of their number is pouring forth, with a perfectly grave face, a succession of imaginary

dialogues between characters, real and fictitious, one exceeding another in humour and drollery" (*Tennyson Memoir*, I, 37, n.2).

[3] Hamlet on Horatio. *Hamlet*, III, 2, 59-60.

[4] EFG's family responsibilities during the summer of 1835 made it most unlikely that he had been in Lincolnshire. Tennyson's "graminivorous" referred to EFG's vegetable diet.

[5] Robert Tennant, an Apostle, wrote to Tennyson in 1833, "May your success in rhyming vary inversely as the number of letters you write" (*Tennyson Memoir*, I, 126).

To W. M. Thackeray

Wherstead, July 1835
Pmk., Ipswich
July 29, 1835

Dear Thackeray,

I was very glad to get your letter last night: for I assure you that I have long been wishing to write to you. But in the letter which I received in Cumberland[1] you seemed to be not very fixed in your abode, especially as your Governor was just coming over: and in your packet which had the drawing in it, and which I only got a month ago, you gave no address: but, so far from it, talked of going to Constantinople. What has become of those Eastern plans?[2] For my part, I am glad that you stay at Paris, and work at your Art. But you tell me that my letters are rather too sensible: and I know well what that means. So I will write in a looser way. Marry then, I have got up at seven o'clock this fine morning to answer your letter: and I am sitting in no other clothes but that ancient red dressing gown, and inditing of this letter upon that capacious but now battered rosewood desk which you must know by this time. But, by the Lord, I feel I am growing hugely sensible—and then again I think that I am a greater fool than ever. These opinions succeed by turns, one naturally drawing on the other. We are going to leave this place, as my Father is determined to inhabit an empty house of his about fourteen miles off:[3] and we are very sorry to leave this really beautiful place. The other house has no great merit. So there is nothing now but packing up sofas, and pictures, and so on. I rather think that I shall be hanging about this part of the world all the winter: for my two sisters are about to inhabit this new house alone, and I cannot but wish to add my company to them now and then. I suppose that I shall occasionally trip up to London, and so forth, to see the ancient Johnny and others. He, poor fellow, has been alarmed about his wife's health: for she has had a cough all the year, and could not get rid of it. I never heard of so much consumption as there is this year—I suppose from the long protracted winter. What has been ailing you? You, who defied all these weaknesses? I wish your shabby scrap of a note had been longer to tell me more about yourself. But you were ever a lazy dog in pen matters: except in that immortal summer of foolscap, which I do not forget: but, having got all your letters of that time, bring back to myself very really. After thinking what I could tell you about other people, and the world at large, I find that myself is the readiest object to enlarge upon. So, you must hear about me to the end of the chapter, I believe. I made a pleasant stay in Cumberland, and then staid a month at Warwick, where I was very happy, being out all day, and wandering about to Stratford Upon Avon, Kenilworth, and such places. It is a seedy thing to attempt to tell you about these things: am I not on the brink of talking about "the immortal Swan of Avon?" I am—and prudence bids me retire from the danger. And now, my dear Boy, do you be very sensible, and tell me one thing—think of it in your bed, and over your cigar, and for a whole week, and then send me word directly—shall I marry? I vow to the Lord that I am upon the brink of saying "Miss ——— do you think you could marry me?"[4] to a plain, sensible, girl, without a farthing! There now you have it. The pro's and con's are innumerable, and not to be consulted: for I have at last come to a conclusion in morals, which is this: that to certain persons of a doubting temper, and who search after much perfection, it is better to do a thing slap dash at once, and then conform themselves to it. I have always been very unmanly in my strivings to get things all compact and in good train. But to the question again. An't I in a bad way? Do you not see that I am far gone? I should be as poor as a rat, and live in a windy tenement in these parts, giving tea to acquaintances. I should lose all my bachelor trips to London and Cambridge, I should no more, oh never more!—have the merry chance of rattling over to see thee, old Will, in Paris, or at Constantinople, at my will—I should be tied down—these are to be thought of: but then I get a settled home, a good companion, and the other usual pro's that desperate people talk of. Now write me word quickly: lest the deed be done! To be sure, there is one thing: I think it is extremely probable that the girl wouldn't have me: for her parents are very strict in religion, and look upon me as something of a Pagan. When I think of it, I know what your decision will be— NO!

How you would hate to stay with me and my spouse, dining off a mutton chop, and a draught of sour, thin, beer, in a clay-cold country. You would despair—you would forsake me. If I know anything of myself, no wife would ever turn me against you: besides, I think no person that I should like would be apt to dislike you: for I must have a woman of some humour lurking about her somewhere: humour half hidden under modesty. But enough of these things—my paper is done, and I must wash myself, and dress for breakfast. This letter is written with dirty fingers, and incomptis capillis.[5] My dear boy, God bless thee a thousand times over! When are we to see thee? How long are you going to be at Paris? What have you been doing? The drawing you sent me was very pretty. So you don't like Raphael! Well, I am his inveterate admirer; and say, with as little affectation as I can, that his worst scrap fills my head more than all Rubens and Paul Veronese together—"the mind, the mind, Master Shallow!"[6] You think this cant, I dare say: but I say it truly, indeed—Raphael's are the only pictures that cannot be described: no one can get words to describe their perfection. Next to him, I retreat to the Gothic imagination, and love the mysteries of old chairs, Sir Rogers etc.—in which thou, my dear boy, art and shalt be a Raphael.[7] To depict the true old English gentleman, is as great a work as to depict a Saint John—and I think in my heart I would rather have the former than the latter. There are plenty of pictures in London—some good Watercolours by Lewis[8]—Spanish things—two or three very vulgar portraits by Wilkie, at the Exhibition: and a big one of Columbus, half good, and half bad. There is always a spice of vulgarity about Wilkie. There is an Eastlake, but I missed it. Etty has boats full of naked backs as usual: but what they mean, I didn't stop to enquire. He has one picture, however, of the Bridge of Sighs in Venice which is sublime: though I believe nobody saw it, or thought about it but myself. The Exhibition was a good one, on the whole, I think. Mr. Hunt[8] filled the Water Colour with boys looking into lanterns, etc. etc. So now I come back to end where I began upon my first side.[9] This brings things round very mystically. And so, farewell, and be a good boy: and let me hear from you soon. You may as well direct to me at the new place, which is "Boulge Hall, Woodbridge, Suffolk."

I am as heartily as ever yours most affectionately,

E. FitzGerald

[1] The letter of [May, 1835] (*Thackeray Letters and Papers*, I, 287).

[2] In his May letter Thackeray had written, "Do you know that I have been applying to the Morning Chronicle for a correspondentship at Constantinople, &

it is not improbable that I shall get this [w^h] will give me a handsome income for a year and fill my sketch book into the bargain."

[3] Boulge Hall, an estate three miles northeast of Woodbridge. The decision to leave Wherstead must have come as a surprise, for EFG had had no inkling of the plan when he wrote to Allen on July 4. It was at Boulge that EFG found the cottage he had been searching for, in which to set up his own establishment.

[4] The "Miss ———" to whom EFG had been attracted was Elizabeth Charlesworth, daughter of the Reverend John Charlesworth, rector of Flowton, Suffolk, who lived at Bramford, near Ipswich. Elizabeth was a friend of EFG's sisters and frequently visited them at Wherstead and, later, at Boulge. He was still toying with the idea of proposing six months after writing to Thackeray (see letter to Allen, Feb. 4, 1836), but in a letter to Donne the following October he was concerned about the "cares and anxieties" involved in marriage. By January, 1837, he appears to have gained control over his "passion" and intended, he wrote Allen, to "wrap myself round with the domestic affections of brothers and sisters and nephews and nieces, and live a quiet life in the country. I am looking out for a horse." As life's ironies would have it, in 1847 Elizabeth married Edward Byles Cowell, EFG's "tutor" in Persian, and, after 1845, one of his intimate friends. For many years thereafter, EFG nursed his secret passion, permitting it at times to sink into adolescent sentimentality; but the attachment in no way ever interfered with his solicitous friendship with both the Cowells. (For this episode see Terhune, *FitzGerald*, chap. x.)

[5] "With hair disheveled."

[6] An entry in Thackeray's diary for June 11, 1835, reads: "Tuesday the Louvre opened . . . the Raphaels do not strike me more than they did before" (*Letters and Papers*, I, 286). In "Levant House Chambers," *Our Street* (1848), Thackeray wrote, "We smoked a couple of pipes, and talked about Raphael being a good deal overrated" (*Christmas Books*, Biographical Edn., II, 44).

[7] EFG had not abandoned his plan to have Thackeray illustrate a volume of Addison's Sir Roger de Coverley essays, first mentioned in the letter to Allen, June, 1834. From Paris, October 7, 1836, Thackeray wrote, "I am surprized you have not got the Sir Rogers," which he had asked two friends returning to England to deliver (*Thackeray Letters and Papers*, I, 323). When EFG's pictures were auctioned for his executors at Christie's, December 8, 1883, "Sir Roger de Coverley and the Inn Sign; and Sir Roger de Coverley's Gamekeeper a-wooing," drawings by Thackeray, brought £5.

[8] After spending the years 1832-34 in Spain, John Henry Lewis (1805-76), equally proficient in oils and watercolors, for several years devoted his art to Spanish subjects. In 1835, four of his canvases, "A Begging Friar, Seville," and pictures of three Spanish girls were shown at the exhibition of the Royal Academy. Six canvases by David Wilkie (1785-1841), three of them portraits, were hung that year. His Columbus picture was "Christopher Columbus explaining the project of his intended voyage for the discovery of the New World, in the Convent of La Rabida." Charles Lock Eastlake (1793-1865) exhibited only his "Italian Scene in the Year of the Jubilee." One of the eight pictures by William Etty (1787-1849) was "The Bridge of Sighs, Venice." Etty was a faulty draughtsman, but through years of study from the nude he acquired "unequalled power of imitating flesh both in colour and texture" (Redgrave, *Dictionary of Artists*). His "Phaedria and Cymochles on the Idle Lake," exhibited in 1835, may have prompted EFG's

comment about "boats full of naked backs." (Sidney C. Hutchison, Librarian of the Royal Academy of Arts, kindly provided data pertaining to the 1835 exhibition of the Academy.) The exhibition of the Royal Academy opened annually the first Monday in May and closed about the middle of July.

The Society of Painters in Water Colours in Pall Mall, East, and the Society of Water Colour Artists in Pall Mall (the *Old* and the *New* societies) held exhibitions during the same period. William Henry Hunt (1790-1864) was one of the creators of the English school of watercolor painting. Both Hunt and Lewis were members of the Society of Painters in Water Colours.

[9] EFG finished his letter at the top of page one.

To John Allen

Boulge Hall, Woodbridge
October 31, 1835

Dear Allen,

I don't know what has come over me of late, that I have not written to you, nor any body else for several months. I am sure it is not from any decrease of affection towards you. I now begin a letter merely on the score of wanting one from you: to let me know how you are, and Mrs. Allen too, especially. I hope to hear good news of her. Many things may have happened to you since I saw you: you may be a Bishop, for anything I know. I have been in Suffolk ever since I saw you. We are come to settle at this place: and I have been enjoying capital health in my old native air. I meant to have come to London for the winter: but my sisters are here, and I do not like to leave them. This parish is a very small one: it scarce contains fifty people: but that next to it, Bredfield, has more than four hundred: and some very poor indeed. We hope to be of some use: but the new Poor Laws have begun to be set afoot, and we don't know who is to stop in his cottage, or who is to go to the Workhouse.[1] How much depends upon the issue of this measure! I am no politician: but I fear that no political measure will ever adjust matters well between rich and poor. I have always thought that the poor have been neglected: and, if the rich will not relieve necessity from their superfluity, believe that the poor have a right to demand it. I would not say this to a poor man: but say so to you, not in the radical spirit of the day, but according to the best of my reason and natural feelings. But enough of this. Talking will do no good.

I have just read Southey's Life of Cowper;[2] that is to say, the first

Volume. It is not a book to be read by every man at the fall of the leaf. It is a fearful book. Have you read it? Southey hits hard at Newton[3] in the dark; which will give offence to many people: but I perfectly agree with him. At the same time, I think that Newton was a man of great power. Did you ever read his life by himself?[4] Pray do, if you have not. His journal to his wife, written at sea, contains some of the most beautiful things I ever read: fine feeling in very fine English. I have read very little all this year: and my little is very little. I have been rather Theological—Mosheim's History[5]—Chalmer's Bridgewater[6] (very weak, eh?) and—the Bible. But what has wholly entranced me was, some very bad translations *from* a French translation of Plato's dialogues: I say there is no use in any new books: for if men won't listen to these, the human mind never can produce anything worth listening to. The best Christian must admit this: for Socrates says nearly all that Christ said: so much so that, as I dare say you know, Origen, Irenaeus,[7] and other Platonical Fathers are blamed by some for declaring that the λόγος was partially revealed to Plato.

You see how I march upon my stilts: I feel ridiculous to myself in having said these things to you; but they are written now, and I dare not begin another sheet. I have not said this as at all detracting from Christianity: which was revealed, I know, not to make new discoveries in morals, but to sanction them, and excite men by the certainty of future judgment. It is said in the Bible that man was made but a little below the Angels:[8] he must therefore be capable of a Wisdom not much under theirs; a wisdom only twice removed from God himself. Indeed, if we were not naturally endowed with a mind of the same *kind* as his, though not in the same *degree*, we should not be responsible to him, nor fall under his judgment.

Do you disagree with all this? or do you understand it at all? Pray, my dear Allen, if you see Spedding give him my best love: as also to Heath, and others that I know. I would write to Spedding if I had anything to tell him of: but I don't think that he would thank me for a long essay like this. If you see Mazzinghi also, tell him that I love him, and have him in mind constantly. I think that I shall be able to manage a letter to him by and bye.

Farewell, my dear Johnny. How are all the Freestonians? What do you think! Thackeray has engaged himself to be married to a young Lady at Paris—a Miss Shawe.[9] I have had two rapturous letters from him about it. He tells me not to divulge this abroad: and I beg you will tell no one: I have told it to nobody but to you.

Pray do write to me: a few lines soon are better than a three-decker a month hence: for I really want to know where and how you are: and so be a good boy for once in your life.

Ever yours lovingly,
E.FG.

[1] Since 1795 the Speenhamland System of poor relief had been in operation. The system served merely to protect the indigent from starvation by supplementing scanty wages with a dole drawn from parish funds. Employers took advantage of the plan to reduce wages to bare minimums. Relief costs soared. "In one parish in Buckinghamshire the rates rose from £10 11s. in 1801 to £367 in 1832" (Spencer Walpole, *A History of England* [in the 19th century], 6 vols., 1890, III, 445). The effect upon labor was to substitute indifference for incentive, and pauperism for independence and self-respect. In 1834 the Speenhamland System was replaced by a new Poor Law which continued home relief for the aged and infirm and established workhouses, "bastilles" as they were called, to which were consigned all able-bodied persons applying for relief. The poor, naturally, resented surrendering their last vestige of independence; but, despite weaknesses, the new system was superior to that which it replaced.

[2] *The Works of William Cowper*, "with a life of the author by the Editor, Robert Southey," 15 vols., 1834-37. Cowper's mother (Anne Donne before her marriage) was a member of the Donne family of Norfolk to which William Bodham Donne belonged. "There is in me, I believe, more of the Donne than of the Cowper," the poet wrote to his cousin, Anne Donne Bodham, February 27, 1790. Mrs. Anne Bodham was W. B. Donne's great-aunt and Cowper's "Cousin Anna Bodham" who sent the poet "My Mother's picture out of Norfolk." The famous lines beginning, "Oh, that these lips had language!" were the result. The portrait was later returned to W. B. Donne and is still treasured by his descendants. Mrs. Bodham, a woman of exceptional intellectual and physical vitality, shared her home with the Donnes at Mattishall, where she died in 1846 at the age of 97. The Donnes aided Southey in writing his biography by providing him with information, letters, and portraits.

[3] John Newton (1725-1807), after a career at sea which terminated when he commanded a slave-trader, prepared for the church and in 1764 was appointed curate at Olney in Buckinghamshire. At Newton's suggestion Cowper and his friends, the Unwins, settled at Olney in 1767. A man of great vigor, and a zealous Evangelical, Newton persuaded Cowper to aid him in parochial duties, and the two also collaborated in writing the *Olney Hymns*, published in 1869. Southey, in his biography, implies that the activities, parochial and creative, into which Newton led Cowper were too strenuous for the poet's weakened mental and physical resources in the period following the death of Cowper's brother in 1770.

[4] *An Authentic Narrative of some particulars in the life* of . . . [John Newton] *in a Series of Letters to Mr. Haweis . . . and by him . . . now made public* (1764). The work has been republished frequently. The "journal . . . written at sea" to which EFG refers subsequently, is *Letters to a Wife* (1797).

[5] Johann Lorenz von Mosheim (1694-1755), German Lutheran divine and church historian, in 1726 published *Institutionum Historiae Ecclesiasticae Libri IV*, a history of the Church from the birth of Christ to the beginning of the 18th

century. Four English translations of the work were published in London between 1806 and 1822.

[6] The *Bridgewater Treatises,* a series of eight works on facets of natural theology provided for by a bequest of £8,000 in the will of the Reverend Francis Henry Egerton (1756-1829), eighth Earl of Bridgewater. The essays, the will stipulated, were to deal with "the Power, Wisdom, and Goodness of God, as manifested in the Creation . . . as, for instance, the variety and formation of God's creatures in the animal, vegetable, and mineral kingdoms . . . the construction of the hand of man, and an infinite variety of other arguments. . . ." Eight writers appointed by the President of the Royal Academy carried out the terms of the bequest. The first of the treatises was that by Thomas Chalmers (1780-1847) in two volumes on the subject, *On the Power, Wisdom, and Goodness of God as manifested in the Adaptation of External Nature to the Moral and Intellectual Constitution of Man.* The entire series of eight essays was published between 1833 and 1836. Sir Charles Bell (1774-1842), professor of anatomy, physiology, and surgery at the College of Surgeons in London and an eminent neurologist of the day, contributed *The Hand: its Mechanism, and Vital Endowments as evincing Design.*

[7] Origen (c.185-c.254), with the possible exception of Augustine, the most influential theologian of the ancient church. Irenaeus (dates unknown), theologian and Bishop of Lyons, known as "the peacemaker" from his efforts to reconcile dissident factions within the Church at the close of the second century.

[8] "For thou hast made him a little lower than the angels, and hast crowned him with glory and honour" (Psalms 8:5; Hebrews 2:7 and 9).

[9] Isabella Shawe, daughter of Colonel Matthew Shawe and Isabella Creagh Shawe. EFG's announcement anticipates by almost six months a letter from Thackeray to Isabella, written April 14, 1836, from which, Dr. Ray tells us, Mrs. Shawe "had taken alarm at Thackeray's abrupt proposal" (*Uses of Adversity,* p. 185).

To John Allen

Boulge Hall, Woodbridge
Pmk., Feb. 4, 1836

My dear Allen,

I have just returned from a dance round my room to the tune of Sir Roger de Coverley,[1] which I dare say you never heard. Why I should write to you, I'm sure I don't know: for I know very well you won't answer, and all I want to know is how your Lady is, and you too. Please to look out for me an Urry's Chaucer. I mean, a folio—not the black letter which is not Urry's, and not readable by my eyes. The little edition which I have by Tyrwhitt[2] may be very fine text and all that, but it is so small and ill-printed that I can't get on with it. Cornish had a very nice Urry last year: but I suppose it's gone long ago. If you see a good copy (none but a good one) please to buy it. My coming to town has been put off: and I don't know when I may go there: but I think very likely towards the end of February. Here we are all wading through mire, owing to the heavy rains: but I dance and sing merrily. Now you must know that there has been staying here for a fortnight the young damsel I have often told you about:[3] and I like her more than ever. She has shewn sense and clearsightedness in some matters that have made me wonder: judging by the rest of the world. Yet have I not committed myself—no, my Johnny, I am still a true Bachelor. What do you think of me? You would like this woman very much, I am sure. She is very pious, but very rational ("poor FitzGerald!" say you internally, with one of those mild shakes of the head that belong to you) she is healthy, and stout, and a good walker, and a gardener, and fond of the country, and thinks everything beautiful, and can jump over stiles with the nimblest modesty that ever was seen. Item, eats very little meat—humph!—drinks no wine—understands good housekeeping—understands children (ill-omened consolation!)—ay, there's the rub. Should I dance round my room to the tune of Sir Roger de Coverley if I were married, and had seven children? Answer me that.

Here's a pretty frame of mind for a man to be in, who is reading the Old Testament—yea, truly, Genesis—another shake of the head, eh?—but excuse the quantity of my oxygen at this time being, which makes me wonder at myself.

It is really a shame to send such a ridiculous letter, which seems to be indited from no deeper source than some tingling volition of the finger tips. If you were a very handsome, good, boy, you would send me a letter to keep me quiet—but you shan't [fill] me with disappointment for I don't [exp]ect one. Remember me very truly to Mrs. Allen and believe me your very affectionate Bachelor

E.FG.

[Written on outside of letter]

Did Raniford ever send you home the *Bayle*?[4] I paid her for it and bid her send it to you.

1 Before Addison and Steele introduced Sir Roger de Coverley as a member of the Spectator Club in 1711, "Roger of Coverly" was the name of both a song and a square dance. Sir Roger's name was subsequently substituted for the original title. The music and directions for the dance are given in Grove's *Dictionary of Music.*

2 *The Works of Chaucer*, begun by John Urry (1666-1715), completed by other editors and published in 1721. Thomas Tyrwhitt (1730-86) in 1775 published the *Canterbury Tales* in five volumes.

3 Elizabeth Charlesworth. See letter to Thackeray, July 29, 1835.

[4] Pierre Bayle (1647-1706), French philosopher and literary critic, noted chiefly for his *Dictionnaire historique et critique* and his *Nouvelles de la république des lettres.*

To W. B. Donne

London
March [21], 1836

Dear Donne,

I thank you much for your kind letter. I was very sorry not to be able to go to Thetford, after being so near the point: but a time will come for Mattishall.[1] As to the sponsorship, I was sure that you and Mrs. Donne would receive my apology as I meant it.[2] Indeed I wish with you that people would speak their minds more sincerely than it is the custom to do; and recoin some of the every day compliments into a simpler form: but this is voted a stale subject, I believe. Anyhow, I will not preach to you who do not err: not to mention that I cannot by any means set up myself as any model of this virtue: whatever you may say to the contrary.

I have consulted my friend John Allen concerning your Ancestor's Sermons:[3] he says that the Book is scarce, and not to be got, generally speaking, under £1.10. I saw a Copy marked in a Catalogue at Brighton for £1 some three months ago: but I suppose it is gone by this time. Are you willing to go so high? I think that you should be possessed of him by all means, considering that you are his descendant. Allen read much of him at the Museum, and has always spoken very highly of him. As to doctrine, I believe Jeremy Taylor has never been quite blameless; but then he wrote many folios instead of Donne's one: and I cannot help agreeing with Bayle[4] that one of the disadvantages of much writing is, that a man is likely to contradict himself. If he does not *positively* do so, he may *seem* to do so, by using different expressions for the same thing, which expressions many readers may construe diversely: and this is especially likely to be the case with so copious and metaphorical a writer as Jeremy.

According to the principles contained in page 1 of this letter I will tell you that I thought the second volume of Southey[5] rather dull. But then I have only read it once; and I think that one is naturally impatient of all matter that does not absolutely touch Cowper: I mean, at the first reading; when one wants to know all about him. I dare say that afterwards I shall relish all the other relative matter, and contemporary history, which seems indeed well done. I am glad that you are so content with the book. We were all talking the other night of Basil Montagu's new Life of Bacon—have you read it? It is said to be very elaborate and tedious. A good life of Bacon is much wanted. But perhaps it is as difficult to find a proper historian for him as for anyone that ever lived.[6] But enough of grave matters. I have been very little to the Play: Vandenhoff's Iago[7] I did not see: for indeed what I saw of him in other characters did not constrain me to the theatre to see his Iago. There is no use asking you to London: else, I am at present in lodgings, and have a spare bedroom which should be perfumed with growing hyacinths if you would come to occupy it. Spedding is just now furnishing chambers in Lincoln's Inn Fields: so that we may look on him as a fixture in London.[8] He and I went to dine with Tennant at Blackheath last Thursday: there we met Edgeworth, who has got a large house at Eltham, and is lying in wait for pupils: I am afraid he will not find many. We passed a very delightful evening. Tennant is making interest for a school at Cambridge:[9] but I do not know if he is likely to succeed. And now I have told all the news I know, except that I hear that Sterling[10] is very ill with an attack on his chest, which keeps him from preaching: and that Trench[11] has been in London. Neither of these men do I know, but I hear of them.

And now farewell, my dear Donne, I have written as tedious a letter as Basil Montagu could: except that it is all text, and not fretted with notes, which is the dismal fashion of his books, and, I dare say, of his letters. His pages look like a perspective of printing: first, the large type: then note B in smaller: then note b, smaller still: then note bb smallest pica, etc., etc. Remember me very kindly to Mrs. Donne, and believe me yours ever affectionately

E. FitzGerald

1 The care of a rapidly growing family had sapped the vitality of Donne's wife, Catharine; so in June, 1835, Donne had taken the family to Cromer on the Norfolk coast for three months. The winter was passed at Thetford. Donne was about to return to his home when EFG wrote.

2 Donne's fourth child, Blanche, had been born in 1835. Evidently EFG had "begged off" from becoming her godfather, though he later accepted that responsibility for one of Frederick Tennyson's sons. Tennyson's approach in offering the honor probably differed from Donne's. When his second son was born in 1854, Frederick wrote, "Sponsors I have succeeded in hooking, one in this manner: A friend of mine called yesterday and introduced a Mr. Jones. 'Sir,' said I, 'happy

to see you. Like to be a godfather?' 'Really,' he said, not quite prepared for the honour, 'do my best.' 'Thank you, then I'll call for you on my way to the church'; so Mr. Jones was booked" (Charles Tennyson, "Tennyson and His Brothers, Frederick and Charles," in *Tennyson and His Friends*, ed., Hallam Tennyson, 1911, p. 42).

[3] A Donne family tradition included John Donne, dean of St. Paul's, among Donne's ancestors. Despite the fact that Cowper speaks of "our forefather Donne," wrote Mrs. Johnson, "the claim cannot actually be proved" (*Donne and Friends*, p. viii).

[4] Pierre Bayle. See letter to Allen, Feb. 4, n.4.

[5] Cowper's biography, in Southey's edition of Cowper's works, then being published.

[6] Montagu's biography, included in his seventeen-volume edition of Lord Bacon's *Works*, published between 1825 and 1837. Much to EFG's regret, as will be seen, Bacon's "proper historian" proved to be none other than James Spedding, who had read Montagu's biography the previous summer and described it as "a work of much labour both on the writer's part and the reader's, but well meant, and if not itself a good one, containing all the materials necessary for a good one, which is saying a good deal" (*Tennyson and Friends*, p. 404). Six years later Spedding resigned his post in the Foreign Office to edit Bacon's correspondence. His search for letters led him to a wealth of neglected manuscript material, and Spedding embarked on his life's work. The result was an edition of Bacon's *Works* in seven volumes, 1857-59, and seven volumes of *Life and Letters*, 1861-74. Spedding published a two-volume abridgement of the latter work in 1878.

[7] EFG saw the Macready-Vandenhoff *Othello*, October 21. See letter to Donne, October 23, for his comments.

[8] Spedding, who never married, lived at 60 Lincoln's Inn Fields until 1867, when he left to make his home with relatives.

[9] After teaching at London University School (now University College School), Robert J. Tennant had become a master at the Blackheath Proprietary School. Aldis Wright conjectured that Tennant may have applied for a position at the Perse Grammar School, Cambridge (*Letters and Literary Remains*, I, 45, n.1).

"Edgeworth," wrote Carlyle, ". . . hoped to find support in preparing young men for the University, in taking pupils to board . . . ignorant that it is mainly the Clergy whom simple persons trust with that trade at present; that his want of a patent of orthodoxy, not to say his inexorable secret heterodoxy of mind, would far override all other qualifications in the estimate of simple persons, who are afraid of many things, and are not afraid of hypocrisy. Poor Edgeworth tried this business for a while, but found no success at all" (*Life of John Sterling*, Library Edn., p. 162).

[10] John Sterling (1806-44), charter member of the Cambridge Apostles, a man, wrote Carlyle, of "darting brilliancies and nomadic desultory ways," who, through force of personality, independence of judgment, and brilliance of intellect exerted an influence on contemporaries far out of proportion to personal achievement. He had been ordained deacon in May, 1834, and served as curate to Julius Hare at Hurstmonceux, Surrey. He never became a priest.

[11] For Richard Chevenix Trench, see Biographical Profile.

From W. M. Thackeray

[*Thackeray was married to Isabella Shawe in Paris, August 20, 1836. On October 7 he wrote to FitzGerald.*]

My dear Edward. Your two letters arrived a day after each other, the first coming last in the order of Scripture. As for the money, you have made me so used to these kinds of obligations, that I dont say a word more, but I feel very much your kind and affectionate letter, and long to have you with me. . . . I intend with your money to buy chairs and tables, to decorate this chamber, for as yet I have only hired them; . . . I shall make Mrs. Tack write to you on this very sheet of paper.

I am sorry to say that I like the newspaper-work very much, it is a continual excitement, and I fancy I do it very well, . . .

But you don't know how happy it is (to return to the marriage business) to sit at home of evenings, and pass pleasant long nights lolling on sofas smoking & making merry: dear Edward do come and see me, it wd do your heart good to see how happy I am.[1]

[1] *Thackeray Letters and Papers*, I, 322-23.

To W. B. Donne

London
Oct: 23: 1836

Dear Donne,

What have you been doing, and where have you been? To the sea side yet? And did Blakesley[1] find you? Pray when you have a spare half hour, and are not disinclined, let me know of your doings. I conclude that you are safe at Mattishall by this time. I have been to Ireland: and after that in Northamptonshire,[2] till last Wednesday when I came to London. Tomorrow I go into Suffolk: where I shall be for a fortnight: in which space of time if you can manage to write to me I shall be glad. My abode, Boulge Hall, Woodbridge.

Spedding is coming back to London this dientical night, so that I shall just miss him—which is a bore. Allen is in town, and as merry as good. Otter, the former Principal of King's College, is made Bishop of Chichester: and he will, I think, give my Divine Doctor a living in the course of time: for he is very fond of him.[3] I always thought Providence would do something for Johnny: and lay an easy pillow in the corner where Johnny was only thinking to hide his head in humility. I am afraid for his wife's health: but I don't know that her friends or Doctors think her in a bad state.

I have been to the play nearly every night since I have been here:[4] and they have really mustered all the strength of England at Covent Garden, even at the present low prices.[5] I have seen King John, and Othello, there. Charles Kemble has lost all his lightness in Falconbridge and Cassio: and is become very burdensome on the stage, I think. Vandenhoff really plays Iago very well: not so well as Young,[6] to my taste: I don't think he has made up his mind so clearly as to Iago's real character. But he plays with great ease, and point. Macready's Othello is fine: in parts, very fine: but not so good as some of his other parts. Miss Helen Faucit is a very considerable bore: and Mrs. W. West persists in softening whore into *whoore*: an old item of stage delicacy. Liston is delicious at the Olympic:[7] he should always be seen at the beginning of a season: for he becomes fagged and careless towards the end of it. He and Mrs. Orger played last night as well as I could wish to see. So now you have heard all that I have seen. When will you come up and see some of these things according to your promise? My movements are not quite certain just now: but I shall be in town again in the middle of November, for I have to go to the Isle of Wight at that time. I should like hugely to sit with you before the green curtain again. I have also got Blake's book of Job[8] for you to see: terrible, awful, and wonderful—and Retsch's[9] Romeo and Juliet, and no end of Epicureanisms in store. I am ashamed of living in such Epicurean ease: and really think I ought to marry, or open a book at a Banker's, that I may not be more happy than my fellows. Seriously, I do not mean to speak disrespectfully of marriage, etc., but I only mean that it must bring some cares, and anxieties. However, don't divulge what I say: for it sounds pert and awkward. Edgeworth is still at Eltham with one pupil, I hear: I am sorry that I have not had time to go and see him. Thackeray is married and happy as the day is long. John Kemble is in town, I believe: but I have not seen him. Now you have heard about men you do know, and about men you know no more of than Alexander the Coppersmith.[10] So now I will bid you good bye: and go to pack up a trunk. But remember me very kindly to Mrs. Donne: why will not she come to London some day? Then we will all go to the Boxes, ye Gods—"which that we may all do, etc."[11] How's Padden?[12]

Yours ever
E.FG.

[1] Joseph W. Blakesley (1808-85), classics scholar, one of the Apostles contemporary with EFG at Cambridge. He entered the Church; was canon of Canterbury, 1863-72; and Dean of Lincoln, 1872 until his death. He served on the committee revising the translation of the New Testament and took a vital interest in social problems of the day. EFG corresponded with him, but only five of the letters have been found.

[2] At this time EFG's father was devoting all his time and energy to his luckless coal-mining venture at Manchester. To Edward fell the responsibility of supervising harvests on the other FitzGerald estates; and for that purpose he had gone to Ireland and Northamptonshire. The estate in Ireland, Little Island (now called The Island), is exactly that, an island of some three hundred acres in the Waterford River, near Waterford. Naseby Wooleys, in Northamptonshire, embraced most of the battlefield of Naseby. (See letter to Allen, Nov. 10, 1830.)

[3] William Otter (1768-1840), friend and biographer of Thomas Malthus, had been principal of King's College, London, from its founding in 1830. Upon being elevated to the bishopric, he appointed John Allen his examining chaplain.

[4] EFG had been to the theater every night but one since his arrival in London, Wednesday, October 19. That evening he saw *King John*, and Friday evening, *Othello*, both at Covent Garden. Saturday he went to the Olympic Theater, managed by Madame Vestris.

[5] Covent Garden, which had emptied Charles Kemble's purse, had taxed the patience and resources of lessees who had succeeded him. D. W. Osbaldiston took over the theater in October, 1835, and cut admissions by about one-half —to 4s, 2s, and 1s—to the dismay of the management at Drury Lane, where attendance fell off sharply while Covent Garden was overpacked. Osbaldiston opened the 1837 spring season with no fewer than eight actors and actresses of the first rank: Charles Kemble (playing his last full engagement), William Macready, John M. Vandenhoff, William Farren, Benjamin Webster, Helen Faucit, Mrs. Julia Glover, and Mrs. W. West.

[6] Charles Young, who had retired from the stage in 1832.

[7] John Liston, leading comedian of the day, who had played at Covent Garden and, later, at Drury Lane, where he received £40 a week. In 1831 Madame Vestris lured him to the Olympic with a weekly salary reported by one authority to be £60, by another £100. He ended his stage career in 1837. Mrs. Mary Anne Orger, subsequently mentioned, was a comedienne. Neither Liston nor Mrs. Orger was named by the *Times* in the cast of *Court Favour*, the main attraction at the Olympic for October 22. They were given ample opportunity to appear, however, for *A Pleasant Neighbour*, *Love in a Cottage*, and *A Gentleman in Difficulties* were also on the program that evening.

[8] Beginning the work in 1820, William Blake devoted the last years of his life to the engraved designs illustrating his *Inventions to the Book of Job*. He died in 1827.

[9] EFG misspells the name of Friedrich August Moritz Retzsch (1779-1857), German painter and etcher noted for his illustrations for Goethe's *Faust* (1812), the works of Schiller, and a number of Shakespeare's plays from 1828-45.

[10] "Alexander the coppersmith did me much evil: the Lord reward him according to his works" (2 Tim. 4:14).

[11] See letter to Aldis Wright, Feb. 22, [1871].

[12] EFG misspells the name of Thomas Paddon (1784-1861), Vicar of Mattishall,

1821-61. Paddon, who took his B.A. at Cambridge in 1806, had been a Fellow of Trinity from that year until 1823 (Venn, *Alumni Cantab.*).

To John Allen

[Geldestone Hall]
January 1, 1837

Dear Allen,

A merry new year to you and yours. How have you been since I saw you?

You remember that I promised to write to you; but I have not been able to write at all. I suppose, you have been down to Chichester by this time to examine youth.[1] I have been spending my Christmas here: but we have not had a very merry one, for all my sister's Children have had bad inflammatory colds, and one little Child has all but died. I was to have gone back yesterday to Boulge to stay with my sisters: but I think this deep snow will keep them from coming there. What have you done in London? When have you shovelled the snow away? People can scarce remember so much. It will put the Poor Law to the test:[2] at present it is so far good that the poor are employed in clearing the roads.

If you can find an old Copy of Taylor's Holy Living and Dying cheap and clean at the same time, pray buy it for me. It is for my old friend Mrs. Schutz:[3] and she would not allow me to give it her: so that I give you her directions. Also, three copies of a pamphlet, published by Pinnock and Maunder,[4] Old Boswell Court, 267 St. Clement's Churchyard, Strand—called, "The Collects for Sundays, and Holy days throughout the Year, with Notes, and some Prayers." Also a book has been published by some bookseller in Lamb's Conduit Street about eight months ago, giving an Account of all the Charities in London. Do not buy this book: but let me hear from you of its size, price, etc. All these things are for my old friend: the remainder of whose life is given up to Charities. She has a book that was published under Lord Brougham's directions giving a history of the Charities and endowments of the *City* of London:[5] but this is quite another work. These things would be troublesome to you; but that the places where they are to be sought lie in your daily haunts. I write in a room full of chattering Children: and so I don't know if I have made myself understood. Jeremy Taylor's book used to be very common indeed.

I am very deep in my Aristophanes, and find the Edition I bought quite sufficient for my wants. One requires a translation of him less than of any of the Greeks I have read, because his construction is so clear and beautiful. Only his long words, and local allusions, make him difficult, so far as I have seen. He has made me laugh heartily, and wonder: but as to your calling him greater than Aeschylus or Sophocles, I do not agree with you. I have read nothing else. What a nice quiet speech Charles Kemble made on quitting the stage: almost the best I ever remember on such an occasion.[6] Did Spedding hear him? My dear Allen, I should often wish to see you and him of an Evening as heretofore at this season in London: but I don't see any likelihood of my coming till February at nearest. We live here the usual quiet Country Life: and now that the snow is so deep we are rather at a loss for exercise. It is very hard work toiling along the roads, and besides so blinding to the eyes. I take a spade, and scuppet[7] away the snow from the footpaths.

To any of my friends you see give my love: call on Spedding especially. I would write to him if I thought I could say anything worth saying: but you see of what scraps this letter is made up. I shall soon be as bad as ever you were in point of correspondence. I have been wishing to write to Thackeray for weeks: but after one abortive effort have almost given it up.

Farewell, my dear Boy. You said you would write: and now that I have asked you to do me some jobs, and to answer some questions, I think you must write: especially as your Christmas holidays are going on. My letter does not ask for a long answer: but a sentence from you will gladden me. The Clergyman of the parish who is a very nice fellow also desires me to ask any friend in London to buy him Scott's Christian Life,[8] if it can be got for seven or eight shillings. This Clergyman is a young man, a year above me at College, I think:[9] very good natured, sensible, charitable, and well read in Church matters and doctrines. We see a great deal of him: and indeed he is more like one of the family. So if you find the book at the said price buy it: and we will devise means for having this and the aforementioned books conveyed hither.

Write to me at Boulge Hall, Woodbridge—for I think that the snows will be passable, and my sisters arrived there, before you will write. There's an insinuation for you. Make my remembrances to Mrs. Allen: and believe me

Yours ever most affectionately,
E. FitzGerald

Tell me if you pay double postage for a sheet of paper folded in this way. I hope not, I am sure.[10]

Another request. Buy me if you can at Pickerings, the 14th Vol. of Montagu's Bacon—it contains the translation of the Novum Organum, and of other Latin pieces. Who translated them, do you know? There are different initials at the end of each.[11]

1 As examining chaplain for Bishop William Otter. See letter to Donne, Oct. 23, 1836.

2 See letter to Allen, Oct. 31, 1835.

3 Mrs. John Bacon Schutz, who lived at Gillingham Hall, a mile east of Geldestone.

4 William Pinnock and Samuel Maunder, compilers and publishers of religious works and popular manuals of instruction.

5 Probably *Endowed Charities of the City of London*, published in 1829. *The Collects for Sundays* has not been further identified.

6 For his farewell appearance at Covent Garden, December 23, 1836, Charles Kemble played one of his most successful roles, Benedick, in *Much Ado About Nothing*. Helen Faucit played Beatrice. Spectators gathered at the theater as early as three o'clock in the afternoon, the London *Times* reported on December 24, "and when the hour for opening the doors arrived, the multitude assembled would have a dozen times filled the space the house affords." Kemble's retirement at this time was purely nominal. He continued to act for short periods for several years thereafter.

7 "Scuppit, dimin. of *scoop* . . . also a common shovel" (Robert Forby, *Vocabulary of East Anglia*, 2 vols., 1830).

8 John Scott (1639-95), for the last four years of his life Rector of St. Giles-in-the-Fields. in 1681 published *The Christian Life from its Beginning to its Consummation in Glory*.

9 John Mainwaring (1806-57), B. A. Cambridge, 1829. He was rector of Geldestone from 1831 until his death but was not resident there after 1837. In a letter to Frederick Tennyson, October, 1841, he reported that his health had improved. "I hope to do duty next summer," he concluded (*Letters to Frederick Tennyson*, H. J. Schonfield, ed., 1930, pp. 51-52). Francis de Soyres, who married EFG's sister Andalusia in 1844, served as Mainwaring's curate at Geldestone from June, 1842, until July, 1844.

10 Instead of folding his letter once, as was the normal practice, EFG folded over the upper and lower thirds of his paper. The experiment did not cost Allen additional postage.

11 The Latin treatises in Basil Montagu's edition of Bacon's works were translated by Francis Wrangham (1769-1842) and William Page Wood (1801-81), who, as Lord Hatherley, in 1868 became Lord Chancellor, "as just and conscientious a man as ever rose to the Woolsack," EFG believed. William Wood married Charlotte, daughter of EFG's boyhood "hero," Major Edward Moor of Great Bealings. (For this, and others of Lord Hatherley's Suffolk connections, see letter to Pollock, Feb. 2, 1869. For Montagu's *Bacon*, see letter to Donne, Mar. [21], 1836, n.6.)

To John Allen

[Boulge Hall]
Tuesday, January 10, 1837

My dear Allen,

Another letter in so short a time will surprise you. My old Lady[1] will be glad of a new edition of Jeremy Taylor, beside the old one. I remember you once gave me a very nice large duodecimo one:[2] are these to be had, and cheap? It must have a good type, to suit old eyes. When you are possessed of these and the other books I begged you to ask for (except the Bacon which is for myself) do me one favour more: which is to book them per Coach at the White Horse, Piccadilly, directed to Mrs. Schutz, Gillingham Hall, Beccles. I should not have troubled you again, but that she, poor Lady, is anxious to possess the books soon, as she never looks forward to living through a year: and she finds that Jeremy Taylor sounds a good note of preparation for that last hour which she looks upon as drawing nigh. I myself think she will live much longer: as she is wonderfully healthy for her time of life—seventy-six.[3] Sometimes I talk to her about you: and she loves you by report. You never grudge any trouble for your friends: but as this is a little act of kindness for an old and noble lady, I shall apologize no more for it. I will pay you all you disburse when I come to London.

I was made glad and sad last night in looking over some of your letters to me, ever since my stay at Tenby.[4] I wonder within myself if we are changed since then. Do you remember that day when we sat upon that rock that runs out into the sea, and looked down into the clear water below? I must go to Tenby one of these days, and walk that old walk to Freestone. How well I remember what a quiet delight it was to walk out and meet you, when you were coming to stay a week with me once at my lodgings.

Whom do you think I had a letter from this morning? from Alfred Tennyson. I wrote to him: and he has written the very kindest possible letter to me. He talks of coming to live near London:[5] which indeed, I think, will be much better for him. I think that, when I am not engaged with my sisters here, I shall go and live with Mr. Kerrich at Geldestone: they are really fond of me, and it will be a good home. I love the country more than London: and I often think that when you have got a living somewhere near Chichester, and are out of London, I should feel strange there ever after. I do not suppose that I shall henceforward make many new acquaintances in town, as I am not in the way to do so: but try and wrap myself round with the domestic affections of brothers and sisters and nephews and nieces, and live a quiet life in the country. I am looking out for a horse. There I stop, and think how the "spirits of the wise may be sitting in the Clouds and mocking me,"[6] and laughing at my shallow resolu[tions an]d[7] anticipations, which I myself may be the fir[st unceremo]niously to disperse. One good thing is, I have learnt by the largest experience never to be astonished at my own vagaries, nor to reckon on any stability in my plans. Oh! the ass that I am conscious I am.

And now, Sir, when you next go to the British Museum, look for a Poet named Vaughan. Do you know him? I read some fine sacred poems of his in a Collection of John Mitford's: he selects them from a book of Vaughan's called "Silex Scintillans," 1621.[8] He seems to have great fancy and fervour and some deep thought. Yet many of the things are in the tricksy spirit of that time: but there is a little Poem beginning, "They are all gone into a World of Light," etc., which shews him to be capable of much. Again farewell, my dear Allen: give my best remembrances to Mrs. Allen, who must think that I write to you as if you were still a Bachelor. Indeed, I think you had best burn this letter suddenly, after you have read my commissions. Βρεκεκεκὲξ κοὰξ κοάξ.[9] There—I believe I can construe that passage as well as Porson.[10]

Yours ever,
E. FitzGerald

I have copied in the verses of Vaughan which I spoke about: which, if you can read, will make my letter worth sending. At least I think so. Nothing *very* fine: but affectionate and Blakeish. This is like one of my old letters, isn't it!

P.S. Here are some of Vaughan's[11]—but I doubt if you can read.

They are all gone into the world of light!
And I alone sit lingering here;
Their very memory is fair and bright,
And my sad thoughts doth clear.

It glows and glitters in my cloudy breast
Like stars upon some gloomy grove,
Or those faint beams in which this hill is drest,
After the Sun's remove.

I see them walking in an Air of glory,
Whose light doth trample on my days:
My days, which are at best but dull and hoary,
Meer glimmering and decays.

O holy hope! and high humility,
High as the Heavens above!
These are your walks, and you have shew'd them me
To kindle my cold love.

Dear, beauteous death! the Jewel of the Just,
Shining no where, but in the dark;
What mysteries do lie beyond thy dust;
Could man outlook that mark!

He that hath found some fledg'd bird's nest, may know
At first sight, if the bird be flown;
But what fair Well, or Grove he sings in now,
That is to him unknown.

And yet, as Angels in some brighter dreams
Call to the soul, when man doth sleep;
So some strange thoughts transcend our wonted theams,
And into glory peep.

[1] Mrs. Schutz, mentioned in the previous letter.

[2] Probably the copy of Jeremy Taylor's *Holy Living and Holy Dying* which Allen gave EFG when the latter left Cambridge in 1830.

[3] Mrs. Schutz lived for another decade and died in December, 1847.

[4] See letters to Allen, [Late Aug., 1832] and Nov. 8, 1833.

[5] From 1837 to 1840 the Tennyson family lived at Beech Hill House (now Beech Hill Park), High Beech, Epping.

[6] "Well, thus we play the fools with the time, and the spirits of the wise sit in the clouds and mock us," observes Prince Hal to Poins (*Henry IV*, Part 2, II. 2. 155-57).

[7] Segment torn out of sheet, where EFG had placed the sealing disc.

[8] EFG erred in assigning Henry Vaughan's *Silex Scintillans*: or *Sacred Poems and private Ejaculations* to 1621. Vaughan (1622-95) published the work in two parts, the first in 1650, the second in 1655.

[9] "Brekkekex, coax, coax," coined by Aristophanes to represent the croaking of frogs for his comedy *The Frogs*.

[10] Richard Porson (1759-1808), famous Greek scholar; Regius Professor of Greek at Cambridge, 1792-1808, though he never lectured, nor did he reside in Cambridge while holding his chair (Venn, *Alumni Cantab.*).

[11] EFG added his transcript of the poem above the heading of his letter, where space permitted him to include only the first seven of Vaughan's ten stanzas. The selection is generally recognized as one of Vaughan's finest lyrics.

To John Allen

Boulge Hall, Woodbridge
[February 12, 1837]

My dear Allen,

Another commission in so short a time is rather too bad: but I know not to whom I can apply but to yourself: for our bookseller here could not get me what I want, seeing that I don't exactly know myself. The book I want is an Athenaeus,[1] but the edition I know not: and therefore I apply to you who know my taste—Black and Young's is the best place, I think for it must be a German edition, as their type and paper suit my eyes. I have seen such an one in three or four Volumes, I think. Lastly, will you bid him pack it up instantly and direct it to me *E.* FG—at Portland Place: for my Father is coming down here on Wednesday and will bring it for me—I send this note to defray the cost for this and the other books you were so good as to get for me: they arrived safe at their proper destination. My Father is going to bring down a Lady here to live as Companion with my sister: so that this will, I think, keep me here rather than at Geldestone.

There is a small Cottage of my Father's close to the Lawn gates, where I shall fit up a room most probably. The garden I have already begun to work in. I hope to come to London soon however, and I have need to go there, besides wishing to see you and others. Have you escaped the Influenza? And has Mrs. Allen? We have escaped it hitherto: but people have been all laid up in the towns about. Sometimes when I have sat dreaming about my own comforts I have thought to myself "If Allen ever would come and stay with me some days at my Cottage if I live there"—but I think you would not: "could not" you will say, and perhaps truly.

I wrote to Thackeray some time ago, but I have not heard from him. Indeed, I don't know where in Paris he lives: and am doubtful if my letter reached him.

I am reading Plutarch's Lives, which is one of the most delightful books I ever read. He must have been a Gentleman. My Aristophanes is nearly drained: that is, for the present first reading: for he will never be dry, apply as often as I may. My sisters are reading to me Lyell's Geology of an Evening:[2] there is an admirable chapter illustrative of human error and prejudice retarding the truth, which will apply to all sciences, I believe: and, if people would consider it, would be more valuable than the geological knowledge, though that is very valuable, I am sure. You see my reading is so small that I can soon enumerate all my books: and here you have them. If Black and Young have the Athenaeus plainly bound, or half bound, I shall like it the better.

Again farewell, dear Allen,—you are constantly in my thoughts. Remember me very kindly to Mrs. Allen.

Ever yours affectionately,
E.FG.

Sunday Evening.

[1] Athenaeus, Greek rhetorician and grammarian, who lived c. 230 A.D., author of *Deipnosophistae*, or *Banquet of the Learned*, a miscellany of quotations from ancient writers, anecdotes, and dialogues. The German edition of the work to which FitzGerald refers is probably that edited by the German scholar, Karl Wilhelm Dindorf (1802-83), 3 vols., 1827.

[2] The *Principles of Geology* by Sir Charles Lyell (1797-1875) proved to be a "best seller" when published. Second editions of the first two volumes (1830 and 1832) were issued before the third volume appeared in 1833. By 1837 five editions of the work had been published. The *Principles*, attributing earth formations to "natural" causes still in operation, revolutionized thought on the creation and age of the earth and profoundly influenced the thinking of laymen and theologians. The chapter to which EFG specifically refers is "Prejudices Which have Retarded the Progress of Geology" (Vol. I, chap. V). The impress of Lyell's disclosures on EFG is attested by passages in letters written to Cowell, Jan. 28, [1845] and [July 24, 1847].

In his letter to Allen, written January 10, FitzGerald had spoken of his intention to make his home with the Kerriches at Geldestone. His decision to occupy Boulge Cottage, just outside the gates of Boulge park, canceled that plan and brought to an end FitzGerald's search for a home of his own—a search he had carried on since his departure from Cambridge. The cottage was a rambling one-story, thatch-roofed dwelling with walls "as thin as sixpence." FitzGerald furnished only three rooms for himself—a dining room and a study on either side of the front entrance, and a bedroom behind the study. (So the editors were informed by a later occupant of the cottage.) The remainder of the house was given over to his housekeeper, Mrs. Faiers, and her husband, a laborer on the estate. For six years FitzGerald occupied the cottage only from spring through autumn, when he would retreat to the Hall for the winter. In 1843 he improved the cottage, and, thereafter, lived there the year round until 1853. Fire destroyed the original structure in November, 1923; but that which replaced it (without thatched roof) conforms to the original design. Thomas Wright in his biography states that FitzGerald occupied only two of the rooms.

Since Frederick Tennyson, Donne, Samuel Laurence, and other friends were sometimes guests at the cottage, three appears to be the more likely number. Although FitzGerald spoke of the cottage as belonging to his father, the Boulge estate was actually part of Mrs. FitzGerald's inheritance.

From Alfred Tennyson

[London]
[Late March, 1837]

My dear Fitz,

We have stopt here for two hours (i.e. I and Sep[1]) and I dare say you will not be at home till 2 or 3 o'clock. I am going home tomorrow morning & as you will not come, after your tonight's deboshments by twelve tomorrow to Mornington Crescent (my quarters) why—I shall not see you—wherefore goodbye

Thine

P.S. I wonder how long you intend to stop in town—if a week or two longer, possibly I may have a chance of seeing you.

P.S.2 Stopt after I had written this—altogether from a quarter past 9 to *do.* past one—very sorry not to have seen you. Servant offered refreshments—did as well as we could.

Goodnight.

[1] Septimus, a brother, seven years the poet's junior. Sir Charles Tennyson recounts that a visitor, upon entering a drawing room in the home of the Hallams, was surprised to see a tall, swarthy man rise from the hearth-rug on which he had been lying. Approaching the newcomer with outstretched hand, the man said in a deep voice, "I am Septimus, the most morbid of the Tennysons" (Alfred Tennyson, p. 199).

To W. B. Donne

Boulge
March 29, [1837]

Dear Donne,

I am just returned from London where I have been staying a month. A joyful month it was, for I found all my friends there, unexpectedly, so that we had all kinds of delights, and smokings and sittings up.

March 1837

The man you ask me about was there: Alfred Tennyson: he lives at No. 12 Mornington Crescent, Hampstead Road. He will not be long there: for his family has taken another house in Lincolnshire,[1] very much to his sorrow. When I spoke to you of inviting him, you comprehend, I am sure, the tone in which I did so: half jokingly not seriously desiring you to fulfil a duty.

Letters look very grave, while all the time there is a smile on the writer's lips: nor will lines of writing represent the modulations of the voice that is speaking half in jest, and half in earnest. Perhaps one might write more intelligibly in waving lines on those recessions.

"Why do you not ask Alfred Tennyson to your house?"

This would at least characterise the wondering and uncertain mood of mind in which we often are: in which I am more than half my life, I believe. Seriously however, I think you will be much enriched with his acquaintance, and he with yours, and one wishes to bind together all good spirits and to dispose an electric chain of intelligence throughout the country. But I suppose I spoke of this chiefly from an instinctive desire we all have to share good things with those we love.

I know John Kemble and his wife, she is a very unaffected pleasing woman.[2] They have a pleasant house at Bayswater, and John is as busy as possible and with all the vigour of mind and body, that I ever knew him possessed of—what a little concentration of energy it is.

Spedding is all the same as ever, not to be improved; one of the best sights in London.

Your ancestor's sermons[3] are coming down into the country among other books. When next I go to Geldestone, I will bring him thither and so forward him to you.

My plans of residence are not yet decided, for while my sister is here I cannot leave, and I do not know but that this may be my chief home for the future.

I have just found the eleventh volume of Cowper, what a Trump is Southey to stick to the first edition of the translation.[4]

As to your Theatricals, I did not wish you to leave Mrs. Donne, for I wished her to see my friend Mac[ready] as well as yourself.[5] Some day or other we will all go together. Farewell my dear Donne.

I am yours ever
E.FG.

Boulge is appended to Woodbridge: now be honest and let Mrs. Donne know that she was in the right.

[1] The Tennyson family moved to High Beech, Epping, not to another location in Lincolnshire, during the summer of 1837. Rooms in Mornington Crescent, Hampstead, were rented for the convenience of members of the family on visits to London.

[2] The previous year, 1836, John Kemble had married Natalie Auguste, daughter of Johann Wendt, professor of philosophy at the University of Göttingen. Their union appears to have been normal and happy as late as 1844, but by February, 1847, they had separated and were later divorced. Mildred, the youngest of their three children, married W. B. Donne's son Charles Edward in 1860.

[3] The "ancestor" John Donne. See letter to Donne, March [21], 1836, n.3.

[4] Cowper's translation of Homer's *Iliad* appears in vols. 11 and 12 of Southey's fifteen-volume edition of Cowper's *Life and Letters* (1834-37).

[5] By "your Theatricals" EFG refers to one of his many attempts to persuade Donne to join him in London so that they might attend the theater together. Mrs. FitzGerald, also a lover of the theater, had entertained William Macready at Wherstead and, one may safely assume, at Portland Place as well. Donne eventually got more than his fill of the theater. From 1857 to 1874 he was Examiner of Plays.

To W. M. Thackeray

Boulge Hall, Woodbridge
Pmk., April 5, 1837

My dear Thackeray,

I send you the Beranger's complete: except the end of the stanza about the demoiselles in the Roi d'Yvetot. If it is wrong pray set it right, or send me a translation of the words, for I cannot construe them. Your wife can, I am sure. I found also the Souvenirs du Peuple, and the Convoi de David: which I send. Do not feel bound to use them because I have sent them:[1] indeed I think the Roi d'Yvetot is the only perfect one: the rest have much of the French sentiment about them. You and I know each other too well to need any ceremony about such matters as these: use them if you choose. If they are printed, the chorus or refrain should always be printed at full length after each verse: for it is a necessary part of the composition, and should not be merely thought of, but absolutely read. I will send your Roi d'Yvetot,[2] if you wish: it is a paraphrase, and a very proper pendant to your Roger Bontem[p]s. If you have some minutes to spare write: and give me the sense of the stanza I ask about.

Yours ever,
E.FG.

P.S. Your Roi d'Yvetot has far more spirit than mine, but is not so literal. You have made a beautiful drawing too, which I should like you to see: but I know you would lose it if I sent it to you. Pray do remember me most kindly to Mrs. Thackeray: for you cannot think how well I remember the very [piece torn out—a word or two missing] of her.

[*The text of the poems as printed here differs in two respects from the MS: 1. FitzGerald was careless in his use of quotation marks, mixing single and double indiscriminately in the dialogue. These have been made consistent. 2. Through caprice he wrote* t'was, t'is, *etc., for* it was, it is, *etc. The editors have shifted the apostrophes.*]

[LE ROI D'YVETOT]

There was a King of Yvetot
  Of whom Renown hath little said:
He let all thoughts of glory go,
  And dawdled half his life abed.
And as every night came round
By Jessy with a nightcap crowned
          Slept very sound.
Sing ha, ha, ha, and he, he, he,
That's the sort of King for me.

2

And every day it came to pass
  Four meals beneath his belt he stowed:
And step by step upon an ass
  Over his dominions rode.
And whenever he did stir
What think you was his escort, Sir?
          Why, an old cur.
Sing ha, ha, ha, and he, he, he,
That's the sort of King for me.

3

His charges ran to no excess
  Save from a somewhat lively thirst:
But he that would his people bless
  Odds fish!—must whet his whistle first.
So for himself a pot he drew
From every barrel opened new,
          As Caesar's due.
Sing ha, ha, ha, and he, he, he,
That's the sort of King for me.

4

Firmly in all the ladies' hearts
  Was this sagacious prince installed:
And with strict justice on their parts,
  "The father of his people" called.
No other soldiers did he raise
But such as might at targets blaze
          On holidays.
Sing ha, ha, ha, and he, he, he,
That's the sort of King for me.[3]

5

Neither by force, nor false pretence,
  He sought to make his kingdom great:
And made, oh princes learn from hence,
  "Live and let live" his rule of state.
'Twas only when he came to die
That the people, who stood by,
          Were known to cry.
Sing ha, ha, ha, and he, he, he,
That's the sort of King for me.

6

The portrait of this best of Kings
  Still does the duty of a sign,
And o'er a village tavern swings
  Famed in that country for its wine.
The people in their Sunday trim
Filling their glasses to the brim
          Look up to him:
Singing ha, ha, ha, and he, he, he,
That's the King, the King for me.

THE GUARDIAN ANGEL

A beggar drawing near his end
  Saw his good Angel at the door:
And said to him, "Now my good friend,
  Trouble yourself for me no more."
Good angels bring one little joy;
But never mind—good bye, my boy.

2

"Am I what people call God's heir,
  Born on a strawheap in a loft?"
"Yes," said the Angel, "I took care
  That the straw was fresh and soft."
Good angels bring one little joy;
But never mind—good bye, my boy.

3

"What had I left me but a face
  And tongue, of brass, to take folks in with?"
"What!" said the Angel, "Of my grace
  An old friar's wallet to begin with."
Good angels bring one little joy;
But never mind—good bye, my boy.

4

"Then, 'listing, to the wars I went,
  And lost a leg e're I got out."
"Well," said the Angel, "be content,
  That leg would soon have had the gout."
Good angels bring one little joy;
But never mind—good bye, my boy.

5

"Then with a pocket I made free,
  And the law got me by the ears."
"Yes," said the Angel, " 'twas through me
  You only were in gaol three years."
Good angels bring one little joy;
But never mind—good bye, my boy.

6

"Then I must needs make Love my game,
  And from the chase retreated sore."
"Yes," said the Angel, "but through shame,
  I always left you at the door."
Good angels bring one little joy;
But never mind—good bye, my boy.

7

"Next a wife I took in tow,
  And never was a worse miscarriage."

"Yes," said the Angel, "but you know
We angels never meddle with marriage."
Good angels bring one little joy;
But never mind—good bye, my boy.

8

"Is this the peaceful end that ought
To crown a life of pain and toil?"
"Yes," said the Angel, "and I've brought
A priest with rag and holy oil."
Good angels bring one little joy;
But never mind—good bye, my boy.

9

"Shall I then to hell go pat,
Or fly away to happier spots?"
"Why," said the Angel, "as to that,
You may—or may not—let's draw lots."
Good angels bring one little joy;
But never mind—good bye, my boy.

10

So this poor soul with faltering tongue
Made the folks merry round his bed:
He sneezed—the Angel as he sprung
Upward for Heaven, "God bless you," said—
Good angels bring us little joy;
But never mind—good bye, my boy.

THE FUNERAL MARCH OF DAVID[4]

"Hold back!—you go no further here,"
They heard the frontier sentry call
Who the dead painter on his bier
Were bearing to his native Gaul.
"Soldier," they answered in their gloom,
"Does France proscribe his memory too?
And you deny his ashes room
Who left eternal fame to you?"

Chorus

Exiled, unfriended and forlorn
He pined beneath a despot's eye:
Thrice happy those who live and die
In the dear land where they were born.

2

"Hold back—you cannot pass, I say,"
  The soldier still in fury cries.
"Soldier, as even in death he lay
  Toward France he turned his dying eyes.
For her alone and all in all
  He wrought in exile and in woe:
And made from many a palace wall
  The genius of her people glow."
Chorus

3

"No, no—hold back—you cannot pass,"
  The soldier somewhat touched returned.
"The man that drew Leonidas
  With equal love of freedom burned—
With him began the bright array
  Of conquest and of art, when France
Spurning the bonds of Kings away
  Rose like a giant from her trance."
Chorus

4

"No, no—I cannot let you on,"
  More gently said the soldier then.
"Soldier, 'twas he that could alone
  Portray the greatest of great men.
While Homer raised his soul above,
  And round the imperial eagle flew,
He seemed elect to picture Love,
  But 'twas Prometheus whom he drew."
Chorus

5

"No, no—you cannot pass the walls,"
  The soldier said in accent mild.
"Soldier, at last the hero falls,
  And the great painter is exiled.
Death reaches him in foreign lands,
  Death—a sad and bitter one—
Oh France, hold forth a mother's hands
  To the great ashes of thy son."
Chorus

6

"No, no—I dare not yield to you,"
  The soldier all in tears replied.
"Well, let us turn—Sweet France, adieu
  Land of our birth, our love, our pride!
Quenched is the glory from whose birth
  The blaze of Roman art decayed.
We go to beg six feet of earth
  Where these great ashes may be laid."
    Chorus

THE GARRET

With pensive eyes the garret I review
  Where in my youth I weathered it so long:
With a wild mistress, a staunch friend or two,
  And a light heart that bubbled into song.
Making a mock of life, and all its cares,
  Rich in the glory of my rising sun,
Lightly I bounded up four pair of stairs
  In the brave days when I was twenty-one.

2

It is a garret—let him know't who will:
  There stood my bed—how hard it was and small:
My table there: and I decypher still
  A halfmade couplet charcoaled on the wall.
Ye joys, that Time hath swept with him away,
  Rise up—ye royal dreams of love and fun:
For you my watch I pawned how many a day
  In the brave days when I was twenty-one.

3

And thou, my little Nellie, first of all—
  Fresh, and fresh drest as daisies, in she flies:
Her little hands already pin the shawl
  Across the narrow window curtainwise.
Along the bed she spreads her flowing gown
  For coverlet, where coverlet was none—
I have heard since who paid for many a gown
  In the brave days when I was twenty-one.

4

One noble evening, when my friends and I
Joined in full chorus round the little board,
A shout of triumph mounted up thus high,
And the deep cannon through the city roared:
We rise: we join in the triumphant strain:
"Napoleon conquers! Austerlitz is won!
Tyrants shall never tread us down again!"
Oh the brave days when I was twenty-one.

5

Let us be gone—the place is sad and strange—
How far, far back those happy times appear!
All that I have to live I'd gladly change
For one such month as I have wasted here.
To dwell in one long dream of love and power
* By founts of hopes that never would outrun
Quaffing of
And concentrate life's essence in an hour
Give me the days when I was twenty-one.

* Which of these is best? [FitzGerald's note]

[LES SOUVENIRS DU PEUPLE][5]

His glory in the land shall grow,
The people's household talk, and song:
The humble cottage hearth ere long
No legend but of him shall know.
Thither the country folk shall meet
And to some aged Grandam say,
"Some tale of bygone times repeat
To while the winter night away.
Though his ambition wrought us ill
The people glory in him still,
Yes, love him still:
Tell us about him, Grandmother,
Tell us a tale of him."

2

"Children, I saw him passing here
With a train of monarchs—oh!

Many, many, years ago—
    It was in my bridal year.
He came on foot, and, trampling o'er
    The very hillock where I sat,
A grey riding coat he wore,
    And little military hat.
I shook with fright to stand so near.
But, quoth he, 'Good day, my dear,
        Good day, my dear!' "
"And he spoke to you, Grandmother,
        He spoke to you here."

3

"After that I went by chance
    To Paris: and I saw him pass
In procession to High Mass
    Followed by the Court of France.
Everyone was glad and gay:
    They gazed upon their King with pride:
Saying, 'What a glorious day.
    Heaven is always on his side.'
A sweet smile was on his face
For God had given him of his grace
        A little boy."
"Ah what a day, that, Grandmother,
        What a day of joy!"

4

"But when ill luck came to the land,
    And her strength [was] overthrown,
He seemed to keep the field alone,
    And fight the battle singlehand.
One night, just as this night might be,
    I heard a rapping at the door:
I open it—Good God, 'tis he,
    Followed by only three or four.
Down sat he in this very chair,
'Poor France! What wars, what wars,' quoth he
        'The country tear.' "
"And so he sat there, Grandmother,
        In that very chair!"

5

" 'I'm hungry,' quoth he. I apace
    Brown bread and wine before him set!
He dried his garments dripping wet,
    And dozed before the fire a space.
He saw me crying, when he woke:
    'Cheer up,' quoth he—'I hasten, dame,
To rescue Paris from the yoke,
    And to avenge my country's shame.'
He went: and I have sacred kept
The glass he drank from e're he slept,
                                        And ever will."
"And still you have it, Grandmother,
                                        And you have it still."

6

" 'Tis here—well, after a long while
    The lion heart was hunted down:
He, whom a Pope was brought to crown,
    Died heartbroke on a barren isle.
Long time we said, 'It cannot be:
    Wait but a little: he will come
Like thunderstorms across the sea,
    And scare the boasting stranger home.'
We waited, waited, till hope fled:
We said despairing, 'He is dead.'
                                        And all was true."
"Well, God be with you, Grandmother,
                                        His blessing be with you."

[1] *The Constitutional and Public Ledger*, for which Thackeray had been serving as Paris correspondent, had suffered from sluggish circulation since the appearance of its first number on September 15, 1836. Through personal investments and sacrifices by Thackeray's stepfather, Carmichael-Smyth, the paper survived for ten months. As an economy measure, the directors named Thackeray managing director, and he had returned to London from Paris in March. EFG's note makes it clear that the Béranger translations were being sent at his friend's request. Thackeray had garnished his former paper, the *National Standard*, with rhymes and verse of his own composition, and it appears that he considered vitalizing the anemic *Constitutional* with a few lively lyrics. The poems, however, were not used. The paper ceased publication with the July 1 issue. EFG sent translations of "L'Ange Gardien" and "Le Grenier," in addition to the three poems mentioned. Although Thackeray made no immediate use of EFG's work, he published "The King of Yvetot" and "The Garret," with alterations, in the

second volume of his *Paris Sketch Book* in 1840; and the selections have been ascribed to Thackeray. (See n.2.) Pierre Jean Béranger (1780-1857), one of the most popular of French lyric poets.

[2] "The King of Brentford" is Thackeray's version of "Le Roi d'Yvetot"; he translated "Roger Bontemps" under the title, "Jolly Jack." These two poems complete the "Four Imitations from Béranger" which may be found, with the French originals, in the Biographical Edition of Thackeray's works, XIII, 135-47.

[3] The last five lines of this stanza are those about which EFG expressed uncertainty in his letter. Thackeray abandoned them, and Béranger as well, when he substituted:

Each year he called his fighting men,
And marched a league from home, and then
  Marched them back again.

The original reads:

D'ailleurs il ne levait de ban
Que pour tirer quatre fois l'an
  Au blanc.

[4] Jacques Louis David (1748-1825), painter to Louis XVI and later to Napoleon. In spite of the king's patronage David became an ardent revolutionist and, as a member of the convention, voted for Louis' death. Upon the return of the Bourbons, he was exiled as a regicide and lived the remainder of his life in Brussels. His friends actually were stopped at the border when they attempted to return with his body for burial in Paris.

[5] EFG did not follow a uniform line-pattern in his transcript of "Les Souvenirs." The editors have selected the form that predominates in the manuscript.

To John Allen

[Boulge Hall, Woodbridge]
Pmk., April 21, 1837

Dear Allen,

Have you done with my Doctor?[1] If you have, will you send him to me here: Boulge Hall, Woodbridge, per Shannon Coach? You may book it at the Boar and Castle, Oxford Street, close by Hanway Passage. This is not far out of your beat. Perhaps I should not have sent for this book (it is Bernard Barton[2] the Quaker who asks to read it) but that it gives me an excuse also to talk a little to you. Ah! I wish you were here to walk with me now that the warm weather is come at last. Things have been delayed but to be more welcome, and to burst forth twice as thick and beautiful. This is boasting however, and counting of the chickens before they are hatched: the East winds may again plunge us back into winter: but the sunshine of this morning fills one's pores with jollity, as if one had taken laughing gas. Then my house is getting on: the books are up in the bookshelves and do my heart good: then Stothard's Canterbury Pilgrims are over the fire-place:[3] Shakespeare in a recess: how I wish you were here for a day or two! My sister is very well and cheerful and we have kept house very pleasantly together. My brother John's wife is, I fear, declining very fast: it is very probable that I shall have to go and see her before long: though this is a visit I should gladly be spared. They say that her mind is in a very beautiful state of peacefulness. She *may* rally in the summer: but the odds are much against her. We shall lose a perfect Lady, in the complete sense of the word, when she dies.[4]

I have been doing very little since I have been here: having accomplished only a few Idylls of Theocritus, which harmonize with this opening of the fine weather. Is all this poor occupation for a man who has a soul to account for? You think so certainly. My dear Allen, you, with your accustomed humility, asked me if I did not think you changed when I was last in London: never did I see man less so: indeed you stand on too sure a footing to change, I am persuaded. But you will not thank me for telling you these things: but I wish you to believe that I rejoice as much as ever in the thought of you, and feel confident that you will ever be to me the same best of friends that you ever have been. I owe more to you than to all others put together. I am sure, for myself, that the main difference in our opinions (considered so destructive to friendship by so many pious men) is a difference in the Understanding, not in the Heart: and though you may not agree entirely in this, I am confident that it will never separate you from me.

Mrs. Schutz is much delighted with the books you got for her: and still enquires if you hurt your health in searching. This she does in all simplicity and kindness. She has been very ill all the winter: but I see by a letter I have just had from her that her mind is still cheerful and the same. The *mens sana in corpore sano*[5] of old age is most to be wondered at.

Farewell, dear Allen: give my kind remembrances to Mrs. Allen; tell her I should like to come and dine with her on Monday next. How easily might this be done, but it is certainly better not to do it. Ever yours most affectionately

E.FG.

Black and Young were to do up a small Aristophanes (the German stereotype edition in three volumes, price 4^{s}) in cloth, and they should have sent it to me before I left London. Will you ask them for it and send it with my Doctor?

[1] Probably EFG's copy of John Donne's works.

[2] See Biographical Profile.

[3] The well-known engraving, "Canterbury Pilgrims setting forth from the Tabard Inn," the original of which was painted by Thomas Stothard (1755-1834). Stothard's picture had been commissioned by Robert Cromek, London publisher and printseller, who had previously offered the commission to William Blake. Blake charged that Cromek approached Stothard after viewing the picture which Blake had begun. The poet-artist recorded his anger in an epigram:

> Cromek loves artists as he loves his meat;
> He loves the art, but 'tis the art to cheat.

The success of the Stothard plate was immediate and remarkable, but the artist received only £60 for his work (DNB and Redgrave, *Dictionary of Artists*).

[4] John's wife died in August.

[5] "*Orandum est ut sit mens sana in corpore sano.*" (Your prayer must be that you may have a sound mind in a sound body.) Juvenal, *Satires*, X. 356.

To W. M. Thackeray

Pmk., Lowestoft
September 1, 1837

Dear Thackeray,

I am glad you are in full employment again:[1] indeed, I don't think you need ever fear of being without it. I have been here ever since I last wrote: but shall soon leave the place, which is a very pleasant place, to my thinking. I am very glad to hear you say you have been drawing: is Dando a good subject?[2] He certainly was a great man: having that inward magnanimity that is independent of fortune and money, so much admired by Ben Jonson in Lord Bacon, and by Lamb in Elliston. I trust he was not crazy: I mean, that I should be very disappointed if his impudence was not the result of deep conviction. His name is a good illustration of sir names going by contraries—Dando a semper recipiendo—but "recipiendo" is too mild a word.

Sir Frizzle Pumpkin seemed to me a painful joke:[3] perhaps it was meant to be so. I do not mean that it was a heavy joke: but that it was more sad than merry. The Hints to Authors were very laughable indeed. The writer must be a humourist, as you describe him. Pray have you seen anything of the Kembles? Jacky is going on swimmingly with his Review, I hear:[4] it certainly is a very cheap one, and as it is supported by Beaumont is independent of the private politics of booksellers. My friend Donne is writing articles in it:[5] and I believe they are good ones. You can tell me nothing of the Tennysons, I suppose: I wish you could. As to my going to see you in London, it is not impossible: I should like to be with you there some days: but I must hear how family plans are settled first. My Father and Mother are going to Paris for a month, like yours.

How very stupidly I write, to be sure: you must not think me tired of you on this account: but I cannot write to anybody now; except to Browne of Bedford, who tells me how many pike he has caught, and how many foxes he has killed, and so on. For now you are married, I dare not write nonsense, and what Mrs. Butler[6] calls "potter," to you: I don't try not to do it: but I instinctively do not do it. Elegant language. I have just written to the said Browne a long and circumstantial account of my proposing to a young Lady: I think he must be taken in: and I look forward with pleasure to the letter of congratulation that he will write. You don't know what a good boy he is: I suppose there are more such than I am aware of: I fancy that the better virtues and characteristics of Englishmen have slipped away from the aristocracy, and settled among the trading classes apart from London, who are yet unspoiled. Is this humbug? As to Carlyle's book I looked into it, but I did not desire to read it. I do not admire the German school of English.[7] What a mistake to suppose that when you write of troublous times and scenes, you must write in that abrupt hurried manner, as if you were carried away by what you have to describe: a writer should feel himself master of his subject—I rub out something that you would hate.[8] We have lost Summer, I fear: what cold days. When shall we go to Rome together, Thackeray? I think I should like to spend this winter there: but it cannot be. Rome ought to be seen: though you would abuse the Frescos famously, to be sure. Spedding is still in London, and to be heard of at the Club in St. James' Square. If you and Mrs. T. are alone in Albion Street,[9] do ask him to come and see you. I shall come and stay with you if I can positively: in the middle of next week I go to Boulge with my sisters. With kind remembrances to your lady believe me ever yours

E.FG.

[1] After the failure of the *Constitutional* in July, Thackeray turned to magazines for a livelihood, selling sketches, tales, reviews, and illustrations wherever he could find a market. The first of his *Yellowplush Papers* appeared in *Fraser's Magazine* in November, 1837.

[2] Thackeray had painted a picture of Dando, an extremely original rogue, the previous January (*Thackeray Letters and Papers*, I, 327) and followed with a

story, "The Professor," in which the man appears. Dando may best be described as a culinary confidence man and oyster thief. Without a farthing in his pockets and with no intention of paying, he would devour raw oysters in oyster shops until his capacity to consume the viand disclosed his identity. "He has been known to eat twenty dozen at one sitting," wrote Dickens, "and would have eaten forty, if the truth had not flashed upon the shopkeeper. For these offences he was constantly committed to the House of Correction." He died in prison—eating oysters ordered for him by a physician (James T. Fields, *Yesterdays with Authors,* Boston and New York, 1900, p. 139).

Robert Elliston (1774-1831), comedian, had played the title role in Lamb's unsuccessful farce, *Mr. H.*, at Drury Lane in 1806. He was a comic off, as well as on, stage. "Magnificent were thy capriccios on this globe of earth, Robert William Elliston," wrote Lamb, then quoting Ben Jonson on Lord Bacon, "I have and do reverence him for the *greatness*, that was only proper to himself."

[3] *The Adventures of Sir Frizzle Pumpkin* by James White (1803-62), a confession by the elderly, conscience-haunted Sir Frizzle, who owed his wife, title, military fame, and fortune to "a confoundedly useful sort of cowardice" which prompted him "always to be terrified at the right time." He recounts the steps by which his timorous valor had elevated him to the rank of national hero. The story, published with other tales in 1836, had originally appeared in *Blackwood's Magazine* in November, 1830. In a letter to Frederick Tennyson dated March, 1846, EFG identifies White as the author also of *Hints to Authors*, a burlesque published in random issues of *Blackwood's* between October, 1835, and May, 1836, followed by a second series in 1841. Thackeray wrote his mother in February, 1840, "White stopped with us one day—and was very much pleased with FitzGerald and Tennyson" (*Thackeray Letters and Papers*, I, 421).

[4] *The British and Foreign Review, or European Quarterly,* established by Thomas W. Beaumont, had begun publication in July, 1835. John M. Kemble has been credited with being the first editor, but it appears that he did not take charge of the journal until a year or more later. In November, 1836, Charles Merivale asked W. H. Thompson, "Have you seen the first specimen of Kemble's editorship? . . . all about Russia and all Kemble-geschrieben" (*Merivale Autobiography*, p. 138). The purpose of the *British and Foreign*, its popular name, was to call attention to the interdependence of Britain and the Continent. Kemble was editor until the quarterly ceased publication in 1844.

[5] The following January Kemble wrote to Donne, "Pocket your money, and hold your jaw, and never look a gift horse in the mouth even though his grinders should be better than you anticipated" (*Donne and Friends*, p. 35). Mrs. Johnson credits Donne with 15 articles in the quarterly.

[6] Mrs. E. W. Butler, Thackeray's maternal grandmother, formerly Mrs. John H. Becher.

[7] Carlyle's *French Revolution*, published in the spring, had been reviewed by Thackeray in the London *Times*, August 3. "The reader will see . . . that it is written in an eccentric prose," Thackeray stated, ". . . but for all this, it betrays most extraordinary powers—learning, observation and humour. Above all, it has no cant."

[8] EFG had crossed out half a line.

[9] Since his return from Paris the previous spring, Thackeray and his wife had made their home with his parents at 18 Albion Street, Hyde Park.

To Bernard Barton[1]

London
April, 1838

Dear Sir,

John, who is going down into Suffolk, will I hope take this letter and despatch it to you properly.[2] I write more on account of this opportunity than of anything I have to say: for I am very heavy indeed with a kind of Influenza, which has blocked up most of my senses, and put a wet blanket over my brains. This state of head has not been improved by trying to get through a new book much in fashion—Carlyle's French Revolution—written in a German style. An Englishman writes of French Revolutions in a German style. People say the book is very deep: but it appears to me that the meaning *seems* deep from lying under mystical language. There is no repose, nor equable movement in it: all cut up into short sentences half reflective, half narrative; so that one labours through it as vessels do through what is called a short sea—small, contrary going waves caused by shallows, and straits, and meeting tides, etc. I like to sail before the wind over the surface of an even-rolling eloquence, like that of Bacon or the Opium Eater. There is also pleasant fresh-water sailing with such writers as Addison; is there any *pond*-sailing in literature? that is, drowsy, slow, and of small compass? Perhaps we may say, some Sermons. But this is only conjecture. Certainly Jeremy Taylor rolls along as majestically as any of them. We have had Alfred Tennyson here; very droll, and very wayward: and much sitting up of nights till two and three in the morning with pipes in our mouths: at which good hour we would get Alfred to give us some of his magic music, which he does between growling and smoking; and so to bed. All this has not cured my Influenza as you may imagine: but these hours shall be remembered long after the Influenza is forgotten.

I have bought scarce any new books or prints: and am not sorry to see that I want so little more. One large purchase I have made however, the Biographie Universelle, 53 Octavo Volumes. It contains everything, and is the very best thing of its kind, and so referred to by all historians, etc. Surely nothing is more pleasant than, when some name crosses one, to go and get acquainted with the owner of the name: and this Biographie really has found places for people whom one would have thought almost too small for so comprehensive a work —which sounds like a solecism, or Bull, does it not?

Now I must finish my letter: and a very stupid one it is. Here is a sentence of Warburton's that, I think, is very wittily expressed: though why I put it in here is not very discoverable. "The Church, like the Ark of Noah, is worth saving: not for the sake of the unclean beasts and vermin[3] that almost filled it, and probably made most noise and clamour in it, but for the little corner of rationality, that was as much distressed by the stink within, as by the tempest without."[4] Is it not good? It is out of his letters: and the best thing in them. It is also the best thing in mine.

With kind remembrances to Miss Barton, believe me,

Yours very affectionately
E. FitzGerald

[1] Quaker poet and bank clerk of Woodbridge, with whom EFG corresponded freely until Barton's death in 1849. See Biographical Profile.

[2] By having his brother John carry the letter to Boulge to be sent from there to Woodbridge by servant, EFG saved Barton 7d. Until pre-payment of postage was made possible by stamps in 1840, such practices and economies were common.

[3] The words, "and vermin," do not appear in the letter as published by Aldis Wright.

[4] William Warburton (1698-1779), Bishop of Gloucester; *Letters from a Late Eminent Prelate to one of his Friends* [Richard Hurd], 1808, Letter XLVI, p. 114. Warburton abandoned the study of law for the Church in 1723 and five years later was granted an M.A. degree by the University of Cambridge to enable him to qualify for a living which had been offered to him. The practice of granting degrees for this purpose persisted into the nineteenth century. Warburton was created a Bishop in 1759.

From Alfred Tennyson

[May 10, 1838]

Dear Fitz,

I cannot dine with you today because I am knockt up with about the 30th cold I have had since I came to Essex.

I am coming to town on Monday and may possibly go with you to Windsor on Tuesday. At any rate do not go thither before I come.

always yours
A. Tennyson

To Bernard Barton

[London]
[June 8, 1838]

Dear Sir,

I have just come home after accompanying my father and Lusia to their starting-place in the City: they are off for Suffolk for some days. I should have written to you by them: but I only just now found your letter on the mantelpiece: there it has lain some days during which I have been ruralising in Bedfordshire. Delicious has it been there: such weather, such meadows, to enjoy: and the Ouse still wandering along at his ease through pretty villages and vales of his own beautifying. I am much in love with Bedfordshire: it beats our part of the world: and I am sure you would like it. But here I am come back to London for another three weeks I suppose.

I should much like to see your Platonic Brother. By your account he must have a very perfect mental organization: or, phrenologically speaking, he must be fully and equally furnished with the bumps of ideality and causality: which, as Bacon would say, are the two extreme poles on which the perfect "sound and roundabout" intellect is balanced. A great deficiency of the causality bump causes me to break short in a long discussion which I meant to have favoured you with on this subject. I hope to meet your Brother one of these days: and to learn much from him. "Guesses at Truth" I know very well: the two Brothers are the Hares:[1] one a fellow of Trinity College, Cambridge; the other Author of some Sermons which I think you had from me this winter. "The Guesses" are well worth reading; nay, buying: very ingenious, with a good deal of pedantry and *onesidedness* (do you know this German word?), which, I believe, chiefly comes from the Trinity Fellow, who was a great pedant. I have just read Mrs. Austin's Characteristics of Goethe:[2] which I will bring for you when I come. It is well worth knowing something of the mind of certainly a great man, and who has had more effect on his age than any one else. There is something almost fearful in the energy of his intellect. I wish indeed you were in London to see all these pictures: I am sure their greatness would not diminish your pleasure in your own small collection. Why should it? There is as genuine a feeling of Nature in one of Nursey's[3] sketches as in the Rubenses and Claudes here: and if that is evident, and serves to cherish and rekindle one's own sympathy with the world about one, the great end is accomplished. I do not know very much of Salvator:[4] is he not rather a melodramatic painter? No doubt, very fine in his way. But Claude and the two Poussins[5] are the great ideal painters of Landscape. Nature looks more stedfast in them than in other painters: all is wrought up into a quietude and harmony that seem eternal. This is also one of the mysterious charms in the Holy Families of Raffaelle and of the early painters before him: the faces of the Madonnas are beyond the discomposure of passion, and their very draperies betoken an Elysian atmosphere where wind never blew. The best painter of the unideal Christ is, I think, Rembrandt: as one may see in his picture at the National Gallery, and that most wonderful one of our Saviour and the Disciples at Emmaus in the Louvre: there they sit at supper as they might have sat. Rubens and the Venetian Painters did neither one thing nor the other: their Holy figures are neither ideal nor real: and it is incongruous to see one of Rubens' brawny boors dressed up in the ideal red and blue drapery with which the early Italians clothed their figures of Christ. But enough of all this. I have seen Trench's Sabbation,[6] and like it much: how do you like those centuries of couplets, which are a German fashion? They are very much in the style of Quarles' Emblems,[7] and other pithy epigrams of that time: only doubtless more artistically polished: perhaps profounder. There were some of the same kind in Blackwood some months ago. My paper is out: and I must again say Good Bye.

[1] *Guesses at Truth* had been published anonymously by Julius and Augustus Hare in 1827. Julius, the younger, took his degree at Cambridge in 1816 and was made Fellow of Trinity two years later. He succeeded an uncle to the living of Hurstmonceaux, Sussex, in 1832, established a reputation as a scholar and theologian and became one of the leaders of the Broad Church movement. Augustus took his degree at Oxford, 1814; later was made Fellow of New College and Rector of Alton Barnes, Wiltshire.

[2] *Characteristics of Goethe from the German of Falk, von Müller, and Others*, by Sarah Austin, 3 vols., 1833.

[3] Perry Nursey (1771-1840), Suffolk artist and friend of EFG; friend, also, of Sir David Wilkie. EFG was sincere and constant in his admiration for Nursey's work, but was unsuccessful in attempts to convince London exhibitors and dealers of the merit of his friend's painting. (See letters to Pollock, Jan. 22, 1872, and Oct. 21, [1872].) Nursey's devotion to art may be judged from the fact that he named five of his children after artists. See Biographical Profile.

[4] Salvator Rosa (1615-73), versatile painter of the Neapolitan school, who, instead of painting the idealized landscapes of Claude le Lorraine and the two Poussins, "made choice of the lonely haunts of wolves and robbers." His canvases "are peopled by assassins, outlaws, and ferocious banditti. . . . He frequently represented battles and attacks of cavalry" (Bryan's *Dictionary of Painters and Engravers*). Salvator Rosa also distinguished himself as a satirical and dramatic poet. He possessed a talent for acting and performed parts in his own plays.

[5] Claude Geleé, usually known as Claude le Lorraine (1600-82), called "The Prince of Landscape Painters." Nicolas Poussin (1594-1665), historical and landscape painter, and his brother-in-law, Gaspar Dughet (1613-75), who studied under Nicolas and assumed his name. Gaspar is chiefly known for his landscapes.

[6] *Sabbation, Honor Neale, and other Poems*, the second volume of poetry by Richard Chenevix Trench (1807-86), was published in 1838. For Trench, who became Archbishop of Dublin, see Biographical Profile.

[7] Francis Quarles (1592-1644), author of *Emblems*, a volume of devotional poems published in 1635. Each *emblem* was based on a scriptural text, followed by quotations from the Christian Fathers, and concluded with an epigram.

To John Allen

Lowestoft, Suffolk[1]
August 28 [1838]

Dear Allen,

Two nights ago I resolved within myself as I lay in bed that I would write to you to know how you and Mrs. Allen were: and yesterday Lusia asked me about you much and desired I would write to enquire. So I have now got up an hour before breakfast to do so. When I left town I went into Bedfordshire and loitered about there and in Northamptonshire till ten days ago: when I came to join my sisters at this watering-place on the Suffolk coast. I have been spending a very pleasant time; but the worst of it is that the happier I am with Browne the sorrier I am to leave him. To put off this most evil day I have brougth him out of Bedfordshire here: and here we are together in a pleasant lodging looking out upon the sea, teaching a great black dog to fetch and carry,[2] playing with our neighbour's children, doing the first five propositions of Euclid (which *I* am teaching him!), shooting gulls on the shore, going out in boats, etc. All this must have an end: and as usual my pleasure in his stay is proportionably darkened by the anticipation of his going, and go he must in a very few days. Well, Carlyle told us that we are not to expect to be so happy. I have thought once or twice how equally happy I was with you by the sea-side at Tenby. You and Browne (though in rather different ways) have certainly made me more happy than any men living. Sometimes I behave very ill to him, and am much ashamed of myself: but enough of this.

I have been to see two shew places lately: Boughton[3] in Northamptonshire, a seat of the Duke of Buccleugh's, of the Versailles or Clare Hall style of building, in a very great park planted with the longest avenues I ever saw. But I thought the whole affair gloomy and deserted. There are some fine pictures: and two cartoons said to be by Raffaelle: of which one is the Vision of Ezechiel[4]—I could not judge of their genuineness. The other place I have seen is Woburn Abbey[5]—the Duke of Bedford's—a fine place but not much to my taste either. There are very fine pictures there of all kinds—one room hung with brilliant Canalettis—and altogether the pictures are better arranged and hung than in any place I have seen. But these kind of places have not much character in them: an old Squire's gable-ended house is much more English and aristocratic to my mind. I wish you had been with me and Browne at an old seat of Lord Dysart's, Helmingham in Suffolk,[6] the other day. There is a portrait there of the present Lady Dysart in the prime of her beauty, by Sir Joshua. She is now 95.

This is a very stupid letter indeed, I am conscious: but I am got quite out of the way of letter writing. If you can say anything to me pray do: at all events the mere notice that you and Mrs. Allen are well will be better than anything I have said or can say [to] you. I am reading Pindar now and then: I don't much care about him I must say: though I suppose he is the very best writer in the Poet Laureate style: that is, writing on occasion for so much money. I see great merits doubtless—a concise and simple way of saying great things, etc., but the subjects are not interesting enough to me. I suppose a good poet could have celebrated Dutch Sam[7] as having been descended from King William the Third just as well as Pindar glorifies his boxers with the mythical histories of the Aeacidae, Heraclidae,[8] etc. But while I have Browne at my side I do not read much: he being very much better than any books in my opinion. I have some new plans and anticipations floating in my head about all of which I should much like to talk with you. I wish you would tell me if you think I do wrong in leading such an idle self-seeking life. Sometimes I am frightened at finding myself in such a state. I wish you would say something about this. And now good bye and remember me as kindly as may be to Mrs. Allen, and all whom I know about you: and write me some lines to answer my questions: and believe me your ever affectionate friend

E. FitzGerald

P.S. If you write within a fortnight's time, direct to the Post Office here: if not to Boulge Hall, Woodbridge.

[1] Lowestoft, Suffolk, North Sea fishing port some 30 miles north of Woodbridge, not yet, in 1838, the popular resort it became with the advent of railways. Geldestone, home of the Kerrich family, lay 13 miles to the southwest.

[2] The dog was probably "Bletsoe," a black retriever which, Thomas Wright states, was given to FitzGerald by W. K. Browne.

[3] Boughton, six miles north of Northampton, formerly the ancestral home of the Montagu family. Robert, first Duke of Montagu (c. 1638-1709) had rebuilt a portion of Boughton after the fashion of Versailles after serving Charles II as ambassador extraordinary at the court of Louis XIV. The estate, when FitzGerald visited it, was the property of Walter Francis Scott, fifth Duke of Buccleugh, whose principal seat was Dalkeith Palace, near Edinburgh. Both seats were noted for their picture collections. The "Clare Hall" buildings to which EFG refers are those of Clare College.

[4] Raphael appears to have made many cartoons of the "Vision of Ezekiel." The actual painting, now in the Palazzo Pitti, Florence, is credited to Giulio Romano (1492-1560), one of Raphael's two favorite pupils.

[5] Woburn Abbey, magnificent mansion 25 miles southwest of Bedford. The "brilliant Canalettis" mentioned by EFG were 12 scenes of Venice by Antonio Canal (1697-1768), usually called Canaletti or Canaletto.

[6] Helmingham Hall, seven miles northwest of Woodbridge, ancient seat of the Tollemache family, one of whom succeeded to the Earldom of Dysart. The Hall, built of red brick about the time of Henry VIII, is still surrounded by a moat with two drawbridges. In 1799 the property had passed into the possession of the Countess of Dysart, to whom EFG refers. She died in 1840. At another of her properties, Ham House, Surrey, near Twickenham, was a second portrait of Lady Dysart by Sir Joshua Reynolds.

[7] Dutch Sam, a prize-fighter.

[8] Aeacidae, descendants of Aeacus, a king of the Myrmidons. Heraclidae, descendants of Hercules. Aeacus and Hercules—called Heracles by the Greeks—were sons of Zeus.

To Samuel Laurence[1]

Boulge Hall
Sept. 10/38

Dear Sir,

William Browne, whose face you will remember, wishes to see John Allen's portrait.[2] He could, I know, have accomplished this without any introductory letter from me, but I am glad of the opportunity of saying a few words to you. I assure you, I have thought with very much pleasure, and a very many times, of the new acquaintance I have made with you; and it is with some such hope that it may not die away, that I am tempted to send you these few lines. When I shall be in London again I cannot say, but I conclude before much time has elapsed. I have been spending all this summer with this identical W. Browne, and sorry I am to part with him. We have been fishing, and travelling about in a gig as happy as needs be. I should like to hear that you had been getting the fresh air in some such holiday-making, for I cannot but think both eye and hand and the directing mind require some such relaxation. All these lose their best impulses by being used too slavishly. But all this you knew before.

I have still a vision of Rome floating before me, and something tells me that if I don't go this winter I never shall.[3] And yet what between my own indecision, and a few cross casualties, I am sure I shall not accomplish it. I have seen two cartoons said to be by Raffaelle: one of the well-known vision of Ezekiel; the other of a Holy Family, both at a place of the Duke of Buccleuch in Northamptonshire.[4] I did not know whether to think them original or not. I suppose a visit to Rome, or an exact technical knowledge of pictures, is very essential. I am sure I can understand the finest part of pictures without doing either.

I sincerely wish you health and all good things, and am yours very truly,

E. FitzGerald

[1] This letter fixes the summer of 1838 as the approximate date of EFG's first meeting with Samuel Laurence, the portrait painter. See Biographical Profile. The text is taken from *The Life of Edward Fitz-Gerald* by John Glyde, 1900, pp. 36-38. Glyde incorrectly hyphenates *FitzGerald*.

[2] The first of a number of portraits of EFG's friends painted for him by Laurence.

[3] EFG did not go to Italy that winter, and his "something" prophesied correctly. He never made the journey.

[4] At Boughton. See letter to Allen, Aug. 28.

W. B. Donne wrote to Bernard Barton, October 29, 1838:

. . . *Edward FitzGerald is, I believe, now at Boulge. Will you deliver him the enclosed note, or if he be not there, put it into the Boulge letter-bag, as it will then be forwarded to him* free?

You may as well tell him that his notions of a letter differ widely from mine. He sent me from Lowestoffe a screed of paper with six lines, and not sealed, and instead of the lines containing letters and words, as you might have concluded, there was something that looked like an exercise in punctuation, e.g., "j:,:? ! :.=x.;".[1]

[1] *Donne and His Friends*, p. 43.

To W. M. Thackeray

[Boulge]
Thursday, November 29, [1838]

Dear Thackeray,

Thank you for your last letter, as also for the former one accompanying a very beautiful drawing, which I take pleasure in looking at. I am very glad you are engaged in a way of life that you like:[1] that is a good thing indeed, which most people miss. It would seem that I ought to be able and willing to write plenty of letters as I have nothing in the world to do: but it is all I can do now to manage one. When you see Spedding pray remember to tell him that I did write him a letter, which I put into the fire because it was pert: and got nearly through another lately which I abandoned because it was all about nothing. He has so much to do, that one has no right to expect any letter from him: but give him my hearty love—all this you will forget, you rascal.

I will exalt your name as a politician forever if you will contrive to persuade me that we have nothing to fear from the domineering Russia. It is not the present fuss made about her that makes me tremble, but I have always been afraid that she was the Power kept in pickle to overwhelm Europe just as men were beginning to settle into a better state than the World has yet seen.[2] If she were out of the question we should [do] very well.

> There is but one
> Whose being we do fear: and under her
> Our Genius is rebuked, as it is said
> Marc Antony's was by Caesar.[3]

Another illustrious Author says "Joy to the Jews, and Russia pays the expense etc."—but this is in the way of Revelations, and therefore inexplicable. I study Clarke's book more and more,[4] and see something new every time. Do you know anything of a second part? The last delicate touch that I became aware of was when, after the catastrophe at Pedaster House, Mrs. Gurley carries off Athanasius in *her gig*, which was waiting for her at the door. You will herewith draw Mrs. Gurley's gig. Thank you for your desire that I should come on a visit to you in London. I have been within an ace of coming up: but I do not think I shall now. Your accounts of Jack are very fine.[5] I have been staying two days with Donne who contributes to his Review, and is a very delightful fellow. If you ask Jack about him I dare say he will inform you in a whisper that he is one of the most distinguished Generals alive. My sisters and brother in law broke out into just praises of your Yellowplush the other day, not knowing who had written it: so I had the satisfaction of insinuating with an air of indifference that I knew the Author well. They are also not quite certain but that I wrote it myself: so that I gain every way. I see poor old Macready toiling away at the Tempest three times a week:[6] the papers talk of there being full houses: but I conclude that that is undoubtedly a lie. Miss Horton must be a pretty Ariel: there is some knavishness in the expression of her face which must be suitable. Now farewell dear Thackeray and make my duty to my Lady, and believe me ever yours

E. FitzGerald

P.S.[7] If you happen to go to Edmonton, or to meet Mrs. Gurley in her gig between that place and London, do not forget to give her my Compt[s].

"Here one of the Bishops was sick, and was obliged to be taken out:—I did *not hear what became of him.*" Who can write like that!

[1] See letter to Thackeray, Sept. 1, 1837.

[2] EFG rarely engages in prophecy; but in this, his first reference to "the Eastern Question," he plays the part of Tiresias rather capably. The "Question," as the problems which evolved from the decay of Turkish power were called, plagued European diplomats throughout the 19th century; and EFG refers to it frequently in his later correspondence. During the reign of Nicholas I, 1825-55, Russia labored to suppress the growth of liberal views within the country and to prevent their intrusion from without. Russia, Prussia, and Austria formed an autocratic "East" under the leadership of Russia, opposed to a liberal "West" led by England and France. Nicholas strengthened Russia's influence over Turkey and occupied new territories in Asia Minor, successes which England viewed with concern. During the decade of the 1830's a diplomatic struggle was waged by the powers to maintain or to recover influence at Constantinople. The British public rallied behind aggressive Lord Palmerston, Minister for Foreign Affairs, and was prepared to quarrel with Russia on any pretext.

[3] EFG adapts *Macbeth*, III.1.54-57 to his topic. Macbeth, brooding on Banquo's virtue and power, and on the prophecy of the witches, declares:

> There is none but he
> Whose being I do fear; and, under him,
> My Genius is rebuked, as, it is said,
> Marc Antony's was by Caesar.

[4] "Clarke's book," from which EFG quotes, is *The Library of Useless Knowledge*, "Part I, Autobiography of the Editor, by Athanasius Gasker, Esq., F.R.S., etc., etc." The "Library" was suggested, we may assume, by the publications of the Society for the Diffusion of Useful Knowledge. Its author, Edward William Clarke (1807-43), was rector of Yeldham, Essex, and son of Edward Daniel Clarke, former professor of mineralogy at Cambridge, who, in his undergraduate days, had also been something of a wag. Young Clarke, of Jesus College, B.A.,

1829, was a friend of William Williams, also a humorist, who had tutored both EFG and Thackeray in Cambridge days.

The "Autobiography," a pamphlet of 52 pages published by Pickering in 1837, is an account of the persecution suffered by Gasker, "possessed of knowledge," in his efforts to impart his learning "to a benighted multitude." Gasker relates three episodes in his life: (1) the means by which he gained recognition in England; (2) the attack by the Church on his six-volume work, *Tenebrae; or, the Invisible Visible*, and his success in breaking up a conclave of clergymen, met to consider his work; (3) an adventure he experienced in an attempt to lecture to the young ladies of Pedaster House Academy on "The Sexes of Facts, and the Economy of Discussion." For his first literary production, *On the Nature of Sounds* (two folio volumes), Gasker said he had been punished at Potsdam because of "an absurd suspicion of the king's, that, in my chapter on 'simple relations,' I alluded to a stupid nephew of his." Despite his "cloth," Clarke states, "I hold the Clergy to be the most extraordinary class of men in this country. They are not ignorant. On the contrary, they know too little. Their knowledge is limited by a circumference, whose radius is so small that they know almost everything; almost everything, that is, within that small circumference. . . . There is the source of infinite calamity . . . dispersing itself perennially from this small seminal circle, the Poppy-Head of the Church." Much of the dialogue is composed of double-talk involving philosophic terms. The action is decidedly slapstick; but this feature, EFG said, held "the great secret" of the book, its "astounding Gravity of Burlesque." Gasker announced that "Part II will contain 'The Nature and Condition of Truth,'" but no sequel appears to have been published. EFG's delight in the burlesque never waned.

"Certainly only you and I and Thackeray understand it," he said, writing to Pollock, May 11, 1842. In notes added to the 1842 letter, Pollock records that Clarke created "a museum of curiosities," which included The Trojan Horse. "This," Pollock wrote, "was a large clothes horse—and he [Clarke] used to show how easy it was to step through the bars and get on the other side of it." We learn regretfully from Pollock's notes that Clarke went mad.

5 John M. Kemble, editor of the *British and Foreign Review* at the time.

6 William Macready, 45 years of age, had been on the London stage since 1816. He had taken over the management of Covent Garden in 1837; his *Lear* of that year and his *Tempest* of 1838 had liberated those plays from the texts of the adaptors whose versions had held the stage for 150 years. When he could find no suitable actor for the part, Macready had cast Priscilla Horton, 20 years old, as Lear's Fool, but the experiment was not successful.

7 Allusions to passages in Clarke's book.

To Frederick Tennyson[1]

Geldestone Hall, Beccles
[April 10, 1839]

My dear Tennyson,

I see in the last Atlas[2] a notice of the first Concert of the Società Armonica[3]—there were you to be found of course seated in black velvet waistcoat (for I hope you remember these are dress concerts) on one of the benches, grumbling at most of the music. You had a long symphony of Beethoven's in B flat—I forget how it goes, but doubtless there was much good in it. The overture to Egmont is also a fine thing.[4] The Atlas (which is the best weekly critic of Music and all other things that I know of) gives great κῦδος to the Società Armonica: especially this season, as the Directors seem determined to replace Donizetti and Mercadante by Mozart and Rossini,[5] in the vocal department. A good change doubtless. I hear no music now: except that for the last week I have been staying with Spring Rice's mother-in-law Mrs. Frere,[6] one of the finest judges of Music I know. She was a very fine singer: but her voice fails now. We used to look over the score of Don Giovanni[7] together, and many a mystery and mastery of composition did she shew me in it. Now then there is enough of Music. I wish you would write me a letter, which you can do now and then if you will take it into your head, and let me know how you and my dear old Morton[8] are, and whether you dine and smoke together as heretofore. If you won't write, tell him to do so: or make up a letter between you. What new pictures are there to be seen? Have you settled yet whether spirit can exist separately from matter? Are you convinced of the truth of Murphy's Almanac this year?[9] Have you learned any more Astronomy? I live on in a very seedy way, reading occasionally in books which every one else has gone through at school: and what I do read is just in the same way as ladies work: to pass the time away. For little remains in my head. I dare say you think it very absurd that an idle man like me should poke about here in the country, when I might be in London seeing my friends: but such is the humour of the beast. But it is not always to be the case: I shall see your good physiognomy one of these days, and smoke one of your cigars, and listen to Morton saying fine and wild things, "startling the dull ear of night"[10] with paradoxes that perhaps are truisms in the world where spirits exist independent of matter. You two men have made great commotion in my mind, and left your marks upon it, I can tell you: more than most of the books I read. What is Alfred about, and where is he? Present my homage to him. Don't you rather rejoice in the pickle the King of the French finds himself in? I don't know why, but I have a sneaking dislike of the old knave. How he must pine to summon up Talleyrand's Ghost, and what a Ghost it must be, wherever it is![11]

[1] This is the earliest known letter to Frederick Tennyson, Alfred's oldest brother and one of EFG's principal correspondents. It appears to have been written soon after the two became acquainted. In subsequent letters EFG addresses his friend

as Frederic. See Biographical Profile. After taking his degree at Cambridge in 1832, Frederick made his home in Italy until 1859. In the spring of 1839 he had returned to England for one of his infrequent visits. The text of this letter is taken from the *Literary Remains*, and the brackets around the date probably indicate a date supplied by the postmark. Aldis Wright did not differentiate between such dates and those which he conjectured.

[2] The *Atlas*, a general newspaper and journal of the arts published Sundays in London from 1826 to 1869.

[3] The Società Armonica, had been founded "about 1827" to give subscription concerts "in which symphonies, overtures, and occasionally instrumental chamber works were intermingled with vocal numbers usually selected from Italian operas." Numerous works by foreign composers were first heard in England in programs arranged by the Società. The concerts were successively held at the Crown and Anchor Tavern in the Strand, Freemasons' Tavern in Great Queen Street, and the Opera Concert room in the Haymarket. The concerts terminated "in or about the year 1850" (Grove's *Dictionary of Music*).

[4] Beethoven's overture from op. 84, his music for Goethe's tragedy, *Egmont*.

[5] Gaetano Donizetti (1797-1848), composer of operas, whose most popular work is, no doubt, *Lucia di Lammermoor*. Saverio Mercadante (1797-1870), composer, and director of the Conservatorio of Naples. Mozart (1756-91). Gioachino Rossini (1792-1868), whom EFG later described as "our dear old Rossini."

[6] Mrs. William Frere (1781-1864), of whom EFG was extremely fond, was the widow of William (Serjeant) Frere (1775-1836), Master of Downing College from 1812 until his death. EFG and his friend Robert Hindes Groome (later Archdeacon) considered her to be the most perfect private singer they had ever heard. Their admiration was justifiable, for Madame Catalini, operatic star of the early 19th century, described Mrs. Frere as "the best unprofessional singer in England." Groome recorded, "She had no particle of vanity in her, and yet she would say, 'Of course, I can sing Handel. I was a pupil of John Sale, and he was a pupil of Handel.' " Mrs. Frere created a stir in Cambridge academic circles by establishing a salon and entertaining with musicals in the Lodge and with private theatricals in the Hall at Downing.

[7] Mozart.

[8] Savile Morton (1811-52), EFG's "wild Irishman," a frequent companion of Frederick Tennyson's in Italy. EFG probably made his acquaintance through Frederick. See Biographical Profile of Morton.

[9] Sensation and admiration had been created the year before by the publication of *The Weather Almanack* "(on Scientific Principles, showing the State of the Weather for every Day of the Year 1838) by P[atrick] Murphy, Esq., M.N.S., i.e., member of no society." For January 20, Murphy had predicted "Fair, probably lowest degree of winter temperature." At sunrise on that day the thermometer read four degrees below zero (centigrade), and 45 editions had been required to meet the demand for the almanack—Murphy's first, incidentally. DNB frigidly notes that the coldest day of the year "generally" occurs about January 20, and points out that Murphy's predictions were "partly" correct on 168 days, but "decidedly wrong" on 197. Murphy continued to publish the almanack until his death in 1847; however, sales were limited after his "best seller" of 1838.

[10] EFG appears to be recalling Milton's "L'Allegro":

> To hear the lark . . .
> . . . singing, startle the dull night . . ."
> (ll. 41-42)

[11] The ministry of Comte Louis Molé had fallen March 31. Efforts to form a replacement were unsuccessful until dissident factions in the Assembly were frightened into agreement by a one-day revolt, May 12. Talleyrand had supported Louis Philippe in the Revolution of 1830 and served the new king as ambassador to Great Britain until his retirement in 1834. He died in May, 1838.

To John Allen

Geldestone Hall, Beccles
[April 28, 1839]

My dear Allen,

Some one from this house is going to London: and I will try and write you some lines now in half an hour before dinner: I am going out for the evening to my old Lady who teaches me the names of the Stars, and other chaste information. You see, Master John Allen, that if I do not come to London (and I have no thought of going yet) and you will not write, there is likely to be an end of our communication: not by the way that I am never to go to London again: but not just yet. Here I live with tolerable content: perhaps with as much as most people arrive at, and what if one were properly grateful one would perhaps call perfect happiness. Here is a glorious sunshiny day: all the morning I read about Nero in Tacitus lying at full length on a bench in the garden: a nightingale singing, and some red anemones eyeing the sun manfully not far off. A funny mixture all this: Nero, and the delicacy of Spring: all very human however. Then at half past one lunch on Cambridge cream cheese: then a ride over hill and dale: then spudding up some weeds from the grass: and then coming in, I sit down to write to you, my sister winding red worsted from the back of a chair, and the most delightful little girl in the world chattering incessantly. So runs the world away. You think I live in Epicurean ease: but this happens to be a jolly day: one isn't always well, or tolerably good, the weather is not always clear, nor nightingales singing, nor Tacitus full of pleasant atrocity. But such as life is, I believe I have got hold of a good end of it. All this is egotistical nonsense, mind you, that I only confide to you: anything to make up a letter, and you will laugh and think it all so very nice. I had a letter from Spedding this morning: long have I teased him for it: humph!—a hint. I suppose Mrs. Allen has heard not unlately from Lusia, who is a vigorous correspondent, I think. She will come to London very soon. Look out for her, and give her tea once or twice, and if she has brought up any new religious phrases from Hastings warn her of them. The last I heard was—*let us make a conscience*, of chewing our meat slow, etccc. Does this abound in London? Oh my dear Allen, my heart turns very sick when I hear these things: but that is absurd, and not worthy a man of universal Charity.

Give my love to Thackeray from your upper window across the street. So he has lost a little child:[1] and moreover has been sorry to do so. Well, good bye my dear John Allen: Auld Lang Syne: my kind regards to your Lady.

> Down to the vale this water steers,
> How merrily it goes:
> 'T will murmur on a thousand years,
> And flow as now it flows.[2]

E.FG.

[1] At this time Allen was living at 36 Coram Street (also called Great Coram Street), near Brunswick and Russell Squares. In March, 1838, Thackeray had moved to No. 13. Thackeray's second daughter, Jane, had died March 14, 1839, at the age of eight months (Gordon Ray, *The Uses of Adversity*, 1955, p. 203).

[2] From "The Fountain," by Wordsworth.

To Bernard Barton
(Fragment)[1]

Geldestone, Sunday
[Spring, 1839]

Dear Sir,

. . . I met Donne a week ago at Norwich. When I shall be back in these shires again I cannot tell: as soon as I can. Never did man less wish to go to London than I do. The country is now in its finest state—buttercup time—the meadows never look so rich as then.

I have been more idle than usual for the last fortnight, having had my Venator, W. Browne, with me. He has shot at rooks and rabbits and trained horses and dogs; and I—have looked at him: and well I may while I can, for his like is not to be seen. Perhaps also he will not be long to be looked at; for there are signs of decay about him: and his very perfection of nature somehow forebodes a short continuance: and as dramatists are said to prematurely kill such characters as they find it difficult to sustain, so it is that Nature cannot or will not carry on her finest creations through the five acts. Indeed, there is something anomalous and perhaps insupportable in the appearance of one perfect character in a world of imperfection and inconsistency.

You do not know this fellow, and I shall probably see less of him year by year. But I have said what I have said—and, as the Doctor says, perhaps I am the better for having said it. Farewell again, dear Sir—thanks for your wishes to see me at Woodbridge.

Ever yours,
E. FitzGerald

[1] The text is from a transcript among the FitzGerald papers in Trinity College Library.

To W. F. Pollock[1]

[Boulge]
[July 20, 1839]

My dear Pollock,

I have not such a pen as yours that can be inspirited to indite a jolly long letter under such circumstances as you describe. My circumstances are not much more enlivening: but then I have the advantage of your letter to begin upon: a great advantage. So here goes for an answer: for though few men have ever sat down with less to say, yet it is good to have such a starting-point as a letter just received. We have more books in our Library here than you found at your lodging in York[2]—an Encyclopedia, a Johnson's Dictionary, Bailey's Navigation,[3] etc., but nothing so new or striking as to make me suppose that you would be interested with any remarks I could make. Have you ever read Smith's Wealth of Nations? I never have. *Smellie's* Moral Philosophy?—Better than his Physical, I should think—Drury's Madagascar, Alison on Taste, Kett's Elements of Knowledge, etc.?[4] All these we have well bound upon the shelves of the room in which I write: and we have had them for years—and shall have them, I dare say: they will never wear out. Grammont we have also, not so visible, however: he is in a private corner of a book case in the drawing-room.[5] I read him once twelve years ago, I believe: and have forgotten all about him. At your recommendation I shall read him again. I have also heard Thackeray speak well of him: but he is naturally prejudiced in favour of the dirty and immoral. I like Horace Walpole:[6] he's capital fun, and the most easy reading in the world: no small praise, for easy reading does not presume easy writing by any means. Walpole I suppose wrote easily: but then it is not easy to have such a head as would write so easily. Q.E.D.

Can you shoot with a pistol, Pollock? Can you hit an oak tree (they grow large in this part of the country) at the distance of about ten yards? I tell you how it is with me: I generally miss—and when I hit, the bullet returns with great violence back upon me. So if you read of an inquest sitting upon me one of these days, don't wonder: I think they'll find it hard to bring in a verdict whether Felo-de-se[7] or Accidental Death. For I go on with my eyes open: though to be sure I am taking the quickest course to put them both out. A worse shot never existed, not omitting that most unfortunate of all marksmen Mr. John Thomas:[8] of whose condition the early part of Der Freyschutz[9] is an Allegory or Parable. Fancy a man's selling his soul to the Devil to be able to satisfy his wife—I'd see her damned first.

Morton recommended me to read Alfieri's Life of Himself.[10] So I bought it in London and have been reading it by bits ever since. It is in very easy Italian, and is entertaining, as far as I have read: just half. He was a very fine fellow, was Alfieri: they say his plays are very dull, and I think the Life becomes duller as he begins the Literary part of it. For he only began to *read* his own language at twenty-five: and his first plays were written first in French Prose and then drafted into Italian verse. What a process! Up to that time of his life he only rode horses over every country in Europe, and kept mistresses: his loves were very heroic and poetical: so perhaps he would have aided the cause of Poetry more by leaving it to others to write about him. I wonder the French Playwrights haven't got hold of him: perhaps they have though. He was such a fellow for Liberty too: he calls Catherine the 2nd *codesta Clitennestra filosofessa*,[11] which words have the whistling of the lash about them, I think. He would have been a capital Middle Age Italian: especially for Dante to put into Hell. But perhaps he'll meet him there yet.

My dear Pollock, this (viz: a dull letter) comes of making such a determination to answer on the spur of the *bobelt*.[12] I am now going to set off to Ipswich which I hope is by this time settling down into quiet after the turmoil of the Election in which you demnition Tories beat us h'alliblasted Whigs.[13] Do you know my story about h'alliblasted? If not ask Spedding to tell it you: or shall I finish my letter with it? I will. Two whores were slanging each other on the Bridge at Bedford: one was fair and the other dark. "Ah (says the fair one) you'd best hold your tongue, you brown bitch." "Better be a brown bitch (says the other) than a damned *halliblasted* beauty like you." That was her idea of *alabaster*. Now this is a true story as you must see from its simplicity: and a very fine one as you *will* see when its esoteric odour steals upon you. Leave it in your mind carelessly, without trying to be much amused at first: you will find it after many days. For it involves a good outward picture, and a good metaphysical confusion in the reaching after language. I deserve to be kicked for pretending to analyze it. Let us say Grace after it in simple Faith, as Lamb recommended. The rule is—Open your mouth and shut your eyes and take what God provides you.

Ever yours
E.FG.

[1] William Frederick Pollock (1815-88), known as Frederick, one of EFG's lifelong friends and correspondents. See Biographical Profile.

[2] Pollock had been called to the bar in January, 1838, and joined the Northern Circuit that spring. Assizes were held at York.

[3] Possibly one of the numerous works of Francis Baily (1774-1844), astronomer, who reformed *The Nautical Almanac*. The title is not listed.

[4] Adam Smith (1723-90), whose *Wealth of Nations* revolutionized thought on political economy, as the subject of economics was originally called. Published in 1776, the work predicts that the American colonies would become "one of the foremost nations of the world." William Smellie (1740-95), Edinburgh printer, publisher, and naturalist. EFG evidently listed the titles from memory, for there is no record of a "Moral Philosophy" by Smellie. He edited and, in great part, wrote the first edition of the *Encyclopedia Britannica*. Robert Drury (fl. early 18th century), forced ashore at Madagascar from a disabled ship, en route from Bengal, was captured by natives and held in slavery until ransomed by his father. In 1729 he published *Madagascar*; or *Robert Drury's Journal during Fifteen Years Captivity there*. Archibald Alison, who had died in May (b. 1757), was the author of *Essays on the Nature and Principles of Taste* (1790), a treatise on aesthetics. Henry Kett (1761-1825), clergyman and miscellaneous writer whose *Elements of Knowledge* (2 vols.) was published in 1802.

[5] Comte de Philibert de Gramont (1621-1707), courtier, wit, and gambler. Exiled from Paris in 1662, he became a favorite at the court of Charles II—a favorite of the king as well as of the king's mistresses. *The Mémoires de la Vie du Comte de Gramont* by his brother-in-law, Anthony Hamilton, published at Cologne in 1713, contains a vivid description of Charles's court. An English edition appeared in 1714.

[6] Perhaps the volumes of Horace Walpole (1717-97) in the library at Boulge Hall included a portion of his letters, five collections having been published by 1839. EFG would not have dreamed that the day would come when his letters, with Walpole's, would be recognized as among the finest the language has produced.

[7] Suicide.

[8] The *Times* for May 23, 1837, reported an inquest on a John Thomas who had committed suicide, but it hardly seems likely that EFG referred to the incident two years later. However, no other John Thomas is mentioned in the newspapers of the time.

[9] *Der Freischütz,* the "free marksman" of German folklore, who received from the Devil seven bullets, six of which unerringly found the target chosen by *Der Freischütz.* The Devil, however, retained control over the seventh. The legend is the subject of the opera of that name (1821) by Carl von Weber (1786-1826).

[10] Vittorio Alfieri (1749-1803), Italian dramatist and poet. His *Vita di Vittorio Alfieri . . . scritta da esso* (2 vols.) had been published in London in 1804. EFG errs in stating that Alfieri did not begin to read his own language until he was 25. EFG's command of Italian was limited, and he could have been misled by a number of statements in the memoir. Alfieri had acquired a mastery of French before he was 14; but "the reading of French romances, the constant society of foreigners, the want of opportunity of speaking or hearing the Italian, had insensibly made me lose the little Tuscan I had acquired" (*Life of Vittorio Alfieri,* Boston, 1877, p. 106). In the same portion of the memoir, however, he speaks of school exercises in translating Latin into Italian while a student at the Academy at Turin. After the production of his first tragedy, *Cleopatra,* in 1775, written after a decade spent in traveling through Europe, Alfieri was dissatisfied with his command of his native speech and concluded that he must "study grammar and the art of composition" (*Life,* p. 200). He wrote *Filippo* and *Polinice,* his second and third tragedies, in French prose before converting them into Italian verse.

[11] Catherine II of Russia (1729-96), of German birth, married to Peter III, was proclaimed empress by the Russian army in July, 1762; and Peter died of "apoplexy" before the month was out. Hence, it would appear, Alfieri's "*codesta Clitennestra filosofessa*"—"That Clytemnestra, female philosopher." Catherine's reputation as a philosopher and a woman of superior intellectual attainments was created largely by flatterers.

[12] "Bobelt" appears to be a corruption of "burbolt" which, according to G. L. Kittredge, is a contraction of "bird-bolt," a flat-headed arrow used in hunting birds. EFG seems to have misinterpreted Beatrice's charge that Benedick had challenged Cupid to an archery duel "at the burbolt" (*Much Ado,* I.1.37-39) to mean "at once" or "on the spur of the moment."

[13] This is the only time, the editors believe, that EFG identifies himself with a political party.

To Bernard Barton
(Fragment)[1]

Bedford
July 24, 1839

Dear Barton,

. . . I have brought down here with me Sydney Smith's Works,[2] now first collected: you will delight in them: I shall bring them to Suffolk when I come: and it will not be long, I dare say, before I come, as there is to be rather a large meeting of us at Boulge this August. I have got the fidgets in my right arm and hand (how the inconvenience redoubles as one mentions it)—do you know what the fidgets are?—a true ailment, though perhaps not a dangerous one. Here I am again in the land of old Bunyan[3]—better still in the land of the more perennial Ouse, making many a fantastic winding and going much out of his direct way to fertilize and adorn. Fuller supposes that he lingers thus in the pleasant fields of Bedfordshire, being in no hurry to enter the more barren fens of Lincolnshire. So he says. This house is just on the edge of the town:[4] a garden on one side skirted by the public road, which again is skirted by a row of such Poplars as only the Ouse knows how to rear—and pleasantly they rustle now—and the room in which I write is quite cool and opens into a greenhouse which opens into said garden: and it's all deuced pleasant. For in half an hour I shall seek my Piscator, and we shall go to a Village[5] two miles off and fish, and have tea in a pot-house, and so walk home. For all which idle ease I think I must be damned. I begin to have dreadful suspicions that this fruitless way of life is not looked upon with satisfaction by the open eyes above. One really ought to dip for a little misery: perhaps however all this ease is only intended to turn sour by and bye, and so to poison one by the very nature of self-indulgence. Perhaps again as idleness is so very great a trial of virtue, the idle man who keeps himself tolerably chaste, etc., may deserve the highest reward; the more idle, the more deserving. Really I don't jest: but I don't propound these things as certain.

There is a fair review of Shelley in the new Edinburgh:[6] saying the truth on many points where the truth was not easily enunciated, as I believe.

Now, dear sir, I have said all I have to say: and Carlyle says, you know, it is dangerous to attempt to say more. So farewell for the present: if you like to write soon, direct to the Post Office, Bedford: if not, I shall soon be at Woodbridge to anticipate the use of your pen.

[1] Text incomplete; taken from *Letters and Literary Remains.*

[2] Sydney Smith (1771-1845), popular clergyman, wit, and, with Henry Brougham and Francis Jeffrey, founder in 1802 of the *Edinburgh Review.* Macaulay described Smith as "the greatest master of ridicule . . . since Swift." Three volumes of his *Works* were published in 1839; the fourth, and last, in 1840.

[3] Elstow, the birthplace of John Bunyan (1628-88), is less than two miles south of Bedford. While imprisoned in Bedford jail as a Dissenter, Bunyan wrote a portion of *Pilgrim's Progress* and all of *Grace Abounding.*

[4] Until his marriage Browne lived at Cauldwell House, Cauldwell Street, Bedford (T. Wright, *Life*, I, 120).

[5] EFG's "Piscator" was W. K. Browne; the village referred to was doubtless Goldington, two miles east of Bedford town hall, where Browne established his home when he married in 1844. Aldis Wright conjectured that EFG referred to Bletsoe. That village, however, is six miles north of Bedford.

[6] *The Poetical Works of Percy Bysshe Shelley*, edited by Mrs. Shelley, 4 vols., 1839; the *Edinburgh Review*, July, 1839, pp. 503-27.

To W. F. Pollock

Boulge Hall
Aug. 14, [1839]

My dear Pollock,

I came here only yesterday, and your letter was brought up into my bedroom this morning. What are you doing at Binfield?[1] rusticating there for fun with your family, or are there Assizes at such a place? And is the juvenile party you speak of assisting at, one of juvenile depredators? Well, I have been in my dear old Bedfordshire ever since I saw you: lounging in the country, lying on the banks of the Ouse, smoking, eating copious teas (prefaced with beer) in the country pot-houses, and have come mourning here: finding an empty house when I expected a full one, and no river Ouse, and no jolly boy to whistle the time away with. Such are the little disasters and miseries under which I labour: quite enough, however, to make one wish to kill oneself at times. This all comes of having no occupation or sticking-point: so one's thoughts go floating about in a gossamer way. At least, this is what I hear on all sides. So you are going with Monteith's party to Ireland.[2] Well, I think you will have a pleasant trip. I think I shall probably be in Ireland all September, but far away from your doings. Not to mention that I shall be on shore and you at sea. You will go and see the North Coast: which I am anxious to see, and shall not unlikely go too about the time of the Equinoctial gales, when such places should be seen. I love Ireland very much, I don't know why: the country and the people and all are very homogeneous: mournful and humorous somehow: just like their national music. Some of Tommy Moore's Irish Melodies[3] (the airs, I mean) are the spirits of the Waterford women made music of. You should see them, Pollock, on a Sunday as they come from Chapel in their long blue cloaks. Don't you think that blue eyes with black hair, and especially with long black eyelashes, have a mystery about them? This day week a dozen poor fellows who had walked all the way from the County Mayo into Bedfordshire came up to the door of the Inn where we were fishing, and called for small beer. We made their hearts merry with good Ale: and they went off flourishing their sticks, hoping all things, enduring all things, and singing some loose things. You must contrive to see something of the people when you go to Ireland: I think that is the great part of the fun. You should certainly go some miles in or on an Irish Stage Coach, and also on a jaunting Car. I never saw Wimpole[4] near Cambridge till the other day when I passed it in my way from Bedfordshire. Did you ever go and see it? People always told me it was not worth seeing: which is another reason for believing nothing that people tell one: it is a very noble old Queen Anne's building of red brick, in the way of Hampton Court (not half so fine, but something in that way), looking down two miles of greensward as broad as itself, skirted on each side with fine elms. I did not go inside, but I believe the pictures are well worth seeing. Houses of that style have far more mark and character than Woburn and the modern bastard Grecian. I see they have built a new chapel at Barnwell—of red brick and very well done. I should think Peacock must have done it. Fancy his being Dean of Barnwell.[5] Cambridge looked very ghastly, and the hard-reading, pale, dwindled students working along the Observatory road looked as if they were only fit to have their necks wrung. I scorn my nerveless carcase more and more every day—but there's no good in talking. Farewell, my dear Pollock: I know this is a very worthless letter: but it is very good of you to write, and I have nothing better to do today than to write ever such vapid stuff. I would ask you if Spedding were still in London if your Yes or No (never very clamorously uttered by you) could reach me from Binfield. But even then I should not be much the better for the Information.

Ever yours,
E.FG.

Miss Mitford is the worst,[6] I think: most to be dreaded.

Fragment, in answer to part of your letter.

[1] Binfield, in Berkshire, about eight miles southwest of Windsor, the home of "Dear E," a cousin to whom Pollock wrote many of the letters published in his *Personal Remembrances.*

[2] On August 22 Pollock, with Robert Monteith and four other friends, put out from Greenock in the *Orion*, a 35-ton cutter, and spent four weeks cruising among the islands off the west coast of Scotland. Pollock's log of the cruise (*Remem-*

brances, I, 139-45) reveals that the party did not cross to Ireland as EFG anticipated it would. Robert Monteith (c. 1812-84) had been at Trinity with EFG and took his degree in 1834. He was the son of Henry Monteith, wealthy owner of a dye and print works at Glasgow.

[3] Thomas Moore (1779-1852), lyric poet, the Irish counterpart of Scotland's Robert Burns. Under contract to a publisher between 1807 and 1834 Moore wrote many lyrics which were set to Irish airs by Sir John Stevenson (1760?-1833), vicar-choral at St. Patrick's and Christ Church, Dublin. The first *Irish Melodies* was published in 1808. Aldis Wright read "Irish Ballads" for "Irish Melodies."

[4] Wimpole Hall, between Royston and Cambridge, owned at that time by the Earl of Hardwicke.

[5] George Peacock, who became Dean of Ely in 1839, had been EFG's tutor at Trinity. He was Lowndean Professor of Astronomy and Geology at Cambridge, 1837-58. At the time EFG wrote, Barnwell, on the eastern border of Cambridge, shared an unsavory reputation with "Castle-End," at the northern border.

The "new chapel" to which EFG refers is Christ Church, consecrated June 7, 1839. In 1846 it became the parish church for St. Andrew-the-Less.

[6] Mary Russell Mitford (1787-1855), novelist and dramatist, chiefly known for her essays, *Our Village, Sketches of Rural Character and Scenery.*

To W. B. Donne

Boulge Hall
August 22, [1839]

My dear Donne,

I had a letter from you nearly three weeks back I think, while I was staying at Bedford. By what you told me then, I conclude you are now at Cromer;[1] but I direct to Mattishall as you desired me. Thank you for your invitations etc., if I were disengaged, I should come over to the sea-side and wander about on the shore with you, but I have come here to *assist* at a kind of family reunion for a time, and believe that I shall go over to Ireland about the beginning of September. The middle of October (at the latest) will find me with all my summer wanderings over, ready to wish myself in cotton and quietude for the winter.

Perhaps however I shall see you some of those days: for an excursion to Norfolk from here, or to Norwich from Geldestone, is not to be accounted in the list of long movements.

I have nothing at all to tell you of, less than ever, as I have even read nothing for months except Dante's Paradisi, which happens to have been published some time. By the way I stumbled upon a Review by Carlyle on some German Memoirs of a certain Rahel Von Ense,[2] in the Westminster which touched me as all his writings do. I suppose one day I shall be converted to be a furious admirer of his French Revolution. All this time I think Carlyle is a one-sided man; but I like him because he pulls one the opposite side to which all the world are pulling one.

Tell Mrs. Donne I read his and a translation of her favourite Quintus Fixlein[3] some weeks ago; the design and the characters are very fine; but rather muddled with sentiment—so I think now: but I hope to be converted by her one of these days.

In the Review I spoke of before, there is an account of Jean Paul in his little home at Baireuth—a very beautiful account of a very noble simple fellow. The Author[4] stays a day with him, "But (as Carlyle says) those candles are blown out, and the fruit platters swept away, and all the living story of that household gone down into the long night."

Have you ever read Carlyle's review of Lockhart's Scott?[5] There is little else but Carlyle in this letter I see.

Pray Donne write to me if you can: and tell me that Mrs. Donne is better. I have resumed my *farming character*,[6] now that Harvest is pending, pending indeed it has been during these rains, but now the weather seems promising fine. Farewell: kind remembrances to all.

Ever yours,
E. FitzGerald

[1] Mrs. Donne was not strong, and her husband several times sought rest and change for her through vacations spent at Cromer, a seaside resort 20 miles north of Norwich.

[2] A review of nine volumes of letters and memoirs of his wife Rahel published by Karl A. Varnahagen von Ense (1785-1858), Prussian diplomat and historian, between 1834 and 1838, which appeared in the *London and Westminster Review*, December, 1838. The review is devoted for the most part to *Denkwürdiskeiten und Vermischte Schriften*, 4 vols., 1837-38. Carlyle and von Ense corresponded, and the Prussian's letters to the Scot were published in 1892.

[3] *Leben des Quintus Fixlein*, an extravaganza both sentimental and humorous, by Jean Paul Richter (1763-1825), published in 1796 and translated by Carlyle in his *German Romances*, 1827.

[4] "The Author," i.e., von Ense. For Carlyle's account of the visit see his Centenary Edition, XXIX, 94-97.

[5] *Memoirs of the Life of Sir Walter Scott*, 7 vols., by his son-in-law, John Gibson Lockhart (1794-1854), had been published 1837-38. Carlyle's review of the first six volumes appeared in the *London and Westminster Review*, Jan., 1838.

[6] For several years EFG supervised the harvests on the family estates.

To Bernard Barton

Halverstown,[1] *Sunday*
Oct. 20, [1839]

My dear Sir,

I am very glad that you lifted yourself at last from your mahogany desk, and took such a trip as you describe in your last letter. I don't think you could have made a better in the same given space of time. It is some years since I have seen the Castle at Windsor, except from Eton. The view from the Terrace is the noblest I know of, taking it with all its associations together. Gray's Ode rises up into the mind as one looks around—does it not?[2]—a sure proof that, however people may condemn certain conceits and expressions in the poem, the spirit of it is genuine. 'Ye distant spires, ye antique towers'—very large and noble, like the air that breathes upon one as one looks down along the view. My brother John told me he thought the Waterloo gallery very fine:[3] the portraits by Sir Thomas almost as fine as Vandyke. You saw them, of course. You say nothing of having seen the National Gallery in London:[4] indeed I rather fear it is closed these two months. This is a great loss to you: the Rubens landscape you would never have forgot. Thank you for the picture of my dear old Bredfield[5] which you have secured for me: it is most welcome. Poor Nursey once made me a very pretty oil sketch of it: but I gave it to Mr. Jenney. By all means have it engraved for the pocket book:[6] it is well worthy. Some of the tall ash trees about it used to be visible at sea: but I think their topmost branches are decayed now. This circumstance I put in, because it will tell in your verse illustration of the view. From the road before the lawn, people used plainly to see the topmasts of the men-of-war lying in Hollesley bay during the war. I like the idea of this: the old English house holding up its enquiring chimneys and weathercocks (there is great physiognomy in weathercocks) towards the far-off sea, and the ships upon it. How well I remember when we used all to be in the Nursery, and from the window see the hounds come across the lawn, my Father and Mr. Jenney in their hunting-caps, etc., with their long whips—all Daguerreotyped into the mind's eye now—and that is all. Perhaps you are not civilised enough to know what Daguerreotype is:[7] no more do I well. We were all going on here as merrily as possible till this day week, when my Piscator got an order from his Father to go home directly. So go he would the day after. I wanted to go also: but they would have me stay here ten days more. So I stay: I suppose I shall be in London toward the end of this week however: and then it will not be long before I pay you a visit. . . .

I have gone through Homer's Iliad—sorry to have finished it. The accounts of the Zoolu people, with Dingarn their king, etc.,[8] give one a very good idea of the Homeric heroes, who were great brutes: but superior to the Gods who governed them: which also has been the case with most nations. It is a lucky thing that God made Man, and that Man has not to make God: we should fare badly, judging by the specimens already produced—Frankenstein Monster Gods, formed out of the worst and rottenest scraps of humanity—gigantic—and to turn destructively upon their Creators—

> But be ye of good cheer! I have overcome the world.[9]

So speaks a gentle voice.

I found here a Number of Tait's Magazine for August last, containing a paper on Southey, Wordsworth, etc., by De Quincey.[10] Incomplete and disproportioned like his other papers: but containing two noble passages: one, on certain years of his own Life when Opium shut him out from the world; the other, on Southey's style: in which he tells a truth which is obvious, directly it is told. Tait seems to be very well worth a shilling a month: that is the price of him, I see. You have bought Carlyle's Miscellanies, have you not?[11] I long to get them: but one must wait till they are out of print before the Dublin booksellers shall have heard of them. Now here is really a very long letter, and what is more, written with a pen of my own mending—more consolatory to me than to you. Mr. Macnish's inscription for Milton is—

> His lofty spirit was the home
> Of inspirations high,
> A mighty temple whose great dome
> Was hidden in the sky.

Who Mr. Macnish is, I don't know. Didn't he write some Essays on Drunkenness once? or on Dreams?[12]

Farewell for the present, my dear Sir. We shall soon shake hands again. Ever yours,

E. FitzGerald.

1 Halverstown, Kilcullen, County Kildare, the home of EFG's paternal uncle, Peter Purcell. EFG's father, born Purcell, assumed the FitzGerald name and arms on the death of his father-in-law, John FitzGerald, in 1818. See Biographical Profile. W. K. Browne accompanied EFG on this trip to Ireland.

[2] "Ode on a Distant Prospect of Eton College" by Thomas Gray (1716-71), the first line of which EFG quotes.

[3] The Waterloo Chamber at Windsor, in which state banquets and theatrical performances are held, is hung with portraits of sovereigns, ministers of state, ambassadors, military commanders, and others involved in events at the close of Napoleon's career. All were painted for George IV by Sir Thomas Lawrence.

[4] The National Gallery in Trafalgar Square had required six years to build and had been opened to the public, April 9, 1838. The Rubens picture to which EFG refers is "Landscape, with a View of the Chateau de Steen," one of 16 paintings given by Sir George Beaumont in 1826 (Cunningham's *Handbook for London*, II, 576, 578).

[5] EFG refers to his birthplace, the *White House* at Bredfield. Comparison of the passage about his old home with his poem, "Bredfield Hall" (*Literary Remains*, VII, 319-22), reveals striking parallels; and the recollections here recorded very likely were the genesis of the poem.

For "poor Nursey" see Biographical Profile. Edmund Jenney, of the Red House in nearby Hasketon, was the owner of considerable property, including the Bredfield estate. The Jenney and FitzGerald families were on the best of neighborly terms, and Squire Jenney shared with EFG's father the cost of maintaining a pack of harriers.

[6] "Pocket Books" or "Ladies Memorandum Books," diaries extremely popular during the nineteenth century. They differed from their modern counterparts in that they contained pages of prose and verse for the entertainment of owners. Some of the selections were reprinted from the works of established authors. The majority of the selections, however, were contributed by local poets and poetasters, for the books were published by provincial printers and stationers. Engraved illustrations were usually excellent, and charades, enigmas, riddles, and conundrums, all in verse, were also features. Solutions would be given the following year. George W. Fulcher of Sudbury, Suffolk, published *Fulcher's Sudbury Pocket Book* and *Fulcher's Ladies Memorandum Book and Poetical Miscellany*. Barton contributed to the *Pocket Book* and was probably responsible for the appearance in that publication in 1841 of EFG's poem, "Chronomoros," written for Barton's daughter Lucy, to be presented with a clock she gave her father as a Christmas gift. "Chronomoros," published anonymously, was reprinted in the *Literary Remains*, VII, 325-28.

[7] On August 2, a bare three months before EFG wrote, the French government had announced the daguerrotype process of photography. Louis J. M. Daguerre (1789-1851), who had perfected the method, agreed to its being made public in return for annuities granted by the government to him and to the heir of his collaborator, J. N. Niepce, who had died in 1833.

[8] *Missionary Journey to the Zoolu Country in 1835*, by Captain Allen F. Gardiner (1794-1851) of the Royal Navy, published in London in 1836.

[9] Jesus, speaking to the Disciples, said, "In the world ye shall have tribulation: but be of good cheer; I have overcome the world" (John 16:33).

[10] "Southey, Wordsworth, and Coleridge," the fifth of Thomas De Quincey's *Lake Reminiscences*, contributed to *Tait's Magazine* between January and August, 1839. The passage on De Quincey's addiction to opium appears in *Collected Writings*, Masson ed., II, 339-40. In the portion on Southey's style (pp. 345-46), De Quincey wrote, ". . . the truth is, that Southey's defects in this particular

power are as striking as his characteristic graces." In passages requiring "splendid declamation" or "impassionate fervour" the style "will immediately betray its want of the loftier qualities" which the content requires.

[11] *Critical and Miscellaneous Essays* in four volumes contains essays Thomas Carlyle had previously contributed to periodicals. The London edition (1839) followed publication in Boston, Mass., the previous year.

[12] The quatrain, which EFG misquotes, appears in "Poetical Portraits by a Modern Pythagorean" (*Blackwood's Magazine*, Apr., 1830, p. 632), by Robert Macnish (1802-37), a Glasgow physician. In the magazine, the lines read:

His spirit was the home
  Of aspirations high;
A temple, whose huge dome
  Was hidden in the sky.

Lapse of memory may have been responsible for EFG's deviations from the original. On the other hand, he was not averse to altering diction or rhythm when quoting passages that invited revision. He was correct in his surmises: Macnish published *The Anatomy of Drunkenness*, 1827; *The Philosophy of Sleep*, 1830; and *Introduction to Phrenology*, 1835.

To Bernard Barton

London, Saturday
[November 23, 25, 1839]

My dear Sir,

I am not indeed coming down to Boulge direct just yet: but I hope that ten days more will see me clear of London—perhaps at Geldestone—and it will not be long before I come Woodbridgewards then. As to Kerrich's drawing, it will bide its time, being in good keeping.

Your verses on Assington Hall I had not only seen and read—but even bought—for passing through Cheapside the other day I saw the print up at a Stationer's window, and for old acquaintance sake went in and bought the Pocket book.[1]

I have got Alfred Tennyson up with me here, and to-day I give a dinner to him and two or three others. It is just ordered: soles, two boiled fowls, and an Apple Tart—cheese, etc. After this plenty of smoking. I am quite smoke-dried as it is. If you drop in you shall be welcome.

I asked young S[pring] R[ice] about your Dream verses[2]—he believes that his Father shewed them to the Queen. R. M. Milnes, Esq., M.P. sent her a Sonnet, which she said she was very much obliged to him for, but she couldn't understand it.[3] We went to Windsor a fortnight ago (did I tell you this before?) and saw her, and the Castle and the pictures. The Vandykes are noble indeed. And what say you to Nelson's Bust on the mainmast of the Victory?

I have bought few new Pictures since I last wrote, and hope I have now done with the Trade for this season. But who can resist, when one sees a thing hanging outside a Pawnbroker's shop, like fruit ready to fall into one's lap—for a pound or two? The most prudent of my purchases is—an *Umbrella.*

Monday. I could not finish my letter on Saturday, and here I sit down to it again—still more smoke-dried and two-o'clock-in-the-morning-fuddled than before. I want A. T. to publish another volume: as all his friends do: especially Moxon, who has been calling on him for the last two years for a new edition of his old volume: but he is too lazy and wayward to put his hand to the business. He has got fine things in a large Butcher's Account book that now lies in my room:[4] but I don't know if any would take you much. A Sir Somebody Hanmer is said to have published some pretty poetry lately:[5] or as Spring Rice calls it inversely "potery." We are all reading Carlyle's Miscellanies—some abusing, some praising: I among the latter. I am glad to hear that nearly all of the edition that came from America is sold.[6] Carlyle has got a horse and rides about Chelsea, and has improved his digestion wonderfully. An Accumulation of undigested matter is worse than an unsold Edition. Dear me, I haven't seen you since I have been in Ireland. A man has just come from Italy, and he stood on one of the Alps and saw at once the moon rising over the Adriatic while [the] sun sank into the Mediterranean. That was a neat sight.[7]

You do not mention Miss Barton: but I conclude she is with you, and trust she is well. Will you be so good as to remember me to her? And now farewell again for the present.

Ever yours,
E.FG.

[1] EFG's comment suggests that *Fulcher's Pocket Book* for 1840 was already on sale. Assington Hall, near Sudbury, Suffolk, was the residence of John Gurdon, member of an old Suffolk family.

[2] Stephen Spring Rice (1814-65), one of EFG's correspondents. See Biographical Profile. Barton's "Dream verses," probably "A Dream" in *Poems and Letters of Bernard Barton*, 1849. Spring Rice's father, Thomas, Chancellor of the Exchequer, 1835-39, had been created Baron Monteagle and Comptroller of the Exchequer in September.

[3] Richard Monckton Milnes (1809-85), created first Baron Houghton in 1863, a contemporary of EFG's at Trinity and a lifelong, though never an intimate, friend. See Biographical Profile.

[4] Tennyson's 1832 volume, *Poems*, had been severely criticized; and for a decade the poet resisted all pressures to appear again in print. EFG was most persistent in urging his friend to break silence and eventually tricked Tennyson into a meeting with Edward Moxon, the publisher, at which time negotiations for the two volumes of 1842 were begun. (See letter to Barton, March 2, 1842.) The "Butcher's Book" and the poems written therein will be referred to frequently in letters of the next few years.

[5] Sir John Hanmer (1809-81) in 1839 published *Fra Cipolla and Other Poems.*

[6] A note by I. W. Dyer in his *A Bibliography of the Writings of Thomas Carlyle* (Portland, Maine, 1928, p. 188) clarifies this comment. James Fraser was the publisher of the 1839 London edition of the *Critical and Miscellaneous Essays*; but, Dyer states, the edition was "in fact, 250 additional copies of the American [1838] printing." Fraser issued a second edition of five volumes in 1840. The *Miscellanies*, declared Emery Neff, was the "pioneer in what became a profitable fashion of collecting fugitive essays" (*Carlyle*, New York, 1932, p. 193).

[7] Probably reported by Savile Morton.

To W. B. Donne

[Geldestone Hall]
Monday [December 30, 1839][1]

My dear Donne,

My stay here is prolonged for ten days more. Are you going to the Sessions at Norwich on Friday?[2] Write me word of that: for if you are, I will strive and get over that day. Kerrich is going: but in Sir E. Bacon's carriage and it is reported that there is no vacant seat for me. So whether I can get over at all is doubtful. But give me a line as to your movements by return of post.

Thompson tells me you are writing a Roman History. But you have not been asked to LECTURE at the Ipswich Mechanics' Institution, as I have—"any subject except controversial Divinity, and party Politics."[3] In the meantime I have begun Livy: I have read one book, and can't help looking at the four thick octavos that remain—

Oh beate Sesti,
Vitae summa brevis spem nos vetat inchoare longam.[4]

But it is very stately reading. As to old Niebuhr,[5] it is mean to attack old legends that can't defend themselves. And what does it signify in the least if they are true or not? Whoever *actively* believed that Romulus was suckled by a wolf? But I have found in Horace a proper motto[6] for those lumbering Germans:

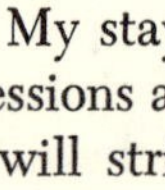

Quis Parthum paveat? quis gelidum Scythen?
Quis Germania quos horrida parturit
Foetus?[x]

[FitzGerald's footnote reads:]

[x]horrida . . . foetus per metasyntaxin:
"horrid abortions."

[1] This letter, published in part by Aldis Wright, was placed by him between letters of December, 1841, and January, 1842 (*Letters and Literary Remains*, I, 117). The date provided here is established by a letter of January 3, 1840, from Donne to J. W. Blakesley. "FitzGerald will probably come home with me to-morrow," wrote Donne. "He is reading Livy, and sends me a most ingenious criticism on Niebuhr, with a wood-cut, as a great humbug! It will make a fine frontispiece for the U.K.S. Roman History, when complete" (*Donne and Friends*, p. 53). "U.K.S.," the abbreviation for the Society for the Diffusion of Useful Knowledge.

[2] The January Court of Quarter Sessions was held the first week after each December 28. Donne, John Kerrich, EFG's brother-in-law, and Sir Edmund Bacon of Raveningham Hall, two miles north of Geldestone, were justices. For most of his life EFG was fond of attending local courts.

[3] EFG here indirectly refers to the Society for the Diffusion of Useful Knowledge and directly to the Mechanics' Institute, two projects undertaken to provide adult education for the rapidly increasing literate laboring class of the time. The U.K.S., established in 1826, proposed to publish each month two sixpenny pamphlets on subjects drawn from the humanities and the sciences. Donne had contracted to write *From the Samnite Wars to Caesar* for a history of Rome. His first pamphlet, for which he was paid £30, was published in 1841 (*Donne and Friends*, p. 51). He did not complete the assignment. Failing to win mass support, the U.K.S. suspended activities in 1846.

The first Mechanics' Institute had been founded in London in 1824 to provide members with vocational instruction and classes for "scientific and useful knowledge." Institutes were quickly formed in many cities and towns. Lecture subjects were not well adapted to the interests of members and, like the U.K.S., the movement failed to achieve its objective. In 1844 the unit at Ipswich, established in 1824, had a membership of between 300 and 400 and a library of some 3,000 volumes (White's *Directory of Suffolk*, 1844, p. 74).

[4] "Happy Sestius, the brief span of life forbids that we enter upon an undertaking that cannot be fulfilled." Horace, *The Odes* I.4.14-15.

[5] Barthold Georg Niebuhr (1776-1831), German statesman and historian. Lectures given at the University of Berlin formed the basis of his *Römische Geschichte*, published in 1812. Niebuhr is credited with being the first writer to approach the history of Rome in a scientific spirit.

[6] "Who fears the Parthian, who the icy Scythian, who the swarms that rough Germania breeds?" (Horace, *The Odes* IV.5.25-27).

To Bernard Barton

[Geldestone]
[January, 1840][1]

My dear Sir,

You tell my Father you mean to write a Poem about my invisibility —and somehow it seems strange to myself that I have been so long absent from Woodbridge. It was a toss up (as boys say—and perhaps Gods) whether I should go now:—the toss has decided I should not. On the contrary I am going to see Donne at Mattishall: a visit, which having put off a fortnight ago, I am now determined to pay. But if I do not see you before I go to London, I shall assuredly be down again by the latter part of February: when toasted cheese and ale shall again unite our souls.[2] You need not however expect that I can return to such familiar intercourse as once (in former days) passed between us. New honours in society have devolved upon me the necessity of a more dignified deportment. A letter has been sent from the Secretary of the Ipswich Mechanics' Institution asking me to Lecture—any subject but Party Politics or Controversial Divinity. On my politely declining, another, a fuller, and a more pressing, letter was sent urging me to comply with their demand: I answered to the same effect, but with accelerated dignity. I am now awaiting the third request in confidence: if you see no symptoms of its being mooted, perhaps you will kindly propose it. I have prepared an answer. Donne is mad with envy. He consoles himself with having got a Roman History to write for Lardner's Cabinet Cyclopaedia. What a pity it is that only Lying Histories are readable. I am afraid Donne will stick to what is considered the Truth too much.

This is a day like May: I and the children have been scrambling up and down the sides of a pit till our legs ache.[3]

[No signature]

[1] Misdated by Aldis Wright, [Jan. 1842] (*Letters and Literary Remains*, I, 118).

[2] Although FitzGerald may have been as fond of toasted cheese as he implies in many letters to Barton, it is also possible that his partiality for the dish was dictated by concern lest his entertainment tax Barton's slender means.

[3] A gravel pit where, on Saturdays, the Kerrich children were permitted to "dirty stockings and frocks as much as they please."

To W. F. Pollock

Hastings
Feb^r 3/40

My dear Pollock,

When I got here I found the letter you had sent after me into Suffolk. I keep it as a perfect specimen of a Penny Post letter:[1] this is meant for a compliment. Not being able to write such a one myself, I send the enclosed advertisement[x] from an Atlas of two weeks ago. A Roman Dictator could not pronounce more emphatically: nor Tacitus relate more concisely. Have you heard if there has been a general Suicide among all the Brown Bread Makers, not to say of London, but of England generally? When I read the last line of the Advertisement, I felt glad I was not a Brown Bread Maker.

There is an excellent Review on Carlyle's Chartism in the same Atlas.[2] Tell Spedding of this. But what will he care? Carlyle is universally believed here to be *the* Carlile—the more decided one, I mean.[3] All the invalids are warned by the Clergymen to be on their guard against him.[4] He is all the more dangerous now that his meaning cannot be discovered. What do you think of Sterling's review of him?[5] Some very good remarks: but I never was so suffocated by words in my life. I declare it gives me a shortness of breath to think of it.

I shall return to London either to-morrow week or fortnight. As I depend on others, I am not certain. Here I have got a good lodging looking on the sea—books, tobacco, etc. But I know nobody,[6] except the Maid—"Knowing" is here used not in the Biblical sense: of which Plato also was unconscious, I think. Indeed he would have classed such knowledge as that more under the head of Doxy than επιστήμη.[7] So much for all things. Good bye, my dear Pollock: I hope we shall smoke a cigar together ere long.

Ever yours
E. FitzGerald

[x]No. 118 Jermyn Street,
Jan. 5, 1840.

Beaufoy's Digestive Bread.—The sale of this article is *discontinued* from this day: any Bread offered under this designation is, therefore, deceptious. Brown Bread, as usually made, and Beaufoy's Digestive Bread, are very different articles.

[1] Penny postage had gone into effect on January 10. The bill authorizing the reduction in postage fees had been submitted to Parliament by Thomas Spring Rice, Chancellor of the Exchequer in 1839 and father of EFG's friend, Stephen Spring Rice (*Annual Register*, "History," 1839, pp. 285, 288). Under the old rates, EFG would have paid 1s 6d for his letter: 8d for postage from London to Woodbridge, and 10d from Woodbridge to Hastings. (Source: Post Office Records Dept., London.)

[2] Carlyle's *Chartism* had been published by James Fraser in December, 1839, post-dated 1840. The first printing of a thousand copies had been followed by a second thousand in January (Dyer *Bibliography*, p. 50). The work was reviewed in the *Atlas*, January 18, 1840, pp. 41-42.

[3] Richard Carlile (1790-1843), freethinker, controversialist, and publisher; one of the army that fought for freedom of the press. After William Hone stopped publication of his parodies of the *Catechism*, the *Litany*, and the *Creed*, he tried unsuccessfully to deter Carlile from printing them to be sold "by all who are not afraid of incurring the displeasure of His Majesty's Ministers, their Spies and Informers, or Public Plunderers of any denomination. . . . Price two-pence" (F. W. Hackwood, *William Hone, His Life and Times*, 1912, p. 116). For his publishing misdemeanors, which included a printing of the works of Thomas Paine in 1818, Carlile spent almost ten years of his life in prison.

[4] Thomas Carlyle.

[5] John Sterling (1806-44), one of Carlyle's intimate friends, had published "On the Writings of Thomas Carlyle" in the *London and Westminster Review* in October, 1839 (pp. 1-68). Carlyle alluded to the essay as "The first generous human recognition" of his work, "expressed with heroic emphasis, and clear conviction visible amid its fiery exaggeration" (*Life of John Sterling*, Library Edition, 1869, p. 235).

[6] Aldis Wright's sense of propriety compelled him to delete the remainder of this, and the sentence which follows, in his version of the letter. The excision was not indicated in the text.

[7] Positive knowledge as opposed to "doxy", or opinion—one of FitzGerald's rare puns.

To John Kerrich[1]

London, Wednesday
[February, 1840]

My dear Kerrich,

I received your note (the double one I mean), and thank you for it. I send you by the coach a kennel for your Lion,[2] which I hope will get safe to you. The iron grating necessary to secure the doorway, to prevent danger to the family from so fierce a beast, I must leave to you to provide. I start to-day for Bedford on my way to Suffolk. I shall be at Boulge on Tuesday, then, I suppose, I shall hear of you. . . . Tell Miss Schutz[3] that I send her Dibden's songs[4] and . . . an Italian Dictionary by this slow coach . . . Thackeray is blooming, and remembers you. We have smoked together as usual. W. Browne thinks of going into the Church[5]—what a pity he should be spoiled. Thackeray, coming in, sends his compliments as below,[x] with which we both bid you heartily farewell.

E.FG.

[x] Miss Kerrich added: "There comes at the foot of the paper a spirited pen-and-ink sketch of a young gentleman, hand on heart, in so-called 'skeleton' trousers and a Toby frill, 'making a leg' as the deferential bow used to be called, to a damsel of haughty aspect who smells a full-blown rose. The simpering idiocy on the boy's face is delightful, and 'Miss,' with her grown-up airs, no less charming."

1 The text of this letter to FitzGerald's brother-in-law is taken from "Edward FitzGerald; a Personal Reminiscence" by Eleanor FitzGerald Kerrich, a grand-niece, contributed to the *Nineteenth Century Magazine*, March, 1909 (p. 466). The deletions were made by Miss Kerrich.

2 Perhaps the name of a dog for which the kennel was provided.

3 A number of times, while in London, EFG bought books for Mrs. Schutz of Gillingham Hall, near Geldestone. (See letter to Allen, Jan. 1, 1837, n.3.) Although one of Mrs. Schutz's daughters was unmarried, Miss Kerrich probably read *Miss* where EFG had written *Mrs.*

4 Charles Dibden published *Collection of Songs*, 2 vols., in 1814.

5 W. K. Browne did not become a clergyman.

To Bernard Barton

Pmk., London
February 17, 1840

My dear Sir,

You will by this time, I dare say, have seen Isabella,[1] who will have told you of my abode etc. for the last month. I expect to be at Boulge very shortly, as I have some things to do there: and I shall be very glad to see you again. Why it is a long time since we met. I left Lusia certainly better at Hastings:[2] and a note I had from her this morning tells me she has been walking about at the rate of two and three hours a day. I really liked Hastings very much: more than any watering-place I ever was at. The seas were very high. I am now come to London to see my friends, to go to a play or two (from which wicked and foolish amusement I am not yet weaned), and to abstain entirely from buying either books or pictures (money failing). If I can pay my lodgings, and for a place in the Pit once or twice I shall do. I went last

Saturday night to see a new play by poor Leigh Hunt,[3] who has at last done something to put a few pounds into his pocket. His Play is very pretty, though not so dramatic as to ensure any long success on the stage: it is very well acted. Poor L. H. is delighted with his new friends the Actors. When I got to my lodgings, I found A. Tennyson installed in them: he has been here ever since in a very uneasy state: being really ill, in a nervous way: what with an hereditary tenderness of nerve, and having spoiled what strength he had by incessant smoking, etc. I have also made him very out of sorts by desiring a truce from complaints and complainings. Poor fellow: he is quite magnanimous, and noble natured, with no meanness or vanity or affectation of any kind whatsoever—but very perverse, according to the nature of his illness. So much for Poets, who, one must allow, are many of them a somewhat tetchy race. There's that great metaphysical, Doric, moral, religious, psychological, poet of the Age, W. Wordsworth, who doesn't like to be contradicted at all: nor to be neglected in any way.

Well, my dear Sir, you are made of a happier compound, and take the world easily. Your nerves will not irritate you with a sense of neglected genius, if I do not quite fill up this sheet to the end. Prepare yourself: take a little Bottled Porter if you have it: I am going to end: no offence intended: now are you ready?—quite ready?—Well then, I am ever yours,

E. FitzGerald

[1] EFG's sister, one year his junior.

[2] Hastings, a vacation and health resort on the Sussex coast. For his sister Andalusia's invalidism, see letter to Allen, Nov. 21, 1832, n.2. Andalusia was his youngest sister.

[3] Leigh Hunt's *A Legend of Florence*, with Ellen Tree and George Vandenhoff in the cast, had scored a success on its opening night, Friday, February 7. EFG saw the play February 15, when, according to the London *Times*, the program included "a grand allegorical and national masque, in honour of Her Majesty's Nuptials," entitled *The Fortunate Isles*; or *The Triumphs of Britannia*. Queen Victoria and Prince Albert had been married the previous Monday, February 10. Hunt's delight in his actor friends is recorded in chap. XXV of his *Autobiography*.

To John Allen

Boulge, Woodbridge
[April 4, 1840]

My dear Allen,

I am just going to set off for Norfolk. I want you to do a little thing for me. The Bookseller here cannot get me a copy of Digby's Godefridus[1]—which I want. I knew that not many copies remained unsold (that, Bohn the publisher told me) but I don't think they can have been exhausted since I saw him. Will you, in the course of your rambles, enquire, and if one is to be got will you buy it and keep it for me?

The country is now showing symptoms of greenness and warmth. Yesterday I walked (not a common thing for me) eleven miles; partly over a heath, covered with furze bushes just come out into bloom, whose odour the fresh wind blew into my face. Such a day it was, only not so warm as when you and I used to sit on those rocks overlooking the sea at Tenby, just eight years ago. I am afraid you are growing too good a Christian for me, Master Allen, if you know what I mean by that. Don't be alarmed however. I have just read the first number of Dickens' new work:[2] it does not promise much, I think.

Love to all Coram Street.[3]

Ever yours,
E. FitzGerald

[1] In 1822 Kenelm Henry Digby (1800-80) had published *The Broad Stone of Honour* or *Rules for the Gentlemen of England*, an exposition of "the origin, spirit, and institutions of Christian chivalry." A greatly enlarged second edition appeared in 1826-27. *Godefridus* is the first of four books in the expanded version. EFG, while writing *Euphranor*, "a Dialogue on Youth," during the 1840's, was strongly influenced by Digby. *Godefridus* is analyzed and discussed by the characters in EFG's dialogue, which could appropriately be called, "a manual for the conduct of the Gentlemen of England."

[2] The first weekly part of *Master Humphrey's Clock* was placed on sale Saturday, April 4, the day the letter is postmarked. Dickens's original plan for a miscellany of essays and brief narratives, similar to Addison's *Spectator*, was abandoned when readers demanded a "continued story." *The Old Curiosity Shop* and *Barnaby Rudge* resulted.

[3] In other words, "Love to the Thackerays," who were living at 13 Coram Street.

To W. F. Pollock[1]

Geldestone Hall
Friday night [May 1, 1840]

My dear Pollock,

I received a second letter of yours from York—how many months ago? certainly when no leaves were out as they are now in a wonderful way for this season of the year. You in London do not know that the country is in great want of rain. What does it signify to you; what effect would it have on your dry wigs,[2] which, like Achilles' sceptre, will never, never bud again? To-day we have been drinking the Duke of Wellington's health,[3] as my brother-in-law is a staunch Tory, and I am not disinclined—so far. Then, after a walk which was illuminated by a cigar—*lanterna pedibus meis*[4]—we are come back to the library: where, after tea, we are in some danger of falling asleep. So I take this sheet of paper and this pen that lie opposite me on the table, and write to you. So far so good.

You told me to read Clarendon[5]—which I have begun to do: and like him much. It is really delightful to read his manly, noble English after Lord Brougham's spick-and-span Birmingham ware in the Edinburgh.[6] Is the article on Sir W. Raleigh by Macaulay?[7] It is not so good as most of his, I think. I never was one of those who cared much for the vindication of Raleigh's character: he was a blackguard, it seems: and the chief defence is that he lived among blackguards—Bacon, for instance. Does Spedding think him immaculate? I think the portraits of Raleigh are not favourable: there is great finesse in his eyes and in the shape of his face. Old James the First was a better man than any of his courtiers, I do believe.

It must be very nearly half-past 9 I am sure: ring the bell for the tea-things to be removed—pray turn the lamp—at 10 the married people go to bed: I sit up till 12, sometimes diverging into the kitchen, where I smoke amid the fumes of cold mutton that has formed (I suppose) the maids' supper.[8] But the pleasant thing is to wake early, throw open the window, and lie reading in bed. Morning, noon, and night we look at the Barometer, and make predictions about the weather. When will Jupiter piss thro' his sieve? as Aristophanes says.[9] The wheat begins to look yellow; the clover layers are beginning to blossom, before they have grown to any height; and the grass won't grow: stock therefore will be very cheap, because of the great want of keep. That is poetry. Have you been down to Kitlands with that mad wag Spedding?[10]

My brother-in-law is fallen fast asleep over Buckland's Bridgewater Treatise[11]—his breathing approaches a snore. Now could I drink hot blood.[12] I will write no more. Clarendon shall wind up the night with me. What do people say of Dickens' new work? I saw the 1st No.—a very seedy framework, I thought:[13] but the little conversation between the Lord Mayor and Mr. Toddyhigh wonderful. Thackeray writes to me that he is going to shew up D. Lardner in a quiz. Have you heard if Dionysius has put Mrs. Heaviside in the Family Library way?[14] Ever yours,

E.FG.

[1] Occasionally in his correspondence EFG indulged in ribaldry such as is found in this letter. The strain is restricted, in extant correspondence, to letters written to bachelor friends and is noted most frequently in those to Pollock, after whose marriage in 1844 it disappears. Virtually all the letters to Spedding (also a bachelor) were destroyed by his sisters, who were shocked, it appears, by passages intended solely for masculine eyes.

[2] An allusion to the wigs worn by barristers during sessions of the courts.

[3] The Duke of Wellington (1769-1852), after the close of his military career one of the leaders of the Tory party, was 71 years old on May 1.

[4] "A lantern to my feet."

[5] Edward Hyde, Earl of Clarendon (1608-74), Royalist, appointed Lord Chancellor on the restoration of Charles II. EFG may refer to his *History of the Rebellion and Civil War in England*, published 1702-04.

[6] Lord Brougham, Lord Chancellor, 1830-34, one of the founders in 1802 of the *Edinburgh Review*, to which, for 30 years, he was a frequent contributor. The aplomb with which he discoursed on a wide range of subjects elicited numerous quips from contemporaries. "If Brougham only knew a little law," Daniel O'Connell is reported to have said, "he would know a little of everything."

[7] The essay on Raleigh appears not to have been written by Macaulay.

[8] EFG was spared the inconvenience, suffered by some Victorian gentlemen, of retiring to the stables when he wished to smoke.

[9] When Strepsiades asks Socrates to teach him to reason, the philosopher invokes the aid of the clouds as deities. "Who causes the rain to fall?" Strepsiades asks; and Socrates replies, "Why these" [the clouds]. "For my part," says Strepsiades, "I always thought it was Zeus pissing into a sieve" (*The Clouds*, l.373).

[10] Kitlands, near Dorking, Surrey, the home of Douglas Heath.

[11] *Geology and Mineralogy considered with reference to Natural Theology*, 1836, by William Buckland (1784-1856), divine and pioneer geologist.

[12] Hamlet's words when summoned to his mother's chambers after having caught "the conscience of the King" by means of his play, "The Mousetrap" (*Hamlet*, III.2.408).

[13] Dickens outlined his "framework" of *Master Humphrey's Clock* in a letter to John Forster: "Then I mean to tell how that he has kept odd manuscripts in the old, deep, dark, silent closet where the weights are; and taken them from thence to read (mixing up his enjoyments with some notion of his clock)" (John Forster, *The Life of Charles Dickens*, 1892, p. 87).

[14] Dionysius Lardner (1793-1859), formerly professor of natural philosophy and astronomy at University College, London, and popularizer of scientific knowledge through writing and lecturing. He edited the *Cabinet Library* (1830-32). After an acquaintance of 13 weeks, in March, 1840, Lardner eloped with Mary Heaviside, wife of Captain Richard Heaviside of Brighton, who sued on the grounds of seduction and gained a verdict of £8,000. Lardner spent the next five years in America where, it is recorded, he made £40,000 as lecturer and writer. In 1849 he divorced his wife, from whom he had been separated since 1820, and married Mrs. Heaviside, whose husband had divorced her in 1845.

Thackeray's "quiz," or lampoon of Lardner, "The History of Dionysius Diddler," was not published until 1864, the year following Thackeray's death. The "quiz" is a fragment composed of nine drawings, with brief text, in which both Lardner and Edward Bulwer-Lytton (1803-73), novelist and dramatist, are caricatured. (See Thackeray Biographical Edition, Vol. XIII, pp. 651-69.)

To Frederick Tennyson

The Corporate Town of Bedford
June 7, 1840

Dear Frederick,[1]

Your letter dated from the Eternal City on the 15th of May reached me here two days ago. Perhaps you have by this time left Naples to which you bid me direct: or will have left it by the time my letter gets there. Had I known where to direct to you, I assure you I should have written long ago: but Morton never could tell me further than that he directed to you under cover to the Signori Tennant:[2] and a certain letter that Morton and I wrote conjointly to you this time year never reached you. (The direction of that having been delivered by your brother Septimus while in a trance.) I had no heart to make another venture till I should have more certain hopes of my vessel reaching its port. Our letters are dated from two very different kinds of places: but perhaps equally well suited to the genius of the two men. For I am becoming more hebete every hour: and have not even the ambition to go up to London all this Spring to see the Exhibitions, etc. I live in general quietly at my brother-in-law's in Norfolk: and I look with tolerable composure on vegetating there for some time to come, and in due time handing out my eldest nieces to waltz, etc., at the County Balls. People affect to talk of this kind of life as very beautiful and philosophical: but I don't: men ought to have an ambition to stir, and travel, and fill their heads and senses: but so it is. Enough of what is now generally called the subjective style of writing. This word has made considerable progress in England during the year you have been away,[3] so that people begin to fancy they understand what it means. I have been striving at it, because it is a very *sine qua non* condition in a book which I have just been reading: Eastlake's translation of Goethe's Theory of Colours. I recommend it to you, when you can get hold of it. Come back to England quick and read my copy. Goethe is all in opposition to Newton: and reduces the primitive colours to two. Whewell,[4] I believe, does not patronise it: but it is certainly very Baconically put together. While you are wandering among ruins, waterfalls, and temples, and contemplating them as you sit in your lodgings, I poke about with a book and a colour-box by the side of the River Ouse—quiet scenery enough—and make horrible sketches. The best thing to me in Italy would be that you are there. But I hope you will soon come home and install yourself again in Mornington Crescent. I have just come from Leamington: while there, I met Alfred by chance: we made two or three pleasant excursions together: to Stratford upon Avon and Kenilworth, etc.[5] Don't these names sound very thin amid your warm Southern nomenclature? But I'll be bound you would be pleased to exchange all your fine burnt up places for a look at a Warwickshire pasture every now and then during these hot days.

I have heard several times from Morton, who has been living as quietly all this year in Devonshire as I in Norfolk: which is a fact not without wonder. But I think he is gone now to see the sights in London. All our other friends there remain in *status quo.* I am going back in a few days to Suffolk: and whenever you are inclined to write, the same direction you used before will be sure to find me. I think if you stay much longer in Italy, you will never return to England: or at least only come over to knock down some Lincolnshire Joint Stock Company, and then go back to solace yourself in a more congenial climate. Yet you must have a lingering love of the old soil if you take such pains to chase your old schoolfellow Mainwaring about. We have not heard of him for a long time: the last was, that he was in Naples. I dare say you will have found him out before this letter reaches you. So now good bye—which I am half sorry to say.

The sun shines very bright, and there is a kind of bustle in these clean streets, because there is to be a grand True Blue dinner[6] in the town Hall. Not that I am going: in an hour or two I shall be out in the fields rambling alone. I read Burnet's History—ex pede Herculem.[7] Well, say as you will, there is not, and never was, such a country as Old England—never were there such a Gentry as the English. They will be the distinguishing mark and glory of England in History, as the Arts were of Greece, and War of Rome. I am sure no travel would carry me to any land so beautiful, as the good sense, justice, and liberality of my good countrymen make this. And I cling the closer to it, because I feel that we are going down the hill,[8] and shall perhaps live ourselves to talk of all this independence as a thing that has been. To none of which you assent perhaps. At all events, my paper is done, and "it is time to have done with this solemn letter." I can see you sitting at a window that looks out on the bay of Naples, and Vesuvius with a faint smoke in the distance: a half-naked man under you cutting up watermelons, etc. Haven't I seen it all in Annuals, and in the Ballet of Massaniello long ago?[9]

Believe me ever yours,

E. FitzGerald

[1] In the earlier years of the correspondence EFG usually drops the *k* from Frederick's name except when writing to others in the Tennyson family.

[2] Robert John Tennant (1809-42), intimate with W. B. Donne, the Tennysons, and others of EFG's friends, had been an Apostle at Cambridge where he took his degree in 1831. In 1838 he married the sister of Francis Edgeworth's wife. (See letter to Allen, July 4, 1835, n.2.) After serving as master at a number of schools in England, Tennant entered the Church and was appointed "British Chaplain at Florence," where he died. A volume of his sermons was published in 1844, *Sermons Preached to the British Congregation at Florence.* (See letter to F. Tennyson, Aug. 31, 1843.)

[3] To demonstrate the early application of "subjective" to literature and art, the NED quotes FitzGerald's letter of [March, 1846] to Frederick: "The whole *subjective* scheme (damn the word!) of the poems I did not like."

[4] Charles Eastlake in 1840 published a translation of Goethe's *Farbenlehre*, or the *Doctrine of Colours*. A portion of Eastlake's work is an aesthetic application of Goethe's theory. Walter A. Phillips, in his article on Goethe in the *Encyclopedia Britannica*, states, "We marvel at the obstinacy with which he, with inadequate mathematical knowledge, opposed the Newtonian theory of light and colour." William Whewell (1794-1866), to whom EFG also refers, was Professor of Moral Philosophy at Cambridge, and, the following year, became Master of Trinity College.

[5] Tennyson had gone to Warwick via Leicester, to which place he had taken a third-class carriage on the railroad. "It is a carriage entirely open, without seats, nothing but a rail or two running across it, something like pens of cattle," he recorded in his diary. "Tho' we did not move very quickly, yet it was liker flying than anything else" (*Memoir*, I, 175). On driving into Warwick on the mail coach the following day, he caught sight of EFG, walking toward Leamington. Tennyson stopped the coach, EFG joined him, and the two spent the evening at the George. In the course of the following days they "tumbled about the ruins at Kenilworth," visited Warwick Castle, and went to Stratford. In the room where, they were told, Shakespeare had been born, they found the wall "scribbled over" with names. "I was seized with a sort of enthusiasm, and wrote mine," Tennyson recorded, "tho' I was a little ashamed of it afterwards: yet the feeling was genuine at the time, and I did homage with the rest" (*ibid.*, p. 176).

[6] "Blue is the colour of the Tory party in Suffolk—Yellow, of the Whig" (EFG's note, *Selections from the Poems and Letters of Bernard Barton*, p. 82).

[7] Gilbert Burnet (1643-1715), Bishop of Salisbury and historian, active in the religious and political controversies of England and his native Scotland from the time of the Restoration until his death. EFG probably refers to Burnet's most important work, *History of His Own Times*, 2 vols., 1724 and 1734.

Ex pede Herculem: "Hercules from his foot," or, "Judge the whole from the part."

[8] This becomes a familiar strain in EFG's correspondence.

[9] *Masaniello*, the title in England of *La Muette de Portici*, a five-act opera by Daniel Francois Auber (1782-1871). A production in three acts had been staged at Drury Lane, May 4, 1829.

The *Annuals* which EFG mentions were illustrated miscellanies of poetry, prose, and general information published as gift books for the Christmas season. Some were elaborate publications. Prices ranged from ten shillings to a guinea.

To John Allen

Boulge Hall
Sunday, July 12/40

My dear John Allen,

I wrote a good bit of a letter to you three weeks ago: but, being nonplussed suddenly, tore it up. Lusia says she has had a letter from Mrs. Allen, telling how you had a troublesome and even dangerous passage to Tenby: but that there you arrived at last. And there I suppose you are. The *veteris vestigia flammæ*, or old pleasant recollections of our being together at that place, make me begin another sheet to you. I am almost convicted in my own mind of ingratitude for not having travelled long ago to Pembrokeshire, to show my most kind friends of Freestone that I remember their kindness, and that they made my stay so pleasant as to make me wish to test their hospitality again. Nothing but my besetting indolence (the strongest thing about me) could have prevented my doing this. I should like much to see Mr. and Mrs. Allen again, and Carew Castle, and walk along the old road traversed by you and me several times between Freestone and Tenby. Does old Penally Top[1] stand where it did, faintly discernible in these rainy skies? Do you sit ever upon that rock that juts out by Tenby harbour, where you and I sat one day seven years ago, and quoted G. Herbert? Lusia tells me also that nice Mary Allen is to be married to your brother—Charles, I think.[2] She is really one of the pleasantest remembrances of womanhood I have. I suppose she sits still in an upper room, with an old turnip of a watch (tell her I remember this) on the table beside her as she reads wholesome books. As I write, I remember different parts of the house and the garden, and the fields about. Is it absolutely *that* Mary Allen that is to become Mrs. Charles Allen? Pray write, and let me hear of this from yourself. Another thing also: are you to become our Rector in Sussex?[3] This is another of Lusia's scandals. I rather hope it is true: but not quite. Lusia is pretty well: better, I think, than when she first came down from London. But the weather is not favorable to healthy or sick, sane or insane.[4] She makes herself tolerably happy down here: and wishes to exert herself: which is the highest wish a FitzGerald can form. I go on as usual, and in a way that needs no explanation to you: reading a little, drawing a little, playing a little, smoking a little, etc. I have got hold of Herodotus now: the most interesting of all Historians. But I find the disadvantage of being so ill-grounded and bad a scholar: I can get at the broad sense: but all the delicacies (in which so much of the beauty and character of an author lie) escape me sadly. The more I read, the more I feel this. But what does it all signify? Time goes on, and we get older; and whether my idleness comprehends the distinctions of the 1st and 2nd Aorist[5] will not be noted much in the Book of Life, either on this or the other side of the leaf. Here is a letter written on this Sunday Night, July 12, 1840. And it shall go to-morrow. My kind remembrances to Mrs. Allen: and (I beg you to transmit them) to all my foreknown friends at Freestone. And believe me yours now as I have been and hope to be ever affectionately,

E. FitzGerald

I shall be here till the end of the month.

N.B. I am growing bald.

[1] FitzGerald, evidently, was recalling Prescelly Top (spelled variously), the highest peak in Pembrokeshire, which rises to 1,760 feet 20 miles north of Tenby. The highest elevation near Penally, a village a mile or so from Tenby, is 250 feet.

[2] Mary Allen married her cousin Charles, who spent the years 1848-56 in the Bengal Civil Service and became a member of the Supreme Council of India under Lord Dalhousie. On his return to Britain he made his home at Tenby.

[3] At Seaford, where the FitzGeralds owned considerable property. Allen was not appointed to a living there.

[4] See letter to Allen, Nov. 21, 1832.

[5] The aorist tense, denoting action which took place in unspecified past time, without implication of continuance. A few verbs have both a first and second aorist, resulting in differing shades of meaning.

To John Allen

Boulge
July 25/40

My dear Fellow,

Many thanks for your kind long letter. It brought me back to the green before the house at Freestone, and the old schoolroom in it.[1] I have always felt within myself that if ever I did go again to Freestone, I should puzzle myself and every one else by bringing back old associations among existing things: I should have felt awkward. The place remains quite whole in my mind: Anne Allen's damask cheek forming part of the colouring therein. I remember a little well somewhere in the woods about a mile from the house: and those faint reports of explosions from towards Milford, etc., which we used to hear when we all walked out together. You are to thank Mary Allen for her kind wishes: and tell her she need not doubt that I wish her all good things. I enclose you as you see a little drawing of a Suffolk farm house close here: copied from a sketch of poor Mr. Nursey.[2] If you think it worth giving to Mary Allen, do: it seems, and perhaps is, very namby-pamby to send this: but she and I used to talk of drawings together: and this will let her know that I go on just the same as I did eight years ago. N.B. It is not intended as a nuptial present.

Now, you need not answer this letter: as you have done remarkably well already. I am living (did I tell you this before?) at a little cottage close by the lawn gates, where I have my books, a barrel of beer which I tap myself (can you tap a barrel of beer?), and an old woman to do for me. I have also just concocted two gallons of Tar water under the directions of Bishop Berkeley:[3] it is to be bottled off this very day after a careful skimming: and then drunk by those who can and will. It is to be tried first on my old woman: if she survives, I am to begin: and it will then gradually spread into the Parish, through England, Europe, etc., "as the small pebble stirs the peaceful lake."[4] Good people here are much scandalized at Thirlwall's being made a Bishop:[5] Isabella brought home a report from a Clergyman that Thirlwall had so bad a character at Trinity that many would not associate with him. I do not think however that I would have made him Bishop: I am all for good and not great Bishops. Old Evans would have done better. I am become an Oxford High Church Divine after Newman: whose sermons are the best that ever were written in my judgment.[6] Cecil I have read:[7] and liked for his good sense. Is the croft at Tenby still green: and does Mary Allen take a turn on it in a riding habit as of old? And I remember a ravine on the horn of the bay opposite the town where the sea rushes up. I mean as you go on past the croft. I can walk there as in a dream. I see Thackeray's book[8] announced as about to be published, and I hear Spedding has written a Review of Carlyle's Revolution in the Edinburgh.[9] I don't know a book more certain to evaporate away from posterity than that, except it be supported by his other works. Parts may perhaps be found two hundred years hence and translated into Erse by some inverted Macpherson.[10] "These things seem strange," says Herodotus, *γένοιτο δ' ἂν πᾶν ἐν τῷ μακρῷ χρόνῳ*."[11] Herodotus makes few general assertions: so when he does make them, they tell. I could talk more to you, but my paper is out. John Allen, I rejoice in you: and am ever yours affectionately,

E.FG.

[1] Recollections of his visits to Allen in 1832 and 1833.

[2] See Biographical Profile.

[3] George Berkeley (1685-1753), Bishop of Cloyne, Ireland. "Having been benefited by the use of tar-water during an attack of nervous colic," Allibone states,

"his active philanthropy induced him to give to the world in 1744, *Siris*, a Chain of Philosophical reflections and Inquiries respecting the virtues of Tar-Water in the Plague." After the publication of *Siris*, tar-water was popularly accepted as a panacea.

[4]
> Self-love but serves the virtuous mind to wake,
> As the small pebble stirs the peaceful lake;
> The centre mov'd, a circle straight succeeds
> Another still, and still another spreads
> Friends, parent, neighbour, first it will embrace;
> His country next; and next all human race;
>
> Pope's *Essay on Man*, IV, 363-68

[5] The appointment of Connop Thirlwall (1797-1875), historian, as Bishop of St. David's had just been made public. Thirlwall, a brilliant scholar, had been named Fellow of Trinity upon taking his degree in 1818. A latitudinarian, he published, while at Cambridge, a translation of Friedrich Schleiermacher's *Über die Schriften des Lukas, ein kritischer Versuch*, one of the first disclosures in English of the application of the "higher" German criticism to the New Testament, and a pamphlet supporting admission of Dissenters to academic degrees. The latter publication resulted in his being compelled to resign his post as tutor at Trinity in 1834. These events probably provided the basis of the report by Isabella, EFG's sister, on Thirlwall's character. As Bishop, he was an effective and fearless liberal in ecclesiastical controversies during his long and active career.

In mentioning "old Evans," EFG referred, not to a rival when Thirlwall was appointed Bishop, but to Robert W. Evans (1789-1866), Vicar of Tarvin, Cheshire, at the time, who had been tutor at Trinity from 1814-36.

[6] John Henry Newman (1801-90), B.A., Oxford, 1826, Fellow of Balliol, 1826-30. From 1828 to 1843 he held the living of St. Mary's, Oxford, where he established a reputation as a powerful and dynamic preacher. Five volumes of his *Parochial Sermons* had been published between 1835 and 1840. His activity and soul-searching as one of the leaders of the Oxford Movement led him to join the Roman Catholic Church in 1845. He was ordained priest the following year and in 1879 was created Cardinal.

[7] Probably Richard Cecil (1748-1810), distinguished and popular evangelical preacher in and near London from 1780 to 1810. A volume of his sermons had been published in 1839.

[8] *The Paris Sketch Book*, Thackeray's first published book, went on sale in July. About half of the tales and sketches that make up the two volumes had already appeared in periodicals. "Imitations of Béranger," vol. II, includes versions of FitzGerald's translations of "Le Roi D'Yvetot" and "Le Grenier" (see letter to Thackeray, April 5, 1837).

[9] EFG had been misinformed. The criticism of Carlyle's *French Revolution* in the *Edinburgh Review* (July, 1840, pp. 411-45) was by Herman Merivale (1806-74), brother of EFG's friend Charles Merivale, who became Dean of Ely. Herman Merivale was professor of political economy at Oxford at the time. He later became Under-Secretary for India.

[10] James Macpherson (1736-96), fabricator of the Ossianic and other poems, published 1760-63, which he claimed to have translated from Erse, the ancient Gaelic language of the Highlands.

[11] "But anything might happen in great length of time." *Herodotus*, V, 9.

To Bernard Barton

Bedford
Aug. 31/40

Dear Sir,

I duly received your letter. I am just returned from staying three days at a delightful Inn by the river Ouse, where we always go to fish. I dare say I have told you about it before. The Inn is the cleanest, the sweetest, the civillest, the quietest, the liveliest, and the cheapest that ever was built or conducted. Its name, the Falcon of Bletsoe. On one side it has a garden, then the meadows through which winds the Ouse: on the other, the public road, with its coaches hurrying on to London, its market people halting to drink, its farmers, horsemen, and foot travellers. So, as one's humour is, one can have whichever phase of life one pleases: quietude or bustle; solitude or the busy hum of men: one can sit in the principal room with a tankard and a pipe and see both these phases at once through the windows that open upon either. But through all these delightful places they talk of leading railroads:[1] a sad thing, I am sure: quite impolitic. But Mammon is blind.

I went a week ago to see Luton, Lord Bute's place;[2] filled with very fine pictures, of which I have dreamt since. It is the gallery in England that I most wish to see again: but I by no means say it is the most valuable. A great many pictures seemed to me misnamed—especially Correggio has to answer for some he never painted.

I am thinking of going to Naseby for a little while: after which I shall return here: and very likely find my way back to Norfolk before long. At all events, the middle of October will find me at Boulge, unless the Fates are very contrary.

[1] Bedford's first railway, connecting that town with Bletchley, was opened November 17, 1846.

[2] Luton Hoo, two miles south of the center of Luton, Bedfordshire, built in 1767 by Robert Adam, one of the family of famous architects, for John Stuart, third Earl of Bute. The Earl, confidant of and Secretary of State under George III, was also a botanist of repute; and Luton Hoo was notable for its botanical gardens as well as for its art collection. It stands on a slight eminence overlooking the River Lea. "Hoo" frequently terminates names of sites on hills (Edward Moor, *Suffolk Words and Phrases*, 1823).

To W. H. Thompson[1]

Bedford
Sept. 4/40

My dear Thompson,

I kept wondering why I did not get a letter from you a fortnight ago, and began to suppose you must have become worse. I am afraid you can scarce be called better if it is necessary that you must undergo another operation: which however I pray may be no painful one, and the last. I am glad you have gone to the best London surgeon.

I have been amusing myself down here as usual, with my friend W. Browne: the best of good fellows, and absolutely wanting in nothing that may become a man. We have been staying at an Inn by the side of the river Ouse: he fishes, etc. I do nothing as usual. A little riding, driving, eating, drinking, etc. (not forgetting smoke) fill up the day. I am now staying for a few days with an old school fellow, and fellow collegian, one W. Airy—brother of the Professor;[2] and I have just come in at half past eleven at night from escorting the aforesaid W. Browne a mile on his road to Bedford. Pretty and interesting all this circumstantiality to you: but positively I have nothing else to tell you of.

I am glad you like Violet: which seems to me happily touched: and, a rare thing, not too much of it. I think the writer must be a man: you say, a woman:—and when I lay down my pen for a minute and think, it seems to me also that a woman it must be. So my first and third thoughts agree: for at first I thought as you do—and Hare says "second thoughts are *not* best"—so toss up—woman!—woman it is.

A sort of devil-may-care man in these parts who does not set up for a wit, enunciated the following theorem the other day: and as he talks very little, and deals still less in general rules, it is worthy of attention. "Every thing that is, is—nothing is right—and main force is the ticket." I laughed very much when he gave it out. He is very grave in his manner, and seemed convinced of his proposition.

That old cut-away Spedding—the interior of Africa[3]—and old Alfred living for a fortnight at a madhouse.[4] We did not want that to finish his education, I think. I went yesterday to see a Clergyman near here who cultivates about 15,000 Dahlias—each with a little pole by its side, with a little flower pot reversed on the top, to catch earwigs in. He empties these earwig pots of their contents every morning. As you may imagine, he is not dangerous. This seems to me a tolerably sane county.

I must tell you I have been to see Lord Bute's place, Luton Park, twenty miles from Bedford. The collection of pictures is almost the best I have seen in England—a noble Cuyp, two fine Tintoretto's (far beyond Paul Veronese), a Valesquez, two grand N. Poussin landscapes, and a very great many others—so many that I was tired with looking. The Flemish and Dutch are counted the best. There is a Raffaelle insured for £15,000—I doubt if I would give 15,000 shillings for it: and I see that Waagen[5] in his book says nothing at all about it.

This is a very dull piece of goods in return for yours. But no reflection would make it better: so it shall go. I am vexed about Allen's Bishop dying:[6] but Johnny can't come to harm. Farewell, my dear Thompson: it was good of you to write to me. I shall make Spedding tell me how you get on in London.

Ever yours
E.FG.

[1] An intimate friend since EFG's undergraduate years. Thompson became Fellow of Trinity, 1832; Regius Professor of Greek, 1853; Master of Trinity, 1866. See Biographical Profile.

[2] William Airy, Vicar of Keysoe, nine miles north of Bedford. See Biographical Profile. He was the brother of George Biddell Airy (1801-92); professor of astronomy at Cambridge, 1828-36; and Astronomer Royal, 1835-81.

[3] Spedding's duties in the Colonial Office, where he served as under-secretary from 1835-41, had evidently taken him to Africa.

[4] While living at High Beech, Epping Forest, Tennyson had made the acquaintance of Dr. Matthew Allen, who, in 1825, had established an asylum for the insane at Fairmead, nearby. Allen had formerly been superintendent of the York Asylum. In 1831 he had published *Cases of Insanity* and, in 1837, *Essay on the Classification of the Insane* (J. W. and Anne Tibble, *John Clare*, New York, 1832, pp. 381-82). Considering the time in which he practiced, the doctor held enlightened theories about care of the insane. He advocated and practiced humane control of patients, for whom he provided normal occupations and diversions. In a letter (which Charles Tennyson assigns to July, 1840) James Spedding wrote to John Allen, "He [Tennyson] has been on a visit to a madhouse for the last fortnight (not as a patient), and has been delighted with the mad people, whom he reports the most agreeable and the most reasonable persons he has met with. The keeper is Dr. Allen (any relation of yours?), with whom he had been greatly taken" (W. Aldis Wright, "James Spedding," *Tennyson and His Friends*, ed. Hallam, Lord Tennyson, 1911, p. 408). Had Dr. Allen restricted his activities to treatment of the insane, he would have spared Tennyson considerable anguish and unhappiness. See letter from A. Tennyson, [February, 1841], n.2.

[5] Gustav Friedrich Waagen (1794-1868), German art historian. EFG no doubt

refers to his *Kunstwerke und Künstler in England und Paris*, 3 vols. (Berlin, 1837-39).

[6] William Otter (1768-1840), Bishop of Chichester, had died August 20. Allen had been appointed chaplain and lecturer in mathematics at King's College, London, in 1833 under Otter, the first principal, who, upon being made bishop in 1836, selected Allen as his examining chaplain. Through the bishop's influence, Allen, in 1839, was appointed one of the three original government inspectors of schools. EFG correctly predicted that "Johnny can't come to harm." John Lonsdale (1788-1867), the third principal under whom Allen served at King's College, was named Bishop of Lichfield in 1843; and in 1846 Allen was appointed Vicar of Prees, Shropshire, in that diocese. The following year he became Archdeacon of Salop.

To Bernard Barton

Holbrook
[October, 1840][1]

Dear Sir,

The faith of man!—it is proverbially bad—I cannot get home till Monday: and the sun of toasted Cheese must set for this week. But next week it shall rise anew, and warm us with redoubled ray—"Foul impious man," etc.[2] Crabbe—toasted Cheese—Gin and Water—what else is wanted but a Pipe—to complete the perfect Square of comfort. One night, devote your little room to *that*: let it be said for once—[3]

Farewell. Ever yours,

E.FG.

When I write this, I *believe* I cannot get away tomorrow: expect me not after 6.

[1] The date is that assigned by F. R. Barton, ed., *Some New Letters of Edward FitzGerald*, 1923, p. 23.

[2] With characteristic abandon, EFG misquotes "Fond impious Man" from Thomas Gray's "The Bard," l.135.

[3] EFG was chaffing Barton, who loathed tobacco, except in the form of snuff. EFG, George Crabbe, Vicar of Bredfield, and others of Barton's friends, however, enjoyed pipes and cigars. "The odour of that room after the first hour or two from the time of lighting up was really awful," Barton once complained to Crabbe after an evening spent at Boulge Cottage. "Have you ever tried the Guano? Marry, I smelt some the other day, and thought it wondrous like the residuary perfume left next morning by pipe, or cigar" (Bernard Barton MS letters to George Crabbe, February 1 and March 24, 1845, British Museum).

To Samuel Laurence[1]

Boulge Hall, Woodbridge
Nov. 9/40

Dear Laurence,

. . . We have had much rain which has hindered the sporting part of our company: but has not made much difference to me. One or two sunshiny days have made me say within myself, "how felicitously and at once would Laurence hit off an outline in this clear atmosphere." For this fresh sunlight is not a mere dead medium of light, but is so much vital champagne both to sitter and to artist. London will become worse as it becomes bigger, which it does every hour.

I don't see much prospect of my going to Cumberland this winter: though I should like to go snipe-shooting with that literary shot James Spedding. Do you mean to try and go up Skiddaw?[2] You will get out upon it from your bedroom window: so I advise you to begin before you go down to breakfast. There is a mountain called Dod, which has felt me upon its summit. It is not one of the highest in that range. Remember me to Grisedale Pike; a very well-bred mountain. If you paint [Hartley Coleridge][3] put him not only in a good light, but to leeward of you in a strong current of air. . . .

Farewell for the present.

[1] Except for the letter of September 10, 1838, the text of FitzGerald's letters to Samuel Laurence, one of his chief correspondents, is taken from the *Letters and Literary Remains*. The original manuscripts appear not to have survived, so the editors have been unable to restore Aldis Wright's numerous deletions. For data on Samuel Laurence, the Victorian portrait painter, see Biographical Profile.

[2] Spedding apparently had invited both FitzGerald and Laurence to visit him at Mirehouse, located on the east shore of Bassenthwaite Lake. Skiddaw looms to 3,053 feet, less than two miles behind the house. FitzGerald had climbed Dod, 1,612 feet, a mile to the southeast, with Spedding and Tennyson while at Mirehouse in May, 1835. Southwestward, across the lake, Grisedale Pike rises to 2,593 feet.

[3] Aldis Wright left a blank at this point in the *Letters and Literary Remains*. In a copy of the 1889 edition in Trinity College Library, a marginal note reads "Hartley Coleridge." The notation was probably made by Wright.

To Bernard Barton

[Geldestone][1]
[November, 1840]

Dear Barton,

My friend W. Browne of Bedford is just about to go off as Surveyor of Taxes to Carlisle—"the city of pleasant waters" as you called it in language more suitable to Cheltenham or Harrogate. Do you know any good folks in that part of the world?[2] Poor fellow, he leaves his old home because his screw of a father won't do anything for him, and cannot be grateful enough that he has begotten a Gentleman. He would have him live on a shilling a day. Henceforth I have no one to call me to the dear old Ouse—bless its idle windings—farewell to Turvey, and Olney, and all the pretty places.[3] Hang me if I couldn't cry, and spit in the face of old Browne at the same time. I will marry or go hang. It is wrong to talk in this way: but really the old gentleman has

> "Like a base Indian thrown a pearl away
> Richer than all his tribe."[4]

For is not the heart of a Gentleman (N.B. not an Esquire) better than the whole Art of Skinning Flints as practised from the earliest ages.

When do you go to Norwich? I shall perhaps pass through it the very end of this week or the beginning of next on my way to Cambridgeshire.

E.FG.

[1] F. R. Barton erroneously conjectured that this letter was written from Halverstown.

[2] Barton was probably of little help in providing FitzGerald with the names of "good folks" in Carlisle. His father had engaged in business there but left Cumberland for London shortly before Barton was born.

[3] It appears that the plan to transform the ideal country gentleman into a Surveyor of Taxes was never carried out. FitzGerald's visits to Browne and Bedford continued without interruption.

[4] "Then you must speak," says Othello to Lodovico, after the death of Desdemona,

> of one whose hand,
> Like the base Indian, threw a pearl away
> Richer than all his tribe. . . .
> *Othello*, V.2.346-48

To Bernard Barton[1]

[Geldestone]
[November 30, 1840]

My dear Barton,

Did you read in the papers that Daddy Wordsworth had been capsized in a gig?[2] What a Sonnet he will make on it—I am going to write one for him.

Ever yours,
E.FG.

On my being upset while driven by my nephew (or son?) John in his Gig—on the night of Nov. (11)[3] 1840.

Late was it when the venerable man,
By pious hands not unattended, sat
In Tilbury[4]—a fort more frail than that
In which the warlike Queen her toils began:[5]
When suddenly, driv'n by some "saucy groom",
With fearful lamps discomfiting the gloom,
The mail against him like a whirlwind ran.

And but that the awful Genius of the Land
Received him softly on her bosom green,
And soothed his forehead with a Mother's hand,
That more than mitred head,[6] that dwells half-seen
In Granta's shades, had vain lamentings made:
Europe had wept:—perchance Lucina[7] stay'd
Her helping hand from England's laboring Queen.
W.W.

1 The text of this letter is taken from a transcript filed among the FitzGerald papers in Trinity College Library.

2 William Wordsworth had been dubbed "Daddy" by EFG while at Cambridge, to the delight of his companions. On November 20, the poet was returning to his home at Ambleside, Cumberland, in a gig driven by his eldest son John, a clergyman. Suddenly, from around a sharp turn in the road a mail coach bore down "at a rattling pace" upon the light carriage. The vehicles collided "with such force that both horse and the gig and the two riders were thrown . . . into the adjoining plantation." The poet, the *Annual Register* recorded, suffered "a slight bruise on the finger" ("Chronicle," 1840, pp. 107-08).

3 EFG appears to have dated the incident from memory, writing "(11)" to indicate uncertainty. The *Annual Register* dates the incident.

4 Tilbury, a light vehicle resembling the two-wheeled gig. At Tilbury, Essex,

on the Thames opposite Gravesend, stands Tilbury Fort, built by Henry VIII and enlarged by Charles II for the defense of the river.

[5] On the advice of her physicians, Queen Victoria had returned to Buckingham Palace from Windsor Castle on November 13. On Saturday, November 21, she gave birth to her first child, Victoria, the Princess Royal.

[6] Christopher Wordsworth (1774-1846), the poet's brother, Master of Trinity, 1820-41. He was not especially popular with the undergraduates of EFG's generation, who irreverently referred to him as "the Mēēserable Sinner."

[7] Lucina, in Roman mythology, the goddess who presided over childbirth.

To W. F. Pollock

Boulge Hall
Feb^r 10/41

PROLOGUE[1]

When dirty Jacobs, thirty years of age,
With greasy gladness trod the early stage,
Astonished Gurlow caught the grace he bore,
And so transplanted it to Albion's shore:
Charmed the fair daughters of our sunny isle
With Sorrow's tear and Joy's Celestial smile.
As dirty Jacobs wreath'd his laurelled brow,
So *we* presume upon your patience now.
When moral James gave way to thumbless Shoots:
When gory Pritchard seiz'd the proffered boots;
When Berdmore bawl'd his sacrilegious verse,
And heedless Phipps upset his Uncle's hearse:
With hiccupped murmurs see their spirits rise,
In fleecy sinews mellowing the skies.
And can they die? Ah no! their transient sway
Still glimmers through the mist of Freedom's day:
The sword revengeful severs and forgets,
And murderer's wrongs are fresh in female threats.
He spits! he bleeds! with anguish slaked he reels!
May Fortune's adverse whirlwind blast his heels!
May the same fire that prompted Isaac Huggans
To kill his wife, and then to eat his young ones,
Purge the dark brotherhood with sorrow's fill—
The dastard fiends that wrought a woman ill.
Pardon expression, gentles—Time may bring

Her calmer hour on circumambient wing:
Fair gales may blow again; but if they slight ye,
Then seek the advised track *Fallentis Vitæ*,
And then *in rure* manifestly *beato*
Cull the fair rose, and dig the brown potatoe:
Or watch at eve beneath the favourite tree
The wily worm, or more industrious bee:
And if on loftier themes you're bent than this,
The beetle's silken metamorphosis—
Joys by which fond simplicity and Truth
Amuse the elder and excite the Youth.
Here in your lone retreat with wife and daughter,
Cold loin of mutton and your rum and water,
When conversation deadens, and the mind
Unconscious casts one fleeting look behind,
Remember Jacobs—and 'mid seas of strife,
Be he the beacon of your future life:
And if a second could increase your hope,
Behold in me an enemy to soap.

E.W.C.

There, Pollock, don't you think I'm a gentleman? Did you expect such treatment from me? Luckily for you, *my farming* is a good deal hindered by these demnition snows and frosts; in fact, we can only thresh in the barn, and hedge and ditch a little—all which, you know, when you have set your men to work, requires but little supervision[2]—so that I have time on my hands to write out Prologues. I have read Gibbon's Decline and Fall till I have got a headache: and live in perfect solitude at present: except for my sister's Bullfinch.

Is the new Tale of a Tub published?[3] I could not hear of it before I left London. In this state of the weather, and of the land—when I cannot cull the fair Rose and dig the Brown Potatoe, when conversation does not so much deaden as not exist—what a pleasure to remember Jacobs. Farewell.

Ever yours,
E.FG.

How goes on old Jemmy Wood's cause?[4]

[1] "In another copy FitzGerald has added, 'Spoken by E. W. Clarke at some private Theatricals in Downing College, Cambridge, Mrs. Siddons looking on'" (Aldis Wright note, *Letters and Literary Remains*, I, 92). The entertainment, it is clear, had been arranged by Mrs. William Frere, wife of the Master of Downing

(see letter to F. Tennyson, April 10, 1839, n.6; for E. W. Clarke, see letter to Thackeray, Nov. 29, 1838, n.4). Persons alluded to in the "Prologue" remain unidentified despite a search.

[2] EFG supervised the family estates at Boulge and Naseby while his father was engaged in his coal mining venture at Castle Irwell, Manchester.

[3] *The New Tale of a Tub*; or, *Adventures in Verse*, by Frederick W.N.B. Bayley (1807-52), was published in the spring of 1841. Bayley, the first editor of the *Illustrated London News*, wrote miscellaneous prose and verse.

[4] Pollock recorded in his *Personal Remembrances*, "After returning to London [in the spring of 1841] I had a very interesting employment in digesting the evidence in the famous Wood's will case—then on appeal before the Privy Council—and went to see the original will and the partially burnt codicil at Doctor's Commons" (I, 174). James Wood, unmarried, draper and banker of Gloucester, had died April 20, 1836, leaving an estate of almost £800,000. Three separate testamentary documents naming different beneficiaries had been submitted to the courts as the will of the deceased. Other papers bearing on the disposition of the estate, it was alleged, had been burned. In 1841, while the case was still in litigation, it was estimated that the value of the estate had increased to almost £1,200,000 (*Annual Register*, "Chronicle," 1840, pp. 184-94; 1841, pp. 74-75).

To W. F. Pollock

[Boulge Hall]
[c. February 15, 1841]

Dear Pollock,

Without losing one single instant, whether you are at meal, at business, or on the W——r-Closet, rush off to some Divan,[1] Club, or Bookseller's, and forcibly read the last sentence of an Article called "The Emperor Nicholas" in the British and Foreign Review.[2] It must annihilate the party in question: he will either die, kill himself, or abdicate. It made *me* tremble. The edict I sent you last year about the Brown Bread Makers is nothing to it.[3] I am bewildered as I write—but God bless you. Ever yours,

E.FG.

P.S. There is also an astonishing Article on Pindar's Odes by Edgeworth: it has quite floored me. Then there's an account of Hallam's Literature, with a deal about *Aesthetics* in it. Oh Pollock! let you and I and Spedding stand out against these damnable German humbugs. You lawyers are pretty safe, I think: so is Spedding constitutionally: and I will swear not to let my unfurnished head to any such foreigneering customers—who never pay for their lodging. I am not unfit for a victim: but I have had warning. Let us read Addison, Fielding etc., and fart without thinking why.[4]

Now that I am about it, I must transcribe for you a charming passage of Gibbon's History. He is describing the two Gordians—Father and Son—who were made Emperors once on a time—"With the venerable proconsul, his son, who had accompanied him into Africa as his lieutenant, was likewise declared Emperor. His manners were less pure, but his character was equally amiable with that of his Father. Twenty-two acknowledged Concubines, and a library of 62,000 volumes attested the variety of his inclinations: and from the productions which he left behind him, it appears that the former as well as the latter were designed for use rather than ostentation."[5] Is not this pleasant reading? Let Empires decline to such a tune. Tell Spedding I have treasured up a small note out of Gibbon for him—it is too *beastly* to insert in a letter to you. Ask him if he does not think Celia's falling in love with Oliver, in As You Like It, a very clumsy contrivance. She might have remained a maid.

[1] Public smoking parlors where newspapers and magazines were available to patrons. See letter to Thackeray, Oct. 10, 1831, n.6.

[2] The sentence reads: "There is *one* man in Europe who on reading this article will acknowledge in his soul that we have spoken the truth, for he is cognizant of the truth in all its hideous horror—that man is the Czar of Russia!" The 48-page essay, which the statement concludes, appeared in the winter issue of Kemble's *British and Foreign Review* (XI, 1840, 543-91). The article, which bears a double title, "The Emperor Nicholas" and "The Present Government of Russia" appraises Nicholas's domestic and foreign policies—"no easy task . . . since it is the nature of despotic governments artfully to conceal one portion of their deeds and to misrepresent the other." For Kemble and the *British and Foreign Review*, see letter to Thackeray, Sept. 1, 1837, nn.4 and 5.

[3] See letter to Pollock, Feb. 3, 1840.

[4] For further comments on the subject, see letter to Thompson, Feb. 18.

[5] *History of the Decline and Fall of the Roman Empire*, H. H. Milman, ed., 6 vols., Philadelphia, 1869, I, 205.

To W. H. Thompson

Boulge Hall, Woodbridge
Pmk., February 18, 1841

Doesn't this name express heavy clay?

My dear Thompson,

I wish you would write to me ten lines to say how you are. You are, I suppose, at Cambridge:[1] and I am buried (with all my fine parts—what a shame!) here: so that I hear of nobody—except that Spedding and I abuse each other about Shakespeare occasionally: a subject on which you must know that he has lost his conscience, if ever he had any. For what did Dr. Allen (A. Tennyson's mad Doctor)[2] say when he felt Spedding's head? Why, that all his bumps were so tempered that there was no merit in his sobriety—then what would have been the use of a Conscience to him: Q.E.D.

Since I saw you, I have entered into a decidedly Agricultural course of conduct: read books about composts, etc. I walk about in the fields also where the people are at work, and the more dirt accumulates on my shoes, the more I think I know. Is not this all funny? Gibbon might elegantly compare my retirement from the cares and splendours of the world to that of Diocletian. Have you read Thackeray's little book—the Second Funeral of Napoleon? If not, pray do; and buy it, and ask others to buy it: as each copy sold puts 7½d. in T.'s pocket: which is very empty just now, I take it.[3] I think this book is the best thing he has done. What an account there is of the Emperor Nicholas in Kemble's last Review—the last sentence of it (which can be by no other man in Europe but Jack himself) has been meat and drink to me for a fortnight. The electric eel at the Adelaide Gallery is nothing to it. Then Edgeworth fires away about the Odes of Pindar, and Donne is very aesthetic about Mr. Hallam's Book.[4] What is the meaning of "exegetical"? Till I know that, how can I understand the Review?

Pray remember me kindly to Blakesley, Heath,[5] and such other potentates as I knew in the days before they "assumed the purple." I am reading Gibbon, and see nothing but this d——d colour before my eyes. It changes occasionally to bright yellow, which is (is it?) the Imperial colour in China, and also the antithesis to purple (*vide* Coleridge and Eastlake's Goethe)—even as the Eastern and Western Dynasties are antithetical, and yet, by the law of extremes, potentially the same (*vide* Coleridge, etc.) Is this aesthetic? is this exegetical? How glad I shall be if you can assure me that it is. But, nonsense apart and begged-pardon-for, pray write me a line to say how you are, directing to this pretty place. "The soil is in general a moist and retentive clay: with a subsoil or pan of an adhesive siliceous brick formation: adapted to the growth of wheat, beans, and clover—requiring however a summer fallow (as is generally stipulated in the lease) every fourth year," etc. This is not an unpleasing style on Agricultural subjects—nor an uncommon one.

Ever yours
E.FG.

[1] Thompson at this time was an assistant tutor at Trinity.

[2] Dr. Matthew Allen, promoter of "pyroglyph," was a phrenologist as well as a physician for the insane. Carlyle had made his acquaintance in 1817 when Allen lectured on phrenology at Kircaldy, Fifeshire. It was through Allen that Tennyson first met Carlyle, possibly in the fall of 1840 (D. A. Wilson, *Carlyle Till Marriage*, pp. 204-05; *Carlyle on Cromwell and Others*, pp. 121-22).

[3] *The Second Funeral of Napoleon*, Thackeray's account of the return of Napoleon's remains from St. Helena for burial in the Hôtel des Invalides, had been published in London early in January. The author wrote from Paris on the 10th that he hoped EFG would buy the book "as 7½ out of the 2/6 will come to me" (*Thackeray Letters and Papers*, II, 4).

EFG's attempt to promote sales of the booklet was one of his many efforts to aid his friend in his struggle for recognition and financial security during his apprentice years. Numerous passages in Thackeray's correspondence of the 1830's and early 1840's contain acknowledgments of sums of money given or lent to him by EFG. In January, 1840, Thackeray, who had "been obliged to spunge" on EFG, "sent him some of the money back: and received a letter in return as follows 'What the devil do you mean?'—my [Thackeray's] £10 note was enclosed in the letter" (ibid., I, 420). After Thackeray's wife suffered a mental breakdown in August, 1840, he placed her in an asylum in France. "A couple of months hence," he wrote to EFG the following January, "I shall ask you to pay my wife's pension for a month, a heavy sum £20" (II, 4). "I must say that I believe Fitz would give W. his last shilling," Thackeray's wife had written July 3, 1839 (I, 388).

[4] "The Odes of Pindar" by Francis Edgeworth is a review of *Pindari Carmina*, edited by L. Dissenius, 2 vols., Göttingen, 1830; W. B. Donne's essay reviews volumes II, III, and IV of Henry Hallam's *Introduction to the Literature of Europe in the Fifteenth, Sixteenth, and Seventeenth Centuries*, published in 1839 (Edgeworth's essay, *British and Foreign Review*, Vol. XI, No. 22, 1840, pp. 510-42; Donne's, pp. 355-416). For Kemble's article, see letter to Pollock, [c. Feb. 15, 1841], n.2.

At the time EFG might well have inquired about the meaning of "exegetical." The *NED* gives 1823 for the application of "exegesis" to "interpretation of the Scriptures," and notes the use of "exegetical" in 1838.

[5] For Joseph Blakesley, see letter to Donne, Oct. 23, 1836, n.1; for Douglas Heath, see letter to Allen, May 16, 1830, n.7.

To Mrs. John Charlesworth[1]

Boulge
Wednesday [? February, 1841]

My dear Mrs. Charlesworth,

Isabella gives us some hope of Miss Charlesworth's Company tomorrow. I do not send the carriage, because I cannot send a close[d] one:—and this is not weather to travel in any other. Had Isabella arranged her plans so as to have let us know of them before today, we could have managed better. But she is pretty generally in a whirl of plans, which the common race of mortals cannot keep pace with.

You must therefore excuse our inhospitality. My only hope is that Miss Charlesworth will guess pretty well at the little obstacles that arise in matters of this kind (more especially at Boulge)—and so pardon. I shall send down to Woodbridge to meet the Shannon: so if she does take the trouble to come by it, she will at least not be left there.

I am always talking of going over to see you: and I really hope to do so *one* day. The reason that one does it not is that one can do it any day: an old human perversity, I understand.

Please to give my kind regards however to Mr. Charlesworth and such of your family as I have the pleasure of knowing.

Ever yours truly
E. FitzGerald

[1] The wife of John Charlesworth, Rector of Flowton, near Ipswich. See Biographical Profile of the Cowells.

From Alfred Tennyson

[Mablethorpe, Alford]
[February, 1841]

Dear old Fitz,

Not on the "western" on the eastern coast. Mablethorpe[1] near Alford in the fat shire of Lincoln is the place where I am. Curse not anything till you see what it brings forth—not even pyroglyphs.[2] I walk about the coast here and have it to myself, sand and sea. You bore me about my book: so does a letter just received from America, threatening, tho' in the civilest terms, that if I will not publish in England they will do it for me in that land of freemen—Damn!—I *may* curse knowing what they will bring forth, but I don't care.[3] I am in great haste waiting for the muffin-man, my only communication with the world, who comes once a week, bringing the produce of his art, and also what letters may be stagnating in the Alford post—waits five minutes and then returns. I have several other letters to write, so farewell. But first—I want to know what has become of your stewardship.[4] Always yours

AT

[1] Mablethorpe, a village on the Lincolnshire coast near Somersby, Tennyson's birthplace, had been a favorite summer resort of the poet's family. EFG wrote in

1863 that Tennyson "should never have left his old Country. . . . He has lost that which caused the long roll of the Lincolnshire Wave to reverberate in the measure of Locksley Hall."

[2] Tennyson's friend, Dr. Matthew Allen, who operated a mental hospital near High Beech (see Thompson letter, Sept. 4, 1840, n.3), in 1840 undertook to promote the Patent Decorative Carving and Sculpture Company to produce carved wood paneling and furniture by machinery at low cost. Allen called his product "Pyroglyph," and convinced Tennyson that investors would reap fortunes when his products were offered for sale at moderate prices. The poet converted all his assets into cash and turned more than £3,000 over to him (C. Tennyson, *Tennyson*, p. 186). The doctor was unsuccessful in efforts to persuade Frederick to risk a like sum in November, 1841; but other members of the family did speculate. In a letter to Frederick dated March 4, 1843, Allen, in anguish, confessed that the venture was a dismal failure, and the Tennysons lost every penny they had staked. Alfred was plunged into despair. "I have," he wrote, "drunk one of those most bitter draughts out of the cup of life, which go near to make men hate the world they move in" (*Memoir*, I, 221). He fell into a state of hypochondria from which he did not fully emerge until he published his "best seller," *In Memoriam*, in 1850. See letter to Barton, Jan. 17, 1845.

[3] Except for an occasional poem contributed under pressure to what he termed "vapid Annuals," Tennyson had published nothing since 1832. Edward Moxon, his publisher, wanted to issue a second edition of the 1832 volume; and most of his friends constantly urged him to venture again into print; but EFG, who was particularly persistent, had reported in 1839 that Tennyson was "too lazy and wayward to put his hand to the business."

The letter from America to which Tennyson refers had been written by Charles S. Wheeler of Harvard, who offered to prepare the old poems for publication in Boston. Before the month was out Tennyson responded that he would "in the course of a few months republish them in England . . . and transmit copies to Little & Brown" (C. Tennyson, *Tennyson*, pp. 188-89). However, another year was to pass; and EFG was compelled eventually to resort to "violence" before Tennyson submitted his manuscript to Moxon. See letter to Barton, March 2, 1842.

[4] By "your stewardship" Tennyson probably refers to EFG's supervision of the Boulge and Naseby estates.

☞ To Frederick Tennyson

For *Mortellari* read *Mortaletti*[1] through this letter.

Boulge Hall, Woodbridge
March 21, [1841]

Dear Frederic Tennyson,

I was very glad indeed to get a letter from you this morning. You here may judge, by the very nature of things, that I lose no time in answering it. I did not receive your Sicilian letter: and have been for a year and a half quite ignorant of what part of the world you were in. I supposed you were alive: though I don't quite know why. De non existentibus et non apparentibus eadem est ratio.[2] I heard from Morton three months ago: he was then at Venice: very tired of it: but lying on such luxurious sofas that he could not make up his mind to move from them. He wanted to meet you: or at all events to hear of you. I wrote to him, but could tell him nothing. I have also seen Alfred once or twice since you have gone: he is to be found in certain conjunctions of the stars at No. 8 Charlotte Street with a little bit of dirty pipe in his mouth: and a particularly dirty vellum book of MSS on the sofa. He lives also in great intimacy, as you may have heard, with one Dr. Allen, a mad Doctor at High Beech:[3] who is very mad himself. All our other friends are in statu quo: Spedding residing calmly in Lincoln's Inn Fields: at the Colonial all day:[4] at the play and smoking at night: occasionally to be found in the Edinburgh Review. Pollock and the Lawyer tribe travel to and fro between their Chambers in the Temple and Westminster Hall: occasionally varying their travels, when the Chancellor chooses, to the Courts in Lincoln's Inn. As to me, I am fixed here where your letter found me: very rarely going to London: and staying there but a short time when I do go. You, Morton, Spedding, Thackeray, and Alfred, were my chief solace there: and only Spedding is now to be found. Thackeray lives in Paris.[5]

From this you may judge that I have no such sights to tell of as you have. Neither do *mortellari* ever go off at Boulge: which is perhaps not to be regretted. Day follows day with unvaried movement: there is the same level meadow with geese upon it always lying before my eyes: the same pollard oaks: with now and then the butcher or the washerwoman trundling by in their carts. As you have lived in Lincolnshire I will not further describe Suffolk. No new books (except a perfectly insane one of Carlyle,[6] who is becoming very obnoxious now that he is become popular), nor new pictures, no music. A game at picquet of two hours' duration closes each day. But for that I might say with Titus—perdidi diem. Oh Lord! all this is not told you that you may admire my philosophic quietude, etc.; pray don't think that. I should travel like you if [I] had the eyes to see that you have: but, as Goethe says, the eye can but see what it brings with it the power of seeing. If anything I had seen in my short travels had given me any new ideas worth having I should travel more: as it is, I see your Italian lakes and cities in the Picturesque Annuals as well as I should in the reality. You have a more energetic, stirring, acquisitive, and capacious soul. I mean all this seriously, believe me: but I won't say any more about it. Morton also is a capital traveller: I wish he would keep notes of what he sees, and publish them one day.

I must however tell you that I am becoming a Farmer! Can you believe in this? I hope we shall both live to laugh over it together. When do you mean to come back? Pray do not let so long a time elapse again without writing to me: never mind a long letter: write something to say you are alive and where. Rome certainly is nearer England than Naples: so perhaps you are coming back. Bring Morton back with you. I will then go to London and we will smoke together and be as merry as sandboys. We will all sit under the calm shadow of Spedding's forehead.[7] People talk of a war with America.[8] Poor dear old England! she makes a gallant shew in her old age. If Englishmen are to travel, I am glad that such as you are abroad—good specimens of Englishmen: with the proper *fierté* about them. The greater part are poor wretches that go to see oranges growing, and hear Bellini[9] for eighteenpence. I hope the English are as proud and disagreeable as ever. What an odd thing that the Italians like such martial demonstrations as you describe—not at all odd, probably—their spirit begins and goes off in noise and smoke. It is like all other grand aspirations. So Milnes' Epics crepitate in Sonnets. All I ask of you is to write no Sonnets on what you see or hear—no sonnets can sound well after Daddy Wordsworth, Milnes,[10] etc., who have now succeeded in quite spoiling one's pleasure in Milton's—and they are heavy things. The words "subjective and objective" are getting into general use now: and Donne has begun with *aesthetics* and *exegetical* in Kemble's review. Kemble himself has written an article on the Emperor Nicholas which must crush him.[11] If you could read it, no salvos of *mortellari* could ever startle you again. And now my paper is almost covered: and I must say Good bye to you. This is Sunday March 21—a fine sunny blowing day. We shall dine at one o'clock—an hour hence—go to Church—then walk—have tea at six, and pass rather a dull evening, because of no picquet. You will be sauntering in St. Peter's perhaps, or standing on the Capitol while the sun sets. I should like to see Rome after all. Livy's lies (as the aesthetics prove them to be) do at least animate one so far—how far?—so far as to wish, and not to do, having perfect power to do.

Oh eloquent, just, and mighty Theory of Mortaletti![12]

Ever yours,
E.FG.

[1] *Mortaletto* (plural, *mortaletti*) means, literally, a small military mortar. It is most commonly applied to the device used to discharge fireworks. Metaphorically, it means an eruption of great enthusiasm or joy. In one of his letters Frederick had evidently described an Italian feast-day celebration. The variations in spelling appear in EFG's MS.

[2] The law maxim reads: "De non apparentibus et de non existentibus eadem est ratio." (The reasoning is the same about what does not appear to exist and what does not exist.)

[3] See letter to Thompson, Sept. 4, 1840, n.4.

[4] Spedding had taken his post at the Colonial Office at a yearly salary of £150, expecting that a permanent appointment would eventually be offered him. "For six years," Sir Henry Taylor wrote in his *Autobiography*, "Spedding worked away with universal approbation, and all this time he would have been willing to accept a post of précis writer with £300 a year, or any other such recognized position. . . . But none such was placed at his disposal" (Quoted from W. Aldis Wright's "James Spedding," *Tennyson and His Friends*, p. 405).

[5] Thackeray had remained in Paris after placing his wife in a mental hospital in France the previous fall. He did not return to England until the summer of 1841.

[6] *On Heroes, Hero Worship, and the Heroic in History*, Carlyle's published version of six lectures which he had delivered the previous spring. Carlyle's struggle for recognition and a livelihood had been long and arduous. The lectures on heroes were the last of four series which he had reluctantly delivered between 1837 and 1840. EFG attended them and reported Carlyle's "agony" while speaking. "He looked very handsome then," EFG wrote in 1876, "with his black hair, fine Eyes, and a sort of crucified Expression."

[7] Spedding's high and impressive forehead is frequently the object of EFG's affectionate banter.

Sandboys: *NED* cites a proverbial phrase, "As merry as sandboys," and adds, "Perhaps a boy who hawks sand for sale."

[8] Since the close of the American Revolution diplomatic relations between Great Britain and the United States had been far from amicable, and threats of war were sometimes uttered. While the bellicose Lord Palmerston served as Minister of Foreign Affairs during the 1830's, friction often marred negotiations between the two nations. In 1840 a fresh crisis had arisen as the result of Britain's claim to the right of search of foreign ships by her naval vessels stationed off the African coast to suppress slave trade. In September, 1841, Palmerston was succeeded in the Foreign Office by Lord Aberdeen, whose more diplomatic methods led to the creation of the Ashburton Commission, which resolved a number of the issues causing ill-feeling.

[9] Vincenzo Bellini (1802-35), composer who wrote *Il Pirata*, *I Puritani*, and other operas EFG mentions in his letters.

[10] Richard Monckton Milnes in 1840 had published two volumes, *Memorials of Many Scenes* and *Poetry for the People and Other Poems*. *Memorials* contained a group of sonnets written during a visit to Italy in 1831. By "Milnes' Epics" EFG probably alludes to his friend's tendency to dwell on particulars and details, which resulted, one critic noted, in an "injudicious expansion." Aldis Wright, prompted by delicacy, omitted Milnes' name from this letter and that of July 26 to F. Tennyson.

[11] See letter to Pollock [c. Feb. 15, 1841], n.2.

[12] In his MS, EFG crossed out *Mortellari* at this point and substituted *Mortalletti.*

To. W. H. Thompson

Boulge Hall, Woodbridge
March 26/41

My dear Thompson,

Thank you for your letter: had I known you were in the middle of a Classical Tripos,[1] I should not have expected an answer. But I am really glad you are so well.

Now that the Examination is done, and you can meditate leisurely on what mistakes and injustices you have committed—will you do me a little or great favour? We are going to build a Church at Woodbridge: by subscription[2]—some people give £100—some 1s.—aren't you in a horrid fright lest I'm going to ask you? But what I want is this: I want the people here (when the proper sum is got) to build a church something like that new red brick chapel at Barnwell: which always remains on my mind as one of the best modern things I have seen. You have a hand in these matters at Cambridge—and perhaps can tell me something about this—how large is the Chapel; how many people it holds—what was the expense of building it?—or do you know of any printed account that will tell one?—or, who is the Architect? that is the shortest way.

After all this, the people here would think such a building very vulgar—all only as people being afraid of red brick. Now red brick is the proper English component—is it not?

I have heard from Donne that Blakesley is about to be m—rr—d one of these days.[3] When are you to be so, Thompson? I am sure you will be: for every man who is worth anything gets married when he can—except Spedding: who is altogether such an anomaly and scoffer that I have done with him.

I had a long letter from Morton the other day—he is still luxuriating at Venice. Also a letter from Frederic Tennyson, who has been in Sicily, etc., and is much distracted between enjoyment of those climates and annoyance from Fleas. These two men are to be at Rome together soon: so if any one wants to go to Rome, now is a good time. I wish I was there. F. Tennyson says that he and a party of Englishmen fought a cricket match with the crew of the Bellerophon on the *Parthenopoean hills* (query about the correctness of this—I quote from memory), and *sacked* the sailors by ninety runs. Is not this pleasant?—the notion of good English blood striving in worn out Italy—I like that such men as Frederic should be abroad: so strong, haughty and passionate. They keep up the English character abroad. Fancy his rage, when asked too much for a watermelon—he used to say to cab men—"if you say any more, I'll mash you."

Have you read poor Carlyle's raving book about heroes?[4] Of course you have—or I would ask you to buy my copy. I don't like to live with it in the house. It smoulders. He ought to be laughed at a little. But it is pleasant to retire to the Tale of a Tub, Tristram Shandy, and Horace Walpole, after being tossed on his canvas waves. This is blasphemy. Dibdin Pitt of the Coburg[5] could enact one of his heroes: he, who in comic parts, always came on the stage with his flap down, to excite harmless merriment. So Thackeray said.

E.FG.

[1] The final honors examination.

[2] St. John's Church, completed in 1843 at a cost of £3,500. EFG's fellow-citizens were not impressed by his preference in architecture: St. John's is Early English.

[3] Joseph W. Blakesley, at the time tutor at Trinity, did not marry until he was appointed to the living of Ware, Hertfordshire, in 1845. He married Margaret Wilson Holmes of Brooke, Norwich.

[4] *Heroes and Hero Worship.* "It smoulders," EFG adds, perhaps recalling a message on the title page of Carlyle's *Chartism*, "It never smokes but there is fire."

[5] George Dibden Pitt, actor and playwright. The Royal Coburg Theater in Waterloo Road, renamed the Royal Victoria in 1833, is now the Old Vic.

To Bernard Barton

London, Saturday
[April 24, 1841]

My dear Barton,

I was at breakfast with my Father at Portland Place this morning when your letter came. In walking back to my own lodgings I have laid out twopence sterling: 1d on a bunch of wall flowers which inspire something of the salubrious country air into this d——d heavy smutty atmosphere—and the other 1d on a pen: with which I may, and do, endite an answer to you. For know, that my heart warms to old Suffolk after this short absence from it—I hate this place—have a confused headache, etc. But this is all personal and offensive. However I can't get back to Woodbridge till Saturday, I believe. I should like well to see your brother:[1] you must make him stay a week with you.

There is a grand article in the new Edinburgh against Newman and Tract 90[2]—not a very good article: what Truth is in it is true, as you may imagine: but it need not have been told. Newman is doubtless a humbug: but Plato expressly asserts that all wise governors may lie a little, seasonably. This is a doctrine which the wiser Egyptians would have kept esoterically, and involved in symbol.

I spent yesterday in walking about in the wet to my favourite pawn brokers. Nothing very bad to be got just now. A sketch by Constable—£3—quite genuine—and not a bit the better for that. Shall I buy you a capital head of Handel by Sir Joshua's master, Hudson[3]—£30? I think seriously of buying the head of an old man for £1. The owner assures me it is the portrait of Stothard:[4] that some of that painter's family came into the shop and identified it. Now why did they not buy it?

Then I went to see the Gallery of Modern Painters in Suffolk St. a sort of sham Exhibition. There was one delicious picture of Jacques sitting by a stream "under the shade of melancholy boughs" contemplating the wounded hart who comes to die there. The branches meet close and dark over his head and far down the river: only at the extremity the forest ends, and you see a glimpse of level pasture land all sunshine. Then there's Miss Helen Faucit, all in black velvet, with a little bit of jessamine in her bosom, which makes one fall in love with her.[5] And lots of pretty things besides. In another hour I shall be again on foot picture-hunting. There is such an odd picture of Christ and his Apostles to be got for £3—so quaint, ugly, and solemn. They are all dwarfs, and very ill made. Yet there is more in them than in West's and Westhall's[6] five foot ten imperturbables. The wind is South West too: how much better for lounging than yesterday's North East.

Enough of this chatter—and farewell

E.FG.

I trust Miss Barton is better—much better.

[1] John Barton, a half-brother. See letter to John Barton, Sept. 17, 1844, n.1.

[2] "Tracts for the Times—Number 90" appeared in the *Edinburgh Review* for April, 1841. In his essay, "Remarks on Certain Passages in the Thirty-nine Articles," John Henry Newman (1801-90) maintained that the Articles of the Anglican Church were directed at popular errors and abuses but not at the authorized creed of the primitive Catholic Church. The reviewer in the *Edinburgh* claimed that Newman and his fellow Tracterians "on all great points which separate Protestants from Roman Catholics . . . side more with the old society than with their own church." The review further charged that *Tract 90* "teaches men to be reckless of what assertions they make . . . provided only verbal sophistry and special pleading may enable them to retain hold of the letter" (*Edinburgh Review*, April, 1841, pp. 271-72 and 297).

Although EFG concludes that "Newman is doubtless a humbug," he described the clergyman's *Apologia pro Vita sua*, when it was published in 1864, as "pathetic, eloquent, and, I think, sincere."

[3] Thomas Hudson (1701-79), chiefly known as the artist to whom Sir Joshua Reynolds was apprenticed and for his portraits of Handel and of George II.

[4] Thomas Stothard, painter and illustrator. EFG appears to have bought this picture for Barton. See letter to Barton, [c. June 1, 1845].

[5] "A Scene from *As You Like It*" by A. J. Woolmer (1805-92), shown in the exhibition of the Society of British Artists. The portrait of Helen Faucit (1817-98), popular Shakespearean actress who played with both William Macready and Henry Irving was by Miss M. Drummond. (Identification of the two pictures was made with the aid of R. J. Murton of the Royal Society of British Artists.)

[6] Benjamin West (1738-1820), Anglo-American historical and portrait painter, at eight years of age received his first lessons in coloring "from a party of wandering Cherokee Indians, who were pleased with his rude drawings" (Bryant's *Dictionary of Painters and Engravers*). After study in Italy, he spent the remainder of his life in England and, in 1792, became president of the Royal Academy. West was the first artist to abandon classical costume in his portrayal of modern subjects, and that feature of his famous "Death of Wolfe" caused a sensation. Richard Westall (1765-1836), chiefly known for his watercolors and book illustrations, also painted in oils but with little success.

To W. F. Pollock

Geldestone Hall, Beccles
May 29/41

Dear Pollock,

Thank you for your advertisement, which was and is very charming.[1] I have waited to see if I could send you back anything so short and so good: but I have scarce read an advertisement since I have been down here, and since the weather has become so delightful. I live in a house full of jolly children: and the day passes in eating, drinking, swinging, riding, driving, talking and doing nonsense: the intervals being filled with idleness. I hear a nephew of eight years old say his Latin Grammar: to-day we said the verb moneo—in this way—moneo, mones, monui, monuorum, monuarum, monuorum—then I thought it was time to stop. But it was a good shot.

When one talks in this sort of way, I am sure it must seem as if one considered oneself very sublimely philosophical, etc.—but I don't—my digestion is very good: and everybody here is very kind and well-behaved, and there never was such fine weather since the world began. Also, I have had Fielding to read, while smoking in the garden.

You see that all this is a mighty pleasant kind of life to lead, but not easy to write about. You must *therefore* (a pretty consequence) write to me: and tell Spedding to do so: and if old Alfred is in London, or at his country house, stir him up. Not that he will be stirred up. But I really do like very much to hear of my friends, and about pyroglyphs,[2] etc. I wish very much also to step into the pit of Drury Lane and to hear Fidelio once a week.

So take pity, and ask others to take pity, on a poor devil who is rather too well off—and let a London letter slide once in a while out of the Beccles post-bag.

Does the word Beccles put you in mind of hooks and eyes? Good bye, my dear fellow—ever yours,

E.FG.

[1] The two men had been exchanging amusing advertisements for more than a year.

[2] Dr. Allen's ill-starred wood-carving venture. See letter from A. Tennyson, Feb., 1841, n.2.

To Bernard Barton

[Lowestoft]
Pmk., June 17, 1841

My dear Barton,

I met Reynolds[1] in the street here to-day. We shook hands, and spoke of you: I said that you had given up writing, and were, I supposed, in a rage: if Quakers can rage except in verse: where what is called poetic rage is not only venial, but even advisable. Reynolds says you are not angry: neither did he look so himself: he was going off to some school or missionary meeting. Neither am I angry—why should I—? So none of us are angry. Why should we?

How did I get here? Why I left Geldestone yesterday to go to Norwich: when I expected Donne to carry me back to Mattishall: no Donne came: so, after sitting seven hours in the commercial Room I got up on the Coach by which I had set out, and vowed in desperation that I would not descend from it till it stopped. It stopped here at the sea. I was satisfied: I felt that it could not reasonably be expected to go further—so here have I spent the day: and like a naughty boy won't go home to Geldestone quite yet.[2] Such fine weather: such heaps of mackerel brought to shore: pleasant flippant Magazines at the Circulating

Libraries—above all an Inn to live in! After living some time at my brother-in-law's expense, there is something very refreshing in launching out at one's own.

I have been reading the account of the Life and the Death of Elizabeth Cullingham—a Pilot's Daughter—written by the Clergyman here—the Revd. F. Cunninghame.[3] And now I shall conclude: without making any remark on that work: except that it costs 6d. No, I won't conclude till I have said that I don't mean the last sentence in satire: quite the contrary: for E. Cullingham was a very good girl: and died more happily than I shall dine perhaps.

But goodbye—I expect to go to Ireland in ten days or so—shall probably return to Geldestone to-morrow.

Reynolds tells me Miss Barton is well: present her my congratulations.

Ever yours,
E.FG.

[1] Osborne Shribb Reynolds (1782-1848), Rector of Boulge and the adjoining parish of Debach from 1817 until his death. His father, Robert, had also been Rector of Boulge.

[2] Donne tells his side of the story in a letter to Bernard Barton. "If E.F.G. is within your reach, pray tell him I was punctual at twelve o'clock where he wots of. That I afterwards went to various public houses, and finally before the mayor and into the prisons in search of him, but I returned disconsolate, and the very skies sympathised with me, and wetted me through. To make matters worse I had in some measure been the cause of my own disappointment, by putting him off coming the week before" (*Donne and his Friends*, p. 69).

[3] Miss Kathleen Sharkey of the Lowestoft Library provided the following information from local records. Elizabeth Cullingham, daughter of James and Alice Cullingham, was christened March 27, 1812. Her *Life and Death* is mentioned in the obituary of her brother Peter (Lowestoft *Journal*, Feb. 20, 1897). No copy of the *Life* has been located. The author, the Reverend Francis Cunningham (not Cunninghame, as EFG spells it), Vicar of Lowestoft, 1830-60, died in 1863.

To Frederick Tennyson

Ireland
July 26, 1841

My dear Frederic,

I got your letter ten days ago in London on my way here. We have incessant rain, which is as bad as your siroccos;[1] at least it damps my energies very much. But people are accustomed to it in Ireland: and my Uncle (in whose house I am staying) is just set off with three of his children—on horseback—cantering and laughing away in the midst of a hopeless shower.[2] I am afraid some of us are too indolent for such things.

I am glad Morton has taken up painting in good earnest, and I shall encourage him to persevere as much as I can. I fear his brother is a ticklish paymaster: Morton's letter to Thackeray gave a very bad account of the prospects of the whole family.[3] But things may not turn out quite so desperate as he at present seems to anticipate.

I have begun to draw a little—the fit comes upon one in summer with the foliage: as to sunshine, so necessary for pictures, I have been obliged to do without that. We have had scarce a ray for a month. One consoles oneself for all with cigars: which are absolutely necessary in these latitudes. I have read nothing, except the Annual Register:[4] which is not amiss in a certain state of mind, and is not easily exhausted. A goodly row of some hundred very thick Volumes which may be found in every country town wherever one goes forbid all danger of exhaustion. So long as there is appetite, there is food: and of that plain substantial nature which, Johnson says, suits the stomach of middle life. Burke, for instance, is a sufficiently poetical politician to interest one just when one's sonneteering age is departing, but before one has come down quite to arid fact. Do you know anything of poor Sir Egerton Brydges?[5]—this, in talking of sonnets—poor fellow, he wrote them for seventy years, fully convinced of their goodness, and only lamenting that the public were unjust and stupid enough not to admire them also. He lived in haughty seclusion, and at the end of life wrote a doating Autobiography. He writes good prose however, and shews himself as he is very candidly: indeed he is proud of the display.

All this is not meant to be a lesson to you who write, everybody says, good sonnets. Sir E. Brydges would have been the same dilettante if he had written Epics—probably worse. I certainly don't like sonnets, as you know: we have been spoiled for them by Daddy Wordsworth, Milnes, and Co. Moxon must write them too forsooth.[6] What do they seem fit for but to serve as little shapes in which a man may mould very mechanically any single thought which comes into his head, which thought is not lyrical enough in itself to exhale in a more lyrical measure? The difficulty of the sonnet metre in English is a good excuse for the dull didactic thoughts which naturally incline towards it: fellows know there is no danger of decanting their muddy stuff ever so slowly: they are neither prose nor poetry. I have rather a wish to tie old Wordsworth's volume about his neck and pitch him into one of the deepest holes of his dear Duddon.[7]

But it is very stupid to write all this to Italy, though it would have done very well to have canvassed with you and Morton over our pipes in Mornington Crescent. I suppose you never will come back to stay long in England again: I have given you up to a warmer latitude. If you were more within reach, I would make you go a trip with me to the West of Ireland, whither I am not confident enough to go alone. Yet I wish to see it. I wonder if I shall ever get to Italy? My Mother and my brother are come back in ecstacies with it. Sir Egerton Brydges thinks that it excites the imaginative faculties greatly: which doesn't entice me at all. You can't imagine how entertaining politics are now: fancy Peel and the Tories with a majority of eighty in the Commons.[8] You never cared much for these things and now, I suppose, you don't care at all. I passed through London ten days ago: Spedding told me that Alfred had gone off to Rotterdam. I am afraid he has been trusting his money too generously to some speculators. I suppose you have heard of his new woodcarving Society.[9] And yet I dare say you have heard nothing about it: these miscalculations about what distant friends know are frequent enough. If you write to ask me about it, I will write to tell you what I know. Direct to me at Boulge Hall, Woodbridge.

Ever yours,
E.FG.

[1] Savile Morton reported in a letter written to EFG on July 20, "I am afraid to say how many Degrees of Heat we have had here in the last Fortnight, but Thermometer-keepers tell me the Temperature has varied . . . from 90 to 108 Fahrenheit" (Trinity College MS).

[2] EFG's uncle was Peter Purcell, of Halverstown, Kilcullen, County Kildare. Mr. Purcell, with a partner, controlled virtually the entire stage-coach transportation in the southern counties of Ireland. When the Dublin and Cashel Railroad was organized in 1844, he became chairman of the board of that company. He was as successful at farming as he was at business. His four-hundred-acre estate, as well-ordered as a garden, was tilled by 110 happy, loyal laborers. The description of "Mr. P's" estate in chapter II of *The Irish Sketch Book* is Thackeray's account of a visit to Halverstown in 1842. The family camaraderie mentioned by EFG was also noted by Thackeray. "Nothing but laughing and sunshine from morning till night," he reported.

[3] The family properties were heavily encumbered, and Savile found it difficult to maintain himself in the manner to which he was accustomed.

[4] *The Annual Register*, "or View of the History and Politics of the Year," published in London.

[5] Sir Samuel Egerton Brydges (1762-1837), bibliographer, genealogist, and

miscellaneous writer who is credited with having written 2000 sonnets in a single year. In 1834 he published *The Autobiography, Times, Opinions and Contemporaries of Sir Egerton Brydges.*

[6] EFG had already touched upon this subject in his previous letter to Frederick (March 21, 1841). When he states subsequently that he would like "to tie old Wordsworth's volume about his neck," he refers to *The Sonnets of William Wordsworth* published in 1838.

Edward Moxon (1801-58), publisher for and companion of many of the leading writers of the first half of the century. His volume, *Sonnets*, published in 1837, had drawn the fire of John Wilson Croker in the *London Quarterly Review* (vol. LIX, 209-17). "The necessity of obtaining the 'imprimatur' of a publisher," observed Croker, "is a very wholesome restraint, from which Mr. Moxon—unluckily for himself and for us—found himself relieved."

[7] A Cumberland river celebrated by Wordsworth in *The River Duddon*, "A Series of Sonnets . . . and Other Poems" published in 1820.

[8] In a general election held in the summer of 1841, Lord Melbourne's administration of "Whig men and Tory measures" was succeeded by a government of "Tory men and Whig measures" led by Sir Robert Peel (1788-1850). EFG reports a majority of 80 in the House of Commons; the *Annual Register*'s tabulation of election returns places the figure at 76 (1841, "History," p. 147).

[9] See letter from A. Tennyson, [Feb., 1841], n.2.

To Bernard Barton

Bray, near Dublin[1]
August 8/41

My dear Barton,

This comes to tell you I am alive—though not wholly well:—having cold, etc. But colds were made for vulgar souls. Here we are in the land of potatoes: having had little but rain, as I understand has been the case with you in England. I am fidgetty about the harvest there: how is it, after all this wet? We are now staying at this very pretty place: it is ten miles from Dublin, upon the sea, and half encircled with the Wicklow mountains. The country is quite beautiful, very varied: and, if I lived much in such places, I should find it hard to bring myself down to the level of Suffolk. This is literal, as you will perceive, and not metaphorical. I am half inclined to travel into the West of Ireland—Galway and Connemara—wild, mountainous, places, bounded by the Atlantic—the ancient abodes of minor kings, still retaining the ruins and wild manners of 2000 years back. I am struck more and more by the Southern, or even Eastern, character of the people even in these parts. I say again, and over and over again, that the English should travel in Ireland.

I make a good many sketches in my walks here: they are said not to be very intelligible to other people. When I was in London, I bought a very clever sketch said to be by Constable—unlike any I have seen of his: but as good. I gave £2 for it: which is my ultimatum—I have read nothing except some novels since I saw you: and a little Dante, who goes well with these black mountain tops. I look with scorn upon Martlesham Hill.[2] I see out of my window the sea, which would be the Atlantic if it hadn't mistaken its way up the Irish Channel: and Bray Head—this kind of thing: [a crude line sketch] up which Isabella[3] and Mrs. Amy Gunn tried to scale yesterday: but it was not to be: they slipped suddenly, and rolled over each other—and so thought it best to descend.

Well, I am going to-morrow to hear O'Connell speak in Dublin:[4] five days hence we go to my brother's: then I am going to see old Miss Edgeworth[5]—and I shan't be back in England till the beginning of September. I shall commission you to buy me some things at the Bazaar: among them, some copies of yours, and the Major's books.[6] I am really sorry not to be at the Bazaar. Is Mr. Harding going to leave Woodbridge? Let me hear from you: direct to me at the Imperial Hotel Dublin "to be left till called for."[7]

Ever yours,
E.FG.

[1] Bray, a seaside resort sometimes called "the Irish Brighton."

[2] An elevation of 100 feet which one descends on approaching Woodbridge from Ipswich.

[3] EFG's sister. Bray Head is a promontory on the coast, two miles south of Bray.

[4] Daniel O'Connell (1775-1847), Irish patriot and statesman known as "The Liberator." Throughout his career he sought to extort Irish reforms from Parliament through constant agitation of the Irish people without resorting to violence. EFG probably heard some first-rate but little fiery oratory when he heard O'Connell, who, then serving as Lord Mayor of Dublin, refrained from fomenting dissension during his term in office.

[5] EFG's younger brother, Peter, lived at Ballysax, Kilcullen, County Kildare, at this time. "Old Miss Edgeworth"—the famous Maria.

[6] The bazaar, held September 2 to raise funds for the construction of St. John's Church at Woodbridge. Major Edward Moor contributed *Bealing's Bells*, published by him for the occasion. The book reports numerous accounts of mysterious and, the Major believed, spectral ringing of house bells. Those in rooms of his home at Great Bealings had rung for a period in 1834. (For Major Moor, see Biographical Profile and EFG's letter to Mrs. Cowell, [April 25, 1856].) Barton had published nothing since 1836.

[7] The Imperial Hotel in Sackville Street was owned by one of EFG's aunts,

a member of the Purcell family. EFG arranged for Carlyle to stay there when the latter visited Dublin in July, 1849, and Carlyle described the hotel as a "fine roomy well ordered place."

To Bernard Barton

Edgeworthstown
September 2/41

My dear Barton,

You must allow I am a good correspondent—this half year at least. This is Septr 2, a most horrible day for a Bazaar,[1] judging at least by the weather here. But you may be better off. I came to this house a week ago to visit a male friend, who duly started to England the day before I got here.[2] I therefore found myself domiciled in a house filled with ladies of divers ages—Edgeworth's wife, aged—say 28—his mother aged 74—his sister (the great Maria) aged 72[2]—and another cousin or something—all these people very pleasant and kind: the house pleasant: the grounds ditto: a good library: . . . so here I am quite at home. But surely I must go to England soon: it seems to me as if that must take place soon: and so send me a letter directed to me at Mr. Watcham's,[3] Naseby, Thornby. Those places are in England. You may put Northampton after Thornby if you like. I am going to look at the winding up of the harvest there.

I am now writing in the Library here: and the great Authoress is as busy as a bee making a catalogue of her books beside me, chattering away. We are great friends. She is as lively, active, and cheerful as if she were but twenty; really a very entertaining person. We talk about Walter Scott whom she adores, and are merry all the day long. I have read about thirty-two sets of novels since I have been here: it has rained nearly all the time.

I long to hear how the Bazaar went off: and so I beg you to tell me all about it. When I began this letter I thought I had something to say: but I believe the truth was I had nothing to do. When you see my dear Major[4] give him my love, and tell him I wish he were here to go to Connemara with me: I have no heart to go alone. The discomfort of Irish inns requires a companion in misery. This part of the country is poorer than any I have yet seen: the people becoming more Spanish also in face and dress. Have you read The Collegians?[5]

I have now begun to sketch heads on the blotting paper on which my paper rests—a sure sign, as Miss Edgeworth tells me, that I have said quite enough. She is right. Good-bye. In so far as this country is Ireland I am glad to be here: but inasmuch as it is not England I wish I were there.

[1] See letter to Barton, Aug. 8, n.6.

[2] Francis Edgeworth, who lived at Edgeworthstown, County Longford, 50 miles northwest of Dublin. Maria, in 1841, was 74 years of age. For Francis Edgeworth, see letter to Donne [Feb. 5 or 12, 1835], n.7; for his wife, letter to Allen, July 4, 1835, n.2.

[3] Charles Watcham, later described by EFG as "an old (not very old) servant of ours: and his family willing and accustomed to wait on us."

[4] Major Edward Moor.

[5] *The Collegians*, by the Irish novelist, Gerald Griffin (1803-40), published in 1829, was extremely popular. The story, a domestic tragedy, is relieved by quiet humor and amusing scenes of Irish life. Dion Boucicault's play *The Colleen Bawn* dramatizes the story; and the novel, also, has been printed under that title. *The Colleen Bawn*, in turn, was converted into an opera, *The Lily of Killarney*.

To Frederick Tennyson

1mo piano. No. o Strada del Obelisco[1]
Naseby
[c. September 15, 1841]

My dear Frederic,

I am surprised you think my scanty letters are worth encouraging—especially with such long and excellent answers as that I have just got from you. It has found its way down here: and oddly enough does your Italian scenery, painted, I believe, very faithfully upon my inner eye, contrast with the British barrenness of the Field of Naseby.[2] Yet here was fought a battle of some interest to Englishmen: and I am persuading farmers to weed well the corn that grows over those who died there. No—no—in spite of your Vesuviuses and sunshine, I love my poor dear brave barren ugly country. Talk of your Italians! why, they are extinguished by the Austrians because they don't blaze enough of themselves to burn the extinguisher. Only people who deserve despotism are forced to suffer it.[3] We have at last good weather: and the harvest is just drawing to a close in this place. It is a bright brisk morning, and the loaded waggons are rolling cheerfully past my window. But since I wrote what is above a whole day has passed: I have eaten a bread dinner: taken a lonely walk: made a sketch of Naseby (not the least like yours of Castellamare):[4] played for an hour on an old tub of a piano: and went out in my dressing gown to smoke a pipe with a tenant hard by. That tenant (whose name is Love, by the bye) was out with his folks in the stack yard: getting in all the corn they can, as the night looks rainy. So, disappointed of my projected "talk about runts" and turnips, I am come back—with a good deal of animal spirits at my tongue's and fingers' ends. If I were transported now into your room at Castellamare, I would wag my tongue far beyond midnight with you. These fits of exultation are not very common with me: as (after leaving off beef) my life has become of an even grey paper character;[5] needing no great excitement, and as pleased with Naseby as Naples. This is not philosophy, nor anything fine: but simply a quiet state of guts. God knows when they may begin to roll again.

I am reading Schlegel's lectures on the History of Literature:[6] a nice just book: as also the comedies of Congreve, Vanbrugh, and Farquhar: the latter very delightful: as also D'Aubigné's History of the Reformation,[7] a good book. When I am tired of one I take up the other: when tired of all, I take up my pipe, or sit down and recollect some of Fidelio on the pianoforte. Ah Master Tennyson, we in England have our pleasures too. As to Alfred, I have heard nothing of him since May: except that some one saw him going to a packet which he believed was going to Rotterdam. Neither have I heard any more of Pyroglyphs: except that the chief projector who bought the patent (not Dr. Allen, but one Wood) has turned out a knave. I much fear for poor Alfred's money.[8] There is a providence over fools and drunkards but not over poets, I fear.

When shall you and I go to an Opera again, or hear one of Beethoven's Symphonies together? You are lost to England, I calculate: and I am given over to turnips and inanity. So runs the world away. Well, if I never see you again, I am very very glad I *have* seen you: and got the idea of a noble fellow all ways into my head. Does this seem like humbug to you? But it is not. And that fine fellow Morton too. Pray write when you can to me: and when my stars shine so happily about my head as they do at this minute, when my blood feels like champagne, I will answer you. How soon is all this paper covered when the pen runs of itself: I am disappointed that more time has not elapsed: it is but half past eight o'clock; I shall soon have done talking to you: and then I must light my pipe.

When you go to Florence, get to see a fresco portrait of Dante by Giotto: newly discovered in some chapel there.[9] Edgeworth saw it, and has brought home a print which is (he says) a tolerable copy. It is a most awful head: Dante, when about twenty-five years old. The likeness to the common portraits of him when old is quite evident. All his great poem seems in it: like the flower in the bud. I read the last cantos of the Paradiso over and over again. I forget if you like him: but, if I understand you at all, you must. Farewell.

Ever yours,
E.FG.

You had best direct to Boulge Hall, Woodbridge.

What have you been doing in the musical way? Morton wrote that you had been applying yourself hard to it. The German opera was very good in London this year: The Italians so stale that I could not go to hear them.[10]

P.S. Just heard from Edgeworth that Alfred is in London "busy preparing for the press"!!![11]

[1] EFG gives his address as "First floor, No. zero, Obelisk Road, Naseby." A monument to commemorate Naseby Battle, which EFG's parents had erected a quarter of a mile from the village beside the Naseby-Clipston Road, accounts for the address.

[2] The FitzGerald estate embraced much of the battlefield at Naseby where, on June 14, 1645, the army of Parliament under General Fairfax and Oliver Cromwell defeated the Royalists under Charles I and Prince Rupert.

[3] After the fall of Napoleon in 1815, and until 1861 when Italy was united under its first king, Victor Emanuel, the greater part of the peninsula was dominated by Austria.

[4] Castellammare di Stabia, a seaside resort in the southeast angle of the Bay of Naples, commands a view of Vesuvius.

[5] EFG had first been attracted to vegetarianism in 1833. Although he adhered to a simple diet for the remainder of his life, he was no food faddist. See letter to Donne, Sept. 27, [1833].

[6] August Wilhelm von Schlegel (1767-1845), German poet, critic, and translator. His lectures on dramatic art and literature, given in Vienna in 1808, were published, 1809-11, under the title, *Über dramatische Kunst und Literatur*. EFG did not read German at this time.

[7] Theodore Agrippa d'Aubigné (1550-1630), French historian. EFG evidently refers to *Libre discours sur l'état présent des Églises reformées en France*, 1625.

[8] See letter from A. Tennyson, [Feb., 1841], n.2. Charles Tennyson states, "By October, 1841, it was reported that the agent, who was to have bought the patent for the promoters, had turned out a rogue . . . having presumably made away with the funds entrusted to him for the purpose" (*Tennyson*, p. 187).

[9] The discovery had been made in the Bargello, or Palace of the Podesta, then being used as a prison. The portrait, found among frescoes on a wall of the Chapel of the Magdalene, had been concealed by whitewash for two centuries. The painting shows Dante in his 35th year, a book in his right hand, a pomegranate in his left. It is now believed that the frescoes, as they survive, are the work of "some well-trained follower," but not by Giotto himself. The Bargello now houses the Museo Nazionale at Florence.

[10] German opera, during this period, was performed at Drury Lane; Italian opera, at Her Majesty's Theater, Haymarket.

[11] Alfred appears to have been less busy than Edgeworth reported. See letter to Barton, March 2, 1842.

To Samuel Laurence
(Fragment)

Naseby
Septr 28/41

My dear Laurence,

. . . Do you know that I wanted you to come down by the railroad and see me here: where there is nothing else to be seen but myself: which would have been a comfort to you. I have been staying here three weeks alone, smoking with farmers, looking at their lands, and taking long walks alone: during which (as well as when I was in Ireland) I made such sketches as will make you throw down your brush in despair. I wish you would ask at Molteno's or Colnaghi's[1] for a new Lithographic print of a head of Dante, after a fresco by Giotto, lately discovered in some chapel at Florence.[2] It is the most wonderful head that ever was seen—Dante at about twenty-seven years old: rather younger. The Edgeworths had a print in Ireland: got by great interest in Florence before the legitimate publication: but they told me it was to be abroad in September. If you can get me a copy, pray do.

[1] P. & D. Colnaghi & Co., Ltd., now of 14 Old Bond Street, in 1841 were printsellers located at 14, Pall Mall East. "Molteno," probably Anthony Molteno, a printseller who, for a brief period, was a partner in the Colnaghi firm (data supplied by P. & D. Colnaghi & Co., Ltd.).

[2] See letter to F. Tennyson, [c. Sept. 15, 1841], n.9.

To Bernard Barton

19 Charlotte St.
Rathbone Place
[November 20, 1841][1]

Dear Barton,

Have I not sent to Flook's Stationery Warehouse over the way, and bought one Quire of Bath Post—and paid a shilling for it—(for they don't like trusting lodgers)—and have I not turned away from the fire to the table, and devoted the end of a pipe, which was consecrated to the Spirit of inactivity, to the inferior calling of letter writing—all for the sake of writing a letter to you?—I have. My Father tells me that you were not well enough to dine with him last week. Now this is not as it should be. Your sound heart should have a sound body to dwell in, Mr. Barton: and in short it is not proper that you should be ill. Seriously, you should take exercise: walk even half an hour in your garden up and down, with a book, or (better still) with a pipe as a companion: you should eat and drink little—except when t-s-t-d cheese is on the table—and be careful of what you do eat and drink—and then you would be well, I am sure: your sound head and heart would do the rest. One can't afford to lose the full use of good men in this world. Now "be by your friends advised, too rash, too hasty Dad."

I am afraid you will be much disappointed with the Constable[2] sketch when you see it: but I have found nothing else that seemed in your way: and I don't like to ransack the pawnbrokers' shops without giving you a specimen of my doings. Three doors off me is a Constable which is worth a journey from Woodbridge to London to see: it is a large one—of Salisbury Cathedral.[3] It was bought at his sale for £200: and the owner adds £100 to its value every year, he tells me: he now wants £600. It is worth it: being as fine as Rubens. It ought to be in the National Gallery. Why don't you come up here and see it: I can give you bed and board.

It is not certain when my sisters will go down to Boulge. I am trying to make my Father keep them in London till Xmas: which, I am sure, would be better for them both: but I know not if I shall succeed. When they go, I shall not be long in following. If we do not go down yet, I will send you your picture: which will do very well to hang in your bedroom: it is not spick and span enough for your state sitting room.

I saw a portrait by Sir Joshua Reynolds so tender and delicious that it almost brought the tears into my eyes—A Lady, with a little child clinging round her neck, passing through a wood: to the left, the branches opening, and the golden Autumn light peeking in. It seemed like the type of all that is fair and gentle and transitory. A. Tennyson and I pass some hours together every day and night: with pipes and Brandy and Water. I hope he will publish ere long. He is a great fellow. But he is ruining himself by mismanagement and neglect of all kinds. He must smoke twelve hours out of the twenty-four.

We are enjoying very fine London fogs, of the colour of sage cheese.

Red herrings are very good just now: don't you like them? Isabella has become a great Oxford Divine:[4] she attends matins, vigils, etc. but she does not fast, which would do her more good than anything. This is the chief news of the day.

Now write to me and tell me you are well, and moreover taking measures to keep so. It is possible I may run down to Bedford to-morrow for two days: but all depends on what my Papa decides: and also on the state of the weather. Please to make my respects and remembrances to Miss Barton: and believe me ever yours,

E.FG.

[1] Although EFG mentions plans for Christmas holidays in this letter, F. R. Barton in *New Letters* assigns it to "April, 1841." The corrected date is supported by a number of allusions which conform to passages in letters of November and December, 1841.

[2] EFG appears to have committed a "slip of the pen." The reference to "a Constable" in the following sentence probably accounts for the error. In the letter to Barton which follows (Nov. 27), EFG identifies the picture being sent to Woodbridge as a Gainsborough.

[3] John Constable (1776-1837) painted two pictures of Salisbury Cathedral: "from the Bishop's Garden," 1823; "from the Meadows," 1831. EFG ran counter to popular taste in praising Constable at this time. The artist had failed to catch public favor while he lived, and critics and public persisted in their indifference after his death. EFG, however, wrote in January, 1842, "Oh, Barton, how inferior are all the black Wouvermans, Holbeins, Rusdaels, etc. to a fresh Constable with the dew on it." Posterity has confirmed many of EFG's judgments that clashed with those of his contemporaries.

[4] His sister Isabella was being attracted by the emphasis on ritualism that the Tractarians had set in train within the Established Church.

To Bernard Barton

London
November 27/41

Dear Barton,

I am afraid you were disappointed last night at finding no picture by the Shannon.[1] Mayhap you had asked Mr. C[hurchyard][2] to come and give his judgment upon it over toasted cheese. But the truth is, the picture has just been varnished with mastick varnish, which is apt to chill with the cold at this season of the year: and so I thought it best to keep it by me till its conveyance should be safer. I hope that on Monday you will get it. But I must tell you that, besides the reason of the varnish, I have had a sneaking desire to keep the picture by me, and not to lose it from my eyes just yet. I am in love with it. I washed it myself very carefully with only sweet salad oil; perfectly innocuous as you may imagine: and that, with the new lining, and the varnishing, has at least made the difference between a dirty and a clean beauty. And now, whoever it may be painted by, I pronounce it a very beautiful picture: tender, graceful, full of repose. I sit looking at it in my room and like it more and more. All this is independent of its paternity. But if I am asked about that, I should only answer on my own judgment (not a good one in such a matter, as I have told you) that it *is* decidedly by Gainsborough, and in his best way of conception. My argument would be of the Johnsonian kind: if it is not by G., who the devil is it by? There are some perhaps feeble touches here and there in the tree in the centre, though not in those autumnal leaves that shoot into the sky to the right: but who painted that clump of thick solemn trees to the left of the picture:—the light of evening rising like a low fire between their boles? The cattle too in the water, how they stand! The picture must be an original of somebody's: and if not of Gainsborough's—whose? It is better painted far than the Market Cart in the National Gallery: but not better, only equal (in a sketchy way) to the beautiful evening Watering Place.[3]

Now I have raised your expectations too high. But when you have looked at the picture some time, you will agree with me. I say all this in sober honesty, for upon my word, whether it be by Gainsborough or not, it is a kind of pang to me to part from the picture: I believe I should like it all the better for its being a little fatherless bastard which I have picked up in the streets, and made clean and comfortable. Yet, if your friend tells you it is by G. I shall be glad you should possess it. Anyhow, never part with it but to me.

I must tell you my friend Laurence still persists it is not by Gainsborough: but I have thrown him quite overboard. Oh the comfort of independent self confidence! Said Laurence also observed that Gainsborough was the Goldsmith of Painters:[4] which is perhaps true. I should like to know if he would know an original of Goldsmith, if I read something to him. He is a nice fellow this Laurence by the way.

Our prospect of going down to Suffolk this year is much on the wane: the Doctor has desired that Lusia should remain in town. Though I should like much to see you and others, yet I am on the whole glad that my sisters should stay here, where they are likely to be better off. I shall stay with them, as I am of use. I may however run down one day to give you a look. I wish you would enquire and let me know how Mr. Jenney[5] is: he was not well when my Father was in Suffolk. Only *don't ask himself*: he hates that. And now farewell. This is a long letter: but look at it by way of notice when the picture comes to you. If it does *not* come on Monday don't be angry: but it probably will.

[1] A daily coach between London and Woodbridge.

[2] Thomas Churchyard, Woodbridge solicitor and artist. See Biographical Profile.

[3] Both these Gainsborough pictures are in the National Gallery.

[4] Probably because of Gainsborough's fondness for painting rural English scenes.

[5] Squire Edmund Jenney of Hasketon.

To Bernard Barton

London
Dec[r] 24/41

Dear Barton,

I am just going off to Brighton to visit my Mother for a week. I should have liked much to have gone down into Suffolk to see all my friends there: but I must put that off for the present. I want to have an evening's chat with you in your snuggery. I want to see Mr. Jenney, who, I understand, is not well. But all this must be put off for a while. I have bought no more pictures: indeed I have spent all my money: and must wait till next quarter before I make a fresh plunge. But I have not seen anything very tempting lately: I flatter myself I have exhausted the pawnbrokers of the probability of anything good in their shops for at least a quarter of a year. Near here is a sweet little sea piece by Morland, £20—and a very clever landscape by some Fleming, £10. But I can live very well without either, now I have got my Titian[1] to feed on. It is cut and come again with him, so far as colour is concerned.

And now for that hatefullest of all places, Brighton: whither if you wish to direct me a letter (do) direct it 129 King's Road. I have not seen the Pocket Book you speak of: but I remember now having heard Mills murmur something about having sent a pen and ink sketch I made of his house to be engraved.[2] We'll have Boulge cottage in the next. Alfred Tennyson, my neighbour, is getting better: and I advise him to go down to his friends for Xmas: To this he seems half inclined: so whether I shall find him here on my return is very doubtful. I shall miss him very much though we squabble and growl like dogs at each other.

I wish you and yours

A Merrie Xmas

and am yours as ever,

E.FG.

[1] One of EFG's pictures, "Flora and Cupid in a Landscape," was identified as a Titian in the sale catalog of EFG's effects. Another picture, "Landscape With Abraham and Isaac," which he believed to be by Titian and which he left to Fitzwilliam Museum, Cambridge, was later identified as the work of Ippolito Scarsella.

[2] The engraving, "Stutton Rectory, Suffolk, from a drawing by Edwd. FitzGerald, Esq.," is one of the illustrations in *Pawsey's Pocket Book* for 1842. Thomas Mills, Chaplain in Ordinary to the Queeen, was patron-incumbent of St. Peter's Church at Stutton, near Ipswich.

To Bernard Barton

Brighton
Dec. 29, 1841

My dear Barton,

The account you give of my old Squire "that he is in a poorish way" does not satisfy me: and I want you to ask Mr. Jones the surgeon,[1] whom you know, and who used to attend on the Squire,—to ask him, I say, how that Squire is. He has been ill for the last two or three winters, and may not be worse now than before. He is one of our oldest friends: and though he and I have not very much in common, he is a part of my country of England, and involved in the very idea of the quiet fields of Suffolk. He is the owner of old Bredfield House in which I was born—and the seeing him cross the stiles between Hasketon and Bredfield, and riding with his hounds over the lawn, is among the scenes in that novel called The Past which dwell most in my memory. What is the difference between what has been, and what never has been, *none*? At the same time this Squire, so hardy, is indignant at the idea of being ill or laid up: so one must inquire of him by some roundabout means. . . .

We had a large party here last night: Horace Smith came:[2] like his brother James, but better looking: and said to be very agreeable. Do you [know] that he gives a dreadful account of Mrs. Southey:[3] that meek and Christian poetess: he says, she's a devil in temper. He told my mother so: had you heard of this? I don't believe it yet: one ought not so soon, ought one?

Goodbye.

[1] Richard Jones of Church St., Woodbridge.

[2] Horace Smith (1779-1849) and his brother James (1775-1839), writers in prose and verse, wits, and popular men-about-town. They achieved fame in 1812 by the publication jointly of *Rejected Addresses*, a volume of parodies on Wordsworth, Scott, Crabbe, and other contemporaries.

[3] In 1839, three years before his death, Robert Southey, the Poet Laureate, married Caroline Anne Bowles (1786-1854), a writer of modest reputation.

To Frederick Tennyson

London
Jan. 16, 1841 [1842][1]

Dear Frederic,

I must be a very remarkable nincompoop to write you a letter on the day after despatching one to Morton: one should divide one's means better. But the cause of this second effusion is very simple: snow which now falls fast and keeps us all in our lodgings. So I am tired of reading and smoking and playing bits of Fidelio on what "the Miseries of Human Life"[2] used to call "a strung tub"—and have nothing to do but write letters. Perhaps they won't ever be finished: the Snow will melt: the Millennium may come.

I have just concluded, with all the throes of imprudent pleasure, the purchase of a large picture by Constable: of which, if I can continue in the mood, I will enclose you a sketch. It is very good: but how you and Morton would abuse it! Yet this, being a sketch, escapes some of Constable's faults, and might escape some of your censures. The trees are not splashed with that white sky-mud, which (according to Constable's theory) the Earth scatters up with her wheels in travelling so briskly round the sun: and there is a dash and felicity in the execution that gives one a thrill of good digestion in one's room, and the thought of which makes one inclined to jump over the children's heads in the streets. But if you could see my great enormous Venetian Picture you would be extonished. Does the thought ever strike you, when looking at pictures in a house, that you are to run and jump at one, and go right through it into some behind-scene world on the other side, as

Harlequins do? A steady portrait especially invites one to do so: the quietude of it ironically tempts one to outrage it: one feels it would close again over the panel, like water, as if nothing had happened. That portrait of Spedding, for instance, which Laurence has given me:[3] not swords, nor cannon, nor all the Bulls of Bashan[4] butting at it, could, I feel sure, discompose that venerable forehead. No wonder that no hair can grow at such an altitude: no wonder his view of Bacon's virtue is so rarefied that the common consciences of men cannot endure it. Thackeray and I occasionally amuse ourselves with the idea of Spedding's forehead: we find it somehow or other in all things, just peering out of all things: you see it in a milestone, Thackeray says. He also draws the forehead rising with a sober light over Mont Blanc, and reflected in the lake of Geneva. We have great laughing over this. The forehead is at present in Pembrokeshire, I believe: or Glamorganshire: or Monmouthshire: it is hard to say which. It has gone to spend its Christmas there.

[*At this point FitzGerald copied his Constable picture. Although he was capable of using watercolors with skill, haste and unsuitable paper resulted in a rough miniature. The Constable,* The Edge of a Wood, *sold at Christie's after FitzGerald's death for 100 guineas.*]

This you see is a sketch of my illustrious new purchase. The two animals in the water are cows: that on the bank a dog: and that in the glade of the wood a man or woman as you may choose. I can't say my drawing gives you much idea of my picture, except as to the composition of it: and even that depends on the colour and disposition of light and shade. The effect of the light breaking under the trees is very beautiful in the original: but this can only be given in water-colours on thick paper, where one can scratch out the lights. One would fancy that Constable had been looking at that fine picture of Gainsborough's in the National: the Watering Place: which is superior, in my mind, to all the Claudes there.[5] But this is perhaps because I [am] an Englishman and not an Italian. So now at least you will have got a drawing for whatever this letter may cost you. And it is now Sunday, and nearly one o'clock, and I am going off to my Papa's in Portland Place to have some luncheon and carry away a lady or two to Church. [I have] bought a new Prayerbook, with which I intend to produce a [page torn] effect at St. James's! You should hear Brookfield preach there:[6] in an authoritative way: and all about submission, loyalty, etc. I suppose he takes this tack because the Bishop of London is often engaged about St. James. Brookfield is just married, to a young and handsome woman, I hear, but not rich: which is odd. Wood carving is going on at such a rate that it is written on a brass plate outside the Office door: Alfred, when he was in London, seemed to me to know just nothing of what was going on: and to be content to "laisser aller." Venables, Chapman, Lushington,[7] and the legal men entertain doubts of Dr. Allen: that is, either of his integrity, or knowledge of business. I can form no judgment of the man, but I certainly wish that Alfred had not ventured all his money in the matter. I will now tell Morton[8] a little pun which I hope will please him. I don't know if it can be called a pun: perhaps it may be called safely a joke. Thackeray and I were dining at the Garrick[9] with a little German composer named Eliason:[10] and were talking about music, operas, etc. I said what bad subjects they chose for librettos: as for instance, the Huguenots.[11] "Yes," said Eliason, "they might as well write one called *the Cocoa nuts*!" Imagine the little pert, dandified Jew-German face, etc. I don't know why this tickles me: I doubt if the humour will bear so long a voyage as to Italy. But no matter—I recommend this to Morton because of that very early specimen of rhyme with which he has enriched my Memory: I mean that of the bellringers in Devonshire. He will know to what I allude. And now goodbye: I did not think to have written such a famous long letter: but am glad I have. Pray write when you can. For however little my letters may give you the idea that I am serious enough to love the arts and all artistical sympathies, yet I assure you I do: only others can tell me more than I can tell them.

Ever yours,
E.FG.

[1] EFG found it difficult to adjust to the passage of time in January, 1842. He dated this letter and one sent to Barton on the 19th, "1841." Frederick's letter is clearly postmarked 1842.

[2] Perhaps Alfred Tennyson, who had fallen into a valetudinarian state after the failure of his wood-carving venture.

[3] An oil sketch of Spedding by Laurence, which EFG describes in a letter of [c. April 12, 1881], written to W. H. Thompson shortly after Spedding's death.

[4] Psalms 22:12.

[5] Claude Geleé (1600-82), "the Prince of landscape painters," also known as Claude le Lorraine.

[6] William Henry Brookfield, at this time Curate of St. James's Church in Piccadilly. He had married Jane Octavia, daughter of Sir Charles Elton, Bart., November 18, 1841. See letter from A. Tennyson, [Summer, 1835], n.2.

[7] George Stovin Venables (1810-88) and Henry Lushington (1812-55), close friends who had met at Charterhouse in days when Thackeray was also a student there. Venables took his degree at Cambridge in 1832; Lushington in 1834. Both had recently been called to the bar from the Inner Temple. Venables, a journalist

as well as a barrister, became a valued contributor to the *Saturday Review* and the *Times*. Lushington published poetry as well as prose. "Chapman" was probably Henry Samuel Chapman (1803-81), barrister of the Inner Temple, who became a judge in New Zealand.

[8] Savile Morton. See Biographical Profile.

[9] The Garrick Club, located at 35 King Street (now Garrick Street), Covent Garden. Thackeray was a member.

[10] Edward Eliason, conductor of the permanent orchestra at Drury Lane. Promenade concerts had recently become established as a popular form of entertainment in Paris. In 1840 Eliason leased Drury Lane, and under his management during the summer of 1840, the colorful and dramatic Jullien embarked on his brilliant London career as a conductor of promenade concert orchestras. (See letter to F. Tennyson, [c. Sept. 25, 1845], n.2.) Eliason's Christian name long defied identification; handbills and books refer to him simply as "Eliason." The riddle was solved by Professor Alan Downer of Princeton University, who noted the name on the original contract between Eliason and Jullien drawn up for their 1841 concert series. The contract is now in the Princeton University Library.

[11] *The Huguenots*, opera in five acts by Giacomo Meyerbeer (1791-1863), libretto by Scribe and Deschamps. The first performance in London was given by a German company on April 20, 1842, at Covent Garden.

To Bernard Barton

London
January [16]/42

Once more, my dear Barton, I sit down to write another chapter in the History of our Dilettantism. It is such pleasant trifling that I hope we shall not bid it quite Adieu with this year. I have been to two Auctions since I wrote to you: at the first of which I bought a huge naked woman—a copy of Raffaelle—as large as life down to the knees—which you will allow is quite enough of her. I bought her at dusk—one of the last lots—when all other bidders had buttoned up their money in their breeches pockets, and made up their minds that nothing more was to be done. The auctioneer himself was tired, and glad to have done: so she was knocked down to me for £3.10. I could scarcely see her: and when I went with Laurence to look at her this morning, expected to find a daub: but it is a very good copy:—only such exhibitions are not fit for Quakers' eyes. I have sent her to Laurence's house to preserve my reputation. He is a married man. At this sale the pictures went cheap. I went to a sale this morning where all went as dear: and the whole concern was a hoax. I saw that fat fellow Rowe of Ipswich[1] at both these auctions. At the last he bought a pretty little landscape at my recommendation. But he gave the full value for it.

Well now about the Poacher. He is bought. He is home. He is d——d ugly.[2] Droll enough, the same man who was about to buy my Constable (No. 2) was also about to buy the Poacher, just when I made up my mind to take them. This was no stratagem of the dealer to sharpen my desire to buy; for he told me of it both times after I had bought. How shall the Poacher go to you? Must he have a box made? I can make no doubt that if you want £3 for him, you will easily get it in Suffolk, when you grow tired of him: indeed he is worth £5 to those who like the subject. Your idea of Peter Bell[3] is a very opposite one indeed.

We have had trouble at home. Captain Allen, Lusia's betrothed lover, is dead with nearly all his crew on the shores of the fatal Niger.[4] He wrote to her in good health and spirits the day before he was taken ill: and lay ill more than thirty days. He was a gallant fellow, true to the cause to the last: for when they proposed to turn back to the River's mouth and take him out of the evil air, he bid them hold on. You may imagine it was a sad thing to break this to poor Lusia, who was sanguine of his return: I shall not easily forget doing it. I knew of what had happened all day, and she was not to be told till night. It is an awful thing to be as it were in the secret of Fate, and see another smiling unconscious of the bolt that you know must fall. She was much benumbed: and finally taking off a golden bracelet which her lover had sent her from Africa, and which she had worn night and day, from the moment she had received it, crushed it into my Father's hand and fell upon his bosom, in a way that no affectation of passion could reach, however novel-like it may seem to read. She has shewn great fortitude and determination to bear up since.

You may wonder how with all this going on I have the heart to run about picture dealing. I cannot however help it: though I wish I had a stronger sense of these afflictions. What I can do for my poor dear Lusia I hope to do now and as long as I live. She is a noble-hearted girl: and should be married to a good fellow.[5] Here is a monstrous letter. And so goodbye.

Oh, Barton, how inferior are all the black Wouvermans, Holbeins, Rusdaels, etc.[6] to a fresh Constable, with the dew on it. Pictures have their ages as men. The darkening shadow of time does not so much injure the effect of figures, especially in religious or dramatic subjects: but all the freshness of colours is required to give the freshness of a landscape.

E.FG.

P.S. Don't bargain about the picture till you see it: I do not say it is anything very fine: but a good bit of Northcote[7] for £2. That is all.

P.S. I really like your picture[8] very much, on looking more at it. *Keep* it. It is a kind of *pendant* to Reynold's Banished Lord—*banished* meaning perhaps *transported.*

[1] Probably G. J. Rowe, artist.

[2] Barton described this picture in a letter of May 14, 1842, to Elizabeth Charlesworth, later Mrs. E. B. Cowell, "Edward will have [it] to be the portrait, by anticipation, of Bill Sykes, in Oliver Twist. I call it Peter Bell! The fellow has, I own, a somewhat villainous aspect, and his arms are brought forward in a way that conveys a fearful suspicion that his hands, luckily not given, are fettered. . . . The broker who sold it to Edward, called it a portrait of a gamekeeper, and said it was by Northcote. I opine it to be by Opie" (*Barton's Poems and Letters*, pp. 70-71).

[3] Peter Bell, a peddler in Wordsworth's poem of the same name, in whose "whole figure and his mien / A savage character was seen."

[4] Commander (not *Captain*) Bird Allen, R.N., brother of John Allen, had been engaged to Andalusia FitzGerald. He had commanded the *Soudan*, one of three small vessels built for the Niger Expedition, an attempt by the British government, in collaboration with the African Civilization Society, to eliminate slave trade by cutting off the supply of negroes at the source.

The expedition entered the Niger, August 15, 1841, and reached Iddah, in the interior, two weeks later. At that point an epidemic of "river fever" broke out among the personnel. Allen took the stricken aboard the *Soudan* and turned downstream. After reaching the coast, he fell ill; he died October 25 (*Annual Register*, 1841, "Chronicle," pp. 547-54).

[5] In 1844 Lusia married the Reverend Francis de Soyres, Curate at Geldestone and at nearby Stockton in Norfolk, 1842-44.

[6] Philip Wouvermans (1619-68), Dutch painter of battle and hunting scenes; Hans Holbein (1497-1543); Jacob Ruysdael (c. 1628-82), Dutch landscape painter.

[7] Identified by Barton as "a portrait of Stothard, the painter, by Northcote" in the letter to Elizabeth Charlesworth quoted in n.2. It had been "picked up," he said, by EFG "in his exploratory visits to brokers' shops about town."

[8] "The Poacher."

To Bernard Barton

London
January 20/41 [1842][1]

Dear Barton,

About my second (that is, smaller) Constable, I can say nothing, because my friend Laurence has in a manner secured the first refusal of it. Besides I would not again let you purchase a picture without your seeing it first, and your friends seeing it:—perhaps I shall bring both my Constables into Suffolk: and then we will pro and con like monkeys together. The second is far inferior in style to the large one:[2] but it is a scene that might please you better: certainly a more Suffolk scene: and it has some things in it as good as can be—the sky, especially. It is about two and a half feet high by two feet wide: and very handsomely framed. Laurence it was who made me buy it: in fact, he would have bought it himself had £7 been lying useless in his pocket. So you see I am bound to him in a way.

You don't say whether you wish to have your Poacher framed or unframed. I told you the terms. He must always be worth £2 I think to some one:—though I should not buy him at any price for my own pleasure: nor would I [want] a real Poacher hung up in my room. It is not a pleasing object. But tastes differ. The dealer had clapt £1 more upon him on my second visit: but still offered to stick to the old price if I was minded to buy. How these devils know how to tempt unwary souls. Can anything be conceived more likely to exalt one in an instant to buying-pitch? Consider of it, and see to what temptations your poor friend is exposed. I am going again to-day to look at some pictures for auction at Phillips'[3]—Oh Lord, Lord.

All my friends, who have visited me in due form after my accouchement of my new Constable, are pleased to express their conviction of the beauty and value of the darling. Why, I say again, don't you come up here for two days and see all these things? Surely you can take charge of some great bag of gold by the Coach, being paid travelling expenses.

As to our money matter, we will settle all when we meet. You bought some things for me at the Bazaar, did you not?

I had some men here last night—we toasted cheese and drank ale and smoked—and they seemed merry. Alfred Tennyson has written to announce he will pay me a visit here: and I have written back to stipulate that it shall be a very short one.

I am going to have my big Constable framed!

Ever yours,
E.FG.

P.S. My dear Barton, keep these letters of mine to yourself—let us fool it only between ourselves.

[1] EFG was still dating 1842 letters "1841." The postmark reads "Jan. 19."

[2] See letter to F. Tennyson, Jan. 16, [1842], in which EFG gives a description of the larger Constable.

[3] There were three auctioneers of this name in London: Harry Phillips, 73 Bond Street; John Phillips, 4 Great Chapel Street, Westminster; and R. Phillips, 35 Chiswell Street.

To Bernard Barton

[London]
Jan. 24/42

Dear Barton,

You mistake. The Poacher was bought in his shell—for £3—did I not name that price?[1] As you desire a packing case, I will order one to-day: and I hope you will have him down on Wednesday, just when your Bank work is over, and you will be glad of such good company. One of my friends thought the picture must have been an anticipation of Bill Sykes:[2] put a cap and feathers on his head and you make him Iago, Richard the Third, or any other aristocratic villain. I really think the picture is a very good one of its kind: and one that you will like.

I am going to get my large Constable[3] very lightly framed, and shall bring it down into Suffolk with me to shew you and others. I like it more and more.

. . . There is something poetical, and almost heroic, in this Expedition to the Niger—the motives lofty and Christian—the issue so disastrous.[3] Do you remember in A. Cunningham's Scottish Songs one called "The Darien Song"?[4] It begins

> We will go, maidens, go,
> To the primrose woods and mourn, etc.[5]

Look for it. It applies to this business. Some Scotch young folks went out to colonize Darien, and never came back.

> Oh there were white hands wav'd,
> And many a parting hail,
> As their vessel stemm'd the tide
> And stretch'd her snowy sail.

I remember reading this at Aldbro', and the sound of the sea hangs about it always, as upon the lips of a shell.

Farewell for the present. We shall soon be down amongst you.

P.S. I think Northcote drew this picture[6] from life: and I have no doubt there is some story attached to it. The subject may have been some great malefactor. You know that painters like to draw such at times. Northcote could not have painted so well but from life.

[1] Although EFG had not specifically named a price, he had previously mentioned sums of £2 and £3. Apparently the £3 included the cost of the frame, for on January 20 he had asked Barton if he wanted the picture "framed or unframed."

[2] Bill Sikes, the burglar in Dickens' *Oliver Twist.*

[3] See letter to Barton, Jan. [16], 1842, n.4.

[4] Allan Cunningham (1784-1842), *The Songs of Scotland, Ancient and Modern,* with an Essay and Notes, historical and literary, 4 vols., 1825, "The Darien Song," III, 318.

[5] EFG substituted "primrose" for "lonesome."

[6] "The Poacher."

To Frederick Tennyson

London
February 6, 1842

Dear Frederic,

These fast-following letters of mine seem intended to refute a charge made against me by Morton: that I had only so much impulse of correspondence as resulted from the receipt of a friend's letter. Is it very frivolous to write all these letters, on no business whatsoever? What I think is, that one will soon be going into the country, where one hears no music, and sees no pictures, and so one will have nothing to write about. I mean to take down a Thucydides to feed on: like a whole Parmesan. But at present here I am in London: last night I went to see Acis and Galatea brought out, with Handel's music, and Stanfield's scenery:[1] really the best done thing I have seen for many a year. As I sat alone (alone in spirit) in the pit, I wished for you: and now Sunday is over: I have been to church: I have dined at Portland Place:[2] and now I come home to my lodgings: light my pipe: and will whisper something over to Italy. You talk of your Naples: and that one cannot understand Theocritus without having been on those shores: I tell you, you can't understand Macready without coming to London and seeing his revival of Acis and Galatea. You enter Drury Lane at a quarter to seven: the pit is already nearly full: but you find a seat, and a very pleasant one. Box doors open and shut: ladies take off their shawls and seat themselves: gentlemen twist their side curls: the musicians come up from under the stage one by one: 'tis just upon seven: Macready is very punctual: Mr. T. Cooke[3] is in his place with his Marshal's baton in his hand: he lifts it up: and off they set with old Handel's noble overture. As it is playing, the red velvet curtain (which Macready has substituted, not wisely, for the old green one) draws apart: and you see a rich drop scene, all festooned and arabesqued with River Gods, Nymphs, and their emblems: and in the centre a delightful, large, good copy of Poussin's great landscape[4] (of which I used to have a print in my rooms) where the Cyclops is seen seated on a mountain, looking over the sea shore. The overture ends, the drop scene rises, and there is the seashore, a long curling bay: the sea heaving under the moon, and breaking upon the beach, and rolling the surf down—the stage![5] This is really capitally done. But enough of description. The choruses were well sung, well acted, well dressed, and well grouped: and the whole thing creditable and pleasant. Do you know the music? It is of Handel's best: and as classical as any man who wore a full-bottomed wig could write. I think Handel never gets out of his wig: that is, out of his age: his Hallelujah chorus is a chorus not of angels, but of well-fed earthly choristers, ranged tier above tier in a Gothic cathedral, with princes for audience, and their military trumpets flourishing over the full volume of the organ. Handel's gods are like Homer's, and his sublime never reaches beyond the region of the clouds. Therefore I think that his great marches, triumphal pieces, and Coronation Anthems, are his finest works. There is a little bit of Auber's[6] at the end of the Bayadère when the God resumes his divinity and retires into the sky, which has more of pure light and mystical solemnity than anything I know of Handel's: but then this is only a scrap: and Auber could not breathe in that atmosphere long: whereas old Handel's coursers, with necks with thunder clothed and long resounding pace, never tire. Beethoven thought more deeply also: but I don't know if he could sustain himself so well. I suppose you will resent this praise of Beethoven: but you must be tired of the whole matter, written as it is in this vile hand: and so here is an end of it. Alfred reappeared lately in London, after having assisted in marrying your sister Emily to a Lieutenant of the navy. She is now Mrs. Jesse.[7] Did you know of all this? He brought up two of his sisters to London: and of course took a lodging where an old and violent madman lived, who woke them all in the night with cries of murder: which cries were answered by a strait waistcoat being clapt on him by three female relatives: Alfred thinking it indecorous to assist. He (Alfred) is now gone to Dr. Allen's. Wood-carving is said to be going on very prosperously: and Lord

Brougham has declared that all England should be made acquainted with it. So it will, I suppose. When do you mean to write me a letter, in return for this rigmarole of mine? And when do you mean to come back to England? Not but that I think you are as well in Italy, for your own sake: especially having Morton with you. My father proposes to spend all next winter in London with my sisters: if he does, I shall certainly be here. If you should happen to be here also, we shall smoke and talk over music together: and buy pictures, too. But you will never endure the November fogs of London again. And now I am going to put on my night-cap: for my paper is nearly ended, and the iron tongue of St. Paul's, as reported by an East wind, has told twelve. This is the last news from the City. So Good night. I suppose the violets will be going off in the Papal dominions by the time this letter reaches you: my country cousins are making much of a few aconites. Love to Morton.

Ever yours,
E.FG.

P.S. I hope these foolish letters don't cost you and Morton much: I always pay 1s. 7d. for them here: which ought to carry such levities to Hindostan without further charge.

[1] Macready's revival of Handel's opera, *Acis and Galatea*, opened at Drury Lane, February 5, 1842, the night EFG attended.

Clarkson Stanfield (1793-1867), marine and landscape painter, had been a scene-painter at Drury Lane, 1822-34. On becoming famous, he gave up scene-painting, but occasionally painted scenes "for friendship's sake," as in the case of *Acis and Galatea.*

[2] The London home of his parents.

[3] Thomas Simpson Cooke (1782-1848), musical director at Drury Lane, 1821-42.

[4] Michael Levey, Assistant Keeper of The National Gallery, supplies the information that there were versions of this composition by Nicolas Poussin at Leningrad, at Madrid, and at Northwick Park, Blockley, Moreton-in-Marsh, Gloucestershire.

[5] Frederick Pollock, who also saw this production, reported, "In it, by the art of Stanfield, scenic effects were carried to their utmost legitimate limits, and the opening scene, with the waves breaking gently along the front of the stage, has never been surpassed" (*Personal Remembrances*, I, 190).

[6] Daniel François Esprit Auber (1782-1871), French operatic composer. The work which EFG mentions is the opera-ballet, *Le Dieu et la Bayadère* (1830), based on Goethe's ballad, "Der Gott und die Bajadere."

[7] Emily (Emilia) had married Richard Jesse the previous autumn. She was the sister who had been engaged to Alfred's friend Arthur Hallam, commemorated in Tennyson's elegy, *In Memoriam.* Hallam had died in 1833.

To Bernard Barton

[London]
Sat: Feb^r 19/42

Dear Barton,

That this wonderful correspondence may not languish till it dies a natural sudden death, I send you such a Report on the Fine Arts as has been laid on your table every Sunday morning, I think, for several weeks. Your temptations have ended in a fall: you have bought the box:[1] well—I have had smaller temptations which I have resisted. In particular, a little bit of Evening landscape by some body: very like what I remember of a village near Cambridge: a small bit of canvas, but well suggestive of the Spirit of the time: that is, of Twilight. £4.10 they want: but the picture has been rubbed in parts, especially in the sky: so that it is not in keeping. I don't know however if I can yet pronounce myself safe: I walk insensibly *that* way: flutter round the shop-window—there it is: meeting my gaze with a kind of ironical quiet. I have also seen a picture of Highland Shooting by Ward:[2] and fortunately recollecting that my Uncle goes every year to shoot in Perthshire, I think I can't do better than lay out £7 for him. What I gain by buying pictures for my friends is the keeping those pictures for a time in my room, and then seeing them from time to time afterward. Besides, the pride of making a good purchase and shewing one's taste: all that contributes to health and long life. I hope you like the Gainsborough still: I shall be really glad to see that little picture again. I knew it would want varnishing soon: indeed it was varnished (by the dealer's mistake) too soon after I had cleaned it with oil. There are three genuine pictures of Gainsborough now to be seen in Conduit St. I understand: the property of some Suffolk man. Laurence saw them: says they are copies of Wynant's manner:[3] do you know whose they are? I dare say Mr. C[hurchyard][4] does. Poor old Nursey[5]—I think I remember his sketch of Bealings Bridge in the good old picturesque days: when little rivers were suffered to run wild.

I have cut down my great Opie,[6] and think I have done well: I am going to paint it on Monday, as it has suffered during the late operation: it will then be cleaned, and left at a dealer's shop to earn what it can. Never was a stupider purchase. I am glad you have got rid of your sham Constable. Only wait till I come down and shew you a real one. You have some picture of a Holy Family, or some sacred subject—people in red and yellow—by Rubens or P. Veronese—which you must get rid of one day. It has no merit if I recollect rightly.

My dear Barton, I hope you keep all this nonsense of mine to yourself. You have a bad habit of reading letters out, have you not?—Pray, pray don't these. I have lost some of my confidence in you since I hear that you read those lines of mine to my Mother! My dear fellow! You have no idea of what FitzGeralds are. If you betray me further, you shall learn what they are by my abusing you like a pick pocket. So look out. Does not your little Nellie[7] laugh at two elderly gentlemen (for am not I 33—which is certainly elderly in a damsel's eyes) corresponding in this way? She hasn't those eyes for nothing—rather mischievous eyes, if I remember. Now goodbye again.

[No signature]

1 Barton was a collector of snuff boxes, and F. R. Barton notes that "he had no fewer than thirty at the time of his death, many of them valuable works of art" (*New Letters*, p. 49).

2 Probably James Ward (1769-1859), noted for his pictures of animals. He sometimes used scenes in Scotland for background.

3 Jan Wynants, 17th-century Dutch painter, one of the founders of the Dutch School of landscape painting.

4 Thomas Churchyard. See Biographical Profile.

5 Perry Nursey, Suffolk artist, had died January 12, 1840. See Biographical Profile.

6 His "Fruit Girl."

7 "Nellie" was Ellen Churchyard, Thomas Churchyard's eldest daughter.

To Bernard Barton

London
February 21/42

I have just got home a new coat for my Constable: which coat cost 33 shillings: just the same price as I gave for a Chesterfield wrapper[1] (as it is called) for myself some weeks ago. People told me I was not improved by my Chesterfield wrapper: and I am vext to see how little my Constable is improved by his coat of Cloth of Gold. But I have been told what is the use of a frame lately: only as it requires nice explanation I shall leave it till I see you. Don't you wish me to buy that little Evening piece I told you of? worth a dozen of your Paul Veroneses put together.

When I rate you (as you call it) about shewing my verses, letters, etc., you know in what spirit I rate you: thanking you all the time for your generous intention of praising me. It would be very hard, and not desirable, to make you understand why my Mama need not have heard the verses: but it is a very little matter: so no more of it. As to my doing anything else in that way, I know that I could write volume after volume as well as others of the mob of gentlemen who write with ease: but I think unless a man can do better, he had best not do at all; I have not the strong inward call, nor cruel-sweet pangs of parturition, that prove the birth of anything bigger than a mouse. With you the case is different, who have so long been a follower of the Muse, and who have had a kindly, sober, English, wholesome, religious spirit within you that has communicated kindred warmth to many honest souls. Such a creature as Augusta—John's wife[2]—a true Lady, was very fond of your poems: and I think that is no mean praise: a very good assurance that you have not written in vain. I am a man of taste, of whom there are hundreds born every year: only that less easy circumstances than mine at present are, compel them to one calling: that calling perhaps a mechanical one, which overlies all their other, and naturally perhaps more energetic impulses. As to an occasional copy of verses, there are few men who have leisure to read, and are possessed of any music in their souls, who are not capable of versifying on some ten or twelve occasions during their natural lives: at a proper conjunction of the stars. There is no harm in taking advantage of such occasions.

This letter-writing fit (one must suppose) can but happen once in one's life: though I hope you and I shall live to have many a little bargain for pictures. But I hold communion with Suffolk through you. In this big London all full of intellect and pleasure and business I feel pleasure in dipping down into the country, and rubbing my hand over the cool dew upon the pastures, as it were. I know very few people here: and care for fewer; I believe I should like to live in a small house just outside a pleasant English town all the days of my life, making myself useful in a humble way, reading my books, and playing a rubber of whist at night.[3] But England cannot expect long such a reign of inward quiet as to suffer men to dwell so easily to themselves. But Time will tell us:

Come what come may,
Time and the Hour runs through the roughest day.[4]

It is hard to give you so long a letter, so dull an one, and written in so cramped a hand, to read in this hardworking part of your week.

But you can read a bit at odd times, you know: or none at all. Anyhow 'tis time to have done. I am going to walk with Lusia. So farewell.

P.S. I always direct to you as "Mr. Barton" because I know not if Quakers ought to endure Squiredom. How I long to shew you my Constable!

Pray let me know how Mr. Jenney is. I think that we shall get down to Suffolk the end of next week.

[1] An overcoat.

[2] His brother John's wife who had died in 1837.

[3] EFG was also fond of piquet and chess.

[4] So observes Macbeth after Ross hails him as Thane of Cawdor, an honor predicted by the witches. *Macbeth*, I.3.146-47.

To Bernard Barton

London
Feb^r 25/42

My dear Barton,

Your reason for liking your Paul Veronese (what an impudence to talk so to a man who has just purchased a real Titian!) does not quite disprove my theory. You like the picture because you like the verses you once made upon it: you associate the picture (naturally enough) with them: and so shall I in future, because I like the verses too. But then you ask further, what made you write the verses if you were not moved by the picture imprimis? Why you know the poetic faculty does wonders, as Shakespeare tells us, in imagining the forms of things unseen, etc.,[1] and so you made a merit where there was none: and have liked that merit ever since. But I will not disturb you any further in your enjoyment: if you have a vision of your own, why should I undo it?

Yesterday I was busily employed in painting over my Opie, which had suffered by heat, or something of that kind. I borrowed Laurence's palette and brushes and lay upon the floor two hours patching over and renovating. The picture is really greatly improved, and I am more reconciled to it. It has now to be varnished: and then I hope some fool will be surprised into giving £4 for it, as I did. I have selected an advantageous position for it in a dealer's shop, just under a rich window that excludes the light.

February 1842

On second thoughts I shall not send you down my Twilight: but bring it with me. I like it much, and do not repent the purchase. As to the difficulty of bringing down so many pictures, I shall travel by the steamer; which will bear any quantity. The great new purchase, spoken of in yesterday's letter, will also go with me: it will be insured at a high valuation before it is entrusted to the Deep, of whose treasures I don't at all wish it to become one. My Titian is a great hit: if not by him, it is as near him as ever was painted. But you would not care six straws for it. The history of the finest theory of colouring lies in those few inches of canvas. But Laurence (who has gone for some days into the country) must see it, and tell me about it. He is so good a judge, that I ought never to talk till I have first heard his verdict.

I was amused at a passage in Clarissa[2] the other day, which gives one some idea of what the average state of the arts was among the gentry of a hundred years ago. Miss Howe, in drawing up a character of her lost Clarissa, says that among other things she had a fine taste for the Pencil: had not time to practise it much, but "was an absolute mistress of the 'should be,'" and then proceeds thus: "To give a familiar instance for the sake of young Ladies: she (untaught) observed *when but a child*, that the Sun, Moon, and Stars, never appeared at once: and were therefore never to be in one piece: that bears, tygers, lions, were not natives of an English climate, and should not therefore have a place in an English landscape: that these ravagers of the forest consorted not with lambs, kids, or fawns: nor kites, hawks, or vultures, with doves, partridges, and pheasants." Such was a prodigy in those days. It is easy to sneer at this passage: but whoever has read anything of the Masques, etc., of James's time, will readily recall what absurdities were brought together, even by the good Scholars of the day: and therefore will not wonder at the imperfect Natural History that was found in young Ladies' Drawings, and samplers. I remember now to have seen wonderful combinations of phenomena in those samplers which are occasionally to be found hung up in the parlours of Country Inns, and Farm houses.

These letters succeed like the ghosts of Banquo's progeny before the eyes of Macbeth. Lucky that time itself draws on too close for this letter to "hold a glass that shews you many more."[3] You did not answer my question about the Gainsboroughs. So I won't ask you another.

SONNET ON MY NEW PICTURE

Oh Twilight! Twilight!!

Rot me, if I am in a poetical humour: I can't translate the picture into words.

[1] *A Midsummer-Night's Dream*, V.1.12-18.

The poet's eye, in a fine frenzy rolling,
Doth glance from heaven to earth, from earth to heaven;
And as imagination bodies forth
The forms of things unknown, the poet's pen
Turns them to shapes and gives to airy nothing
A local habitation and a name.
Such tricks hath strong imagination.

[2] EFG never tired of reading Samuel Richardson's *Clarissa Harlowe.*

[3] *Macbeth*, IV.1.119-20.

To Bernard Barton

[London]
Pmk., March 2, 1842

And now, Barton, know that I really have made my last purchase in the picture line for the season—today at Phillips' I fell—my virtue fell under the Auctioneer's hammer—an early Venetian picture the seducer—a Holy Family[1]—to think such Families should be painted to allure unwary youths into Sin! There they sit collected in a quiet group just outside the walls of Nazareth, or Bethlehem—sweet St. Catherine with the palm in her hand, her yellow hair encircled with a row of pearls. The child is an ugly swollen child: but I skip him. This picture pleases me hugely. But my encouragement to buy afresh has been this: that Mr. Browne the elder[2] (long life to him!) came to town yesterday: eat a meat tea at my rooms: and was pleased to express himself laudatorily of my Opie Fruit Girl: I said nothing then: but I hope to make him buy her for what I gave—£4. She has cost me some shillings more in getting her curtailed: and then have I not painted her myself? Besides this I understand a man at Bedford has offered to buy a picture I have there: good fellow: so he shall: and then I shant have to borrow monies this quarter, shall I? And as for the future, I utterly scorn it—I bought the best picture in to-day's auction: and that over the dealers' heads: who had agreed the picture had been painted on:—"Look there—there's a patch," etc.—whereas the picture has been *rubbed*, not re-painted, and probably was but a sketch at first. I exult over the whole tribe.

Alfred Tennyson suddenly reappeared in town to-day: I carried him off to the auction: and then with violence to Moxon's: who is to call on him to-morrow, and settle the publishing of a new volume.[3] And only think: two new volumes are just coming out: one by Daddy Wordsworth:[4] another by Campbell—the Daddy's Tragedy!—what a lamentable one it will be—and Campbell's book is to get money. Then Trench is coming out!—such wonders is this Spring to call forth. Milnes talks of a popular edition of his poems![5]—poor devil, as if he could make one by any act of typography.

Goodbye. Given under our hand in the exultation of a new purchase this second or first day of March in the year 1842

E. FitzGerald

[1] "The Holy Family" with St. Catharine and St. John by P. de Inganatis, "signed and dated 1548," is listed in the Little Grange Sale Catalogue as Item 59. The picture sold for £19 19s.

[2] Joseph Browne, father of W. K. Browne.

[3] EFG long had urged Tennyson to publish a new edition of his poems; and in February, 1841, the poet had told C. S. Wheeler of Harvard that he would do so "in the course of a few months" (see letter from Tennyson to EFG [Feb., 1841], n.3). However, the poems had not as yet appeared. EFG's "strong-arm" method at this time resulted in the 1842 edition, published by Moxon in May.

[4] In 1842 Wordsworth published *Poems, Chiefly of Early and Late Years.* The volume included "The Borderers," a tragedy which Wordsworth had written in 1795-96.

[5] Thomas Campbell (1777-1844), *The Pilgrim of Glencoe, and other Poems*; Richard Chenevix Trench's third volume of poetry, *Poems from Eastern Sources*; Richard Monckton Milnes did not publish until 1844. Both Trench and Milnes were friends of EFG.

To Bernard Barton

London
March 5, 1842

My dear Barton,

Before the cavalcade and suite of Hardinge's[1] (a melancholy procession) reaches you, I think this letter will. You need not envy me my purchases, which are imprudent ones: both because I can't well afford them, and because I have no house to put them.[2] And yet all this gives a sense of stolen enjoyment to them. I am yet haunted with the ghost of a Battle-piece[3] (little in my way) at a shop in Holborn: by whom I know not: but so good as to be cheap at £4:10s., which the man wants for it. My Twilight *is* an upright picture: about a foot wide, and rather more than a foot high.

Mr. Browne has declined taking my Opie, unless in conjunction with some others which I won't part with: so the Fruit Girl[4] must set up her stall at a Broker's. I doubt she will never bring me the money I gave for her. She is the only bad speculation of the season. Were she but sold, I should be rejoicing in the Holborn Battle Piece. After this year however I think I shall bid complete adieu to picture-*hunting*: only taking what comes in my way. There is a great difference between these two things: both in the expense of time, thought, and money. Who can sit down to Plato while his brains are roaming to Holborn, Christie's, Phillips's,[5] etc.?

My Father talks of going down to Suffolk early next week. Whether I shall accompany him is not certain. Do you remember what a merry Good Friday you and I passed last year? I suppose I shall find the banks covered with primroses, the very name carries a dew upon it.

As one who long in populous city pent,[6] etc.

Good-bye. I am going to pay my compliments at Portland Place, and then to walk in a contrary direction to Holborn.

1 Probably a box of books sent to Woodbridge from London. George Hardinge (1743-1816), "the waggish Welsh Judge, Jefferis Hardsman" of Byron's Don Juan, whose *Miscellaneous Works in Prose and Verse* (1818) were doubtless the "melancholy procession." The three volumes contain the judge's "solemn" charges and speeches, his poetry (of inferior quality), and his miscellaneous prose.

2 EFG meant that the limited wall space at Boulge Cottage would not accommodate all of his pictures.

3 The picture continued to haunt him until September, when he bought it.

4 Misread by Aldis Wright, "*Forest* Girl."

5 Picture dealers and auctioneers.

6 Milton, *Paradise Lost*, IX.445.

To Bernard Barton

London, Saturday
[March 12, 1842]

Dear Barton,

Being in a sort of bilious medicated state today, I have no great mind to write a letter:—but here goes for a short one. My Papa is gone down to Ipswich by the Steamer[1] today: and I suppose he will be at Boulge the beginning of next week. He then goes off to Geldestone. I expect to go down either the end of next week (I mean the week that begins to-morrow) or the very beginning of the week after: and am now casting about to stow my pictures away—books, etc. I have bought no new pictures: and have escaped the Battle piece hitherto. I take care not to go near the field of action. Yesterday I saw a very graceful Sir Joshua Portrait—an early, and rather thin-bodied, one—sold for £4.

My last Venetian purchase[2] is my favourite: I don't know if you would admire it: and I don't know if I can give you an opportunity of doing so: for it is painted on a heavy panel. But the Constable[3] shall go down among the East Angles.

And now I must finish my letter—I am going to get a mouthful of fresh air at Lewisham[4] today: and indeed that is all the medicine I want.

Ever yours,
E.FG.

[1] Two steam packets plied between London and Ipswich, the *Orion* and the *Orwell.*

[2] His "Holy Family." See letter to Barton, March 2, 1842.

[3] See letter to F. Tennyson, Jan. 16, [1842].

[4] To visit Stephen Spring Rice, at this time a Commissioner of Customs. See Biographical Profile.

To Bernard Barton

[London]
Pmk., March 17, 1842

Dear Barton,

I went for two days to see my friend Spring Rice at Lewisham: the fresh air made me a new man, but my return to London has knocked me up again. When I can stow away all these pictures and books I shall be off to good old Suffolk. I have sold a pony which I had in Bedfordshire,[1] and which I have relied on as something to fall back upon. If I happen to go down Holborn, I shall scarce be able to resist the Battle Piece now. However, as one sees more pictures, one becomes more fastidious: and I hope to be less tempted another year. I could part with three or four that I have without caring: my Constable, my Venetian Holy Family, and my Twilight, are all I greatly wish to keep. I saw a portrait by Sir Joshua sold for £46 the other day—very good—but not worth that.

Your verses to Mrs. H are very kindly: and you will much improve them by a little condensation of expression. Poor Tennyson has got home some of his proof sheets:[2] and, now that his verses are in hard print, thinks them detestable. There is much I had always told him of—his great fault of being too full and complicated—which he now sees, or fancies he sees, and wishes he had never been persuaded to print. But with all his faults, he will publish such a volume as has not been published since the time of Keats: and which, once published, will never be suffered to die. This is my prophecy: for I live before Posterity.

I don't know that you will care much for most of his poems, which are in the heroic way: but there are some on quieter themes which you cannot fail to like. "Lady Exeter" is among them: and an English Eclogue called "Dora," which comes near the Book of Ruth. To add to the list of Poets who are to be seen altogether above the horizon this Spring, is Henry Van Artevelde Taylor.[3] He has got a Saxon story: which will be a d——d bore, I should think.

I have been given five bottles of wine: and tomorrow night four artists are coming to drink them quite up. And now goodbye. If you want any masterpieces before I leave London, you must write soon.

Ever yours,
E.FG.

[1] At W. K. Browne's.

[2] For his 1842 volumes. Tennyson at the time was staying in Spedding's rooms in Lincoln's Inn Fields where the poet and EFG prepared the manuscript for the printer and read proofs. EFG recorded: "The poems to be printed were nearly all, I think all, written out in a foolscap folio parchment-bound blank book . . . which I used to call 'The Butcher's Book.' The poems were written in A.T.'s very fine hand . . . toward one side of the large page; the unoccupied edges and corners being often stript down for pipe-lights. . . . These pages of MS from the Butcher's Book were one by one torn out for the printer, and, when returned with the proofs, were put in the fire" (*Tennyson Memoir*, I, 198). EFG salvaged a few pages which he subsequently gave to Trinity College Library.

[3] EFG coined this name for Henry Taylor (1800-86) from *Philip Van Artevelde*, the title of a closet drama in verse published by him in 1834. EFG here refers to *Edwin the Fair*, an historical drama in verse. Taylor (later Sir Henry) married Stephen Spring Rice's sister, Theodosia Alice.

To Bernard Barton

London
March 26/42

My dear Barton,

I really expect to be down in Suffolk by the middle of next week: but it is not certain. Some of my enormous pictures I have sent off to my friend Laurence who gives them harbour: the rest are to follow. I meant to have sent down my Twilight this day by Warren in the steamer: but could of course get no packing case made for it yesterday. I see tempting sales advertised in the papers: but I think my work is done for this year: and perhaps next year one will be wise enough not to want to have pictures at all. The Battle piece is still to be got, I dare say—but shall it be said that I who have resisted so long shall fall at last? I am going this morning with Tennyson to Dulwich: when we get there of course the Gallery will be shut because of Easter.[1] Well, then we shall go in a bad humour to dine at a tavern: get heartily sick of each other: and so back to town. His printing gets on very slowly: but the world will have its reward for waiting. Can I be mistaken in supposing some of these poems so good as to endure? I doubt if I have the merit of being so partial a friend as to be blinded so far. To be sure, a bad judgment may make up for deficiency of cordiality.

So now goodbye. I must change my shirt, and put myself in order. A fine blowing day—Trench's book is out:[2] seemingly a very tiresome affair. If I could have written it I should have had too much wit to publish it.

E.FG.

[1] The art gallery, built in 1812 at Dulwich College, particularly noted for its paintings by Dutch masters.

[2] Richard Chenevix Trench, *Poems from Eastern Sources.*

To Frederick Tennyson

[London]
Pmk. March 31, 1842

Dear Frederic,

I have written more letters in the last two months, I think, than in the two preceding years. So much has the dissipated dilettantism of

London diluted my formerly-not-too-closely-compacted habits of thought. One sees shops and pictures, and hears barrel organs and Milneses,[1] etc., till one catches up just impetus enough to write a letter about it all, and to think seriously of nothing. I may congratulate you on finding that an accession of company has had the contrary effect of contenting you without your having to put forth your feelers to other lands. Write when you will: your letters are always most welcome to me: and probably tell me all I shall ever know of Italy. Sometimes I much wish to be with you: but the journey thither and back daunts me entirely. I expect really to be in good old Suffolk in another fortnight: and then Italy will seem twice the distance off that it does now.

My Constable is a delightful picture,[2] and my sketch gives you a very poor idea of it. I have lately bought for a very few pounds an early Venetian picture which pleases me greatly: but, after your excommunication of old Saints, etc., I know not if you would tolerate it. One day, it is to be hoped, we shall talk it over as it hangs before us. It is probable I shall spend all next winter in town and I suppose that, love Italy as you may, you must come over into our latitudes some day or other.

Concerning the bagwigs[3] of Composers. Handel's was not a bagwig, which was simply so named from the little stuffed black silk watch-pocket that hung down behind the back of the wearer. Such were Haydn's and Mozart's—much less influential on the character: much less ostentatious in themselves: not towering so high, nor rolling down in following curls so low as to overlay the nature of the brain within. But Handel wore the Sir Godfrey Kneller[4] wig: greatest of wigs: one of which some great General of the day used to take off his head after the fatigue of the battle, and hand over to his valet to have the bullets combed out of it. Such a wig was a fugue in itself. I don't understand your theory about trumpets, which have always been so little spiritual *in use*, that they have been the provocatives and celebrators of physical force from the beginning of the world. "*Power*," whether spiritual or physical, is the meaning of the trumpet: and so, well used, as you say, by Handel in his approaches to the Deity. The fugue in the overture to the Messiah expresses perhaps the thorny wandering ways of the world before the voice of the one in the Wilderness, and before "Comfort ye my people, etc." Mozart, I agree with you, is the most universal musical genius: Beethoven has been too analytical and erudite: but his inspiration is nevertheless true. I have just read his Life by Moscheles:[5] well worth reading. He shewed no very decided preference for music when a child, though he was the son of a composer: and I think that he was, strictly speaking, more of a thinker than a musician. A great genius he was somehow. He was very fond of reading: Plutarch and Shakespeare his great favourites. He tried to think in music: almost to reason in music: whereas perhaps we should be contented with *feeling* in it. It can never speak very definitely. There is that famous "Holy, Holy, Lord God Almighty, etc.," in Handel: nothing can sound more simple and devotional: but it is only lately adapted to these words, being originally (I believe) a love song in Rodelinda.[6] Well, lovers adore their mistresses more than their God. Then the famous music of "He layeth the beams of his chambers in the waters, etc.,"[7] was originally fitted to an Italian pastoral song—"Nasce al bosco in rozza cuna, un felice pastorello, etc."[8] That part which seems so well to describe "and walketh on the wings of the wind" falls happily in with "e con l'aura di fortuna" with which this pastorello sailed along. The character of the music is ease and largeness: as the shepherd lived, so God Almighty walked on the wind. The music breathes ease: but words must tell us who takes it easy. Beethoven's Sonata—Op. 14—is meant to express the discord and gradual atonement of two lovers, or a man and his wife: and he was disgusted that every one did not see what was meant: in truth, it expresses any resistance gradually overcome—Dobson[9] shaving with a blunt razor, for instance. Music is so far the most universal language, that any one piece in a particular strain symbolizes all the analogous phenomena spiritual or material—if you can talk of spiritual phenomena. The Eroica symphony[10] describes the battle of the passions as well [as] of armed men. This is long and muddy discourse: but the walls of Charlotte Street[11] present little else—especially during this last week of Lent—to twaddle about. The Cambridge Dons have been up in town for the Easter vacation: so we have smoked and talked over Peacock, Whewell, etc.[12] Alfred is busy preparing a new volume for the press: full of doubts, troubles, etc. The reviewers will doubtless be at him: and with justice for many things: but some of the poems will outlive the reviewers. Trench, Wordsworth, Campbell, and Taylor, also appear in new volumes this Spring: and Milnes,[13] I hear, talks of publishing a *popular* edition of his poems. He means, a cheap one. Nothing has been heard of Spedding: but we all conclude, from the nature of the case, that he has not been scalped.[14]

We went two days ago to see Greenwich Fair. The People ran and rolled down the hill, and in the evening, every one is on speaking and (as it seemed to me) *hand*ling terms. The good English! Very little invention is there in their jokes and sports, but a good broad humour.

The only joke of the evening was that every one bought a small wooden crake,[15] costing a penny, which being rubbed suddenly down a person's back (for the first time in his life) makes him fancy his coat is rent. But the whole company doing this, as well as enduring it, no one is deluded. Very different all this from your Moccoletti[16] and sugar plumbs. To see the elderly Cockneys on the alert at this sport—inflicting fishy kisses on the women caught in the act—was very good. This letter is finished almost a fortnight after it was begun, and as soon as I have sealed it, I am going to pay some bills, buy packing boxes, wind up all affairs, and—as I believe—to start for Suffolk by a steamer on Saturday—the day after tomorrow.

Alfred and I are going to dine at some tavern this very day, March 31—my birthday—33 years old: wherefore I will drink your health. Pray remember me to H. Lushington,[17] if he is still at Rome. Write to me in Suffolk, and believe me ever yours,

E.FG.

[1] In Benjamin Disraeli's *Tancred* Milnes appears as Mr. Vavasour, whose "life was a gyration of energetic curiosity . . . he was everywhere and at everything."

[2] Described in letter to F. Tennyson, Jan. 16, [1842]. For his Venetian picture purchase, a "Holy Family," see letter to Barton, March 2, 1842.

[3] An 18th-century wig, with the back hair enclosed in a bag.

[4] Sir Godfrey Kneller (1646-1723), originally Gottfried Kniller, portrait painter.

[5] *The Life of Beethoven*, including his correspondence with his friends, English translation by Ignaz Moscheles, 2 vols., 1841. The original, by Anton Felix Schindler, violinist, who had served as secretary to Beethoven, was *Biographie von Ludwig van Beethoven* (Münster, 1840). Grove's *Dictionary of Music*, states, "This is the book which was translated or adapted by Moscheles, strange to say with no mention of Schindler on the title-page."

[6] It *was* a song in *Rodelinda*, an opera by Handel composed in 1725. Alfred Whittingham, in a pamphlet, *Life and Works of Handel*, writes, "The charming air—Dove sei amato bene—maintained its hold upon the musical world for a great length of time. This air has been by various adapters set to English words, and is now known as 'Holy, Holy, Lord God Almighty' to which words it was adapted by Arnold [Samuel Arnold (1740-1802), organist to the Chapel Royal, Westminster Abbey] in his *Redemption*" (1786) (William Reeves' *Music Primers*, Biographical Series, No. 2, London, p. 13). Arnold's "Holy, Holy, Lord God Almighty" is not the hymn, "Holy, Holy, Holy," etc., which is familiar today. Music for the latter was written in 1861 by the Reverend John Bacchus Dykes (1823-76) for words by Bishop Reginald Heber.

[7] *Psalms* 104:3.

[8] From Handel's opera, *Il Pastor Fido* (1712), in "Caro amor," Act II, sung by Ezio; libretto by Rossi, based on a pastoral play by Battista Guarini.

[9] William Dobson (1809-67), Cambridge B.A., 1832; Fellow of Trinity, 1834-41; Vicar of Tuxford, Notts., 1840-48; and Principal of Cheltenham College, 1845-59.

[10] The *Eroica*, third of Beethoven's symphonies, was originally entitled *Bonaparte*. When Napoleon declared himself emperor, the composer angrily changed the name.

[11] Where EFG frequently rented lodgings.

[12] George Peacock, Dean of Ely, formerly Tutor at Trinity. William Whewell had become Master of Trinity in 1841.

[13] See letter to Barton, March 2, 1842.

[14] EFG implies that scalping would be impossible, a reference to Spedding's bald head.

Early in February Spedding had gone to the United States as secretary of the commission under Lord Ashburton which concluded the Webster-Ashburton Treaty, settling the vexing problem of the Maine boundary and providing for concerted efforts by the two nations to suppress African slave trade. The treaty was signed August 9. EFG's correspondence indicates that Spedding returned to his Cumberland home about mid-September.

[15] The "crake," a noise-maker that, when rolled over a surface, creates a harsh, grating sound.

[16] *Moccoletti*, "sugar plums."

[17] Henry Lushington (1812-55), Cambridge B.A., 1834; chief secretary to the government of Malta, 1847-55, published verse and prose. Tennyson dedicated *The Princess* to him, 1847. Lushington's brother Edmund married Tennyson's sister Cecilia.

To W. F. Pollock[1]

[Boulge]
[May 1-3, 1842]

Dear Pollock,

I have this Sabbath morning received the enclosed Temperance Report. There is nothing good in it: but I send it to you as a memento. Cast your eye over it *as you sit*: and then———.

As to Miss Clough,[2] you or I are in a muddle: I never said, or never meant to say, that I chose writings least like the writer in their character, but in their meaning: as for instance, A. Tennyson's: that was like all his hand-writing: but a little unlike his way of going on. Perhaps the best way would be to make every one write out a scrap of quotation: and the same scrap. I have not at all lost faith in Miss Clough: on the contrary, I am going to send her some more writings: I say that it is perhaps impossible for her to judge of the writings without her mind being a little coloured by the contents. Q.E.D.

Tuesday

I mislaid this sheet in rushing off in a hurry—to church—not to where you supposed. I should perhaps have carried it with me had I been going as you thought.

If you have got the 2nd Edition of that momentous work by Bacon Helps,[3] Esqre., here is a motto which I have just read in his progenitor's Essays, and which, in my Edition, where the substantives are printed in capitals, seems an absolute prophecy of his successor. Spedding might affirm it was. It is in the Essay to persons in Great Place. "Embrace and invite Helps, and Advices, touching the execution of thy place, and do not drive away such as bring thee information as Medlers: but accept of them in good part." To think of the early wisdom of some men: and there was poor Charley Lamb, crazy, drunk, and making puns all his life: and dying with a vision of roast turkey in his head. Did you ever notice his pun (not a very good one to be sure) in his letters (which perhaps you never read). In writing to Gillman about Coleridge he says, "You and I have too much sense to trouble ourselves with Revelations: marry, to the same in Greek you may have something professionally to say."[4] This struck me this morning—what a discovery! My eye! Goodbye: pray give me a line when you can: for we never see a paper even here. How does Tennyson get on with his book? I wish you would tell me that.

Ever yours,
E.FG.

1 EFG wrote this letter on stationery engraved with "A View of Woodbridge" by G. J. Rowe, Ipswich. Beneath is printed Bernard Barton's poem, "On a Vignette of Woodbridge from the Warren Hill."

2 Miss Clough, who professed to read character from handwriting and to whom EFG submitted samples of manuscripts of some of his friends. He sent nine of her analyses to W. K. Browne—those of A. Tennyson, Thackeray, Barton, Savile Morton, Francis Edgeworth, W. K. Browne, Arthur Malkin (a schoolfellow at Bury St. Edmunds), Mrs. Kerrich, and a man named Livesey, probably Joseph Livesey, a classmate at Trinity. Thomas Wright mistook the analyses for character sketches written by EFG and published them as "Word Portraits" (*Life*, II, 225-26), thereby misleading many subsequent writers. EFG was intrigued later by the analysis of his own handwriting by one "Warren." (See letter to Crabbe, Oct. 22, 1849.)

3 Arthur Helps (later Sir Arthur) (1813-75), whom EFG had known at Cambridge. EFG calls him "Bacon" because the previous year he had published *Essays Written in the Intervals of Business.* Helps had been private secretary to Thomas Spring Rice, Stephen's father, and he served as clerk of the Privy Council, 1860-75. Although chiefly known as an essayist, his miscellaneous writings cover a wide range of subjects. Queen Victoria respected his talents and enlisted his aid in preparing some of her writings for publication.

4 Lamb's friend, Dr. James Gillman, Highgate physician who took S. T. Coleridge into his home and cared for him, helping him to break the opium habit. For Lamb's letter, March 8, 1830, see *Works of Charles and Mary Lamb*, E. V. Lucas, ed., 7 vols., New Haven, 1935, III, 252.

To W. F. Pollock

Boulge Hall
May 11/42

Dear Pollock,

Thank you for your letter which gave me more news of London than I have heard for a long while. In return I can only tell you that we have had some fine rains down here, and that the country is as beautiful and pleasant as it can be. As to the Squeezibition[1]—it must be like many of its predecessors—Maclise theatrical,[1] I suppose—none of these fellows have education enough to be good painters. As to Laurence, I begged him not to send that portrait of your Papa,[2] which was the worst-coloured thing of his I ever saw. I don't know what earthy propensity mixes with all Laurence's colours—he sees the beauty of colouring in others. It is wonderful to me that when men have pure crimson, ultra-marine, yellow etc. on their pallettes they contrive to mix them up so abominably. Brick dust red, lead blue, and such yellow as a man would take medicine if he voided.

I have just been reading the great Library of Athanasius.[3] Certainly only you and I and Thackeray understand it. When men like Spedding quote to me such a passage as "Athanasius alas is innocent of many smiles, etc.," they shew me they don't understand it. The beauty—if one may dare to define—lies more in such expressions as "adjusting the beaks of the macaws, etc." I have laughed outright (how seldom one does this alone!) at the Bishops' meeting. "Mr. Talboys—that candle behind Dr. Allnut—really that I should be obliged—." I suppose this would be the most untranslatable book in the world. I never shall forget how I laughed when I first read it.

Have you seen a book called "Tendrils Cherished,"[4] an Essay on Education I suppose. It sounds well. The report about the alcoholic Sacrament[5] I saw: and marked, did I not? It struck me as quite a new view of the liquor-case. But what chiefly pleased me was that brother who "came down hot and heavy on the people." Athanasius is not dead.

I am going to my brother-in-law's, Geldestone Hall, Beccles, the day after tomorrow. I hope you will send me a line there now and then. And I am now going to smoke a pipe out of doors, while those fellows are mowing the grass plot. So Good-bye, ever yours,

E.FG.

I shall certainly send to Miss Clough[6] again when I have made up a pound's worth of writing.

[1] The exhibition at the Royal Academy opened regularly on the first Monday in May and closed about the middle of July. Daniel Maclise (1806-70), historical painter. The review of the exhibition in *Blackwood's Magazine*, July, 1842, stated, "Maclise . . . dares to tell the whole of a story, some will say, do say, theatrically—that we consider no dispraise." The critic described Hamlet in Maclise's "Play Scene in Hamlet" as "an ungentlemanly ruffian" and Ophelia as "little better than a barmaid . . . we are at first sight reconciled to her drowning."

[2] In 1842 Laurence exhibited his portrait of Sir Jonathan Frederick Pollock, attorney-general in Peel's administration. From 1844-66 Sir Frederick was Chief Baron of the Exchequer, and in 1866 was created baronet.

[3] *The Library of Useless Knowledge*, by Athanasius Gasker (see letter to Thackeray, Nov. 29, 1838, n.4).

[4] *Tendrils Cherished*; or Home Sketches, by "E.B.," 1842, a "Book for Young People."

[5] The "Temperance Report." See letter to Pollock, May 1-3, 1842.

[6] The handwriting analyst.

To W. F. Pollock

[Geldestone Hall]
Pmk., May 22, 1842

Dear Pollock,

I did not tell you, did I, that I got a note from Spedding ten days ago:—the impudentest thing ever written even from America[1]—saying he had received one of mine, and desiring more—and that was all. Was there ever such an old humbug? The Americans will learn all the particulars of every single person in the embassy. As to Spedding's baldness, that to be sure speaks for itself. I defy the most hardened sceptic to doubt of that. By the bye I was given a very elaborate sermon of Chalmers[2] to read the other day: one of the first sentences talks of "sifting the walks of Nature"[3]—which I take to be rather a loose metaphor. There are four sermons delivered by Harness[4] at St. Mary's, Cambridge, last year that beat all I have ever seen for badness. I mean to try them. In the country, you know, one is obliged to borrow a book or two to subsist on now and then: and sermons are all I can find. They fortunately don't require much attention; and a certain number of pages can be turned over of them as of other books. So Alfred is come out.[5] I agree with you quite about the skipping-rope, etc. But the *bald men* of the Embassy would tell you otherwise. I should not wonder if the whole theory of the Embassy, perhaps the discovery of America itself, was involved in that very Poem. Lord Bacon's honesty may, I am sure, be found there. Alfred, whatever he may think, cannot trifle—many are the disputes we have had about his powers of badinage, compliment, waltzing, etc. His smile is rather a grim one. I am glad the book is come out, though I grieve for the insertion of these little things, on which reviewers and dull readers will fix; so that the right appreciation of the book will be retarded a dozen years.[6] "And what the hell does that signify?"—as we say hereabouts.

The rain will not come and we are burnt up, and in despair. But the country never looked more delicious than it does. I am as happy here as possible, though I don't like to boast. I am going to see my friend Donne in ten days: he is writing the dullest of histories—one of Rome. What the devil does it signify setting us in these days right as to the Licinian Rogation, and Livy's myths?[7] Every school-boy knew that Livy lied; but the main story was clear enough for all the purposes of experience; and, that being so, the more fabulous and entertaining the subsidiary matter is the better. Tell Thackeray not to go into Punch yet.[8] Here we see no paper but a thrice-a-week filtration of the Times—we have seen that Good is to be executed on Monday:[9] that is our latest news. Therefore expect none from me except this, that turnips and beet can't be got in. You are very good to write to me—to merit it I write these tell-nothings.

Ever yours,
E.FG.

1 Spedding was in America with the Ashburton Commission.

2 Thomas Chalmers (1780-1847), Scottish divine, whose works were published in more than 30 volumes. He is best remembered for his refutation of Hume's objection to the truth of miracles.

3 Someone, probably Pollock, has inserted an asterisk at this point and noted at the end of the letter, "gravel walks, I suppose."

4 William Harness (1790-1869), divine, author, and editor, at this date Perpetual Curate of St. Peter's, Regent Square, London, and Clerical Registrar to the Privy Council.

5 *Poems*, 1842, published May 14. "The Skipping-Rope," a feeble jingle omitted by Tennyson from later editions. "The bald men of the Embassy" refers to Spedding.

6 On the whole the volumes were well received. (See Edgar Shannon, *Tennyson and the Reviewers*, Harvard, 1952, pp. 60-81.)

7 Licinius, Roman tribune. His *Rogations*, laws passed in 367 B.C., ended the struggle between plebeians and patricians. In his history of Rome Livy's primary objective was to write an entertaining narrative. He omitted facts at will and assumed little responsibility for checking his sources.

8 Despite EFG's warning, Thackeray, three weeks later, told his mother, ". . . I've been writing for . . . a very low paper called Punch, but that's a secret—only its good pay, and a great opportunity for unrestrained laughing sneering kicking

and gambadoing" (*Thackeray Letters and Papers*, II, 54). Thackeray did not become a member of the staff of *Punch* until 1844.

[9] Daniel Good, a middle-aged Irish coachman living at Roehampton. The police, seeking him after he had committed a petty theft, found the dismembered and mutilated remains of a woman, Jane Good, reputedly his wife, in a stable on the estate where he was employed. Arrested two weeks later at Tonbridge, Good was found guilty of murder and was hanged at the Old Bailey, May 23 (*Annual Register*, "Chronicle," 1842, pp. 64-68).

To Samuel Laurence
(Fragment)

Geldestone Hall, Beccles
Sunday, May 22/42

My dear Laurence,

. . . I read of the advertisements of sales and auctions, but don't envy you Londoners while I am here in the midst of *green idleness*, as Leigh Hunt might call it. What are pictures? I am all for pure spirit. You have of course read the account of Spedding's forehead landing in America. English sailors hail it in the Channel, mistaking it for Beachy Head. There is a Shakespeare cliff, and a Spedding cliff. Good old fellow! I hope he'll come back safe and sound, forehead and all.

I sit writing this at my bedroom window, while the rain (long-looked for) patters on the window. I prophesied it to-day: which is a great comfort. We have a housefull of the most delightful children: and if the rain would last, and the grass grow, all would be well. I think the rain will last: I shall prophesy so when I go down to our early dinner. For it is Sunday: and we dine children and all at one o'clock: and go to afternoon church, and a great tea at six—then a pipe (except for the young ladies)—a stroll—a bit of supper—and to bed. Wake in the morning at five—open the window and read Ecclesiasticus.[1] A proverb says that "everything is fun in the country."

My Constable has been greatly admired, and is reckoned quite genuine by our great judge, Mr. Churchyard.[2] Mr. C. paints himself: (not in *body* colours, as you waggishly insinuate) and nicely too. He understands Gainsborough, Constable, and old Crome.[3] Have you ever seen pictures by the latter? some very fine. He was a Norwich man.

[1] In the *Apocrypha*.

[2] The lawyer-artist was, in fact, a competent judge; and his careful study of

Constable's landscapes is manifest in his own pictures. EFG and Churchyard were pioneer admirers of Constable, for whose pictures there was little demand when he died in 1837.

[3] John Crome (1768-1821), founder of the Norwich Society of Artists, was another landscape painter, then little known, whose work EFG and Churchyard admired. "Young Crome," his eldest son, also painted landscapes.

To W. F. Pollock

[Geldestone]
[June, 1842]

Dear Pollock,

I think the man who shot at the dear little Queen must have been mad.[1] Surely no sane man would choose such a place as he did for his purpose: I mean, where he was sure to be taken whether he succeeded or not. What is your Uncle doing in India? I see manifestoes by General Pollock:[2] but I always hope to be told the result of Politics by some good friend.

I have been on a visit to my friend Donne. He is very busy with his history: which must inevitably be a great bore. This I regret: for Donne has fun in him, only when he gets a pen in his hand he forgets it all. So his style is of the Quaker-coat cut.

I read at his house Venables' Article on Carlyle.[3] I thought it most admirable. He seems to me in the first rank of Reviewers: and I hope we shall see much more. I also read his Hegel, which I did not so much admire: but then the subject is a more perplexed one: and I suspect Venables is more at home in matters of the understanding than of the Arts. And how did you and Thackeray like Penshurst?[4] I should like well to have seen it. We are calling out for rain loudly here: no hay: corn looking yellow. This does not touch you in London: except that I suppose the Opera is rather too hot at times. You see what a lofty sense of rustic superiority I can assume. As to your sea trip,[5] I wish it all success: it is a pity you are not about it now with these long cheery days, and a fine steady breeze always blowing. Perhaps, however, autumn weather has more variety and excitement about it. I should like one good toss on the sea again, not in a steamer: but somehow or other I seldom get far from my kennel. Pray ask Thackeray if he has done anything for poor Pandurang Hari[6]—I wish he could. Is Alfred in town still? I have got his books. It is a pity he did not publish the new volume separately.[7] The other will drag it down. And why reprint the Merman, the Mermaid, and those everlasting Eleanores, Isabels,—which always were, and are, and must be, a nuisance, though Mrs. Butler[8] (who recognised herself in the portrait, of course) said that Eleanore (what a bore) was the finest thing he ever wrote. She has sat for it ever since, I believe. Every woman thinks herself the original of one of that stupid Gallery of Beauties. The sonnet to J.M.K. also remains: there's a beauty too.

Goodbye,
E.FG.

[1] As Queen Victoria approached the gates of Buckingham Palace with Prince Albert in an open barouche about 6 P.M., May 20, 1842, she was shot at by John Francis, 19-year-old son of a machinist at Covent Garden Theater. The Queen was not injured and attended the opera that evening. No motivation for the attack was established. The sentence of death handed down at Francis' trial was commuted, at the Queen's request, to transportation (*Annual Register*, "Chronicle," pp. 96-99, 121). The attack by Francis was the second of three attempts to assassinate the Queen between 1840 and 1842. The third occurred on July 3. Carlyle wrote to his mother the next day, "The people are sick of their misgovernment, and the blackguards among them shoot at the poor Queen" (*Letters of Thomas Carlyle to his Youngest Sister*, C. T. Copeland, ed., 1899, p. 128).

[2] Major General George Pollock (1786-1872), field marshal, was appointed in January, 1842, to command the operation for the relief of Jalálábád, which he reached, after heavy fighting, in April. Instructed by Lord Ellenborough, then governor-general of India, to withdraw from Afghanistan, General Pollock remonstrated, convinced that he should continue his advance to Kabul, the capital. He was permitted to proceed at his own discretion and occupied the city in September. The "manifestoes" to which FitzGerald refers were evidently General Pollock's dispatches to civil authorities published in the *Annual Register*, "Chronicle," 1842, pp. 405-97.

[3] G. S. Venables' review of *Chartism*, *British and Foreign Quarterly Review*, XII, 1841; his essay on Hegel, ibid., XIII, 1842.

[4] Penshurst Place, near Tonbridge, Kent, seat of the Sidney family. Thackeray had found Penshurst "splendid" outside "but in the most woebegone condition within" (*Thackeray Letters and Papers*, II, 52).

[5] To the Hebrides. The cruise was canceled.

[6] William Browne Hockley (1792-1860) wrote, among other works of Anglo-Indian fiction, *Pandurang Hari*, or *Memoirs of a Hindoo* (1826), described as a "vivid picture of Mahratta life." In 1846 EFG was on intimate terms with Hockley's brother, a retired major living in Ipswich. This passage suggests that he was acquainted with the major in 1842.

W. B. Hockley, after attending the East India Company School at Haileybury, was sent to Bombay in 1812. He filled civil positions of increasing responsibility until 1821 when charges of bribery were lodged against him. On his return to England in 1824 he was dismissed by the company. Thereafter, he lived for a time with his mother and two sisters at Bury St. Edmunds, his birthplace, and, later, in London where, one source states, he gradually sank into poverty. *The Memoirs of a Brahmin*, the last published work ascribed to him, appeared in 1843, the year after EFG wrote his letter. All Hockley's books were published anonymously and have been attributed commonly to a "Captain Ottley." The Advocates Library in Edinburgh assigns the works to "Captain Thomas Henry Ottley," commissioned in the Bombay Native Infantry in 1821. Ottley's Christian name creates an intriguing web of association, for Hockley's Ipswich brother was Major Thomas Henry John (1790-1878), who had served in the Madras Artillery. After retiring in 1833, Major (later Lt. Col.) Hockley settled in Ipswich. EFG's friend, E. B. Cowell, began reading Persian with the Major in 1842 (*Cowell Biography*, p. 184), and EFG may have made Hockley's acquaintance through Cowell. The major later aided EFG in his Persian studies.

[7] Tennyson had published his *Poems* in two volumes. The first contained revisions of about half of the poems published in 1830 and 1832; the second, poetry written during his "ten years' silence."

[8] Mrs. Butler—Fanny Kemble—who, in 1840, had returned from America with her husband, Pierce Butler, of Philadelphia, for a visit. The Butlers remained in England until May, 1843. The FitzGerald and Kemble families were friends of long standing. "J.M.K.," to whom EFG subsequently refers, is Fanny's brother John.

To Samuel Laurence
(Fragment)

Boulge Hall
June 19/42

My dear Laurence,

Keep the head of Raffaelle as long as you please. I am glad that one of the three pictures at all events is worth something. I anticipated that Morton's friend would spoil them in the carriage: friends always do. Keep them all, like my other pictures, at your house: and make what use of them you please. The head of Dante is, I suppose, the same as the one L. Hunt shewed us engraved in a book: a theatrical one, I thought. . . . Have you been to any auction-rooms? I have forgot all about them: and can live very well without pictures. I believe one loses all one's tastes in the country: and one is not the less happy. We have had glorious weather: new pease and young potatoes—fresh milk (how good!) and a cool library to sit in of mornings. . . .

June 1842

To W. F. Pollock

Geldestone
June 24/42

Dear Pollock,

Are you being circumcised for a Peer that you never send me a line now? There is that poor fellow Thackeray gone off to Ireland:[1] and what a lazy beast I am for not going with him. But except for a journey of two days, I get as dull as dirt. I wish somebody had gone with him. But he will find lots of companions in Ireland.[2] What is become of A.T.?[3] You never told me that, nor how his book went on: about which I have really a curiosity. I see the advertisement of Edwin the Fair[4] in the papers: something about the Heptarchy, I suppose; a stupid time, whenever it was. And my dear Daddy's Tragedy too; has any one read it?

We have been burnt up here, but to-day (the grass being just mowed) it rains pitch-forks, which might be useful if not coming in such great numbers. But our garden is full of roses and all capital things. I wish trade was going on well: and that we could be left as we are.

I have written a note to Spedding, such an one as he sent me, a ruffian—I have the pleasure of abusing some of his idols in it. A man on the coach the other day told me that all was being settled very easily in America, but stagecoach politicians are not always to be trusted. I propose that we leave Spedding as a hostage in the hands of the Americans. They must send over Willis[5] or some one of their great men.

When do you set off on your trip to the Hebrides? or your yachting, wherever it is? I mean to go to Blenheim to see a Raffaelle[6] this year, and that is all I propose to do. No sights recompense the often undoing and doing up of a carpet-bag. What then is the stamping down, strapping, and locking up of a trunk, with all the blood in your head! If one were rich, and travelled with a valet to do all, it would be well. The only other alternative is to travel with nothing but the clothes on one's back.

Sic cogitabat.

Yours ever,
E.FG.

[1] Thackeray had contracted to write *The Irish Sketch Book*, published in 1843.

[2] Among the companions Thackeray found were EFG's uncle, Peter Purcell, at

Halverstown, Kilcullen, and EFG's younger brother, Peter, in County Meath. On July 29 he wrote to his mother, "Well, I made a most delightful trip with Peter Purcell and his family, as noble a fellow as I ever came near, nothing but laughing & sunshine from morning till night . . . and when I parted from them, I felt as if I had known them all my life." He described Peter, with whom he spent three days near Drogheda, as "the honestest best creature that ever was born" (*Thackeray Letters and Papers*, II, 69, 80).

[3] Alfred Tennyson.

[4] Henry Taylor's drama in verse, and Wordsworth's *The Borderers.*

[5] Nathaniel P. Willis (1806-67), American miscellaneous writer who had lived in England for a time during the thirties and married there. His *Inklings of Adventure*, stories descriptive of American life, was well received when published in London in 1836.

[6] "Virgin Enthroned."

From Alfred Tennyson

[June, 1842]

My dear Fitz,

If you had known how much I have gone thro' since I saw you,[1] you would pardon perhaps my ungracious silence in return for so many kind letters: if you had known—but then I don't mean to tell you: you will very likely know soon enough: you have been a very good fellow to remember me in your correspondence; but then I know you like writing which I hate mortally: I have seen you scribble to B.B. and others for the mere love of scribbling, and so perhaps I have not been so grateful for your notice as I might have been.

Don't abuse my book: you can't hate it more than I do, but it does me no good to hear it abused; if it is bad, you and others are to blame who continually urged me to publish. Not for my sake but yours did I consent to submit my papers to the herd—d——n em! and all reproach comes too late.

I don't know whether the Dulwich days were good days:[2] something good no doubt about them, but I don't look back with *much* satisfaction on them: I have not had a good day, a perfect white day, for years; I think I require delicious scenery to make a perfect day as well as friends. I don't know.

Edwin the fair I have not read: people say it is a weaker Philip.[3] You are unjust in calling the latter a solemn humbug: there is some very good stuff in it, tho not of the highest class. I do not know that I can make any expeditions this year: for I have neither money nor credit. Blenheim[4] I should certainly like to see with you—O that glorious old chase! The great oaks are fresher in my recollection than the Raffaelle; indeed I had not much time to study the latter: I was just getting into it when the old Duke sent a special blue-plush to me to turn me out.

that is a fac-simile of the nib of my pen. The ink has twice spurted right into the apple of my eye—therefore

good bye, old Fitz
Lest I lose my wits

never more my own than when

Yours
A.T.

Hoovery! Doovery! etcc. etcccc.

[1] His dismal investment in Dr. Allen's Pyroglyphs was causing him concern. In September he wrote to a friend, "What with ruin in the distance and hypochondriacs in the foreground, 'God help all'" (C. Tennyson, *Alfred Tennyson*, p. 198).

[2] See letter to Barton, March 26, 1842.

[3] *Edwin the Fair*, a drama in verse published that spring by Henry Taylor. In "a weaker Philip," Tennyson alludes to Taylor's verse play, *Philip van Artevelde*.

[4] Blenheim, near Woodstock, Oxfordshire, a palace erected by Parliament for the Duke of Marlborough in recognition of his victory at Blenheim. "Virgin Enthroned," the Raffaelle to which Tennyson refers, is now in the National Gallery.

To Frederick Tennyson

Bedford
August 16, 1842

Dear Tennyson,

I have been long hoping for a letter from you: it has come this morning, and repays me for all waiting. While you and Morton write to me about Italy I shall never go to see it. And yet your account of Cicero's villa,[1] I confess, gives me a twinge. But of this I am sure: if I saw all these fine things with the bodily eye, I should but see them as a scene in a play, with the additional annoyance of being bitten with fleas perhaps, and being in a state of transition which is not suitable to me: whereas while you see them and will represent them to me, I see them through your imagination—and that is better than any light of my own. This is very true, I assure you: and you and Morton have given me quite a different view of Italy to what I had before: a much more enchanting one, but not the more likely to seduce me into making the false step of trying to realize it for myself. Like the Lady of Shalott I should be dished if I turned to gaze at the truth. There is another young Lady upon record who in an excess of transport of some kind, cried out, "Well, there's nothing like the real thing, after all!" But I am not of her kidney.

In the mean time how tired and bored would you be to take one of my travels—a voyage of eight miles from Bedford perhaps—travelled twenty times before—every winding of the river, every church-spire, every country pot house and the quality of its beer, well known. No surprise at all. Nil admirari—I find that old Horace is a good fellow-traveller in England: so is Virgil. It is odd that those fellows living in the land they did live in should have talked so coldly about it. As to Alfred's book, I believe it has sold well: but I have not seen him for a long while, and have had no means of hearing about the matter except from Thompson,[2] who told me that very many copies had been sold at Cambridge, which indeed will be the chief market for them. Neither have I seen any notice of them in print except that in the Examiner[3]—and that seemed so quiet that I scarce supposed it was by Forster. Alfred himself is, I believe, in Kent at present. And now, my dear Frederic, why do you think of returning to England? Depend upon it you are better off as you are. You will never turn magistrate nor bean-dibbler, nor make yourself of use in the country, and therefore why should you not live where you like to live best? When I read of your laughing and singing and riding into Naples with huge self-supplying beakers full of the warm South I am sure you had best stay where you are. I should indeed be very glad to see you again: but then I should miss hearing from you: and you would only come here to abuse us all and go back again. You Tennysons are born for warm climates. As to poor England, I never see a paper, but I think with you that she is on the go. I used to dread this: but somehow I now contemplate it as a necessary thing, and, till the shoe begins to pinch me sorely, walk on with some indifference. It seems impossible the manufacturers can go on as they are: and impossible that the demand for our goods can continue as of old in Europe: and impossible but that we must get a rub and licking in some of our colonies—and if all these things come at once, why then the devil's in it. I used to think as you do about France and the French: and we all agreed in London that France should be divided among the other powers as Poland was: but Donne has given me pause: he says that France is the great counteracting democratic principle to Russia. This may be: though I think Russia is too unwieldy and rotten-ripe ever to make a huge progress in conquest. What is to be thought of a nation where the upper classes speak the language of another country, and have varnished over their honest barbarism with the poorest French profligacy and intrigue? Russia does not seem a whole to me.[4] In the mean time, all goes on toward better and better, as is my firm belief: and humanity grows clear by flowing (very little profited by any single sage or hero)[5] and man shall have wings to fly and something much better than that in the end. But all this you will think frowzy twaddle: and indeed one should keep it to oneself.

I draw a very little, and think of music as I walk in the fields: but have no piano in this part of the world. If you come to England we shall at least have some palaver about that. I shall be at Boulge probably a good deal in the winter, but also some time doubtless in London. Have you ever tried the Accordion? It is a nice thing to carry about with one.[6] I never tried it till the other day; it is easy enough. One day I shall buy one. I hear there is a fine new Symphony by Mendelssohn,[7] who is by far our best writer now, and in some measure combines Beethoven and Handel. I grow every day more and more to love only the old God save the King style: the common chords, those truisms of music, like other truisms so little understood in the full. Just look at the mechanism of Robin Adair.[8]

Now pray write to me again when you can. You don't know how much I rejoice in your letters. And believe me

Yours ever truly
E. FitzGerald

[1] At Tusculum, 15 miles southeast of Rome. The exact location of the villa has not actually been identified. See letter to Allen, Aug. 29, 1842.

[2] W. H. Thompson.

[3] The review of Tennyson's poems in the *Examiner*, May 28, pp. 340-41, was generally favorable. John Forster was literary critic of the periodical.

[4] A letter written to Frederick in 1852 concludes, "Don't write Politics—I agree with you beforehand." EFG's professed indifference to domestic and foreign affairs has obscured the fact that his comments on current topics and problems were often incisive and prophetic.

[5] EFG is evidently challenging Carlyle's view of "heroes." The comment was written just a month before the two men met.

[6] The passage about the accordion is not included in Aldis Wright's text. It is typical of many passages revealing EFG's homely interests, which Wright seems to have considered inappropriate for publication. The portion about the Lady of Shalott in this letter was also deleted.

[7] *The Scotch Symphony*, 1842, dedicated to Queen Victoria.

[8] An Irish folk air that became popular in England during the latter half of the 18th century.

To Samuel Laurence
(Fragment)

Bedford, Thursday
[August, 1842]

Dear Laurence,

. . . I have heard from Morton and F. Tennyson; the letter of the latter very descriptive and fine. He is summering at Castellamare, and Morton at Sorrento. What must Italy be if we are complaining of heat here!

I have just been naming all Mr. Browne's pictures for him. This he has insisted on for three years, and at last this very hot day after an early dinner pens and paper were brought out and I have been writing down awful calumnies about Cuyp, Both,[1] etc. Who could have painted Catharine of Medicis, do you know? We are afraid to call it Vandyke, as he lived (I believe) a century after her: and Mr. B. won't give up its being Catharine's portrait. So here we are in a fix. I went to see Lord Northampton's place Castle Ashby[2] a week ago: expected pictures, and saw very bad ones. The house is very handsome, built by Inigo Jones.

I weigh 14 stone—fact.

[1] Albert Cuyp, and the brothers John and Andrew Both, all 17th-century Dutch painters.

[2] Castle Ashby, six miles due east of Northampton on the road to Bedford. Although experts, with reservations, attribute parts of the mansion to Inigo Jones, the original design, early Renaissance, is credited to Henry Compton.

To John Allen

[Keysoe]
[August, latter half, 1842]

My dear John Allen,

I have now been in Bedfordshire nearly a month, and hoped to have seen you at my friend Airy's[1] before now: but you have put off your visit till after harvest: so I shall probably not see you. And yet if I knew you were coming very soon into these parts I would e'en delay my departure: that we might spend a day together on the banks of the Ouse. Therefore be a good boy and write me a line by return of post to Bedford, and let me hear all about it. I have just come to visit Airy for a day, before his departure on a tour. I should have written to you before had I known how to direct to you: and lo! how simple it is.

I am much *entêté* at present about one Matthews,[2] a preacher at Bedford, who would do very well for Manchester in opposition to Chartists, etc. If you are here on a Friday or a Sunday go and hear him. I would gladly subscribe to remove him from Bedford. All this you will think absurd; and so perhaps it is.

I have been reading Stobaeus' Anthology[3] as I saunter in the fields: a pretty collection of Greek aphorisms in verse and prose. The bits of Menander and the comic poets are very acceptable. And this is really all I have looked at all this summer. I stayed two days at Cambridge on my way here, and saw Thompson in his robes of Proctor.[4] He was very kind to me and we did very well together. I ought to have gone to travel with Thackeray in Ireland: and here I am to say that "I ought." But do you come down here quickly: for though it seems I cannot go to look for an old friend, I can wait for his coming to me. So come and come quickly. We will get Laurence down from London.

Yours as ever, my dear fellow,

E.FG.

[1] The Reverend William Airy. EFG had expected Allen to visit Keysoe, Airy's home, as inspector of schools.

[2] The Reverend Timothy R. Matthews (1795-1845), for 12 years curate at Colmworth and Bolnhurst, Bedfordshire, later evangelical preacher, whose followers built a chapel for him in Bromham Road, Bedford. While visiting Browne, EFG often attended services at Matthews' chapel and was present at his funeral in 1845. EFG's brother John, a man of non-conformist leanings, aided Matthews in his evangelical mission and for a time after the preacher's death carried on the work at the chapel.

Simmering labor unrest erupted into violence in the manufacturing areas of England during the summer of 1842. The People's Charter, a mammoth petition submitted to Parliament on May 2, had been ignored by the legislators. Rioting broke out among the restive, poverty-stricken laborers near Manchester on August 4. The following day the rioters moved into the city. Although military forces as well as police opposed the demonstrators, order was not restored in the area until August 24 (*Annual Register*, 1842, "Chronicle," pp. 133-34).

[3] Joannes Stobaeus (late 5th century A.D.), compiler of extracts from Greek authors. Stobaeus quotes from more than five hundred writers, poets, historians, orators, philosophers, and physicians. It is to him that we owe many important fragments from the dramatists, especially Euripides.

Menander (342-291 B.C.), Greek dramatist, author of more than a hundred comedies. Menander wrote the familiar line, "Whom the Gods love, dies young."

[4] The proctors at Cambridge and Oxford are young M.A.s charged with a variety of functions, particularly the discipline of students. Clad in academic robes, they patrol the streets in pairs after sundown accompanied by two college servants who are fleet of foot and are dubbed "bulldogs" by the students.

To John Allen

Bedford
August 29/42

My dearest Fellow,

Your letter reached me this morning and gave me much pleasure. An old acquaintance is not the worse for its wear, I think. This very time ten years ago we were in Wales together: I at Mr. Rees' boarding house at Tenby:[1] and there I made chance acquaintance with the whiskered man at whose house I am now staying—then a boy of sixteen.[2] He is now a man of business, of town-politics, and more intent on the first of September than on anything else in the world. I see very little of him.

I have written you two letters: one enclosed in Airy's: the other, not indeed a letter but a note, sent to your house in London. For, by what I heard from Laurence, I supposed you were there. And so you are looking at the mountain-tops of N. Wales: higher than Penally[3] Top which we used to look at ten years ago from those fields about Freestone.[4] I have become quite a divine of late: and listen to Mr. Matthews preach in the open street. He is a good man for the multitude: I rather want to get him to Manchester.[5] Did I tell you that?

I occasionally read sentences about the Virtues out of this collection of Stobaeus[6]—and look into Sartor Resartus, which has fine things in it: and a little Dante and a little Shakespeare. But the great secret of all is the not eating meat. To that the world must come, I am sure. Only it makes one grasshopper foolish.[7] I also receive letters from Morton and F. Tennyson full of fine accounts of Italy—finer than any I ever read. They came all of a sudden on Cicero's villa—one of them at least, the Formian—with a mosaic pavement leading thro' lemon gardens down to the sea, and a little fountain as old as the Augustan age bubbling up as fresh, Tennyson says, "as when its silver sounds mixed with the deep voice of the orator as he sate there in the stillness of the noon day, devoting the siesta-hours to study." When I first read of these things I wish to see them: but, on reflection, I am sure I see them much better in such letters as these.

I have seen one good picture about here: a portrait of O. Cromwell by Lely[8]—so said—unlike other Lelys, but very carefully painted: and, I should think, an original portrait. I went to see Lord Northampton's place[9] which is handsome outside—built by Inigo Jones—but has not a good picture in it. I rather think of going to Luton[10] once to see the fine collection there again. I read about the pictures at the Foundling[11] the other day—I can't think where. Hogarth always declared that his portrait was the best there.

I also read Hayley's Life of Romney[12] the other day. Romney wanted but education and reading to make him a very fine painter: but his ideal was not high nor fixed. How touching is the close of his life! He married at nineteen, and, because Sir Joshua and others had said that marriage spoilt an artist, almost immediately left his wife in the North, and scarce saw her till the end of his life: when, old, nearly mad, and quite desolate, he went back to her, and she received him, and nursed him till he died. This quiet act of hers is worth all Romney's pictures: even as a matter of Art, I am sure.

Whether this letter will ever reach you, I don't know. I am going in two days to Naseby for a little while, and shall then find my way home to Suffolk for the greater part of the Winter and Spring, I suppose.

O beate Sesti,
Vitae summa brevis spem nos vetat inchoare longam.[13]

I think of hiring a house in some country town like this, but nearer Suffolk, and there have my books, etc. I want a house much: and a very small one will content me, with a few old women close by to play cards with at night. What a life, you will say!

His virtues walked their humble round,
Nor knew a pause, nor felt a void:
And sure the Eternal Master found
His single talent well employed.[14]

That was not in playing picquet, I doubt. What fine lines of Johnson's these!

[1] See letter to Allen, [Late Aug., 1832], n.1.
[2] W. K. Browne.
[3] Written in error for Prescelly.
[4] Home of Allen's cousins.

[5] See preceding letter, n.2.

[6] *Virtues and Vices*, treated as a pair, subject of the third of the four books of Stobaeus.

Carlyle's *Sartor Resartus*, rejected by London publishers in 1831. Portions of it appeared in *Fraser's Magazine* at intervals from July, 1833, to August, 1834. First published entire in three volumes in Boston, April, 1836, it was not published in England until 1838.

[7] EFG had persisted in his modified vegetarian diet for almost a decade. See letters to Donne, Sept. 27, [Oct. 25], and Nov. 19, 1833.

[8] Sir Peter Lely (1618-80), portrait painter who came to England from Holland in 1641, attracted by Charles I's patronage of the fine arts. He painted Charles I; later, Oliver Cromwell; and after the Restoration, Charles II, who knighted him in 1679.

[9] See letter to Laurence, [Aug., 1842], n.3.

[10] Lord Bute's seat in Bedfordshire. See letter to Barton, Aug. 31, 1840, n.2.

[11] The Foundling Hospital, Guilford Street, London, originally founded in 1739 by Captain Thomas Coram as "an hospital for exposed and deserted children." In 1760 it was changed from a foundling hospital to one for illegitimate children of the poor whose mothers were known. The portrait of the founder by Hogarth is the one referred to by EFG. The artist declared it to be "the best portrait in the place, notwithstanding the first painters in the kingdom exerted all their talents to vie with it." Most of the famous pictures at the Foundling were gifts, among them works by Gainsborough, Sir Joshua Reynolds, Richard Wilson, and others.

[12] William Hayley (1745-1820), poet, whose close friendship with George Romney (1734-1802), painter, began in 1777. Hayley's *Life of George Romney, Esq.* was published in 1808. After reading this paragraph on Romney in EFG's *Letters and Literary Remains*, first published in 1889, Tennyson wrote the poem "Romney's Remorse," which appeared in *Demeter and Other Poems* later in the year. He quoted EFG's remarks as a note on the poem. (See *Tennyson Memoir*, II, 366.)

[13] Horace, *Odes* 1.4.14-15.

[14] FitzGerald quotes from memory, with characteristic alterations, the seventh stanza of Samuel Johnson's elegy, "On the Death of Dr. Levett." Levett, Boswell states, was "an obscure practicer of physic amongst the lower people" and, for almost 20 years, had been one of Johnson's pensioners. Johnson's lines read:

> His virtues walk'd their narrow round,
>   Nor made a pause, nor left a void;
> And sure th' Eternal Master found
>   The single talent well employ'd.

To W. F. Pollock

London
Septr 17 [16]/42

My dear Pollock,

What reason I have to give for not having written to you these two months I don't know. I grow so fat and selfish, I believe, only conceive—14 stone.[1] I have come up to London for two days on a false errand: and am therefore going back in a pet—to Naseby. But in the beginning of October I shall be at Boulge—and set in there for the winter, I suppose. I enquired at Spedding's rooms today: he is expected by the 20th which is near.[2] Laurence is the only person I know in town: and he tells me he has seen you lately. Let me hear of you. He and I went to see Carlyle at Chelsea yesterday. That genius has been surveying the field of battle of Naseby in company with Dr. Arnold—who died soon after, poor man.[3] I doubt (from Carlyle's description) if they identified the very ground of the carnage. I have also just bought a tragedy for sixpence—with wonderful things in it. It is called "Philo"[4] who is the hero: and who, after describing his mistress' beauty in a general way—proceeds.

> But let me speak minutely—Her head, 'tis something
> Peculiar in itself. It is visible
> That within it resides the far expanding mind
> Controlling, as a monarch rules his Vassals,
> The Body's arts, surpassing all I ever saw,
> Or shall see but in Heaven, and to there God give
> Me speed!—But 'tis form'd as if 'twas more than human
> And the desire 'pon seeing it, if it would not
> Hurt the creature, would be to feast upon the brains.
> And, oh! that bust! etc.

This (and like passages) is really in the serious Second Edition of the Tragedy of Philo: which I rejoice in possessing. One day we will read *the whole Play* together. The versification is the most astonishing thing.

I have heard nothing of Thackeray for these two months. He was to have visited an Irish brother of mine: but he has not yet done so.[5] I called at Coram St. yesterday, and old John seem'd to think he was yet in Ireland. I hear your sea-cruise has been given up—capital weather for it. Alfred Tennyson is reported to have appeared in town some days ago. He enquired in a wild way for Aubrey de Vere,[6] who had invited him to Ireland: Aubrey de Vere having been hunting for Tennyson in the same way. I don't know where you are: but shall send this to your Chambers to take its chance.

Ever yours,
E.FG.

[1] EFG was six feet tall.

[2] From his American trip with the Ashburton Commission.

[3] Thomas Arnold (1795-1842), headmaster of Rugby School and father of Matthew Arnold. He was appointed Regius Professor of History at Oxford in 1841. Carlyle and Dr. Arnold had visited Naseby the first week in May. Arnold died five weeks later.

[4] *Philo*, a tragedy, London, 1836. No author is given in the British Museum copy.

[5] Thackeray visited EFG's brother Peter at his home near Drogheda for three days at the beginning of October. "Old John," Thackeray's factotum.

[6] Aubrey de Vere, Irish poet, son of Sir Aubrey de Vere, also a poet.

To Bernard Barton

London
Friday, Sept[r] [16] 1842

Dear Barton,

Have you supposed me dead or what? Well, so far from it, I have grown more fat than ever, which is quite as much reason for not writing. I have been staying at Naseby, and, having come up here for two days, return to that place by railroad to-morrow. I went to see Carlyle last night. He had just returned from the neighbourhood of Bury. He is full of Cromwell, and, funny enough, went over from Rugby to Naseby this spring with poor Dr. Arnold. They saw nothing, and walked over what was not the field of battle. I want him to go down with me: but he thinks it would be too expensive. So I have engaged to collect what matter I can for him on the spot. At the beginning of October I expect to be back in East Anglia for the winter. Frail is human virtue. I thought I had quite got over picture-dealing, when lo! walking in Holborn this day I looked into a shop just to shew the strength of my virtue, and fell. That accursed Battle Piece—I have bought it[1]—and another picture of dead chaffinches, which Mr. C[hurchyard] will like, it is so well done: I expect you to give high prices for these pictures—mind that: and begin to economize in household matters. Leave off sugar in tea and make all your household do so. Also write to me at Naseby, Welford, Northampton. That's my direction—such a glorious country, Barton. I wrote you a letter a week ago, but never posted it. So now goodbye. I shall bring down the Chaffinches with me to Suffolk. Trade has been very bad, the dealers tell me. My Fruit Girl[2] still hangs up at a window—an unpleasant sight. Nobody is so hard set as to bid for her.

[1] For EFG's struggle to resist the "Battle Piece," see letters to Barton, March 5, 12, 17, and 26, 1842.

[2] His "Opie" picture, left at a dealer's to be sold.

To Thomas Carlyle

39, Portland Place
[September 16, 1842]

Dear Sir,

I am going tomorrow to Naseby—where I shall be for ten days or so. I will ask the folks there to tell what they know: and, if you send me a list of questions, will get them answered as well as I can. I cannot but wish you would come down yourself, while I am there to do the honours of the place. Rail-road to a station called Crick—13 shillings, 2nd class—which is pleasant enough in fine weather. At Crick, what is called a farmer's *Buggy* meets you and conveys you slowly to the place: where I could give you bed and board and cheese. But this I suppose you will not do. I and the farmers shall make horrid blunders in the topography, depend upon it. But we will do as well as we can.

Yours very truly
E. FitzGerald

Address—
Naseby, Welford
Northampton

Since taking up residence in Chelsea in 1834, Thomas Carlyle had won recognition through the publication of a number of strange books. Readers were startled by their content and puzzled by their style. FitzGerald, by turns, praised and condemned works and author, but his interest was kindled because Carlyle "pulls one the opposite side to which all the world are pulling one."

During the summer of 1842 FitzGerald had been "generating" increased interest in Carlyle. In June he was favorably impressed by George Venable's review of Chartism; *and he found "fine things" in* Sartor Resartus, *which he read in August. On September 1 FitzGerald went to Naseby. About 12 days later he made an unexpected trip to London where he fell in with Samuel Laurence who, over the previous five years, had painted an oil portrait and drawn three portrait-sketches of Carlyle. FitzGerald may have mentioned his interest in Carlyle's works for on Thursday the 15th Laurence took him to meet the writer. The meeting proved to be most fortunate for Carlyle as the correspondence attests. Letters written by him to guide FitzGerald in what the latter called "bone-rummaging" on the site of the last major battle between the armies of Charles I and Parliament were saved by FitzGerald and are now in Trinity College Library. Misled by the concluding paragraph of a letter of October 1, 1842, FitzGerald credited Thackeray with first having taken him to Cheyne Row. The error appears in notes, supplied by FitzGerald, which serve as a preface to the correspondence. The preface, published in part in the* Letters and Literary Remains, *is given here in full.*

About the middle of September, 1842, W. M. Thackeray took me to tea with Carlyle whom I had not previously known. He was then busy with Cromwell; had just been, he told us, over the Field of Naseby in company with Dr. Arnold of Rugby, and had sufficiently identified the Ground of the Battle with the contemporaneous Accounts of it. As I happened to know the Field well—the greater part of it then belonging to my Family—I knew that Carlyle and Arnold had been mistaken—misled in part by an Obelisk which my Father had set up as on the highest Ground of the Field, but which they mistook for the centre-ground of the Battle. This I told Carlyle, who was very reluctant to believe that he and Arnold could have been deceived—that he could accept no heresay Tradition or Theory against the Evidence of his own Eyes, etc. However, as I was just then going down to Naseby, I might enquire further into the matter: and *Letter I* was to direct me in the Search.

The inclosure (afterward written, I think) was incorporated in Carlyle's Second Edition.[1]

On arriving at Naseby, I had spade and mattock taken to a hill near half a mile across from the "Blockhead Obelisk," and pitted with several hollows, overgrown with rank Vegetation, which Tradition had always pointed to as the Graves of the Slain. One of these I had opened; and there, sure enough, were the remains of Skeletons closely packed together—chiefly teeth—but some remains of Shin-bone, and marks of Skull in the Clay.[2] Some of these, together with some sketches of the Place, I sent to Carlyle, who acknowledges the receipt of my Intelligence in Letter II.

"Our Scotch Friend" named therein, was a very intelligent Tenant on the Estate, who "assisted" at the Digging, and (I suppose) suggested what practical use it might be made of.

Letter III. The "pretty story" was that when the Parliamentary Troops were marching through Naseby the day before the Battle, one of the Troopers took up a little Boy who was in the Road, and lifted him over a mud wall out of harm's way.

Letter IV. The "Cold Ashby Tradition" was, I think, of some Skeletons found there, quite away from any point of Conflict but perhaps not of *pursuit*: being on the road from Daventry to Harboro' whither Charles retreated from the Enemy.[3]

Letter X. [October 26, 1844] "Dry as dust" was D. E. Davey, Esq., of Ufford, near Woodbridge, who, at my Request, furnished Carlyle with all the Information he wanted about some Long Parliament Election at Ipswich, and was duly rewarded with this Distinction. He was a very polite Antiquary—a model Sylvanus Urban—and bequeathed more than eighty folios of Suffolk History to the British Museum.

The Naseby Monument, already advised by Carlyle, was not executed at the time:[4] and somehow or other was not again talked of till 1855 when the Estate was to be sold from us. I was told however by the Lawyers, etc., that it was better not to interfere while that Business was going on. So the Scheme went to sleep again till 1872, when, Carlyle renewing the subject in some Letter, I applied to the Agent of the Estate who was willing to help us in getting permission to erect the Stone, and to a neighbouring Mason to fashion it as Carlyle desired. We had some difficulty in this latter point, but at last all was settled, when suddenly Agent and Lawyer informed us the thing must not be done —for one reason, that Stone and Inscription were considered too plain.

FitzGerald's letters from Naseby have been bound and are now in the University of Cambridge Library. His sketches, frequently referred to, are water-color views of Naseby field and countryside, on which are located sites mentioned in records of the battle. Eight sketches, including the one given in the letter of September 23, 1842, have been preserved with the correspondence.

Carlyle's brief description of the battlefield and the action which took place there, included in Cromwell's Letters and Speeches, *illuminates the correspondence which passed between Naseby and Chelsea. The passage precedes Cromwell's report of the action sent to Parliament immediately after the battle.*[5]

The old Hamlet of Naseby stands yet, on its old hill-top, very much as it did in Saxon days, on the Northwestern border of Northamptonshire; some seven or eight miles from Market-Harborough in Leicestershire; nearly on a line, and nearly midway, between that Town and Daventry. A peaceable old Hamlet, of perhaps five hundred souls; clay cottages for labourers, but neatly thatched and swept; smith's shop, saddler's shop, beer-shop, all in order; forming a kind of square, which leads off, North and South, into two long streets: the old Church, with its graves, stands in the centre, the truncated spire finishing itself with a strange old Ball, held up by rods; a "hollow copper Ball, which came from Boulogne in Henry the Eighth's time,"—which has, like Hudibras's breeches, "been at the Siege of Bullen." The ground is upland, moorland, . . . Avon Well, the distinct source of Shakespeare's Avon, is on the Western slope of the high grounds; Nen and Welland, streams leading towards Cromwell's Fen-country, begin to gather themselves from boggy places on the Eastern side. The grounds, as we say, lie high; and are still, in their new subdivisions, known by the name of "Hills," "Rutput Hill," "Mill Hill," "Dust Hill," and the like, precisely as in Rushworth's time: but they are not properly hills at all; they are broad blunt clayey masses, swelling towards and from each other, like indolent waves of a sea, sometimes of miles in extent.

It was on this high moor-ground, in the centre of England, that King Charles on the 14th of June, 1645, fought his last Battle; dashed fiercely against the New-Model Army, which he had despised till then; and saw himself shivered utterly to ruin thereby. "Prince Rupert, on the King's right wing, charged *up* the hill, and carried all before him;" but Lieutenant-General Cromwell charged downhill on the other wing, likewise carrying all before him,—and did *not* gallop off the field to plunder, he. Cromwell, ordered thither by the Parliament, had arrived from the Association two days before, "amid shouts from the whole Army:" he had the ordering of the Horse this morning. Prince Rupert, on returning from his plunder, finds the King's Infantry a ruin; prepares to charge again with the rallied Cavalry; but the Cavalry too, when it came to the point, "broke all asunder,"—never to reassemble more. The chase went through Harborough; where the King had already been that morning, when in an evil hour he turned back, to revenge some "surprise of an outpost at Naseby the night before," and give the Roundheads battle. ******

The Parliamentary Army stood ranged on the Height still partly called "Mill Hill," as in Rushworth's time, a mile and half from Naseby;[6] the King's Army, on a parallel "Hill," its back to Harborough;—with the wide table of upland now named *Broad Moor* between them; where indeed the main brunt of the action still clearly enough shews itself to have been.[7] There are hollow spots, of a rank vegetation, scattered over that Broad Moor; which are understood to have once been burial *mounds*;—some of which have been (with more or less of sacrilege) verified as such. A friend of mine has in his cabinet two ancient grinder-teeth, dug lately from that ground,—and waits for an opportunity to rebury them there. Sound effectual grinders, one of them very large; which ate their breakfast on the fourteenth morning of June two hundred years ago, and, except to be clenched once in grim battle, had never work to do more in this world!—"A stack of dead bodies, perhaps about one hundred, had been buried in this Trench; piled as in a wall, a man's length thick: the skeletons lay in courses, the heads of one course to the heels of the next;—one figure, by the strange position of the bones, gave us the hideous notion of its having been thrown in before death! We did not proceed far:—perhaps some half-dozen skeletons. The bones were treated with all piety; watched rigorously, over Sunday, till they could be covered in again."[8] Sweet friend for Jesus' sake forbear!—

Carlyle himself was "the friend of mine" in whose cabinet the teeth were stored. With the teeth were at least three musket balls and a shinbone, all sent from the battlefield by FitzGerald. The relics have a curious history.

In the spine of the slip-cover protecting the volume of FitzGerald's Naseby letters is a small drawer that once contained two of the musket balls. Unfortunately, the bullets had been removed before the letters were acquired by the university. Bound with the letters is an envelope on which Carlyle had written: "Two jaw teeth, dug from a burial-mound (near Cloisterwell) on Naseby Battlefield, on 23rd Sept[r]*., 1842, [actually the 22nd] and sent to me by E. FitzGerald. T.C." A notation records: "One given to J. Childs of Bungay, 18 Feb*[y] *1848." Childs printed the* Cromwell Letters and Speeches. *A third note: "bigger one left here." A fourth note states: "other tooth (and bullet) given to Mr. [name indecipherable] of the 'Bookplate' 23rd. Jan*[y] *1853."*

Carlyle books and memorabilia have been prizes sought by Norman H. Strouse, a bibliophile of New York City, formerly president of the Grolier Club. While in Chicago one day in 1966, he inquired of a dealer if he had any Carlyle letters to offer. "A couple," was the reply, "but we have something else of Carlyle's you might find interesting," and he produced a silver box. Within, were a tooth and a bone "under glass." In the box cover were mounted two notes in Carlyle's script identifying the contents as having been sent from Naseby "by Edward FitzGerald; now presented to John Childs of Bungay 18 February 1848."[9] *The relics were included in Mr. Strouse's gift of his Carlyle collection to the library of the University of California at Santa Cruz.*

[1] Not written later. Appendix 8 of the 1846 Edition of *Cromwell* includes the notes on Naseby Battle sent with Carlyle's letter of Sept. 18. The substance was drawn from early published sources and Carlyle's survey of the field with Thomas Arnold.

[2] The site is marked on Ordnance Survey Map, No. 133, at a point just off the Naseby-Welford road and about a half-mile north of Naseby Wooleys, the manor house on the FitzGerald estate. The obelisk is almost two miles to the southeast, not "near half a mile" as FitzGerald states. A second monument to commemorate the battle has been placed by the Cromwellian Association on Broad Moor, a mile east of the grave and adjacent to the Naseby-Clipston road. The grave still lacks identifying stone or monument.

[3] Daventry and Cold Ashby are both southwest of Naseby. While retreating from Daventry toward Naseby, two days before the battle, the king had passed through Cold Ashby, closely pursued by General Ireton.

[4] Carlyle proposed that he and FitzGerald place an inscribed stone to mark the site of the grave.

[5] First edition, 1845, I, 211-14, preceding Letter XIII.

[6] Mill Hill is less than a mile north of the village.

[7] Carlyle erred. Broad Moor, an area of lower elevation, lies between the hills, a mile apart. The Royalists crossed Broad Moor and engaged the enemy on hilltops before Naseby village. EFG identifies the hill where he opened the grave as Cloisterwell. The name does not appear on the Ordnance Map.

[8] The closing paragraph paraphrases portions of EFG's despatches but includes misstatements which, without success, EFG later urged Carlyle to revise.

[9] Address by Mr. Strouse at the dedication of the Mayfield Library, Syracuse University, May 20, 1966.

Carlyle to FitzGerald

Chelsea, 18 Sept^r, 1842

My dear Sir,

Profiting by the unexpected fact that *you* are now master of Naseby Battlefield, I have gone over the whole matter once more, probably for the twentieth time; I have copied you my illegible pencil-notes, and re-verified everything,—that so, if you can understand the meaning (which will be difficult, I fear), you may append to it what commentary, collected on the spot, you may judge edifying. Let me, however, again impress upon you that these statements and descriptions are actual *facts*, gathered with industry from some seven or eight eye-witnesses, looking at the business with their own eyes from seven or eight different sides; that the present figure of the ground, in my recollection, corresponds very tolerably well with the whole of them;—and that no "theory," by what Professor soever, can be of any use to me in comparison. I wish you had Sprigge's[1] complete Plan of the Battle: but you have it not; you have only that foolish Parson's,[2] very dim copy of it, and must help yourself with that.

The things I wish you to give me are first: the whole story of your Blacksmith, or other oral Chronicler, be it wise and credible, be it absurd and evidently false. Then you can ask, whether there remains any tradition of a Windmill at Naseby? One stands in the Plan, not far from North of the village, probably some 300 yards to the west of where the ass of a Column now stands: the whole concern, of fighting, rallying, flying, killing and chasing, transacted itself to the *west* of that,—*on* the height, over the brow of the height, down the slope, in the hollow, and up again to the grounds of Dust Hill, where the *final* dispersion took place. Therefore, again, pray ask.

Where precisely any dead bodies are known to have been found? Where and when the *last*-found was come upon; what they made of it,—whether no Antiquarian kept a tooth; at any rate, a button or the like? Cannon-balls ought to be found, especially musket-balls, down in that hollow, and on the slope thitherward: is any extant cabinet master of one?

Farther, are there, on the high ground N.W. or W. of Naseby Village, any traces still discoverable of such names as these: "Lantford hedges" (or perhaps "hedge"; a kind of thicket running *up* the slope, towards the western environs of Naseby Village, nearly from the North;—Fairfax had dragoons hidden here, who fired upon Rupert's right, as he charged upwards): "Rutput Hill"; "Fanny Hill" (according to Rushworth, "Fanny Hill" in Sprigge),—probably two swellings in the ground, that lie between the south end of Lantford Hedges and the Village; "Lean Leaf Hill"[3] seemingly another swelling, parallel to these, which reaches in with its slope *to* the very village—from the west: "Mill Hill" farther to the east (marked as due west from the windmill, which of course must have stood upon a part of it), lying therefore close upon the north part of the village? Is it possible, in spite of all ditching and enclosure bills, there may still some vestige of these names adhere to some fields or messuages; the exact position of which it would be satisfactory to fix. You can also tell me whether Burrough Hill is visible from Naseby, and "what it is like"; and what the Sibbertoft height, on the other side, and the Harboro' Height are like! I suppose one sees Sibbertoft steeple, but no houses, from Naseby Height? Also that it was undoubtedly Clipston (as the good Dr. Arnold and I supposed) that we saw there. Dr. A. and I came,[4] as I find, thro' Crick, West Hadden, Cold Ashby; and crossed the Welford and Northampton road perhaps some three miles from Naseby.

On the whole, my dear Sir, here seems to be work enough for you! But after all is it not worth your while on other accounts? Were it not a most legitimate task for the Proprietor of Naseby, a man of scholarship, intelligence and leisure, to make himself completely acquainted with the true state of all details connected with Naseby Battle and its localities? Few spots of ground in all the world are memorabler to an Englishman. We could still very well stand a *good* little book on Naseby! *Verbum sapienti.*

As for myself, had I the wings of an eagle, most likely I should still fly to you, and to several other quarters; but with railways and tub-gigs, and my talent for insomnolence, and fretting myself to fiddle-strings with all terrestrial locomotion whatsoever—alas, alas!

Believe me always,
My dear Sir,
Very truly yours,
T. Carlyle.

[1] Joshua Sprigg, or Sprigge (1618-84), in 1647 published *Anglia Rediviva: England's Recovery*, "being the History of the Motions, Actions, and Successes of the Army under his Excellency Sir Thomas Fairfax."

[2] EFG added a note: "There were two Parsons who wrote accounts of Naseby —Mastin in 1792, and Locking in 1830."

John Mastin, Vicar of Naseby, *History and Antiquities of Naseby*; Henry Lockinge, Curate of Naseby and Kelmarsh, *Historical Gleanings on the Memorable Field of Naseby*, which contains a plan of the battle.

[3] In EFG's letter of Sept. 23 will be found corrected or variant forms of these place names.
[4] From Rugby, about 15 miles southwest of Naseby by road.

To W. F. Pollock

Naseby, Welford, Northampton
Sept. 20/42

My dear Pollock,

I hope that before this you have got a note from me, written when I was in London three days ago, and when I had not yet received yours. So I am not so bad as might be—to wait for the absolute kick on the backside before I make the amende honorable. London was very close and nasty: so I am glad to get down here: where, however, I am not (as at present proposed) to stay long: my Father requiring my services in Suffolk early in October. Laurence has made a sort of promise to come and see me here next Saturday: I wanted him to come down with me while the weather was fine. The place is very desert, but a battle was probably fought here 200 years ago, as an Obelisk planted by my Papa on the wrong site intimates. Poor Carlyle got into sad error from that deluding Obelisk: which Liston[1] used to call (in this case with truth) an Obstacle. I am afraid Carlyle will make a mad mess of Cromwell and his Times: what a poor figure Fairfax[2] will cut! I am very tired of these heroics: and I can worship no man who has but a square inch of brains more than myself. I think there is but one Hero: and that is the Maker of Heroes.

Here I am reading Virgil's delightful Georgics for the first time. They really attune perfectly well with the plains and climate of Naseby. Valpy (whose edition I have) cannot quite follow Virgil's plough—in its construction at least. But the main acts of agriculture seem to have changed very little, and the alternation of green and corn crops is a good dodge. And while I heard the fellows going out with their horses to plough as I sat at breakfast this morning, I also read—

> Libra die somnique pares ubi fecerit horas,
> Et medium luci atque umbris jam dividit orbem,
> Exercete, viri, tauros, serite hordea campis
> Usque sub extremum brumae intractabilis imbrem.[3]

One loves Virgil somehow—was he much of a b——? Not that that can touch us now.

I was glad to hear at Moxon's that Tennyson's book sold very well. I also saw an article on it in the Quarterly: a very stupid article, I thought. Some one said Milnes was to write an article there—but it did not seem to me to be his. At all events the Quarterly has been forced to change its tone.[4] The note about The Sleeping Beauty being cribbed from Maclise's picture must have been by Lockhart himself.[5] Alfred T. is (I suppose) gone to Ireland.

And now here is a long note: perhaps repeating what I said in my other. But never mind: it shews zeal. I enquired at 60 Lincoln's Inn Fields,[6] and was told that they had orders to be ready by the 20th which is today—so the μετώπιον[7] may be even now in a brothel at Wapping. Now I have told you what I have not been doing: tell me what you have been doing. Ever yours,

E.FG.

[1] John Liston, comedian. See letter to Donne, Oct. 23, 1836, n.7.

[2] Thomas Fairfax (1612-71), third Baron Fairfax of Cameron, appointed commander-in-chief of the Parliamentary army in 1645.

[3] Virgil's *Georgics*, a didactic poem on cultivation of the soil and raising cattle and bees, I.208-11.

> When Libra equal makes the day and night,
> And cuts in twain the shadows and the light,
> Your oxen work; strew barley now, my swains!
> E'en to the pelting of the brumal rains.
>
> Translation by William Stawel

[4] The article, written by John Sterling, had appeared in the September issue of the *Quarterly Review* (pp. 385-416). The critique, which apportioned praise and censure about equally, exposed a decided change in the editorial tone of the periodical that had published J. W. Croker's savage attack on Tennyson's 1832 volume (April, 1833, pp. 81-96). EFG condemned Sterling's article as "stupid," probably because the reviewer regretted that Tennyson had not dealt with "matter . . . of more earnest meaning" and had taken too little note of the revolutionary changes occurring in the world.

The *Westminster Review* published a criticism by R. M. Milnes in October (pp. 371-90).

[5] The footnote to which EFG refers reads in part: "It is difficult to suppose that the poem was written before the exhibition [at the Royal Academy in 1841] of Mr. Maclise's picture of 'The Sleeping Beauty'" (*Quarterly Review*, p. 402). The editor need not have been confronted by any "difficulty." Tennyson had published "The Sleeping Beauty" in 1830. In 1842 it formed a portion of "A Day-Dream." John Gibson Lockhart, editor of the *Quarterly Review*, 1825-53.

[6] Spedding's quarters at Lincoln's Inn, being prepared for his return from America.

[7] "Forehead."

To Bernard Barton

[Naseby]
Septr 22/42

My dear Barton,

The pictures are left all ready packed up in Portland Place, and shall come down with me, whenever that desirable event takes place. In the mean while here I am as before: but having received a long and interesting letter from Carlyle asking information about this Battlefield, I have trotted about rather more to ascertain names of places, positions, etc. After all he will make a mad book. I have just seen some of the bones of a dragoon and his horse who were found foundered in a morass in the field—poor dragoon, much dismembered by time: his less worthy members having been left in the owner's summer-house for the last twenty years have disappeared one by one: but his skull is kept safe in the hall: not a bad skull neither: and in it some teeth yet holding, and *a bit of the iron heel of his boot,* put into the skull by way of convenience. This is what Sir Thomas Browne calls "making a man act his Antipodes."[1] I have got a fellow to dig at one of the great general graves in the field: and he tells me to-night that he has come to bones: to-morrow I will select a neat specimen or two. In the mean time let the full harvest moon wonder at them as they lie turned up after lying hid 2400 revolutions of hers. Think of that warm 14th of June when the Battle was fought, and they fell pell-mell: and then the country people came and buried them so shallow that the stench was terrible, and the putrid matter oozed over the ground for several yards: so that the cattle were observed to eat those places very close for some years after. Every one to his taste, as one might well say to any woman who kissed the cow that pastured there.

Friday, 23rd. We have dug at a place, as I said, and made such a trench as would hold a dozen fellows: whose remains positively make up the mould. The bones nearly all rotted away, except the teeth which are quite good. At the bottom lay the *form* of a perfect skeleton: most of the bones gone, but the pressure distinct in the clay: the thigh and leg bones yet extant: the skull a little pushed forward, as if there were scanty room. We also tried some other reputed graves, but found nothing: indeed it is not easy to distinguish what are graves from old marl-pits, etc. I don't care for all this bone-rummaging myself: but the identification of the graves identifies also where the greatest heat of the battle was. Do you wish for a tooth?

As I began this antiquarian account in a letter to you, so I have finished it, that you may mention it to my Papa, who perhaps will be amused at it. Two farmers insisted on going out exploring with me all day: one a very solid fellow, who talks like the justices in Shakespeare: but who certainly was inspired in finding out this grave: the other a Scotchman full of intelligence, who proposed the flesh-soil for manure for turnips. The old Vicar, whose age reaches half-way back to the day of the Battle, stood tottering over the verge of the trench. Carlyle has shewn great sagacity in guessing at the localities from the vague descriptions of contemporaries: and his short *pasticcio* of the battle[2] is the best I have seen. But he will spoil all by making a demigod of Cromwell, who certainly was so far from wise that he brought about the very thing he fought to prevent—the restoration of an unrestricted monarchy.

[1] "To keep our eyes open longer, were but to act our *Antipodes*. The Huntsmen are up in *America*, and they are already past their first sleep in *Persia*" (*The Garden of Cyrus*, chap. V, par. 14).

[2] The account enclosed with Carlyle's letter of Sept. 18.

To Thomas Carlyle

Naseby, Welford
Sept[r] 23, [1842]

Dear Sir,

I took a walk over the Field with my Blacksmith yesterday, and wished you had been with us: you would then have seen every thing very clearly. All the questions in your letter I cannot yet answer: but some I can and will, so that you may apply to your map with perhaps some clearer light. But I cannot help saying again I wish you would come here: Laurence talks of coming here on Saturday. Besides the country itself, I have found a great map of the *Lord*ship[1] at the Vicar's: this map drawn in 1800—before the enclosure—with *all* the old names, *some* positions of the army, of the graves of the dead, etcc. If I come to town I will bring it with me: but I cannot send it. All the old names of the localities are in present use—and none other. What you write "*Lantford* hedges" is "*Langfordy* hedges"—that is, the long hedge that runs all the way from near to *Rutpit* Hill to Broadmoor, and divides the Lordship of Sulby from that of Naseby. The hedge itself is generally called "Sulby Hedge": but the land on our side of it, is called always "*Langfordy*". "Fanny" or "Famny Hill" is "*Fenny* Hill" which rises out of *Rutpit* Hill, and runs eastward toward the village. "Lean Leaf" is "Lean Leys" (I suppose *leys* or *lays* of grass—as people now talk of clover-lays, etcc., and these "leys" are *lean* enough, as I can testify; of a coarse grass, and marshy) is a slightly rising pasture that reaches *to* the hill on which the village is built toward the west: which hill (wonderful to say) has no name in particular, and so may be called Lean Leys Hill.

About Mills. Once upon a time there were *two* Mills, the marks of whose foundation-posts in the sward my Blacksmith remembers: one on Mill Hill, of whose complete being however there is no record, so that it may have disappeared (and probably did) from the Field *before* the Battle, and left its foundation-marks and name only to the Hill it stood on: and 2ndly a Mill which stood where the Obelisk now stands, and which my blacksmith's grandmother remembers standing and being burnt down some hundred years ago. Nearly every separate swelling of ground in this part of the world has its distinct name. But the principal ridges of Hills (subdivided into divers names) run almost parallel from east to West something in this way:

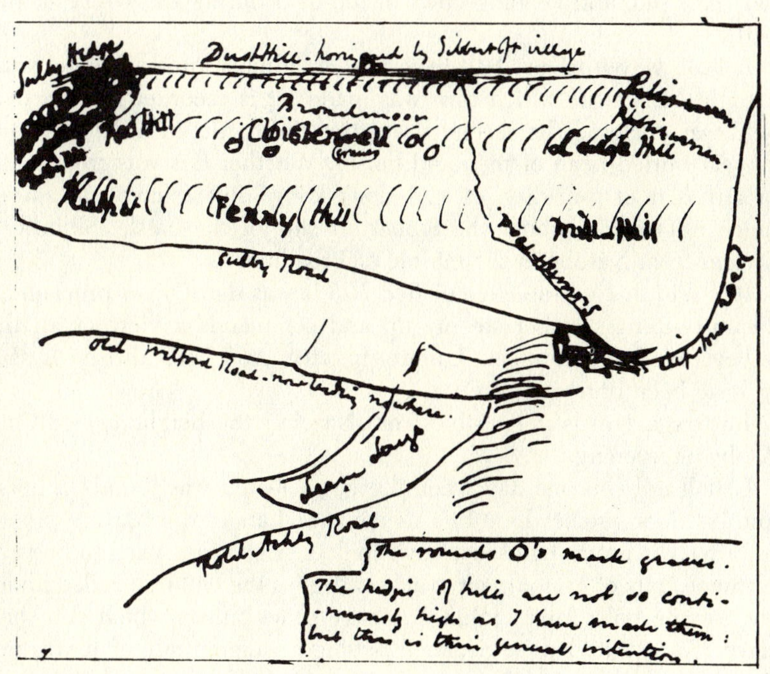

I only draw this very rudely to show how these ridges run, all pretty much of the same height: so that when you stand just to the North of Naseby Church, you see scarce above Mill Hill: when you get on Mill Hill, you see but to Cloisterwell and Lodge Hill (except the topmost trees of the next ridge and the blue distance toward what you call Infinite space beyond) and when on Cloisterwell and Lodge Hill, then at last you see the Broadmoor: which lies between Cloisterwell, etc., (where Fairfax drew up) and Dust Hill, where Charles. This Broadmoor is more than a mile from Naseby village.

I fear this wearies you: but the maps do not express the *rising* of the ground: and no one could judge from the old map how far Broadmoor is from the village.

Most graves are to be traced in and about Cloisterwell and down by Langfordy: some of the holes would (before the field was enclosed) have taken twenty loads of earth to fill up. You will find in the Histories of Naseby how an old man (living in 1792 when the book was written) describes how the dead were buried "very shallow" so that the putrid matter oozed out over the ground several yards, etcc.—he heard it from his Grandfather, who was a "strong boy, about nine or ten years old, and keeping cows in the field during the whole of the battle".

A little way *up* Dust Hill from the Broadmoor runs a hedge, with a slight turn in it: which turn was made (it is recorded) when that field was enclosed the second year after the battle, in order to avoid a great buried heap of men and horses. Whether this was from piety or any fear of putridity, etcc., I don't know. But I have not as yet much information about the Sibbertoft side of the battle. Sibbertoft divides from Naseby in the middle of Broadmoor.

It is said that on the edge of *Red Hill* it was that Oliver proclaimed Victory—it rises rather steeply up and commands a view of all the valley round—Broadmoor, Langfordy, etcc. And here also he is said to have been buried. Q.E.D.

Burrough Hill is *not* visible from Naseby: the height (!) of Cold Ashby intervening.

I shall tell you one day when the last skeleton was found—a horse and his rider—somewhere in a marsh near Langfordy; but my proper informant is not at hand just now. Bullets of all kinds used to be very common: bits of armour: my blacksmith says the children rolled about the cannon balls for playthings. I have some bullets which you shall have, if you like. I once declined buying a cannon ball, as it was not so portable as one could wish. Bones and skulls also *used* to be not uncommon: and a very solid farmer has assured me he is not sure if a skull may not yet be had. Also three buttons, out of nine found, with a crown and "*N.Y.I.*" engraved on each, are in the cabinet of the Vicar. The initials are said to mean *North* York Infantry—which sounds rather pleonastic, does it not?

The old fish ponds marked in the maps, yet remain. They are fed, among other Springs, by the Spring of the Avon, which rises in the village and runs down with a stream "No bigger than the tap of a barrel" (so says blacksmith) to these fish-ponds—and then in a ragged straggling cleft down by Lean Leys, and called Lean Leys Gutter, or Vicarage Gutter. A Pretty beginning.

Here is enough for once. Is it too much? If you won't come here, and I may go off any day to Suffolk, I must tell all I can. But, really, if you cannot see the place itself, or the map I have found, I will make a little sketch of it for you, and some sketches of the hill-tops about.

Yours truly
E. FitzGerald

P.S. In my map, I have not drawn Rut-pit quite right: it rises a little to the North of Fenny, and swells up into it: as the old map rudely represents.

Do you know Bridge's History of Northamptonshire?[2] I do not: but there is such a book, I am told. It might enlighten you.

P.S. (2) Having ordered one of the reputed graves to be opened near Cloisterwell—a soil of animal matter mixed with crumbling jaw-bones, arm-bones, skulls, etc., is found about four feet under the surface. Only the teeth perfect: plenty of them. The Scotchman[3] is digging hard now this late:[x] and proposes the whole matter as a manure for turnips.

I will open one or two more places.

[x] 1/2 past 8 P.M.

[1] Property owned by a lord.

[2] John Bridges (c. 1666-1724), antiquarian, who accumulated a wealth of material for a history of Northamptonshire. The work was not published complete until 1791 when it appeared in two volumes edited by Peter Whalley.

[3] A Naseby farmer named Love.

Carlyle to FitzGerald

Chelsea, Saturday, 25 [24][1] *Sept^{r}, 1842*

My dear Sir,

You will do me and the Genius of History a real favour, if you persist in these examinations and excavations to the utmost length possible for you! It is long since I read a letter so interesting as yours of yesterday. Clearly enough you are upon the very battle-ground;—and I, it is also clear, have only looked up towards it from the slope of Mill Hill. Were not the weather so wet, were not, etc., etc., so many *etceteras*, I could almost think of running up to join you still! But that is evidently *un*feasible at present.

The opening of that burial-heap blazes strangely in my thoughts: these are the very jawbones that were clenched together in deadly rage, on this very ground, 197 years ago! It brings the matter home to one, with a strange veracity,—as if for the first time one saw it to be no fable and theory but a dire fact. I will beg for a tooth and a bullet; authenticated by your own eyes and word of honour!—Our Scotch friend too, making turnip manure of it, he is part of the Picture. I understand almost all the Netherlands battlefields have already given up their bones to British husbandry; why not the old English next? Honour to thrift. If of 5000 wasted men, you can make a few usable turnips, why, do it!

The more sketches and details you can contrive to send me, the better. I want to know for one thing whether there is any *house* on Cloisterwell; what house that was that I saw from the slope of Naseby height (Mill-hill, I suppose), and fancied to be Dust Hill Farm? It must lie about North by West from Naseby Church, perhaps near a mile off. You say, one cannot see Dust Hill at all, much less any farm house of Dust Hill, from that Naseby Height?

But why does the Obelisk stand there? It might as well stand at Charing Cross; the blockhead that it is! I again wish I had wings: alas, I wish many things; that the gods would but annihilate Time and Space, which would include all things!

In great haste, Yours most truly, T. Carlyle.

[1] Saturday was the 24th.

To Thomas Carlyle

Naseby, Welford
Septr 27/42

Dear Sir,

I am glad my first batch of communications did anything for you. I write to you what I have heard more—not much—that no heap may gather formidably big. Don't trouble yourself to write answers unless you have questions to ask—I dare say you hate it. We opened part of the grave[x] I told you of—a trench about 7 feet long and 3½ wide—6 deep—the remains of seven or eight poor chaps in this space, as we thought: but a rule of three Men would tell one exactly how many men of given dimensions could be packed in such an area. They lay east and west alternately—as they pack fish—the bones (such as remained) as porous as sponge almost—the skulls (those not porous) not enduring the heaving of the spade round the clay that hooded them—the teeth quite good. I send you samples—such as argued (our Scotchman said) stout owners. One skeleton lay across the rest, jammed in it seemed: the jaw desperately protruded from the skull and the arms pinched up to the chin. The last (as we thought) of the batch. I mean the last in depth—was pretty perfect in form—then we left him—a heavy rain fell in the night and washed away his ribs: his thighs and legs still extended in corpse-like propriety, looking upward too.

We tried three other little valleys about that Cloisterwell ground, and found—nothing. The truth is that little marle-pits, etcc., have become confounded with the graves: so it is only by chance (now the ground has been so often ploughed over) that you get upon a grave. I shall have two more diggings—one down at Langfordy—one over the Broadmoor on Charles' side. As to the site of the Battle there can be no doubt—my Professor[1] (whom you rather sneered at) only made out the written account to be right: he took us *to Broadmoor*, which was the middle ground between the two Armies. It chanced that when I first went over the ground with him, we took as a Guide the only man in Naseby who knew nothing of the matter—a new tenant. About this same Cloisterwell have most bullets been found: not most cannon-balls: Charles had enough of them on the other side of Broadmoor. Langfordy has now bits of pond and swamp in it, which shew what a state that ground was in at the time of the battle: the account tells how the Parliament left wing were impeded in their movements by it. A man at Welford who used to rent Langfordy has the bones of a

Dragoon who was found with his horse, saddle, etcc., in one of these little bogs twenty years ago. He has lost by carelessness greater part of these bones: but I saw the Dragoon's skull, and the iron heel of his boot, which is kept in his skull for convenience. This is what Sir Thomas Browne calls "a man acting his Antipodes."[2] Same man at Welford has a gallant iron sword dug up from Broadmoor.

I send you three sketches of the appearance of the hills as you go due North from the Village towards Broadmoor. If I said to you in my last that when on Mill Hill you could not see Dust Hill, I lied. You can see just the top—what I meant was, that you did not see the whole field of battle, Broadmoor, Dust Hill, etcc., till you had surmounted two ranges of Hill to the North. Did you walk along the road by the Obelisk? I do not quite know which way you went, so I cannot tell you which was the Farm house you ask about. Perhaps you will recognize it in the second drawing. *Mill Hill* is not Obelisk Hill, you know. The Obelisk was put in its place as being the highest ground: and I think reasonably enough. It is a pity you will not come and see it all for yourself in four hours: I am very happy to tell you what I can, but after all I shall confuse you. However, you can always come here when you like: there is always room in this farm house:[3] and the people are civil: will send for you to the Railway, and shew you the field (I mean if I am not here) and not bother.

A man here used to be told by his Grandfather that that Grandfather's Grandfather knew a man who, when a child of five or six, was toddling up Naseby Street when the troopers came riding along: he was almost under the horse's feet, when the foremost trooper leaned down, took him up, and put him gently over the low mud wall of a rick yard. Oh mighty beginning and little conclusion—yet I know you will like this little kindly story, which seems to me to sparkle from the very number of hands it has passed through. One would not care to have a man tell of it as happening to himself at Brussels on the day before Waterloo. Even the name of this child has come down, being a native.[4] But the jolly trooper, whether Dragoon or Life Guard, or what, passed on nameless.

We have the oak table at which the King's Life Guards were surprized at their supper by Ireton's party on the night before the Battle.

They shew you a place in a field, a good deal to the North East of Naseby, a little out of the Clipstone road, where it is said the Parliament Army heard prayers and a sermon on the morning of the 14th. The text was the 22nd verse of the 22nd Chapter of Joshua.[5] They say also that an Aidecamp (what was he called in those days?) was sent thence to reconnoitre: he rode to the brow of Mill Hill, and went back to say that the King's army was showing over from Sibbertoft. The Rebels might have rested in such a place to breakfast, etcc., if they were chasing Charles to Harborough. The Clipstone road leads there.

You ask what village you saw, etcc. If you walked on the Clipstone road (past the Obelisk) and looked due East (at right angles to the road) you saw Hazlebeech: if more North, Kelmarsh Church among the woods: if straight along the road, and walking a long way forward, Clipstone. I do not think you can now see Sibbertoft from the Obelisk —because of trees.

As to "Gilling," Mastin[6] says there was an old House so called two miles south of Naseby: but no one else has heard of it. One must suppose Guilsborough is meant: as both the despatches to Parliament write it so.

I send you also a sketch of Naseby, something as Rupert saw it when he dashed with his horse over Fenny Hill. There were, I suppose, fewer trees and hedges about the houses. I suppose his eye caught the Church as he was going and then pell mell right on. I suppose the Rebels' Train and Baggage nestled under that stubble Hill, between that and Lean Leys? Or did people get under hills on such occasions? I shall be here (I dare say) to the end of the week, if you have more queries.

I enclose a cast of the button—which I hope will not break. The old Vicar cannot tell about its digging up. It may after all be one from the jacket of some New Yeomanry Infantry who displayed upon these hills.

You mistook about the weather, for see how fine it is. Never did the country about here—I mean just beyond our Field which serves as a lofty foreground—look more noble. For this is a noble country. I shall remain here till Thursday or Friday; and then (having received a summons) go into Suffolk. If you come I shall be happy to entertain you as well as I can: and most of all by leaving you to yourself, which I think is good hospitality to one on your errand. But, as I said, you will always find room, etc., whether I am here or not. I will make one or two more sketches if I can. Red Hill you know (one side of it) in my last—which drawing is pretty correct in outline, but not in colour: Red Hill is further off than it looks in my drawing—Broadmoor sweeping round toward the South to the Sulby Road. I expect to be made your Landscape Painter in Ordinary.

Thackeray calls Oliver Cromwell, Oliver Crummles.

The steam-trains that touch at Crick (nine miles from here) are two:

the first leaves at eight in the morning: the second at one-half past one, p.m. If you give me an inscription (not like that of the Count in Sartor)[7] I will put up a stone at Cloisterwell. How many men were killed in the fight?

[No signature]

P.S. Bullets and shin-bone by first opportunity. The teeth I swear I saw picked out of the grave.

[x] N.B. The whole grave (they said) might have contained above a hundred men.

[1] Carlyle refers to this shadowy person in the first paragraph of his September 18 letter.

[2] See letter to Barton, Sept. 22, 1842, n.2.

[3] The home of Charles Watcham, a former servant of the FitzGerald family.

[4] In his letter of Oct. 7, 1842, EFG gives the name of the boy as "Ringrose."

[5] "The Lord God of gods, the Lord God of gods, he knoweth, and Israel he shall know; if *it be* in rebellion, or if in transgression against the Lord, (save us not this day.)"

[6] One of Carlyle's sources. See Sept. 18, 1842, letter from Carlyle, n.2.

[7] Teufelsdröckh, in *Sartor Resartus*, maintained that "lapidary inscriptions . . . should be historical rather than lyrical." An epitaph composed in Latin at the request of the Zähdarm family translates, in part: "Here lies Philip Zähdarm, surnamed the Great, Count of Zähdarm, . . . Knight of the Golden Fleece, of the Garter . . . , and of the Black Vulture. Who during his sublunary existence, shot five thousand partridges: A hundred million hundredweights of foods of various kinds, through himself, and through his servants, quadrupeds or bipeds, not by any means without racket in its course, he openly converted into manure" (*Sartor Resartus*, Book II, chap. 4).

To Samuel Laurence
(Fragment)

Naseby
Sept[r] *28/42*

My dear Laurence,

I am sorry you did not come, as the weather has become fine, and this wild wide country looks well on these blowing days, with flying shadows running over the distance. Carlyle wrote me a long letter of questions concerning the field of Battle, its traditions, etc. So I have trotted about, examined the natives, and answered a great many of his queries as fully, but as shortly, as I could. However I suppose he growls superciliously at my letter, which was necessarily rather a long one. I have also, in company with two farmers, opened one of the reputed graves in which the killed were said to be reposited: and there sure enough we found decayed bones, skulls, arms, legs, etc., and very sound teeth—the only sound part. For many bodies put together corrupt one another of course, and 200 years have not contributed to their preservation. People had often dug about the field before and found nothing; and we tried two or three other spots with no success. I am going to dig once more in a place where tradition talks of a large burial of men and horses. . . .

How long I shall yet be here I know not: but not long I doubt. I dare say I shall pass through London on my way to Suffolk: and then perhaps see the trans-Atlantic Secretary.[1]

Don't trouble yourself to write answers to my gossip. I have just been at our Church where we have had five clergymen to officiate: two in shovel-hats. Our Vicar is near ninety; we have two curates:[2] and an old Clergyman and his Archdeacon son came on a visit. The son having a shovel-hat, of course the Father could not be left behind. Shovel-hats (you know) came into use with the gift of Tongs.[3]

[1] Spedding.

[2] William Marshall served as vicar at Naseby from 1829 until his death in 1847. T. H. Manning is the only curate given in the 1842 *Clergy List*.

[3] EFG's remark appears to involve a pattern of association worthy of an Elizabethan conceit. The *NED* cites 1829 for the origin of the term, "shovel hat." "Shovel" seems to have suggested "tongs." Edward Irving, the popular Scottish preacher, in 1829 revived the belief in "the Gift of Tongues" among members of his congregation at the Caledonian Chapel in London.

From Thomas Carlyle

Chelsea
29 Sept^{r}, 1842

My dear Sir,

Had the weather held up today as it promised yesterday to do, the chances are I should have written, in time for the post, to request the favour of the Farmer's Gig at Crick tomorrow, that I might join you in the field, after all, and see with my own eyes! There is a horrible impressiveness in these jaw-teeth; a stern matter of fact that there *was* a Fight at Naseby, and that you are now on the very arena of the same. To think that this grinder chewed its breakfast on the 14th of June 1645, and had no more eating to do in the world, or services further there—till now, to lie in my drawer, and be a horror! For one thing, I wish you would not open any more mounds till I can be there too: it would have been worth a longer journey to see those poor packed skeletons; that "last of the batch" (or *first*, first-buried, I suppose he must have been) lying flat on his back; and that one lying across the rest, jammed in, as you describe! Pray explain *him* a little better: was he atop, near the middle, or where? He must have lain north and south, I suppose, and you got but half of him, and that all indistinct.

I want no more bones, shin or other; but pray continue to send me as many details as you can; I will write only if I have something new to ask,—as I have at present, on one or two points.

Your Sketches recall to me perfectly the physiognomy of the ground; I now see where I was, and that the house I inquire after was that in sketch No. 2 which stands at the west end of Lodge Hill: this the Dr. and I had agreed to consider as *Dust Hill*, which latter also we must have noticed, tho' far off our route, was past the Obelisk a little way; then down to the left by a field-lane (the first we could find, I think, and near a small three-cornered speck of something like plantation if I remember); down this field-lane we proceeded a pretty way; opening a gate or gates, and holding on with varieties of level, but without suspicion of new "Hills", till I think we had come nearly to the bottom of the ground there, and saw *Lodge Hill* house (is that the name of it?) nearly opposite to us: we then scrambled along *westward*, without descending farther; by the roots of high hedges, rough dingles, briars and young wood, thro' ditches, sometimes on the edge of ploughed fields, and often on very spongy ground,—discerning at intervals what must have been the Sibbertoft road, and a good way to the N. E. of that and of Lodge Hill house, a clear red distinct village, which I consider to have been Clipstone: we got at length into open field-paths or cart-tracks, and returned conveniently into Naseby right thro' the Farmer's yard, as our last course led us! We were never on the proper side of the Sibbertoft road at all; nor I fancy within more than sight of Broadmoor and Cloisterwell, if even that. I mean to visit the place once more,—along with you, if you will let me in good weather.

But now for the questions I have in view:[1]

1. Can you mark on one of these Plans where specially the place is from which you dug these two jaw-teeth? Is Cloisterwell the foreground of No. 3: the grave is somewhere on that, is it not?

2. The three buttons are altogether insignificant, but their "N.Y.I." is becoming altogether a riddle to me. The names of perhaps 20 regi-

ments are given in Books, and not one of them has any title even distantly resembling that, or, as it were, reconcilable with that. "Infantry" is not a word used much in those days,—and perhaps never in official language. The regiment is always "Colonel *Something's* of Foot," Colonel Something's Tertia etc., etc. Yet N.Y.I. must mean something; there it is! Could you give me a clear stamp of it in wax,—and assure yourself that these 9 buttons were actually found on the battle-field, and did belong to a soldier.—I do not discern at present that there was a single York *Infantry* man there; Sir Marmaduke Langdale (on the King's left wing) had Northern Horse, some of whom I doubt not were Yorkshire men;—them (and not the King's lifeguard) were they that Ireton beat up in Naseby the night before. They were not in the best humour next morning; wanting rather to be off towards Pontefract, to raise the siege there, and be within scent of their own hearth smoke—"N.Y.I."? On the whole, it is but an inanity if one did know it: but riddles of that kind fasten occasionally on the inquiring mind!

3. Do not forget to give me the traditional name of the little Boy whom the Horseman flung gently out of harm's way into the cabbage garden. It is very pretty.

4. Will you copy me the inscription on the Obelisk.—I trust in Heaven it was not you or any of your Ancestors that put it up! For verily I still must astonish myself that it did not stand *on* the battlefield, instead of a mile from it,—a vain rival to Naseby Steeple, which *already* stood conspicuous there. Let some charitable mortal clap an index hand upon it, at least, and write "Yonder!" Seriously I think some stone ought to be set up on the place where you dug the skeletons or thereabouts; and if I had charge of the Obelisk, I would pray to have it carted thither.

5. Were I not getting ashamed of myself, I would ask finally about the Bells of Naseby Church: they were put up new some years before the Battle; one of them has on it an inscription *Auspice regno*, which fairly baffle my Latin, if Latin and sense are to go together,—unless it be a *misprint* of the Vicar's, and the poor metal Bell carry on it *Auspice Rege*? How can the *Kingdom* be any Bell's *Auspex*,—nay for that matter, the *King* is straitened enough to be it! There runs in my head some sad feeling that I have not yet asked all; but at present nothing more presents itself, therefore you are free. Do not trouble yourself with these trivialities further than you like, for really to me also they are trivial, tho' I *would* ask them of Friar Bacon's brass Head,[2]—a machine, alas, whose absence I must forever regret, in this world!

I adjure you send me back my Sketches at least:—nay who knows but you will make more by and by! Red Hill, Oliver's supposed grave,[3] —one of the real graves as it now looks: all, and each would be welcome.

Yours most truly
T. Carlyle

Is it in the Farm House in Naseby village that you now lodge, or where? Tell me also your man's name, in case I had any message to him in your absence.

[1] EFG answers Carlyle's questions in his letter of Sept. [Oct.] 2, 1842.

[2] A head, possessing power to "tell out strange and uncouth aphorism," created by the two friars in Robert Green's play, *Friar Bacon and Friar Bungay*.

[3] Cromwell died September 3, 1658, and was buried in the Chapel of Henry VII in Westminster Abbey. On January 30, 1661, the first anniversary of the execution of Charles I after the Restoration, his body was exhumed and hanged on the gallows at Tyburn near the Marble Arch of modern London. In the evening the body was cut down, the head was severed from it, and the trunk was cast into a pit beneath the gallows. Legends variously name Naseby, Westminster Abbey, and Newburgh Abbey as the site of Cromwell's grave.

To Thomas Carlyle

[Naseby]
[September 30, 1842]

Dear Sir,

You will hope, I think, that this is the last packet you will receive on the subject of Naseby: and I think it is. I have asked every body about it, till people begin to think I mean to insult them. As I hold what I hear very badly in my head I think it best to tell it to you at once.

First then, they say there is a book called Nicholl's History of Leicestershire,[1] which tells a great deal about the Civil Wars, as connected with these counties. Nicholls, I hear, went about, lived with the country gentlemen, heard and put down anecdotes, etc. The book is scarce and dear: but is doubtless to be found at the British Museum. I went over to Guilsborough, but could not see Borough Hill from any part of it, high as it is: nor could I learn that it was to be seen. But it might have been perhaps, before the brow of the hills towards Daventry was planted. Borough Hill is to be seen from a spot close to Cold Ashby. I hear of traces of an army passing through Cold Ashby, but not through Thornby, which is the *more* direct road from Guilsborough to Naseby: But neither are the *directest* road, as you will see by any map. I should therefore suppose that it was more probably the Royalist than the Parliament army, since Cold Ashby certainly lies between Borough Hill and Naseby. One story indeed yet extant at Cold Ashby tells of *both* armies: that the Royalists were busy eating the good man's bacon at the Inn, in his absence: he returned suddenly, and the fellows asked him where the Rebels were: he said, close behind him: on which they decamped and he saved his bacon.

Between Cold Ashby and Guilsborough (in a valley, close by a marshy place) were found—in a gravel pit—two perfect skeletons of soldiers *sitting*, rather hunched together: their helmets sticking to their skulls, and bits of chain (like curbs of bridles, I was told) still remaining: some part of their accoutrements, I suppose. These figures were dug up twenty-five years ago by my friend Mr. Faux of Thornby, whose brother told it to me. There was some device partly to be seen on the helmets, but of course people forgot all one wanted to know. Mr. Faux kept the skulls in his house till the last six or seven years, when, selling his estate, the new possessor (I believe) carried off these relics elsewhere. This is the oddest excavation I have heard of. I was told that there were graves at a place called Marston woods—about three miles, or rather less, from Broadmoor—on the way to Harborough. I drove to these woods, and saw a country indeed where a flying army might have got a check from the steep declivity of the ground, but I could not hear more of graves. I send you a sketch of these hills, to show you the look of them. I then went on to Marston itself: which has a story to tell. The Royalists fled, and were pursued thither, and a great slaughter made. And I, without having heard the story, found myself entrapped in my progress exactly as they were. I drove my gig into Marston, straight along the road from Sibbertoft, to the Church: where, at the very church yard gate, the road stopped: went no farther.[2] Had a fellow with a drawn sword been behind me, I must have turned and stood at bay, or received an inglorious wound. And in this plight exactly the Royalists found themselves. This end of the town is called, and has always been called Pudding-bay-end—it is a "cul-de-sac": and was much more so 200 years ago, when it was completely blocked up by a great mansion of the Trussells (the village is called now Marston Trussell) with a moat, out-courts, etcc., and a moor behind that, and all on one side of the Church. *Marston* means (I hear) Marsh Town. So here the Royalists stood at bay, and there was a grand scrimmage: so that a little paddock just under the Church yard is called Slaughford: which the parson told me meant Slaughter ford. However this may be, Slaughford is the name of the place. As to proofs of the slaughter, my parson's father was digging in the churchyard many years ago to found a vault for his own family: and he came upon a heap of decayed bodies (just like that I lit upon) in the very place where tradition had always pointed out the grave of the slaughtered to be, and which was marked by that sinking in of the ground, which always follows a heap of bodies buried shallowly. Such are the Naseby graves: cavities, in which water stands. One of the diggers in this Marston place was more scrupulous than we are: he found multitudes of fine strong teeth: and thought he might sell them to advantage: so he carried a heap to Harborough for the purpose of doing so: but being struck all of a sudden with a vision of the Furies of the teeth-owners pursuing him, he carried them all back, and opening a hole in the Church wall, closed them up in it. All this I heard from the Clergyman of the place: who saw me in my perplexity at the Church gate: and came out to relieve me. Tradition also tells of a great ravishment of women in the fields about here: but of that no decisive evidences remain. My parson told me of it with a scream of defiance. Is it true that women, officers' wives, etcc., were killed? This Marston is the place most worth going to see about here: it almost requires to be seen. It is but three miles from Harborough: and as I came down those Marston Hills, and saw Harborough steeple just blinking at me in the distance over the side of another hill, I thought I was very well off in my Farmer's gig, with nobody behind me.

At Lubbenham (the next village to Marston) they have still the chair in which Charles sat—in that Inn room—the night before Naseby Battle. Mastin tells you of the old House—belonging to a Major Hawksworth; standing in 1792 (when Mastin wrote) and called Old Hall House.

There is yet one more village near Clipstone, that, I am told, bears some record of the Flight, but I know not if I shall have time to visit it. I ought now to be on my way to Ireland to join Thackeray in a tour there—but I hate moving almost as much as you seem to do. Still a very earnest letter from that best of good fellows would draw me over: unless I am obliged previously to go into Suffolk. An idle man has, after all, most calls upon him: and fit it is it should be so.

I send you a view from Dust Hill, to complete my set of hill-tops. They are pretty correct in outline: can you make them out? They would be more intelligible if not so divided into arable partitions of various colours. So I thought when too late to remedy. I hope you got my other packet with the teeth. You can give me *one line* to say you have received these things all: can I do any more for you?

Yours truly
E. FitzGerald

[1] John Nichols, *The History and Antiquities of Leicester*, 8 vols., 1795-1815.
[2] A road now runs through Marston Trussell to join the road from Husbands Bosworth to Market Harborough.

From Thomas Carlyle

Chelsea
1 Oct^r, 1842

My dear Sir,

Thanks anew for your new Sketches and Details: you have anticipated nearly all I wanted in the Sketch way; had I my Sketches N°s. 2 and 3 safe back, it were about all right on that side. Pity, indeed, that these two are on the same paper—somewhat. One might spread out the whole on the table at once, and construct for study a perfect panorama of the ground from them. You have proved yourself, I must be allowed to say, a most brave Investigator in this matter; had I anticipated any such harvest of results I should certainly have gone with you, rain and all.

Your Marston-Trussel graves are very likely to be authentic. The chase lasted all the way to Harborough: the King, feeling himself unsafe there, fled on to Ashby de la Zouch that night; and even there rested only a few hours. There was no "ravishing of women"—far other fish to fry on that occasion: besides the Fairfax soldiers were no ravishers; even the stealing of a goose was punished with instant hanging. Prince Rupert's chivalry indeed—But you can judge whether they would be in a ravishing humour on that occasion!

That we could not see Burrough Hill from Guilsborough is all as it should be; for Sprigge's error in that name is manifest, and the place he means, there can be no doubt even from his own content, is Kislingbury: it was from the environs of Flower (near Weedon)—somewhere between Flower and Kislingbury—that Fairfax, on the Friday morning early, saw the King's forces hurrying away from Burrough Hill and their tents on fire. He got to Guilsborough that night—and if "Gilling" be not a misprint or mistake for that, it is to the *present* Antiquarian clearly a nonentity, having totally vanished out of that region.

The Cold Ashby tradition is likewise very credible, almost probable. For Ireton with light horse hung all that Friday upon the King's rear, scuffling with them; finishing off his day's work at Naseby, on Langdale's Northern Horse. It is as good as certain the King would go thro' Cold Ashby—I suppose he was marching on *all* the practicable roads that led up towards Harborough; Ireton keeping him close company on the main road. Ireton therefore we conclude was the saviour of the Ashby bacon: he would not eat it without paying for it! The two sitting skeletons of troopers would most likely be killed in this skirmishing pursuit;—and the chance rather is, since they were *not stript*, that they might be soldiers of his own; buried by their friends, pushed into any hole, and at least hidden from insult? Or perhaps not so? One would have liked to see the traces of the inscription on their caps. The "bridle-chains" were probably chin-straps for keeping their helmets on.

Fairfax, as I interpret, would not go thro' either Thornby or Cold Ashby, on Saturday morning, from Guilsborough; but straight up by the nearest road and roads he could fall in with. He took two hours: from 3 till 5 in the morning. By the way, there was no sermon at Naseby; but there were exhortations, prayers, and psalm-singing: that text from Joshua may well enough have been in many mouths and hearts that morning.

On the whole I am really much gratified with the first of this little antiquarian campaign of yours; and have, for my own share, a real obligation to you for it. But a man who owns Naseby Field in 1842 ought verily to know what is knowable about that bit of ground in 1645. Few more memorable spots are on the Earth's surface,—I do not say England's surface alone: perhaps nowhere else in the world, at no other time in the world, was such a Host gathered together as that of Fairfax, with such a cause as theirs. Charles called them "Rebels;" but he was very far mistaken in that word. It was he, poor Scarecrow, that has been found now to have been *rebelling*—rebelling against God Almighty and the whole true Universe, little as he dreamt of that! Finally, tho' I advise no man to become an Author, I again say that if you drew up these details into due shape, and studying the matter effectually, made a treatise of it, and printed it, you would do not ill, but *well.* At all events I will preserve what you have written to me, as a valuable thing.

And so farewell till we meet again,—if this is to be the last of Naseby at present. I will commend myself heartily to the brave Thackeray, Fitzboodle or whatever he is called, and wish him and you a speedy reappearance here.[1]

Yours always truly
[No signature]

[1] Samuel Laurence, it will be recalled, had taken EFG to Chelsea September 15, when Carlyle enlisted his aid in the Naseby research. The reference to Thackeray probably caused FitzGerald to state, 30 years later, that Thackeray had introduced him to Carlyle. From about July 1 to the end of October, Thackeray was in Ireland gathering material for his *Irish Sketch Book.*

To Thomas Carlyle

Naseby
Sunday Sept^{r} [October] 2/42

Dear Sir,

The Letter I packed off the day before yesterday will have answered your question as to the site of the Grave I opened. The spot is not included in the sketches you have returned: and the other I forget.[x] I dug once at the crook in the hedge I have marked: but no bones: nor marks of the earth having ever been moved under two feet in depth. A common farmer soon discovers this: or a common labourer.

If ever you come down, you will find all ready and at your service here: and the farmer who went digging with me will carry you to the place. Make him also shew you Langfordy, and the reputed graves there which you can open as you will. You must certainly come down to see Marston. It must be seen.

The Farm House I live at is in possession of one Charles Watcham: an old (not very old) servant of ours: and his family willing and accustomed to wait on us. I keep a store of tea, candles, brandy etc., here: which use—come when you will. But, when you desire him to send for you, write two or three days before, directing to him, Naseby, *Thornby*. He has a lad who will drive you about in that pew-upon-wheels he calls a Gig. Your Countryman also, Love, (whose Farm-yard you passed through, I think, in returning from your walk) is a very clever fellow: and will go with you. He has great sagacity in these researches: and floored me terribly once or twice. His proposition about manure was half in jest: said laughingly as he was digging away at the grave. He is a very generous fellow, and excellent company to smoke with, I find: worth all the ladies and gentlemen. You saw the back-side of Cloisterwell—so to speak.

The Inscription on the Obelisk (which really is what Liston used to call "an Obstacle")—raised by my Papa, and by him inscribed, runs thus:[1] "To commemorate that Great and Decisive Battle, fought in this field on the 14th Day of June, 1645, between the Royalist Army, commanded by his Majesty King Charles the 1st. and the Parliamentary forces, headed by the Generals Fairfax and Cromwell, which terminated fatally for the Royal Cause, led to the subversion of the Throne, the Altar, and the Constitution, and for years plunged the nation into the horrors of Anarchy and Civil War—leaving a useful lesson, etccc." I shall not go on with it, for you will but grimly smile at it: and it can be of no use to you.

October 1842

The Inscription on the Bells, I quote from Mastin's History[2]—with a comment on that which troubles you by the present Vicar.

1st Bell. Treble.

Round the skirt—"God save the King" and on a kind of medal one inch and half diameter, this Inscription round the King's Arms—Auspice Regno. 1633. Comment. Mastin did not know that these medals were half-crowns of Charles 1. let into the molten metal: the motto being on one side "Christo Auspice regno"—On the other Charles on horseback, etcc., as follows on the others (i.e. [I suppose] medals for halfcrowns) of the same size round King Charles on horseback—"Carolus D.G. Mag. Britan. Fran. et Hib. Rex 1633."

2nd Bell.
I.H.S. Nazarenus Rex Judeorum Fili Dei Miserere Mei. 1640.
3rd Bell.
Same inscription. 1633.
4th Bell.
Cum sono, si non vis venire
Nunquam ad preces cupies ire. 1633.
5th Bell.
(This like the Bears in the Child's story)

In old Saxon Characters—"Statu tum est omnibus semel mori. 1633."

There—Griffith would be an honest chronicler, only he copies from book, without ascending the steeple.

It was a good notion of our ancestors to make their bells μεροπηΐς.[3]

Mastin says that on very uncommon days, BOSTON DEEPS may be seen from the Church tower: these deeps sixty miles off: nearly N.E., etcc. This ought to be true. He talks of the aid of "a good glass"—perhaps two or three glasses.

The copper ball at the top of the snub-nosed spire was brought by Sir Gyles Allington[4] from Boulogne when that place was taken by the English Ann: Dom: 1544. Sir Gyles put it on the cupola of his house at Horseheath in Cambridgeshire. It was sold, when that house was pulled down, to Mr. Ashby[5]—former owner of Naseby: and by him stuck up on the church. All which is certainly not relevant to the Battle. The Ball did not see that: but it can contain (the proud Vicar relates) sixty gallons, ALE measure!

That cramped-up disgusted-looking skeleton, was about halfway down the heap—North and South—his under half, I suppose, still under the ground we did not dig.

Lodge Hill is so called because there was once an old Lodge upon it: the present farmer-tenant dug up the foundations thereof some years ago: and found some coin of Elizabeth's time: which I have not seen. Between that Lodge Hill, and Mill Hill, is a little hillock planted with firs (whose tops appear in my Sketch 2.) called—Colonel Worseley's—or, Colonel Ouseley's—hill—one cannot make out which from the folks here, who have a sort of arbitrary Digamma,[6] or Damned-gabber, which has set me wrong many times. Was there any such Colonel or Man at Arms at the Battle?

You saw undoubtedly, *Clipstone.* I know the lane and the ground you went over, etcc., between Mill Hill and Lodge Hill. Lodge Hill Farm is the name of the house you mistook for Dust H[ill] Farm. Of the teeth, etcc., I must say that we took only such as lay loose tumbled about, or falling from fragments of ruined jaws. The poor fellow who was pretty whole, though put in so against the grain, was gently put aside, and the deepest-down also suffered to lie at length under the harvest moon—for three nights—but the rains washed away some of him, and the folks went on Sunday to pick him to pieces, as I hear. It is queer (or not queer) that we felt backward at discomposing what at all approached to the whole figure of man. On the contrary, we moralized according to our capacities on it—and the solid English Farmer wore a mysterious brow for three days: kept watch like a dog near the spot, which is on his farm: and it was (as I said) only on an unlucky Sunday when he was safe in his pew, pointing hard at the Preacher, that profane men deformed what shape there was. This farmer's name is Watts: his theories are all very substantial: and his disputes with the Scotchman about the Battle very genuine. My Blacksmith has had a slight cholera: but I am happy to say, was at work mending the teeth of a scarifier yesterday. He also extracts human teeth from such as wish it.

[No signature]

[x] P.S. I remember now: the other sketch is Mill Hill, etcc. And in this 3rd Sketch, I see it written that the Grave is *behind* the sketches. The view *is* taken from Cloisterwell: which name does not run along the whole hill to the road, but changes to Bull's Back—pronounced *Bull's bitch.* I did not want to plague you with subdivision.

[1] FitzGerald does not give the complete inscription, which reads as follows:

TO COMMEMORATE
THAT GREAT AND DECISIVE BATTLE
FOUGHT IN THIS FIELD
ON THE XIV DAY OF JUNE MDCXLV,

BETWEEN THE ROYALIST ARMY
COMMANDED BY HIS MAJESTY
KING CHARLES THE FIRST,
AND THE PARLIAMENT FORCES
HEADED BY THE GENERALS FAIRFAX AND CROMWELL,
WHICH TERMINATED FATALLY
FOR THE ROYAL CAUSE,
LED TO THE SUBVERSION OF THE THRONE,
THE ALTAR, AND THE CONSTITUTION,
AND FOR YEARS PLUNGED THIS NATION
INTO THE HORRORS OF ANARCHY
AND CIVIL WAR:
LEAVING A USEFUL LESSON TO BRITISH KINGS
NEVER TO EXCEED THE BOUNDS
OF THEIR JUST PREROGATIVE,
AND TO BRITISH SUBJECTS
NEVER TO SWERVE FROM THE ALLEGIANCE
DUE TO THEIR LEGITIMATE MONARCH.
THIS PILLAR WAS ERECTED
BY JOHN AND MARY FRANCES FITZGERALD,
LORD AND LADY OF THE MANOR OF NASEBY:

A.D. MDCCCXXIII.

[2] EFG does not quote Mastin verbatim. The vicar records: "At the west end is an embattled tower, in which are five fine maiden bells, having never been chipt, or wrought upon with a chissel, from their first casting. The tenor, eighteen hundred weight, hangs considerably above the others, the tower being too small to contain them all in the same frame-work."

[3] "Famed for learning."

[4] Sir Giles (d. 1586) was an avid collector of bulky mementoes. Sir Bernard Burke records: "Mr. Alington appears to have attended King Henry VIII as master of the ordnance at the siege of Boulogne, by the inscription of a clock which he brought from that siege, and affixed over the offices at Horseheath Hall, in which was the alarum bell of the garrison of Boulogne" (*A Genealogical History of the Dormant, Abeyant, Forfeited, and Extinct Peerages of the British Empire*, 1883).

[5] George Ashby, Lord of Naseby Manor, had novel ideas on ecclesiastical architecture. The spire on Naseby Church had been "snub-nosed," as EFG puts it, since 1450. Construction of a new spire was abandoned at that time after only 12 feet had been built. It was discovered that the walls would not support the planned superstructure. In 1791 Ashby placed his copper ball at the top of the truncated spire. A full spire was built in 1859, and the ball is now on a stone pedestal at its base (information supplied by the Reverend J.W.S. Mansell, Vicar of Naseby).

[6] The sixth letter of the original Greek alphabet, a consonant probably equivalent to the English *w*. It is no longer used.

From Thomas Carlyle

Chelsea, Monday (3 Oct^{r}, 1842)

My dear Sir,

The companion of this Note should have been the forerunner of it; being written, in great haste, on Saturday afternoon; triumphantly carried out in my breast-pocket, and then—forgotten till near seven o'clock, when I pulled it out, seeking for my catalogue in an Old Book shop in Holywell Street! Today I can add this to it; with a certificate that your last packet also has arrived,—the button-seal unbroken, the sketch not injured by its journey. You shall be appointed Topographer-General when I come to be King.

You have not sent me the Boy's name (Trooper-and Cabbage-yard Boy's); but if you mark it down on paper, nothing will run away with it; and at present it is not in the least wanted. God knows if it ever will be, for any solid purpose—alas, alas!

No Worsley or Ouseley that I can get trace of was present as a Colonel at Naseby. A Sir Charles Wolseley (ancestor, I think, of the present or late ultra radical) gets himself occasionally named; and became ultimately one of Oliver's Council of State: but (tho' my *Sprigge*, which contains a list of Fairfax's Army, is gone back to Cambridge) I have little or no doubt he was *not* a Colonel there, or at all there. The name therefore remains enigmatic. There was a Colonel Okey,[1] future Regicide, formerly a "Brewer's Stoker in Southwark," who might well enough have left his name: . . . it was at his advance, with a sputtering of shot and other dangerous features of conduct, that the King's Horse broke finally away and fled. He was, I think, the most audacious fighter then going, on either side. Alas, I fear your county *Digamma* will not stretch to the length of Colonel *Okey*; whose name it would have been interesting to find on that ground.

The buttons, I am very glad to consider as new and spurious; for the N.Y.I., indisputable there, is altogether unintelligible otherwise. The stamp indeed looks quite new; far too fresh to have lain two centuries. Besides I rather think they used horn-buttons in those days, and of far larger size.

The accounts of the number killed are very vague. The Parliament-Commissioners dispatch (written however that same evening) says, "On the King's side 600, on ours not one hundred;" Cromwell, also on the same evening, says, killed and taken about 5000; which agrees with Chronicler Heath's[2] account, that the number of Prisoners, marched off on the Monday from Harborough towards London, was

4500. There is a list of all the Officers taken. Perhaps 600 in all may be a fair guess for the number killed on both sides. Battles at that time were not [a] fourth-part so deadly as now: their muskets were great clumsy things, with *rests* to stick in the ground when you fired, bullets carried in your *mouth*, etc.: I suppose a man with percussion-caps and cartridges could fire at least ten times as often in a given time. The number engaged at Naseby seems to have been about 10,000 on each side: the Parl[t] took 8,000 stand of arms; and most of the Horse doubtless got off. The chase lasted thro' Harborough, till within sight of Leicester steeple.

By the bye, the "little chair" does not belong to Lubbenham; it and the "little low room" are at Harborough!

Thanks heartily for your offer of the new column at Cloisterwell: it must decidedly be done one day! But unless the very Fates forbid, I mean to be there with you next summer, when the Hills are all green again.

We had Spedding last night, home from Yankee-land; by whom and to whom was honourable mention of you. He goes Northward in about a week. The Yankees have not discomposed him; nothing in this world can. He comes home raying forth the same quiet candid light,—white light, or gray mildly contemplative twilight—as when he went.

Adieu, with lasting thanks
T. Carlyle

[1] John Okey (d. 1662), Colonel of Dragoons at Naseby, 1645, signed Charles I's death warrant, 1649; opposed the protectorate; and was cashiered for circulating a petition against it.

[2] James Heath (1629-64), royalist historian, published *A Brief Chronicle of the late Intestine War in the three Kingdoms of England, Scotland, and Ireland*, 1661; and *Flagellum*, or *The Life and Death, Birth and Burial, of Oliver Cromwell, the late Usurper*, 1663.

To Thomas Carlyle

Naseby
Oct[r] 7/42

Dear Sir,

More last words and drawings. I am very glad to have been of use to you. The buttons, I saw very clearly, were modern: the crown not of the old shape; having ermine edge (to make it sit more easy, I suppose). The Vicar has however a plate, or button (as he says) of about this size: of some plated metal, rubbed a good deal: the *eye* (by which a button is sewed on) worn off. The Half-crown from which he supplied the missing word on the Bell was found in the field. I drove yesterday to a village called Farndon, two miles from Clipstone, on the Harborough road. It stands on a hill with a Roman-looking entrenchment: and looks down on a noble expanse: Harborough lying most city-like and desirable under it: as if one's horse could jump from the brow of the hill down within one rich pasture of the city of refuge—never to be reached perhaps. There is record of Royalist women being slain and buried here: and I saw a falling in of the ground in the Churchyard just like the graves at Naseby and Marston. The Clerk (who knew about it) was out: the Parson (who knew very little about it) knew however that some thirty bodies were found together in the Churchyard some years ago. But, you will not hear of any ravishing or murdering, by the Parliament—an Act of Parliament indeed.

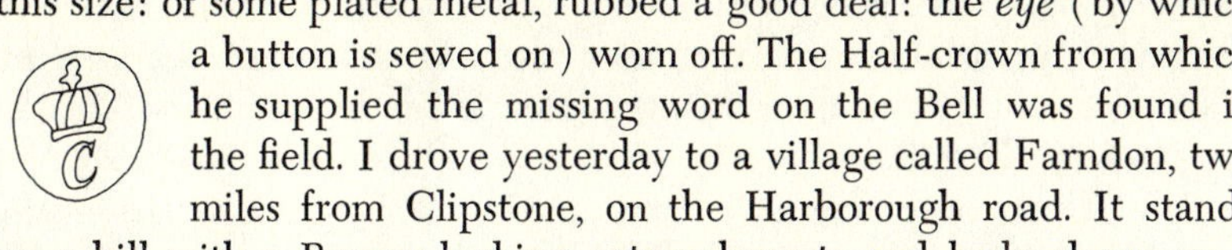

The boy's name was "Ringrose"—a name that flourishes much here: and the trooper is recorded to have been a *Rebel.* Record also is of an old man who told of his having to scamper over the field after the army with Oliver's *portmantle.* One sees how all the "myths" and stories gather about Cromwell—about Oliver, as all call him. The English bear a good-natured grudge against him. There is just enough to abuse in him: but they wouldn't hear a Frenchman say a word against him. For my part, I think the common opinion to which two centuries have come is a just enough one: you scorn it. Why did not Oliver cripple hereditary monarchy for life, instead of sanctifying it by cutting off the King's head? Or was there any use in Scotching a Stuart? The unheroic Somerses[1] of 1688 managed better after all. Oliver must surely (with all his sagacity) have sadly mistaken the temper of the English to suppose them civilized enough to do without, or to wish to do without, their hereditary "scarecrow"[2] in his day: we only now begin to let it dangle without repair: and is not that the best way? This very battle of Naseby ended but in bringing back Charles 2nd *without restrictions* (as I think Clarendon[3] repentantly confesses) the revulsion of the popular feeling enduring no conditions. In spite of your great men the greater world will have its way, and wag to and fro till it is tired.[4]

Pardon mouldy remarks. I have got four mouldy bullets for you, which is much better: and will leave them with Laurence when I go through London toward Suffolk next week. I cannot bring up the Vicar's old map: as he thinks it part of the Regalia of the place: but perhaps you don't want it. I have bought a cannon-ball of twelve pounds: not without suspecting that such big shot were not used on such occasions at that time. But the poor fellow had carried it all the way from Sibbertoft.[5]

You talk of "next summer when the hills will be green again"—they are green now, I assure [you]: I never saw the country look nobler, and the weather prime October. They are about to erect a great telescope on the Church for some Government survey: then for Boston Deeps![6]

I have marked a little pudding hill as, strictly speaking, the Burrough Hill: but I suppose the Shuckburgh range may be, or was, called so. Charles' men and horses would have been sharp-set (as Lamb said) on the little hill.

Perhaps after all Oliver lies at Red Hill[7]—under four feet of earth, as the story goes. The possibility of it gives a soul to the place—and so, nolus-bolus, we confess ourselves worshippers of the ignotum if not of the heroic. There was a Naseby wit feeding his flock in the field on the day of the battle: some soldiers drove up to him with drawn swords, and asked him "which side he was"—to which the Keeley[8] of the day answered, "What, have you been quarrelling?" People now remember well the bare field as it was: no hedges: plenty of bogs: dead sheep (starved with cold and lost in drifted snow, etc.) stenching the air: and these old shepherds in long grey coats standing here and there, motionless as stone figures. In those days the bells of the Church rang in the winter nights—and in great hazes—to warn people when to find their homes.

And now this really is all I have to tell you. Do not think it has been any trouble. This little antiquarian campaign, as you call it (quite unwonted to me certainly) has been done in health, good humour, and fresh air. Besides (though I fear I am not a great hero-worshipper) yet I am glad to gather what little materials I can to set the brains at work which have moved mine, and (wonderful to say) really, I believe, done me some good. Some Dilettanteism I have been warned by you to hide at least: and hidden Dilettanteism is pretty innocent, is it not? If you had done no more than set up old Johnson[9] on his proper pedestal forever (as we call it) in the eyes of Englishmen, we should be grateful to you, or to whatsoever gave you your extra square inch of brains, heart, stomach, or Soul. So pray write about Cromwell: don't make very contemptuous mouths at Clarendon, Hampden, and Falkland:[10] and we will read you, and abuse you, and—read you again—which is saying all.

Meantime, may not digestion suffer:[11] a great wish from your fat, idle, euperistaltic well wisher.

E. FitzGerald

[1] John Somers (1651-1716), Lord Chancellor of England, who opposed the tyrannical measures of Charles II and James II; promoted the Glorious Revolution; and was chairman of the committee which framed the Declaration of Rights.

[2] In this passage on Cromwell, EFG alludes to doctrines found in Carlyle's *Hero Worship* and *Sartor Resartus*. Carlyle submits his "clothes philosophy" in *Sartor*. Were it not for clothes, observes Carlyle, it would be impossible to distinguish kings from cart-drivers. "It will remain to be seen," he states at the conclusion of the chapter, "Adamitism," "in how far the SCARECROW, as a Clothed Person, is not also entitled to benefit of clergy, and English trial by jury: nay perhaps, considering his high function (for is not he too a Defender of Property, and Sovereign armed with the *terrors* of the Law?), to a certain royal Immunity and Inviolability."

[3] Edward Hyde (1609-74), first Earl of Clarendon, whose *History of the Rebellion*, "begun in 1641," was first published under supervision of his son Rochester in three volumes in 1702-04. Long regarded as an important source, the *History* is not considered reliable by modern historians.

[4] Carlyle, 14 years EFG's senior, was 47 years old at this time. He had become a celebrity. Acquaintances, and many of his friends, deferred to the weight and finality of his convictions and his characteristic brusque and sometimes gruff manner. EFG's readiness to cross swords with him, as he does in this paragraph, and his bold honesty of opinion were qualities which appealed to the Scot.

[5] The "poor fellow" had lugged his cannon ball more than three miles.

[6] See letter to Carlyle, Sept. [Oct.] 2, 1842.

[7] See letter from Carlyle, Sept. 29, 1842, n.3.

[8] Robert Keeley, comedian (1793-1869).

[9] In "Boswell's Life of Johnson," *Fraser's Magazine*, May, 1832, and published in all editions of Carlyle's *Miscellanies*.

[10] John Hampden (1594-1643), cousin of Oliver Cromwell's, prominent in the third parliament of Charles I; Lucius Cary, second Viscount Falkland (1610?-43), was persuaded by Clarendon to join the Royalist cause but his sympathies were on the side of freedom; for Clarendon, see n.3.

[11] An allusion to Carlyle's persistent ailment, dyspepsia, the subject of frequent plaints and tirades in his correspondence. "As to myself," he wrote to Gavan Duffy in 1868, "I know sadly, at all moments, *dyspepsia* to be the frightfullest fiend that is in the pit, or out of it; the accursed brutal nightmare that has ridden me continually these fifty odd years" (*Conversations with Carlyle*, 1892, p. 234).

To Thomas Carlyle

Naseby
Octr 9/42

Dear Sir,

A Mr. Baker who published some numbers of a History of Northamptonshire[1]—which got no great success—is going to sell off his books, curiosities, etcc., at Northampton in ten days. In the Catalogue I see one lot, 1158. "Orders established the 14th. January 1646 (at North:ton) by Sir Thomas Fairfax for regulating the Army." 4to. 1646. 1159. (Among other papers) "A more exact and perfect Relation of the great Victory obtained by Sir Thomas Fairfax in Naiseby Field. 14 June 1645". 4to. 1645. "A more particular and exact relation of the same" 4to 1645. "Papers of the Desires[2] of the Army, etcc., and also some passages concerning the King (at Holdenby)" 4to. 1647. "Mr. St. John's[3] speeches, etc., 1641-2."

Now I am going through Northampton on my way to London about noon on Tuesday, and could leave some order about bidding for these books if there were use. Do you know them? Are these in the British Museum—is there any worth in them? I suppose they are very short (like accounts, upon a sheet, of executions, etcc.) since so many go to make up a lot. Also "a curious powder-horn found on Naseby Field"—Nichol's Leicestersh. Bridges Northampt:re also to be sold. Have you a word to say about any of these things?

You see what it is when once you set a Dilettante to work. "You have set a dangerous stone a rolling". But now I am about it, I will do what I can.

What a good picture one could make of the early morning of that 14th. June—the Parliament soldier on his horse standing high up on Mill Hill to look out, the mist curling up from Broadmoor, and Charles' army just peeping and glittering over Dust Hill. I can see it all—if I could but draw it.

Yours ever
E. FitzGerald

[1] George Baker, *History of Northamptonshire*, 2 vols., 1838.
[2] Desire: "A wish as expressed; a request, petition."
[3] Oliver St. John (1598?-1673), chief justice during the Commonwealth.

From Thomas Carlyle

Chelsea, 10 Oct^{r}, 1842

My dear Sir,

It is a good sign of you that you are set "a-rolling;" I bid you, Roll, roll! There ought to be a correct, complete, and every way *right* and authentic Essay, or little Book, written about Naseby as it now is and as it *then* seems to have been,—with the utmost possible distinctness, succinctness, energy, accuracy and available talent of every sort:—I leave you to consider, whether the actual Owner and Heaven's-Steward of Naseby ought to have no hand in that!

As to the Pamphlets at Northampton, they are not very momentous, and will all be dreadfully dull reading, yet to a Northamptonshire man, I should think that first especially (No. 1158, "Fairfax's Orders at Northamp^{n}"), and the two "accounts of Naseby," might be worth something. The usual price of such pamphlets, in the old shops here, is from half-a-crown to 5/ apiece; they come sometimes as low as 1/ or 1/6;—but you cannot always find them when you want them. Suppose you offer half a crown for each of the three; with instructions to rise to the sublimity of five shillings for the *first*, if it cannot otherwise be had?—the rest, "Desires of the Army," etc., are in *Rushworth* and elsewhere, *usque ad nauseam*, considering what terrible stuff they are. "St. John's *Speeches*" and the like,—avoid them as you would the ooze of Lethe! . . .

Of Nichols' Leicestershire or the other County History I know nothing, except what you now tell me, or before told me. The Naseby Powder-*horn* I would look on both sides of before I bought it: the soldiers in 1645 did not carry *horns* (so far as I know or guess); their powder hung in little tiny *Canns* (or bottles one may say), each holding a charge, and all suspended by a belt called the *bandelier*,—hanging like a strop of onions from the soldier's shoulder to his haunch, and rustling as he rode or walked! He lifted off each *Cann* or case, opened the lid of it, and, having emptied it, hung it on again by the hook. He had to carry lighted match in his hand, poor fellow, and often got his powder wet, etc. "Pray to the Lord, and keep your powder *dry*!"[1]

By the by, as to those *women* said to be killed in your villages, I ought to have mentioned that there did usually follow Prince Rupert's Troopers a formidable body of "Irish whores with long skean knives," who occasionally fought like furies, and of course might get themselves killed in fight,—nay it was only their petticoats that saved them from being hanged *after* fight; such was then the acknowledged law for "Irish Papists"; which nobody seemed to think very unfair; neither perhaps was it, such a squad had they become—with no truth in their tongue any more, no pity or justice in their heart any more; a kind of hyaena-demon, *fit* only to be *hanged* when you could catch them! Whitlocke expressly enumerates "100 Irish Queans" among the Naseby Prisoners; and another blockhead, Rycraft, says there were "300" of them killed.

Cannot you come down hither, in your way? I am at home every night after 5 o'clock.

Yours always
T.C.

[1] Cromwell is credited with warning his troops before the battle of Edgehill as they were about to cross a river, "Put your trust in God; but mind to keep your powder dry!" (Lt. Col. Valentine Blacker, "Oliver's Advice," in E. Hayes, *Ballads of Ireland*, 2 vols., 1834, I, 191).

To Bernard Barton

[London]
[c. October 15, 1842]

Dear Sir,

Tomorrow the most amiable of his sex will put himself on the top of the Blue Coach,[1] and he trusts reach Woodbridge rather late at night: too late to look for you. But next week! Lay in a Double Gloucester[2]—I start by the Shannon at 9 A.M. to be dropped at the gates of New Hall Convent,[3] where I am to see my heretical Cousins for an hour: then be taken up by the Blue: and so homeward. Say, shall this rich Argosy ever reach its port! What patient thought has been expended on providing for the voyage. Shall it be well accomplished? Put on your laurel, and pray to Apollo by the remembrance of his own Phaeton that wheels and horses may run lightly and well. If it rains hard, I shall hold on my course by the Shannon and come in early: but New Hall if possible.

I have much and momentous to tell you of. Indeed I wrote to you the other day. Did you get the letter! Perhaps not, as I think I did not post it. But the Naseby Epic is in store for you. Such deeds "as made the Tenants weep"[4]—

I have bought a pretty picture of an ugly boy for £1. All the purchase I have made. Farewell. Put on your laurel directly, and tell Vertue[5] to blow his nose.

E.FG., or say classically
Philocaseotostus:[6] which is
a Love of Toasted Cheese.

[1] Three coaches ran daily between Woodbridge and London: the *Original Blue*, the *Shannon*, and the *Retaliator*. The trip took five hours; the fare was 10s. At the beginning of the century the trip had cost three times that sum and had required 13 hours.

[2] A cheese made in Gloucestershire.

[3] A Roman Catholic convent about three miles northeast of Chelmsford on the road to Colchester and Ipswich. His cousins were probably members of his father's family, the Purcells of Ireland.

[4] man, proud man
Dress'd in a little brief authority,
. . .
Plays such fantastic tricks before high heaven
As makes the angels weep;
Measure for Measure, II.2.117

[5] Probably one of Barton's clerks in Alexander's bank. White's *Directory* (1844) lists "Simon Vertue, clerk."

[6] EFG coins the term from the Greek form *philo*, meaning "loving, fond of" and *caseolus*, Latin for "a small cheese."

To the Reverend John Charlesworth[1]

Boulge Hall
Oct[r] 22/42

Dear Sir,

Lusia tells me you have got a book[2] about some of Oliver Cromwell's family—especially of that *Mrs. Bates*[3] (is that her name?) Ireton's grand-daughter, from whom the Bernerses descend. I may perhaps have read this book in the British Museum, perhaps not, as no one seems to remember the exact name: will you do me the favour to send it to me? or if it is too precious to be entrusted to Coach or carrier, write me the title of it? Does it contain the *whole* of the narrative[4] of that Dissenting Clergyman who knew the she-Cromwell?

I who am naturally no great searcher of such records am searching now for a friend who has an image of a Life of Cromwell in his head. So I have dug up dead bodies on Naseby Field for him: and other pleasant things.

I trust you and your Family are well. I have only just come down here and find Lusia much as usual. Isabella has not yet appeared in person to me: but I am told she lives and is hearty.

Believe me truly yours,

E. FitzGerald

[1] Rector of Flowton, near Ipswich, 1814-44, and of St. Mildred's, London, 1844-62. See Biographical Profile of the Cowells.

[2] A notation on the MS identifies the book as *Memoirs of the Protectorial House of Cromwell* by the Reverend Mark Noble, 2 vols., Birmingham, 1784. Noble (1754-1827), Rector of Barming, Kent, was a genealogist and "historical compiler."

[3] The descendant of Cromwell from whom the Bernerses of Ipswich descended was not a "Mrs. Bates," but Mary Bendish (sometimes spelled Bendysh), great granddaughter of Lt. Gen. Henry Ireton, Cromwell's son-in-law and companion in arms, who married William Berners. Frederick Spalding recorded in his diary, October 24, 1869, "talking of the Berners of Woolverstone Park Mr. FG said they are descended from Mrs. Bendish—the grand-daughter of Cromwell—and have been famous for their fat, heavy Cromwell-like features to this time."

[4] Noble's book on the Cromwells (see n.2) does contain "the whole narrative" of Mrs. Bridget Bendish, granddaughter of Oliver Cromwell, written by "the dissenting clergyman," Samuel Say (1676-1743) of Ipswich, together with an account by Dr. Hewling Luson of Lowestoft and a third by Dr. J. Brooke (II, 329-46). An uncle of Say's wife had married a Cromwell, and Say had known Bridget Bendish when he served at Yarmouth. His sketch of her character was first written in 1719; was published in the *Gentleman's Magazine* for August, 1765, p. 357; and was frequently reprinted.

To John Allen

[Boulge Cottage]
Novr 18/42

My dear Allen,

It was very good of you to write to me. You did not tell me however whether you remain in town till Xmas—but I suppose, from what you say of your present rest and of a Report to prepare, that you will remain. I am about, I believe, to leave this place for a time, and I would willingly go where some friend is to be found. Do you know that I am really going to look out for some permanent abode,[1] which I think I am well qualified to decide on now. But in this very judgment I may be most of all mistaken. I do not love London enough to pitch my tent there: Woodbridge, Ipswich, or Colchester—won't one of them do?

However, sufficient for the day: about the beginning of next week I mean to go somewhere: perhaps to Cambridge. I suppose Laurence is going to Cumberland if not gone. "What have I been reading?" You may fancy it all: for I have no new books—except Boz's America[2] which is very good. Arnold's Lectures[3] I have always desired: but they seemed to me in such magnificent type that I thought it better to wait till one could borrow the book. I mean one day to buy a cheap copy of Barrow's Sermons. I have been reading Burton's Anatomy lately: a captivating book certainly. That story of his going to the bridge at Oxford to listen to the bargemen's slang, etc., he reports of the old Democritus, his prototype: so perhaps biographers thought it must be Burton's taste also. Or perhaps Burton took to doing it after example. I cannot help fancying that I see the foundation (partly) of Carlyle's style in Burton: one passage quite like part of Sartor Resartus. Much of Burton's Biography may be picked up out of his own introduction to the Anatomy.

Maurice's Introductory Lecture I shall be very glad to have. I do not fancy I should read his Kingdom of Christ[4]—should I? You know.

I have had bad cold and cough which still hang about me: this damp cottage is not good for a cure.

We have now a large party here: all of us, indeed, except my Mother. Lusia sends her love. And now goodbye.

Ever yours
E.FG.

[1] When EFG took possession of Boulge Cottage in 1837, he considered it only as a temporary residence. His proposal at this time to establish his residence elsewhere in a "house" came to naught.

[2] Charles Dickens, *American Notes*, 1842. Dickens had toured in America the first half of 1842, giving readings from his novels. His book, an account of his trip, had been published October 18.

[3] Thomas Arnold, *Oxford Lectures on Modern History*, published after his death. For Isaac Barrow, see letter to Allen, [Nov. 27-28], 1832, n.2.

[4] Frederick Denison Maurice (1805-72), son of a Unitarian minister, after attending both Cambridge and Oxford, was ordained in the Anglican Church in 1834. EFG probably refers to his initial lecture delivered after Maurice's appointment to the chair of English literature and history at King's College, London, in 1840. A revised edition of his *Kingdom of Christ*, first published in 1838, was issued in 1842. Although one of the most devout of men, Maurice's liberal theological views repeatedly elicited charges of heterodoxy and resulted, in 1853, in his dismissal as professor of divinity at King's College.

To Frederick Tennyson

Geldestone Hall, Beccles
[January, 1843]

Dear Frederic,

I am glad you are back[1]—and perhaps sorry. But glad let it be, for I shall be in London, as proposed, in another fortnight—more or less—and shall pig there in a garret for two months. We will go to picture sales and buy bad pictures: though I have scarce money left. But I am really at last going to settle in some spooney quarters in the country, and would fain carry down some better forms and colours to put about me. I cannot get the second or third best: but I can get the imitations of the best: and that is enough for me.

What is become of Alfred? He never writes—nor is heard of.

Your letter found me poring over Harrington's Oceana:[2] a long-shelved book—its doctrine of Government I am no judge of: but what English those fellows wrote! I cannot read the modern mechanique after them—"This free-born Nation lives not upon the dole or Bounty of One Man, but distributing her annual Magistracies and Honours with her own hand is herself King People." Harrington must be a better writer than Milton. One finds books of this kind in these country houses: and it is pleasant to look them over at midnight in the Kitchen, where I retire to smoke.

Now you are come to England again, one takes to note sheets. When do you go to town? How you will laugh at my picture purchases: Alfred used to scorn them.

Your old school-fellow Mainwaring has lately made a strange match:[3] proving more and more what you once said that he always was the greatest Fool that breathed.

Farewell till I see you one of these days.

E.FG.

[1] From Italy.

[2] In 1656 James Harrington (1611-77) published *Oceana*, a political romance set in a reconstructed England, the government of which was a free but distinctly aristocratic republic.

[3] John Mainwaring had married Jane-Susannah, oldest daughter of the Reverend W. J. Carver, of Sprowston Hall near Norwich, Rector of Winfarthing, Norfolk. The marriage had taken place on August 31, 1842, at All Souls' Church, Langham Place, Marylebone, London (record of marriage, General Register Office, Somerset House). For John Mainwaring, see letter to Allen, Jan. 1, 1837, n.9.

To Bernard Barton

13 Coram St.[1]
Tuesday [Mid-February, 1843]

My dear Barton,

If Mr. Churchyard says that the sketch is either Reynolds or Gainsborough, I beg you to buy it for me for £5 directly. As to Wodderspoon's[2] own opinion of its genuineness, I can have no reliance on it as I don't know his genuineness. Is the sketch of the size of life? Pray let me hear this. I have yet bought no pictures, which makes me more bold about the sketch. You have the money, and can pay it at once. You see that I attributed your delay in writing to illness: desk work is better than that anyhow.

I got a slap on the back from Carlyle yesterday as I was walking up Regent St. with a Cigar in my mouth,[3] (N.B.—a very misty day)—"There you are going along quite at your ease." He was dressed in a coat called a *Zephyr.*[4] Farewell.

E.FG.

[1] Except for short trips afield, EFG stayed at 13 Great Coram Street until, about mid-May, Thackeray vacated the premises.

[2] John Wodderspoon, miscellaneous writer living at Ipswich, was a friend of Bernard Barton's.

[3] EFG was spurning convention. Propriety did not sanction smoking on the streets until well after mid-century.

[4] A topcoat of light material.

To Bernard Barton

[London]
[March, 1843]

Dear B.B.

I am glad you have definitely written about the sketch: which, relying on Mr. C's[1] opinion, I wish to possess. As to the monk (a monk it is) by Northcote, remember it is as large as life:—it cost but £3—for which account I must own I chiefly bought it: it is the best Northcote I have seen however: and would look well on your Staircase in place of the Nigger. 'Tis the sort of picture you would like. But how to send such a sized picture. N.B. It has no frame: and wants none. At an auction the other day I saw a Venetian picture for which I was near offering £20 last year: it has been damaged since, though not vitally and sold for £7. My friend W. Browne bought it, to my surprise: and now I am loth to let him run off with it. He would let me have it, but I know not how in honour to claim it, as it was he who made the venture. It is in a most splendid carved frame that must have cost £80. I send you a little sketch of the Tassi[2] the middle distance is the chief merit in the picture: but all its air has vanished in my pen and ink.

Ever yours,
E.FG.

[1] Thomas Churchyard.

[2] Agostino Tassi (fl. 1600), Italian artist who, after serving a sentence in the galleys, became noted for his maritime pictures. He is credited with being the teacher of Claude Lorraine.

To Mrs. Stephen Spring Rice[1]

13 Coram St.
Tuesday [March, 1843]

Dear Mrs. Spring Rice,

Will you be so good as to read and like the little book I enclose. It is written by one John Allen,[2] a parson: one of the best men in the world. He is too modest to print anything but such a tract as this for children. S. Rice will translate you the Greek names: by the bye I hope said S.R. got home safe, having lost no toes or fingers.

Yours truly
E. FitzGerald

[1] This is the earliest letter in the Spring Rice correspondence in the Cambridge University library. For Stephen Spring Rice, see Biographical Profile.

[2] John Allen had published *Sermons for Children* in 1842.

To Frederick Tennyson

London
Friday [March, 1843]

Dear Frederic,

The first intimation I had of your having returned from High Beech was the note you left in my room on the day of your departure for Boxley: and that note turned up quite by chance last night from a heap of odd papers into [which] old John had plunged it. John *never* mentions to one that anybody calls: so another time you must leave your card and address. As to my being offended, etc., you see that was not the case: and is very unlikely ever to be the case. I own I was sorry to hear you went to High Beech. Depend upon it, all the world is right about Dr. Allen:[1] he is not a man to be trusted. But you Tennysons have the obstinacy of mules. Now you may be offended. Come back soon to town: I am going on Tuesday (as I believe) into Suffolk for a week or ten days: and then shall return here. Farewell. Love to Alfred, and Compliments to the ladies of your family.

E.FG.

Just off to dine with Carlyle—on sheep's head.

[1] The promoter of pyroglyphs. See letter to Thompson, Sept. 4, 1840, n.2. The project collapsed at this time.

To Bernard Barton

[13 Great Coram Street]
[London]
[April, 1843]

My dear Barton,

The day before yesterday I reached London after a very pleasant stay in Cambridgeshire with Mrs. Frere.[1] We went to Ely on a visit to the Dean, Dr. Peacock: there we were entertained with High Church honours of all sorts from Chaunted Litanies to still Champagne. It was very pleasant: fine weather:—a verger in canonicals waiting at dinner: choristers to sing glees for us at night. Then there was Cromwell's house[2] to be visited—two miles from Ely: I made a drawing of it for Carlyle. You see his new book is out:[3] I am now reading it: you will also read it I suppose: or if not, read what he has written before and that is the same thing. Here I find all my pictures spread out before me as when I left: huge purchases! I begin to be rather frightened with their size, now that the time of disposing of them draws near. I hope to be in town but three weeks or so, and then to go to Ireland.[4] Not that I want so much to go to Ireland as to get away from this hot hole. Thackeray's book will soon be out:[5] the last proof sheets were just now brought him at the tail of our breakfast. Then he will spread his wings for Paris. Why won't you come up and see me? The bugs are just beginning to bite: Thackeray says he was bit last night, and I hear old John taking down the curtains from his bed in the floor over this. Tell me of your Norwich trip: you had bad weather, I doubt. Farewell. Compts. to Miss Barton.

Ever yours,
E.FG.

[1] Widow of William Serjeant Frere, Master of Downing College from 1812 until his death in 1836. See letter to F. Tennyson, April 10, 1839, n.6.

[2] In 1636 Cromwell, heir of his maternal uncle, Sir Thomas Steward, moved to Ely and succeeded his uncle as farmer of the cathedral tithes. Carlyle records, "It is reasonable to believe that he [Sir Thomas], and Oliver after him, occupied the House set apart for the Tithe-Farmer there; . . . Of this House, for Oliver's sake, some Painter will yet perhaps take a correct likeness:—it is needless to go to Stuntney . . . as Oliver's Painters usually do; Oliver never lived there, but only his Mother's cousins!" (Carlyle's *Cromwell*, 1845, I, 135-36). EFG was one of "Oliver's Painters," misdirected to Stuntney. See letter to Mrs. Spring Rice, Sept. 28, 1843.

[3] *Past and Present*, published early in the month. EFG's own copy, with portions deleted, and rebound, is now in the Syracuse University Library.

[4] EFG did not arrive in Ireland until July 11. See letter to Laurence, July 11, 1843.

[5] *The Irish Sketch Book*, published about May 4, 1843.

To W. K. Browne
[Fragment]

[London]
[April, 1843]

Dear Stubby,[1]

. . . Alfred [Tennyson] is just left us in a cab: he, like me, has had and has yet the damned influenza. To-night I go with my mamma to the Opera. We get on very well together, by help of meeting very little. Lusia had her eyelid cut by Guthrie. As to your picture, I will not send it till Laurence has seen if something cannot be done to it. As I have such abundance of pictures I shall not be solicitous to keep it for myself, much as I like it, that is, I will leave it quite to your papa's will without saying a word. I have lately had a very charming head by Reynolds sent up from the country. You would like it much. Give me some account of the house you spoke of at Bedford. Is there any sitting-room looking out to the back? I went on Thursday with

Alfred and Thackeray to drive with Boz.[2] He is like Elliott,[3] only rather on a smaller scale—unaffected and hospitable. You never would remark him for appearance. A certain acute cut of the upper eyelid is all I can find to denote his powers, but you would doubtless see much more than I do. . . .

[1] Browne was five feet, seven inches tall.

[2] This was EFG's only meeting with Dickens. The men returned to Dickens's home for dinner and played cards afterward. (See letters to the Tennysons, [Dec., 1872] and Nov. 2, 1873, and to Cowell, [Late March, 1873].)

[3] Robert Elliott, whose sister Elizabeth Browne married in 1844.

To Richard Monckton Milnes

73 Newman St.
[June, 1843]

Dear Milnes,

Will you let me introduce to you one Morris Moore,[1] an artist who has lived nearly all his life in Italy, and has now come back to show what he can do in London. He seems to me to be the best colourist we have: but he has not yet had opportunity to produce any large work. He is rather a violent fellow in his opinions about art: but then he is for the most part right, and knows well what he is talking about. I wish you would go and see a portrait he has painted at 10, Robert Street, Hampstead Road: an out of the way place: but you will see a portrait that might almost pass for a Titian, in strength of character and colour. Eastlake says, they are the right thing: but not suited to English eyes. Perhaps so: but as the man has genuine power about him, he ought to be known and encouraged. There are some smaller heads by him at the Exhibition: which you must break your back to look at. You need not buy any of his pictures: but you may perhaps give him a little finger of encouragement and patronage. The man is a little of a bear: but quite honest and independent. Spedding will confirm what I say. Look at the portrait he has painted first, and you will be sure the painter must have some "vis" in him.

Yours truly,
E. FitzGerald

[1] Morris Moore (1812-85), rather "violent" as EFG states, took part in the Greek war for independence in 1830 and spent much of the remainder of his life

in Italy. Failing to win recognition as an artist, he became a critic and was an authority on Raphael. He published *Apollo e Marsias opera di Raffaello Sanzio da Urbino*, Milan, 1860; and *Raphael's Apollo and Marsyas*, "a European Scandal," Edinburgh, 1884. He also wrote *Abuses of the National Gallery*, 1847, and *Revival of Vandalism at the National Gallery*, 1853. Moore died in Rome. EFG's appeal for aid on his behalf is one of the many letters of the kind received by Milnes, who was a willing sponsor and advocate of talented unknowns struggling for recognition in the arts.

To Samuel Laurence
(Fragment)

Dublin
July 11/43

My dear Laurence,

We got here this morning; most of us sick, but not I: not evidently sick, I mean. Here the sun shines, and people go about in their cars or stand idle, just the same as ever. "Repeal"[1] is faintly chalked on a wall here and there. I have been to see a desperate collection of pictures by the Royal Academy: among them old unsaleables by Maclise and Uwins.[2]

What I write for however is to say that the first volume of Titmarsh's Ireland[3] is at 39 Portland Place; and that I wish you would ask for it there and get it. Keep the two volumes for a time. It is all true.[4] I ordered a bath here when I got in: the waiter said it was heated to 90°, but it was scalding: he next locked me up in the room instead of my locking him out.

Keep an eye on the little Titian, and I shall really make the venture of borrowing £30 to invest in it. Tell Rochard[5] you must have it. I may never be able to get a bit of Titian in my life again: and I shall doubtless learn to admire it properly in time.

[1] "Repeal," the slogan for the Home Rule movement revived in 1842 by the *Nation*, a newspaper founded that year by Gavan Duffy (1816-1903) and other young Irishmen. The "Repealers" agitated for dissolution of the 1801 union with England and restoration of the Irish Parliament. Daniel O'Connell, who had permitted his efforts for Home Rule to languish for a decade, declared that 1843 should be the Repeal year.

[2] Daniel Maclise; see letter to Pollock, May 11, 1842, n.1. Thomas Uwins (1782-1857), painter in oils and watercolors; later, Keeper of the National Gallery, 1847-55.

[3] *The Irish Sketch Book.* Thackeray wrote under the pseudonym of Michael Angelo Titmarsh.

[4] An allusion to Thackeray's description of life on the estate of EFG's paternal uncle, Peter Purcell, at Halverstown, in chapter II of *The Irish Sketch Book.* See also letter to F. Tennyson, July 26, 1841, n.2; and to Pollock, June 24, 1842, n.2.

[5] Either Simon Jacques Rochard (1788-1872) or his brother François Theodore (d. 1858). Both were painters and both were living in London at this time.

To Frederick Tennyson[1]

Halverstown, Kilcullen, Ireland
[July, 1843]

Dear Frederic:

This is to certify that we all got over to Ireland in safety, though most of us very sick. I did not disgrace myself by vomiting: which I believe I avoided by laying in a store of brandy and cold boiled beef!

You would rave at this climate which is wetter far than that of England. There are the Wicklow hills (mountains we call them)[2] in the offing—quite high enough. In spite of my prejudice for a level, I find myself every day unconsciously verging towards any eminence that gives me the freest view of their blue ranges. One's thoughts take wing to the distance. I fancy that moderately high hills (like these) are the ticket—not to be domineered over by Mont Blancs, etc. But this may be only a passing prejudice.

We hear much less of Repeal here than in London: and people seem amused at the troops and waggons of gunpowder that are to be met now and then upon the roads.

Let me hear from you one of these days: especially before you make any move abroad. But that will not be yet, surely. I suppose you will soon leave London for Boxley,[3] however.

Farewell—no more to say.

E.FG.

[1] EFG "illuminated" his manuscript with the line drawing of a shamrock.

[2] East of County Kildare. The highest peak, Lugnaquilla, is 3,039 feet.

[3] Boxley, Kent, near Maidstone, home of the Tennyson family from 1841 to 1843.

To Thomas Carlyle

Halverstown, Kilcullen
[c. July 16, 1843]

Dear Carlyle,

I came to Ireland nearly a week ago, and shall be here, I suppose, six weeks or so. Then back to England, and to Naseby—will you come to that place then, or shall you be away in Scotland or elsewhere? I write about the matter now, because I know you generally leave London for the Autumn—September is a good time, I think, for visiting agricultural countries. You will see a rich attorney shooting partridges over Naseby field.

Nothing but wet, wet, here. As to Repeal, etc., one hears more about it in England. The word is faintly chalked on one or two walls in Dublin, to the exclusion perhaps of lighter topics. People seem rather amused at the soldiers and ammunition that are seen occasionally upon the dreary roads hereabout. I have got your last book here,[1] which reads with much zest upon the top of a broken stone wall in this waste do-nothing country. A landlord may really be a great man here, and see great effects from very little exertion:—the poor still retaining their feudal veneration for the rich. (What an abuse of terms! But I don't know what else they venerate in those who are called their betters.)

Yours truly
E. FitzGerald

[1] *Past and Present.*

To Richard Monckton Milnes

Ballysax
Kilcullen } *both Arcadian*
August 9/43

Dear Milnes,

I hear from Moore[1] you were so good as to pay him a visit, which much gratified him: and that you liked some of his pictures—which doubtless gratified him more. He wants to know if you dare send old Rogers, or other lucrative connoisseur, to him? I dare say he has asked you this himself. All I can say is that such folks would do well to encourage a man who can *colour* better than any one now alive—*may* draw better, for what I know: and certainly impresses a character of earnestness and vigour into such heads as he has done beyond the reach of modern artists. Don't you think so? He really pitches himself into the canvass somehow.

I heard Dan O'Connell two days ago at Baltinglass. Judging by that meeting, I should say that the papers had much exaggerated, if not the numbers, the enthusiasm, of the folks assembled on such occasions. The people seemed to me too starved to be capable of much action, or even of much cheering. But for a chap who stood behind Dan, and waved his hat after Dan's long sentences, they would not have cheered at all: and only some twenty starved boyish voices cheered, when they did cheer. When I laughed at some of Dan's fine promises, they laughed too: and seemed to think it fun. But when he asked if they would meet him again, if he should call for them, certainly multitudes of right hands were held up. But there was none of the deep purpose of a good English mob in them. Why doesn't the Queen come over this Autumn? I think that would be a politic trip.

Yours ever
E. FitzGerald

[1] Morris Moore. See letter to Milnes, [June, 1843].

From Thomas Carlyle

Scotsbrig, Ecclefechan
16 August, 1843

Dear FitzGerald,

Your letter found me amid the mists, rain-tempests, slate-chasms and other intricacies of a Welsh Tour, on which enterprise I had embarked some weeks before.[1] I have now got home to my Mother's Cottage, heartily tired, meaning to rest here for a week or two, and see what will come of that. All sight of waterfalls and such like, almost all speech of men, shall be far from me for a while! I do literally nothing: I saunter along the slopes of the high grounds, wide grassy expanses, bare of wood, tenanted only by sheep which need no shepherd, where all is silent, in this noble Autumn weather, "as if Pan *slept*." At evening I can see the windows of Carlisle, twenty miles off, gleaming against the setting sun; and westward and southward an endless sea of mountains, not one of them speaking an impertinent word to me,—and so I rove about, and like Alexander Selkirk, for the time being, am monarch of all I survey.

My purpose to visit Naseby holds firm as ever. Nothing is fixed with me as to movements farther, except that I do not return to Babylon till this month of August and its heats be over. If your projects continue firm, perhaps the end of your "six weeks" might almost suit the time of my return southward: in that case it would be right pleasant for me to pause at Crick, and spend a couple of days with you at Naseby; terminating my travels in a worthy manner. But it is not worth while to alter anything on my account: if you have not returned as I pass, we will wait for some other opportunity. Write, some time soon, how it is. I shall be here yet for a week or ten days; here or appointed to return hither.

Were my travelling faculty a shade better, I should be tempted to run up to Dunbar;[2] and see if on the spot it were possible, what by all books and study it has never hitherto been, to form some rational conjecture about the manner of the Fight there. I went about a hundred miles out of my way to see Gloucester and Worcester,—and made mighty little of them when I did see them! The "crowning mercy"[3] I could only look at from Severn Bridge, with a poor labourer out of work for guide, who "wished to God we had another Oliver, Sir, times is so cruel bad!" I wished it too, but knew not where to find him. One wanders in vain over battlefields and antiquarian works seeking the man; he is not here, he is gone to his place—and has left Peel Russel and Comp^y [4] behind him.

Spedding's Brother wishes me over to Skiddaw and his Lake Country which is about forty miles off. It is uncertain whether I shall be equal to going. The charms of *sitting still* are great! Yet Thomas Spedding is a chief favourite of mine; I sit not still without regret. James S., it seems, is shooting partridges in Yorkshire, and shortly expected at his Brother's.

As to the Picturesque, I have been dreadfully annoyed with it ever since I left home. Not properly with *it*, for I rather like big rocks, high mountains, swift rivers, etc., as I suppose all mortal men since the beginning of the world have done; but the eternal cackle and babble about it from all persons, even sensible persons, in these times, is truly distressing to me. It is like a human being uttering to me, "Cuck-*oo*! Cuck-*oo*!" with a tongue that might speak real *words*. Far more shocking than you think!—This among other things attracts me rather to these bare solitudes: the grand meaning of *them* too is that

God Eternal made them, that they are still solitary of all but the needful fourlegged sheep!

Well; I bid you enjoy the Green Island, I bid you pray daily you could cure what is ragged and awry in it, by *Repail* or otherwise;—and forget not to say when you are leaving it.

Yours in hope of meeting,
T. Carlyle

[1] Carlyle had been in Wales, July 7-21.

[2] Near Edinburgh, the site of Cromwell's victory (Sept. 3, 1650) over the Scots who had opened hostilities after the execution of Charles I.

[3] Quoted from Cromwell's letter of Sept. 4, 1651, to William Lenthall, Speaker of the Parliament of England, reporting the victory at Worcester on the River Severn the previous day. The passage reads, "The dimensions of this mercy are above my thoughts. It is, for ought I know, a crowning mercy" (*Cromwell's Letters and Speeches*, 1st ed., II, 146).

[4] Lord John Russell, at this time Member of Parliament for the City of London, succeeded Robert Peel as Prime Minister in 1846.

To Bernard Barton

Ballysax,[1] *Kilcullen*
August 17/43

My dear Barton,

. . . That old Suffolk comes over here sometimes, as I say; and greets one's eyes with old familiar names: Sales at Yoxford, Aldeburgh, etc., regattas at Lowestoft, and at Woodbridge. I see Major Moor turning the road by the old Duke of York; the Deben winding away in full tide to the sea; and numberless little pictures of this kind.

I am going the day after to-morrow to Edgeworth's,[2] for a week, it may be a fortnight before I set sail for England. Where shall I pitch my tent? that is the question. Whither shall those treasures of ancient art descend, and be reposited there for ever?

I have been looking over the old London Magazine. Lamb's papers come in delightfully:[3] read over the Old China the night you get this, and sympathize with me. The account of the dish of green pease, etc., is the true history of lawful luxury. Not Johnson nor Adam Smith told so much. It is founded not on statistics but on good humanity.

We have at last delightful weather, and we enjoy it. Yesterday we went to Pool-a-Phooka,[4] the Leap of the Goblin Horse. What is that, do you suppose? Why, a cleft in the mountains down and through which the river Liffey (not very long born from the earth) comes leaping and roaring. Cold veal pies, champagne, etc., make up the enchantment. We dabbled in the water, splashed each other, forded the river, climbed the rocks, laughed, sang, eat, drank, and were roasted, and returned home, the sun sinking red.

[*A note by Aldis Wright—"A pen and ink sketch"*]
This is not like Pool-a-Phooka.

[1] Where his brother Peter was living, about three miles southwest of Kilcullen, County Kildare.

[2] The home of his Trinity friend Francis Edgeworth, at Edgeworthstown, County Longford.

[3] From 1820 to 1823 Lamb was a regular contributor to the *London Magazine*; the first series of his "Essays of Elia" appeared there. Barton and Lamb had been friends and correspondents.

[4] Pool-a-Phooka, on ordnance maps spelled Pollaphuca, ten miles east of Ballysax.

To Frederick Tennyson

Ireland
August 31/43

Dear Frederic,

I know not if I asked you *to answer* Mrs. Tennant's[1] query, which I put in my last letter from Edgeworthstown. She spoke to me again about it, and hoped I should hear from you, and let her know. Write to me a line of answer then, and direct it to me at Naseby, Welford, Northamptonshire. I set sail from Dublin tomorrow night, bearing the heartfelt regrets of all the people of Ireland with me.

Where is my dear old Alfred? Sometimes I intend to send him a quotation from a book: but do not perform the same. Are you packing up for Italy? I had a pleasant week with Edgeworth. He farms, and is a justice: and goes to sleep on the sofa of evenings. At odd moments he looks into Spinoza and Petrarch. People respect him very much in those parts. Old Miss Edgeworth is wearing away: she has a capital bright soul which even now shines quite youthfully through her faded carcase. She has made great exertions to promote the Subscription for Tennant's Sermons: the Archbishop of Canterbury is to be on the list: the Bishop of London declines appearing but will take three copies [I] understand—and pay for them, it is to be hoped. I think one ought to subscribe for three copies oneself. That is, *I* ought: who knew Tennant, and know all the Edgeworths. *Mrs.* T. is not quite well, and at times seems downcast: but her Spanish eyes[2] let out the merry devil now and then. She is a noble kind of woman: and would look very handsome out of a detestable widow's cap she wears.

I had the weakest dream the other night that ever was dreamt. I thought I saw Thomas Frognall Dibdin[3]—and that was all. Tell this to Alfred. Carlyle talks of coming to see Naseby: but I leave him to suit the weather to his taste. Farewell—but write.

Ever yours
E.FG.

They are going to put up a monument to Tennant at Florence!

[1] Mrs. Tennant, widow of Robert Tennant, minister of the English Church in Florence, and a sister-in-law of Francis Edgeworth. Tennant had died the previous year in Florence, and Mrs. Tennant was publishing a volume of her husband's sermons. The letter to which EFG refers has apparently not survived.

[2] Mrs. Tennant and Mrs. Edgeworth were daughters of Don Antonio Eroles, of Catalonia, Spain.

[3] Thomas Frognall Dibden (1776-1847), clergyman, prolific bibliographer, and author of miscellanies of travel.

To Thomas Carlyle

Saturday Morning
on board of the L'Urgent
[September 2, 1843]

Dear Carlyle,

If you cross the Solway waters this night, I hope you will have as good a passage as I am just arriving at the close of. We are sailing along the hills of Wales at half past six, I believe: and I have had but a little doze on the sofa of the cabin since I shook hands with my Irish friends in the Kingstown harbour last night.

The weather has brightened up so the last three days (and with it, I hope, your spirits) that I rather fancy you will go to Dunbar, etcc., and so home to London. Therefore, I shall not wait to catch a glimpse of you at Liverpool, but step out of this boat upon the railroad, and so to Naseby. I leave it entirely to your pleasure when and how you follow me there: only repeating that I shall be very glad to see you. Any letter may be directed to Naseby, *Welford*, Northton, etc. You remember what I wrote you about the stations of Rugby and Crick?

September 1843

I hear there are many tokens of Cromwell at Waterford. One day you must see Ireland with your eyes.

My Father, after spending £100,000 on a colliery, besides losses by everlasting rogues, runaway agents, etc., has just been drowned out of it by an influx of water.[1] So end the hopes of eighteen years; and he is near seventy, left without his only hobby! He may perhaps be able to let it to a Company at a low rent, that they may pump out the water. But he is come to the end of his purse. Naseby might have had many a draining tile but for that d——d Colliery.

To make amends for this, my brother has just had nineteen people baptized in the Naseby Reservoir—1500 looking on.[2] That is his hobby —not *so* expensive.

Yours ever
E. FitzGerald

P.S. I have brought a gallon of capital whiskey in my carpet bag. I hope the Steward is not looking over my shoulder.

[1] In the late twenties Mr. FitzGerald had begun to mine coal at Pendleton, near Castle Irwell, the family estate at Manchester. His superintendent was Robert Stevenson, whose more famous brother, George, became one of the directors of the Pendleton Colliery Company which FitzGerald, Sr., founded in 1836. Subterranean waters, and dishonest employees and agents at the minehead had encumbered operations almost from the start. The flooding that EFG reports brought ruin to the company and swept Mr. FitzGerald into bankruptcy five years later. John Kerrich of Geldestone Hall was one of the investors who lost heavily. (See Terhune, *FitzGerald*, chap. XIV.)

[2] John FitzGerald was a zealous and extremely sincere evangelical lay preacher. Despite an impediment in his speech and eccentric mannerisms on the platform, he attracted large assemblies, in neighboring counties as well as in Suffolk, when he preached or lectured. "John is giving at our theatre here a series of Lectures on the Prophecies every Tuesday and Friday evening to most overflowing audiences," Barton wrote to Donne from Woodbridge, March 21, 1844 (*Donne and His Friends*, p. 80).

To Thomas Carlyle

Naseby, Welford
Septr 9/43

Dear Carlyle,

I sent a note as you directed to Liverpool.[1] Perhaps it was never delivered. Though I am sorry you have not been here this noble weather, I am glad you have not failed to see Dunbar. You are now,

I conclude, returned to London. I will leave it entirely to yourself when you come here: you must not feel bound to do so because we have agitated it so long. It is a thing to be done at any time. Towards the end of next week I think of going to Bedford to pay a long-promised visit.

Have you read the Romance of Oliver Cromwell—by a Mr. Herbert,[2] who also has written Marmaduke Wyvil—as the papers must have told you more than once. I remember him a scapegrace at Cambridge—an active fellow.

We have had such weather as farmers, as well as poets, must call glorious: and Naseby Field has looked very fine covered with ridges of good corn. Tonight the harvest moon is full. We cannot expect such weather to last much longer. I am no longer at my old lodgings, but with some people called Watts. I command another bed, and a bit of bacon, for you when you like to come.

Did I tell you that Oliver has left marks of himself about another bit of land of my Papa's in Ireland?—near Waterford. So I hear: but I was not at Waterford to see.

Fece assai col spada,   con lo senno.

This is a line somewhere in Dante[3] that would do for Oliver's tomb—if he had one.

I would beg Compliments to Mrs. Carlyle, if they meant anything. I declare I don't know what they mean. Well, then, I hope to hear her converse one of these days in Chelsea again.[4]

Yours truly
E. FitzGerald

[1] No doubt the note written September 2 on board the *L'Urgent*.

[2] Henry William Herbert (1807-58) published *Cromwell*, "an Historical Novel," 2 vols., 1837. Herbert, son of William Herbert, Dean of Manchester, took his degree at Cambridge in 1830 and the following year emigrated to America. His *Marmaduke Wyvil, or the Maid's Revenge* (3 vols.) appeared in New York and London in 1843. A prolific writer, Herbert used many pseudonyms, most frequently, Frank Forester. His subjects covered a wide range: biography, history, fiction, and sports. He committed suicide in New York in 1858. A volume of his poems was published in 1888.

[3] Dante's *Divine Comedy*, "Inferno," Canto XVI, 39: "fece col senno e con la spada" (he achieved much with wisdom and with the sword).

[4] Gavan Duffy, one of the younger Irish leaders and a founder of the *Nation*, described Jane Carlyle as a hostess, after his first call at Cheyne Row, where he had gone in April, 1845, with two of his fellow patriots. "She is one of the most natural, unaffected, fascinating women I ever encountered, and O'H. and P. declare they would rather cultivate her acquaintance than the philosopher's. She

is no longer handsome, but full of intellect and kindness blended gracefully and lovingly together . . . we came away at eleven o'clock at night, delighted with the man and woman. She bantered the philosopher in the most charming manner on his style and his opinions" (*Conversations with Carlyle*, 1892, pp. 4, 5).

To Bernard Barton

Naseby, Welford
Sept[r]
Pmk., September 12, 1843

Dear Barton,

I have been suffering for these last four days with an attack, which I partly attribute to my having walked to Thornby[1] under a burning sun, then eaten unripe peaches, and then gone to sleep upon long wet grass! A pretty mixture—I have paid for it: and am even now in a state of water gruel, shiverings, headache like a thundercloud over the eyes, etc. The Doctor told me my tongue was very white: I told him the tongues of all Suffolk men were said to be white. He looked rather as if he was affronted. Haven't you heard this before, as a saying?

We have had a famous harvest at Naseby. Today a little rain begins to fall: but we are nearly all safely housed. I talk of going the end of this week to Bedford, at the Post Office of which place a letter will find me. I do not mean to wait for Carlyle. He did not return from Scotland by Liverpool, but by Edinburgh packet, etc. and I doubt if he will be much inclined to set off here again soon. Still he writes that he is very earnest so to do: since he has been to see the field of Dunbar, and verified all its position. He stood on the spot where Cromwell stood when the sun broke out, and Oliver broke out too with "Arise O Lord," etc.[2] and led such a charge as won the battle. "Worthy man!" Carlyle calls him.

When I got home I found my brother married and come down here. These little surprises are common in our family. She seems a decent woman. We have other rumours of marriage afloat too:[3] but what the issue will be nobody knows. The wind bloweth where it listeth.

You should have stated the reason why Mr. Churchyard left off smoking, for the benefit of survivors. Why did he? Let him leave off cigars: that is good: but pipes! Not that I can boast, for I believe some of my headache originates from them.

I am glad our dear Major[4] has taken up the Privy Council—as a wit once called it. Do you also read the book and see if it is not more interesting than Gaieties and Gravities.[5] "The health of the whole world!" Is not this a poetical subject? Poetry has done its duty by daisies, heart-breakings, etc.—it must now turn to the real views of mankind at large—or be lost. The ideal and the actual are about to meet! Therefore be wise in time and send me a sonnet to a Privy in return for mine. The diver may be a night man, and he may bring up a fragrant treasure which may tell him how it became so fragrant. Farewell.

E.FG.

A diver springing darkly to the brim
Of the full sapphire river as it rolled
Under palm shadows over sands of gold
Along the balmy vale of Almahim:
Brought up what seem'd a piece of common mould,
But of so rare a fragrance that he cried—
"Mine eyes are dim with diving—thou'rt no piece
Of common earth, but musk or ambergrease."
"I am but common earth," the clod replied—
"But once within my dusky bosom grew
The Rose, and so insinuated through
Her aromatic fibres day by day,
That time her virtue never will subdue,
Nor all the rambling water wash away—"

This I found in my desk tonight. I remember versifying it out of a passage in one of old D'Israeli's books[6]—when, I forget. But it turned up opportunely as a counter stench to the subject of the last part of my letter. The last line is a good one. But my poetical farthing candle is almost burnt out. Is your *Liar* silent?

[1] Two miles southwest of Naseby.

[2] Carlyle reports that when the Royalist army was routed, one of Cromwell's men heard him say, "They run! I profess they run!" And, Carlyle continues, as the sun rose over St. Abb's Head and the German Ocean, the soldier "heard Nol say, in the words of the Psalmist, 'Let God Arise, let His enemies be scattered.' " Cromwell was quoting Psalm 68:1, "Let God arise, let his enemies be scattered; let them also that hate him flee before him" (*Cromwell's Letters and Speeches*, 1st ed., II, 39-40).

[3] John, who had married Hester, daughter of William Haddon. The marriage being rumored was that of his sister Isabella to Gaetano Vignati, which took place October 18, 1843. See letter to F. Tennyson, Oct. 15, 1843.

[4] Major Moor.

[5] *Gaieties and Gravities* (1825), three volumes of prose and verse by the hu-

morist Horace Smith, mainly reprinted from the *London* and *New Monthly* magazines.

[6] Isaac D'Israeli (1766-1848), author, father of Benjamin, Lord Beaconsfield. The passage from which EFG "versified" is in D'Israeli's *Mejnoun and Leila, the Arabian Petrarch and Laura* (1797). This portion of the letter is not with the Barton MSS at the University of Virginia library.

To Frederick Tennyson

Naseby
Septr 12/43

My dear Frederic,

I got your letter this morning here. I will not write to inform Mrs. Tennant[1] till you have heard and written all that is to be told about the drawings. When did I ever call Mrs. T. a *dirty* person? Never, I am sure. I used not to like her regular features so well as her sister's irregular ones: but now I like them better. Why will she wear that horrid widow's cap? I only quarrelled with her for pretending to look grave on Sunday night. But the noble woman spoke out several times: no sham there. The Edgeworths seemed very fond of her. Old Miss Edgeworth has got some great names for the Subscription. Perhaps I told you this.

Here I have been for a week, and stay till the end of this week: then go to Bedford for ten days. I have been suffering with a slight touch of cholera which has made me weak. I think of no great guns but mine own now, I assure you. I am glad to hear so helpful an account of your affairs with that Old Serpent.[2] Edgeworth asked me much about him, and is about to remove his brother from the Asylum. Allen had stuffed his ears with *his* whole version of the wood carving, etc., and all his dealings with you and your family—your assaults on him, etc.[3] I told Edgeworth that whatever his brother's opinion might be (that brother being yet under Old Allen's enchantment) I could swear that Allen was a damned scoundrel on the best authority. So here I think the old wretch will lose a patient. Mrs. A. had been quite as loquacious on the subject as the Doctor.

You say nothing of going abroad yet. After having been at Bedford, I rather think of going to the Eastern coast for a while: I mean, a town there close to my own home, but right on the Sea. Let me hear from you: your letters give me great pleasure.

E.FG.

1. Mary Frances FitzGerald (EFG's mother) by Sir Thomas Lawrence

2. John FitzGerald (EFG's father) by Richmond

3. EFG and his two brothers (John, Edward, Peter, right to left) by Sir Thomas Lawrence

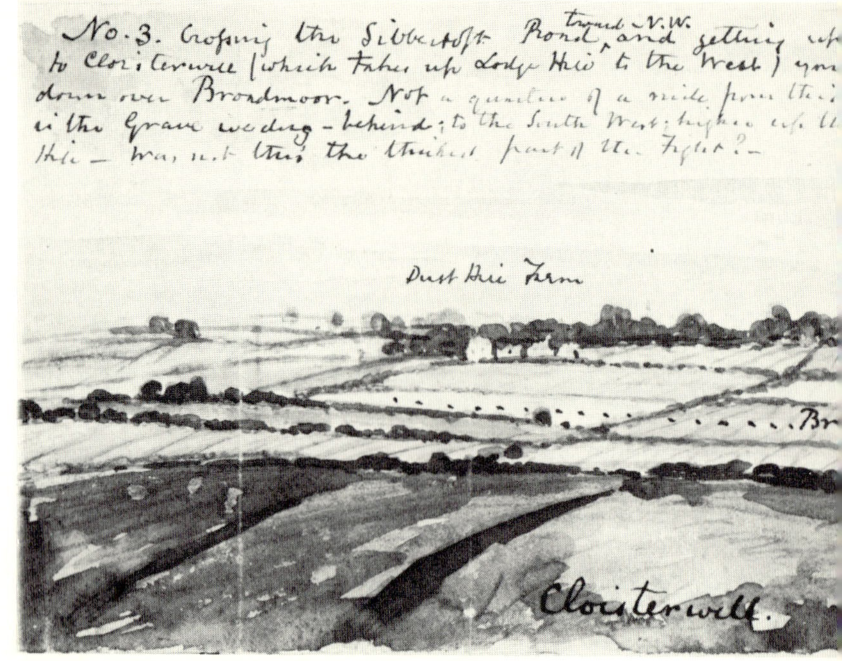

4. and 5. Wash drawings by EFG of scene of Naseby battlefield included with letter of September 27, 1842 to Thomas Carlyle

The crook in the hedge where dead are said to be.
Sibbertoft Road.
written in the map (1800)

No. 2 — Looking thus North from Mill Hill to Lodge Hill.
Lodge Hill

6. Pencil sketch of EFG by James Spedding

7. EFG as a young man by W. M. Thackeray

[1] See letter to F. Tennyson, Aug. 31, 1843.

[2] Dr. Matthew Allen. See letter from A. Tennyson, [Feb., 1841], n.2.

[3] As a young man Frederick possessed anything but a placid personality. His resentment of discipline and his indifference to attendance at chapel led to his being rusticated by Trinity College for three terms. He was described, while at Cambridge, as "sinister in aspect and terrific in manner, even to the discomfiture of elderly dons" (C. Tennyson, *Tennyson*, p. 60). On one occasion when angered by Frederick, his father, an embittered and irascible man, turned the young man over to the constable. Frederick, moreover, maintained a running conflict with his grandfather, who was also his benefactor. EFG reports his threat to cab men, "If you say any more, I'll mash you." Dr. Allen probably had good cause to complain of "assaults"—probably threatened—while he and Frederick were attempting to settle the tangled affairs of pyroglyphs.

To Mrs. Spring Rice

Bedford
Septr 28/43

Dear Mrs. Spring Rice,

It is very good of you to enquire about me and my drawings. Your letter, after making a tour to Ireland, found me here within fifty miles of London. My summer ramble is over, it is to be hoped: and I am positively looking out for a residence in some country town. In such is it my ambition to live. Ipswich, Woodbridge, Beccles, and, last not least, *Bungay*:[1] these fate has left me to choose out of. Bedford is better than all, and one is on the spot now: but friends and relations lie further East.

I expect to go to London before long to see F. Tennyson before he sets out for Italy again. You did not mention how Mrs. Frere was progressing. My Mama is ill of gout at Richmond just now: my Father has just lost a Colliery: and a match is on the *tapis* in our family exceeding all that we have ever attempted yet. I will not tell you of it till it is done: it may never be done, though there are but eight days now fixed to intervene between the design and the fulfilment.[2] So altogether the scutcheon of the Squeers's[3] seems likely to set in the ocean wave. Is it not time to look out for a garret in Bungay? My copies of Titian shall console me for the bothers of life. Then again I have got a terrific cold: and am at last given to understand by a silly physician here that persons of middle age cannot safely sit down on wet grass banks—especially about autumn time. Unripe pears, melons etc. he thinks also not fit for persons of mature years. Well, well. As to the drawings, I sent Carlyle the sketch of Cromwell's house, which after all was *not*

Cromwell's house, but belonged to his uncle, a Mr. Page (no ancestor, I believe, of the gentleman we used to know in Woodbridge). Such as it is, it shall be copied for you when I arrive in town, if you please: or some other drawing made in the days when one could sit on wet grass given as an equivalent. I do not expect to be long in town: but will make a day's excursion to Lewisham if it is convenient to you. Then you shall hear all about the marriage and all. Read the lists of such things in the papers for the next ten days.

Love to S. Rice. Have you all got bad colds?

Yours very truly
E. FitzGerald

[1] Beccles and Bungay, six miles apart, both on the Waveney River which forms a portion of the Suffolk-Norfolk border, offered attractive lures to EFG. Geldestone Hall, home of the Kerriches, was almost equidistant from the two towns. Lowestoft, one of his favorite seaside haunts, was within easy reach to the east. Both were flourishing market towns, stirred by the bustle of rural business EFG loved to observe.

[2] Isabella's marriage did not take place until October 18.

[3] EFG likens the misfortunes which had overtaken the FitzGeralds to the lot that fell to Wackford Squeers and his family in Dickens' *Nicholas Nickleby*. The parallel in no way applies to personalities.

To Samuel Laurence
(Fragment)[1]

[Geldestone]
[October, 1843]

. . . I purpose to live the winter in Ipswich. You must come and see me at Christmas. I shall be able to get you a commission or two, for I am considered rather an authority in these parts.

[1] This fragment is taken from *The Life of Edward FitzGerald* by John Glyde, 1900, p. 40. The date is Glyde's.

To Frederick Tennyson

Geldestone
Octr 15/43

Dear Frederic,

Don't scorn me for a heartless vagabond for not going to shake hands with you in London before you start for Italy—for Heaven knows how long. I could not go to town just now. My sister (not the one you saw) has made a desperate match, which is to be solemnized perhaps next Tuesday at St. Martin's Church.[1] I could not be present: and should have had to lie perdu had I gone to London. The Man she has chosen is—1st an Italian. 2nd a converted Catholic Monk! 3rd is not all this enough without more? He was teaching Italian, without a decent coat on his back, and without a penny in the coat he had. You will think I am of the English persuasion, thinking no one can be worth a straw who is not worth a thousand a year. This is not so—could I know that he were an honest and sensible man who could manage her, he would not be without my approval—but I can scarce think this: and, knowing my sister as I do, I have every reason to fear the issue on all accounts. She may kick over the traces, and say "No" at the foot of the altar: but at present the marriage is to take place early next week. I will say no more about it.[2] Take this as an excuse for my not going to see you, as I proposed. I wished to go to London on other accounts.

You spoke in your last of starting on the 16th. If you do, this letter will hardly reach you. But people don't go such journeys on the very day appointed. Write me a line if you have time—and take all my hearty good wishes whenever and wherever you go.

I had a letter from old Morton a fortnight back. He wrote from Tivoli, where he had hired a lodging for a month. That month has expired by this time (his letter was dated Septr 14) and I suppose he will get back to Rome for the winter. Do you go there? Tell him I sent him a letter to the Poste Restante at Rome, as I knew not how to direct to him in Tivoli.

Pray write to me when you are in Italy. There is no man I wish more to hear from than yourself. You will be over in England some of these days, won't you? Then we will celebrate more salads and Cigars in Cardington St. I am not well, and am a man of paper altogether. Farewell.

Ever yours as I hope
E.FG.

[1] The wedding did not take place until Wednesday.

[2] EFG's fears proved to be unfounded. Isabella's marriage to Gaetano Vignati turned out happily and EFG came to like him.

To Bernard Barton

Geldestone
Octr 21/43

My dear Barton,

I have just returned from Norwich, where I assisted (a French phrase) at a Ball and a Concert. Also bought a picture of course—a fine head, either by Giorgione, or a Flemish copyist. But as I am not particular, I call it Giorgione: and shall sell it to old Rogers[1] at a vast profit.

Rossi, the dealer of whom I bought it, told me that Mr. Churchyard had been at Norwich lately, and bought two Cromes of him. I suppose you have been tempted with these before now. Rossi showed me another: which I did not consider a good specimen. The Lake scene you have is (taking it all in all) the best Crome I ever saw—it is the most poetical. That cold fishy mere![2]

I hear 'tis as hard to find a lodging at Ipswich as at Woodbridge. Where is a single gentleman to rest the sole of his foot! Norwich looked not unamiable this time. Anywhere so it be somewhere!

Farewell. It will not be long before I move toward you. Isabella was married on Wednesday: and sailed to the Continent next day.

Ever yours,
E.FG.

[1] Samuel Rogers (1763-1855), banker, poet, and connoisseur of the arts.

[2] E. V. Lucas, in *Bernard Barton and His Friends*, describes this picture as "an Old Crome, a masterpiece of this great painter, depicting a rain cloud bursting over a peaceful mere at evening, full of that peculiar mellow softness which is now associated with the name of Corot" (p. 56).

To Bernard Barton[1]

73 Newman Street
Oxford Street [London]
[November, 1843]

My dear Barton,

About half an hour ago I came in from a *wet-through* ride from Hatfield[2]—whither I escorted Lusia on Friday. A pleasant day this! But my clothes are changed: the fire lighted: paper, pens, and ink lie invitingly on the table: and I will tip you a pennyworth. But how have you been silent all this long time? You may to be sure have written a letter that remains at Portland Place: if so, well: if not, why well, too. It is too wet to think of going out till better times: especially since my new cotton umbrella was left of course outside the stage coach this morning. Well then, let us be thankful it was but a cotton one: never in this mortal life will I buy a silk one again. My Bassano Holy Family having been carefully varnished is really a capital picture, and is, I believe, the only one of my purchases this season that I will keep. The other mysterious Bassano and the Northcote shall to the hammer. You groan. But they are very large: the Bassano not so mysterious as the Magi of last year. There are two very fine little Constables to be seen in Charlotte St. but both far above my figure: indeed, above their worth, as I think. Things that sold at his sale[3] for £5 will now fetch £20.

Hatfield is a very pretty place: Lord Salisbury's house[4] very noble in a grand dismal park: no one allowed to see inside the house now. Here's a haristocracy for you, as Mr. Vincent would say. But the cheery inside of a wayside pothouse is worth all such places. Mid pleasures and palaces though we may roam, give me a pot of porter all in a foam, cruets, a vast pan of toasted cheese smoking etc. . . .

E.FG.

1 This letter, incomplete, taken from a transcript in Trinity College Library.

2 A town in Hertfordshire, 19 miles north of London.

3 After Constable's death in 1837.

4 Hatfield House, early 17-century mansion, built by Robert Cecil, first Earl of Salisbury.

To Frederick Tennyson

Boulge Hall, Woodbridge
Sunday, Dec[r] 10/1843

Dear Frederic,

Either you wrote me word yourself, or some one told me, that you meant to winter at Florence. So I shall direct to the Poste Restante there. You see I am not settled at the Florence of Suffolk, called Ipswich, yet—but I am perhaps as badly off—being in this most dull country house quite alone—a grey mist, that seems teeming with half formed snow, all over the landscape before my windows. It is also Sunday morning—ten of the clock by the chime now sounding from the stables. I have fed on bread and milk (a dreadfully opaque diet) and I await the morning Church in humble hope. It will begin in half an hour. We keep early hours in the country. So you will be able exactly to measure my aptitude and fullness for letter writing by the quantity written now, before I bolt off for hat, gloves, and prayer-book. I always put on my thickest great-coat to go to our Church in: as fungi grow in great numbers about the communion table. And now, to turn away from Boulge, I must tell you that I went up to London a month ago to see old Thackeray, who had come there to have his eyes doctored. I stayed with him ten days and we were as usual together.[1] Alfred came up "in transitu" from Boxley to Cheltenham: he looked, and said he was, ill:[2] I have never seen him so hopeless: and I am really anxious to know how he is. But he would scarcely see any of us, and went away suddenly: so I know not where to direct to him. Are our poetical nerves to come to this? Must a man vegetate like a beast to keep himself well and hopeful? I doubt poets are an ill-starred race—that is, poets who deal in their own susceptibilities. Yet Alfred might be fairly well if he would do as he should, but that again he does not do for the very reason he is a poet. Horatio[3] was with him, and seemed rather unused to the planet. One day he was to go to Cheltenham—another to Plymouth—then he waited for an umbrella he thought he had left somewhere—so where he is now I have not a notion. And how does your charge[3] get on? How do you all pig, quarrel, and agree together? I remember the days of the summer when you and I were together, quarrelling and laughing—these I remember with pleasure. Our trip to Gravesend[4] has left a perfume with me. I can get up with you on that everlastingly stopping Coach on which we tried to travel from Gravesend to Maidstone[5] that Sunday morning—worn out with it, we got down at an inn, and then got up on another coach—and an old smiling fellow passed us holding out his hat—and you said, "That old fellow must go about as Homer did"—and numberless other turns of road and humour, which sometimes pass before me as I lie in bed.

I had a long letter from Morton a few days ago. He is yet in Rome. I will put in his direction before I close my letter. He talks of coming to England if his brother Ned comes home from Nova Zembla or some such place, and if he gets £100—which he has some hope of. I doubt his affairs are as badly off as ever; and if he gets his £100, it seems to me he had better make the most of it where he is than just run back to see his brother. But there may be more in it than I know of. He (Savile) has been ill of a fever, and inflammation, and such convulsion of bowels as made him feel (he says) "like Stromboli with its crater downwards."[6] I hear there is a great deal of *grippe* abroad. Have you had it?

You wished to know the event of my sister's marriage.[7] Well, she married the Italian, and away they went to Brussels, she vowing she never wished to see England again. But she now writes that she must come back. She cannot endure the police and espionage abroad, it app[ears] in truth, she must ever be changing. [She will want] to change her husband very soon.

That man whose pictures you took such an extraordinary fancy for—Morris Moore[8]—has now quarrelled with everybody—still reserving a little hanging out rag of acquaintance with me. The fact was I began to quarrel with him—insofar as I told him what an ass he was for quarrelling with others. So how it will end I neither know nor care a half penny. But I most particularly beg of you that you will not cut me—but on the contrary, that you will write me a long letter forthwith, and tell me all about yourself and about Italy. Now before I turn over, I will go and see about Church—as I hear no bell—pack myself up as warmly as I can—and be off. So goodbye till twelve o'clock. 'Tis five minutes past twelve by the stable clock[9]—so I saw as I returned from Church through the garden. Parson and Clerk got through the Service see-saw like two men in a sawpit. In the garden I see the heads of the snowdrops and crocuses just out of the earth. Another year with its same flowers and topics to open upon us. Shenstone somewhere sings,

> Tedious again to mark the drizzling day,
> Again to trace the same sad tracts of snow:
> Or, lulled by vernal airs, again survey
> The selfsame hawthorn bud, and cowslips blow.[10]

I rely on you and all your family sympathizing in this. So do I sometimes—anyhow, people complimenting each other on the approach of Spring and such like felicitations are very tiresome. Our very year is of a paltry diameter. But this is not proper language for Mark Tapley,[11] whose greatest bore just now is having a bad pen—but the letter is ended. So he is jolly and yours as ever.

[No signature]

Morton's direction: 5 Monte Catino.
1mo Rome.

[1] During this visit, Bryan W. Procter (1787-1874), better known as Barry Cornwall, wrote to Thackeray on November 18, "Next Tuesday is my birthday—I shall be 27 on that day—Will you & Messrs FitzGerald and Tennyson come & dine with me at ¼ before 7, therefore, on Tuesday. I shall try to get one or two

men whom you all know" (*Thackeray Letters and Papers*, II, 127). Procter, it will be observed, would have been 56 years old that year. Both solicitor and miscellaneous writer, Procter was the beloved friend of many prominent men of the time.

[2] The Tennysons moved from Boxley to 6 Belle Vue Place, Cheltenham, late in the year. Satisfaction derived from the relative success of his 1842 volumes aided Tennyson little in contending with pressures which created despondency and frayed nerves. Since the death of his father in 1831, responsibilities of the head of a numerous and difficult family had fallen largely on his shoulders. His engagement to Emily Sellwood, contracted in 1838, had been broken off two years later by Emily's father. The loss of his own and family funds in the pyroglyph speculation had proved to be "sorrow's crown of sorrow," to quote Tennyson's own words in "Locksley Hall."

[3] Horatio, youngest member of the Tennyson family, was 24 years old; Frederick's "charge," subsequently mentioned by EFG, was Septimus, 28. None of the younger members of the family had received a university education. A proposal that Horatio enter the navy after the death of his father was soon abandoned. The boy was only 11 at the time. Septimus, "a clever, sharp fellow," was articled to a solicitor in 1832; but before 1834 he had abandoned that vocation and was apprenticed to a country doctor. Medicine, likewise, failed to appeal to him; and in 1837 he and Horatio considered emigrating to Demerara in British Guiana. That plan ended with Horatio's going alone to farm in Tasmania, a venture that failed. Septimus, in the meantime, "was unable to settle to any employment." Hence, in 1843, as EFG reports, Horatio was again in England. Septimus, "suffering seriously from some nervous ailment" (C. Tennyson, *Tennyson*, p. 199), had gone to Italy with Frederick.

Much of the eccentricity characteristic of members of the Tennyson family should be attributed to tumultuous home influences. Their father, the Reverend George Clayton Tennyson, was an elder son who had been disinherited by his wealthy father in favor of the younger son, Charles. In compensation, George was given three livings, including that of Somersby, where he "reluctantly and rather defiantly" settled down to the life of a country rector, a role for which, by temperament, he was ill-suited. He was proud and sensitive. His sense of injustice at being passed over by his father, the cares of a large family—11 children—and envy of the easy lot of the brother who had supplanted him, made him an embittered man, subject to morbid moods and irritability. He began to drink heavily. In 1829 Mrs. Tennyson, who had patiently borne previous abuse, left her husband, taking her children to her father's home. Tennyson was sent by his father to the Continent for a change of scene and remained there a year. He died at Somersby a year after his return home.

[4] Trips on excursion boats which plied the Thames between London Bridge and Greenwich, Gravesend, and Margate were among EFG's favorite diversions while in town. For further reminiscences of this outing, see letter to F. Tennyson, Feb. 24, 1844.

EFG entered the memorandum of a trip from Gravesend to London, taken the previous year with Alfred Tennyson, on the title page of his copy of the poet's 1832 volume, *Poems*. Below the title FitzGerald added the word "BY," and below that pasted a slip of paper on which he had written

Mr. A. Tennyson
(next door)

On the reverse side of the page is pasted a silhouette of the poet. Below, EFG wrote, "Done in a Steamboat from Gravesend to London. Jan: 1842" The silhouette, EFG wrote to Fanny Kemble in February, 1878, "though not inaccurate of outline, gave the idea of a respectable apprentice." (EFG's copies of Tennyson's 1830 and 1832 publications, bound in a single volume, are now in Trinity College Library.)

With the coming of steam, excursion boats on the Thames carried on a thriving business. During the summer four or five boats daily made the London-Gravesend trip. In 1836 the fare, on some, was 1s (John H. Brady, *Guide to London and its Environs*, 1838, p. 269). During holidays, such as Whitsun, competition sometimes drove the fare down to 6d.

5 En route to the Tennyson home at Boxley.

6 The still-active volcano on Stromboli, one of the Lipari Islands north of Sicily.

7 See letter to F. Tennyson, Oct. 15, 1843.

8 See letter to Milnes, [June, 1843].

9 The same clock was still on the stable after Boulge Hall was demolished in 1955.

10 William Shenstone (1714-63). His "Elegy XI," Stanza 14, reads:

> Tedious again to curse the drizling day!
> Again to trace the wint'ry tracts of snow!
> Or, sooth'd by vernal airs, again survey
> The self-same hawthorns bud, and cowslips blow!

11 Frederick had dubbed EFG "Mark Tapley"—perhaps in the course of their London-Gravesend-Maidstone odyssey. Mark, the servant and companion of Martin in Dickens' *Martin Chuzzlewit*, was invariably cheerful.

Evidence of EFG's wit and jocosity is frequently found in reminiscences of those who knew him. Even as a child he had been an entertaining companion. Sarah F. Spedding, niece of James Spedding's, wrote a few months after EFG's death. "A year or two ago . . . I saw an old letter written by his father . . . from France, in which he speaks of 'little Edward' . . . keeping the whole party in good spirits by his unfailing fun and droll speeches." John de Soyres, a nephew, recorded that EFG "sent us little ones into fits of laughter by his stories." Mary S. Crowfoot of Beccles recalled "how often the servant waiting at table when he dined with us found it impossible to repress an outburst of laughter and left the room to conceal." (The three passages quoted are in letters among the FitzGerald papers in Trinity College Library.)

To Samuel Laurence
(Fragment)

Boulge, Woodbridge
Decr 21/43

My dear Laurence,

I hope you got safe and sound to London:[1] as I did to this place yesterday. Those good Tetter people! I have got an attachment to them somehow. I left Jane in a turmoil as to which picture of W[ilkinson] she was to take. I advised her to take a dose of Time, which always operates so gently.

I have been down to Woodbridge to-day and had a long chat with Churchyard, whom I wish you had seen, as also his Gainsborough sketches. He is quite clear as to Gainsborough's general method, which was (he says) to lay all in (except the sky, of course) with pure colour, quite unmixed with white. The sketch he has is certainly so; but whether it ever could have been wrought up into a deep finish, I don't know. C. says yes it could: that Gainsborough began nearly all his pictures so. He has tried it over and over again (he says) and produced exactly the same effect with pure colour, laid on very thin over a light brown ground: asphaltum and blue producing just such a green as many of the trees in this sketch are of. The sky put in afterwards.

He thinks this the great secret of landscape painting. He shewed me the passage quoted by Burnet[2] from Rubens' maxims (where and what are they?) "Begin by painting in your shadows lightly, taking care that *no* white be suffered to glide into them—*it is the poison of a picture except in the lights.* If ever your shadows are corrupted by the introduction of this baneful colour, your tones will no longer be warm and transparent, but heavy and leaden. It is not the same in the lights: they may be loaded with colour as much as you think proper."

Here is a technical letter, you see, from a man who is no artist, and very ignorant, as you think, I dare say. Try a head in this way. You have tried a dozen, you say. Very well then.

I will send up your cloak, which is barely bigger than a fig leaf, when I can. On Saturday I give supper to B. Barton and Churchyard. I wish you could be with us. We are the chief Wits of Woodbridge. And one man has said that he envies our conversations! So we flatter each other in the country.

[1] From Holbrook where Laurence had painted a portrait of the Reverend J. B. Wilkinson, husband of EFG's sister Jane.

[2] John Burnet (1784-1868), engraver and painter, who wrote *Practical Hints on Light and Shade in Painting* in 1826; the quotation appears on pages 25 and 26.

The Wits of Woodbridge also included the Reverend George Crabbe, son of the poet Crabbe, whose vicarage at Bredfield was less than a mile across the fields from Boulge Cottage. He had been appointed to the living about the time the FitzGeralds took possession of Boulge Hall. A scrap among the FitzGerald papers at Trinity College

Library bears what was obviously the draft of an invitation to a meeting of the Wits. The note reads:

Dear Crabbe,

When from your walk you're rested
And your dinner's half digested,
Prithee, then set off again
Through the dirty roads and rain,
And win your way with courage here
To smoke cigars and drink small Beer.
Churchyard I expect, and Barton;
But should they fail—here's I for sartain;
Who, as e'en my foes do boast,
Am always in myself "a host."
And so expecting you to see
I'm your obedient E.F.G.

Thanks to Bernard Barton, Crabbe's reply has survived. He had recently seen the vicar at the Cottage, Barton wrote to Donne in June, 1847. "Edward had axed him to meet one or two of us there, and his acceptance of the invitation ran thus, as nearly as my memory serves:

As sure as a gun
I'll be in at the fun;
For I'm the old Vicar
As sticks to his liquor;
And smokes a cigar
Like a jolly Jack Tar:
I've no time for more,
For the Post's at the door;
But I'll be there by seven,
And stay 'till eleven
For Boulge is my Heaven!"

Barton's correspondence yields accounts of two meetings of the Wits. To an Ipswich friend he wrote: "Tom Churchyard drove me last night to a symposium given by Edward FitzGerald to us two and Old Crabbe—lots of palaver, smoking, and laughing. Edward was in one of his drollest cues, and did the honours of his cottage with such gravity of humour that we roared again. It was the oddest melange. Tea, porter, ale, wine, brandy, cigars, cold lamb, salad, cucumber, bread and cheese; no precise line of demarcation between tea and supper. It was one continuous spread, something coming on fresh every ten minutes till we wondered whence they came and whither they could be put. 'Gentlemen, the resources of the cottage are exhaustless,' shouted our host. 'Miss Faiers, the salad there, the cucumber here, oil at that corner, vinegar and pepper yonder; there put the cream, and that glass of butter in the middle, push those wine and brandy bottles close together.'—Certes, it was rare fun." (Quoted in the Suffolk Chronicle, *May 7, 1900.) Barton detested the smell of cigars. On February 1, 1845, he wrote to George Crabbe of Bredfield, "I hereby give you notice that after a reasonable time given to your Cigar Divan—I mean to bolt, and fly for refuge to the purer atmosphere of the Drawing room. I cast no reflections on the hearty hospitalities of our Nero of the Cottage. His Mutton was capital—his Wild Ducks—ditto—the Port fine—Porter prodigiously potent—his Pickles had the true Bredfield pungency—but the odour of that room after the first hour or two from the time of lighting up was really awful. Talk of my tippling Port! marry the clouds such a trio as yours can and do blow would do more to make me drunk than all the Wine I could ever be induced to swallow" (Barton-Crabbe Correspondence, British Museum Add. 36,756).*

Crabbe's older son, also named George, who later became one of FitzGerald's most trusted friends, recorded his recollections of FitzGerald at Boulge Cottage. The following passage, originally published by Aldis Wright,[1] is taken from the younger Crabbe's notes, now at Trinity Library. One statement, "No one was, I think, resident at the Hall," has been deleted by the present editors from the account as published by Wright. FitzGerald and Barton refer a number of times in letters to the presence of the family at Boulge, and the Hall was FitzGerald's Suffolk residence from 1835 to 1837. From the latter year until 1843 he occupied the cottage the major part of each year but, except for trips to London, spent the winter months in the Hall with other members of his family. The cottage became his year-round home in 1843. Young Crabbe reported:

> FitzGerald was living at Boulge Cottage when I first knew him: a thatched cottage of one storey just outside his Father's Park. His mother would sometimes be there a short time, and would drive about in a coach and four black horses. This would be in 1844 when he was 36.[2] He used to walk by himself, slowly, with a Skye terrier.[3] I was rather afraid of him. He seemed a proud and very punctilious man. I think he was at this time going often of an evening to Bernard Barton's. He did not come to us, except occasionally, till 1846. He seemed to me when I first saw him much as he

was when he died, only not stooping: always like a grave middle-aged man: never seemed very happy or light-hearted, though his conversation was most amusing sometimes. His cottage was a mile from Bredfield. He was very fond, I think, of my Father; though they had several coolnesses which I believe were all my Father's fault, who took fancies that people disliked him or were bored by him. E.F.G. had in his cottage an old woman to wait on him, Mrs. Faiers; a very old-fashioned Suffolk woman. He was just as careful not to make her do anything as he was afterwards with Mrs. Howe.[4] He would never ring the bell, if there was one, of which I am not sure. Sometimes he would give a little dinner—my Father, Brooke,[5] B. Barton, Churchyard—everything most hospitable, but not comfortable.

In 1846 and 1847 he does not seem to have come much to Bredfield. Perhaps he was away a good deal. He was often away, visiting his mother, or W. Browne, or in London, or at the Kerriches'. In 1848, 1849, and 1850 he was a great deal at Bredfield, generally dropping in about seven o'clock, singing glees with us, and then joining my Father over his cigar, and staying late and often sleeping. He very often arranged concerted pieces for us to sing, in four parts, he being tenor. He sang very accurately but had not a good voice.

While E.F.G. was at Boulge, he always got up early, eat his small breakfast, stood at his desk reading or writing all the morning, eat his dinner of vegetables and pudding, walked with his Skye terrier, and then often finished the day by spending the evening with us or the Bartons. He did not visit with the neighboring gentlefolks, as he hated a set dinner party.

1 *Letters and Literary Remains*, I, 175-77.

2 EFG was 35 in 1844.

3 The terrier was Ginger. At this time EFG also had a retriever which had been given him by Browne, Thomas Wright says (*Life*, I, 161). He named this dog Bletsoe after a village near Bedford, one of the favorite haunts of the two friends.

4 His housekeeper at Little Grange in Woodbridge, where EFG lived the last years of his life.

5 Francis Capper Brooke, of Ufford Place, Ufford, was a wealthy friend and neighbor. Brooke is never mentioned by any of the "Wits" as being one of the group.

From Thomas Carlyle

Chelsea, 9 Jany 1844

Dear Fitzgerald,

Your letter comes to me in a "good hour,"—makes for me what the French call a *bonheur*! I am sunk in inexpressible confusions; and any kind voice of encouragement is right welcome. Surely if ever I do get this *Book of Cromwell* finished, we will smoke a pipe of triumph over it, and rejoice to remember difficulties undergone! Alas, for the present I cannot so much as get it begun. In my whole life, I have found myself in no such hideous situation: a ghastly labyrinth, created for me by the stupidities of England accumulating for two hundred years;—vacant Dullness glaring on one everywhere, with torpedo look, in this universal "dusk of the gods," saying with a sneer: "Thou? Wilt thou save a Hero from the Abysses, when dark Death has quietly hidden him so long?" It is frightful.[1] But on the whole we must hold on; we must not spend our strength in execrating, in complaining! It is really something like the *sixth* time, that I have burnt considerable masses of written attempts at commencing the unwriteable; and to this hour it remains properly uncommenced. And it must be commenced, and (if God please) finished; I shall have but a poor time of it otherwise! Let me be silent; let my next Note to you say: I *am* launched; by the blessing of Heaven, I hope to sail, to arrive! Surely there was no such business as the writing a Life of Oliver Cromwell for the present race of Englishmen, in the present distracted darkness of the whole subject, ever before laid upon a human sinner?

One of the things I have at length got to discern as doable is the gathering of all Oliver's Letters and Speeches, and stringing them together according to the order of time: a series of final *rock*-summits, in the infinite ocean of froth, confusion, lies and stupidity, which hitherto constitutes the "History" of Cromwell, as Dryasdust[2] has printed it and read it. This I am at present doing; tho' this is not what I have the real difficulty in doing. I have made considerable progress; time has eaten up most of Oliver's utterances; but a fraction still remains: these I can and will see printed, set in some kind of order.[3]

Directly on receiving your Note I shot off a missive to "A. Cromwell Russell," etc.:[4] no answer yet; you shall hear of it, if I ever get an answer: but I hardly expect one, or at any rate one that will be better than none. Various are the applications of a like sort that I have made; always with the one answer, Nothing available here; something once *was*, or was said to be, but, etc., etc. In the British Museum I find the original of the Letter about Naseby: written from Harborough that very night of the battle: I tried hard to find some shiver in the hair-strokes, some symptom that the man had been bearding Death all day; but there is nothing of that sort there; a quite composed letter, the handwriting massive, steadfast, you would say almost firmer than usual.

I like that account of Lawrence's about the Portrait,* and must see farther into it. Do you ever go to Lincolnshire? I wish you had some errand thitherward, to get me a right account of those places. Oliver's first scenes of real fight,—of setting life against life in that Cause of his. Grantham, somewhere near that; then Gainsborough, where George Cavendish was killed in the bog; thirdly Winsby Field some miles from Horncastle: these are the three.[5] My stupid Topographies, etc., are silent, some of them *worse*. But I hope to know the real transactions yet; I must know them. Did you ever hear of Sir Symonds d'Ewes of Stow Langtoft in Suffolk, a member of the Long Parliament, Historian, Antiquary and much else? There are ten volumes of written reports and Notes by him about the Long Parl[t], which I accidentally discover, which Dryasdust has never once turned his dull eye upon! *Ex uno disce omnes.*[6] A right Editor of d'Ewes[7] might do an acceptable feat. Adieu dear Fitzgerald; Heaven love you.

Yours very truly and sorrowfully,
T. Carlyle

*Of Cromwell, by Cooper. E.FG.

[1] The passage duplicates those in many letters written by Carlyle while in the throes of beginning a new work.

[2] Carlyle applied the name "Dryasdust" collectively and individually to unmethodical and uncritical compilers of fact, error, and fiction whose tomes and pamphlets he searched in writing his historical works. "Alas, what mountains of dead ashes, wreck and burnt bones, does assiduous Pedantry dig up from the Past Time, and name it History and Philosophy of History; till, . . . over your Historical Library, it is as if all the Titans had written for themselves: DRY RUBBISH SHOT HERE!" ("St. Edmundsbury," *Past and Present*, Book II, chap. II). For a tirade on a specific Dryasdust, see the comments on Mark Noble in "Biographies of Oliver," *Cromwell*, chap. II.

[3] Carlyle set about to write "some kind of book on Oliver Cromwell and the English Civil Wars and Commonwealth. It is the ungainliest enterprise I ever tried," he informed his German friend, Varnhagen von Ense, December 3, 1843. His intended approach was to be biographical; but in January he wrote EFG that he had burned "considerable masses" of manuscript, "something like" six times, and the book remained "properly uncommenced." To bring order out of chaos, Carlyle then began to arrange Cromwell's letters and speeches in chrono-

logical sequence. A year later he decided that these should form a separate work. "The *Life* must follow when it can," he wrote to EFG in February, 1845. The result was *Oliver Cromwell's Letters and Speeches.*

[4] Artemidorus Cromwell Russell (b. 1803). See letter from Carlyle, Feb. 10, 1844, n.1.

[5] Not George but Charles Cavendish (1620-43), Royalist general, second son of the Earl of Devonshire. He was killed at Gainsborough where Cromwell, on July 28, 1643, routed Cavendish and his reserves. At Grantham, May 13, 1643, Cromwell defeated, with twelve troops, twice that number of Royalists. At Winceby Cromwell won another battle, October 11, 1643.

[6] Virgil wrote "Ab uno disce omnes" (*Aeneid* II. 65). "From one learn all."

[7] Sir Symonds D'Ewes (1602-50) took an active part as a member of the moderate party in the opposition to the king's arbitrary government in the Long Parliament of 1640. His *Diaries* from 1621-24 and from 1643-47, the latter valuable for the notes of proceedings in Parliament, are often the only authority for incidents and speeches during those years. Carlyle's interest in D'Ewes resulted in October, 1844, in his article "An Election to the Long Parliament" in *Fraser's Magazine.* The idea of editing the D'Ewes papers was not the only suggestion of the kind that Carlyle made to EFG.

To Bernard Barton

Boulge, Tuesday
[January 30, 1844]

Dear Barton,

My Papa, Lusia, Mrs. Kerrich and others come here today—till Thursday. A tale hangs to their coming (which you will know ere long)[1] and I cannot well leave the party tomorrow evening, especially as I have no horse to bring me back at night. So you must be content to be sixty without my aid. I will drink your health cordially, and wish you all the goods that lie in the lap of the Gods. We don't know what is best to wish: and our wishes don't get very far upwards I doubt. One cannot even promise one's own constant regard to a man: but so far as I can promise this small advantage I do: and am, and hope to be, while we curvet upon this horizon

Yours ever,
E. FitzGerald

How are all your colds? My throat is still a very scrannel pipe. Mrs. Smith[2] had a severe cold the other night: but her maid set her bed on fire (this is fact) by way of antidote. No harm done, but some curtains burnt.

[1] The family probably met to consider the engagement of EFG's sister Andalusia to the Reverend Francis de Soyres.

[2] Mrs. Job Smith, wife of the agent and principal tenant-farmer on the Boulge estate.

From Alfred Tennyson

[Cheltenham]
Pmk, February 2, 1844

My dear Fitz,

It is very kind of you to think of such a poor forlorn body as myself. The perpetual panic and horror of the last two years had steeped my nerves in poison: now I am left a beggar but I am or shall be shortly somewhat better off in nerves. I am in an Hydropathy Establishment near Cheltenham (the only one in England conducted on pure Priessnitzan principles).[1] I have had four crisises (one larger than had been seen for two or three years in Grafenberg—indeed I believe the largest but one that has been seen)—much poison has come out of me, which no physic ever would have brought to light. Albert Priessnitz (the nephew of the great man officially at this establishment) and very quick and clever he is and he gives me hopes of a cure in March: I have been here already upwards of two months. Of all the uncomfortable ways of living sure an hydropathical is the worst: no reading by candlelight, no going near a fire, no tea, no coffee, perpetual wet sheet and cold bath and alternation from hot to cold: however I have much faith in it.

My dear Fitz, my nerves were so bad six weeks ago that I could not have written this and to have to write a letter on that accursed business[2] threw me into a kind of convulsion. I went thro' Hell. Thank you for inquiring after me. I am such a poor devil now I am afraid I shall very rarely see you no more trips to London and living in lodgings hard penury and battle with my lot.

Good bye
Yours very truly
A.T.

You are the only one of my friends who has asked after me and I really feel obliged to you. I shall go over I think to Italy—I cer[tainly] cannot live in England and be comfortable. I hear that Frederic Arthur and Septimus live well on eight shillings a day and are all very happy.

Write to me again. I shall be glad to hear from you: and direct as before 6 Belle Vue Place Chelt:

[1] The water-cure had become established at Cheltenham, Malvern, and other watering places in England. Hydropathy, as a formal system, had been developed about 1829 by Vincenz Priessnitz (1801-51), a farmer of Gräfenberg, Austria, who had converted his father's home into a water-cure establishment. The treatment consisted of alternating hot and cold baths, compresses, the consumption of large quantities of water, and other practices. Hydropathy became immensely popular, both in Europe and in America during the nineteenth century, although there were those who were skeptical of the efficacy of the cure. Frederick Pollock, for example, replied to a cousin who had recommended the treatment, "Upon the faith of your representations, [I] will begin with the universal element, advancing by degrees from wine-glasses to tumblers, and from them to bowls, until my practice reaches the proper number of bucketsful." A fortnight later, he wrote, "I hold M. Priessnitz to be a humbug of the first water" (*Remembrances,* I, 193 and 195). Tennyson resorted to hydropathy again in both 1847 and 1848.

[2] Pyroglyphs.

To John Allen
(Fragment)

Holbrook,[1] *Monday*
[February 4, 1844]

My dear Allen,

It seems a waste of life, and of the few good things that turn up in it, that I pass three months without seeing or hearing of you. I have often intended to write: three months indeed have gone in intending! I am now staying at this place with Lusia who has told you she has engaged herself to be married.[2] She shewed me a few lines from you. I should be glad to have a line from you: though you have some reason for not writing, which I have not. Is Mrs. Allen still angry with me for being so impatient at missing my way to her house? Give her my kind regard notwithstanding.

I expect to go to London sometime this Spring for a month: and then I hope to see you. Let me know when you are likely to be most stationary in town. I have been reading a good deal, but nothing new, except the Athenaeum every week. I find this a very good paper, and it keeps one a little up with the goings on in the world. I wish you could one day come down to see me in my Cottage—but you have no time nor taste for extra excursions. You and two or three more are the only friends (of the College kind) I even want to see again. Spedding I live in hopes of seeing also: and I heard this very morning from A. Tennyson, who is going through a system.

[1] The home of his sister, Jane Wilkinson.

[2] To the Reverend Francis de Soyres, Curate at Geldestone. Lusia had been engaged to Bird Allen, John's brother, who died while on the Niger expedition in 1841. See letter to Barton, Jan. [16], 1842.

From Thomas Carlyle

Chelsea 17 feb^{y}, 1844

Dear Fitzgerald,

There is unfortunately, if also fortunately, not the smallest haste in this Lincolnshire business; the Fates, I believe, have too clearly said that the child *Cromwell* cannot be born this year,—alas, they still say they know not in what year, or whether at all! As you remark, he is a devil of a foetus to carry about with one!

The rule of the matter, therefore, is: If you be at any rate going to Lincolnshire, go at your own time, and do this thing for me so as to amuse and instruct yourself with it; at least not so as to bore and burden yourself with it: any result you get out of it will be better than the round cipher I at present have; the smallest contribution shall be welcome. My notion is, that all tradition of the thing is utterly gone,—far farther than you found it about Naseby: but I think perhaps the *whereabouts* of these transactions might still be discovered by an ingenious eye, and the picture such a one could give me of the ground would be decidedly worth something.

I have never yet been in Ireland with Oliver; and will not go, except cursorily, if I can help it. The Irish department of our Civil War requires to be done *in little* throughout; and Oliver's cutting off of the great fungous gangrenous horror that had grown together there, tho' one of his best pieces of surgery, will not invite us to expatiate, I hope! Besides I never *saw* a square inch of Ireland with my mind's eye, and do not know it at all. Oliver's own Letters, I hope, which are very copious in that season, will suffice. Did you ever see Temple's Hist^{y} of the Irish Rebellion in '41,—Sir John Temple,[1] Lord Palmerston's ancestor? It is a small contemporary quarto, of which certain pages are well worth preserving.

If your Brother[2] can speak to the Duke of Manchester, certainly it will be worth doing. Prior to 1644, it is almost indubitable there must have many letters gone between the Duke's ancestor[3] and Oliver; they had even a Controversy in a House of Commons Committee (of which Clarendon has left a story, that I have got some glimmering of light upon), but in the Spring of '44, in the time of the Selfdenying Ordinance,[4] they had an open public quarrel, and I suppose never corresponded more. The Committee Clarendon refers to treated (as I believe) of the Manor of "Somersham near St. Ives":[5] your Brother might ask the Duke, whether this property still belongs to his family, or is certainly known to have ever done so? The Earl of Sandwich might also have many Letters; his Ancestor[6] was in a good deal of hard service at Oliver's right hand: to him I shall have good access by and by.

And now enough, enough! Get done with your influenza straightway, and come to London, to Chelsea, that we may see and hear you.

Yours ever
T. Carlyle

[1] Sir John Temple (1600-77), Master of the Rolls in Ireland, wrote *History of the Irish Rebellion* in 1646.

[2] John.

[3] The Duke's ancestor was Edward Montagu (1602-77), second Earl of Manchester, one of the leaders of the Rebellion, in the House of Lords during the Long Parliament. For a time Cromwell served under his command in the Eastern Counties. He later took a leading part in negotiating with Charles I and opposed the trial of the king. Cromwell broke with him in November, 1644, when the Earl disapproved continuation of the war.

[4] Selfdenying Ordinance—an act stipulating that no member of Parliament should hold any civil or military office.

[5] Cromwell had espoused the cause of his neighbors at Somersham where common lands had been enclosed and sold to Lord Manchester. Cromwell induced the Commons to appoint a committee of inquiry.

[6] The ancestor of the Earl of Sandwich was another Edward Montagu (1625-72), first Earl of Sandwich, who in 1643 raised a regiment for the Parliamentary party. He distinguished himself at the battles of Naseby and Marston Moor and at the siege of Bristol.

To Frederick Tennyson

Boulge, Woodbridge
February 24/44

My dear Frederic,

I got your letter all right. But you did not tell me where to direct to you again—so I must send to the Poste Restante at Florence. I have also heard from Morton, to whom I despatched a letter yesterday: and now set about one to you. As you live in two different cities, one may write the same things to both. You told me of the Arno being frozen, and even Italian noses being cold: he tells me the Spring is coming. I tell you that we have had the mildest winter known: but as good weather, when it does come in England, is always unseasonable, and as an old proverb says that a green Yule makes a fat kirkyard, so it has been with us: the extraordinary fine season has killed heaps of people with influenza, debilitated others for their lives long, worried everybody with colds, etc. I have had three influenzas: but this is no wonder: for I live in a hut with walls as thin as a sixpence: windows that don't shut: a clay soil safe beneath my feet: a thatch perforated by lascivious sparrows over my head. Here I sit, read, smoke, and become very wise, and am already quite beyond earthly things. I must say to you, as Basil Montagu once said, in perfect charity, to his friends, "You see, my dear fellows, I like you very much, but I continue to advance, and you remain where you are (you see), and so I shall be obliged to leave you behind me. It is no fault of mine." You must begin to read Seneca, whose letters I have been reading: else, when you come back to England, you will be no companion to a man who despises wealth, death, etc. What are pictures but paintings—what are auctions but sales! All is vanity. Erige animum tuum, mî Lucili,[1] etc. I wonder whether old Seneca was indeed such a humbug as people now say he was: he is really a fine writer. About three hundred years ago—or less—our divines and writers called him the divine Seneca; and old Bacon is full of him. One sees in him the upshot of all the Greek philosophy, how it stood in Nero's time, when the Gods had worn out a good deal. I don't think old Seneca believed he should live again. Death is his great resource. Think of the *rococity* of a gentleman studying Seneca in the middle of February 1844 in a remarkably damp cottage.

I have heard from Alfred also, who hates his water life—*βίος ἄβιος*[2] he calls it—but hopes to be cured in March. Poor fellow, I trust he may. He is not in a happy plight, I doubt. I wish I lived in a pleasant country where he might like to come and stay with me—but this is one of the ugliest places in England—one of the dullest—it has not the merit of being bleak on a grand scale—pollard trees over a flat clay, with regular hedges. I saw a stanza in an old book which seemed to describe my condition rather—

> Far from thy kyn cast thee:
> Wrath not thy neighbour next thee,
> In a good corn country rest thee,
> And sit down, Robin, and rest thee.[3]

Funny advice, isn't it? I am glad to hear Septimus is so much improved. I beg you will felicitate him from me: I have a tacit regard of the true sort for him, as I think I must have for all of the Tennyson build. I see so many little natures about that I must draw to the large, even if their faults be on the same scale as their virtues. You and I shall I suppose quarrel as often as we meet: but I can quarrel and never be the worse with you. How we pulled against each other at Gravesend![4] You would stay—I wouldn't—then I would—then we did. Do you remember the face of that girl at the Bazaar, who kept talking to us and looking all round the room for fresh customers—a way women have—that is, a way of doing rather gracefully? Then the gentleman who sang Ivy green;[5] a very extraordinary accentuation, it seemed to me: but I believe you admired it very much. Really, if these little excursions in the company of one's friends leave such a pleasant taste behind in the memory, one should court them oftener. And yet then perhaps the relish would grow less: it is the infrequency that gives them room to expand. I shall never get to Italy, that seems clear. My great travel this year will be to Carlisle. Quid prosit ista tua longa peregrinatio, etc.[6] Travelling, you know, is a vanity. The *soul* remains the same. An amorem possis fugare, an libidinis exsiccari, an timorem mortis depellere?[7] What then will you say to Pollock's being married![8] I hear he is to be. Ad matrimonium fugis? Miser! Scaevola noster dicere solebat, etc.[9] Excuse my overflowing with philosophy. I am going this evening to eat toasted cheese with that celebrated poet Bernard Barton. And I must soon stir, and look about for my greatcoat, brush myself, etc. It blows a harrico, as Theodore Hook[10] used to say, and will rain before I get to Woodbridge. Those poor mistaken lilac buds there out of the window! and an old Robin, ruffled up to his thickest, sitting mournfully under them, quite disheartened. For you must know the mild winter is just giving way to a remarkably severe spring. I expect a woman in this house to be confined every half hour. I have nothing to do with her situation. She is our cook married to a groom. I wish you were here to smoke a pipe with me. I play of evenings some of Handel's great choruses which are the bravest music after all.[11] I am getting to the true John Bull style of music. I delight in Handel's Allegro and Penseroso. Do you know the fine pompous joyous chorus of "These pleasures, Mirth, if thou canst give, etc."?[12] Handel certainly does in music what old Bacon desires in his Essay on Masques, "Let the songs be loud and cheerful, not puling, etc."[13] One might think the Water music[14] was written from this text. Now it is time and place to say farewell—which I say, asking you always to write when you can—

and let me see all I ever shall see of Italy in your letters. When shall we go to Gravesend again?

Ever yours
E.FG.

[1] "Lift up your spirit, my Lucilius." EFG was reading Seneca's *Letters to Lucilius*.

[2] "Life without life."

[3] Quoted in *Reliquiae Antiquae*, "Scraps from Ancient Manuscripts illustrating Early English Literature and the English Language," Thomas Wright and James O. Halliwell, eds., 2 vols., 1841, 1843, I, 233. EFG's copy, with his autograph, is in Trinity College Library.

[4] See letter to F. Tennyson, Dec. 10, 1843.

[5] "The Ivy Green," a lyric written by the clergyman of Dingley Dell in Dickens' *Pickwick Papers*, was set to music by Henry Russell (1812-1900) and became a popular song.

[6] "What profit would your long journey be?"

[7] "Would you be able to flee from your love, or get rid of your lusts or dispel your fear of death?"

[8] Pollock married Juliet, daughter of the Reverend Henry Creed, Vicar of Corse, Gloucestershire, March 30, 1844.

[9] "You flee to matrimony? Wretched! As our Scaevola was accustomed to say."

[10] Hook (1788-1841), novelist, wit, and popular man-about-town endowed with a gift for improvising in verse and music. He was co-founder and first editor of *John Bull*; later edited the *New Monthly*.

[11] While an undergraduate at Cambridge, EFG cultivated a love for Handel as a member of Camus, a musical society composed of students and senior members of the colleges. The group met in college rooms and five times each term gave vocal and instrumental concerts, each opening with a Handel overture. EFG was one of the pianists.

[12] Charles Jennens, who arranged Milton's *L'Allegro* and *Il Penseroso* for Handel's composition, combined the two poems, with lines of his own added, in the form of a Greek ode. EFG quotes neither man verbatim.

[13] "Let the *Songs* be *Loud*, and *Cheerefull*, and not *Chirpings*, or *Pulings*. Let the *Musicke* likewise be *Sharpe*, and *Loud*, and *Well Placed*" (Bacon's *Essays*, "Of Masques and Triumphs").

[14] The twenty-five selections, known as Handel's "Water Music," were played during a royal fete on the Thames. Handel himself conducted the orchestra in a barge which followed that of George III.

To Mrs. John Charlesworth[1]
(Fragment)

[Boulge Cottage]
March/44 [c. the 1st]

. . . But as Carlyle is like to make good use of what we can find him, and make a good English Hero of Oliver—something of a Johnsonian figure—I hope you will try and pester these Lincoln ladies and gentlemen. I wrote to Livesey:[2] who once, he says, had a butler named Oliver Cromwell. That is the nearest approach to history I make through him.

My brother John, after being expected every day this week, wrote positively to say he could not come to-day: and accordingly was seen to drive up to the Hall two hours ago.*

Believe me, dear Mrs. Charlesworth, yours thankfully,

E. FitzGerald

* N.B. I am not at the Hall: but in the Cottage. Pray give my compliments to all your party.

[1] In the spring of 1844 EFG, at Carlyle's request, enlisted the aid of Elizabeth Charlesworth of Bramford, who had relatives in Lincolnshire, in obtaining information on Cromwell's campaign in that county in 1643. Propriety complicated communication somewhat. Carlyle sent his queries to EFG, who forwarded them to Mrs. Charlesworth, because, he explained, "I being unmarried, all her information has to come through *her Mother*."

[2] Probably Joseph Livesey, of Trinity, who took his degree at Cambridge in 1835. His home was Stourton Hall, Lincolnshire.

From Thomas Carlyle

Chelsea, Sunday
[March 3, 1844]

Dear FitzGerald,

With real reluctance I have written that Note to the Lincoln Doctor;[1] which, I think, you will perhaps be as wise to burn as to forward: —beforehand I know almost for certain that there will nothing come of it but bad corresponding and botheration. Nobody does "know" anything,—especially as to that unfortunate subject! However, that you may not call me cross and wilful, there is for you; do as you like.

What is become of your influenza; and when are you coming to Town? My work is still sticking fast in bottomless clammy mud, and Sloughs of Despond!

I dare not borrow anybody's horse, tho' I study always to ride conscientiously, and our Livery-Stable people seemed very careful: I dare not borrow;—and *who*, as you say, dare buy? My health seems sometimes to grow better, and then suddenly again it grows worse than ever: I am in the medium state at present.

The Town is getting terribly throng; the sky more and more vernal; —one wishes one had wings! Fly you the *other* way tho'!

Yours ever truly,
T. Carlyle

[1] W. Cookson, M.D. of Lincoln.

To Mrs. John Charlesworth

Boulge
March 5/44

Dear Mrs. Charlesworth,

I have heard again from Carlyle who has sent me a letter for Dr. Cookson, which I am to burn or send, as I think best. Before I do so, I should be glad to speak to Miss Charlesworth on the matter again: and as my brother is going off on one of his comet excursions tomorrow (at least so he purposed an hour ago) I shall go with him to Ipswich, unless it snows, etc., and shall walk to Bramford. My humble request therefore is nothing more than that you will be so good as to lock up Miss C. till I have come and consulted as to what is best to be done: and how best to address this Doctor: whom I conclude she knows.

However, I only mean that if the day is pretty fair I may hope to find some of you at home: and Mr. Charlesworth well again.

Yours very truly,
E. FitzGerald

To Mrs. John Charlesworth

Boulge
[c. March 10, 1844]

Dear Mrs. Charlesworth,

Contributions from the fens or anywhere else will be good. We must get out all from the Allenbys.[1] I think I remember in Carlyle's notes that *the hill* in Winsby (where the farm house is) was the scene of a daring attack of Cromwell's: but my memory is bad. Your correspondent says that bones, spurs, and *urns* have been found there: the latter look rather as if the hill were of *Roman note.* I should like it to be clearly told, *exactly where* the relics were dug up: whether on the hill or on the level said to extend from the hill to the west. Mrs. Allenby's first letter says *that* was probably the field of battle: her son says the hill itself was. Also, *exactly what the relics were.* These two points are the chief I can see to need thorough sifting. I sent Carlyle the letter: he is now I dare say groaning over it. I have threatened to turn the correspondence entirely into his hands: so Miss Charlesworth may expect that. I go to town (I hope for a very short time) next week. John is yet here: we all like his wife much.[2]

Farewell. Yours ever thankfully,

E. FitzGerald

Poor old Mrs. Chaplin is dead![3] I have found an old Lady here to replace her.

[1] Lincolnshire friends of the Charlesworths.

[2] John's second wife, Hester Haddon, whom he had married the previous summer.

[3] Mrs. Chaplin, who lived at Wherstead near his former home, is the first of EFG's "pensioners" to be mentioned in the correspondence. Throughout his life EFG contributed small sums of money at regular intervals to a number of needy elderly persons.

To Mrs. John Charlesworth

Boulge, Friday
[March 15, 1844]

Dear Mrs. Charlesworth,

I am sorry for the trouble you have. But I must hope that all that is to be got from such good authority as the Allenbys will be got, as to Winsby. *Slash Lane* promises very well. From the Allenbys let us be content to reap Winsby field *only*: as it seems they once farmed it: and let us get as good an account as possible of the look of the field, Slash Lane, the records and traditions of the place, and what remains were dug up, and *exactly where*; for that generally shows where the stress of the battle was. It is best to keep people to one point: else they wander off into generalities: as for instance what the Lady tells of War Scythes hung up in Horncastle Church: which, cruel as Oliver was, we must refer back to an earlier warfare than his, I doubt. Pray thank Miss Charlesworth: and believe me yours ever,

E. FitzGerald

To Thomas Carlyle

Boulge
March 20/44

Dear Carlyle,

That you may see some hope of a little visitage, I send you the enclosed map, which comes from the hands of one of the Allenbys, who once farmed all Winsby Field: and have relics, etcc. These you shall hear of in time. You will see perhaps the uncertainties, etc., which always attend these descriptions: could the *field of battle* have been on rising ground? Or was this the hill you wrote about which Cromwell *did* take? Dr. Cookson has got all my memory.[1] Slash Lane promises well. Another note from another of the family describes the hill as "high, or rather steep—a line of Wold Hills to the East: the ground flatter toward the West, though generally undulating. Slash Lane and a *few adjoining fields quite level.*" If Slash Lane lies as in the map, it must be level in one part, and run up the hill in another. Both accounts agree that in Slash Lane bones, etc., have been found: was it not in such a place the two armies dogged each other all night?

I have not sent you all these letters for fear of too much: I shall be in town next week, and then you shall see. She who has processed all this for you is a very famous girl (now 30) with whom I used to be slightly in love as I supposed.[2] She wrote by chance to Allenby: and Allenby was Lord of Winsby! When your book is published you must send one to *Miss Charlesworth*; who has always been a very understanding admirer of you, and will do what she can to pick up information.

Ever yours,
E. FitzGerald

P.S. Sketches are promised—do you want *any particular sketch*, I am asked. I really think you will have to begin to write to Miss C. herself: for, I being unmarried, all her information has to come through *her Mother*. Or would you have us marry at once, to explore Winsby Field conveniently?

[1] "Memory: a record, a history." EFG refers to the notes he had sent to Dr. Cookson.

[2] See letter to Thackeray, July [29], 1835, n.4.

To Bernard Barton

19 Charlotte St.,
Rathbone Place
[April 7, 1844]

Dear Barton,

I got here but yesterday, from Bedford, where I left W. Browne in train to be married to a rich woman.[1] When I heard that they could not have less than five hundred a year, I gave up all further interest in the matter: for I could not wish a reasonable couple more. W. B. may be spoilt if he grows rich: that is the only thing could spoil him. This time ten years I first went to ride and fish with him about the river Ouse—he was then 18—quick to love and quick to fight—full of confidence, generosity, and the glorious spirit of Youth. . . . I shall go to Church and hope he mayn't be defiled with the filthy pitch. Oh! if we could be brought to open our eyes. I repent in ashes for reviling the Daddy who wrote that Sonnet against damned Riches.[2]

I heard a man preach at Bedford[3] in a way that shook my soul. He described the crucifixion in a way that put the scene before his people —no fine words, and metaphors: but first one nail struck into one hand, and then into another, and one through both feet—the cross lifted up with God in man's image distended upon it. And the sneers of the priests below—"Look at that fellow there—look at him—he talked of saving others, etc." And then the sun veiled his face in Blood, etc. I certainly have heard oratory now—of the Lord Chatham kind,[4] only Matthews has more faith in Christ than Pitt in his majority. I was almost as much taken aback as the poor folks all about me who sobbed: and I hate this beastly London more and more. It stinks all through of churchyards and fish shops. As to pictures—well, never mind them. Farewell!

In the chapel opposite this house preaches Robert Montgomery![5]

[1] Browne married Elizabeth Elliott of Bedford, July 30, 1844.

[2] Wordsworth's "October, 1803," sonnet concluding:

> What do we gather hence but firmer faith
> . . .
> That virtue and the faculties within
> Are vital—and that riches are akin
> To fear, to change, to cowardice and death!

[3] The Reverend Timothy R. Matthews, a Nonconformist.

[4] The elder Pitt (1708-78), first Earl of Chatham, ranked with the greatest orators, ancient and modern.

[5] Robert Montgomery (1807-55), popular minor poet who wrote chiefly on religious subjects, ordained in the Established Church in 1835, became minister of Percy Chapel, Percy Street, Rathbone Place, in 1843.

To Bernard Barton

19 Charlotte St
April 11/44

Dear Barton,

I am still indignant at this nasty place London. Thackeray, whom I came up to see, went off to Brighton the night after I arrived, and has not re-appeared: but I must wait some time longer for him. Thank Miss Barton much for the *kit*; if it is but a kit: my old woman is a great lover of cats, and hers has just *kitted*, and a wretched little blind puling tabby lizard of a thing was to be saved from the pail for me: but if Miss Barton's is *a kit*, I will gladly have it: and my old lady's shall be disposed of—not to the pail. Oh rus, quando te aspiciam?[1] Construe that, Mr. Barton.—I am going to send down my pictures to Boulge, if I can secure them: they are not quite secure at present. If they vanish, I snap my fingers at them, Magi and all—there is a world (alas!) elsewhere beyond pictures—Oh, oh, oh, oh—

I smoked a pipe with Carlyle yesterday. We ascended from his dining room carrying pipes and tobacco up through two stories of his house, and got into a little dressing room near the roof:[2] there we sat down: the window was open and looked out on nursery gardens, their almond trees in blossom, and beyond, bare walls of houses, and over these, roofs and chimneys, and roofs and chimneys, and here and there a steeple, and whole London crowned with darkness gathering behind like the illimitable resources of a dream. I tried to persuade him to leave the accursed den, and he wished—but—but—perhaps he *didn't* wish on the whole.

When I get back to Boulge I shall recover my quietude which is now all in a ripple. But it is a shame to talk of such things. So Churchyard has caught another Constable. Did he get off our Debach boy that set the shed on fire? Ask him that. Can'st thou not minister to a mind diseased, etc.[3]

A cloud comes over Charlotte Street and seems as if it were sailing softly on the April wind to fall in a blessed shower upon the lilac buds and thirsty anemones somewhere in Essex; or, who knows?, perhaps at Boulge. Out will run Mrs. Faiers, and with red arms and face of woe haul in the struggling windows of the cottage, and make all tight. Beauty Bob[4] will cast a bird's eye out at the shower, and bless the useful wet. Mr. Loder will observe to the farmer for whom he is doing up a dozen of Queen's Heads,[5] that it will be of great use: and the farmer will agree that his young barleys wanted it much. The German Ocean will dimple with innumerable pin points, and porpoises rolling near the surface sneeze with unusual pellets of fresh water—

> Can such things be,
> And overcome us like a summer cloud,
> Without our special wonder?[6]

Oh this wonderful wonderful world, and we who stand in the middle of it are all in a maze, except poor Matthews of Bedford, who fixes his eyes upon a wooden Cross and has no misgiving whatsoever. When I was at his chapel on Good Friday, he called at the end of his grand sermon on some of the people to say merely this, that they believed Christ had redeemed them: and first one got up and in sobs declared she believed it: and then another, and then another—I was quite overset:—all poor people: how much richer than all who fill the London Churches. Theirs is the kingdom of Heaven!

This is a sad farrago. Farewell.

[1] "Oh country, when shall I see you?" (Horace, *Satires* II.6.66).

[2] Not Carlyle's famous soundproof room; that was not constructed until the fall of 1853.

[3] *Macbeth,* V.3.40.

[4] EFG's parrot.

[5] John Loder, bookseller, occasional publisher, and stationer, in the Thoroughfare, Woodbridge. Loder's son, also John, who succeeded his father in the business, later became one of EFG's Woodbridge friends. The "Queen's Heads," a common stationery.

[6] *Macbeth,* III.4.110-12. Shakespeare wrote "summer's cloud."

To Mrs. John Charlesworth

[19 Charlotte Street,
Rathbone Place]
London, April 11/44

Dear Mrs. Charlesworth,

I last night smoked a pipe with Carlyle. He has had two large packets from Dr. Cookson,[1] who shows alacrity enough to do what is asked, and may turn up something. But he has chiefly spoken of Winsby: and your Allenbys had so well cleared all that matter up with their map, etc., that the Doctor was going over needless ground. I hope we may be as successful with some other field: or rather that Cookson will anticipate us and save us all trouble.

London is very hateful to me. I long to spread wing and fly into the kind clean air of the country. I see nobody in the streets half so handsome as Mr. Reynolds[2] of our parish: all clever, composed, satirical, selfish, well-dressed. Here we see what the World is. I am sure a great City is a deadly Plague: worse than the illness so called that came to ravage it. I tried to persuade Carlyle to leave his filthy Chelsea, but he says his wife likes London. I get radishes to eat for breakfast of a morning: with them comes a savour of earth that brings all the delicious gardens of the world back into one's soul, and almost draws tears from one's eyes.

With renewed thanks believe me ever yours,

E. FitzGerald

[1] Of Lincoln.

[2] The Reverend Osborne Shribb Reynolds, Rector of Boulge and Debach.

To Mrs. John Charlesworth

19 Charlotte St., etc.
Saturday [April 20, 1844]

Dear Mrs. Charlesworth,

Thank you over and over again for your letters. The last packet with sketches, etc., came all safe yesterday: and Carlyle is much pleased. We may say that Winsby Field is exhausted now. I should like however to have some sketch of the *relics*: the shape of the stone jugs: their size specified. The *helmet* could be identified with the military fashion of some reign, as represented in prints, pictures, etc. But on the whole, the Allenbys have done capitally: and so have you: and so have I: and so I hope will Carlyle one day. He begs seriously to thank you and the Allenbys.

He was much distressed at Dr. Cookson's death:[1] and said how he should feel it when he came to think of it alone. Such is the man: he will call all the wits in London dilettanti, etc., but let a poor fellow die, and the Scotch heart flows forth in tears.

If any one can be found to do half as much for Gainsborough (which was an important battle) as has been done for Winsby, why, the Lincolnshire campaign will be handsomely reported. At Grantham there is no such great interest, it appears.

I hope to get out of London to my poor old Boulge next week. I have seen all my friends so as to satisfy them that I am a duller country fellow than I was, and so we shall part without heart-breaking on either side. It is partly one's fault not to be up to the London mark: but as there is a million of persons in the land fully up to it, one has the less call to repent in that respect. I confess that Mr. Reynolds is a better sight to me than old rouged Lady Morgan[2] and all such.

I hope it will not be long before I visit you at Bramford. In the mean while believe me with best regards to all your family, yours ever very truly,

Edward FitzGerald

[1] Dr. Cookson died April 12, 1844.

[2] Sydney, Lady Morgan (1783?-1859), Irish-born novelist, wife of Sir Thomas Morgan, physician and writer. "On her well-known evenings of reception, she loved to see congregated . . . all the lions of the hour, artistic, scientific, and literary" (William Bates, *The Maclise Portrait-Gallery*, 1891, p. 318).

To Bernard Barton

London, Wednesday
April [24, 1844]

My dear Barton,

This is to say that the Magi, an Italian nobleman's head, a Holy Family, and some heathen Gods, went down in a very large packing box yesterday by Smith's waggon to Woodbridge, where I conclude they will arrive tomorrow—Thursday. Will you on Thursday afternoon step down to the Royal Oak (I think it is) and see if such a box has arrived: and if our Farmer Smith[1] have not sent for it, be so good as to order that it be *kept under cover* till he does. Do not *you* open it: much as your fingers tingle to do so: the whole affair had best roll up altogether like a cloud to Boulge, till I come down with screw driver, hammer, and all authority, to explode the thing. Alas! there is so little to be seen! do not quickly shame the poor little Yarrow you have dreamt of these three years. I hope soon to get down to Boulge: and then we will have a grand field day and house warming at the Cottage, and see the pictures, and know for the thousand and first time that all is Vanity.

April 1844

Thank Miss Barton for taking charge of the kit. It shall grow a Cat, and flourish. I am now looking over and partly transcribing a heap of old letters from Italy: these are to furbish up into an article for Fraser's Magazine and bring the writer £10.[2] How do you like the quality of this letter paper? It necessarily makes the author who writes upon it one-sided.[3] I buy no pictures: I go to no plays: I see few friends: why, Fitz, thou hast played thy fill, and eat and drank: 'tis time to be going.[4] What sort of *feller* is Mr. *Meller*? does he befit ye better than Witty?[5]

Our dear Major[6]—I hear at Portland Place he is coming to town the end of this week. And Dr. Lynn[6] has had paralysis—and we all live in a ridiculous parenthesis of Time[7] on a shelf made by insects and planted by stray sea mews. Farewell.

ever yours,
E.FG.

1 Tenant farmer at Boulge.

2 EFG was editing a portion of his letters from Savile Morton. Late in 1846 Thackeray submitted the correspondence, without success, to *Fraser's* and *Blackwood's* magazines; *Blackwood's* capped its rejection by losing the manuscript. Convinced that the letters were exceptional, EFG later edited the remainder and during the 1870's sent the second portion to a number of friends, observing to each that the letters "should" be published. They never appeared in print. This transcript, now among the FitzGerald papers at Trinity College Library, bears the title, "Fragments of some Letters from an ill-starred Man of Genius."

The letter in which Thackeray reported the rejection of the first manuscript to EFG, dated "February? 1846" in the *Thackeray Letters and Papers* (II, 227), states also that Thackeray had "resigned at the Morning Chronicle." Thackeray mentions his resignation in a letter of January 5, 1847, to Mrs. Caroline Norton (II, 264). Other evidence fixes the end of 1846 as the time of Thackeray's futile effort to place the manuscript.

3 The letter is written on translucent paper.

4 "You've played, and loved, and ate, and drank your fill.
Walk sober off." Pope, *Imitations of Horace*
Book II, Epistle 2, 322-23

5 Thomas William Meller (1808-71), served as Rector of St. Mary's, the Woodbridge parish church, from 1844 until his death. John Francis Wittey (so spelled in directories), curate at St. Mary's.

6 Major Moor; his daughter Charlotte and her husband, William Page Wood, later Lord Hatherley, lived in Westminster. George Doughty Lynn, M.D., of Woodbridge, Major Moor's brother-in-law.

7 "The created world is but a small parenthesis in eternity."
Sir Thomas Browne, *Christian Morals*
III, xxix

The following allusion to "shelf . . . insects and . . . sea mews" is probably a recollection from EFG's reading of Lyell's *Principles of Geology*.

To Bernard Barton

[London]
[April 26, 1844]

My dear Barton,

While waiting for some books in the British Museum, I have the honour of informing you that, having enquired of the Saracen himself at Aldgate,[1] he swears my pictures *did* go down last Tuesday, and would arrive at Woodbridge on *Wednesday*. It is possible therefore that Smith having a waggon at market may have taken back my pictures by way of ballast when the corn was disposed of. I hope so. But if the box exploded by the way—if the Holy Families were laid in the dirt—if the Magi, forbearing to stop at Woodbridge as they ought, chose to go on foolishly to Halesworth—why—I say again, I snap my fingers at them. I will buy no more things that cause me to go to Aldgate such a morning as this.

I have not seen Churchyard: had I known his put-up I would have called on him. I saw his Linnell's[2] sketch for sale at Christie's,[3] as also a true Constable—Salisbury Cathedral: which he would have liked. Indeed I think he had seen it somewhere, and spoke to me of it.

We hear Major Moor is come back no better to London. I shall go down to Westminster to hear of him this evening. Are John's[4] Lectures over at Woodbridge?

Ah—your trees are coming out, hedges and willows I know. But I shall soon be down to welcome them and introduce them with all good-will to my garden at Boulge. My heart sucks at the fresh air from afar. I have seen nobody here, and all I want is to go away from the detestable dunghill. This is true, in spite of what the Squire says—I was obliged to come up to see Thackeray. I have scarce seen him.

My books come, and so I must make the best of the time and bid you farewell. You can write long letters: but are not you inspired with beakers full of the warm South wind that breathes of sweet briar and violets. The fishmongers' shops here are nearly as bad as the churchyards. Farewell.

ever yours,
E.FG.

[1] The Saracen's Head, one of the principal inns of London, probably the London terminus for Smith, the Woodbridge carrier.

[2] John Linnell (1792-1882), portrait and landscape painter.

[3] Christie, Manson, & Woods, famous auction house for works of art, King Street, St. James's, where sales were held between April and July.

[4] John, EFG's brother. See letter to Carlyle, [Sept. 2, 1843], n.2.

To Bernard Barton

19 Charlotte St.
Pmk., April 27, 1844

My dear Barton,

Thank [you] for the pains you have taken to ascertain the safe arrival of my goods. They *have* arrived safe, Smith writes me word: and are now in the Servants' hall at Boulge, only waiting the hand of the Enchanter to blossom into [1] I assure you it is not my own desire that keeps me yet in London: next week I devoutly hope to be free of it. No one will believe that an idle man has anything to do or to think about—but it is not so easy to get a lamp-post down into the country.

Yet no pictures bought—no new pictures—"I fix an unreverted eye" away from them. Yet is there a Gainsborough to be sold at Xty's[2] cool and peaceful as the Evening.

I went to see our dear Major yesterday. He was glad to see me, I think: but he is very unlike the man he was: whose like we never shall see again unless himself becomes himself again. But he will, surely. He sits idle, moping, eyes on the ground, dozing every now and then—and to smile is an act of courtesy with him. I am to dine with him at the Phillipps' tomorrow. Tonight I entertain Fradelle and a fierce painter[3]—Tea, brandy, a cold tongue, etc. If Mr. Churchyard had returned with me, tell him, he would have had this tongue to eat. But he would not. Yesterday at a tavern I drank a poor man's week's wages in a bottle of Champagne. It was scarcely my fault—but what beastly wickedness! Till all this is set right, I shall look on Revolutions to be as just alteratives as Morison's Pills.

Ever yours,
E.FG.

[1] EFG left a portion of the line blank, evidently failing to find an appropriate word or phrase which he intended to supply before sealing the letter.

[2] Christie's.

[3] Henry Joseph Fradelle (1778-1865), English historical and subject painter of French birth. One of his best known pictures is "Milton Dictating *Paradise Lost* to his Daughter." The "fierce painter" was probably Morris Moore.

To Bernard Barton

[Boulge]
[May, 1844]

Dear Barton,

Pray thank Miss Barton for taking the trouble to write to me. I shall be with you tomorrow, though perhaps not till the Evening—or late in the afternoon.

I am going to send back a heap of your books I have had this long while.

Yours ever,
E.FG.

By the bye, about the *kit.* I forgot to mention it is a *Tom*: which some people don't like: I don't; I cannot conceive a Cat other than feminile. Miss Barton is not to take the kit therefore, unless she like it on due reflection. The Kit is a handsome one, and now quite qualified to go alone—to lap—and playful enough. It does credit to Mrs. Faier's education.

To Samuel Laurence

[Boulge]
May, 1844

Dear Laurence,

I hope your business is settled by this time. I have seen praise of your picture[1] in the Athenaeum, which quoted also the Chronicle's good opinion. I am very glad of all this and I hope you will now set to work, and paint away with ease and confidence, forgetting that there is such a hue as bottle-green in the universe (it was tastefully omitted from the rainbow, you see); and, in spite of what Moore[2] says, paint English people in English atmospheres. Your Coningham was rather orange, wasn't he? But he was very good, I thought. Dress your ladies in cheerful dresses, not quite so vulgar as Chalon's.[3] . . . I heard from my sister that you had finished Wilkinson to the perfect content of all: I had charged her particularly not to allow Mrs. W. to intercede for any smirk or alteration whatever.

My Venetian pictures look very grand on my walls, which previously had been papered with a still green (not bottled) on purpose to receive them. On my table is a long necked bottle with three flowers just now in it . . . a tuft of rhododendron, a tuft of scarlet geranium, and a tuft of white gilliflower. Do you see these in your mind's eye? I wish you could come down here and refresh your sodden eyes with pure daylight, budding oak trees, and all the changes of sky and cloud. To live to make sonnets about these things, and doat upon them, is worse Cockneyism than rejoicing in the sound of Bow Bells[4] for ever so long: but here one has them whether one will or no: and they are better than Lady Morgan and ——— at a rout in Harley Street.[5] Maclise is a handsome and fine fellow, I think: and Landseer[6] is very good natured. I long for my old Alfred portrait[7] here sometimes: but you had better keep it for the present. W. Browne and Spedding are with me, good representatives one of the Vita Contemplativa, the other of the Vita Attiva. Spedding, if you tell him this, will not allow that he has not the elements of Action in him: nor has he not: nor has not the other those of contemplation: but each inclines a different way notwithstanding. I wish you and Spedding could come down here: though there is little to see, and to eat. When you write you must put *Woodbridge* after Boulge. This letter of yours went to Bury St. Edmunds, for want of that. I hear Alfred Tennyson is in very good looks: mind and paint him *quickly* when he comes to town; looking full at you.

1 A portrait of William Coningham (1815-84) in the exhibition of the Royal Academy (see letter to Laurence, July 4). Coningham served as Liberal M.P. for Brighton, 1857 and 1859. At one time he had "what was probably the largest private collection of Italian Old Masters in the British Isles" (letter from Frank Miles, Esq., compiler of *Samuel Laurence. A Catalogue Raisonné*, a gift to the National Portrait Gallery).

EFG appears to have attributed to the *Athenaeum* a review published in some other periodical. On June 1 the weekly named Laurence and three other portrait painters, briefly commenting on their pictures in general terms. It reviewed the exhibition in issues from May 11 to June 8, but in none is there any reference to the *Chronicle*.

2 See letter to Milnes, [June, 1843], n.1.

3 Alfred Edward Chalon (1780-1860), portrait painter in watercolors. See letter to Laurence, July 4.

4 The bells of St. Mary-le-Bow in Cheapside. "Cockney" is sometimes defined as one born within the hearing of Bow Bells.

5 Harley Street, one of the "fashionable" avenues south of Regent's Park. Portland Place and Wimpole Street are in the same area. For Lady Morgan, see letter to Mrs. Charlesworth, April 20.

6 Landseer, either Edwin (1802-73), painter of animals, or his brother Charles (1799-1879), historical painter. For Maclise, see letter to Pollock, May 11, 1842, n.1.

7 Tennyson's portrait, painted for EFG by Laurence—"the only one of the old days, and still the best of all to my thinking," wrote EFG in 1871. A copy of the

picture, now in the National Portrait Gallery, serves as the frontispiece of the first volume of the *Tennyson Memoir.* It is not known when the portrait was painted. This allusion *could* mean that it had recently been done and was still in Laurence's studio. "Old" does not refer to the portrait. "Old Alfred" was EFG's favorite epithet for the poet. Laurence did not paint the portrait of Tennyson—full-front—that EFG suggests at the close of his letter.

When EFG writes that "W. Browne and Spedding are with me," he refers to his portraits of those men, also painted by Laurence. This passage misled Thomas Wright into stating that Browne and Spedding were visiting EFG when he wrote (*Life*, I, 188). The letter reveals, however, that Spedding was in London at the time.

To Mrs. Charlesworth

Boulge
May 7/44

Dear Mrs. Charlesworth,

I received your last packet just as I was setting off for Suffolk. I sent part of it to Carlyle. I enclose you what answer he makes me this morning. If Miss Charlesworth will take the pains to read his dispatch of Gainsboro' Fight, and can possibly rake out some information on the doubtful points, we shall help to lay that unquiet spirit of history which now disturbs Chelsea and its vicinity. Please to keep the paper safe: for it must have been a nuisance to write it.

I lament your renewed misfortune: but I cannot wonder at it. These things are not got rid of in a year. Isabella[1] is in England with her husband, at Hastings.

Believe me yours ever thankfully,

E. FitzGerald

[1] See letter to F. Tennyson, Oct. 15, 1843.

To Frederick Tennyson

Boulge, Woodbridge
May 24/44

My dear Frederic,

I think you mean never to write to me again. But you should, for I enjoy your letters much for years after I have got them. They tell me all I shall know of Italy, beside many other good things. I received one letter from you from Florence, and as you gave me no particular direction, I wrote to you at the Poste Restante there. I am now inditing this letter on the same venture. As my location is much more permanent, I command you to respond to me the very day you get this, warmed into such faint inspiration as my turnip radiance can kindle. You have seen a turnip lantern[1] perhaps. Well, here I continue to exist: having broken my rural vegetation by one month in London, where I saw all the old faces—some only in passing, however—saw as few sights as possible, leaving London two days before the Exhibition[2] opened. This is not out of moroseness or love of singularity: but I really supposed there could be nothing new: and therefore the best way would [be] to come new to it oneself after three or four years' absence. I see in Punch a humorous catalogue of supposed pictures—Prince Albert's favourite spaniel and boot-jack, the Queen's Macaw with a Muffin, etc., by Landseer, etc., in which I recognize Thackeray's fancy.[3] He is in full vigour, play and pay in London—writing in a dozen reviews, and a score of newspapers: and while health lasts he sails before the wind. I have not heard of Alfred since March: but I saw Moxon[4] in London, who was just going down to Cheltenham with some money for him—the continued produce of his book. I suppose you know something of Morton—nay, you may be with him at the time you get this letter. Spedding devotes his days to Lord Bacon in the British Museum: his nights to the usual profligacy. Poor Tennant's volume of Sermons[5] is come out: I have paid for my copy, but have not yet claimed it at the publisher's. I suppose Mrs. Tennant is in England—did you fall in with her at Florence? My dear Frederic, you must select some of your poems and publish them: we want some bits of strong genuine imagination to help put to flight these Milneses, etc.[6] Publish a book of fragments, if nothing else but single lines, or else the whole poems. When will you come to England and do it? I dare say I should have stayed longer in London had you been there: but the wits were too much for me. Not Spedding, mind: who is a dear fellow. But one finds few in London *serious* men: I mean *serious* even in fun: with a true purpose and character whatsoever it may be. London melts away all individuality into a common lump of cleverness. I am amazed at the humour and worth and noble feeling in the country, however much railroads have mixed us up with metropolitan civilization. I can still find the heart of England beating healthily down here, though no one will believe it.

You know my way of life so well that I need not describe it to you, as it has undergone no change since I saw you. I read of mornings—

the same old books over and over again, having no command of new ones: walk with my great black dog of an afternoon, and at evening sit with open windows, up to which China roses climb, with my pipe, while the blackbirds and thrushes begin to rustle bedwards in the garden, and the nightingale to have the neighbourhood to herself. We have had such a Spring (bating the last ten days) as would have satisfied even you with warmth. And such verdure! white clouds moving over the new fledged tops of oak trees, and acres of grass striving with buttercups. How old to tell of, how new to see! I believe that Leslie's Life of Constable[7] (a very charming book) has given me a fresh love of Spring. Constable loved it above all seasons: he hated Autumn. When Sir G. Beaumont[8] who was of the old classical taste asked him if he did not find it difficult to place *his brown tree* in his pictures, "Not at all," said C., "I never put one in at all." And when Sir George was crying up the tone of the old masters' landscapes, and quoting an *old violin* as the proper tone of colour for a picture, Constable got up, took an old Cremona, and laid it down on the sunshiny grass. You would like the book. In defiance of all this, I have hung my room with pictures, like very old fiddles indeed: but I agree with Sir George and Constable both. I like pictures that are not like nature. I can have nature better than any picture by looking out of my window. Yet I respect the man who tries to paint up to the freshness of earth and sky. Constable did not wholly achieve what he tried at: and perhaps the old masters chose a soberer scale of things as more within the compass of lead paint. To paint dew with lead!

I also plunge away at my old Handel of nights, and delight in the Allegro and Penseroso, full of pomp and fancy. What a pity Handel could not have written music to some great Masque, such as Ben Jonson or Milton would have written, if they had known of such a musician to write for.

And now here I am at my last words—and end as I began by desiring you will write. Tell me all about yourself, and how Septimus and Arthur are. It is three months since I heard from you. I am not thinking of moving from here just yet: certainly not to London: neither do I contemplate much removal over the summer. My friend W. Browne is about to be married: this time ten years ago I first went to fish with him near Bedford. I hope to retain my acquaintance with him, however, in spite of a wife's hatred of the particular friend. I shall hear of your being married some day.[9] Tell me when you are likely to come to England and believe me yours as ever

E.FG.

1 A turnip hollowed out for use as a lantern.

2 Of the Royal Academy. The exhibition opened annually the first Monday in May.

3 "Academy Exhibition," *Punch*, May 11, p. 200:

> 691. Portrait of the Hat of His Royal Highness Prince Albert; with His Royal Highness's favourite boot-jack. His Royal Highness's Persian wolf-dog, Mirza, is lying on the latter, while the former is in the possession of His Royal Hig[h]ness's diminutive spaniel, Miss Kidlumy.—Sandseer, R.A. . . .
>
> 996. Parroquet with a Muffin, (the property of the Queen of the Belgians).

Readers may find a far superior brand of humor in Thackeray's criticism of the annual exhibition contributed to *Fraser's Magazine* between 1838 and 1845. These did not amuse the artists. See letter to F. Tennyson, June 12, 1845.

4 Edward Moxon, Tennyson's publisher.

5 *Sermons Preached to the British Congregation at Florence*, 1844. See letter to F. Tennyson, Aug. 31, 1843, nn.1 and 2.

6 The name was deleted by Aldis Wright.

7 *Memoirs of John Constable*, R.A., 1843, by Charles Robert Leslie.

8 Sir George Howland Beaumont (1753-1827), art patron and landscape painter. He took an active part in establishing the National Gallery.

9 Frederick had been married since 1839. His wife was Maria Giuliotti, daughter of the chief magistrate of Siena, Tuscany.

To J. B. Alexander[1]

[Boulge Cottage]
Friday, June 7/44

Dear Sir,

With reluctance I say—Let the farmer have the pony.

This I decide from no fault I can find or hear of the pony. The principal fault—that of shying—seeming to diminish, not to increase, as he is in use. But I am doubtful as to his faring well under my keep and use, after his being in yours: and about his being intrusted to others beside oneself to drive; which I should feel bound to allow—especially during my long absences and intervals of journies.

Two or three days would have settled down all these things into a surer decision: but there is no time left: so the pony must go—and I be left lamenting. I am vexed to have given you trouble: pray let me know when I come to Woodbridge the expenses of sending the pony, etc., which are mine in all law. I must thank you for having allowed me so much choosing time: and am yours very truly,

E. FitzGerald

Will you not drive up Barton tomorrow afternoon (if it be fine) and have a game of chess and some tea?

[1] J. B. Alexander, Barton's employer at Alexander & Co.'s bank, Church Street, Woodbridge.

To Bernard Barton

19 Charlotte St., Rathbone Place
[June 13, 1844]

Oh, Barton man! but I am grilled here. Oh for to sit upon the banks of the dear old Deben, with the worthy collier sloop going forth into the wide world as the sun sinks! I went all over Westminster Abbey yesterday with a party of country folks, to see the tombs. I did this to vindicate my way of life. Then we had a smoke with Carlyle and he very gloomy about the look of affairs, as usual. I am as tired this morning as if I'd walked fifty miles. Morton, fresh from Italy, agrees that London is not fit to live in. I can't write, nor can you read perhaps. So farewell. Early next week (unless I go round by Bedford) I expect to see good Woodbridge.

To W. B. Donne

Boulge, Woodbridge
[Latter half, June, 1844][1]

Dear Donne,

Procter[2] is the only literatus I have seen in London that I care to see again (saving Tom Carlyle) as he has the heart of a good fellow about him: and as I think his songs poor Cockney things that had better never have been printed, I would not for the world have to say so. Besides, his wife made me a present of the new little volume.[3] I never could understand how Barry, being what he is and always must have been, could have written such things: but no one of his day escaped the Cockney twang then rising—Keats *only* just managed to carry off his share of it. I wish the B[ritish] and F[oreign] would leave Barry alone: but I suppose many men will be found who will admire the poems and praise them in excellent English.

Go fetch to me a pint of wine,
  And fill it in a silver tassie:
For I maun drink before I go
  A bumper to my bonnie lassie![4]

Could one find a stanza like that in the whole book one might cry "Well Done": but yet not be able to write an article on it: for God only, who made the rose smell so, knows why such verses are from the heart, and go to it.

I am glad you are yet in Norfolk:[5] for little advantage as I take of your being so near yet I am always glad to think you are there: which shews there is something in it. I really mean to go to Norwich before long: not to Geldestone yet.

Are you dried up in Norfolk?[6] We are beginning to cry out here: but in other parts of England people are worse off. Is Vipan[7] still in England?

Ever yours,
E. FitzGerald

1 Dated by Hannay [1845?]. The 1844 date is definitely established by evidence in the footnotes that follow.

2 Bryan Waller Procter (Barry Cornwall).

3 *English Songs and Other Small Poems*, 3rd ed., 1844.

4 EFG quotes from memory a portion of Robert Burns's "My Bonnie Mary." Burns wrote:

> Go fetch to me a pint o'wine,
> An' fill it in a silver tassie;
> That I may drink, before I go,
> A service to my bonnie lassie;

The version in *A FitzGerald Friendship* differs from the manuscript in minor points.

5 Donne's wife had died December 7, 1843. He then proposed to leave Mattishall and take up residence in a town where he could enter his three sons in a superior public school. However, he was not able to carry out his plan until 1846, when he moved to Bury St. Edmunds, where he made his home for eight years.

6 Donne wrote to Bernard Barton, June 17, [1844], "Are you parched up with drought in Suffolk as we in Norfolk?" (*Donne and Friends*, pp. 81-82).

7 David Vipan. See letter to Donne, Sept. 27, 1833, n.5.

To Samuel Laurence

Boulge
July 4/44

Dear Laurence,

I have but lately returned from Holbrook, where I saw your last portrait of Wilkinson. It is very capital, and gives my sister and all her neighbours great satisfaction. Jane indeed can talk of nothing else.

I will say this however, with my usual ignorance and presumption, that I think the last day's sitting made it a little heavier than when I left it unfinished. Was it that the final glazing was somewhat too thick? I only mention this as a very slight defect, which I should not have observed had I not seen its penultimate state, and were I not a crotchetty stickler for lightness and ease. But I hope and trust you will now do all your future sketches in oil in the same way in which this is done: the long brush, the wholesome distance between canvas, painter, and sitter, and the few sittings. For myself, I have always been sure of this: but I can assert it to you with more confidence now, seeing that every one else seems to agree with me, if I may judge by the general approval of this specimen of the long brush. Besides, such a method must shorten your labour, preserve the freshness of your eye and spirit, and also ensure the similitude of the sitter to himself by the very speediness of the operation.

Mills[1] was very much delighted at W.'s portrait. What will you say of me when I tell you that I did not encourage him to have his wife painted by you, as he seemed to purpose! You will pray heaven to deliver you from your friends. But notwithstanding this, I am sure this last portrait will bring you sitters from this part of the country. Perhaps you will not find it easy to forgive me this. I must tell you that Mrs. Mills, who sets up to be no judge of pictures, but who never is wrong about anything, instantly pitched on your portrait of Coningham as the best in the Exhibition, without seeing who it was by:[2] and when she referred to the Catalogue, called out to her husband "Why this is by E.F.G.'s friend Mr. Laurence."

July 18. You see that all up to this was written a fortnight ago. I did not finish, for I did not know where to direct. And now I shall finish this portrait of my mind, you see, in a different aspect perhaps to that with which I set out. On looking over what I wrote however, I stick to all I said about the painting: as to Mrs. Mills, whose case seems to require some extenuation on my part, I fancied she was one of those persons' faces you would not take to: and so not succeed in. It is rather a pretty face, without meaning, it seems to me: and yet she has meaning in her. Mills has already had one portrait of her, which discontents all, and therefore it was I would not advise any painter who did not understand the art of *Millinery* well: for if the face does not wholly content, there is the dress to fall back on. I fancy Chalon[3] would do the business.

I hear you have been doing some brother or brother in law of Mrs.

Lumsden.[4] Mind what I have told you. I may not be a good judge of painting, but I can judge of what people in general like. . . .[5]

[1] The Reverend Thomas Mills, Rector at Stutton, Suffolk.

[2] In "May Gambols," his critique of the 1844 exhibition of the Royal Academy written for *Fraser's Magazine*, Thackeray censured the Academicians for hanging Laurence's portrait of William Coningham "away out of sight," and added, "You are right to keep the best picture in the room out of the way, to be sure; it would sternly frown your simpering unfortunates out of countenance" (Thackeray Biographical Edition, XIII, 440). The Academicians were often charged with hanging their own pictures at the most favorable height for viewing.

[3] Alfred Chalon is identified by Redgrave as "the most fashionable portrait painter in water-colours" of the period, the draperies and accessories in his pictures being drawn "with great spirit and elegance, imitations of all the vagaries that fashion can commit in lace and silk" (*Dictionary of Artists*).

[4] The wife of Henry Thomas Lumsden, Perpetual Curate of St. Peter's, Ipswich.

[5] Thus in *Letters and Literary Remains.*

To John Allen

[Boulge Cottage]
[c. July 16, 1844][1]

My dear good Allen,

Let me hear from you, if even but a line, before you leave London on your summer excursion, whithersoever that is to be. I conclude you go somewhere—to Hampshire, or to Tenby.[2] When I saw you at King's College last, I went there with the purpose of going home with you: but seeing you had got two other men with you, I thought that was quite enough for a Sunday party. I left London soon after, as I indeed only went up to see Morton who had just arrived from Italy. W. Browne is to be married, he says, on the 30th. of this month!

Let me know whither you go this summer. I meditate a little trip somewhere, and now my old summer swallow is going to pair off, I must look for fresh quarters. Such is the state of a bachelor whom his partners desert one by one, you see.

You are to tell Mrs. Allen that I had got into a cab and was going along the New Road on my way to take tea with her (as I hoped) one evening after I saw you, when I saw one of my poor friends the Nurseys[3] turning down their dingy lane that leads out of the N.W.—got out to speak—and being carried to their house, could not get away till it was too late to go further.

I have nothing to tell you of myself. Here I exist, and read scraps of books, garden a little, and am on good terms with my neighbours. The Times paper is stirring up our farming society to the root, and some good will come of it, I dare say, and some ill. Do you know of any good books on *Education*?—not for the poor or Charity schools, but on modern Gentlemen's grammar schools, etc. Did not Combe[4] write a book? But he is the driest Scotch Snuff. I beg leave to say that this letter is written with a pen of my own making: the first I have made these twenty years. I doubt after all it is no proof of a very intelligent pen-Creator, but only of a lucky slit. The next effort shall decide. Farewell, my dear Fellow. Don't forget unworthy me. We shall soon have known each other twenty years—and soon thirty—and forty—if we live a little while.

Ever yours,
E.FG.

[1] Allen's notation.

[2] Tenby was near Allen's boyhood home. His wife was from Hampshire.

[3] The family of Perry Nursey, the Suffolk artist. See Biographical Profile.

[4] Probably George Combe (1788-1858), one of the founders of the Phrenological Society, 1820, and the *Phrenological Journal*, 1823, who published pamphlets on education and social ethics.

From Thomas Carlyle

Chelsea, 29 July, 1844

Dear Fitzgerald,

I am very glad to hear of you again;—you from the green odoriferous Summerfields, I here amid the choking heat of Babylon and the baked bricks!

Alas, it seems to me I shall hardly get out into the Country this year at all. I have succeeded so dreadfully ill with my working affairs, I feel as if my conscience would forbid me to enjoy any rural thing. Besides, I found last year so sorry a result from nearly three whole months of roving and restless wandering,—nothing but increase of sadness, of stupidity and every sort of darkness supervening thereupon: I really think I must try what sitting still will do for me this year.[1] My one poor hope for the present, at least, is that the beautiful Quality will all go about their business in a week or two;[2] and that then we shall have a Quiet Town, where a poor wretch may be left alone to try if he *can* get any work done: he will at least be more solitary than anywhere else, and may meditate on the error of his ways, if he can do no better. I could envy you your beautiful excursions, beautiful to a healthy heart, but I will honestly wish you happiness in them, new health from them and many merry days. I do not envy anybody anything,—that really is true at present: I am as a *drowned mouse*, to whom additional rains or the brightest sunny weather are very literally all one! Such is the "Curse of Cromwell" resting on me, for the time being.

I never give up, but I make almost no way. Such an element of brutal dulness and every form of incoherent Ignorance and Falseness and Stupidity, no man ever worked in before! I go plunging about, in a very desperate manner, in that villainous Quagmire of History; and on some sides find a little progress possible; on most sides none.—I am fast gathering Oliver's Letters together; have a big Heap of them copied with my own hand, and tolerably elucidated. I find it very useful work; the Letters themselves stript of their ragged misspellings, etc., become quite lucid and even lucent. The ground grows always a little firmer as I work in that quarter.

Last week I took a violent resolution that the whole of Cromwell's battles ought to be elucidated for the whole world: maps like the Winceby one, *exact* portraiture of the face of the ground as it now is, with judicious selection of the contemporary testimonies as they now are; *faithful* effort, in short, by a human being of the year 1844 to put down what he *can* know of those things 200 years back, which will be memorable for 1000 years to come. Alas! I went to the Booksellers to give me an estimate of costs; the name of a fit artist, first of all: this they will do;—but there I fear the matter will stick. Suppose *you* try your hand at Naseby, and another or two! *Woodcuts* no bigger than an octavo page,—the Ordnance Survey and utmost geographical correctness lying at the bottom of them. The Portrait of the Place in Wood.

A poor Scotchman coming to me near starved, I gave him a guinea to copy for me certain particulars of an Ipswich Election: this if I find means, I have some thoughts of printing as a Magazine Article somewhere.[3] You will find enough of it in the enclosed Paper;—if you can throw any light on it, you will. Adieu, dear F.

Yours ever truly
T. Carlyle

[1] EFG appears to have invited Carlyle to visit him in Suffolk.

[2] "The Long Vacation (when London is most empty)" extends from early August to late October (Cunningham, *Handbook*, I, xix).

[3] Carlyle's essay, "An Election to the Long Parliament," was published in *Fraser's Magazine*, October, 1844, pp. 379-93.

To Bernard Barton

Geldestone
August 22, 1844

My dear Barton,

You will think I have forgot you. I spent four pleasant days with Donne: who looks pale and thin, and in whose face the grey is creeping up from those once flourishing whiskers to the skull. It is doing so with me. We are neither of us in what may be called the first dawn of boyhood. Donne maintains his shape better than I do, but sorrow I doubt has done that: and so we see why the house of mourning is better than the stalled ox. For it is a grievous thing to grow poddy: the age of Chivalry is gone then. An old proverb says that "a full belly neither fights nor flies well."

I also saw Geldart[1] at Norwich. He paints, and is deep in religious thoughts also: he has besides the finest English good sense about him: and altogether he is a man one goes to that one may learn from him. I walked much about Norwich and was pleased with the old place.

Here I see my old friend Mrs. Schutz,[2] and play with the children. Having shown the little girl the prints of Boz's Curiosity Shop, I have made a short abstract of Little Nelly's wanderings[3] which interests her much, leaving out the Swivellers, etc. For children do not understand how merriment should intrude in a serious matter. This might make a nice child's book, cutting out Boz's sham pathos, as well as the real fun; and it forms a kind of Nelly-ad, or Homeric narration of the child's wandering fortunes till she reaches at last a haven more desirable than any in stony Ithaca.

Lusia is to be married[4] on the 2nd, I hear; and I shall set out for Leamington where the event takes place in the middle of next week. Whether I shall touch in my flight at Boulge is yet uncertain: so don't order any fireworks just at present. I hear from Mr. Crabbe he is delighted with D'Israeli's Coningsby,[5] which I advised him to read. Have you read it? The children still wonder what Miss Charlesworth meant when she said that she didn't mean what she said. I tell them it is a new way of thinking of young England. I have exercised the children's minds greatly on the doctrine of Puseyitical reticence (that is not the word) but I find that children, who are great in the kingdom of Heaven, are all for blurting out what they mean. Farewell for the present.

Ever yours,
E.FG.

If war breaks out with France, I will take up arms as a volunteer under Major Pytches.[6] Pytches and Westminster Abbey!

[1] Joseph Geldart (1808-82), Norfolk artist, friend of Samuel Laurence's.

[2] See letter to Allen, Jan. 1, 1837, n.3.

[3] EFG's MS of his "Nelly-ad" is in the library of Trinity College. It has been published in *A FitzGerald Medley*, Charles Ganz, ed., 1933, pp. 150-90.

[4] To the Reverend Francis de Soyres. He had served as Curate for John Mainwaring, Rector of Geldestone, from June 12, 1842, to July 28, 1844.

[5] *Coningsby, or the New Generation*, a political novel by Benjamin Disraeli, published in 1844.

[6] Thomas Pytches, landowner, of Melton, adjacent to Woodbridge. The annexation of the Society Islands in the South Pacific by a French naval officer in November, 1843, had led to "the Tahiti incident." The following March, one Pritchard, an English missionary who had been serving as British consul at Tahiti, was arrested by the French commandant. British ire flared. The threat of war, brought on by the blundering of minor officials, was removed when, at Pritchard's own suggestion, the French government granted him indemnity for the treatment he had received (Walpole, *History*, V, 344-49). Charles Greville wrote in his diary, "For some time it was a toss-up whether we went to war or not." France never paid the Pritchard claim (*The Greville Memoirs*, 3 vols., 1885, II, 252 and 253, n.1).

To Bernard Barton

Tavistock Hotel, Covent Garden
Tuesday, Septr 17/44

My dear Barton,

I know not if I shall be in town till you arrive in it. I came up yesterday from Winchester: and am going to see poor Isabella[1] today: to do which is indeed my only motive to stay in this filthy ditch. I am located you see in a vegetable quarter: but not the sweeter for that. Give me a line (on venture) by return of post to say when you go—when you pass through London. I am going to send my friend John Allen to see your brother[2] for a day—next Tuesday—but I shall of course write to Leigh first to see if such a visit be acceptable.

Ever yours,
E.FG.

[1] His sister.

[2] See following letter to John Barton.

To John Barton[1]

Tavistock Hotel, Covent Garden
Tuesday, Septr 17/44

Dear Sir,

My friend, John Allen, goes school inspecting in Hampshire next week: beginning with Havant next Tuesday. I am sure you would like him: and I am sure he would like you: and therefore I write to ask if you would choose to entertain him for an afternoon—namely, that of Tuesday. Now mind, I can only do this out of one motive: that I think it may do pleasure to you both; but if you do not anticipate this, or should have your house full, or any other just impediment: you will, of course, say so. I will also admit that Allen is very apt (as who would not) to be much wearied with his day's school work, and not to show to much advantage in company afterwards. Indeed he is generally glad to get to his ease at an Inn. But as you found out the beauty of Spedding's portrait (which you saw at Woodbridge) so will you see (I am sure) the Humour, Wonder, and Observation that lies in John Allen's eyes and eyebrows, though he should not say a word. Indeed those faculties are most of all compatible with Silence.

I came here yesterday: and will get out of the nasty place as soon as I can. Will you give me one line by return of post? Do, please. I think with great satisfaction of Leigh,[2] and its wise, polite, and agreeable household.

Carlyle did not find us out after all, though he came in a grand nobleman's carriage[3] to see Winchester Cathedral. There's a pretty fellow to write democratic books for you.

Well, believe me yours very truly
E. FitzGerald

[1] John Barton, Bernard Barton's half-brother, a churchman of independent means who lived on an estate at Eastleigh, three miles north of Southampton. F. R. Barton, in *Some New Letters of Edward FitzGerald* (1923, p. 88), places "East Leigh near Havant, in Hampshire," 20 miles southeast of Eastleigh. E. V. Lucas, in *Bernard Barton and His Friends* (1893, p. 62), states that John Barton lived at "Stoughton, near Chichester, Sussex."

[2] EFG had visited John Barton earlier in the month.

[3] Carlyle was paying his first visit to Lord and Lady Ashburton at The Grange, near Winchester.

To Bernard Barton
(Fragment)

Leamington
Sept. 28/44

My dear Barton,

. . . I expect to be here about a week, and I mean to give a day to looking over the field of Edgehill,[1] on the top of which, I have ascertained, there is a very delightful pot-house, commanding a very extensive view. Don't you wish to sit at ease in such a high tower, with a pint of porter at your side, and to see beneath you the ground that was galloped over by Rupert and Cromwell two hundred years ago, in one of the richest districts of England, and on one of the finest days in October, for such my day is to be?

In the meanwhile I cast regretful glances of memory back to my garden at Boulge, which I want to see dug up and replanted. I have bought anemone roots which in the Spring shall blow Tyrian dyes, and Irises of a newer and more brilliant prism than Noah saw in the clouds. I have bought a picture of my poor quarrelsome friend Moore,[2] just to help him; for I don't know what to do with his picture.

[1] Edgehill, in Warwickshire, where Charles I was defeated, October 23, 1642, by the Earl of Essex in the first major battle of the Great Rebellion.
[2] See letter to Milnes, [June, 1843].

To W. B. Donne

Boulge, Woodbridge
Oct[r] *10/44*

My dear Donne,

How are you—and where are you? After fruitless rambles in the midland counties I am come back here to my Den for the winter and I was asked some while ago to send your address to MacPherson of King's College Glasgow[1]—who was supposed to want to treat with you on some school or College matter. Have you heard from him?

I spent a few days in London, and saw no one but Carlyle, and Thompson[2] who had just landed from Germany. In the last Fraser (for this October) you will find an article called "An Election for the Long Parliament"—headed and tailed by Carlyle, in his perculiar tasty way.[3] Is it true that Kemble and Beaumont have split?[4] So I heard in London.

Spedding is yet up in the mountains. I went one night to the Haymarket to see Vanbrugh's Confederacy[5]—but it was Vanbrugh castrated within an inch of his life; and all the obsolete intrigue story left. Farren looked admirable, and sipped coffee from a little cup just as you see one of the quality doing in one of Marriage a la Mode pictures.[6]

Pray let me have a line from you. One day also I hope to see you again. Is Charles[7] gone to School? Kerrich has been unwell: but is now better. He is here just now—but returns to Geldestone tomorrow to preside at some Beccles Quarter Sessions.[8]

And now you will not grieve that I stop this bad pen on its worse paper. Farewell for the present.

Ever yours,
E.FG.

Have you called on Geldart?[9] I told him you meant to do so.

[1] Probably Hugh MacPherson, father of EFG's contemporary at Trinity, William Macpherson. EFG errs in speaking of the elder MacPherson as being at Glasgow. He taught Greek at King's College, Aberdeen.

[2] W. H. Thompson.

[3] See n.3, letter from Carlyle, July 29, 1844.

[4] Bruce Dickins in *J. M. Kemble and Old English Scholarship* (Gollancz Memorial Lecture, 1939) states that Kemble's *British and Foreign Review* "came to an abrupt end with the first number of vol. xviii in 1844" (p. 15).

Thomas Wentworth Beaumont (1792-1848), wealthy, liberal politician, had been a co-founder of the *Westminster Review* before establishing the *British and Foreign.*

[5] *The Confederacy*, by John Vanbrugh, at the Theatre Royal, with Madame Vestris, Priscilla Horton, Charles Matthews, and William Farren in the cast.

[6] By Hogarth.

[7] Charles Edward Donne (1832-1907), Donne's oldest son, later Vicar of Faversham, Kent. In September, 1844, Donne had written R. C. Trench that he intended to send Charles to study with a clergyman, a Mr. Calvert, near Norwich (*Donne and Friends*, p. 84).

[8] His brother-in-law, John Kerrich, was justice of the peace for Geldestone.

[9] Joseph Geldart.

To Frederick Tennyson

Boulge, Woodbridge
Oct. 10/44

My dear Frederic,

You will think I have wholly cut you. But I wrote half a letter to you three months ago; and mislaid it; spent some time in looking for it, always hoping; and then some more time despairing; and we all know how time goes when [we] have got a thing to do which we are rather lazy about doing. As for instance, getting up in a morning. Not that writing a letter to you is so bad as getting up; but it is not easy for mortal man who has heard, seen, done, and thought, nothing since he last wrote, to fill one of these big foreign sheets full as a foreign letter ought to be. I am now returned to my dull home here after my usual pottering about in the midland counties of England. A little Bedfordshire—a little Northamptonshire—a little more folding of the hands—the same faces—the same fields—the same thoughts recurring at the same turns of road—this is all I have to tell of; nothing at all added—but the summer gone. My garden is covered with yellow and brown leaves; and a man is digging up the garden beds before my window, and will plant some roots and bulbs for next year. My parsons come and smoke with me, etc. "The round of life from hour to hour"[1]—alluding doubtless to a mill-horse. Alfred is reported to be still at Park House,[2] where he has been sojourning for two months, I think; but he never writes me a word. Hydropathy has done its worst; he writes the names of his friends in water. But 'tis the nature of the beast; and I hope to see him one of these days. I spent two days in London with old Morton about five weeks ago; and pleasant days they were. The rogue bewitches me with his wit and honest speech. He also staid some while at Park House, while Alfred was there, and managed of course to frighten the party occasionally with some of his sallies. He often writes to me; and very good his letters are all of them.

When do you mean to write me another? Morton told me in his last that he had heard from Brotherton[3] you were gone, or going, to Naples. I dare say this sheet of mine will never get to your hands. But if it does, let me hear from you. Is Italy becoming stale to you? Are you going to travel to Cairo for fresh sensations? Thackeray went off in a steamboat about the time the French were before Mogadore;[4] he was to see those coasts and to visit Jerusalem! Titmarsh at Jerusalem will certainly be an era in Christianity. But I suppose he will soon be back now. Spedding is yet in his highlands, I believe, considering Grouse and Bacon.

I expect to run up to London some time during the winter just to tell over old friends' faces and get a sup of music and painting. I have bought very few more pictures lately; and [heard] no music but Mendelssohn's M. Night's Dream.[5] The overture, which was published long ago, is the best part; but there is a very noble triumphal march also.

Now I feel just in the same fix as I did in that sheet of paper whose fate is uncertain. But if I don't put in a word more, yet this shall go, I am determined. Only consider how it is a matter of necessity that I should have nothing to say. If you could see this place of Boulge! You who sit and survey marble palaces rising out of cypress and olive. There is a dreadful vulgar ballad, composed by Mr. Balfe,[6] and sung with the most unbounded applause by Miss Rainforth,

"I dreamt that I dwelt in marble Halls,"

which is sung and organed at every fifth corner in London. I think you may imagine what kind of flowing 6/8 time of the last degree of imbecility it is. The words are written by Mr. Bunn! Arcades ambo.[7]

I say we shall see you over in England before long: for I rather think you want an Englishman to quarrel with sometimes. I mean quarrel in the sense of a good strenuous difference of opinion, supported on either side by occasional outbursts of spleen. Come and let us try. You used to irritate my vegetable blood sometimes: but I bore it like a martian.[8]

Ever yours,
E.FG.

[1] From the last line of Tennyson's poem, "Circumstance," "So runs the round of life from hour to hour."

[2] The home near Maidstone, Kent, of Edmund Law Lushington, husband of Tennyson's sister Cecilia. The garden at Park House is the setting of the Prologue to Tennyson's *Princess*.

[3] Augustus Brotherton, artist friend of Frederick Tennyson, who lived in Rome. Mary Brotherton, his wife, practiced "automatic writing" and believed in spiritualistic phenomena. She may have been responsible for Frederick's interest in spiritualism.

[4] Mogadore, Moroccan port on the Atlantic, bombarded by the French in a dispute arising out of the partitioning of Algeria in 1830. In August Thackeray had begun his tour of the Mediterranean which provided the material for his *Notes of a Journey from Cornhill to Grand Cairo*, published in January, 1846.

[5] In 1844 *A Midsummer Night's Dream* was included in the program of the Philharmonic Society. Mendelssohn himself conducted the last five concerts.

[6] Michael William Balfe (1808-70), baritone and composer.

Elizabeth Rainforth (1814-77), soprano at Covent Garden and Drury Lane. She scored a marked success as Arline in Balfe's *Bohemian Girl* at its premiere at Drury Lane in November, 1847.

Alfred Bunn (1796?-1860), for a quarter of a century director and lessee of Drury Lane, noted particularly for his efforts to establish an English opera. He was author and adaptor of many plays.

[7] "Arcadians both" (Virgil, *Eclogue*, VII.4).

[8] EFG was born, "under the influence of Mars," March 31. In the Portuguese epic, *The Lusiad*, by Camoens, Mars typifies divine fortitude.

From Thomas Carlyle

Chelsea, 26 Oct^{r}, 1844

Dear Fitzgerald,

I have sent your Name to the Library:[1] so soon as any Committee-meeting is, your business will be completed, and Cochrane the Librarian will announce fact to you and demand money. You will find it a very real convenience, I do expect, to be admitted freely to such an extent of Book-pasturage. In regard to all but the ephemeral rubbish, which are in great demand, and which you can well dispense with, the access to Books (I believe) is very fair; certainly there are many good Books in the Collection: bad rubbish Books too you can get, French novels, etc., etc., in very great abundance; but you must be on the spot,—nay I believe you must even be a Lady—for that. Do not therefore attempt that!

You may depend upon it Dryasdust* is highly gratified with the notice taken of him. Pray sound him, from the distance, and ascertain: I have still a great many Suffolk questions that I could ask him. I am getting a little better with my poor *Cromwell* in these days; I really must have done with it, if only to save my own life. It is still very frightful,—a dark Golgotha as wide as the World; but here and there it does begin to get luminous, to get alive. Courage! I think it will be the joyfullest feat for me I ever did, when the last tatter of it is fairly shaken off my finger, and I am free again.

One day we had Alfred Tennyson here; an unforgettable day. He staid with us till late; forgot his stick: we dismissed him with *Macpherson's Farewell.*[2] Macpherson (see Burns) was a Highland robber; he played that Tune, of his own composition, on his way to the gallows; asked, "If in all that crowd the Macpherson had any clansman?" holding up the fiddle that he might bequeath it to some one. "Any

Kinsman, any soul that wished him well?" Nothing answered, nothing durst answer. He crushed the fiddle under his foot, and sprang off. The Tune is rough as hemp, but strong as a lion. I never hear it without something of emotion,—poor Macpherson; tho' the Artist hates to play it. Alfred's dark face grew darker, and I saw his lip slightly quivering! He said of you that you were a man from whom one could take money;[3] which was a proud saying, which you ought to thank Heaven for. It has struck me as a distinctly necessary Act of Legislation, that Alfred should have a Pension of £150 a year.[4] They have £1200 every year to give away. A hundred and fifty to Alfred, I say; *he* is worth that sum to England! It should be done, and must.

Yours ever truly
T. Carlyle

*[FitzGerald's MS notation added at the head of the letter:] "Dryasdust," of next page, was D. E. Davy Esq: of Ufford, a polite handsome old Gentleman, who had collected over 80 folios of Suffolk History, which he finally bequested to the British Museum. He supplied Carlyle (at my request) with all the particulars he wanted about an Election of County Members at Ipswich 1640 and—was thanked in print under the name "Dryasdust."

[1] Irked by the difficulty of obtaining historical sources while writing the *French Revolution*, Carlyle had raised the question, "Why is there not a King's Library in every town? There's a King's gallows in every one." Books in the British Museum do not circulate, and the popular circulating libraries restricted their lists for the most part to current novels, biography, and travel. In January, 1839, Carlyle set about to enlist the aid of influential friends in establishing "a lending library for the use of scholars." Carlyle was named secretary of a founding committee which issued a prospectus written by James Spedding. In May, 1841, the library opened at 57 Pall Mall. Three years later, under its present name, the London Library, it moved to its present site, 12 St. James's Square. The membership fee was six guineas; annual subscription, two guineas. The first librarian was succeeded in 1852 by W. B. Donne.

[2] Actually "Macpherson's Lament," a ballad adapted by Burns as "Macpherson's Farewell." James Macpherson, daring Scotch outlaw, after holding three counties for years in lawless bond, was tried and sentenced to death in November, 1700. An accomplished violinist, he is said to have composed ballad and music while awaiting execution. His song began:

I've spent my time in rioting,
  Debauched my health and strength;
I squandered fast as pillage came,
  And fell to shame at length.
    But dantonly and wantonly,
      And rantingly I'll gae;
    I'll play a tune, and dance it roun'
      Beneath the gallows-tree.

[3] After their visit to Spedding at Mirehouse in 1835, EFG had offered to give

Tennyson money when the poet found himself in need. (See letter to Tennyson, July 2, 1835.) Since that time EFG had been aiding Thackeray financially, and Carlyle's comment suggests that Tennyson, also, availed himself of "Old Fitz's" generosity. Thirty years later Carlyle told C. E. Norton that for many years "in Tennyson's poor days" EFG gave the poet £300 a year (*Letters of Charles Eliot Norton*, Sara Norton and M.A.D. Howe, eds., 2 vols., 1913, I, 465). Carlyle was nearly 80 when he talked with Norton, and his recollection is questionable. An annual gift of £300, in addition to other benefactions, would probably have overtaxed EFG's resources at that time of life. However, in his account of Tennyson's marriage, Hallam Tennyson wrote, "Moxom now advanced £300—so my Uncle Charles told a friend,—at all events £300 were in my father's bank in his name; and with this and their united small incomes . . . they decided that they could brave life together" (*Memoir*, I, 238). Perhaps there is a link between the mysterious deposit and the sums that lodged in Carlyle's memory.

[4] Carlyle's conviction, Sir Charles Tennyson believes, is the origin of proceedings which resulted in Tennyson's being granted a Civil List pension of £200 a year later. See letter to Barton, [c. Nov. 1, 1845].

To Mrs. Charlesworth

[Boulge]
[Late October, 1844]

Dear Mrs. Charlesworth,

I have heard something about you, and your change of life that is to be,[1] from the Bartons. I can only hope it will be a pleasant change; and whatever people say about fresh breezes, violets, thrushes etc., I find that every one soon falls into a London life after a little time, and in his heart prefers the cheerfulness, the stir and the many social conveniences, of London to all that poets have sung of the Country. We talk about seasons down here; but in London it is always one season—an eternal summer of books, pleasant people, shops etc. So you are not to be pitied.

But we who are left are to be pitied; first, as I say, because we are not going to London; and next because we lose all of you out of the Country; which last makes the first worse, you know. You are going to add yourselves to that immense mass of people, and to subtract yourselves from us scattered sheep who want you so much. You shall be plagued, like Wordsworth's Poor Susan,[2] with visions of Bramford; and the Gipping shall seem to flow through the vale of Cheapside with a delusive momentary glitter. The cry of *Old Clothes*[3] shall break the charm. But I will not be severe upon you. Why couldn't you have come to Woodbridge, by way of a lively metropolis?

The paper on Sir S. D'Ewes in Fraser[4] is Carlyle's—and good in his way. Pray send me what paper you have about the Knight. Who can now be angry with that harmless Justice now dead these hundred fifty years and more?

I should like to see you all at Bramford once more; before that quiet little house which takes the sunshine so kindly shall be left tenantless. But I am partly expecting a call into Norfolk; though not for any very long while.

With kind remembrances to Mr. Charlesworth and your ladies believe me yours very truly

Edward FitzGerald

John and his family are here; and all well.

[1] At the end of 1843, her husband, the Reverend John Charlesworth, Rector of Flowton, near Ipswich, had been appointed to the Rectory of St. Mildred's, Bread Street, London. However, the family did not move at once.

[2] "Poor Susan," to whom, in London, the song of a thrush, "At the corner of Wood Street," evokes visions of the rural home which she has left. She sees

> Bright volumes of vapour through Lothbury glide,
> And a river flows on through the vale of Cheapside.
>
> Green pastures she views in the midst of the dale,
> Down which she so often has tripped with her pail;
> And a single small cottage, a nest like a dove's
> The one only dwelling on earth that she loves.
>
> The Reverie of Poor Susan

The River Gipping flows past the village of Bramford, where the Charlesworths lived. At Ipswich, three miles distant, the stream becomes the River Orwell.

[3] A street cry.

[4] *Frasers Magazine*, Oct., 1844, pp. 379-93.

To Mrs. John Charlesworth

[Boulge Cottage]
[Late October, 1844]

Dear Mrs. Charlesworth,

I know not if I can get from here on Monday; though toward the middle of the week I shall be on my road to Holbrook. But if I do get off, I will assuredly go to Bramford that day, and see the last of the Autumn with you. I will write a line on Sunday evening to say whether I go or not; but anyhow you will not, to be sure, put yourselves at all out of the way. And I flatter myself that my arrival causes no stir in the larder nor in the cellar—which is a just comfort to me and to my hosts.

I am planting and ordering my garden, and I know not if I can get it all set up in winter trim so early as Monday. These are the great causes of these great suspenses.

Miss Barton told me she was expecting Miss Charlesworth at Woodbridge. As to Barton himself, he has now been out for a fortnight's holidays—a thing which only happens once in three years—and I doubt if he could get away on a Monday. You know his least busy days are at the end of the week.

Believe me truly yours,
Edward FitzGerald

To Bernard Barton

Geldestone
Novr 20/44

Dear Barton,

I am here, as you say, in some glory—and I am going this afternoon to Beccles with a train of five children to buy *bull's eyes* (dost thou remember them?) and other sweetmeats. The children here are so simple by nature, and simply brought up, that a visit to Beccles is to them something what a visit to London is to others. My heart always sinks within me when I see them really interested in the piddling shops here, and think of the unutterable staleness of all such things to oneself.

I shall be back at Boulge next week, I believe. And then we will arrange all about Xmas. I will bring Arnold with me:[1] he was a noble fellow. Ginger[2] came with me here and takes great delight in the rabbit burrows which belong to this sandy soil. We have no rabbits at Boulge: and the dog's talents go to waste. I am not permitted to have him in the room; so he lives in the stable, and will lose some manners in consequence, which Mrs. Faiers and I shall have to restore at our leisure.

I have had a long letter from Crabbe, all written with the freshness of one of twenty-five—nay of one yet younger. I believe he would go with us today to Beccles, and look into the shops with as much interest as the rest of us. He was sixty some days ago.

November 1844

How will Miss Barton get on at Holbrook?[3] She *must* admire Wilkinson however; an unique specimen of a man who really does *all* he thinks he ought to do.

We have here a very pleasant new neighbour—a Mrs. Jones[4]—niece of Lady Morgan, and wife of a Clergyman who has the curacy of this village for a while; but whose Rectory is that of Bawdsey. She sings, plays, talks and is silent, all in harmonious order; and loves society. What will she do at Bawdsey![5] Even the shooting Squires here have more ear than the howling German sea on one side, and the dreary desert *Walks* on the other. We must make much of this little Lady when she comes among us.

Yours ever,
E. FitzGerald

[1] A. P. Stanley, *The Life and Correspondence of Thomas Arnold*, 1844.

[2] EFG's Skye terrier.

[3] Lucy Barton was planning a visit to the Wilkinsons whom Lucy later described, in a letter to Elizabeth Charlesworth, as "very kind and pleasant. Mrs. W. *most gracious*, not patronizing—*he* was like an angel" (MS letter, Cambridge University Library, May 3, 1845).

[4] Edward Inwood Jones apparently served as interim curate at Geldestone after the marriage of the former curate, Francis de Soyres, to EFG's sister Andalusia in September.

Mr. Jones, Vicar of Bawdsey, Suffolk, 1841-46, appears not to have taken up residence there immediately. No incumbent is listed for the Bawdsey living in White's *Suffolk Directory* for 1844. The church had been gutted by fire (ignited by boys setting off fireworks) in 1841 and was not repaired until 1843. EFG mistakenly alludes to the Bawdsey "Rectory."

Mrs. Jones was the daughter of Sir Arthur Clarke, of Dublin, and niece of Lady Morgan. (For Lady Morgan, see letter to Mrs. Charlesworth, April 20, 1844, n.2.)

[5] Bawdsey, a village seven and one-half miles southeast of Woodbridge and less than a mile from the coast, lies in an area described as "the wildest tract of country along the Suffolk coast" (W. A. Dutt, *The Norfolk and Suffolk Coast*, 1909, p. 30).

The "Walks" are open tracts, originally common lands (W. G. Arnott, *The Place-Names of the Deben Valley Parishes*, Ipswich, 1946, p. 75). Several such tracts, covered with bracken and gorse, lie between Woodbridge and the coast.

To Bernard Barton

[Geldestone]
[November 27, 1844]

Dear Barton,

My return to Boulge is delayed for another week, because we expect my Father here just now. But for this, I should have been on the Union

Coach this day. The children here are most delightful; the best company in all the world, to my mind. If you could see the little girl dance the Polka with her sisters! Not set up like an Infant Terpsichore, but seriously inclined, with perfect steps in perfect time.

We see a fine white frost over the grass this morning; and I suppose you have rubbed your hands and cried "Oh Lauk, how cold it is!" twenty times before I write this. Now one's pictures become doubly delightful to one. I certainly love winter better than summer. Could one but know, as one sits within the tropic latitude of one's fireside, that there was not increased want, cold, and misery, beyond it!

My Spectator tells me that Leigh Hunt has published a good volume of Poem-selections;[1] not his own poems, but of others. And Miss Martineau has been cured of an illness of five years standing by Mesmerism! By the help of a few passes of the hand following an earnest Will, she, who had not set foot out of her room, for the chief part of those five years, now can tread the grass again, and walk five miles! Her account of the business in the Athenaeum is extremely interesting.[2] She is the only one I have read of who describes the sensations of *the trance*, which, seeming a painful one to the wide-awake looker-on, is in fact a state of tranquil glorification to the patient. It cheers but not inebriates![3] She felt her disease oozing away out at her feet, and as it were streams of warm fresh vitality coming in its place. And when she woke, lo, this was no dream!

1 *Imagination and Fancy*; "or Selections from the English Poets."

2 Harriet Martineau (1802-76), miscellaneous writer, states in her autobiography that through mesmerism she had been cured of a tumor from which she had long suffered. Six letters written "to lift up the subject [mesmerism] out of the dirt into which it had been plunged, and to place it on a scientific ground, if possible," were published in the *Athenaeum* between November 23 and December 30. *Letters on Mesmerism* was published by Moxon in 1845. (See Miss Martineau's *Autobiography*, I, 475-77.)

3 Cowper's *The Task*, in which the poet speaks of tea as "the cups / That cheer but not inebriate. . . ."

[On Samuel Rogers][1]

My Cot is by St. James's[2] hill,
The hum of Pall Mall soothes mine ear;
Whose endless crowd flows onward still
While many a cab-stand lingers near.

The Witling underneath my thatch
Oft twitters out his little jest:

And Lansdowne[3] often lifts my latch,
And I lift his—a welcome guest.
Around my breakfast table springs
Each happy soul that breathes my praise:
And Moore[4] at my piano sings
The amorous songs of other days.

St. James's Church, where Bishops ease
The conscience of each high-born sinner
With merry murmur swells the breeze
And points with golden hand *to dinner*—

[1] It is impossible to assign these verses to a specific date. They are taken from a MS among the letters to Bernard Barton at the University of Virginia and, therefore, must have been written before 1849.

EFG parodies "A Wish" by the banker-poet Samuel Rogers, who made a practice of entertaining at breakfast. The original poem of four quatrains reads in part:

Mine be a cot beside the hill;
A bee-hive's hum shall sooth my ear
. . .

The swallow, oft, beneath my thatch,
Shall twitter from her clay-built nest:
Oft shall the pilgrim lift the latch,
And share my meal, a welcome guest.

The poem concludes:

The village church, among the trees,
Where first our marriage-vows were given,
With merry peals shall swell the breeze,
And point with taper spire to heaven.

[2] Rogers lived at 22 St. James's Place.

[3] Henry Petty FitzMaurice (1780-1863), third Marquess of Lansdowne, statesman and art patron.

[4] Thomas Moore, Irish lyric poet.

To Frederick Tennyson

Boulge, Woodbridge
Dec[r] 8/44

My dear Frederic,

What is a poor devil to do? You tell me quite truly that my letters have not two ideas in them, and yet you tell me to write my two ideas as soon as I can. So indeed it is so far easy to write down one's two ideas, if they are not very abstruse ones; but then what the devil encouragement is it to a poor fellow to expose his nakedness so? All I can say is, to say again that if you lived in this place, you would not write so long a letter as you have done, full of capital description and all good things; though without any compliment I am sure you would write a better than I shall. But you see the original fault in me is that I choose to be in such a place as this at all; that argues certainly a talent for dullness which no situation nor intercourse of men could much improve. It is true; I really do like to sit in this doleful place with a good fire, a cat and a dog on the rug, and an old woman in the kitchen. This is all my live stock. The house is yet damp as last year; and the great event of this winter is my putting up a trough round the eaves to carry off the wet. There was discussion whether the trough should be of iron or of zinc; iron dear and lasting; zinc the reverse. It was decided for iron; and accordingly iron is put up.

Why should I not live in London and see the world? you say. Why then *I* say as before—I don't like it. I think the dullness of country people is better than the impudence of Londoners; and the fresh cold and wet of our clay fields better than a fog that stinks *per se*;[1] and this room of mine, clean at all events, better than a dirty room in Charlotte St. If you, Morton, and Alfred, were more in London, I should be there more; but now there is but Spedding and Allen whom I care a straw about. I have written two notes to Alfred to ask him just to notify his existence to me; but you know he is obstinate on that point. I heard from Carlyle that he (Alfred) had passed an evening at Chelsea much to C.'s delight; who has opened the gates of his Valhalla to let Alfred in.[2] Thackeray is at Malta, where I am told he means to winter;[3] and old Morton yet abides with his Mother and sisters at Plymouth; which I am very glad of. He writes to me, and complains as you do of my dull letters; so you see I don't pour out all my Treasures to him; for in fact I have none to pour.

As I have no people to tell you of, so have I very few books, and know nothing of what is stirring in the literary world. I have read the Life of Arnold of Rugby, who was a noble fellow;[4] and the letters of Burke, which do not add to, or detract from, what I knew and liked in him before. I am meditating to begin Thucydides one day; perhaps this winter.

The same post which brought your letter from London here, brought one from poor Moore,[5] who still struggles on in London. I cannot think how he subsists—he and his wife. He has sold nothing: and has quarrelled with all who would have bought, or made others buy. Did I tell you all this in so many words before? Was it one of those two ideas which went to fill my last letter?

Old Seneca, I have no doubt, was a great humbug in deed, and his books have plenty of it in word; but he had got together a vast deal of what was not humbug from others; and, as far as I see, the old philosophers are available now as much as two thousand years back. Perhaps you will think that is not saying much. Don't suppose I think it good philosophy in myself to keep here out of the world, and sport a gentle Epicurism; I do not; I only follow something of a natural inclination, and know not if I could do better under a more complex system. It is very smooth sailing hitherto down here. No velvet waistcoat and ever-lustrous pumps to be considered; no bon mots got up; no information necessary. There is a pipe for the parsons to smoke, and quite as much bon mots, literature, and philosophy as they care for without any trouble at all. If we could but feed our poor! It is now the 8th of December; it has blown a most desperate East wind, all razors—a wind like one of those knives one sees at shops in London, with 365 blades all drawn and pointed; the wheat is all sown; the fallows cannot be ploughed. What are all the poor folks to do during the winter? And they persist in having the same enormous families they used to do; a woman came to me two days ago who had seventeen children! What farmers are to employ all these! What Landlord can find room for them! The law of Generation must be repealed. The London press does nothing but rail at us poor country folks for our cruelty.[6] I am glad they do so; for there is much to be set right. But I want to know if the Editor of the Times is more attentive to his devils, their wives and families, than our squires and squiresses and parsons are to their fellow parishioners.[7] Punch also assumes a tone of virtuous satire—from the mouth of Mr. Douglas Jerrold![8] It is easy to sit in arm chairs at a club in Pall Mall and rail on the stupidity and brutality of those in High Suffolk.[9]

Come, I have got more than two ideas into this sheet; but I don't know if you won't dislike them worse than mere nothing. But I was determined to fill my letter. Yes—you are to know that I slept at Woodbridge last night, went to Church there this morning, where every one sat with a purple nose, and heard a dismal well-meant sermon; and the organ blew us out with one grand idea at all events—one of old Handel's Coronation Anthems; that I dined early, also in Woodbridge; and walked up here with a tremendous East wind blowing sleet in my face from over the German Sea, that I found your letter when I entered my room; and reading it through, determined to spin you off a sheet incontinently, and lo! here it is! Now or never! I shall now have my tea in, and read over your letter again while at it. You are quite right in saying that Gravesend excursions with you do me good; when did I doubt it? I remember them with great pleasure; few of my travels so much so. I like a short journey in good company; and I like you all the better for your Englishman's humours. One doesn't find such things in London; something more like it here in the country, where every one, with whatever natural stock of intellect endowed, at least grows up his own way, and flings his branches about him, not stretched on the espalier of London dinner-table company. When shall I see you again? When, even, do you talk of coming to England? I shall never go to Italy! Write when you can.

Ever yours,
E.FG.

P.S. Next morning. Snow over the ground. We have our wonders of inundation in Suffolk also, I can tell you. For three weeks ago such floods came, that an old woman was carried off as she was retiring from a beer house about 9 P.M., and drowned. She was probably half seas over before she left the beer house.

And three nights ago I looked out at about ten at night, before going to bed. It seemed perfectly still; frosty, and the stars shining bright. I heard a continuous moaning sound, which I knew to be, not that of an infant exposed, or female ravished, but of the sea, more than ten miles off! What little wind there was carried to us the murmurs of the waves circulating round these coasts so far over a flat country. But people here think that this sound so heard is not from the waves that break, but a kind of prophetic voice from the body of the sea itself announcing great gales. Sure enough we have got them, however heralded. Now I say that all this shows that we in this Suffolk are not so completely given over to prose and turnips as some would have us. I always said that being near the sea, and being able to catch a glimpse of it from the tops of hills, and of houses, redeemed Suffolk from dullness; and at all events that our turnip fields, dull in themselves, were at least set all round with an undeniably poetic element. And so I see Arnold says; he enumerates five inland counties as the only parts of England for which nothing could be said in praise.[10] Not that I agree with him there neither; I cannot allow the valley of the Ouse, about which some of my pleasantest recollections hang, to be without its great charm. W. Browne, whom you despised, is married;[11] and I shall see but little of him for the future. I have laid by my rod and line by the willows of the Ouse for ever. "He is married, and cannot come."[12] This change is the true meaning of those verses,

Friend after friend departs—
Who has not lost a friend?[13]

and so on. If I were conscious of being stedfast and good humoured enough, I would marry tomorrow. But a humourist is best by himself.

[1] The 1844 autumn fogs had been especially dense. Smoke from homes, factories, breweries, locomotives, and steamboats poured into moisture-laden air to produce fogs, sometimes white, often "pea-soup." On November 21 "the worst fog within the memory of man descended on London" (John W. Dodds, *The Age of Paradox*, New York, 1952, p. 191). Omnibuses were kept off the streets and river traffic was suspended.

[2] See letter from Carlyle, Oct. 26, 1844. When EFG speaks of Carlyle's letting Alfred enter his "Valhalla," he does not mean that this is Tennyson's first visit but that Carlyle has accepted him wholeheartedly as a friend. Tennyson and Carlyle first met in 1840.

[3] Thackeray did not break his Mediterranean tour to winter at Malta. He arrived at the island on his return journey on October 27 and spent 19 days there—15 of them required by the quarantine regulations.

[4] Many writers of memoirs of the time speak of their great admiration for Arnold, after reading Stanley's *Life*.

The Correspondence of Edmund Burke, 1744-1797 had just been published. It was edited by Charles William Wentworth, Earl Fitzwilliam (1786-1857), assisted by Sir Richard Bourke (1777-1855), a relative of Edmund Burke's.

[5] See letter to Milnes, [June, 1843].

[6] EFG was speaking not of specific articles in the *Times* and *Punch* but of numerous articles and letters appearing at this time that exposed and attacked conditions among agricultural workers.

[7] Unfortunately for FitzGerald, the position of the landowners, it appears, was vulnerable. When the potato crop failed the following autumn, the Council of the Royal Agricultural Society advised farm laborers that bones could be bought from butchers for 2d and even with a third boiling would provide some nutriment (Walpole, *History*, V, 130, summarizing a statement in the *Times* of Oct. 24, 1845).

[8] Douglas Jerrold (1803-57), miscellaneous author and dramatist, a constant contributor to *Punch* from 1841 to 1857.

[9] Britain experienced a severe depression during the decade which has aptly been called "The Hungry Forties." An agricultural England was being converted into an industrial and commercial England. Discontent and criticism were manifestations of a complex pattern of group interests which crystallized during the transformation. Growing industrial and commercial groups challenged privileges held by the landed classes. The hapless laboring classes, grossly underpaid and inarticulate, were championed by humanitarians who clamored for the redress of poverty and suffering. The emphasis placed on the plight of farmers and agricultural workers resulted from the fact that the Corn Laws were under direct fire in the controversy. The laws were attacked by reformers and malcontents and zealously defended by the landowners, who held a majority in Parliament.

The Corn Laws fixed duties on grains and controlled their importation. Prices were kept artificially high whether domestic crops were good or lean. Landowners profited, non-agricultural groups complained, laborers suffered. "I be protected," one laborer declared, "and I be starving" (Walpole, *History*, V, 54). The Anti-Corn-Law League agitated for repeal. Nationwide discontent and the failure of the potato crop in Ireland and of grain in England forced Robert Peel, who had taken the office of Prime Minister as a conservative and protectionist, to repeal the Corn Laws in 1846. EFG, understandably, speaks as one of the landed gentry when, in a letter to Barton in November, 1845, he calls Peel "a humbug."

10 The five counties: Warwick, Northampton, Huntingdon, Cambridge, and Bedford. "Suffolk," Arnold added, "which is otherwise just as bad, has its bit of sea-coast" (Stanley's *Life and Correspondence*, I, 53).

11 Browne was married July 30 to Elizabeth Elliot of Bedford.

12 In Christ's parable of "the great supper," one of the invited guests refuses, saying, "I have married a wife, and therefore I cannot come" (*Luke* 14:20).

13 From "Friends," by James Montgomery (1771-1854), popular minor poet.

To Bernard Barton

Brighton
Decr 29/44

Dear Barton,

I sit here at home this very wet Sunday; and having looked over a volume of Blackwood, will now endite you a note all about nothing. I had yesterday a letter from Crabbe, to whom I had written about some parish business. Tell him if you see him, or write to him, that he is too severe on our poor Beauty.[1] He wishes "God may soon take him to himself!" The poor Beauty.

Well and did my turkey eat well[2]—and were you merry? Who dined with you? or were you all alone? I called on the Procters[3] and saw Mrs.—and left a bird for them—and on the day I came here, I was touched on the shoulder, and when I turned, there was my dear little Barry, all muffled up from the cold, and his kind blue eyes, come to thank me. I was sorry I could not go to eat with him.

I return to London on Thursday, and shall be there for near a week; as I have a heap of engagements to fulfil. But in the middle of the week after this, I shall be borne down into Suffolk again, and tell you all the wonders I have met. How do you like Vestiges of Creation?[4] Are you all turned infidels—or Atheists, as Mrs. Jarley[5] was minded to become. I have not thought very much of the *Acarus Crossii*[6] since I have been here; but I shall meditate upon it again when I get to Suffolk. Here one's thoughts are quite enough occupied with the phenomenon of living with the roaring unsophisticated ocean at one side, and four miles length of idle, useless, ornamental population on the other.

I find in these older Blackwoods some fine papers by DeQuincey, as I suppose. Surely no one else can roll out such sentences as I find here —a style which has not yet quite subsided from the Opium agitation.

And now I am going to eat some lunch and go to Church. It rains cats and dogs. We are all pretty well here. On *Thursday* I shall be at 19 Charlotte St., Rathbone Place—mind that.

And now I am ever yours,

Edwd. FitzGerald

[1] EFG's parrot, Beauty Bob.

[2] EFG had considered spending Christmas with Barton but joined his mother at Brighton instead.

[3] For Procter, Barry Cornwall, see letter to F. Tennyson, Dec. 10, 1843, n.1. EFG later made a practice of sending the Procters a brace of pheasants each Christmas season.

[4] *Vestiges of the Natural History of Creation*, an anonymous work in which a theory of evolution was expounded, created a sensation when published in October, 1844. The author, Robert Chambers (1802-71), a member of the Edinburgh firm which published *Chamber's Encyclopedia*, was a competent though self-taught geologist. His book raised a storm of controversy. It was violently attacked by the clergy as "atheistic." Leading scientists, with good reason, condemned it for its fallacies. There was much that was sound in the book; much that was unscientific. Chambers often ignored recognized authorities and drew naively on unreliable and even popular sources. The public, incapable of judging the work on scientific grounds, read the book avidly. Four printings were sold in six months. By drawing the fire of the reactionary orthodox, *Vestiges* prepared the way for Darwin, fifteen years later, a service that Darwin acknowledged in the preface to the 1872 edition of *The Origin of Species.* (A study of Chambers and his book may be found in *Just Before Darwin* by Milton Millhouser, Middletown, Conn., 1959.)

[5] Mrs. Jarley, proprietress of the traveling waxworks in Dickens' *Old Curiosity Shop.* When Little Nell, whom she has sent to distribute handbills at Miss Montflathers' boarding and day school for young ladies, reports Miss Montflathers' threat to have "the genuine and only Jarley" put in the stocks, Mrs. Jarley's wrath "passed all description." "I am a'most inclined," she said, "to turn atheist when I think of it" (chaps. 31 and 32).

[6] *Acarus Crossii,* a mite which caused a great stir in 1837. Andrew Crosse (1784-1855), a pioneer in electrical research, announced that he had produced an arachnid by passing an electric current through a solution of silicate of potash. Crosse's mite was soon identified as *acarus horridus,* a form "which flourishes in the rubbish of chemists' shops" (*Just Before Darwin,* p. 94). Chambers alludes to *acarus Crossii* in *Vestiges* in his chapter on "Origin of the Animated Tribes." Despite authoritative identification of Crosse's arachnid, Chambers clung to *acarus Crossii* as a demonstration of spontaneous generation, a phenomenon which would account for the origin of animal life.

To Bernard Barton

19 Charlotte St.
Rathbone Place
Jany 4/45

Dear Barton,

Clawed hold of by a bad cold am I—a London cold—where the atmosphere clings to you, like a wet blanket. You have often received a letter from me on a Sunday, haven't you? I think I used to write you an account of the picture purchases of the week, that you might have something to reflect upon in your silent meeting. (N.B. This is very wrong, and I don't mean it.) Well, now I have bought no pictures, and sha'n't; but one I *had* bought is sent to be lined. A Bassano of course; which nobody will like but myself. It is a grave picture; an Italian Lord dictating to a Secretary with upturned face.[1] Good company, I think.

You did not tell me how you and Miss Barton got on with the Vestiges.[2] I found people talking about it here; and one laudatory critique in the Examiner sold an edition in a few days. I long to finish it. I am going in state to the London Library—*my* Library[3]—to review the store of books it contains, and carry down a box-full for winter consumption. Do you want anything? eh, Mr. Barton?

I went to see Sophocles' tragedy of Antigone done into English two nights ago.[4] And yesterday I dined with my dear old John Allen who remains whole and intact of the world in the heart of London. He dined some while ago at Lambeth, and the Lady next him asked the Archbishop if he read Punch. Allen thought this was a misplaced question: but I think the Archbishop ought to see Punch: though not to read it regularly perhaps. I then asked Allen about the Vestiges—he had heard of it—laughed at the idea of its being atheistical. "No enquiry," said he, "can be atheistical." I doubt if the Archbishop of Canterbury could say that. What do you think of Exeter?[5] Isn't he a pretty lad?

1 After EFG's death, this painting was listed as "Bassano [Item] 52 A Venetian Nobleman and his Secretary" in the Christie sale catalogue. A notation gives the selling price at the auction, held December 8, 1883, as £2 2s. Another of EFG's Bassanos, "The Adoration of the Shepherds," brought £21 at the same sale.

2 *Vestiges of Creation* by Robert Chambers. See letter to Barton, Dec. 29, 1844, n.4. The review to which EFG subsequently refers appeared in *The Examiner*, Nov. 9, 1844, pp. 707-09.

3 Probably his first visit to the Library. He had been proposed for membership by Carlyle in October.

[4] First produced in London with Mendelssohn's music on January 2, 1845, the night EFG attended. For details of the performance, see letter to F. Tennyson, Feb. 6, 1845, n.4.

[5] Henry Phillpotts (1778-1869), named Bishop of Exeter in 1831, was a staunch champion of High Church. EFG favored Low Church. "The most polemical of bishops," as Exeter is called by Spencer Walpole, vigorously opposed all liberal measures proposed in Parliament. As a legislator, he evolved strange interpretations of the faith he espoused. When a municipal reform bill for Ireland was passed in 1840, he protested that "by this wilful and deliberate abandonment of the cause of true religion . . . we have provoked the justice of Almighty God, and have given too much reason to apprehend the visitation of Divine vengeance for this presumptuous act of national disobedience" (Walpole, *History*, IV, 207). EFG is probably alluding to efforts by the Bishop to impose ritualism on evangelical congregations.

To Bernard Barton

London, Saturday
Pmk., January 11, 1845

Dear Barton,

My illness has been no more than a cold—which made me snivel for three days—and is now gone. Thank you for your enquiries however. Land is in sight! Yo ho!—in the middle of next week I shall form a trio with dog and cat in the cottage parlour! I have waited here chiefly for my Father; whom I have just left till dinner time. He dines with the Woods[1] tomorrow. I am going to call on them today—now—in half an hour.

I spent one evening with Carlyle, but was very dull somehow, and delighted to get out into the street. An organ was playing a polka even so late in the street: and Carlyle was rather amazed to see me polka down the pavement.[2] He shut his street door—to which he always accompanies you—with a kind of groan. He was looking well—but he says he gets no sleep of nights. This comes of having a great idea, which, germinating once in the mind, grows like a tape worm, and consumes the vitals. What a nasty idea.

Last night I went to hear Handel's Messiah—nobly done. But here again I was glad to get into the street before it was half over. So I doubt I can't hold out the heroic long. "Let me plant cabbages!" was the well considered prayer of Panurge;[3] and it is rather mine. But honour to the Carlyles, who, giving up their own prospect of cabbages, toil and sweat in the spirit that we may plant ours in peace.

Don't you like to get a letter upon a Sunday more than on any other day in the week? Have you read a foolish looking letter by Mr. Edge[4] in the Ipswich Journal? It is about Dissent. I say foolish-looking, because I only looked at it in Portland Place just now. So I am the fool, by that logic. But Edge combats an ultra Churchman who asserted that a Dissenting Chapel was the cradle of all vice; and the Edge says it is not *quite* so bad as that. This is a wretched position to take. And he says "Let us be just before we are logical"!!! My powers! What would Plato say to this! As if justice were not the very outcome of logic. The old saying "Be just before you are generous"[5] distinguishes this well.

I don't think this letter is heroic enough to make *you* dance the Polka when you've got through it. And now it is high time for you to be off to your meeting: so mind you don't *polk* there. That would be worse than a Quaker murdering. You ought not to be ashamed of one murderer: your community should keep his body in a glass case for ever.

Farewell. Ever yours,
E.FG.

1 William Page Wood, son-in-law of the FitzGerald's Suffolk neighbor, Major Moor.

2 EFG, "a beautiful dancer," according to his sister Mrs. Wilkinson, had apparently fallen victim of the polka fad which had "spread like an infection" from Bohemia, where it had been "discovered" among the folk dances. *Punch*, on April 14, 1844, under the title, "The Polka Mania," reported that the *Times* "teems with the advertisements" of individuals "prepared to instruct the public in the mysteries of the Polka" (p. 169). A week later, the *Sunday Times* recorded, "This dance, which has lately driven the Parisians almost crazy, and is likely to do the same with many of John Bull's offspring, was introduced . . . two years ago into this country from Baden-Baden" (quoted in *News from the Past, 1805-1887*, Yvonne Ffrench, ed., n.d., p. 333). At its height, the fad begot the polka hat and polka jacket, a tight-fitting garment, usually knitted, for women; and the polka necktie for men. A vestige of the polka craze survives in the still familiar polka dots.

3 The witty, cowardly buffoon in Rabelais' *Gargantua and Pantagruel.* He utters his panegyric of the cabbage planter during a storm at sea in Book IV, Section 18. See letter to Cowell, Jan. 28, [1845], n.3.

4 The Reverend William Edge was Rector of Naughton and Nedging, a few miles north of Hadleigh, Suffolk.

5 So Charles Surface advises Rowley, an old servant, in Sheridan's *School for Scandal* (1777), IV, 1.

From Alfred Tennyson

10 St James' Square, Cheltenham
Tuesday Night, Jan. 14th, 1845

My dear Fitz,

I *had* heard the news.[1] No gladness crossed my heart but sorrow and pity: that's not theatrical but the truth; wherefore bear with me, tho' perhaps it may seem a little out of the tide of things. Now will you be at 19 C[harlotte] S[treet] tomorrow or the day after? I am coming up to see you, and shall arrive most probably between 9 and 10 P.M., when I trust I shall find you well and thriving.

Ever yours,
A.T.

[1] News of the death of Dr. Matthew Allen. After the failure of the pyroglyph venture, Edmund Lushington, Tennyson's brother-in-law, took out an insurance policy on Allen in favor of Tennyson. Lushington's wife, Cecilia, had written to Frederick in December, 1844, "I suppose thou knowest that Alfred will get most of his money back . . . to secure this Edmund pays some eighty pounds a year for him" (*Letters to Frederick Tennyson*, p. 58). Carlyle told EFG that the policy was for £2,000. (See letter from Carlyle, Feb. 6, 1845.)

To Bernard Barton

19 Charlotte St., etc.
Friday
[January 17, 1845]

Dear Barton,

I was all prepared for going into Suffolk today: but I got a note from A. Tennyson yesterday, saying he was coming to London, and wished to see me. So I waited: and last night he came: looking much better: but a valetudinarian almost:—not in the effeminate way; but yet in as bad a man's way. Alas for it, that great thoughts are to be lapped in such weakness. Dr. Allen, who had half swindled his money, is dead: and A. T. having a Life insurance, and Policy, on him,[1] will now, I hope, retrieve the greater part of his fortune again. Apollo certainly did this: shooting one of his swift arrows at the heart of the Doctor; whose perfectly heartless conduct certainly upset A. T.'s nerves in the first instance.

I have sent your letter and its enclosure to Mrs. Jones:—for you do not specify *what* the situation is. But I hope she will enquire directly, and satisfy herself. It is very good of you to remember her. Ah! I shall be glad to be back in the land where such little offices are thought of! Could it be offered to me to write another Iliad, or to live down to my three score years and ten (if it is for me to fulfil that number) in the daily remembrance of such small charities, I should not hesitate which to choose. Of all sayings, none is to me so touching as that of the good Emperor Titus—"I have lost a day!"[2] I always wonder Dante did not expatiate more on one who certainly was so Christian at heart.

I have bought two heads lately: for thirty shillings a piece—one Venetian as usual: the other a very sweet sketch by Harlow, or Sir T. Lawrence[3]—as I think. The latter is much injured and must be repaired. You shall see it one day: and you will like it much. Tell Churchyard I am *angry* he did not come and see me. There he was gadding over London for three days.

Farewell. Next Monday or Tuesday! On them I fix my eyes. Ever yours,

E.FG.

Thackeray travels in the East: I send you one of his Punch sketches[4] concerning his travels.

[1] See previous letter (from A. Tennyson), n.1.

[2] The lament of Roman Emperor Titus (A.D. 40-81) at supper one day when he had failed to find a single recipient for his lavish generosity, "Amici, hodie diem perdidi." ("Friends, today I have lost a day.")

[3] George Henry Harlow (1787-1819), portrait and historical painter, who was an opponent of the Royal Academy. He had spent eighteen months in the studio of Sir Thomas Lawrence.

[4] Thackeray's drawing is of a man, with nightcap, sitting up in bed. He is picking a bug off the bedclothes, while a half-dozen mosquitoes fly about his head. The caption reads, "Arabian Nights' Entertainments" (*Punch*, Jan. 11, 1845, p. 35). For Thackeray's Eastern trip, see letter to F. Tennyson, Oct. 10, 1844, n.4.

To E. B. Cowell[1]

Boulge, Woodbridge
Janr^{y} 28, [1845]

My dear Sir,

I was very happy to receive your letter: and also that I was able to construe your French, and your Greek. As I hope, at least: for I am a very superficial scholar: having much neglected to learn when I was at school: and having but in the last ten years dug out of dictionaries and grammars just enough to give me some insight into the great Authors —long dead. This kind of Scholarship lies much on the surface—soon come soon gone: I believe that I have got some of the substance of these great Authors into my head, and am able to estimate what room they fill in the learning of the world—but the languages they wrote in slide and slide away from my head: and I know not if I shall have time or patience in future to keep up a serviceable amount of Latin and Greek. And yet how easy to read Homer every year: and three or four Greek Plays: and some Plato—some Tacitus; all Virgil's Georgics!

Your man Sallust[2] I had never heard of. His Quotation is good: but does it tell you much? That it is the nature of God to be God—that he cannot help being God—etc. This I dare say comes from the Hindoos —perhaps through earlier Greeks—as does probably the passage about Dreams from Rabelais: which is Plato's, I think. The Rabelais passage is beautifully written, and illustrated. Surely I never denied him merit; I only said he had been over-rated. I think he might well drop out of the world now—his task is done! Surely the heap of trash and filth, which may have allegorized or adumbrated evils which have now got rectified or exploded, surely these are in the proportion of twenty to one to the good or beautiful in Rabelais. The passage about Thelema[3] which you tell me is *θέλημα*, is surely no great stretch of fancy—it is all included in the name—the people of "What-you-will" do what they will.

If you will needs however exhaust your eyes over books which are now pushed back in the shelves that others may stand more conveniently for use before them, mind you make extracts of what there *is* good, either in thought or expression. And then we will keep that, and push the books further back, out of sight if possible. For what is the world to do, if books go on accumulating? I think the only way is to read the best man of his Age on his own matter, and to suppose that he speaks the best sense of all. The present day teems with new discoveries *in Fact*, which are greater, even as regards the Soul and prospect of Man, than all the disquisitions and quiddities of the Schoolmen. A few fossil bones in clay and limestone have opened a greater vista back into Time than the Indian imagination ventured upon for its Gods: and every day turns up something new. But no new discovery can give us a Homer, or an Aeschylus: we must take these in first of all. It is right these should be taught at School; and *not* Useful Knowledge. For the Useful Knowledge we can learn at any time: but not so with the Ancient History and Epic, the foundation of so much Reverence and Imagination.

Mine, you see, is a longer letter than yours; but then it is as a first avowal of the whole subject. I shall not expatiate thus in future: but notice what I can of the extracts you send me. Keep a good Commonplace book.[4] I read a novel of George Sand a month ago: and thought it very clever, and very immoral. But one must see what all the world is doing in France. I only wish so many London ladies would not have her (George S.) on their drawing room tables.

One day I hope to see you over here: and that you will have a great deal to tell me.

Yours truly
Edward FitzGerald

[1] This is the first of more than three hundred letters to Edward Byles Cowell, who, in 1852, persuaded EFG to learn Persian. Cowell had previously coached his friend in Spanish. See Biographical Profile.

[2] Sallust (c. 86-34 B.C.), Roman historian, who modeled his work on Thucydides.

[3] In Rabelais' *Gargantua and Pantagruel*, Thelema is the abbey which Gargantua and his father built to reward Friar John for his valor in their war with Picrochole (I, 52, et seq.). The abbey was intended to be the opposite in every way of ordinary monasteries and convents. There were no confining walls, for example, and the library was filled with the works of the Humanists. The only rule was "Fay ce que vouldras." ("Do what you like.") The novel satirizes warfare, monasticism, education, the professions, etc. θέλημα means "will."

[4] Throughout his life EFG filled notebooks with extracts culled from his wide reading. Some were devoted to specific topics; most of them contained miscellaneous excerpts; to some, he gave titles. Into the "Paradise Book" he copied favorite passages of poetry. A "Museum Book" was compiled from reading in the British Museum. One volume bears the title, "Half Hours with Obscure Authors"; another is filled with portions of debates in Parliament. EFG also made up scrapbooks. Ten of these, the gift of his grandniece, Mary Eleanor FitzGerald Kerrich, are now in the Christchurch Mansion Museum, Ipswich.

To W. B. Donne

Boulge
Jan[y] 29/45

My dear Donne,

How do you thrive? I have been away for five weeks—two at Brighton[1] and three in London: during which latter I saw many old friends—Spedding, Thompson, Blakesley and other Collegians. Also

A. Tennyson suddenly came up, fresh from Water Cure, and drinking a bottle of wine daily.[2] The man who swindled his money died suddenly —and A. T. is come in (I hope) for a Life Insurance, or Policy, or what the Devil they call it, so that Apollo seems to have directly interfered, and slain the offending Doctor[3] with one of those sudden painless darts which Homer tells of. A. T. has near a volume of poems—elegiac—in memory of Arthur Hallam.[4] Don't you think the world wants other notes than elegiac now? Lycidas is the utmost length an elegiac should reach.[5] But Spedding praises: and I suppose the elegiacs will see daylight—public daylight—one day. Carlyle goes on growling with his Cromwell: whom he finds more and more faultless every day. So that *his* paragon also will one day see the light also—an elegiac of a different kind from Tennyson's—as far apart indeed as Cromwell and Hallam.

Barton comes and sups with me to-morrow, and George Crabbe, son of the poet, a capital fellow. We shall smoke and drink and tell dirty stories. When do you mean to come and see me? When the fine weather comes. Kerrich is, I hear, better: he is coming over here in a few days: and I suppose in a few weeks I shall go to Geldestone—with perhaps a detour to Norwich—which I have now got a regard for.

Farewell. Is Charles gone to School?[6] Believe me ever yours,

E. FitzGerald

[1] Where he spent Christmas with his mother.

[2] The wine Tennyson favored was port, and the daily bottle appears to have been his normal portion for most of his life. This, EFG believed during the 1840's at least, was more than the poet's state of health warranted; and so he implies in a number of letters. For EFG's diagnosis of the reasons for Tennyson's drinking, see letter to Spring Rice, Oct. 24, 1853.

[3] Matthew Allen. See letter from A. Tennyson, Jan. 14, 1845, n.1.

[4] Tennyson had been writing the poems since the death of his friend Hallam in 1833. Although EFG did not think highly of them, their publication under the title *In Memoriam* in 1850 established Tennyson as Britain's foremost poet and led to his being named Poet Laureate later in the year.

[5] Tennyson greatly admired Milton's "Lycidas" and called it "a touchstone of poetic taste," EFG wrote to Fanny Kemble in 1880.

[6] Donne's sons received their earlier education at home. Charles Edward, his eldest boy, 13 years old, was sent to school at Norwich in 1845.

To Frederick Tennyson

Boulge, Woodbridge
Feby 6, 1845

My dear Frederic,

I hope my last letter, which contained all the ideas I could pick up or invent, got safe to you at Florence. But you, in your proper anxiety to write the direction well, wrote it so ill, that I doubt if I copied it right after all. But I will again let fly upon the same tack. You like to hear of men and manners. Have I not been to London for a whole fortnight—seen Alfred, Spedding—all the lawyers and all the painters—gone to Panoramas of Naples by Volcano-light[1] (Vesuvius in a blaze illuminating the whole bay, which Morton says is not a bit better than Plymouth Sound, if you could put a furnace in the belly of Mount Edgecumbe)[2]—gone to see the Antigone of Messrs. Sophocles and Mendelssohn at Covent Garden—gone to see Infant Thalia—now as little of an Infant as a Thalia—at the Adelaide Gallery?[3] So! you see all things go on as when you were with us. Only the Thalia has waxed in stature: and perhaps in wisdom also: but that is not in her favour. The Antigone is, as you are aware, a neatly constructed drama, on the French model: the music very fine, *I* thought—but you would turn up your nose at it, I dare say. It was horribly ill sung, by a chorus in shabby togas, who looked much more like dirty bakers than Theban (were they?) respectable old gentlemen. Mr. Vandenhoff[4] sat on a marble camp-stool in the middle, and looked like one of Flaxman's Homeric Kings[5]—very well. And Miss Vandenhoff did Antigone. I forget the name of the Lady who did Ismene; perhaps you would have thought her very handsome: but I did not—nor was she generally considered at all remarkable, as far as I could make out. I saw no pantomimes:[6] and all the other theatres were filled with Balfe[7]—whom perhaps you admire very much. So I won't say anything about him till you have told me what you think on his score.

And Dr. Allen is dead![8] Did you know this? He died of disease in the heart. Let no man say henceforth that anything is made in vain. Alfred came up to London, smitten with some sorrow. But he took no steps concerning the matter, and I left him in London—smoking, as when first I saw him.[9] The water business would do him good if he gave it fair chance—but he smokes, and drinks a bottle of wine a day. He looks however twice as well as he did a year ago; and is certainly in better spirits. I suppose he will go over to Italy one day, won't he? Perhaps he ought to do so.

Well and have you read "Eothen" which all the world talks of: and do you know who it is written by? Why by Devil Kinglake,[10] to be sure. So now Herbert is a great novelist, and the Devil is a great Oriental Traveller. Poor Milnes' "Palm Leaves"[10] (or as Thackeray pronounces it "Burn leaves") are quite faded by the side of the Devil's reckless, magnanimous, Byronic, adventures. Young England[11] sentiment stands no chance beside of him. The Devil stays a fortnight in Cairo while all but himself die of the plague—he sits and smiles on it all, like Melmoth—the Wanderer.[12] Milnes has never done such a thing as that. What a series of sonnets he would [have] made on the Plague! but all the series of Sonnets I have ever seen lean that way.

Then Eliot Warburton[10] has written an Oriental Book! Ye Gods! In Shakespeare's day the nuisance was the Monsieur Travellers who had "swum in a gundello";[13] but now the bores are those who have smoked *tschibouques*[14] with a *Peshaw*! Deuce take it: I say 'tis better to stick to muddy Suffolk.

Last night I read that when James the First went to open a Parliament in 1620—the first for seven years—he was very gracious to the people in the street, as he wanted money. He kept calling out "God bless ye. God bless ye." as he went along—whereas his usual exclamation on such occasions used to be "Pox take ye. Pox take ye." Even now, as he passed, he saw some ladies dressed in yellow bands at a window. And then he called out "Pox take ye, etc." to them—at which they all retired in confusion. I suppose he hated women in yellow, as he was a very crotchetty prince. I read all this in a journal of the time. Does it amuse you? Is it not an idea?[15] Well, if it is not, then I know nothing else to give you. I must come to my garden—my damp house—the bad cold I have got, etc. Snow covers the ground. Allow me to state that one fact: and no more of local news. The river has not inundated again since I last wrote. Has yours? Give my kind remembrances to Septimus and to Arthur, whom I am not sure that ever I saw. But all the Tennysons are to be wished well. And fare you well, and write me a long letter one day with ever so few ideas. I'll be hanged if this is not [a] thundering big letter. Morton still dwells at Plymouth.

Ever yours
E.FG.

[1] Created by Robert Burford (1791-1861) and exhibited in Leicester Square. "The view is taken from the bay . . . The Castle receives the full blaze of the flames of Vesuvius . . . The more distant parts of the picture are lighted by the

tender rays of the moon, and a fine contrast of effect is afforded from the conjunction of these two lights" (*The Gentleman's Magazine*, Feb., 1845, p. 175). Burford, who made a career of painting panoramas, also exhibited at the Royal Academy.

The panorama and its variants provided a popular form of Victorian entertainment. In a panorama the scene was painted on canvas which covered the inner wall of an immense cylindrical structure. Spectators viewed it as from a fixed point. At the Colosseum in Regent's Park, the panorama was of London as seen from the top of St. Paul's. The spectator saw "a sublime and magnificent view of the metropolis," as well as a minutely accurate picture "of every particular house that can be discerned" from the Cathedral. The scene covered 46,000 square feet of canvas (Cunningham's *London*, I, 230). The space between spectators and the panorama was filled with actual objects, with proportions artfully graduated so that foreground blended into the picture. Admission to the Colosseum was 1s.

Daguerre, before he perfected his photographic method, painted and exhibited panoramas, and with a partner devised the diorama, a complex panoramic mutation. Spectators of a diorama sat on a revolving platform from which they observed views seen through apertures or windows. One diorama produced "The Earthquake at Lisbon." The city was first shown bathed in sunshine, then clouds gathered, a thunderstorm broke, the river flooded, and repeated tremors, with appropriate sound effects, demolished buildings (M. Wilson Disher, *Pleasures of London*, 1950, p. 195). Contemporary sources also mention cycloramas, cosmoramas, udoramas, and stereoramas.

[2] A promontory about 450 feet high, on the west shore of the Sound, opposite the city of Plymouth.

[3] The Royal Adelaide Gallery, Lowther Arcade, Strand, offered variety entertainment, including that by various "Infants." Later in 1845, the *Illustrated London News* (June 28) announced that "the performance of the Infant Sappho will take place," alternating with a "Lecture on Character—Mr. J. Russell . . . with Musical Illustrations."

[4] John Vandenhoff and his daughter Charlotte played Creon and Antigone. The part of Ismene was taken by Mrs. J. Cooke (whose name EFG could not remember). The critics agreed with EFG in his estimate of the chorus. The *Globe* critic wrote, "Half these learned Thebans of the chorus might be dispensed with, the remainder drilled into something like precision of voice, and especially of gesticulation." However, it appears that the music director, George Macfarren, had followed instructions from Mendelssohn. In sending regrets that he could not cross to England to see the performance, the composer wrote, "Pray have very good solo voices to sing the quartet, and a very powerful chorus; and let them sing the choral recitatives with great energy, and *not in time*, but quite as a common recitative, following each other, and thus keeping together. It sounds as if impossible, but is very easy thus (*Annals of Covent Garden Theatre*, II, 176).

[5] John Flaxman (1755-1826), sculptor, completed his 80 designs in illustration of Homer, the *Iliad* and the *Odyssey*, in 1793. He published *Engravings to Illustrate Homer* in 1805.

[6] Attending a pantomime is still one of the principal events in the Christmas holiday program of British families. Audience participation at identical points in the action delights the young and amuses the old year after year.

[7] See letter to F. Tennyson, Oct. 10, 1844, n.6.

[8] See letter from A. Tennyson, Jan. 14, 1845, n.1.

[9] Mrs. Carlyle said in 1845 that Tennyson was "unlikely to marry, as no woman could live in the atmosphere of tobacco-smoke which he makes about him from morn till night" (Duffy's *Conversations with Carlyle*, p. 5).

[10] Alexander W. Kinglake, Henry W. Herbert (pseudonym, Frank Forester), Richard Monckton Milnes, and Eliot Warburton, all referred to in the following passage, were EFG's contemporaries at Cambridge but were not among his intimate friends, although he corresponded with Milnes. Herbert had published *Marmaduke Wyvil* in 1843. Kinglake, Milnes, and Warburton, in 1844, had published books based on travels in the Near East. Milnes's *Palm Leaves* had resulted from a journey to Constantinople and Cairo in 1835. Kinglake's *Eothen*, a superficial but witty account of a journey the same year, proved to be extremely popular and went through many editions. Warburton had traveled in the East in 1843. His *Crescent and the Cross* achieved fame comparable to that of *Eothen*. He dedicated the book to Milnes.

[11] "Young England" was the faction in the Conservative Party, led by Benjamin Disraeli, which opposed Peel as he moved toward free trade and repeal of the Corn Laws. The times, the group maintained, called for new leaders and enlightened policies. The youth of the nation, declared Disraeli, were the "trustees of prosperity." Young England sought to cancel the rising power of middle-class industrialists, as represented by the Manchester School, and to restore the political prestige of the old, landed aristocracy. The poverty and suffering of the laboring class were to be relieved through a revival of the traditional Tory benevolence of pre-industrial Britain.

[12] *Melmoth the Wanderer* (1820) by Charles R. Maturin, Irish novelist and dramatist. *Melmoth*, which combines the Faust and Wandering Jew legends, is considered to be one of the most powerful of the tales of terror and mystery popular in the early 19th century. Its influence is manifest in the works of numerous writers, both British and Continental.

[13] "Farewell, Mounsieur Travellor," says Rosaline to Jacques, "Look you lispe, and wear strange suites . . . be out of love with your nativity . . . or I will scarce think you have swam in a gundello" (*As You Like It*, IV.1.33-38, First Folio).

[14] Chibouk or chibouque (from Turkish *chibuq*), a Turkish tobacco pipe with clay bowl and a stem four or five feet long. The German spelling is *Tschibuk*, the French, *chibouque*; for the entertainment of his editors, EFG combined the two.

[15] EFG had written on December 8, 1844, "You tell me quite truly that my letters have not two ideas in them, and yet you tell me to write my two ideas as soon as I can."

From Thomas Carlyle

Chelsea, 6 feb^{y}, 1845

Dear Fitzgerald,

Here is a most polite Note from the Duke of Manchester; and indication withal that there *is* one Letter of Oliver's at Kimbolton available to us! I have answered with all politeness, with many thanks; but rolling over upon *you* and the Lady Olivia[1] (without any travelling of mine) the charge of getting me a Copy of this Letter, and even of examining slightly whether there are any more,—what more there otherwise is. You will be helpfully busy in this, according to opportunity? I have said so! It will unfold itself farther when the Duke returns to England, if no sooner. I have said that the Letter would not be wanted 'for a month.' How in the meanwhile you can keep up your relation to the Lady Olivia; how you can proceed duly in general; and, at the soonest possible, *end by giving me a Copy of the Oliver Letter*, —all this is left to your own friendly discretion, with my progress added; I have no other help to add!

Alfred went away on Sunday, I think; twice I met him, the fiery Son of Gloom. There seems no doubt but he will now get hold of £2,000 by Allen's death: I wish he would straightway buy himself an Annuity with it.

I have *three* Booksellers all busy examining *Cromwell's Letters*, and hope to force one of them into some reasonable bargain about it without farther haggling, in a day or two.

Yours ever truly
T. Carlyle

[1] For FitzGerald's note identifying "Lady Olivia," see Carlyle's note on his letter, following.

From Thomas Carlyle

Chelsea, 8 feb^{y}, 1845

Dear Fitzgerald,

I have expressly named you and the Lady Olivia[x] to His Grace, as the benevolent persons who, under Providence and him, are to *get me a Copy* of that Paper or Letter of Oliver's, without further travel or trouble of mine! My own visit to Kimbolton, thankfully acknowledged, and not refused forever, is postponed into the vague distance,—to the rear of this publication of *Oliver's Letters* at least. So pray bestir yourself, and think what can be done! For the thing will be soon wanted. I have, this morning, after infinite higgling to and fro, definitively settled that the Letters and Speeches are actually to be proceeded with as a separate Book Straightway. The *Life* must follow when it can. The *Letters* themselves, I compute, with bits of light kindled at the corners of them, will prove readable to serious rational men; and may tend to clear away much sordid rubbish out of my road, especially to put the controversy about Oliver's "character," "Hypocrisy," etc., etc., asleep forever and a day. So look to the Gainsborough business,[1] look to the Kimbolton business; and help me what you can!

If the Lady Olivia is resident at Kimbolton, and if you were within four miles of her with your friend there,[2] it would not be difficult to get your eye upon the Paper itself, perhaps, and get me the copy of it, the instant the key of the repository were turned. This latter, I suppose, cannot happen till His Grace in person arrive? We must be patient; that date, "a month hence," will still do for me.

I am so weakly, sleepless and unwell at present, I begin thinking of a Horse again.[3] For I am to be very busy. With a long-legged Horse I could ride beautifully up to Kimbolton in summer weather; and see a great many pleasant things there and by the way!

We are very shivery here; grey, dusty and cold.

Yours ever truly
T. Carlyle

[x] Lady Olivia Sparrow; Aunt, I think, to the then Duke of Manchester.

[1] Part of the Lincolnshire campaign.

[2] William Airy, Domestic Chaplain to the Duke of Manchester at Kimbolton Park, three miles north of Keysoe where he was vicar.

[3] Carlyle, a voluble victim of indigestion and insomnia, at times resorted to horseback-riding to overcome his afflictions.

To Bernard Barton

[Boulge Cottage]
[c. February 8, 1845]

Dear Barton,

Going jauntily into a house the other day with the last £20 I had of you in my pocket, I called for a bill which I supposed would come to about £7—leaving me a handsome remainder to pay other accounts due. I therefore cast my eye carelessly on the account produced, and lo! the amount was £19. I did not change countenance, or faint: but with true greatness of mind called for my £1 change, buttoned it up with a smile, and with a cheerful "Good Day" left the house. But the mind—the inward mind—could not in total peace endure. However, I say no more. Silence is great. So is a £20 note.

But no more—no more of that.

In the meanwhile another £20 has become mine at Coutts's[1]—will you kindly get it for me; and keep it ready for me; for have I not Gall, Issitt, Burton of Ipswich, Clark of Bredfield, and Mallett of Woodbridge—to pay for their damned repairs here?[2] I have. And I have got a very bad cold—and a new Grate—a Register—is put up in my room—a Capital thing.[3] When Peel said "Register—Register—Register!"—I now see what he meant.

Carlyle has had a handsome invitation from his Grace of Manchester to go and inspect MSS at Kimbolton.

I shall come to Woodbridge when I can.

Ever yours,
E.FG.

I send three volumes of Pepys for your Lady.[4] Send me back your Xr. North's Recreations,[5] please. Shall you be at home tomorrow?

[1] The banking house.

[2] George Gall, ironmonger; John Issett, hardware dealer, both of Woodbridge; John Clark, Bredfield, "joiner and wheelwright"; Mallett (there were two, John and William), painters, plumbers, and glaziers of Woodbridge. F. R. Barton had difficulty reading EFG's script; he misread Gall, *Gale*, and Issett, *Ipitt* (EFG used the German double *s*) (*New Letters*, p. 78).

[3] The improvements were made to convert the cottage into a year-round home. Until this time EFG had lived at the Hall during winter months.

[4] "Your Lady" was Barton's daughter, Lucy, whom EFG, unhappily, married in 1856.

[5] John Wilson, "Christopher North," *The Recreations of Christopher North*, 3 vols., Edinburgh, 1842.

To W. B. Donne

[Boulge]
[February 27, 1845]

My dear Donne,

I was very glad to hear of you; and glad to hear you say you will come and see me this Spring. I dare say it will be in London then: for I doubt I shall have to go there for some time. This will be no evil to you, however; and indeed it will be better you should make your little holiday there, as you are a Londoner at heart; and we shall see all our friends together.

I had not heard of Geldart's paper:[1] and as for him, he never writes. He must be a very odd man. I suppose it is a religious paper, is it?

If one could have good Lyrics, I think the World wants them as much as ever. Tennyson's are good: but not of the *kind* wanted. We have surely had enough of men reporting their sorrows: especially when one is aware all the time that the poet wilfully protracts what he complains of, magnifies it in the Imagination, puts it into all the shapes of Fancy: and yet we are to condole with him, and be taught to ruminate our losses and sorrows in the same way. I felt that if Tennyson had got on a horse and ridden twenty miles, instead of moaning over his pipe, he would have been cured of his sorrows in half the time. As it is, it is about three years before the Poetic Soul walks itself out of darkness and Despair into Common Sense.[2] Plato would not have allowed such querulousness to be published in his Republic, to be sure: and when we think of the Miss Barretts, Brownes, Jewsburys,[3] etc., who will set to work to feel friends' losses in melodious tears, in imitation of A. T.'s—one must allow Plato was no such prig as some say he was.

I saw Antigone:[4] but, as Vipan[5] says, the music, etc., which was what I went to hear, was execrable. The Audience seemed pleased with the plot and dialogue; I can only say it would have been fine if properly done. It should be done in the Senate House at Cambridge.

You are very good not to hate me for hinting to you what I did about your boys.[6] If one had seen sickly mopes, one would not have troubled oneself about what they wore and what they did—but your boys are handsome, lusty, and spirited. If they are let out free, they run all sorts of hazards to be sure; but then if they don't run these hazards they wil[l] be worth nothing. Have you ever read *Andrew* [Combe's] Book on Physiology and Education?[7] It is not very good: but better than other books: and so all ought to read it.

Where is Vipan? Well, come and see me in London. I will give you due notice of my going thither and place of abode. I shall be very sorry to leave the Country just when the fine weather is coming.

Ever yours,
Edward FitzGerald

[1] For Geldart, see letter to Barton, Aug. 22, 1844, n.1.

[2] The poems commemorating Arthur Hallam had been written over a period of almost seventeen years. In preparing to print them as the elegy, *In Memoriam*, Tennyson arranged the lyrics to indicate the passage of three years, during which the mourner emerges from his initial despair and doubt and achieves hope and faith.

[3] Elizabeth Barrett (1806-61) had already established a reputation as a poetess, and in the following year eloped with Robert Browning.

Miss Browne was probably Mary Anne Browne (1812-44), minor poetess, a niece by marriage of James Hogg, the Ettrick Shepherd. EFG was unaware that she had died the year before.

Maria Jane Jewsbury (1800-33), promising poetess who had been highly praised by Wordsworth and Christopher North, had died of cholera in India; but new editions of her works appeared in 1844 and 1845. She was an older sister of Geraldine Jewsbury, novelist and miscellaneous writer, friend of the Carlyles.

[4] See letter to F. Tennyson, Feb. 6, 1845, n.4.

[5] David Vipan. See letter to Donne, Sept. 27, 1833, n.5.

[6] Donne had three sons: Charles, 13; William Mowbray, 12; and Frederick Clench, 11.

[7] *Principles of Physiology* "applied to . . . physical and mental education," Edinburgh, 1834. "Combe's" has been torn from the MS. Data supplied by Mrs. Neilson C. Hannay.

To Bernard Barton
(Fragment)

Geldestone
April 3/45

My dear Barton,

. . . I have been loitering out in the garden here this golden day of Spring. The wood-pigeons coo in the covert; the frogs croak in the pond; the bees hum about some thyme, and some of my smaller nieces have been busy gathering primroses, "all to make posies suitable to this present month." I cannot but think with a sort of horror of being in London now: but I doubt I must be ere long. . . . I have abjured all Authorship, contented at present with the divine Poem which Great Nature is now composing about us. These primroses seem more wonderful and delicious Annuals than Ackerman ever put forth. I suppose no man ever grew so old as not to feel younger in Spring. Yet, poor old Mrs. Bodham[1] lifted up her eyes to the windows, and asked if it were a clear or a dull day!

[1] Mrs. Anne Donne Bodham, W. B. Donne's great-aunt, with whom the Donnes lived at South Green House, Mattishall. She died the following January at the age of 97. See letter to Allen, Oct. 31, 1835, n.2.

From Thomas Carlyle

Chelsea
April 4, 1845

Dear FitzGerald,

I am got to Naseby—among my letters. I dare not open the big packet, fruit of our joint investigations long ago. I do it from memory, being in haste, double and treble. And so I want you with your best eyes to revise this, which I have got copied for you, and to correct it where you find need. The Main "Hill" you see I have forgotten, and trust to you for.[1]

I have a note off to his Grace of Man$^{\text{tr.}}$,[2] but as yet no answer. In great haste—great and perpetual,

T. Carlyle

[1] Carlyle never altered his initial account of the battle. See letter to Barton, May 14, n.2.

[2] George Montagu (1799-1855), sixth Duke of Manchester, whose ancestor, Edward, second Earl of Manchester, commanded Parliamentary forces in the early years of the Rebellion.

To E. B. Cowell
(Fragment)

[Boulge]
[c. May 1, 1845]

This subject has long been a hobby of mine; and, had I knowledge sufficient, I have the impulse to enlarge on it. It is all talking against myself; for I am as unstrung as any μαθύτης before the φροντιστύριον.[1] Optat ephippia bos piger.[2] My comfort is, I am no longer young.

I set no high value on Selden.[3] His merit is, the putting a discretionary commonsense policy into lively figure. It is not a book fitted for the young—perhaps not for any age!

Well, I have written a long letter after all—which I dare say is half unintelligible.

Farewell
E.FG.

Come and see me in London. I will let you know where I am to be found.

1 "Learner" before the "thinkery"—an allusion to a passage in Aristophanes' satire on the Sophists, *The Clouds* (1.94). Strepsiades, an old man with many debts, applies for admission to Socrates' "thinkery" in order to learn the method of false reasoning so that he can evade paying his just debts.

2 "The ox covets the horse's trappings" (Horace, *Epistles* 1.14.43).

3 The *Table Talk* of John Selden (1689). EFG owned a copy of the 1777 edition. Despite his reservations about Selden, he annotated his copy in preparation for publication. See letter to William Pickering, London publisher, [April, 1846].

To Bernard Barton
(Fragment)

39 Norton St.
FitzRoy Sqr.
[May 14, 1845]

Dear Barton,

You see my address. I only got into it yesterday, though I reached London on Friday, and hung loose upon it for all that interval. I spent four days at Cambridge pleasantly enough; and one at Bedford where I heard my friend Matthews preach.

Last night I appeared at the Opera,[1] and shall do so twice a week till further notice. Friends I have seen but few; for I have not yet found time to do anything. Alfred Tennyson was here; but went off yesterday to consider the sea from the top of Beachy Head. Carlyle gets on with his book which will be in two big volumes. He has entirely misstated all about Naseby, after all my trouble. . . .[2]

Did Churchyard see in London a picture at the address I enclose? The man's card, you see, proclaims "Silversmith," but he is "Pawnbroker." A picture hangs up at the door which he calls by "Williams," but I think is a rather inferior Crome;[3] though the figure in it is not like Crome's figures. The picture is about three feet high by two broad; good in the distance; very natural in the branching of the trees; heavy in the foliage; all common to Crome. And it seems painted in that fat substance he painted in. If C. come to London let him look at this picture, as well as come and see me.

I have cold, head-ache, and London disgust. Oh that I could look on my Anemones! and hear the sighing of my Scotch firs. The Exhibition is full of bad things: there is a grand Turner, however;[4] quite unlike anything that was ever seen in Heaven above, or in Earth beneath, or in the waters under the Earth.

The reign of primroses and cowslips is over, and the oak now begins to take up the empire of the year and wear a budding garland about his brows. Over all this settles down the white cloud in the West, and the Morning and Evening draw toward Summer.

[1] To hear Bellini's *Il Pirata* given "for the first time in six years" at Her Majesty's Theatre, May 13, 1845.

[2] Carlyle wrote, "There are hollow spots . . . scattered over that Broad Moor; which are understood to have once been burial *mounds*; some of which have been . . . verified as such." Although EFG excavated at least six locations, he found only one grave, that on Cloisterwell, a hill about a mile from Broad Moor. He also reported, September 27, 1842, "About this same Cloisterwell have most bullets been found." Other statements in Carlyle's sketch of the battle in the first edition of *Cromwell* (I, 211-14) distort items in EFG's reports. Revisions in the second edition failed to satisfy him.

[3] For John Crome, see letter to Laurence, May 22, 1842, n.4. EFG may refer to Edward Williams (1782-1855), landscape painter.

[4] Joseph M. W. Turner (1775-1851), still painting at the age of seventy, exhibited three pictures at the Royal Academy in 1845: "Venice," "Morning," and "Whalers." EFG admired the free use of color and indifference to specific detail that characterize Turner's later work—an admiration many art lovers and critics failed to share. To Thackeray, Turner was "a great and awful mystery" in 1845. "Go up and look at one of his pictures, and you laugh at yourself and him," *Titmarsh* wrote in "Picture Gossip" (Thackeray Biographical Edition, XIII, 458).

To Bernard Barton

[London]
[May 18, 1845]

My dear Barton,

Had not your second note arrived this morning, I should surely have written to you; that you might have a little letter for your Sunday's breakfast. Do not accuse me of growing enamoured of London; I would have been in the country long ago if I could. . . . Nor do I think I shall get away till the end of this month; and then I *will* go. I am not so bad as Tennyson, who has been for six weeks intending to start every day for Switzerland or Cornwall, he doesn't quite know which. However, his stay has been so much gain to me; for he and John Allen are the two men that give me pleasure here.

Tell Churchyard he must come up once again. . . . I saw a most lovely Sir Joshua at Christie's a week ago; it went far far above my means. There is an old hunting picture in Regent St. which I want him to look at. I think it is Morland;[1] whom I don't care twopence for;

the horses ill drawn; some good colour; the people English; good old England! I was at a party of modern wits last night that made me creep into myself, and wish myself away talking to any Suffolk old woman in her cottage, while the trees murmured without. The wickedness of London appals me; and yet I am no paragon.

[1] George Morland (1764-1804), prolific painter of domestic subjects and rural scenes. His pictures faithfully portray lowly English life, but their merit frequently failed to match their popularity. Morland led a life of prodigality and dissipation and died while confined for debt. He suggested, as his epitaph, "Here lies a drunken dog."

To Bernard Barton

[London]
[May 28, 1845]

My dear Barton,

I have been hoaxing Crabbe with letters artfully contrived; but which he has defeated by the simple means of not reading what seemed not intended for his eyes. Deuce take him. Well; I really look to be back in Suffolk next week! Yea, really! I want to see my new roses, how they like their new quarters. My Father is now in Ireland with my poor Uncle, whose death may now be expected daily.[1] Anyhow, by the end of this week I shall consider myself free of all engagements, and go my own ways.

When I wrote to you last, or what I wrote to you about, has wholly escaped my memory. Tell Churchyard I am sorry he is not coming to London. I could give him bed all the end of this week if he would even yet come. I have as yet bought no picture. Tell him that at the she-dragons where the early Gainsborough was last year, there is now (as I think) an early Wilson; of the same size—not *quite* the thing, but rising up towards the aerial effects of later years. £30. But I have not looked close to it. Some charming Sir Joshua's were sold last week at Christie's. What is the exact size of your Dell?[2] I meant to have asked you this a month ago. Is it exactly the common portrait size? and what is that! I have seen one or two frames lately that might suit your picture well.

All the world is gone to Epsom races today.[3] I was offered a seat in a gay barouche; but such is not for me. I hate Epsom, roaring with Cockneys.

Well, now have you any last commands to me in this City—Going, going, going—soon will be, Gone! Tomorrow to fresh fields, and pastures new! I gulp the country air in anticipation—

Farewell—yours ever,
E.FG.

[1] Peter Purcell of Halverstown, his father's brother. He did not die until May 25, 1846.

[2] In a letter to John Wodderspoon of Ipswich, Barton refers to a caustic criticism by Morris Moore, of his "Dell" by Constable (British Museum MSS—Add 37,032).

[3] Derby Day; in 1845, Wednesday, May 28.

To Bernard Barton

39 Norton St., Portland Place
[c. June 1, 1845]

My dear Barton,

You know what I think about your book[1]—you go on the principle of gathering together all you can of hitherto unpublished; I should select about one third of all I had ever published. So, we shall never agree. But I wish you peace and success in all things.

I have bought a shilling print of old Stothard, which proves the genuineness of your portrait.[2] I will bring it down with me for you. Some splendid pictures were sold at Christie's on Saturday. I bid for a little admirable sketch by Wilson,[3] and had not courage to go beyond £6. So I did not get it, and am sorry now. Two small finished Gainsboro's went for over £30 a piece. They were not of his best kind.

Tell Churchyard that if he comes to London, I can shew him a Constable as good and as large as Salisbury Cathedral. He may buy it for £600—which is just £400 too much for it. And the best Morland[4] I have ever seen for £25—not very large—but of capital colour and character—I mean *capital* for the man; who is no very capital performer to my thinking.

I have been so busy in attendance at Portland Place that I have seen but little of my friends.[5] Now I mean to have a week's holiday with them. I have not lost a very fair month in the Country; May is but a young month, and a sad coquette. April is scarce out of the nursery and one expects her to be giddy; but May ought to know better.

Ever yours,
E. FitzGerald.

[1] Barton's last volume of poetry, *Household Verses* dedicated to Queen Victoria, being prepared for the press.

[2] Bought for Barton by EFG.

[3] Although subsequently recognized as among England's greatest painters of landscape, Richard Wilson (1714-82) was one of the neglected artists of the eighteenth century. His work was admired by leading artists of the Continent but English critics failed to understand his style and the English public refused to buy his pictures. He lived a life of penury. Wilson's failure to win recognition has been attributed partly to the jealousy of fellow artists, partly to his own asperity. See letter to Barton, [Early Jan., 1847], n.1.

[4] See letter to Barton, May 18, 1845, n.1.

[5] After EFG visited Mattishall in the autumn of 1838, W. B. Donne wrote to their friend, J. W. Blakesley, "He was, when he left me, under marching orders for Hastings to convoy certain sisters. He has some of the inconveniences of marriage even in his state of innocence—and among them I should reckon not the least that of accompanying Mrs. FitzGerald the round of the theatres" (*Donne and Friends*, p. 47).

To Frederick Tennyson

Boulge, Woodbridge
June 12/45

Dear Frederic,

Though I write from Boulge you are not to suppose I have been here ever since I last wrote to you. On the contrary, I am but just returned from London, where I spent a month, and saw all the sights and all the people I cared to see. But what am I to tell you of them? Spedding, you know, does not change: he is now the same that he was fourteen years old when I first knew him at school more than twenty years ago; wise, calm, bald, combining the best qualities of Youth and Age. And then as to things seen; you know that one Exhibition tells another, and one Panorama[1] certifieth another, etc. If you want to know something of the Exhibition however, read Fraser's Magazine for this month; there Thackeray has a paper on the matter, full of fun. I met Stone in the street the other day; he took me by the button, and told me in perfect sincerity, and with increasing warmth, how, though he loved old Thackeray, yet these yearly out-speakings of his sorely tried him; not on account of himself (Stone), but on account of some of his friends, Charles Landseer, Maclise, etc.[2] Stone worked himself up to such a pitch under the pressure of forced calmness that he at last said Thackeray would get himself horse-whipped one day by one of these infuriated Apelleses. At this I, who had partly agreed with Stone that ridicule, though true, needs not always to be spoken, began to laugh: and told him two could play at that game.[3] These painters cling together, and bolster each other up, to such a degree, that they really have persuaded themselves that any one who ventures to laugh at one of their drawings, exhibited publickly for the express purpose of criticism, insults the whole corps. In the mean while old Thackeray laughs at all this; and goes on in his own way; writing hard for half a dozen Reviews and Newspapers all the morning; dining, drinking, and talking of a night; managing to preserve a fresh colour and perpetual flow of spirits under a wear-and-tear of thinking and feeding that would have knocked up any other man I know two years ago, at least. . . .

Alfred was in London the first week of my stay there. He was looking well, and in good spirits; and had got two hundred lines of a new poem in a butcher's book.[4] He went down to Eastbourne in Sussex; where I believe he now is. He and I made a plan to go to the coast of Cornwall or Wales this summer; but I suppose we shall manage never to do it.[5] I find I must go to Ireland; which I had not intended to do this year.

I have nothing new to tell you of Music. The Operas were the same old affair; Linda di Chamouni, the Pirata, etc. Grisi coarse, . . . only Lablache great. There is one singer also, Brambelli, who, with a few husky notes, carries one back to the days of Pasta. I did not hear "Le Désert";[6] but I fancy the English came to a fair judgment about it. That is, they did not want to hear it more than once. It was played many times, for new batches of people; but I doubt if any one went twice. So it is with nearly all French things; there is a clever showy surface; but no Holy of Holies far withdrawn; conceived in the depth of a mind, and only to be received into the depth of ours after much attention. Poussin must spend his life in Italy before he could paint as he did; and what other Great Man, out of the exact Sciences, have they to show? This you will call impudence. Now Beethoven, you see by your own experience, has a depth not to be reached all at once. I admit with you that he is too bizarre, and, I think, morbid; but he is original, majestic, and profound. Such music *thinks*; so it is with Gluck; and with Mendelssohn. As to Mozart, he was, as a musical genius, more wonderful than all. I was astonished at the Don Giovanni lately. It is certainly the Greatest Opera in the world. I went to no concert, and am now sorry I did not.

Now I have told you all my London news. You will not hear of my Cottage and Garden; so now I will shut up shop and have done. We have had a dismal wet May; but now June is recompensing us for all, and Dr. Blow may be said to be leading the great Garden Band in full chorus. This is a pun, which, profound in itself, you must not expect to enjoy at first reading. I am not sure that I am myself conscious of the full meaning of it. I know it is very hot weather; the distant woods steaming blue under the noonday sun. I suppose you are living without clothes in wells, where you are. Remember me to your brothers;[7] write soon; and believe me ever yours,

E. FitzGerald

As to going to Italy, alas! I have less call to do that than ever: I never shall go. You must come over here about your Railroad land.[8]

[1] See letter to F. Tennyson, Feb. 6, 1845, n.1.

[2] Since the publication of "Strictures on Pictures," *Fraser's Magazine*, June, 1838, Thackeray had been writing art criticism for the magazine. His reviews were often seriocomic, the comic element highly spiced with ridicule directed at the sentiment, vacuity, and "namby-pambyism" he found in contemporary art. His principal target was the Royal Academy "which consists . . . of thirty-eight knights and esquire Academicians, and nineteen simple and ungenteel Associates" ("A Second Lecture on the Fine Arts," June, 1839). Thackeray's 1845 criticism, "Picture Gossip," was somewhat less caustic than that which had preceded it. Daniel Maclise is not mentioned; but of the figures in Charles Landseer's "Charles I before the Battle of Edgehill" Thackeray wrote, "nobody seems to have anything to do except the Royal martyr, who is looking at the bone of ham that a girl out of the inn has hold of. Now this is all very well, but . . . you don't want the *Deus intersit* for no other purpose than to look at a knuckle of ham." The critic praised a "devotional picture" by the more famous Edwin Landseer because "the numbers and variety of attitude and expression in that flock of sheep quite startle the spectator."

Gordon Ray states that the artists "of whom he [Thackeray] felt fondest were Frank Stone and George Cruikshank" (*The Years of Adversity*, p. 169). The feebleness of Stone's attachment to Thackeray when he met EFG is easily understood. He had recently read in *Fraser's*: "By far the prettiest of the maudlin pictures is Mr. Stone's 'Premier Pas.' It is that old, pretty, rococo, fantastic Jenny and Jessamy couple, whose loves the painter has been chronicling any time these five years, and whom he has spied out at various wells, porches, etc. . . . The picture is very nicely painted, according to the careful artist's wont. The neck and hands of the girl are especially pretty. The lad's face is effeminate and imbecile, but his velveteen breeches are painted with great vigor and strength."

[3] Thackeray, over six feet tall, was well-built.

[4] *The Princess*, not *In Memoriam*, of which he had spoken, though not by name, in his letter to Donne, January 29. By 1845, Tennyson had written far more than 200 lines of the elegy. *The Princess* was published in November, 1847.

Tennyson seems to have preferred to write out his poems on the long pages of merchants' account books or, as EFG called them, "butchers' books."

[5] The friends succeeded in not making the trip. See letter to Allen, July 4, 1845.

[6] The *Times* reported that Denizetti's opera, *Linda di Chamouni* was given on

May 24 at Her Majesty's Theatre "for the first time these two years" with Luigi Lablache and Marietta Brambilla (not "Brambelli") in the cast. Bellini's *Il Pirata* was offered "for the first time these six years" at the same theater with Giulia Grisi as Imogene.

Le Désert, symphonic ode, by M. Félicien David, prominent French composer, in which he gives his impressions of the desert, gathered while traveling in the Near East. The composition consists of three parts divided into vocal and orchestral movements, each portion introduced by a descriptive recitation. It was immensely popular in both London and Paris, where it had first been produced on December 8, 1844.

[7] Arthur and Septimus.

[8] From his grandfather Frederick had inherited property at Grimsby, near the mouth of the River Humber, while the town was still only a minor Lincolnshire fishing port. During the 1840's harbor and docks were improved and the town was linked by railroad with thriving Manchester. Grimsby became an east-coast port of considerable importance, and Frederick became a rich man. "I am glad to hear," wrote his sister Cecilia, December 11, 1844, "that Railways have or will double thy income" (Schonfield, *Letters*, p. 58). Frederick returned to England in June and remained for several months. For further comments by EFG on the Grimsby property, see letter of June 19, 1849.

To E. B. Cowell

[Boulge]
[c. June 12, 1845]

Dear Sir,

I returned from London four days ago; and should have given you notice of my doing so, but that I was afraid of being called away again almost as soon as arrived. That danger is not yet over; I may have to go tomorrow. But if I do go, it will really be but for four or five days; so that the end of next week is sure to find me at this place again. And then I hope you will come over and see me for a day or two. My cottage is very dry now; my garden beginning to show roses; and I will cause a piece of lamb to be roasted which, with the help of salad, shall serve us for dinner. Will that do for you? You shall bring your share of the entertainment in the better shape of quotations from old books which I shall never read; your Greek cup of tears and laughter is very delightful, and will grace any table. Sir Edward Bulwer's[1] lines I cannot so well admire. The παράδειγμα[2] of Timaeus may, I suppose, be rendered "antitype"—but I declare I am not sure what is the current meaning of the word. The words *example*, *copy*, and *model*, have all come somehow to fluctuate indeterminately between the original and the reflection.

No doubt it is not easy to write a book without some one good thing in it; but that is a poor excuse for writing books except one has a strong inward sense of pregnancy (this is Plato's phrase—κύων)—or a very sincere feeling that some truth needs to be told. And verse is more apt to blunder into some one good thing than prose; the rhyme helps many a man to a lucky thought; and the very current even of blank verse will be sure to turn into some graceful expression. There are good phrases in the Revd Richard Cobbold's Valentine Verses;[3] which is a wonderful book too.

Carlyle is very busy and in a great muddle with editing his Cromwell Letters. He meant to have illustrated them but by a few words of his own to each letter; but he finds he cannot say a little on matters so near his heart; so that the book swells to two volumes; time runs away; and the bookseller, whose contract was for Carlyle's few words, will get too many in for his bargain; which is not a pleasant consideration to any Scotchman's heart. Don't suppose Carlyle is a screw;[4] a sense of Justice, and equal balance, and fair wages for fair work,[5] etc. is at the bottom of these scruples in him and many other Scotchmen.

Quintus Fixlein[6] I am going to buy. It is very beautiful. When you come you will find it here to read. Let me hear about your coming; even if I go to town your note will follow me.

Yours truly
Edward FitzGerald

[1] EFG had not kept up to date. Edward George Earle Lytton Bulwer (1803-73), novelist, poet, dramatist, and M.P., knighted in 1838, in 1844 had assumed the additional name and the arms of Lytton and was known thereafter as Bulwer-Lytton. He was created Baron in 1866.

[2] "Model" or "example." *Timaeus*, a dialogue by Plato intended to be the introduction to a work including the *Critias* and *Hermocrates*. The project was never completed.

[3] The Reverend Richard Cobbold (1797-1877), Ipswich writer; *Valentine Verses*, 1827.

[4] "Screw," EFG's favorite censorious term, "a stingy, miserly person." EFG applies it to men of means who combined stinginess with snobbishness or other disagreeable traits.

[5] EFG read Carlyle with care. Labor's demand for "A fair day's-wages for a fair day's-work" is assessed a number of times in *Past and Present*. "It is as just a demand as Governed men ever made of Governing. It is the everlasting right of man. . . . The progress of Human Society consists even in this same—The better and better apportioning of wages to work. . . . Pay to every man accurately what

he has worked for, what he has earned and done and deserved. . . ." (Book I, chap. III, "Manchester Insurrection," *passim*).

[6] Johann Paul Friedrich Richter (1763-1825), usually called "Jean Paul," German humorist, wrote *Leben des Quintus Fixlein* in 1796. Until Carlyle discovered and translated Richter into English, he had been translated only in fragments. *Quintus Fixlein* appeared in volume III of Carlyle's anthology of German fiction, *German Romances*, 4 vols., 1827.

To E. B. Cowell

[Boulge]
[June 15, 1845]

Dear Cowell,

Wednesday, and any hour of Wednesday, will suit me perfectly. As to dinner, I dine at all hours; and sometimes at none; but you shall dine at any hour you please, for I have got a little joint of lamb which I believe shall be roasted, so that we may have it cold, when we please, with a fresh salad. When you see my old woman, you will be aware that she cannot succeed in the pastry or confectionary line; she has no head for "subtilties." But you are young; and though I hear it said that literary people love good eating; yet, on the score of my superior years, I shall satisfy my conscience in treating you as plainly as possible.

I hope you will stay over Thursday at all events. Your one clean shirt will be quite clean enough for that. Here is no one to note dress.

Come at what hour you please.

Yours ever
E.FG.

From Thomas Carlyle

Chelsea, 27 june, 1845

Dear Fitzgerald,

The Horse,[1] I believe, does me on the whole some essential good; for I ride him two hours daily, about six times every week, and see the green fields by means of him: but at bottom he is still rather a dangerous piece of goods for me! He improves in strength; has excellent paces (when he likes to put them forth), hoofs of brass; is fleet as a roe;—neither do I think the creature has any radical vice or ill-nature in him: but he is in fact *unbroken*; and would require to be ridden half a year by a man far more expert than I am in the delicacies of that business, and with far more *time* than I have at present to attend to the whims of such an animal. He has "decided preferences" as to the roads he wishes to go; needs occasionally to be forcibly flogged and kicked along or he will not go at all;—goes then, as the Scotch say, like a Cat travelling on hot iron! He has never got me off him again; but once or twice has, at a careless moment, approached that result. The day before yesterday, to ease my long legs I had got the stirrups lengthened a hole; and twice over was very nearly in the dirt;—some explosion of a start, at something, at nothing,—the pace a walk. I was glad to dismount, and shorten my stirrups again.—On the other hand, yesterday I had a most glorious view of Richmond Park in the June sunshine, by means of this poor brute! So stands the account balanced.

On the whole, I think of asking you by and by to ask Browne to take him away from me again,—to sell him or buy him; and leave me to crawl along on *two* feet again.[2] I am so overwhelmed with confusion and Printers' Devils in these weeks I really have no moment to bestow on anything. For which reason too I have never yet got Browne's money lodged with his City Banker, but it still lies *here* in the shape of Bank Notes nearby;—I have no Banker of my own nearer than Dumfries, cannot *ride* into the City on such mounting, cannot get leave to go; and have daily been expecting some man *with* a Banker who could do the business instead of me.

Oliver is now made *Protector*—God be thanked! I know the *Iter Carolinum* and the Fife *Memorials*,[3]—a very wooden piece the last.

Good be with you, dear F.

Yours always truly
T. Carlyle

Will you have a Copy of a certain *Life of Schiller*,[4] which is not worth reading? If yea, mention how it can be sent.

1 Carlyle had written to his brother Alexander in Canada on June 17, ". . . I have got a horse according to your advice! . . . A benevolent friend [EFG] of these parts undertook it for me:—a very smart horse, a gelding of six years, black, long-tailed, high and thin,—swift as a roe . . . the price of him was £35; would be very dear in Dumfries." He had been selected by W. K. Browne, probably from his own stable.

For Black Duncan, as the horse was first called, Carlyle eventually substituted the name, Bobus. "Bobus Higgins of Houndsditch, Sausage-maker on the great scale," in *Past and Present* represented members of the middle class who, content with the trappings of newly acquired wealth, were materialistic and superficial and mouthed the catchwords and theories of political and social leaders.

[2] On July 10, Bobus "promises to be one of the best quadrupeds in this part of England!" (*Carlyle's Letters to His Youngest Sister*, p. 178).

[3] [Edward Walker?], *Iter Carolinum*, "being a succinct Relation of the necessitated Marches, Retreats and Sufferings of his Majesty, Charles the First, from January 10, 1641, till the time of his Death, 1648. Collected by a daily Attendant upon his sacred Majesty during all the said time." The preface is signed "Thomas Manley," believed to have been a pseudonym. The work, printed in 1660, was reproduced by Sir Walter Scott in Somers Tracts, 2nd ed., 13 vols., 1809-15, V, 263.

The Fife Memorials, "sculpturings," some dating back to the Bronze Age, others to the Early Christian Era, on the walls of caves along the coast of County Fife in Scotland. George B. Deas, in "The Sculpturings on the Caves of Wemyss" (*Rothmill Quarterly Magazine*, Oct. 1948), reports that there were at one time nine such caves along the coast of Fife but that only three "caves with markings" exist today.

[4] Carlyle's *Life of Friedrich Schiller*, 2nd ed., 1845.

To John Allen

Boulge, Woodbridge
July 4/45

My dear good Allen,

Let me have a line from you one day. I mean in the course of a fortnight—and let me know something of your plans regarding Wales —*when* you go, and to what places. I believe I shall go to Ireland toward the end of this month; and after three weeks or so could surely find my way home by Wales, and "sit upon a promontory"[1] with you, and talk of old times. Alfred Tennyson was to have gone with me to the coast; but I have not the least idea where he is now abiding; and, if I did, he would not write me a line to fix on anything; and if he wrote to fix, he would not do it. One can only rely on Chance for meeting with him.

I have been enjoying the shade of trees, and the grass to walk upon. Lusia and her husband are at the *Hall*,[2] to which my cottage is but a lawn-lodge. She yet bears up well; and walks and drives about. I shall be sorry to move from this place; but one must go.

Have you any news of Newman—is any large batch moving over to Rome?[3] I hear of nothing down here. We have just heard about the murder in Cavan[4] a fortnight ago. I am reading, or rather looking over, Cobbett's Parliamentary History;[5] a book you will wonder how I can be amused with it. But I am. Perhaps when we sit upon one of those old rocks, and look over the Atlantic, you and I shall talk of it. Thirteen years ago we were talking of Herbert's Poetry there.

Give my best remembrances to Mrs. Allen; and believe me

Your loving old friend
Edward FitzGerald

[1] As they had done at Tenby in 1832 and 1833.

[2] Lucy Barton had written Elizabeth Charlesworth a few weeks before, "Lusia and her husband come to Boulge in June for the summer. She is expecting her confinement in July" (MS letter, Cambridge University Library).

[3] John Henry Newman was received into the Roman Catholic Church October 9, 1845. Ten days later the *Sunday Times* reported that five other Oxford men had "been received into the Roman-catholic Church in the course of the last few days. . . . It is stated confidently that other clergymen, also members of the University of Oxford, are preparing to take a similar step."

[4] The *Times*, June 25, 1845, published reports from Cavan County, Ireland, giving accounts of the murder on June 22 of a Protestant Magistrate, George F. Bell Booth, of Drumcarbin, who was returning home from church with his children. A man with a "horse pistol" stepped casually up to the carriage and shot the magistrate through the head. *The Illustrated London News* reported on June 28 (p. 414) that the murder was generally believed to be the work of the Molly Maguires, a secret faction formed in 1843 to resist the payment of rent.

[5] William Cobbett, *Parliamentary History of England to 1803*, 12 vols., 1806-20.

To John Allen

Halverstown
Kilcullen, Ireland
Pmk., July 28, 1845

My dear Allen,

I behaved very shabbily in not going to see you in London, where I was two days. But in those two days I whirled about a good deal; and I thought to be sure I should see you in Wales before long. For that is my design. Only, I would know accurately from you as to when I had best meet you. You say they would be pleased to see me at Bosherston and Freestone; but is that so sure? especially in regard to the latter place, where my only visit is connected with painful thoughts.[1] The general good will of all these relatives of yours towards me I have no doubt of—but one may easily be one too many in a family visit. Perhaps I could so manage as to be with you some days at these two places; and then go on to St. David's;[2] which I have a fancy to see. You mean to be in Pembrokeshire about the 16. Augst. Before that time you can give me a line to say how the land lies.

I got here yesterday after a fair voyage by land and sea. I find my Uncle[3] very ill: I scarce knew him. But they say he is not worse.

One of my evenings (which in fact I had purposed to you) was divided between some duty at P[ortland] Place and poor Mrs. Jones,[4] whom I found ill in town. She said Mrs. Allen had been so good as to ask her to dinner. If you ever hear of any lady looking out for a companion; or of any place for Matron, or such like; pray do not forget her; for I can vouch for her worthiness.

Kind regards to Mrs. A.

Ever yours,
E.FG.

[1] Freestone was the home of Anne Allen, who had died soon after EFG's visit in 1833.

[2] St. David's, in the South Wales peninsula, noted for its cathedral, said to date from the 13th century.

[3] Peter Purcell.

[4] EFG refers to a number of *Mrs. Joneses* in his correspondence, and it is sometimes impossible, as here, to determine to which he refers.

To Bernard Barton

Halverstown, Kilcullen
August 2/45

My dear Barton,

I will write you a line, if it be but a line. For you must know I never felt less able to spin out even a notesheet of the thinnest gossamer. I think this climate lazifies one; you know that is the character of the Irish. I have just written to Crabbe[1] as much as I can write to you; it would not be decent to repeat what I have said to him word for word to you; and I protest I exhausted all that would come into my head.

Only this—tell Churchyard I saw the Crome.[2] I wrote him a note about it (did he get it?). I saw that Crome, I say, go for £9. I did not think it worth more. All the pictures were going very cheap, they said; I bought a good portrait for £7, but not for myself. I should suppose the large Constable would go for under £100—as the sale was so close on the end of the season, and people impoverished and tired of buying. Churchyard will remember Archbutt's[3] large Constable; it was to be sold the day I left London.

Well, and how does your stereotype[4] get on; and when are you to come forth? Let me hear some news of yourself and of Suffolk. I hope you have lost all your lumbago.

This is a wretched letter, to be sure. But then the merit of writing ever so little quite against the grain is as great as that of writing ever so much when the pen runs before a steady impulse of communication. So take will for deed; and believe me yours ever,

Edward FitzGerald

[1] Of Bredfield.
[2] John Crome. See letter to Laurence, May 22, 1842, n.4.
[3] A picture dealer.
[4] The printing of *Household Verses*, published in 1845.

To Bernard Barton

Ireland
August 15/45

My dear Barton,

Tomorrow I leave Paddyland and draw homeward, staying some while at Bedford. I may also go to Naseby for a day or two. But my easily-wearied heart yearns to be at home again. I was to have gone to meet Allen in Wales; but I have refreshed myself with the opal tints of the Wicklow hills here, and I want no more. A line of distant hills is all we want in Suffolk. A landscape should have that image of futurity in it.

I had a very queer hyppish note from Crabbe;[1] lamenting that he could only interest himself in one subject, which would not interest me, viz, the truth of the Evangelical doctrine; and still harping on *my* pride etc. I fancy he has these occasional seasons of doubt etc. I have written to laugh at him; which I hope he wont take ill; for I regard the man too much to risk a quarrel with him. Where would one find such another in any other country but England? How honest and determined his obstinacy!

I suppose Carlyle's book must be on the point of appearing.[2] At all events he must have almost done *his* part. He told me that he had done so much for the illustration of Cromwell's letters etc. that he doubted if he should ever write any further Life of him. So get this;

it is sure to have much more good than bad in it. I told C. that the more I read of Cromwell the more I was forced to agree with the verdict of the world about him. Carlyle only grunted and sent forth a prodigious blast of tobacco smoke. He smokes indignantly.

You say nothing of the state of harvest etc. in Suffolk. The crops about here are very good,[3] and only want sunshine now to crown a full cup of harvest. Ireland is wonderfully improved (this part of it, at least) in the last two years even.

Is your book out?[4] Are you come out in imperishable hot press yet?

Here is a story for you to tell in company. It will do when the conversation happens to turn on toll gates, women, or breeches. Then, pull out your snuff box, take a pinch, and relate this authentic story; that Dr. Welsh of Naas[5] told us. He stopped in his gig at a toll gate the other night; the toll man could not get on his breeches quickly. Next day, Welsh passed the same way; the good woman then opened the toll gate, and Welsh joked with her about her husband's inaptitude in putting on his breeches etc. "Ah plase your honour, its no wonder," said she, "sure he hasn't worn them at all at all for this long while."

Ever yours,
E.FG.

Direct to the P.O. Bedford if you write.

[1] In his recollections of EFG, George Crabbe, Jr., wrote that "coolnesses which I believe were all my Father's fault," occasionally developed in the friendship between the vicar and FitzGerald. A year later, after another tiff "on the old score of *Pride*," EFG reported to Barton, "I am dropped out of his Category of Heroes for ever! he shall always be right glad to see me, he says: but he never can be disappointed in me again! How much the best footing is this to be upon with all one's friends."

[2] *Cromwell's Letters and Speeches.* The work did not appear until November 22.

[3] Only a week before EFG wrote his letter, reports had reached Sir Robert Peel, first from the Isle of Wight, later from Kent and Sussex, that a blight had attacked the potato crop. Similar intelligence came from the Continent. At first, reports from Ireland were favorable; but early in October the blight was discovered there, also. By the middle of the month the news from Cork was "alarming." Peel's *Memoirs* record that half the population of Ireland depended exclusively on the potato for subsistence. Reduction of the crop in 1845 was merely the prelude to more severe failures in 1846 and 1847, and famine was added to the already hapless lot of the Irish poor.

[4] *Household Verses.*

[5] Naas, a town in Kildare nine and one-half miles northeast of Halverstown. F. R. Barton misread the name as "Noas."

From Thomas Carlyle

Chelsea, 18 Aug^{t}, 1845

Dear Fitzgerald,

You will do me a real favour if you can, thro' your Friend Browne or any other eligible channel, procure me a winter requiem for this horse of mine.[1] I hope to have finished my affairs here in about a fortnight; am off then towards Scotland:—and should be very glad to *annihilate* the Horse till the end of February next. He is really a good Horse; has now got to reverence and love me very sincerely; and rides for most part in a very exemplary manner. Does not like railway-trains, and miracles of that nature; but is in general as composed as a Justice of the Peace,—and far livelier, and speedier of foot than any justice! In short an eligible animal. I believe he can leap too, and could hunt: but I have small skill to try him in that way. You must write to Browne about it (since you undertake so kindly), and see what can be done.

If Browne, or any benignant Friend and Subduer of Horses, would take and ride him, hunt him or what else, all winter, I should expect he would come back to me much improved in his paces, and perfect in all manner of equine behaviour, in the Spring:—but that, I suppose, does not lie within the possibilities: we must therefore look to grass or straw-yard, or some cheap form of *annihilation*;—in fact to what Browne, at your request, shall decide to be best. I am now ready to part with the horse at any time; and shall *want* to be rid of him about the first of Sept^{r} —I know not what good he has done to my health: I am very poorly; but suppose I should have been much worse otherwise. At all events I tried my best; and that was very fit to be done.

Cromwell's own things[2] are now all out of my hands,—the last this very day: but there is a conclusion to do, an Index, etc., etc.: there is still certainly a fortnight's work in the business. You will get the Book to try your hand upon in October (so the Booksellers arrange):[3]—a very tough job of reading; but if you read well, I hope, it will shew you more of Cromwell than you have fallen in with hitherto. I reckon it to be like the letting of the Brook upon the Augean Stables; it is meant to tell the whole world what Cromwell is, and move their attention and exertions towards him:—there will be mountains of *dung* swum away in this manner by and by, and the real face of Oliver's History will at length become apparent to Men.[4]

Write to me again whither you go. I am ashamed to mention Naseby again; but really should like to see it,—and bury the *shin-bone* then.

Yours ever truly
T. Carlyle

[1] See letters from Carlyle, June 27 and Aug. 23, 1845.
[2] i.e., Cromwell's actual letters and speeches.
[3] The two volumes did not appear until November 22.
[4] In 1846, he wrote, "Considering the frivolous humour of most men, it is matter of great surprise to me how so many have taken to read this Book; and how very universally my character of [Cromwell] has been recognised as actually [correct]. So I must not grudge my labour upon it. In all probability this is the usefullest business I shall ever get to do in the world; this of rescuing the memory of a Noble and Thrice Noble Man from its disfigurement, and presenting him again to a world that stands much in need of the like of him: I do not know any worthier work a poor son of Adam that pretends to write at all could *do*, in the writing way!" Again, "I fancy in fact it will far survive all my other Books. . . ." (Carlyle, *New Letters*, II, 17 and 21).

From Thomas Carlyle

Chelsea, 23 Aug^{t}*, 1845*

Dear Fitzgerald,

Many thanks for your arrangements in behalf of the horse.[1] The substance of the matter promises to do altogether well; and for the details, of time, etc., we will leave those, look, and give due warning when the day approaches nearer. Heaven knows I ought not and wish not to continue here; but that I shall actually be able to shake the London dust off my feet in 8 days' time seems almost too proud a hope! I am under a kind of obligation also to ride down into Bedfordshire myself, to Sir H^{y} Verney's,[2] a place called Claydon: I must look on the map, and see how localities agree;—the ride, I doubt, will hardly take effect, if they go away. Nay perhaps Claydon is in *Bucks*; I must examine: if I had once a moment's time. —Meanwhile thank your friend Browne for me very handsomely;—and pray send me his Address, which you have forgotten, hitherto; unless Bedford itself be it?

Moreover (for there is no end to me), here is another small job for you. It seems a possibility at present that I may put in somewhere, by way of Appendix, those Anecdotes of Mrs. Bendysh,[x] [3] which are in Noble (II, 329). Now will you read those pages of Noble, once more, carefully over, with an eye that way. You will find one does not learn *where* Mrs. Bendysh lived ('near Yarmouth somewhere'), what her or her husband's business was, or anything about their economic peculiarities and earthly localities;—so that the whole matter looks then very much like a thing in Drury Lane.

Now I want you to ask the Essex Archdeacon,[xx] [4] or whoever he or she is that descends from this Mrs. Bendysh, whether there is not in the Family any certain knowledge as to all these points, any clear Tradition even—*any* light to be had that would complete what you see to be wanting in the business. You have a *Noble* have you not? Or can get one about Bedford? I could cut you out those leaves and send them by post. Perhaps that will be best? You will then at once see what is wanting in general there. For the rest, the thing, if at all will be needed in a day or two. —So here go the leaves at a venture! Edit them yourself (make them ready for editing): that is a task I set you! *Till this day week*:—then return them to me with what you have made out.

Laurence,[5] I am told, is now down in that quarter; actually gone thither with commission to take the Portrait.[xxx]

Yours ever truly
T. Carlyle

[x] Cromwell's Grand-daughter by Ireton [EFG's note]

[xx] Berners, of Woolverstone, Suffolk [EFG's note]

[xxx] [Of Oliver, done in miniature by Cooper,[6] in possession of Archdeacon Berners aforesaid; Laurence's Copy of it being engraved as Frontispiece to Carlyle's Book] EFG

1 W. K. Browne had consented to care for the horse for the winter.

2 Sir Henry Verney (1801-94) assumed the surname Verney in place of Calvert, 1827, on succeeding to the Verney estates at Claydon, Buckinghamshire.

3 For Mrs. Bendysh, see letter to the Reverend John Charlesworth, Oct. 22, 1842, nn.3 and 4. For Noble, ibid., n.2.

4 Henry Denny Berners (1769-1852), Archdeacon of Suffolk (not Essex), lived at Woolverstone Hall, near Ipswich.

5 Samuel Laurence.

6 Samuel Cooper (1609-72), noted for his miniature portraits of celebrities of the Commonwealth and Restoration. Credited with being "the greatest miniature painter who ever lived."

To John Allen

Bedford
August 27/45

Dear good Allen,

I doubt you must have given me up as a very light fellow, for having drawn off from going to meet you in Wales, after so much protestation on my part. But if you got a note which I wrote you on leaving Ireland, you found the true cause why I did not join you—

really the true cause; and no backwardness from further travel; certainly, no disinclination to your society. Indeed part of the reason lay in this, that I supposed, from the many calls of the rest of your family, that I should see very little of yourself.

I came here a week ago—and am paying my usual visits at the Brownes' and at Airy's.[1] I also purpose going to Naseby for two days very soon; and after that I shall retire slowly homeward; not to move, I suppose (except it be for some days to London) till next summer comes again!

I am just now staying with W. B. and his wife. He seems very kind to her; and really domestic—which latter is more than I thought would be. She is a very good, quiet, unaffected, sensible, little woman. They live with very little company; and seem to desire none.

W. B. has told me of his proposals to you about the Bedford School.[2] The Committee debate and debate about it, he tells me: and there is a Dissenting Bookseller, White, who is vehement against any Established Govr Divine being called into their Councils. The thing will be decided in a month, I think; happily you do not care which way!

The Father and Mother of Mrs. W. Browne bought old Mrs. Piozzi's[3] house at Streatham thirty-five years ago—all the Sir Joshua portraits therein, which they sold directly afterward for a song; and all the furniture, of which some yet helps to fill the house I now stay in. In the bedroom I write in is Dr. Johnson's own bookcase and secretaire; with looking glass in the panels which often reflected his uncouth shape. His own bed is also in the house; but I do not sleep in it.

I am reading Selwyn's Correspondence,[4] a remarkable book, as all such records of the mind of a whole generation must be. Carlyle writes me word his Cromwell papers will be out in October; and that then we are all to be convinced that Richard had no hump to his back. I am strong in favour of the hump; I do not think the common sense of two Centuries is apt to be deceived in such a matter.

Now if your time is not wholly filled up, pray do give me one line to say you have not wholly given me up as a turncoat. I would rather have sat with you on the cliffs of St. David's than done anything I have done for the last six months. Believe that, please. And now good bye, my dear fellow.

The harvest promises very well here about; but I expect to find less prosperity at Naseby.

Ever yours
Edward FitzGerald

Give my kind remembrance to your wife and to any of your family I may know.

Write to me at Boulge.

[1] With the Brownes at Bedford and William Airy at Keysoe.

[2] Suggestions probably made to Allen, as government inspector of schools, on a recent trip to Bedford.

[3] Hester Lynch Piozzi, formerly Mrs. Henry Thrale, whose home, Streatham Park, Surrey, was a second home for Samuel Johnson. Robert Elliott, Mrs. Browne's father, bought Mrs. Piozzi's house at auction in 1816.

[4] *George Selwyn and His Contemporaries* had been published in 1843 by John H. Jesse. George Augustus Selwyn (1719-91), M.P., wit, and man-about-town.

To Bernard Barton
(Fragment)

Bedford
Septr 8/45

Dear Barton,

On Thursday I move towards Norwich; where I see Donne, hear some music, and go to Geldestone. But before this month is over, I hope to be at my Cottage again, where I have my garden to drain, and other important matters.

Do you know I have been greatly tempted to move my quarters from Boulge to this country; so exact a place have I found to suit me. But we will wait.

My noble Preacher Matthews is dead![1] He had a long cold, which he promoted in all ways of baptizing, watching late and early, travelling in rain, etc., he got worse; but would send for no Doctor, the Lord would raise him up if it were good for him, etc. Last Monday this cold broke out into Typhus fever; and on Thursday he died! I had been out to Naseby for three days, and as I returned on Friday at dusk I saw a coffin carrying down the street: I knew whose it must be. I would have given a great deal to save his life; which might certainly have been saved with common precaution. He died in perfect peace, approving all the principles of his life to be genuine. I am going this afternoon to attend his Funeral. . . .

Cromwell is to be out in October; and Laurence has been sent to Archdeacon Berners's to make a copy of Oliver's miniature.[2]

[1] The Reverend Timothy R. Matthews died September 6, 1845. See letter to Allen, [Aug., latter half, 1842], n.2.

[2] See letter from Carlyle, Aug. 23, 1845.

To W. B. Donne

Geldestone
Septr 23/45

Dear Donne,

I left one volume of your Swift with good Mrs. Johnson at Norwich; and the other with your Mother at Worship's[1] house in Yarmouth. So I trust you are in a fair way to get them again.

I sat through one Concert and one Oratorio;[2] and on Thursday went to Yarmouth, which I took a great fancy to. The sands were very good, I assure you; and then when one is weary of the sea, there is the good old town to fall back on. There is Mr. Gooch the Bookseller too; he and his books a great acquisition. I called on D[awson] Turner,[3] and in an incredibly short space of time saw several books of Coats of Arms, Churches, Refectories, pyxes, cerements, etc. He looks older, though; and his mind seems to hobble also.

Manage to read De Quincey's Article on Wordsworth in the last number of Tait's Magazine.[4] It is very incomplete, like all De Quincey's things, but has grand things in it; grand sounds of sense if nothing else. I am glad to see he sets up Daddy's[5] early Ballads against the Excursion and other Sermons.

I intend to leave this place the end of this week; and go, I suppose, to Boulge—though I have yet a hankering to get a week by the sea, either at Yarmouth or Southwold. I have now got a very bad cold—blocking nose, eyes, and sense in general. So I must and will bid you Good bye for the present.

Don't you think £3 very cheap for a fine copy of Rushworth's Collections—eight volumes folio?[6] I was tempted to buy it, if only for the bargain; for I only want to look through it once.

Yours ever,
E.FG.

[1] Widow of the Reverend John Johnson, Cowper's "Johnny of Norfolk," related to the poet and the Donnes. The Donnes and Worships were old family friends.

[2] At the Norwich Festival, held triennially.

[3] Yarmouth banker, botanist, antiquary, bibliophile, and collector of manuscripts and autograph letters. In 1853, five years before his death, a portion of his library was auctioned at Sotheby's for £4,560. Five volumes of manuscripts bearing on the history of Great Britain were sold separately to the British Museum for £1,000.

[4] "On Wordsworth's Poetry," Sept., 1845, pp. 545-54.

[5] "Daddy Wordsworth," as EFG, while an undergraduate, had dubbed the poet.

[6] *Historical Collections of Private Papers of State . . . in Five Parliaments*, by John Rushworth, 8 vols., 1659-1701.

To Frederick Tennyson

Boulge, Woodbridge
Thursday
[September 25, 1845]

Dear Frederic,

You were a shabby fellow not to let me know of your being in England before. As I was in London a month ago, and could have timed my visit there to meet you as well now as then. But now I do not think I will go up. For I have only just got back here from Norfolk; and to Norfolk I must go again in another fortnight. How long do you remain in London? I suppose you are tired of writing to me; for I have not heard from you from Italy this year. I suppose we all get lazy and careless. I begged Thackeray to tell me in just so many words whether Morton was yet in London, or was gone off to Stamboul as he called it;[1] but can get no answer to this. Will *you* tell me?

I went to hear Jullien's Band[2] when I was in London. They then played a delightful bit of Mozart or Beethoven every night; so well worth a shilling. Have you read Holmes' Life of Mozart?[3] It is very well spoken of in Reviews, etc.

Does Alfred think of returning with you to Italy? I hear nothing of him. In short, unless one lives in London, one hears nothing of anybody. I heard, when I was there, that you were to be enriched by Railroads;[4] which I hope is the case. Come now and live in England, and then we shall see you. For though I do not go to London now, I do wish to see you; it is really your fault if I let my wishes sleep a little.

Well Good bye, in all ancient good fellowship.

Ever yours,
E.FG.

[1] When the London *Daily News* was founded (in 1846), Savile Morton became its correspondent at Istanbul, French form, *Stamboul.* He later represented the paper successively at Athens, Madrid, and Vienna.

[2] Louis Jullien (1812-60)—the man had 36 given names—conductor *extraordinaire* of French birth, who, for 29 years, delighted Britons from all walks of life by combining music and showmanship in his promenade concerts at Drury Lane, Covent Garden, and other leading theaters. His objective was to provide "entertainment, relaxation, and instruction for the masses" by offering programs combining "the most sublime works with those of a lighter school." For his first London concert, June 8, 1840, he led an orchestra of 100 and engaged 26 vocalists. On March 18, 1845, at Covent Garden he conducted an orchestra of more than 500, including the elite of the Opera and Philharmonic musicians. For each of his annual concert series, Jullien composed a quadrille, rhythmical and melodious, celebrating some patriotic or dramatic theme. For these he augmented his orchestras by as many as four of the leading military bands. Leading British and Conti-

nental vocalists took part in his concerts. Admissions normally were 1s and 2s 6d.
Jullien's success was due in great part to his magnetic personality and flair for theatrics. He conducted all Beethoven selections with jeweled baton, and donned "a pair of clean kid gloves, handed to him at the moment on a silver salver" (Grove's *Dictionary*). He decorated Covent Garden with pink, white, and gold draperies for the summer concerts in 1846, a characteristic embellishment.
The failure of an attempt to establish English opera at Drury Lane in 1847 plunged Jullien into bankruptcy. Other financial reverses followed. He gave his last concerts in England in 1859 and returned to France, where he was placed under arrest on the score of old debts. He died penniless the following year (principal source, Adam Carse, *The Life of Jullien*, Cambridge, Eng., 1951, pp. 5-42 *passim*).

[3] Edward Holmes, *Life of Mozart, including his Correspondence*, 1845.

[4] See letter to F. Tennyson, June 12, 1845, n.8.

To E. B. Cowell

Boulge
Saturday [October 4, 1845]

My dear Cowell,

I have received both your letters; for which I ought to thank you, written on such an occasion. You are a happy man and [I envy you].[1]

I read in bed this morning the twentieth Book of the Iliad, Achilles' re-appearance in arms. It is often hinted that while he was in the field, the Trojans never dared to leave the walls of Troy: and Hector taunts Polydamas (I think) for having always kept them back. If this be so, there was not much to tell of in the nine years warfare preceding Achilles' sulky retirement. The ὁμôιος ἐν πολέμῳ,[2] fit for an epic, begins only when he disappears; and closes again at his return. We do not find it mentioned by Homer that any of the great chiefs of either party had been slain before the Iliad opens; and all this corresponds with Thucydides' account of the war, which was of so dilatory a kind that the Greeks sent half their men about foraging for stock, tilling the ground etc.

I am just finishing also the third book of Thucydides; that is, the first Volume of Arnold's first Edition.[3] The other two volumes I have lost; if you should hear of two such odd Volumes as you pass through London, I wish you would buy them for me. The work was published volume by Volume, I think. Or if not that, let me know what I can buy a copy of the whole work second-hand [for].

As for Nature and Books, you remember what Bacon says—of Poetry rounding off the harsher forms of things and events into a shape more congenial with the diviner impulses and aspirations of Man.[4] Doubtless, as Nature is only beautiful at all as reflected in our senses and souls, so she is most beautifully reflected in the most beautiful senses and souls; i.e., those of the Poets, Painters etc—so that as they teach us how to see Nature best, we cannot help referring to them when we receive any living impulse from her. On reading this over, I see it is very like a bit of *Taylor's* Plato.[5]

And now farewell. My best remembrances and regards to your Lady.

Ever yours
E.FG.

[1] Two segments have been torn from this letter, written to acknowledge one in which Cowell had told EFG of his engagement to Elizabeth Charlesworth. Although a portion was torn from the page at this point, enough of the script remains to recognize that EFG had written, "I envy you." A postscript was also torn from the sheet.

Cowell was 19 years old in 1845. His fiancee, 14 years his senior, was the "plain, sensible girl" to whom EFG had considered proposing marriage ten years before (see letter to Thackeray, July 29, 1835, n.4). However, the "cares and anxieties" involved in marriage had deterred him from declaring his love. Elizabeth and Cowell were married in 1847.

This letter serves to identify as a myth a legend handed down in the Cowell family that when Cowell informed his friend of the engagement, EFG exclaimed, "The deuce you are! Why! you have taken my Lady!" (George Cowell, *Life and Letters of Edward Byles Cowell*, 1904, p. 41).

[2] "Just as in war" (*Iliad* XII, 270).

[3] Thomas Arnold, *Thucydides, Peloponnesian War*, 3 vols., 1830-35.

[4] EFG appears to be summarizing ideas found in Bacon's *Advancement of Learning*, Book II, chap. XIII, "On the Second Principal Part of Learning, namely, Poesy."

[5] Thomas Taylor (1758-1835), called "The Platonist."

To Frederick Tennyson

Boulge, Woodbridge
[October, 1845]

My dear Frederic,

I do beg and desire that when you next begin a letter to me you will not tear it up (as you say you have done some) because of its exhibiting a joviality insulting to any dumps of mine. What was I complaining of so? I forget all about it. It seems to me to be two years since I heard from you. If you had said that my answers to your letters were so barren as to dishearten you from deserving any more I should understand that very well. But if you really did accomplish any letters and not send them, I say, a fico for thy friendship! Do so no more.

It is not quite impossible I may yet run up to see you before you leave. I find I shall not have to go to Norfolk till February; but I must make a little jaunt elsewhere in the meanwhile. Be sure not to leave London, or change your habitat *in* London, without letting me know.

Poor Elizabeth's story[1] is sad; Morton found her very innocent and religious. What can he do to make her amends! I used to feel angry with him sometimes: but he is scarcely a responsible man, I think. God knows.

The finale of C ♭[2] is very noble. I heard it twice at Jullien's.[3] On the whole I like to hear Mozart better; Beethoven is gloomy. Besides incontestably Mozart is the purest *musician*; Beethoven would have been Poet or Painter as well, for he had a great deep Soul and Imagination. I do not think it is reported that he showed any very early predilection for Music; Mozart, we know, did. They say Holmes has published a very good life of M.[4] Only think of the poor fellow not being able to sell his music latterly—getting out of fashion, so taking to drink and whore[5] and enact Harlequin at Masquerades! When I heard Handel's Alexander's Feast at Norwich[6] this Autumn I wondered; but when directly afterward they played Mozart's G minor Symphony, it seemed as if I had passed out of a land of savages into sweet civilized Life.

Poor Alfred! The water really did him good; but he would go on smoking and drinking.[7] That one cannot put a dram of a mean man's prudence into all that great Soul of his, hang him!

Now don't forget to write. I shall run up if I can.

Ever yours,
[No signature]

[1] Elizabeth—never otherwise identified—was one of the victims of Savile Morton's lust. Many years later EFG wrote that Morton's affairs with women were "his quite conscientious habit. He really felt *hurt* at my undue harshness in remonstrating with him on any such score" (letter to Norton, May 19, 1877). One of Morton's amours led to his being stabbed to death. (See Biographical Profile.)

[2] In German musical nomenclature ♭ was formerly used to express "minor."

[3] See letter to F. Tennyson, [Sept. 25, 1845], n.2.

[4] Edward Holmes, *Life of Mozart.*

[5] This bit of information was deleted by Aldis Wright.

[6] *Alexander's Feast*, an "ode" of Handel's to Dryden's poem, and Mozart's G-Minor Symphony were included in the program of the Norwich Festival, Sept. 16, 1845.

[7] Someone has printed between the lines, "(his pint of port)."

To Bernard Barton

[Boulge Cottage]
[c. November 1, 1845]

Dear B.B.

Come by all means tomorrow, an thou wilt. Do not come if it rains like this. I will ask Crabbe, who I have no doubt will come; for though Woodbridge is far for him to go out to in the Evening, we may reckon Boulge as a midway place where happy spirits may alight between Bredfield and Woodbridge.

I have a letter from Cowell. Perhaps he also will ride over tomorrow.

Bring up with thee a pound of Derby Cheese, for a toast; and some oysters, with knives; that thou mayst eat. And I will pay thee the cost—I have a fowl hanging up; and if my Father's cook arrive,[1] as I think she will, tonight, she shall handsel her skill on my fowl. For I doubt Mrs. Faier's powers of Bread-sauce—I doubt she would produce a sort of dumpling. But Sarah knows about these things.

Only think. Robert Peel has given A. Tennyson £200 pension[2]—I suppose so much a year.

I don't think him the less a humbug for this.[3]

Yours,
E F.

1 The cook at Boulge Hall; she did not often come to the cottage.

2 "Something in that word 'pension' sticks in my gizzard," Tennyson wrote to a friend. EFG recorded, "A. T. hardly liked it at first: but said with some grim humour—[when Barton was granted a pension of £100 the following year] 'Well, come—I am at least worth two Bernard Bartons.' " Tennyson predicted that the ire of many people would be stirred by the award—a prophecy that was fulfilled. See *Tennyson Memoir*, I, 224-28, and Sir Charles Tennyson's *Tennyson*, pp. 206-10.

3 The effects of the 1845 potato crop failure were being felt in Britain. The nation was alarmed, and Peel was being forced to recommend repeal of the Corn Laws, a legislative act that few of the landed gentry could accept with equanimity. EFG, understandably, was an agricultural protectionist and resented the Prime Minister's conversion to Corn Law repeal. See letter to F. Tennyson, Dec. 8, 1844, n.9.

To Bernard Barton

18 Charlotte St.
Rathbone Place
[November 22, 1845][1]

Dear Barton,

I returned from Brighton to this City on Tuesday. And here I shall be, I suppose, till Tuesday next. After that, I know not what should keep me from getting into Suffolk again; unless it be that confounded London Library,[2] which will not open when one wants it.

I have scarce seen a picture since I have been here—much less bought one. I walk down Wardour St. and bid its "temptations pass me heedless by." Tell Churchyard that my Wilson sketch is going into a frame twice too big for it. But then every one will think it a precious thing when it is almost lost in its setting. Tell him also I have but just recovered [from] his toasted Cheese—Wretch that I was—to eat as if I had the stomach of an Ostrich.

London whirls and bothers me as usual. But there will soon be an end of all that. I am just going off to Kensington to see poor Isabella,[3] who is in all sorts of troubles. I have seen some of my friends; but have not been to visit the God of Chelsea yet. His book comes out this very day, I believe.

This is a very poor note, but I have no wits. Let me hear how you are, and if the Deben[4] holds its Current still. I will beg Spring Rice[5] not to make a Creek of it. Farewell.

E F.

[1] Misdated *1843* by F. R. Barton. EFG was not a member of the London Library until January, 1845. Furthermore, Carlyle's *Cromwell's Letters and Speeches*, mentioned later, was published November 22, 1845.

[2] See letter from Carlyle, Oct. 26, 1844, n.1.

[3] His sister, Mrs. Gaetano Vignati.

[4] The river on which Woodbridge is situated.

[5] Stephen Spring Rice was a Commissioner of Customs, later deputy chairman of the Board of Customs. Responsibilities of the Board included supervision of coastal waters and harbors.

To Bernard Barton

Geldestone, Monday
[December 29, 1845]

Dear Barton,

Thanks for your letter. I am glad Turkey and Sausage did so well. We had our Feast here also, which did as well as most things of the kind. The children mostly eat as much as they could, and more than was good for them, and looked paler all next day in consequence.

I expect to be home by the end of this week, or early in next week. I want to see how my draining at the Cottage goes on. One may rejoice, I think, in the Snow forbearing us so long. What a day, however, was this day week, when I came hither!

This note is but to acknowledge yours; for I have positively nothing to say. Such total bankruptcies will happen in men's wits every now and then. I have sat over this little sheet of paper a quarter of an hour, looking up and asking intelligence of the ceiling, the furniture of the room, and the lawn before the window. But no thought reducible to paper comes. Take will for deed, and believe me yours as ever,

Edward FitzGerald.

Do give the enclosed paper to Daddy Loder, and bid him get me the book.

To Thomas Carlyle

[Boulge]
[January, 1846][1]

Dear Carlyle,

I find one of your letters acknowledges the receipt of a sketch by me pointing out the exact locality of the grave we opened.[2] Now as the situation of this goes to identify the place of the great *tussle*, will you not, having my papers, just look at that one sketch, and no more, if you want to be *quite* sure? I noted on your proof-sheet that the graves were on the "Parliamentary *slope*"; I believe they are; but I am sure much nearer the crown of the hill than the bottom of it; certainly not in the Broadmoor.[3]

I remember now that I opened a place, said to be a grave, the bottom of Charles' Dust Hill; but I found no signs of burial.

I am sorry to bother you; but you wish to be quite exact; and I will not swear whether my memory maintains an exact level of the ground.

Yours
Edward FitzGerald

Do put in the sketch of the Battle; you see you *must* alter your present account. Stick in an appendix, if the printer cannot now nudge in an extra page.[4] "Okey" should have a word; he is ambushed with his Dragoons, I think, behind Langfordy hedges, at the Western extremity of the lines of Battle; old Skippon will fight, when wounded; Fairfax rushes about, helmet off; and Charles is seen to charge "with more than usual vigour".

[1] Notation on MS: "Post m'k Jany 1846."

[2] Carlyle was preparing the second edition of his *Cromwell* and had asked EFG to identify the location of the grave the latter had opened on Naseby battlefield in 1842.

[3] In his account of the battle Carlyle states that the grave had been opened on Broad Moor, which is almost a mile from the site of the excavation.

[4] Carlyle's "sketch of the Battle" is a reference to notes on the action sent to guide EFG in his search for the "center" of the field. Carlyle responds in his letter of April 8, 1846. EFG closes his comments with an attempt to "nudge" Carlyle into describing the battle in the vivid manner employed in his *French Revolution*.

From Thomas Carlyle

Chelsea, 19 jan^y, 1846

Dear Fitzgerald,

You see you are not to get off. Here are the Two Leaves on Naseby;[1] and as you are, in small matters and in great, a friend to light and correctness, and an enemy to darkness and error,—I will bid you rectify the phraseology in that bit of printing till, if it cannot convey the right impression, it at least convey no wrong one to the uninstructed reader. There! ——— ———[2] And as the Printer is coming on, you may as well lose no time about it. For the rest, as I have another Copy of the leaves here, do not mind how you blot them,—correct them at large, and at your ease (explaining to *me* what you mean): I will adopt what of your suggestions is adoptable, and send it to the Printer on my own shape, on a diff^t paper.

Those 'new Letters'[3] and botherations are really very distressing to me: intrinsically hardly of any importance;—yet requiring to be adopted in some Appendix if not elsewhere;—requiring me to plunge again into those hateful Abysses, now when my coat was all brushed and I had sat down to make a pipe in peace!

How do you like the Corn-law aspects?[4] I live here in a profound seclusion from all strife in the matter; but do honestly wish, for the sake of the Aristocracy itself, our 'noble'—men would without more noise quit forever that beggarly position they have taken up. —Cobden says, if they do *not*, he in a year's time, he and the huge ready-money Cottonmen will fling them on their back and wrench the power from their hands forever and a day![5] I believe it; and do not want to see such an issue.

By the bye is old Davy living, excellent old man![6] Can he tell me anything about a 'Sir John Burgoyne Bar^{t}';[7] to whom Cromwell writes on the 10 April 1643, as to a Commander for the Parl^{t} somewhere in the Eastern Association? A Bedfordshire man, I believe; Father of Sir Roger d^{o}: both of them "recruiters"[8] to the Long Parl^{t}—otherwise to me dark as night. Ask the noble old Davy, if you can or dare

Yours ever truly
T. Carlyle

1 Carlyle's note on Naseby battle in the first edition of his *Cromwell*, I, 211-14.

2 Thus in original MS.

3 Cromwell letters which came to Carlyle's attention after publication of the first edition.

4 In December members of Peel's cabinet had refused to support his proposal to repeal the Corn Laws. He resigned on the 9th, but the Whigs failed to form a government. Peel resumed office on the 20th and introduced the Repeal Bill on January 27.

5 Richard Cobden (1804-65), named by Sir Robert Peel as the man chiefly responsible for repeal of the Corn Laws.

6 David Elisha Davy, Suffolk antiquarian, who, through EFG, had aided Carlyle at times while the latter was writing his *Cromwell*. See note added by EFG to letter from Carlyle, Oct. 26, 1844.

7 In his note to the letter Carlyle identified Sir John as "the Burgoyne of Potton in Bedfordshire, Chief Committee man in that County, not a member of our Association."

8 Puritans and Independents, elected in 1645 to fill vacancies in Parliament, were dubbed "Recruiters" by the Royalists.

To Thomas Carlyle

Boulge
Thursday [January 22, 1846]

Dear Carlyle,

I should have written to you before about Naseby; but I was on the point of going to London, so that I could have spoken to you on the matter. I shall not however go if I can help it; and as your proof-sheets are come, I send them back as well corrected as could by word of mouth.

The *Square* of Naseby consisting of "beershop-smith's shop," etc., consists also, and that mainly, of *farm-houses*; which I doubt you mistook for labourers' Cottages. We do not shine in timber and houses at Naseby; my Papa began with a good work of enclosure; but a great Colliery elsewhere has devoured all means of further improvement.

I thought it a pity you did not give some more graphic sketch of Naseby battle, seeing that the scheme of it was to be made out pretty distinctly. Since I added my corrections to your text, I have sorted out your Naseby letters from a distant box, and I enclose you one paper which you sent me as a chart of general instruction, and which *does* give a very good and spirit-stirring brief of the battle. Can you not stick this in, with a very little alteration? I can easily imagine how, after the toiling through Rushworthian Infernos, etc.,[1] for four or five years, you sicken at the thought of retracing your steps; but here now I send you what you wrote on the subject before you were sick of it. Pray stick it in: it ought to go in. I have super-added in this confounded red ink (I have no other now) a jot or two of circumstance, which may or may not seem useful. At all events, mind you keep the paper safe, and return it to me; for it reminds me well of that pleasant autumn I passed at Naseby.

I have one or two piddling queries to ask you in return for the heaps of half-answered things you have asked me. But if the answers do not lie quite on the surface to you, do not think of troubling yourself about them: sufficiently bothered as you are with your second Edition. I am rejoiced your Book has made such way. I am content to take your Hero, whole and without a flaw. What will Hallam[2] and the other Dryasdusts say in the Edinburgh?

By the by, I must not forget Roger Burgoyne.[3] Davy is sure to know nothing about him as Roger is Bedfordshire—of Potton, as you must know. I wish you did not know the verses about "I, John of Gaunt." Do you?

I, John of Gaunt,
Do give and do grant
To Roger Burgoyne
And the heir of his loyne,
Both Sutton and Potton
Until the world's rotten.

Don't be very indignant if you *have* heard all this since you were a child, as I have; but any local history of Bedfordshire or Cambridgeshire (I am not quite sure in which Potton is) will tell you all about so famous a family.

As to Corn Laws, I have on this as on so many matters no opinion of my own; but stick to that of the wisest, so far as I can know them to be wise. They all say the Corn Laws must go—so, down with them.

I hear your horse does well;[4] you will have to pay the horse-doctor something—which you must not mind, as these casualties will happen. I am sure W. B[rowne] has done his best for you. He is very little of a reader; but he is grateful to you for your "Past and Present," which has helped to make him make himself of use among the poor.

What a farrago of a letter! It beats Rushworth. I shall add my little queries[x] which you will not spend any thought or memory about; and so with a wish of good New Year to you and Mrs. Carlyle remain

Yours as ever
Edward FitzGerald

[x] They all relate to the Civil War time, and may be answered by Yes or No, or the date of a Year.

1. Was the Board of Presbyters called "The Parity"?
2. Which public oath began "Whereas I believe in my conscience, etcc.,—I will aid and assist," etcc.?
3. Was there any proposal for a *National Synod*, either while the regular high Church Convocations were sitting, or the Presbyterian Assembly?
4. Was the *rack* ever used in Charles' time?
5. Was there ever any talk of *50* subsidies being given!!
6. Pray, what is the meaning of the Lord's "*giving protection*" to people; "that such an one is his servant, and employed by him; when perhaps he never saw the man in his life, or heard of him"?
7. When or how, during that time, did the Irish Lords "*take upon themselves*" in Parliament?

[1] John Rushworth (1612-90). EFG refers to his *Historical Collections, 1618-1648*, 8 vols., 1659-1701.

[2] Henry Hallam (1777-1859), historian, father of the Arthur Hallam immortalized by Alfred Tennyson in *In Memoriam.* Henry Hallam was a contributor to the *Edinburgh Review.*

[3] Son of Sir John Burgoyne, both father and son Parliamentary commanders.

[4] See letter from Carlyle, June 27, 1845, n.1.

To W. B. Donne

Boulge, Thursday
[January 29, 1846]

My dear Donne,

Your Speech,[1] and your letter, came in due order. I liked many parts of the Speech much; Barton and some Woodbridge people were so charmed with it that they all determined to devote their sixpences toward the possession of it.

Thank you for your invitation now, and at so many times before. When I write to you that I am going into Norfolk, I do not do so in order that you may as a matter of course, be bound to invite me; but, doubtless, when I get so near, I am glad to run over from time to time and shake hands with you. I shall be going to Geldestone somewhere about the beginning of next week, I suppose. If you go to Yarmouth, let me know; perhaps I may see you there. Or could you not come over to Geldestone to see me?

So you really think of going with your boys to Bury St. Edmunds[2]—where we ourselves were so lately, as it seems, at school. So Time brings about his revenges.

I heard from Spedding a week ago; but he says nothing of Mrs. Rhode's death,[3] nor of his new Seignories. He is got back to London. Carlyle's Cromwell is getting to a second Edition: which surprises me, coming so soon. But I am glad of it. Have you seen Dickens' new paper?[4] and what do you think of the "Cricket"?

So now let me hear of your movements, and believe me

Yours ever truly,
Edward FitzGerald

[1] A pamphlet published by the Norwich Athenaeum containing an address delivered by Donne at a meeting of the society, October 17, 1845. He had been asked to speak on the benefits of literature to the individual and to society.

[2] Donne had shared his home at Mattishall with his great-aunt, Mrs. Anne Donne Bodham, who had died January 3 at the age of 97. In July he moved to Bury St. Edmunds where he maintained his residence until 1854, two years after he was appointed Librarian of the London Library.

[3] Spedding's elderly aunt, a member of the household at Mirehouse.
[4] *The Daily News*, a liberal paper founded and briefly edited by Dickens, began publication January 21. On February 9 the novelist relinquished the editorship to his friend John Forster.
The Cricket on the Hearth, Dickens' Christmas Book for 1845.

To Bernard Barton

[Boulge]
[Late January, 1846]

Dear Barton,

I send a book for Miss Barton. I have marked with a bit of brown paper where, I think, her subject begins. It is a fine book altogether: but then it is a quarto!

Will you send me back your four Volumes of Carlyle's Miscellanies? by Allen.

Beg Miss Barton to mark with pencil in this and other books good passages, etc.

Ever yours
E.FG.

I had a smoke with Crabbe last night. He abused Moses.

To Bernard Barton

Boulge
Monday morning
[February 2, 1846]

Dear Barton,

I wish you would send back by our phaeton—if not that, by Allen's boy tomorrow morning—the three other volumes of Carlyle—that is, if you will allow me to take them to Geldestone with me. I will engage to take care of them.

I send you a funny paper concerning the Epics, Odes, etc., of one Abraham Heraud,[1] a tremendous mystical Epical donkey, whose stray pieces you may have noticed in Athenaeum, etc. There is some fun in this quiz. Return the paper by Allen's boy tomorrow: I return to Geldestone tomorrow at noon.

Yours ever
E.FG.

[1] John Abraham Heraud (1799-1887), miscellaneous writer and dramatic critic for the *Athenaeum*. His *Descent into Hell* (1830) and *Judgment of the Flood* (1834) were two misguided attempts at epic poetry.

To Bernard Barton

Geldestone, Beccles
Sunday [February 8, 1846]

My dear Barton,

I positively have nothing to say but that I am but just come back from Church very cold. You would have me write in a week, and here is a week gone and here is a letter from me. Yesterday I had a note from my friend Moore apprising me of two delightful Venetian pictures that seemed likely to go at a low figure; but his letter (going to Boulge first) got to me too late. Perhaps it is as well. I want one Venetian Holy Family; or Unholy Family. What did Churchyard get for his pictures? I doubt, little.

I have written to Donne to ask him over here for a day; but I suppose he won't come. This day week you and I made that propitious journey over to Crabbe. Did he go to see Margaret Catchpole?[1] I have been looking over Nelson's Letters;[2] very hearty, unaffected, and clear. I don't know that they make a deep impression; time only lets one know what *has* made a deep impression. I had a note (wonderful to relate) from Alfred Tennyson. He is not well, and does not love the world much now that he is only allowed two glasses of wine daily.

Now I *have* written half a sheet—to my own surprise. Kind remembrances to Miss Barton, please; and yours to command

E. FitzGerald

[1] The portrait, no doubt, now in Christchurch Mansion Museum, Ipswich, painted "from memory" by Richard Cobbold, Rector of Wortham, Suffolk. Cobbold (1797-1877) wa, also author of *The History of Margaret Catchpole, A Suffolk Girl* (1845), a romantic account of the checkered career of a servant in the Cobbold home near Ipswich at the turn of the century. Margaret's love for a smuggler involved her in scrapes which led to her deportation and provided Suffolk with a legend.

[2] N. Harris Nicolas, ed., *Lord Nelson's Letters and Despatches*, 7 vols., 1844-46.

To Bernard Barton

Geldestone, Saturday
[February 14, 1846]

My dear Barton,

If you should chance to expect a letter from [me] *this* Sunday morning, lo! you are not disappointed. I believe Sunday is a good day to get letters on. I had a letter from Crabbe yesterday, which I answered forthwith. His verses show the feeling which he has deep in him; and feeling is half of the poetic element at least. Practice would have made him turn out his thoughts in a clearer shape: but practice is just the thing which *us* unprofessional poets (I mean such as I and Crabbe) want.

Now answer me this. Are you or any Woodbridge men or women going to Kesgrave[1] on Thursday? I am axed from that day till Saturday; shall go for the Friday at least. Does Meller[2] go? or any other of the tragedians?

I am not surprised at the sale of Churchyard's pictures: except as regards your little Wilson; for which I should have thought £2 a good sum. His Morland deserved more; but was very likely not to get more, because of its size. I think those Cupids met with their deserts.

I wrote to Donne to ask him here for a day on his road to Yarmouth, whither he talked of going to stay with Dawson Turner. But I have heard nothing of him; and now it will be too late; for I must get back to Boulge as early next week as I can.

One cannot pity Mrs. Sheppard. I suppose no one *does.* I went to call on Lord Berners[3] the other day,—but he was out. And now I must go out: for a covey of children with bonnets on are waiting for Uncle Edward to take them to a great gravel-pit in the middle of a fir-wood, where they may romp and slide down at pleasure. This is Saturday, and they may dirty stockings and frocks as much as they please.

My sister begs her kind remembrances to you and Miss Barton; and I am yours ever,

Edward FitzGerald.

[1] Kesgrave Hall, near Woodbridge, home of Robert Newton Shawe, chairman of the Board of Magistrates at Woodbridge. Barton's *Poems and Letters*, 1849, was dedicated by Barton's daughter to Mr. and Mrs. Shawe.

[2] Rector of St. Mary's in Woodbridge.

[3] The Reverend Henry William Wilson (1762-1851), Rector of Kirby Cane, Norfolk, who had succeeded as tenth Baron Berners in 1838.

To Bernard Barton

[Boulge Cottage]
[March, 1846]

Dear B. B.

Will you further this Athenaeum to DeSoyres when you have read it? I went to Crabbe's last night, and discussed mysteries.

Yours,
E.FG.

To W. B. Donne

Boulge, Sunday
March 8/46

My dear Donne,

I was very sorry you did not come to us at Geldestone. I have been home now near a fortnight; else I would gladly have gone to Mattishall with you yesterday. This very Sunday, on which I now hear the Grundisburgh bells as I write, I might have been filled with the bread of Life from Paddon's[1] hands.

Our friend Barton is certainly one of the most remarkable men of the Age. After writing to Peel two separate Sonnets, begging him to retire to Tamworth and not alter the Corn Laws, he finally sends him another letter to ask if he will be present at Lord Northampton's soiree next Saturday; Barton himself being about to go to that soiree, and wishing to see the Premier. On which Peel writes him a most good humoured note asking him to dine at Whitehall Gardens on that same Saturday! And the good Barton is going up for that purpose.[2] All this is great simplicity in Barton: and really announces an internal Faith that is creditable to this Age, and almost unexpected in it. I had advised him not to send Peel many more Sonnets till the Corn Law was passed; the Indian war arranged; and Oregon settled: but Barton sees no dragon in the way.

We have actors now at Woodbridge. A Mr. Gill who was low comedian in the Norwich [company] now manages a troop of his own here. His wife was a Miss Vining; she is a pretty woman, and a lively pleasant actress, not vulgar. I have been to see some of the old Comedies with great pleasure; and last night I sat in a pigeon-hole with David Fisher[3] and "revolved many memories" of old days and old plays. I don't think he drinks so much now: but he looks all ready to blossom out into carbuncles.

We all liked your Athenaeum address much; which I believe I told you before. I have heard nothing of books or friends. I shall hope to see you some time this spring: and so am yours ever,

Edw[d] FitzGerald

1 The Reverend Thomas Paddon, Vicar of Mattishall, 1821-61.

2 EFG erred somewhat. Lord Northampton invited Barton for March 21; Peel's invitation was for the 14th. See Barton's account of the evening spent as Peel's guest, *New Letters*, pp. 108-15. Shortly before resigning as Prime Minister in June, 1846, Peel recommended the pension of £100 granted to Barton that year.

3 Retired actor and co-owner of a theater circuit established by his father in Suffolk and Norfolk. The Woodbridge theater had been one of the Fisher houses.

To Frederick Tennyson

Boulge, Woodbridge
[March, 1846]

Dear Frederic,

I have been wondering some time if you were gone abroad again or not. I go to London toward the end of April—can't you manage to wait in England? I suppose you will only be a day or two in London before you put foot in rail-coach or on steamer for the Continent; and I excuse my own dastardly inactivity in not going up to meet you and shake hands with you before you start, by my old excuse; that had you but let me know of your coming to England, I *should* have seen you. This is no excuse; but don't put me out of your books as a frog-hearted wretch. I believe that I, as men usually do, grow more callous and indifferent daily: but I am sure I would as soon travel to see your face, and my dear old Alfred's, as any one's. But beside my inactivity. I have a sort of horror of plunging into London; which, except for a shilling concert, and a peep at the pictures, is desperate to me. This is my fault, not London's; I know it is a lassitude and weakness of Soul that no more loves the ceaseless collision of Beaux Esprits, than my obese ill-jointed carcase loves bundling about in coaches and steamers. And, as you say, the dirt, both of earth and atmosphere, in London, is a real bore. But enough of that. It is sufficient that it is more pleasant to me to sit in a clean room, with a clear air outside, and hedges just coming into leaf, rather than in the Tavistock or an upper floor of Charlotte Street. And how much better one's books read in country stillness, than amid the noise of wheels, crowds, etc., or after hearing them eternally discussed by no less active tongues! In the mean time, we of Woodbridge are not without our luxuries; I enclose you a play-bill just received; *I* being one of the distinguished Members who have bespoken the play. We shan't all sit together in a Box, but go dispersed about the house with our wives and daughters.

White I remember very well. His Tragedy[1] I have seen advertised. He used to write good humorous things in Blackwood—among them, Hints to Authors, which are worth looking at when you get hold of an odd volume of Blackwood. I have got Thackeray's last book,[2] but have not yet been able to read it. Has any one heard of old Morton, and of his arrival at Stamboul, as he called it? And poor Elizabeth![3]

Now it is a fact that as I lay in bed this morning, before I got your letter, I thought to myself I would write to Alfred. For he sent me a very kind letter two months ago; and I should have written to him before, but that I have looked in vain for a paper I wanted to send him. But, find it or not (and it is of no consequence) I will write to him very shortly. You do not mention if he be with you at Cheltenham. He spoke to me of being ill. I am not well, and am medicating; but let neither that nor my being forced to wear a truss make you suppose I am in such a dismal condition that a cheerful letter would be an insult. A red face[4] and fourteen stone weight, repudiate such suspicion. It always must give me great pleasure to hear from you. I think you should publish some of your poems. They must be admired and liked; and you would gain a place to which you are entitled, and which it offends no man to hold. I should like much to see them again. The whole *subjective* scheme (damn the word!) of the poems I did not like; but that is quite a genuine mould of your Soul; and there are heaps of single lines, couplets, and stanzas, which would consume all the Milneses, Taylors, and DeVeres,[5] like stubble. N.B. An acute man would ask how I should like *you*, if I do not like your own genuine reflex of *you*? But a less acute, and an acuter, man, will feel or see the difference.

So here is a good sheet full—and at all events, if I am too lazy to travel to you, I am not too lazy to write such a letter as few of one's contemporaries will now take the pains to write to one. I beg you to remember me to all your noble family, and believe me yours ever,

Edw[d] FitzGerald

[1] James White published *The Earl of Gowrie* in 1846. His *Hints to Authors* appeared in *Blackwood's Magazine* October, 1835-May, 1836, and January-December, 1841, both passim.

[2] *Journey from Cornhill to Grand Cairo*, published in January, 1846.

[3] See letter to F. Tennyson, [Oct., 1845], n.1.

[4] "FitzGerald had lost a good deal of his high colour and was very good and rational—I got to like him," Mrs. Carlyle wrote in May, 1849 (*Jane Welsh Carlyle's Letters to her Family*, Leonard Huxley, ed., New York, 1924, p. 333).

[5] Richard Monckton Milnes, Henry Taylor, and Aubrey de Vere. "Milneses, Taylors, and DeVeres" deleted by Wright.

From Thomas Carlyle

Chelsea
8 April 1846

Dear Fitzgerald,

I have now put the little Sketch of Naseby Fight, rough and ready, into its place in the Appendix:[1] it really does pretty well, when it is fairly written out; had I had time for that, it might almost have gone into the Text,—and perhaps shall, if I ever live to see another Edition. Naseby Field will then have its due honour;—only you should actually raise a Stone over that Grave that you opened (I will give you the *shin-bone* back and keep the *teeth*):[2] you really should,—with a simple Inscription, saying merely in business English: "Here, as proved by strict and not too impious examination, lie the slain of the Battle of Naseby. Dig no farther. E. FitzGerald, ——— 1843."[3]—By the bye, *was* it 1843, or 2, when we did those Naseby feats? tell me, for I want to mark that in the Book. And so here is your Paper again, since at any rate you wish to keep that. I am serious about the Stone!

You sent me several Queries; of hardly above one of which could I at the moment say anything satisfactory: wherefore, being in huge haste, and known by you to be in such, I said nothing;—waiting till you came to Town, and we could at leisure discuss the several affairs, by word of mouth, and clean pipes and good tobacco! Several things may be explained then!

I have had again a most distressing business with this Book of Cromwell, and the new Letters for it: but I must not grudge; Labour, I think, is *well* invested there, a very safe place. These *Letters* will most probably survive all my other Books, and my contemporaries' other Books;—and do more good perhaps than anything I ever tried or could try in the "literary" way. That is no extravagant supposition. If they put poor mortals off that thrice accursed notion of theirs, that every clever man in this world's affairs must be a bit of a liar too, the consequences would be invaluable! A truly accursed Notion; all false too; and a "Doctrine of Devils," if there ever was one! Witness Peel, poor fellow, this day,—to go no farther. I hope to do a little towards kicking that Notion into Chaos yet: we have had quite enough of it here in the terrestrial European regions for a couple of centuries past!

W. Browne, the most courteous and obliging of men, has sent me back my Horse: I was on the brute today for the first time;—thin and rough, but airy as a Kangaroo: too airy, and be hanged to it! I think of yoking it into some old shandrydan, and setting my Wife to tame it by driving; I really do. —When are you coming up to Town? I expect to be well thro' with the weight of this Printing business in a week or two: in about a month, they ought to have the Book *out.*

Adieu dear Fitzgerald.

Yours ever truly
T. Carlyle

[1] Appendix 8 of the 1846 edition of *Cromwell's Letters and Speeches.*

[2] See pp. 345-46.

[3] EFG ignored the suggestion. The two men failed in efforts to set up a stone in 1855 and again in 1873.

To Bernard Barton

60 Charlotte St.
Rathbone Place.
[April, 1846]

My dear Barton,

I have been very bilious and very resentful of this London atmosphere. And all epistolary power has left me. I have been able to manage no book but Mrs. Trollope's novels; of which one, "the Robertses on their Travels"[1] is very entertaining and, I think, instructive. I wish our good folks who go abroad yearly to stare, make fools of themselves, and learn much less good than evil, would read and take to heart the true picture of so many of them drawn in that novel.

I sent Churchyard a note some days ago, apprizing him of my locality, and hoping I should see him ere long. I keep all my picture expeditions till he comes up. Indeed, I have lost all appetite for such sight[s]: and I think would go farther to see a bit of clear blue sky over a furze-blossomed heath than any Titian in the world.

On Thursday I dined with a large party at Portland Place; among the company your friend *Ainsworth*[2] figures: and your other friend *Wilson* comes to sing to us in the evening. Ainsworth is, in my opinion, a *Snob*; but I don't reveal my opinion at P.P. Tennyson and I sometimes get a walk and a talk together. He is no Snob. He has been lately standing as Godfather to one of Dickens' children—Count d'Orsay being the other Godfather—insomuch that the poor child will be named "Alfred d'Orsay Tennyson Dickens"! proving clearly enough, I think, that Dickens is a *Snob.*[3] For what is Snobbishness and Cockneyism but all such pretension and parade? It is one thing to worship Heroes; and another to lick up their spittle.

I expect Edward Cowell to-day. He comes to London to see his Lady, and to buy Persian books. I shall be glad to see him; he will bring up a waft of Suffolk air with him—O! the bit of salmon I eat yesterday! I feel it within me like churchyard fat. I scratch out a capital C because I mean a burial place and not any person. Farewell for the present.

Ever yours,
E.FG.

1 The novel satirized the English tourist on the continent. The book, observed Michael Sadleir in 1927, might be distributed "today . . . it contains little . . . that is really out of date" (*Anthony Trollope, A Commentary*, p. 89).

2 Harrison Ainsworth (1805-82), hard-working editor and popular Gothic novelist; a social lion, despite the storm of indignant criticism which had broken after publication in 1839 of his *Jack Sheppard*, a novel based on the career of a common thief who twice escaped from Newgate Prison before he was hanged.

3 A snap judgment later canceled by EFG. He found Dickens unaffected and modest when they met; and in 1874 he wrote, "Dickens . . . did not love Humbugs." Thackeray had begun his series of essays on "The Snobs of England" in *Punch*, February 21, 1846.

To William Pickering

60 Charlotte St., Rathbone Place
[April, 1846]

Sir:

It has been for some time almost impossible to get a copy of Selden's Table-talk.[1] Surely the book deserves, and would repay, reprinting. It is the only one of Selden's that can be said to survive now; well exemplifying what Clarendon says of him—that in his books he was somewhat harsh and obscure; "but in his conversation he was the most clear discourser, and had the best faculty of making hard things easy, and presenting them to the understanding of any man that hath been known." Johnson, whose fame rests on somewhat the same foundation, said this little book was worth all the French "*ana*" put together.

But the Table-talk wants re-editing, as well as re-printing. It was originally ill-printed in 1689—and succeeding editions have done little to rectify the errors of the first. Some colloquial phrases need explanation; some (as not being absolutely Selden's own words, but those of his Editor) may even be altered. In some cases absolute nonsense has been re-printed over and over again, for want of a little attention and alteration. Some things were evidently spoken upon other topics than those under which they are now noted; and a still farther sub-division of some of the longer articles is always an advantage in books of this kind.

But the great need of re-editing lies in this. Milward, who records all these sayings during a twenty years acquaintance with Selden, dedicates the books to Selden's executors, and warns them "to *distinguish times*, and in your fancy to carry along with you the *when* and *why* many of these things were spoken—this will give them the more life, and the smarter relish." Most certainly; and this was easy to those whom he addressed, as they had lived in those very times and had known Selden so well. They would immediately refer each saying to its proper occasion, and see it in its proper light. But this is not so with us; we must either come to the book prepared beforehand with some historical knowledge of the man and his times; or else a date, or note of the circumstances, should be appended to any saying that needs it. For Milward has often gathered up under one head (as in the case of "Bishop," "King," etc.) allusions and opinions which, owing to the revolution of things in that day, *seem* contradictory; and some which, owing to the peculiar humour of Selden, *are* so. For Selden did not go the whole length of either party, but agreed and disagreed with both in turn. He was against Bishop and King when they were supreme; and against Parliament and Presbyter when they ruled the roost. Perhaps he hated the latter most as being "parvenus" and pressing hardest upon him toward the end of [his] life. Surely all this requires a little annotation; and a little re-arrangement so as to mark the progress of event and opinion; keeping still to the old alphabetical order of topics, which perhaps is best.

I leave with you my copy in which some attempt at this revision is made, but by no means completed. Some notes also must be added concerning old Law, and old Customs; easily supplied by those conversant with the subject.

I should be glad to hear if you see reason to approve my design[2]—and remain, Sir,

Your obedient Servant,
Edward FitzGerald

[1] John Selden (1584-1654), Orientalist, jurist, and member of Parliament, a man of wide learning whose advice was sought by James I and Francis Bacon. *Table-Talk: Being the Discourses of John Selden, Esq.*, compiled by his secretary, Richard Milward, was published in 1689.

[2] We may wonder what further negotiations ensued after Pickering received EFG's letter. The following year, 1847, the publisher issued *The Table-Talk of John Selden, Esq.*, "with a biographical preface and notes by S. W. Singer, Esq." Preceding the notes in the edition appears the statement, "Part of the following Illustrations were kindly communicated to the Editor by a gentleman to whom his best thanks are due, and whom it would have afforded him great pleasure to be allowed to name."

FitzGerald's copy of Milward's work, later given to Aldis Wright, was a 1777 edition. On the flyleaf was written, "E. FitzGerald Norwich June 16/41." The copy had been carefully re-edited and many pages bear marginal notes in EFG's handwriting. In the *Letters and Literary Remains* Wright comments on Singer's indebtedness to the unidentified gentleman: "It might have been said with truth that the 'greater part' of the illustrations were contributed by the same anonymous benefactor, who was, I have little doubt, FitzGerald himself." The annotations in EFG's copy of the *Table-Talk*, Wright adds, "are almost literally reproduced in the Notes to Singer's Edition."

Neither Pickering nor Singer should be suspected of any double-dealing in the transaction. EFG's contribution to the work was undoubtedly used with his full knowledge and consent. After the labor of preparing a manuscript, he invariably shrank from the ordeal of seeing a book through the press; and he sought, always and zealously, to maintain anonymity in any activity that could draw public attention to him.

To Bernard Barton

60 Charlotte St.,
Rathbone Place
Pmk., May 5, 1846

My dear Barton,

You will think me very negligent. Crabbe, I suppose, will think I am offended with him. For I owe him and you a letter this long while, I think. But I have no wits to write with in this London, where, positively, I have not enjoyed one hour's clear health since I have been in it.

Tomorrow Tennyson and I are going to get a pint or two of fresh air at Richmond: and we are to wind up our day at Carlyle's by way of a refreshing evening's entertainment. I met C. last night at Tennyson's; and they two discussed the merits of this world, and the next, till I wished myself out of *this*, at any rate. Carlyle gets more wild, savage, and unreasonable every day; and, I do believe, will turn mad. "What is the use of ever so many rows of stupid, fetid, animals in cauliflower wigs—and clean lawn sleeves—calling themselves Bishops—Bishops, I say, of the Devil—not of God—obscene creatures, parading between men's eyes, and the eternal light of Heaven," etcccccc. This, with much abstruser nonconformity for two whole hours! —and even as it was yesterday, so shall it be to-morrow, and the day after that—in saecula saeculorum!

I met Ainsworth at P. P. but had not much talk with him, and did not give him your love. He works very hard at gentility now. Churchyard has doubtless told you of his jaunt with me: and I suppose you have fallen greatly in love with his two little fruit pieces. I have seen nothing since. Indeed, I don't go into the streets now, but get out by the Regent's Park to Primrose Hill, where the air is a little purer.

Thank Miss Barton for the book extracts she sent me. And drive over round by Boulge Cottage one afternoon and tell me if my anemones and irises are in full glow. My heart would leap up to see them.

Farewell. Ever yours,
E.FG.

To Thomas Carlyle

[Boulge Cottage]
Pmk., June 5, 1846

Dear Carlyle,

I find that I did not enclose W. Browne's very off-hand Bill; but here it is. I think you must have mourned at the inefficiency of Men when you got my letter with the Hamlet omitted.

I enclose also a bit of a letter from my wild friend Morton, who is Correspondent to the Daily News at Constantinople. He tells a story of one *Longworth*, Correspondent of the Chronicle at the same place; and I think the pocket handkerchief adventure must entertain you. It is a little drama; quite enough for the French to make a pleasant piece of. I should not have presumed to send you this foolery had Cromwell been yet in hand; but as he is now done with, it may go. You can keep the letter till I see you again.

We have noble hot weather with a fine breeze always blowing: not what I call too hot, on that account. There is no thunder, nor sultriness. Rain is wanted; but I always stick to the old Proverb that "Drought never did harm in England."

Yours truly
Edward FitzGerald

[W. Browne's bill read:]

Expenses of keeping the Horse	6£
bringing to London	1.10.
Horse being attended for the accident	– 1.10.0
	9.0.

Morton's Longworth, no doubt, was G. A. Longworth who in 1840 had published A Year among the Circassians. *According to Morton, Longworth was fired with a desire to ally himself with the Circassians, one of the last of the peoples of the Caucasus to succumb to the domination of Russia. At the British Legation in Constantinople, he sought out an official by the name of Urquhart, reputed to be extremely popular among the Circassians, and requested a letter of introduction to the warring chiefs. Urquhart gave Longworth a large silk handkerchief or scarf with three stars on one portion and three arrows on the other. "This," he said with a lordly gesture, "will be worth all the letters in the world. Tell them that Daoud Bey [Urquhart's Circassian* nom de guerre*] sends them that for their national banner. The arrowheads symbolize their heroic resistance to the Russians, and the stars that heavenly justice which is looking down on their cause. This will rally about you all Circassia." When Longworth reached Circassia, he narrowly avoided execution as a Russian spy because he could offer no identification. He presented Urquhart's scarf, which was ignored by all except the daughter of Longworth's host, who begged for the piece of silk. When Longworth next saw the "banner," it had been converted into a girdle; and, wrote Morton, "was flirted with an innocent vanity on the tail of a Circassian belle. The stars and arrowheads, distributed with admirable symmetry, shown conspicuous on either stern quarter."*

To W. B. Donne

Boulge Hall, Woodbridge
[c. June 8, 1846]

My dear Donne,

I don't know which of us is most to blame for this long gulph of silence. Probably I; who have least to do. I have been for two months to London; where (had I thought it of any use) I should have written to try and get you up for a few days; as I had a convenient lodging, and many beside myself would have been glad to see you.

I came back a week ago; and on looking in at Barton's last evening he showed me your letter with such pleasure as he is wont to receive your letters with. And there I read all the surprising story of your moving to old Bury.[1] When I passed through Cambridge two months ago, Thompson said (I think) that he had seen you; and that you had given up thoughts of Bury. But now you are going. As you say, you will then be nearer to us than you now are at Mattishall; especially when our Railroad shall be completed.[2] In my journeys to and from Bedfordshire, I shall hope to stay a night at the good old Angel, and so have a chat with you.

I saw very little of Spedding in London; for he was out all day at State paper offices and Museums; and I out by night at Operas, etc., with my Mother. He is however well and immutable. A. Tennyson was in London; for two months striving to spread his wings to Italy or Switzerland. It has ended in his flying to the Isle of Wight till Autumn, when Moxon promises to convoy him over;[3] and then God knows what will become of him and whether we shall ever see his august old body over here again. He was in a ricketty state of body; brought on wholly by neglect, etc., but in fair spirits; and one had the comfort of seeing the Great Man. Carlyle goes on fretting and maddening as usual. Have you read his Cromwell? Are you converted—or did you ever need conversion? I believe I remain pretty much where I was. I think Milton, who is the best evidence Cromwell has in his favour, warns him somewhat prophetically at the end of his Second Defence against taking on him Kingship, etc., and in the tract on the State of England in 1660 (just before it was determined to bring back Charles the Second) he says *nothing at all* of Cromwell, no panegyric; but glances at the evil ambitious men in the Army have done; and, now that all is open to choose, prays for a pure Republic! So I herd with the flunkies and lackies, I doubt—but am yours notwithstanding—

E.FG.

1 Donne moved to Westgate Street, Bury St. Edmunds, in July.

2 The railroad from Ipswich to Bury St. Edmunds was opened for passenger service the following December. The distance by rail from Ipswich was 26 miles.

3 Tennyson spent August on the Continent with his publisher, Edward Moxon.

From Thomas Carlyle

Seaforth House, Liverpool
26 july, 1846

Dear Fitzgerald,

After much futile consultation with myself, about walking in the Chiltern Hills and other equally promising speculations, Naseby having failed, and Suffolk lying on the wrong side of the Country for me,—I decided last Monday morning that I was too much of a spooney at present for any of those adventures; that I ought once for all to stow myself like luggage, which was my real character, into the Liverpool train, and so be bowled off straight to my destination, with no effort but that of packing my boxes, and paying so much cash. On Monday accordingly I did, not without an effort, get seated in the mail train, and that same afternoon, was honourably carried hither,—safe so far, and without exertion more than even a spooney was equal to. That is the history of my travels hitherto; which I meant to have given you some days sooner, had not indolence still prevailed. In fact I do nothing here, but smoke a good deal of tobacco, bathe once daily in the messy brine, dawdle about among the shady groves, and listen to the great voice of the Sea and the winds. An extremely indolent man indeed.

Suffolk and Boulge House I do by no means score out of my Books, tho' on this occasion I could not entertain the kind offer. Such hospitality as you describe really seems as if it would suit me right well, and at some other time the thought of running out from Cockneydom thither will certainly strive to realize itself;—a good time, which we hope *is* coming at no very great distance.[1]

The beautiful fresh air and quiet are nerving me here a little before getting into Scotland, in about a week hence, I think of a flying glance at Ireland,—over to Dublin, then up the Coast to Belfast, and so home:[2]—but we shall see whether that proves executable or not! After that, for aught I know, I am in Scotland till I go to Chelsea again. "Scotsbrig, Ecclefechan N.B." is always a central address for me in those regions, should you or your thoughts by good chance happen to wander thitherward.

Heaven love you.

Yours very truly
T. Carlyle

My Horse (Bobus we call him) goes across with me to Scotland; ends his career there. Greathurst[3] has been most helpful and faithful in all manner of emergencies connected with the Bobus department. A really worthy man.

[1] The "good time" did not arrive until August, 1855, when Carlyle spent ten days with EFG at Farlingay and Bredfield.

[2] Carlyle left Liverpool to visit his mother at Scotsbrig, Dumfriesshire. In September he crossed to Belfast and spent a week in Dublin.

[3] The FitzGerald coachman, who had arranged transportation of Bobus to Scotland.

To E. B. Cowell[1]
(Fragment)

[Boulge]
[Summer, 1846]

Dear Cowell,

I am glad you have bought Spinoza.[2] I am in no sort of hurry for him: you may keep him a year if you like. I shall perhaps never read him now I have him. Thank you for the trouble you took. . . .

Your Háfiz[3] is fine: and his tavern world is a sad and just idea. I did not send that vine leaf[4] to A. T. but I have not forgotten it. It sticks in my mind.

In Time's fleeting river
The image of that little vine-leaf lay,
Immovably unquiet—and for ever
It trembles—but it cannot pass away.

I have read nothing you would care for since I saw you. It would be a good work to give us some of the good things of Háfiz and the Persians; of bulbuls and ghuls[5] we have had enough.

Come and bring over Spinoza; or I must go and bring him.

[1] This is the first letter in the Cowell correspondence published by Aldis Wright. It is also the first in which the subject of Persian literature is mentioned. MS has not been located.

[2] The *Opera Posthuma*, which contained a selection of Spinoza's letters. See letter to Cowell, Sept. 15, 1846.

[3] An ode translated by Cowell but not published. Háfiz, Persian lyric poet of the 14th century, is noted for his *Díwán*, a collection of ghazals, lyric poems with a fixed rhyme scheme. Some scholars consider Háfiz to be the Anacreon of Persia; others, a Súfí and therefore a mystic. The disagreement raises the question of literal or allegorical interpretation of allusions by Háfiz to wine, women, love, and passion. The problem also arises in the interpretation of some quatrains in the *Rubáiyát*, but few scholars identify Omar with the Súfís.

[4] Lines from "Mosella," a descriptive poem on the Moselle River, in *Idyllia* by Ausonius:

> Tota natant crispis juga motibus, et tremit absens
> Pampinus, et vitreis vindemia turget in undis.

In a comment on identification of the passage in the *Letters and Literary Remains* (I, 235, n.1) Cowell recorded, "Aldis Wright adds in his note, 'FitzGerald used to admire the break in the line after *absens.*' I have no doubt he got that from some remark of mine. FitzGerald showed the passage to Tennyson soon afterwards" (Cowell biography, p. 423).

In the quatrain that follows, EFG paraphrases lines in Shelley's "Evening, Ponte al Mare, Pisa:"

> Within the surface of the fleeting river
> The wrinkled image of the city lay,
> Immovably unquiet, and forever
> It trembles, but it never fades away.

[5] "Nightingales and roses." ("Ghul," usually transcribed "gul" or "gol.")

To E. B. Cowell

Boulge
July 28/46

Dear Cowell,

I forget if it was *this* week you proposed to come to me; or whether I said anything about it when I wrote to you. But if not, silence meant to say that *here* I should be, and always glad to see you. I believe I shall be at liberty all next week also. I hope you found all well in London.

Yours ever
E.FG.

To E. B. Cowell

Bedford
Septr 15/46

Dear Cowell,

Here I am at last, after making a stay at Lowestoft, where I sailed in boats, bathed, and in all ways enjoyed the sea air. I wished for you upon a heathy promontory there, good museum for conversations on old poets, etc. What have you been reading, and what tastes of rare Authors have you to send me? I have read (as usual with me) but very little—what with looking at the sea with its crossing and recrossing ships, and dawdling with my nieces of an Evening. Besides a book is to me what Locke says that watching the hour hand of a clock is to all; other thoughts (and those of the idlest and seemingly most irrelevant) will intrude between my vision and the written words; and then I have to read over again; often again and again till all is crossed and muddled. If Life were to be very much longer than is the usual lot of men, one would try very hard to reform this lax habit, and clear away such a system of gossamer association—even as it is, I try to turn all wandering fancy out of doors, and listen attentively to Whately's *Logic*,[1] and old Spinoza still! I find some of Spinoza's Letters very good, and so far useful as that they try to clear up some of his abstrusities at the earnest request of friends as dull as myself. I think I perceive as well as ever how the quality of his mind forbids much salutary instinct which widens the system of things to more ordinary men, and yet helps to keep them from wandering in it. I am now reading his Tractatus Theologico-Politicus,[2] which is very delightful to me because of its clearness and acuteness. It is fine what he says of Christ—"*nempe*," that God revealed himself in *bits* to other prophets, but he *was* the mind of Christ. I suppose not new in thought or expression.

Let me hear from you, whether you have bits of revelations from old poets to send, or not. If I had the Mostellaria[3] here, I would read it; or a Rabelais, I would do as Morgan Rattler advised you.

Farewell.

Yours ever,
E.FG.

Direct to the Post Office here.

[1] Richard Whately (1787-1863), Archbishop of Dublin. His *Elements of Logic* (1826) is a treatise which limits the scope of logic to deduction.

[2] In his *Tractatus theologico-politicus*, Spinoza defends freedom of speech,

thought, and conscience in speculative matters. The work was roundly condemned when it was published anonymously in 1670.

[3] *Mostellaria,* a comedy of intrigue by Plautus.

To Bernard Barton

Bedford
Septr 19/46

Dear Barton,

I got here some days ago: and here I am likely to be for another fortnight. After that, a week at Cambridge, may be: after *that,* deponent sayeth not. But long ere winter I shall be making up my dormitory in Boulge, there to abide till another Year shall open new prospects—fresh fields and pastures new.

As you write to Crabbe, pray tell him where I am got to: and that I desire an answer to my *second* letter, which I sent him from Lowestoft. He attacked me most furiously on the old score of *Pride,* on which the man is distracted: and so I told him.[1] He may have written to Lowestoft after I left it. But if he be not too far gone in indignation with me, he will do no hurt by writing yet again. I am dropped out of his Category of Heroes for ever! he shall always be right glad to see me, he says: but he never can be disappointed in me again! How much the best footing is this to be upon with all one's friends.

Tell Churchyard that I saw at Beccles the large Collection of Pictures belonging to Mr. *Delf,*[2] with whom you bargained for your Piper and Evelyn. His pictures are all richly framed, and highly varnished: and contain some indubitable Titians, Rembrandts, and Raphaels. For the rest, I saw about three small Flemish pictures which I thought worth having. A small Jan Steen: and an old woman smelling at a pink, by one of the Teniers school: capital, I thought. Delf wants £14,000 for the whole collection: I should suppose £150 to be the fair price. Would Churchyard be so kind as to hang up, or let you hang up, my little Stothard landscape, so as to keep it out of mischief, and *in* the light? If I should pass through London, I might chance upon a frame that would suit it. Also ask C. what is the price of the Wotton horse-piece,[3] which he showed me before I left. I wish C. could be here; as the river Ouse shows some pretty things, and I should be so happy to entertain him if he came.

This note I write before breakfast: but the good Alderman Browne now descends in his dressing gown, and his broiled bacon lies upon its toast ready for him. Yesterday we dined under the ruins of a noble old place at Ampthill.[4] The last stupid Duke of Bedford dismantled it, as he does many others, in order that Woburn may be the only great gun in Bedfordshire. Farewell; pray give my kind remembrances to Miss Barton (how does the Scripture History go on?)[5] and believe me

Yours ever,
E.FG.

Direct me at Alderman Browne's
Caldwell Street
Bedford.

[1] In his notice of Crabbe's death, contributed to the *Gentleman's Magazine* in November, 1857, EFG mentioned his friend's "rashness in judgment and act, liability to sudden and violent emotions, to sudden and sometimes unreasonable like and dislike" (*Letters and Literary Remains*, VII, 422-23).

[2] The household effects of William Delf of Ballygate, Beccles (also of London), were sold at auction September 30 and October 1, 1846. Works of art advertised were "fine and genuine productions" by Blake, Guardi, Morland, Ruysdael, and others; but no Titians, Rembrandts, or Raphaels were included. However, the notice listed "Several clever pictures after Cuyp, Jan Steen . . . Rembrandt, P. P. Rubens, Teniers, etc., etc." (*Norfolk Chronicle and Norwich Gazette*, Sept. 19, 1846).

[3] EFG doubtless refers to a painting by John Wootton, 18th-century artist noted for his pictures of horses and dogs.

[4] Ampthill, a town near Bedford, site of an old castle where Catherine of Aragon had resided during her trial.

[5] In 1849, Lucy Barton published *Bible Stories for Children* with which EFG had helped her. Drafts of the stories of Joseph and David in his handwriting are among the FitzGerald manuscripts, formerly owned by the Barton family, now in the Tracy W. McGregor Collection, Alderman Library, University of Virginia. Miss Barton had published *Scripture History for the Young* in 1838.

From Thomas Carlyle

Chelsea
22 Sept^r^, 1846.

Dear FitzGerald,

Your letter finds me *here*; where I have been for some ten days now,—mostly *asleep*, for I arrived in a very wearied state. There is therefore nothing to be said about any further wandering, for a good while to come!

My Pilgrimage, so far as immediate improvement in health or spirits went, was none of the successfullest: I was dreadfully knocked about with one tumult and another; and indeed in the whole course of my journeyings, could find no place half as quiet for me as Chelsea, with an empty London behind it, now is.

After a couple of weeks in Lancashire, I went across to Scotland; saw rainy weather, rotten potatoes, brutal drunken *Navvies*,[1] and other unpleasant phenomena; went no further North than Dumfriesshire;—at length, with a dead-lift effort, decided to pass over into Ireland, by Ardrossan and Belfast, not with any hope of profit or enjoyment at all, but merely to redeem a promise I had given in those quarters. For some days accordingly I did see a bit of Ireland; roamed over the streets of Dublin, a little among the Wicklow Hills; saw Daniel[2] in his green cap in Conciliation Hall (the hugest *palpable* Humbug I had ever set eyes on); listened to Young Ireland[2] (with hope that *it* might yet turn to something); regretted much you were not with me to look on all that;—finally, by Liverpool and the swiftest power of Steam, had myself tumbled out here, and so winded up the matter. My Wife, who had not gone farther than Lancashire, was here to receive me a fortnight before: much improved in health she; I too expect to feel myself a gainer by these painful locomotions by and by. The thinnest-skinned creature cannot be left *always* to sit covered under a tub; must be pitched out, from time to time, into the general hurly burly, and ordered to bestir himself a little.

From Moxon I heard the other day that Tennyson and he *had* just been in Switzerland; that T. was actually at that time in Town, his address unknown; Moxon was himself just bound for Ramsgate,—undertook to send Alfred to me if he could; but has not succeeded hitherto. Thackeray I have heard of at Boulogne or Brighton; Spedding I missed in Cumberland: I think there is nobody yet here whom you know; but indeed I keep out of all people's way as much as may be. Do you know Poet Browning? He is just *wedded*, as his card testifies this morning; the *Mrs.* Browning still an enigma to us here.[3] "Conciliation Hall" appeared to me to be on its last legs. Tell Browne, with compliments, my Horse was sold in Annandale, £35 to a much admiring neighbour of my Brother's there. Come you and see us, speedily, and hear all the news.

Ever yours,
T. Carlyle.

[1] In 1848 these laborers employed to build railroads and canals formed a corps of lawless itinerants numbering almost 200,000 (Arthur Bryant, *Pageant of England*, 1941, p. 81).

[2] Daniel O'Connell's leadership was being challenged at the time by the mili-

tant Young Ireland Party led, with others, by Gavan Duffy, Carlyle's host in Dublin. O'Connell died the following May.

[3] Robert Browning and Elizabeth Barrett had been secretly married on September 12. After the ceremony the bride returned to her home and remained there until the 19th, when the couple left for the Continent. Carlyle, greatly admired by both Brownings, had been acquainted with Robert since 1840.

To Bernard Barton

Goldington House
Bedford
[September 24, 1846]

My dear Barton,

Thank you for your long and kindly letter. My stay here draws to a close: winds begin [to] blow cold and gusty, as you say, and leaves to fall; and it is time to draw homewards. I had intended to go and visit some Cities in the West, where I yet look one day to reside. A reason, I assure you, beyond love of change, draws me, or will one day draw me (if I have resolution to move) beyond Suffolk.[1] At least, so I now believe: but I would give much it were otherwise. But time will prove this and many more important things. I make a kind of inward groan—which I will not put down on paper as Carlyle does. I had a note from that worthy a few days since, which I enclose, though there is not much in it. Do not be at the trouble of returning it, for I do not want it.

Thank Miss Barton heartily for her kindness to good Mrs. Faiers. I only doubt she will make her too proud by such honours. I am just about to write a note home about my garden. After I leave this place, I shall go to Cambridge for [a] while. But all this I think I told you before.

Tell Churchyard I will be glad to buy his picture for the sum he names: because W. Browne, with whom I now am, would be very much delighted with it in case I should not desire to keep it. As you say, it is the old English life of it that makes it interesting: and I fancy I should like a few such memorials of the last century. These are to be found in all English country seats, and are constantly selling dirt-cheap at auctions, hung up in garrets, etc. They are historical things to us. Two or three of those pictures at Easton[2] touched me livelily.

I have been looking over parts of Croker's Edition of Boswell, and cannot but think that Carlyle has dealt unjustly with it.[3] Surely it *is* a good edition. The last two volumes besides contain anecdotes of Johnson from other people—anecdotes I had never seen before. Miss Reynolds (Sir Joshua's sister) describes the nervous gesticulations he used in the street, and before entering a room—a sort of penance-exercise, it seemed. Does Boswell describe this? As usual, when once I took up the magical book, I could have sat down and read it all through right on end: but I found it at a clergyman's house[4] near here, where I was staying for two days, and so could only devour two days' worth of it. Carlyle did a great work when he cleared away all the confusion of opinion that was abroad about this book—about Johnson and Boswell themselves—and settled the question for ever: setting up Johnson as a good representative of the English character—solid sense—dogmatic prejudice—veneration—melancholy temperament etc.

This is a short and meagre letter, returning you no such news as you sent me. But take the will for the deed. I write in a cold room, *wishing* for a fire, but of course not able to command, or hint, one in a friend's house. I believe, as you say, Crabbe has forgiven me; but I heartily hope he will never replace me on the pedestal from which he so lately took me down. "I would not rise, and so shan't fear to fall."[5]

And so from my happy station on the common mortal ground I salute you and him.

Yours ever,
E.FG.

[1] The reason was his father's financial reverses.

[2] Easton Park, one of the seats of the Duke of Hamilton, seven miles north of Woodbridge. The books and pictures at Easton, collected by Alexander Hamilton Douglas (1767-1852), realized £397,562 in 1882.

[3] In a review Carlyle had severely attacked John W. Croker's edition of *Boswell's Life of Johnson* published in 1831. After praising Croker's diligence, Carlyle wrote, "Herewith, however, must the praise unfortunately terminate." It is evident "from a very early stage of the business," Carlyle continued, how much the editor "is from within unfurnished with means for forming to himself any just notion of Johnson, or of Johnson's Life." The review, included among Carlyle's *Critical and Miscellaneous Essays*, first appeared in *Fraser's Magazine*, May, 1832.

[4] William Airy's at Keysoe.

[5] EFG was probably recalling Sir Henry Wooton's "Character of a Happy Life":

This man is freed from servile bands,
Of hope to rise, or fear to fall . . .

See letter to Barton, Sept. 19, 1846.

To Bernard Barton
(Fragment)

[Cambridge]
[October 18, 1846]

My dear Barton,

Though my letter bears such frontispiece[1] as the above, I am no longer in Bedford, but come to Cambridge. And here I sit in the same rooms in which I sat as a smooth-chinned Freshman twenty years ago.[2] The same prints hang on the walls: my old hostess does not look older than she did then. My present purpose is to be about a week here: then to go for a day or two to Bury, to see Donne; and then to move homewards. It is now getting very cold, and the time for wandering is over.

Why do you not send me your new Poem? Or is it too big to send as a letter? Or shall I buy it? which I shall be glad to do. . . .

All the preceding was written four days ago; cut short by the sudden entrance of Moore,[3] whom I have been lionizing ever since. He goes away to London today. . . .

Moore is delighted with a Titian and Giorgione at the Fitzwilliam.[4] I have just left him to feed upon them at his ease there, while I indite a letter to you.

[1] An engraving of Trinity Church, Bedford (Aldis Wright note).

[2] No. 19 King's Parade opposite King's College Chapel. His "old hostess" was Mrs. Jane Perry.

[3] Morris Moore, art critic. See letter to Milnes, [June, 1843], n.1.

[4] The Fitzwilliam collection of art, books, and manuscripts bequeathed to the University in 1816 was first housed at Cambridge in a room in the Perse Grammar School. In 1842 it was moved to the University Library, then located in the Old Schools. The present Fitzwilliam Museum was not opened until May, 1848. The exhibition room at the Perse School was sometimes referred to as "Fitzwilliam Museum," and EFG's letter indicates that the name was also applied to the corresponding room at the Library. The "Giorgione" is now attributed to Sebastiano del Piombo (data provided by L. A. Holder of FitzWilliam Museum).

To E. B. Cowell

Bury St. Edmunds
Thursday, Oct. 29 [1846]

My dear Cowell,

At last I am getting toward home. I have been for a fortnight to Cambridge: for a week here: and tomorrow I go to Ipswich. If you can, be at home about one o'clock or so: for I shall come to look for you then. I must one day bring you acquainted with the man I am with here—Donne.

Farewell. Tomorrow I hope to see you.

E.FG.

To W. B. Donne

Boulge Hall, Woodbridge
Pmk., October 31, 1846

My dear Donne,

If you would smoke my Cigars, I should be so glad you should keep those I left at your house. But as you will not, I shall be glad if you can forward them to me here, whether as *letter*, or coach parcel. Whatever you disburse in furtherance of this, let me know. I left the Cigars at the back of a sort of book-stand in your dining room: I put them on purpose there, *out of the boy's way.*

I only got home to-day: and found one letter on my table from Ireland. I did not notice it had a black edge and seal: saw it was from Edgeworthstown: written in the hand of Edgeworth's wife, who often wrote down from his dictation since his eyes became bad. But she tells me that he is dead after twelve days illness![1] I do not yet feel half so sorry as I shall feel: I shall constantly miss him.

Farewell. Thanks for all the hospitality you showed me: kind regards to all your family.

Ever yours,
E.FG.

I only send for the Cigars because without them I have not a decent one to give Crabbe.

[1] Francis Edgeworth, half brother of Maria, the novelist, died in Dublin, October 12, 1846, at the age of 37. See letter to Donne, [Feb. 5 or 12, 1835], n.7.

From Alfred Tennyson

Nov. 12, [1846]
10 St. James Square
Cheltenham[1]

My dear Fitz,

Lovely lines[x]—but I knew them before, the first, ages ago, the two last, two years ago in Schudewin's or Schneidewin's great fragments[2]—

a book Frank Lushington had and which I have ever since intended to get—I fancy those last two lines have only been lately recovered.

Why should you say that it is in vain to expect a line from me? don't you know that I esteem you one of those few friends who would still stick to me tho' the whole polite world with its great idiot mouth (wider than ever was a clown's at a fair, staring at a show) howled at me:[3] if I write not, it is not because I do not love and remember, but from some small absurd cause of not having pen, or paper, or ink, or Queen's head within reach: How do you? You are a beast in this, that you never tell one of your well-doing and really one desires sometimes to know. I got your letter an hour ago. I have to answer (ought to do it tonight but won't) a young lady, an old gentleman, a middleaged gentleman, and a young one—yet I write to you old Fitz—after that say I won't write.

Well, I went to Switzerland[4]—saw Blanc—he was very sulky—kept his nightcap on—doff'd it one morning when I was knocked up out of bed to look at him at four o'clock—the glance I gave did not by any means repay me for the toil of travelling to see him. Two other things I *did* see in Swissland, the stateliest bits of landskip I ever saw—one was a look down on the valley of Lauterbrunnen while we were descending from the Wengern Alp—the other a view of the Bernese Alps from the end of the Gemmi Pass—don't think that I am going to describe them. Let it suffice that I was so satisfied with the size of crags that Moxon being gone on before in vertigo and leaning on the arm of the guide—I *laughed* by myself. I was satisfied with the size of crags: but mountains, great mountains disappointed me. I couldn't take them in I suppose, crags I could. The Swiss people—no words can describe their lowness in the scale of man, gaingreedy, goitred, miserable-looking poor devils. The serfs of Russia, I doubt not, are princes to these republicans. The Canton of Berne where the land is flatter and more fertile is I believe an exception—but this I past thro' by night.

You will be in town this or that side Xmas. I have got two invitations for Xmas. One to Whites, Isle of Wight, one to Tom Taylors, now forlorn of Wigans,[5] who had gone for their holidays to Paris—consequently he has a bed for me, perhaps—perhaps—I shall go. Can't tell. You know he has a joint house with the Wigans at Brompton—if I go shouldn't I be glad to see you?

I called on Dickens at Lausanne who was very hospitable, and gave us biscuits (a rare luxury on the Continent, not such as are sweet and soft, but unsweet and hard) and a flask of Liebfraumilch, which is being interpreted "Virginis lac," as I dare say you know.

November 1846

Goodbye I write in vast
haste to save the
nights post just
starting
Ever thine
A. Tennyson

I have just got Festus;[6] order it and read. You will most likely find it a great bore, but there are really *very grand* things in Festus.

I have heard that your friend Barton has got 100 per ann from Peel pensionwise. I am consequently nearly reconciled to mine. Certainly I am twice a Barton in verse.

[x] *Ὀιον τὸ γλυκύμαλον*, etc. Sappho

[1] Tennyson's mother lived at Cheltenham from 1846 to 1850.

[2] FitzGerald inserted the "x" and the MS note in Greek. The lines Tennyson refers to are from the "Bridal Songs" of Sappho:

> *Οἷον τὸ γλυκύμαλον ἐρεύθεται ἄκρῳ ἐπ' ὕσδῳ ἄκρον ἐπ' ἀκροτάτῳ λελάθοντο δὲ μαλοδρόπηες, οὐ μὰν ἐκλελάθοντ', ἀλλ' οὐκ ἐδύναντ' ἐπίκεσθαι.*

"As the sweet-apple blushes on the end of the bough, the very end of the bough, which the gatherers overlooked, nay overlooked not but could not reach." H. T. Wharton, *Sappho*, 1908, p. 132.

Friedrich Wilhelm Schneidewin, German classical scholar, published *Delectus poesis Graecorum elegiacae, iambicae, melicae* (1838-39), in which fragments from the lyric poets were for the first time given in a convenient form.

[3] Tennyson alludes to criticism which had followed the granting of his pension of £200 a year before. Sir Edward Bulwer Lytton had violently attacked Tennyson in *The New Timon*, a romance introducing leading figures in British public life. The passage concludes with the observation that Peel had pensioned Tennyson "while starves a Knowles." (Actor and dramatist.) Tennyson retaliated with "The New Timon and the Poets," published in *Punch*, February 28, 1846. The antagonists later became friends.

[4] A portion of this letter, strangely altered, is given in the *Tennyson Memoir*, I, 233-34. Tennyson had visited Switzerland in August with Edward Moxon, his publisher; and the *Memoir* version begins, "Well, Moxon went to Switzerland; saw Blanc, he was very sulky. . . ."

[5] For James White, author who lived at Bonchurch, Isle of Wight, see letter to Thackeray, Sept. 1, 1837. Tom Taylor, dramatist and editor of *Punch*; Alfred Wigan, actor and playwright.

[6] *Festus*, by Phillip Bailey, a rambling verse drama of 20,000 lines when first published in 1839. Bailey published successive expanded editions until, in 1889, the poem was more than twice its original length. The work, which imitates Goethe's *Faust*, is a philosophical and theological treatise; EFG, indeed, found it a bore. As Tennyson remarked, "grand things" are to be found in *Festus*; but Hugh Walker observes that it is doubtful "whether the grains of wheat are worth the search through all the chaff."

To W. F. Pollock

Boulge, Woodbridge
Wednesday [November 18, 1846]

My dear Pollock,

I was glad to hear from you; and I congratulate you on having secured stedfast office and revenue[1] that will put you at ease, and end all trouble and disappointment. Henceforth you may sit on your bench and look down complacently on the *mare magnum* of wigs all striving which shall rise topmost. And, as you say, you can now set about finding out what to do with much spare time; a thing hard to do at all times (how tiresome was a whole holiday at school!), but most hard to men who have for the greater part of their lives been accustomed to a regular day-full of work. And all must leave it at some time. I have been all my life apprentice to this heavy business of idleness; and am not yet master of my craft; the Gods are too just to suffer that I should.

Since I saw you I have been here, except going for a month to Bedford, and a fortnight to Cambridge. At Cambridge I saw Thompson, whose mind is bunged up with Lecture and Tutor work; and Merivale,[2] who looks fat, and grows grey, and was quaint and pleasant as usual. I have seen no new books: and have even neglected to get down my due box-full of old ones from the London Library. Have you seen Festus?[3] Tennyson writes word there are very fine things in it. He is come back from Switzerland rather disappointed, I am glad to say. How could such herds of gaping idiots come back enchanted if there were much worth going to see? I think that tours in Switzerland and Italy are less often published now than formerly: but there is all Turkey, Greece, and the East to be prostituted also; and I fear we shan't hear the end of it in our lifetimes. Suffolk turnips seem to me so classical compared to all that sort of thing.

I believe I shall be in London shortly before, or after, Christmas: and shall assuredly look for you. Do you ever see Thackeray? I read some pretty verses of his in Mrs. Norton's Drawing Room Scrap Book;[4] and *such* a copy of verses to her Ladyship by Sir Edward![5] It is impossible to read worse in sense or sound. And how Mrs. Norton could admit such vulgar flattery! I am afraid the Suffolk turnips are better than her too; and they are not particularly good this year.

Yours ever
E.FG.

[1] Pollock had been appointed a Master in the Court of Exchequer in August, at the age of 31. He had been reluctant to forego the excitement which circuit

life provided but found the leisure "for literary and scientific pursuits," which the new post offered, too great a temptation to resist.

[2] W. H. Thompson, tutor at Trinity; Charles Merivale, Fellow at St. John's.

[3] See letter from Tennyson, Nov. 12, n.6.

[4] "The Anglers," one of Thackeray's delightful semi-comic "ballads," published in *Fisher's Drawing Room Scrap-Book*, edited by Caroline Norton (London and Paris, 1847). The selection, one of the more polished of Thackeray's poems, appears in the Biographical Edition (XIII, 76-77), with the title "Piscator and Piscatrix."

[5] Edward Bulwer-Lytton, novelist and dramatist, whose contribution, "The Hon. Mrs. Norton," was the last selection in the gift book. The first stanza reads:

> The Queenly spirit of a Star,
> That long'd to tread the earth,
> Pass'd into mortal mould—the hour
> Made holy by thy birth;
> And kept its lustre and its power,
> To teach the earth,
> The wondering earth,
> What shapes immortal are!

To E. B. Cowell

[Boulge Cottage]
[November, 1846]

Dear Cowell,

The weather is so ungenial, and likely to be so, that I put off my journey to Ipswich till next week. I do not dislike the weather for my part: but one is best at home in such: and as I am to stay two days with the Hockleys,[1] I would fain have tolerably fair days, and fair ways, for it: that one may get about and so on. One does not mind being cooped up in one's own room all day. I think of going on Monday. Shall you be at home next week?

I have read Longus[2] and like him much. Is it the light easy Greek that pleases one? Or is it the story, the scenery, etc.? Would the book please one if written in English as good as the Greek?

The lines from Nonnus[3] are very beautiful. It is always a pleasure to me to get from you such stray leaves from gardens I shall never enter.

I have been doing some of the dialogue,[4] which seems the easiest thing in the world to do but is not. It is not easy to keep to good dialectic, and yet keep up the disjected sway of natural Conversation. I talk, you see, as if I were to do some good thing: but I don't mean that.

But any such trials of one's own show one the art of such dialogues as Plato's, where the process is so logical and conversational at once: and the result so plain, and seemingly so easy. They remain the miracles of that Art to this day: and will do for many a day: for I don't believe they will ever be surpassed—certainly not by Landor.[5]

Yours ever,
E.FG.

[1] Major Thomas Henry Hockley and his sister Mary, of St. Matthews Street, Ipswich. For Major Hockley, see letter to Pollock, (c. mid-June, 1842), n.6.

[2] Longus (c. A.D. 200), Greek Sophist and author of *Daphnis and Chloë*, a pastoral romance which approaches the modern novel in psychological analysis. Cowell had published an essay on the story in *Wade's London Review* in February.

[3] Nonnus of Panopolis (early 5th century) who wrote a poem on Christ but is chiefly known for *Dionysiaca*, an epic in 48 books. "But his poetry seems more remarkable for quantity than quality," writes F. L. Lucas. "Like Ovid, he is too clever; but he is not so clever as Ovid (*Greek Poetry for Everyman*, 1951, p. 368).

[4] His *Euphranor, A Dialogue on Youth*, not published until 1851. EFG had long been critical of the effect of English university education on students, and in 1839 wrote that those at Cambridge "looked as if they were only fit to have their necks wrung." After his visit to Cambridge in October, 1846, he decided "to do something . . . against a training system" of which he "had seen so many bad effects" (letter to Pollock, March 15, 1854).

[5] Walter Savage Landor's *Imaginary Conversations*.

To E. B. Cowell

Boulge, Saturday
[November, 1846]

Dear Cowell,

This note will be too late for this night's post—but will perhaps catch you before you start on Monday. I don't know that I want any books; I am sure I can't afford them—I have scarce had heart to go on with Spinoza, such *sieves* as the preliminary definitions are which have to contain the whole system. But my Eyes have been so indifferent, I have read very little: have therefore hired a gig in which I drive at six miles an hour looking over the corn fields, and catching far off views of the old Sea. I shall be very glad to see you whenever you come; I am not going out anywhere at present as far as I know. Bring over heaps of good bits and *cram* me. Farewell.

Yours ever,
E.FG.

To Bernard Barton

60 Charlotte St.
Fitzroy Square
[Early January, 1847]

My dear Barton,

Lest you should begin to consider that I had forsook you, like so many other faithless correspondents—I will endite to you this morning:—notwithstanding my head aches, and I feel (as usual in London) disinclined to the business of composition. If I see any frame such as you want, I will book it for you: but I have had no time for picture-hunting. What with people coming to see me, and I going to see them. I took a look in at Christie's yesterday, in passing: but there was nothing worth looking at—much less buying. Pray tell this to Churchyard; who wished to know about it. I ought not to forget to say however that there was *one* picture: an early Wilson: a view of Sion House:[1] true, pure, and in some respects admirable.

I find my friends here all kind and well as usual. John Allen swears he means to come into Suffolk: and Thackeray also: so you will see the latter potentate in course of time. I saw Carlyle yesterday: he foams about Ireland at present: on Sunday I shall perhaps see him again.

My Father seems pretty well; my Mother remarkably so.

Don't you see how tardily my news retails itself? Shall I not quickly put an end to this worthless epistle? I had a note from Mrs. Shawe[2] inviting me to Kesgrave on Wednesday: but I was not *sure* of my return on that day. I was obliged to write "nay" in reply. But I *hope* to be down about the middle of the week. So now Goodbye for the present.

Yours,
E.FG.

[1] Richard Wilson. (See letter to Barton [c. June 1, 1845].) The picture of Sion House, near Brentford, Middlesex, is said to have cost him royal patronage. The landscape, painted for George III, was submitted to the King by Lord Bute, who subsequently protested that Wilson's fee, 60 guineas, was too high. Wilson replied that if the King could not pay the entire sum at once, he would accept payment in installments.

[2] Of Kesgrave Hall, near Woodbridge.

To E. B. Cowell

Pmk., Woodbridge
January 13, 1847

Dear Cowell,

I am always delighted to see you whenever you can come, and Friday will do perfectly well for me. But do not feel bound to come if it snow, etc. In other respects I have small compunction, for I think it must do you good to go out, even to such a desert as this.

I have not got Phidippus[1] into any presentable shape: and indeed have not meddled with him lately: as the spirit of light dialogue evaporated from me under an influenza, and I have not courted it back yet. Luckily I and the world can very well afford to wait for its return. I began Thucydides two days ago! and read (after your example) a very little every day, *i.e.* have done so for two days. Your Sanscrit sentences are very fine. It is good for you to go on with that. We hear Mr. Nottidge[2] is dying: who can be sorry for him!

Yours,
E.FG.

[1] EFG's first book, *Euphranor, a Dialogue on Youth*, published in 1851. Until the eve of publication FitzGerald referred to the work as "Phidippus," the name of one of the speakers. While reading proof, he substituted the name of Euphranor, another character, who takes a more active part in the dialogue.

[2] The Reverend John Thomas Nottidge, Rector of the united parishes of St. Clement and St. Helen, Ipswich, 1821-47, called "The Father of the Clergy" at Ipswich. He died January 21, 1847.

To W. M. Thackeray

[Boulge]
[January, 1847][1]

My dear old Thackeray,

I have intended to write to you twenty times since my return from London. First, I meant to tell you how it was I did not go to your house as I have agreed to do one Sunday; we were to have dined and gone to Gurlyle's: but I was so stupified with cold I thought the best thing was to go to bed. And next day I left London. By this time my apology comes rather late: for doubtless you have forgot the occasion of it.

Secondly I wanted to tell you I have (shall have by the 10th.) £5 for that poor Elizabeth if you think this a proper season to give it her in. Have you heard of Morton?

I read in some paper that you Punches have been caricaturing the Irish distresses,[2] which I hope is not true. The Times does what it can to prevent people giving privately—as if there were any danger of their doing so too much! I cannot believe the Times's is good Political Economy; good Charity I am sure it is not. What they say of Ireland may as well be said of the poor in England; let the Government do all —a very comfortable doctrine; but I thought it had become almost exploded.

What a wretched affair is the Battle of Life,[3] scarce even the few good touches that generally redeem Dickens. I see your Perkins[4] greatly extolled in Spectator and Athenaeum. Dickens' last Dombey has a very fine account of the over-cramming Education System; worth whole volumes of Essays on the Subject if Big-wigs would believe that laugh[t]er may tell truth. The boy who talks Greek in his sleep seems to me terrible as Macbeth.[5]

I, in company with many people here, have got an influenza that makes me now feel as if I had walked forty miles and then been beaten for my pains. On Friday I am going to assist at a rent-dinner—no tenants of mine or my Father's—but of an old Squire's[6] who persists in thinking I can help to entertain the farmers.

Pray put the Honorable Julia into Punch; she is fair game. I doubt a Lord Lindsay becomes troublesome. Remember [me] to all yours I know little and great and believe me yours ever

Edward FitzGerald

[1] In a letter dated by Dr. Ray "February ? 1846" Thackeray wrote about raising money for "poor honest Elizabeth" (*Thackeray Letters*, II, 227). Internal evidence, including Thackeray's statement that he had resigned from the *Morning Chronicle*, fixes the 1847 date. His resignation took effect in January, 1847 (Ray, *The Uses of Adversity*, p. 323).

For Elizabeth, see letter to F. Tennyson, [Oct., 1845].

[2] *Punch* adopted an editorial flippancy in its comments on Ireland during the 1846 potato famine.

[3] Dickens' Christmas Book for 1846.

[4] *Mrs. Perkins's Ball*, Thackeray's first Christmas Book, 1846. Reviewed in *The Spectator*, Dec. 19, 1846, p. 1218; in *The Athenaeum*, Dec. 19, 1846, pp. 1290-91.

[5] *Dombey and Son*, part IV, Jan., chap. 12.

[6] Probably Squire Jenney of Hasketon.

To Thomas Carlyle

[Boulge]
[c. February 8, 1847]

Dear Carlyle,

When I go into Norfolk, which will be some time this Spring, I will go to Yarmouth and see for Mr. Squire,[1] if you like. But if he is so rusty as you say, and as I also fancy, I doubt if he will open his treasures to any but to you who have already set him creaking. But we shall see. Some of his MS. extracts are curious and amusing. He writes himself something like Antony Wood,[2] or some such ancient bookworm. It is also curious to hear of the old proud angry people about Peterboro', who won't show their records.

I have not seen the lives of the Saints you spoke of in a former letter. But when I go to London I must look out for a volume. I have begun to read Thucydides, which I never read before, and which does very well to hammer at for an hour in a day: though I can't say I care much for the Greeks and their peddling quarrels; one must go to Rome for wars.

Don't you think Thackeray's Mrs. Perkins's Ball very good? I think the empty faces of the dance room were never better done. It seems to me wonderful that people can endure to look on such things: but I am forty, and got out of the habit now, and certainly shall not try to get it back ever again.

I am glad you and Mrs. Carlyle happen to be in a milder part of England during this changeable and cold season. Yet, for my own sake, I shall be sorry to see the winter go: with its decided and reasonable balance of daylight and candlelight. I don't know when I shall go to London, perhaps in April. Please to remember me to Mrs. Carlyle.

[1] William Squire, of Yarmouth, had written Carlyle late in January that he had 35 Cromwell letters in his possession. For EFG's excellent report on his meeting with Squire, see his letter to Carlyle, June 29, 1847.

[2] Anthony Wood, or Anthony á Wood, as he later called himself (1632-95), Oxford antiquary and historian.

Bernard Barton wrote to W. B. Donne, March 29, 1847,[1] *"His birthday is on the 31st, and just before he went to Geldestone, he made me a present of a pretty little jug to hold hot water, at my nightly symposiums. As he is ever and anon giving me some little memorial of this sort, Lucy, all unknown to me, . . . knitted a silken purse, which the chances are a hundred to one he will never use; however, I'm to send it, and I mean to send the following with it, for fun. I should say that FitzDennis is his 'other Name' with us from his criticizing my Verses, as he is wont to do, and the last line has reference to Scott's 'Pirate,' which we have lately been reading together.*

FOR MAISTER FITZDENNIS[2]

these

FitzDennis, FitzDennis, thou'st given me a jorum,
Hot water to hold, when I moisten my clay;
So I, who am called *of the Muses own Quorum,*
Would fain, in some measure, thy kindness repay.

Besides, 'tis thy Birthday! with joy, not with sorrow,
I drink to thy health ere the grog can grow cool:
What a mercy it chanced not to fall on the morrow,
To make thee, by Birth-right, a mere April fool!

Poets seldom make presents, because they've no Money!
Could I give thee a reason more trite or more terse?
So, in true Irish fashion, 'I send ye, my Honey!'
Fitting gift for a Poet, a poor empty Purse!

But a plague on all Pelf! I say not on all Purses;
My rhymes are exhausted, my time, too, is gone:
Here's health to FitzDennis! to bear with my Verses,
And to Minna! and Brenda! and glorious John!

Claud Halcro"[3]

[1] *Donne and Friends*, pp. 119-20.

[2] Suggested by the name of the critic, John Dennis (1657-1734), frequent target of Pope's rancor and ridicule.

[3] Minna, Brenda, and Halcro, characters in *The Pirate*. Halcro is a poet who, like EFG, greatly admired "Glorious John" Dryden.

To Bernard Barton

[Geldestone]
Pmk., March 31, 1847

Dear Barton,

I would return your compliments in verse if I could do so by return of post. But my Muse is a slow coach. In honest prose then let me foremost thank Miss Barton for her very handsome purse—and you for all your good wishes—and your good verses; which, even in my character of Dennis, I must admit to be easy and pleasant as such verses should be.

Your allusion to the Pirate (at the end of the verses) makes me confess my peccadillo:—that the other night, being possessed with a desire to see what became of the Zetlanders, I hunted all over Kerrich's Library for the book: but (very properly, as you may think) did not find it—so I must even wait to finish the journey with you. I shall leave this place on Monday or Tuesday: be at Earl Soham[1] for two days: and toward the end of the week, be in a condition (I hope) to read with you what remains to be read of the pleasant book.

You may imagine I have seen this house under happier circumstances than at present;[2] Kerrich is gone with his brother to London for a while: Eleanor has acted, and acts, with great sagacity and firmness. She has to learn to put off the yoke of submission to which she has so happily subjected herself for twenty years, and to be the *Master*: for a time at least: a thing not agreeable to the good feminine nature: but necessary here, and in so many cases beside. Her present to me on my birthday was a pair of plain cloth gloves! more touching to me, as coming out of the small funds of a large family, than if they were filled with gold.

And now farewell for the present, my dear Barton. Again let me thank Miss Barton for her royal purse: and believe me,

Yours very truly,
Edward FitzGerald.

[1] To visit his friend, R. H. Groome, the rector.

[2] An allusion to financial problems and emotional tension resulting from the failure of the Pendleton Colliery Company in which John Kerrich was a partner.

To E. B. Cowell

60 Charlotte St.
Rathbone Place
[May 7, 1847]

Dear Cowell,

I have been for ten days in London; and mean to return next week. You have been here, it seems, at the same time with myself. I still beat my breast with anger at not going to see the Charlesworths:[1] but what with men coming to my rooms, and being hauled about to theirs: and formal visits to my own home; I live in a fever of intending to do so many things and doing nothing. I shall get back to Suffolk without again filling my box with London Library books, I think.

For the last month I have read *nothing*: scarce looked into a book: leaving Pericles blowing up the Athenians in the second year of the war: just before he died. Homer sticks fast in the fifth book. The causes of this interruption are trivial, and not worth detailing. "C'est égal." When I get back to Suffolk I shall set to work again, with the music of the new leaves about me, and the humming of bees who come to make their first visits to the new-awakened flowers. (Leigh Hunt all over)[2] Your Swallow verses must be pretty; but I see the English won't do for them. Like the burden of a song, which is more for its sound than its sense, those children's verses are untranslatable. The Solomon story is very grand indeed: new to me, as most things are: I will hang that pearl in Tennyson's ear this very evening.

Tennyson is now in London; ill and dispirited. He has finished his University of Women:[3] and read me three Books of it the other night: I was tired with hacking about London, and slept as he read; so that I cannot speak of it. And yet what I did hear did not charm me wholly. I thought it rather monotonous, and that his old fault of talking big on a common matter was more apparent. But I do not assert this by any means; first, I was knocked up: and also I may be fast growing out of my poetical age. Everyone likes the poem. Carlyle exists and even prospers in his way: at present his chief desire is to exterminate the Irish nation. I have scarce seen him since I have been in town: and a visit to Chelsea is one of the things *yet to be done!*

I don't think I saw the DeQuincey you speak of: though I did see one lately with some wretched attempts at humour in it. There was a bad paper about Tennyson by Gilfillan.[4]

I have not seen Phidippus[5] since you saw him; till next winter he must sleep. As to publishing: I doubt if the good it would do would be a set off to my own private inconvenience. I feel strongly on the subject: and I sometimes think the best thing to do would be to save £100, and propose it publickly as a prize to the best essay written on the subject. Much nonsense would be written: and the best Essay a poor thing perhaps: but people would hear of it, and begin to consider the matter.

I hope to see you soon on my return: that you will come over to me, and eat Mrs. Faiers' bread, and launch me into the Homeric *μέγαν ῥόον*[6] (if that is the right gender). More and more do I find myself fit only for the country, and for country people: London is very pestiferous.

Yours
E.FG.

[1] Mrs. Cowell's parents, who were living in London.

[2] In other words, "Cockney School prose."

[3] *The Princess*, published in November.

[4] George Gilfillan (1803-78), miscellaneous writer, whose critique appeared in *Tait's Edinburgh Magazine*, April, 1847.

[5] *Euphranor*, the dialogue in which EFG attacks weaknesses in English public school and university education.

[6] "Mighty stream."

To Bernard Barton

[London]
[May 7, 1847]

Dear Barton,

I suppose you have already concluded that (in spite of all my protestations) I never really do mean to go back to Suffolk. But still I verily do mean it: and moreover should be glad to be there now. But still I have not done all I wanted to do: and probably shall leave much undone. My books from the London Library are not got: your frame has not been inquired for; this and that friend has not been visited—for what with the visits to some, and the visits of some to me, days and nights have rolled away. I must go to Chelsea once more.[1] I believe, to-morrow: I am to dine with the Woods,[2] if possible, on Sunday—Major Moor is said by all to be better: *much* better than he was this time two years. He is silent in company, but, they say, not *sad.* William Wood is going to stand for Oxford.[3] A better member of Parlt. can not well be.

I find now that Alfred Tennyson is at his very dirty hotel in Leicester Square: filled with fleas and foreigners. He looks thin and ill: and no wonder, from his habits.[4]

Thus far I wrote yesterday: but a man came in: made me lay down my letter, and took up my time till I was forced to go out. And now things so fall out that you will get my letter on a Sunday: when perhaps you are most pleased to get it. As far as I see now, I mean to leave London on Monday; perhaps go for two days to Bedford: and then home. I am not yet clear about future Geldestone arrangements: but at present Kerrich and Eleanor are at Holbrook;[5] he something better, they think.

Farewell for the present.

Yours,
E.FG.

[1] To see the Carlyles.

[2] Major Moor's daughter and her husband, William Page Wood.

[3] He was elected for the City of Oxford as a Liberal and served from 1847-53.

[4] EFG frequently mentions the poet's "general mismanagement." A bottle of port a day was Tennyson's portion of wine; moreover, said EFG, he "must smoke twelve hours out of the twenty-four." Carlyle, also fond of his pipe, wrote that Tennyson was "one of the powerfullest" of smokers.

[5] Visiting his sister Jane and her husband, the Reverend John B. Wilkinson.

EFG's rhymed invitation to Crabbe of Bredfield and the Vicar's response, to be found on page 413, belong, chronologically, at this point in the correspondence. The date of both is [Early June, 1847].

To E. B. Cowell

Boulge
Tuesday [June 15, 1847]

My dear Cowell,

I went to Brooke's[1] for you: and had a look with James for Calderon: but to no purpose—the whole Library has been discomposed—is not yet re-composed—and James knew by certain tokens that Calderon was not yet *placed.*

If you vehemently desire this extract, James will hunt up Calderon out of the yet undigested heap.

I shall not leave home this week, having two engagements that detain me. Next week perhaps I may move; shall assuredly pay my respects to you whenever I do so: and then shall give Donne a look.

Yours ever,
E.FG.

[1] Francis Capper Brooke, of Ufford Place, owner of an exceptionally fine library.

To Samuel Laurence

Geldestone Hall
Beccles
[June 20, 1847]

My dear Laurence,

I have had another letter from the Bartons asking about your advent. In fact Barton's daughter is anxious for her Father's to be done, and done this year. He is now sixty-three; and it won't do, you know, for grand-climacterical people to procrastinate—nay, to *proannuate*—which is a new, and, for all I see, a very bad word. But, be this as it may, do you come down to Woodbridge this summer if you can; and that you can, I doubt not; since it is no great things out of your way to or from Norwich.

The means to get to Ipswich are—A steamboat will bring you for five shillings (a very pretty sail) from the Custom House to Ipswich, the Orwell steamer; going twice a week, and heard of directly in the fishy latitudes of London Bridge. Or, a railroad brings you for the same sum; if you will travel third class,[1] which I sometimes do in fine weather. I should recommend *that*; the time being so short, so certain: and no eating and drinking by the way, as must be in a steamer. At Ipswich, I pick you up with the washerwoman's pony and take you to Woodbridge. There Barton sits with the tea already laid out; and Miss about to manage the urn; plain, agreeable people. At Woodbridge too is my little friend Churchyard, with whom we shall sup off toasted cheese and porter. Then, last and not least, the sweet retirement of Boulge: where the Graces and Muses, etc.

I write thus much because my friends seem anxious; my friend, I mean, Miss Barton: for Barton pretends he dreads having his portrait done; which is 'my eye.' So come and do it. He is a generous, worthy, simple-hearted, fellow: worth ten thousand better wits. Then you shall see all the faded tapestry of country town life: London jokes worn threadbare; third rate accomplishments infinitely prized; scandal removed from Dukes and Duchesses to the Parson, the Banker, the Commissioner of Excise, and the Attorney.

Let me hear from you soon that you are coming. I shall return to Boulge the end of this week.

P.S. Come if you can the latter part of the week; when the Quaker is most at leisure. There is a daily coach from Woodbridge to Norwich.

[1] Ipswich had been linked with London by rail in 1846 when the Eastern Union Railway built a line joining the Eastern Counties Railway at Colchester. By December the road was extended to Bury St. Edmunds. In 1847 the two companies merged and in 1849 completed the line to Norwich. The railroad between Ipswich and Norwich, through Woodbridge, opened in 1859 (Lillian J. Redstone, *Ipswich Through the Ages*, Ipswich, 1948, p. 44, and Jack Simmons, *The Railways of Britain*, 1961, p. 198).

Tennyson described a third-class railway journey in 1840: "I got into the third class of carriages in the train at Leicester. It is a carriage entirely open, without seats, nothing but a rail or two running across it, something like pens of cattle" (Tennyson, *Memoir*, I, 175).

To Thomas Carlyle

Boulge
June 29/47

Dear Carlyle,

Last week I went over to Yarmouth and saw Squire.[1] I was prepared, and I think you were, to find a quaint old gentleman of the last century. Alas for guesses at History! I found a wholesome, well-grown, florid, clear-eyed, open-browed, man of about my own age! There was no difficulty at all in coming to the subject at once, and tackling it. Squire is, I think, a straightforward, choleric, ingenuous fellow—a little mad—cracks away at his family affairs. "One brother is a rascal—another a spend-thrift—his father was of an amazing size—a prodigious eater, etc.—the family all gone to *smithers*," etc. I liked Squire well: and told him he must go to you; I am sure you will like him better than the London penny-a-liners. He is rather a study: and besides he can tell you bits of his Ancestor's journal; which will indeed make you tear your hair for what is burned—Between two and three hundred folio pages of MSS. by a fellow who served under Oliver; been sent on secret service by him; dreaded him: but could not help serving him. Squire told me a few circumstances which he had picked up in running over the Journal before he burnt it; and which you ought to hear from himself before long. Dreadful stories of Oliver's severity; soldiers cut down by sabre on parade for "violence to women"—a son shot on the spot just before his Father's house for having tampered with Royalists—no quarter to spies—noses and ears of Royalists slit in retaliation of a like injury done to Roundheads;—many deeds which that ancient Squire witnessed, or knew for certain, and which he and his successor thought severe and *cruel*:—but I could make out nothing unjust—I am very sure *you* would not. The Journalist told a story of Peterboro' Cathedral like yours in your book about Ely—Oliver marching in as the bells were ringing to service: bundling out canons, prebendaries, choristers, with the flat of the sword; and then standing up to preach himself in his armour! A grand picture. Afterwards they broke the painted windows which I should count injudicious;—but that I sometimes feel a desire that some boys would go and do likewise to the Pusey *votive* windows; if you know that branch of art.

Ancestor Squire got angry with Oliver toward the end of the Journal; on some such account as this—Cromwell had promised him a sum of money; but the ancestor got taken prisoner by pirate or privateer before he went to claim the money; had to be redeemed by Oliver; and the redemption money was subtracted from the whole sum promised by Oliver when payment-time came. This proceeding seemed to both Squires, living and dead, shabby; but one not belonging to the family may be permitted to think it all fair.

On the whole, I suspect you would have used Ancestor Squire as you have used many others who have helped you to materials of his kind; like a sucked orange: you would have tossed him into the dirt carelessly, I doubt; and then what would Squire minor have said? Yet he himself did not like all his Ancestor had done; the *secret* service, which our Squire called "*spyage*"; going to Holland with messages and despatches which he was to deliver to some one who was to meet him on the quay, and show him a gold ring; the man with the gold ring supposed to be the Stadtholder! I tried to persuade our friend there was no great shame in being an agent of this sort; but he said with a light rap on the table that *he* wouldn't do such a thing.

I have now told you something of what remains in my head after our conference; but you must see the man. What gave us the idea of his being old was his old-fashioned notions; he and his family have lived in Peterboro' and such retired places these three hundred years; and amazing as it may seem to us that any people should be ashamed that their ancestors fought for Low Church, yet two hundred years are but as a day in a Cathedral Close. Nothing gives one more the idea of the Sleeping Palace than that. Esto perpetua! I mean, as long as I live at least. When I expressed wonder to Squire that his wife's friends, or his Peterboro' friends, should be so solicitous about the world's ever knowing that their ancestors had received letters from Cromwell, he very earnestly assured me that he knew some cases in which persons' advancement in public life had been suddenly stopt by the Queen or her ministers, when it got wind that they were related in any way to Cromwell! I thought this a piece of dotage, as I do now; but I have heard elsewhere of some one not being allowed to take the name of Cromwell; I mean not very many years back; but more likely under a George than under a Victoria.

I think Squire must be a little crazy on this score; that is, the old dotage of a Cathedral town superstition worked up into activity by a choleric disposition. He seems, as I told you, of the sanguine temperament; and he mentioned a long illness during which he was not allowed to read a book, etc., which looks like some touch of the head. Perhaps brain fever. Perhaps no such thing, but all my fancy. He was very civil; ordered in a bottle of Sherry and biscuits: asked me to dine, which I could not do. And so ends my long story. But you must see him.

Yours,
E.FG.

He spoke of a portrait of Oliver that had been in his family since Oliver's time—till sold for a few shillings to some one in Norwich by some rascal relation. The portrait unlike all he has seen in painting or engraving: very pale, very thoughtful, very commanding, he says. If he ever recovers it, he will present you with it; he says if it should cost him £10—for he admires you.

1 William Squire, claiming descent from a Samuel Squire who had served under Cromwell, wrote to Carlyle late in January, 1847, that he possessed 35 letters written to his ancestor by Cromwell, and a journal which Squire had kept during his period of service. Carlyle wrote to EFG on February 8, asking him to call on Squire at Yarmouth. In June Squire mailed transcripts of the alleged Cromwell letters to Carlyle and later stated that he had burned the originals, which information Carlyle forwarded to EFG, urging him to see Squire. EFG's account of the interview is excellent reporting.

"Thirty-five Unpublished Letters of Oliver Cromwell," contributed by Carlyle to *Fraser's Magazine* for December, 1847, raised a storm. Carlyle asserted that the documents were "of indubitable authenticity." Not all readers agreed. Macaulay branded them as forgeries. Henry Hallam accepted them as genuine. Carlyle included them as an appendix in the 1849 edition of *Cromwell*, granting in his preface, however, that they "must remain of doubtful authenticity." EFG remained convinced of their genuineness until the end of his life. Subsequent writers on Cromwell have refused to accept the letters as genuine.

To E. B. Cowell

Boulge
[July 24, 1847]

Dear Cowell,

Your letter was welcome. That which you wrote me at Geldestone I duly received, with all its good things in it. I have been back from Norfolk a fortnight: but have had a painter from London[1] staying with me a week, and a little invitation for every day beside; so that I have had no time to read, or write scarcely. I was in Ipswich last week, to put my painter upon the railroad: but I had not time to look for you: as I had a Lawyer to see. Somewhere about the beginning of June[2] I shall start upon a little trip; to York perhaps: and shall be out some six weeks. Can't you give me a look in here next week; I can drive you back to Ipswich, if not hither from it; or vice versa. Try.

I am only got half way in the third book of Thucydides: but I go on with pleasure; with as much pleasure as I used to read a novel. I have also again taken up my Homer. That is a noble and affecting passage where Diomed and Glaucus, being about to fight, recognize each other as old family friends, exchange arms, and vow to avoid each other henceforth in the fray.[3] (N.B. and this in the tenth year of the war!) After this comes, you know, the meeting of Hector and Andromache—which we read together; altogether a truly Epic canto indeed.

Yes, as I often think, it is not the poetical imagination, but bare Science that every day more and more unrolls a greater Epic than the Iliad—the history of the World, the infinitudes of Space and Time! I never take up a book of Geology or Astronomy but this strikes me. And when we think that Man must go on to discover in the same plodding way, one fancies that the Poet of today may as well fold his hands, or turn them to dig and delve, considering how soon the march of discovery will distance all his imaginations, [and] dissolve the language in which they are uttered. Martial,[4] as you say, lives now—after two thousand years—a space that seems long to us whose lives are so brief; but a moment—the twinkling of an eye—if compared (not to Eternity alone) but to the ages which it is now known the world must have existed, and (unless for some external violence) must continue to exist. Lyell, in his book about America,[5] says that the falls of Niagara, if (as seems certain) they have worked their way back southwards for seven miles, must have taken over 35,000 years to do so, at the rate of something over a foot a year! Sometimes they fall back on a stratum that crumbles away from behind them more easily: but then again they have to roll over rock that yields to them scarcely more perceptibly than the anvil to the serpent. And those very soft strata which the Cataract now erodes contain evidences of a race of animals, and of the action of seas washing over them, long before Niagara came to have a distinct current; and the rocks were compounded ages and ages before those strata! So that, as Lyell says, the Geologist looking at Niagara forgets even the roar of its waters in the contemplation of the awful processes of time that it suggests. It is not only that this vision of Time must wither the Poet's hope of immortality—but it is in itself more wonderful than all the conceptions of Dante and Milton.[6]

As to your friend Pliny, I don't think that Time can use his usual irony on that saying about Martial. Pliny evidently only suggests that "at non erunt aeterna quae scripsit" as a question of his correspondent; to which he himself replies "Non erunt *fortasse*."[7] Your Greek quotations are very graceful. I should like to read Busbequius.[8] Do *you* think Tacitus *affected* in style, as people now say he is?

Yours ever
E.FG.

[1] Unidentified. Samuel Laurence did not go to Woodbridge until August 2.

[2] EFG wrote June in error for August. The date of this letter is definitely fixed by that which follows.

[3] *Iliad*, book VI.

[4] Latin poet and epigrammatist of the first century A.D.

[5] The passage to which EFG alludes appears in *Travels in North America*, 2 vols., 1845, I, 32-34. EFG enlivens Lyell's well-written account of the formation of the gorge.

[6] Tennyson's "Parnassus," included in *Demeter and Other Poems*, appears to be a denial of EFG's vision of Time destroying the poet's hope of immortality. The volume, published in December, followed the appearance of FitzGerald's *Letters and Literary Remains* in 1889. Tennyson acknowledged that "Romney's Remorse," another poem in the selection, was suggested by a passage about the artist in EFG's letter to Allen, August 29, 1842.

[7] Writing at the time of Martial's death, Pliny questioned the chances for immortality of Martial's poetry; but he added, "still, no doubt, he composed them upon the contrary supposition" (*Epistularum*, III, 21).

[8] Latin name of Augier Ghislain de Busbecq (1522-92), Flemish writer, diplomat, and traveler.

To E. B. Cowell

[Boulge Cottage]
[July 26, 1847]

Dear Cowell,

I wrote you a long letter on Saturday;[1] and somehow mislaid it so as to defy all search of myself and Mrs. Faiers. So, I only send a line now; to say I have received your letter; that I have been back from Norfolk a fortnight; have had a painter staying with me who is now gone; that I shall set off on a little trip perhaps next week. Can't you come over here and see me before I go?

I said many things about books in the letter I wrote: which I have not time to recapitulate. I liked all your quotations, and wish to read Busbequius; whose name would become an owl. Try and come over here: and believe me yours

E.FG.

If I lay my hand on my letter, you shall have it.

[1] The preceding letter. July 26, 1847, was a Monday.

To Lucy Barton

[Boulge Cottage]
[Late July, 1847]

Dear Miss Barton,

I enclose Laurence's note received this morning. I shall write to tell him to put off no longer—unless you and your Father should very much prefer *after* Wednesday. I can stay here till Monday week, I believe.

I had got into a muddle about the *price*. It appears that I told you £15, which it is; but, not being content with wholesome intuition, I took to consider what figures I fancied were written up in Laurence's painting room as announcing the price of a crayon drawing: and then I thought I saw the figures "£20" all written in Laurence's hand. I thought it looked more certainly his writing than £15. Such is human imagination!

Yours truly
E.FG.

If you want to say anything to Laurence his note carries his address.

To E. B. Cowell

[Boulge]
[July 30, 1847]

Dear Cowell,

On Monday I expect a painter from London to draw Barton's phiz:[1] and I have long promised to play the agreeable to sitter and sittee during the operation. So I shall scarcely be at home for three days; after that I shall be engaged, I believe, with my Father here; and at the very beginning of the week after next, I fly for my trip—not to see Donne (who is gone away somewhere for the holidays)—but to see York, and one or two places of repute lying thereabout in the North.[2] I usually take some little excursion of this kind in a summer; and a very little satisfies me.

I was in hopes you would have come here yesterday, that we might have had a talk together. Perhaps if I go to Ipswich next week, I may get a glimpse of you. If not, we must wait till Autumn.

As to my Epic theory, I do not say that the duration of the bodily fabric of the world is a greater interest *than the Soul* of man; but that it is of greater interest than most other subjects *in* the Soul of Man. Surely the mere *affections* of the Homeric Heroes are not so august as the expanse of intellect by which we men take in these vast computations of History and Change and Time! We have not only tradition (Religious and other) but positive scientific demonstration that Man's foot did not walk this Earth for *yogas* and *yogas*,[3] while Great Nature was as it were trying her prentice hand on large and blundering shapes of creatures, who gradually disappeared away from the catalogue of living things as the more complex and perfect being Man was ready to be born into the World. You say that time is nothing: that Mahomet's moment's submersion was indeed as 1000 years. Well—be it so—still it was *an act* of Mahomet's; an act done in one moment of Eternity, and I care not how long or how short an act, so as you admit at the same time that men had gone on *acting* before Mahomet's time, and beasts and strange creatures acting and plunging about before *Men*; and the fabric of Earth rolling round the Sun before Beasts were; and Earth itself one with the Sun before that; and so on. If men, beasts, Earth, etc., have acted and moved in some continuous series of movements from a date we cannot ascertain, and cannot approach to determine, your 1000 years may be crushed into a moment; but then there was a moment before that, and a moment before that, ad infinitum; so that somehow or other "sands do make the mountain" at last, and moments the *yoga*. You say Time is subjective merely: but unless you call Action itself, and "Before and After" subjective also, you must admit some objective succession of events and acts, which succession we call Time; and however short each act may be, if they are endless, it is all the same as if each act did take up 1000 years. It does not signify whether Eternity be made up of moments or yogas. Therefore I think that Geology which has certainly discovered to us so much of the Past—and the Being of this Earth when *we were not*; is a more wonderful, grand, and awful, and therefore *Poetical*, idea than any we can find in our Poetry. For it is a FACT! Milton's Pandemonium rises "like an exhalation" and so remains in our imagination; we see all that is in it; there is nothing behind. But the *facts* of Man's history, beyond even his own appearance, recorded in granite rocks, and reaching the World we walk on and contemplate into a Past of which we can just fathom so much as to know that it is unfathomable; this really fills, and immeasurably over-fills, the human Soul, with Wonder and Awe and Sadness! There is no end to looking into this Vista. The Intellect, and the Feelings, and Intuitions and Hopes and Aspirations of Man, all rouse to look on this, and never to be satisfied!

I think that the little Greek things you like please *because they are commonplace.* It touches us to find men of 3000 years (or, if you like, three moments ago) making up nosegays of flowers, and moralizing over them just as we do now this summer of 1847. And then these feelings of ours reflected back upon us form a little crystal mirror of pure Greek verse.

Yours,
E.FG.

[1] Samuel Laurence spent August 2-4 at Barton's home while drawing a crayon portrait of him. EFG relieved the tedium of the sittings by reading *Pickwick* aloud.

[2] Within a week EFG revised his itinerary. Barton wrote to Crabbe of Bredfield on August 17, "After all the planning of his friend Brown[e] and himself the former could not go; so instead of going Northward with Wm Brown[e] he went Westward alone" (British Museum, Add. 36, 756). EFG spent August in the West Country, went thence to Leamington, visited Browne at Bedford, and did not return to Boulge until October 8.

[3] A term from Hindu chronology. The *yoga* is a unit of time of approximately 26 hours. EFG seems to have thought it a synonym for aeon.

To Samuel Laurence
(Fragment)

[London]
[c. August 9, 1847]

Dear Laurence,

. . . I assure you I am deeply obliged to you for the great trouble you have taken, and the kindness you have shewn about the portrait. In spite of all our objections (yours amongst the number) it is very like, and perhaps only misses of being quite like by that much more than hairbreadth difference, which one would be foolish to expect to see adequated. Perhaps those painters are right who set out with rather idealising the likeness of those we love; for we do so ourselves probably when we look at them. And as art must miss the last delicacy of nature, it may be well to lean toward a better than our eyes can affirm.

This is all wrong. Truth is the ticket; but those who like strongly, in this as in other cases, love to be a little blind, or to see too much. One fancies that no face can be too delicate and handsome to be the depository of a noble spirit: and if we are not as good physiognomists as we are metaphysicians (that is, intimate with any one particular mind) our outward eyes will very likely be at variance with our inward, or rather be influenced by them. Very instructive all this!

I wish you would come to me to-night for an hour at ten: I don't know if any one else will be here.

To Bernard Barton
(Fragment)

Exeter
August 16/47

My dear Barton,

. . . Here I am at Exeter: a place I never was in before. It is a fine country round about; and last evening I saw landscape that would have made Churchyard crazy. The Cathedral is not worth seeing to an ordinary observer, though I dare say Archaeologists find it has its own private merits. . . .

Tell Churchyard we were wrong about Poussin's Orion.[1] I found this out on my second visit to it. What disappointed me, and perhaps him at first sight, was a certain stiffness in Orion's own figure; I expected to see him stalk through the landscape forcibly, as a giant usually does; but I forgot at the moment that Orion was *blind*, and must walk as a blind man. Therefore this stiffness in his figure was just the right thing. I think however the picture is faulty in one respect, that the atmosphere of the landscape is not that of *dawn*; which it should be most visibly, since Morning is so principal an actor in the drama. All this seems to be more addressed to Churchyard, who has seen the picture, than to you who have not.

I saw also in London panoramas of Athens and the Himalaya mountains. In the latter, you see the Ganges glittering a hundred and fifty miles off; and far away the snowy peak of the mountain it rises from; that mountain 25,000 feet high. What's the use of coming to Exeter, when you can see all this for a shilling in London? . . . And now I am going to the Cathedral, where the Bishop has a cover to his seat sixty feet high. So now goodbye for the present.

[1] "The Blind Orion Searching for the Rising Sun," exhibited at the annual summer showing of Old Masters at the British Institution in Pall Mall. The picture is now in the Metropolitan Museum of Art, New York.

Orion, loved by the dawn goddess, Eos, according to one legend, was blinded by the father of Merope, whom he had violated. Orion sought out the palace of Eos, where his sight was restored.

To W. B. Donne

Somersetshire
August 22/47

My dear Donne,

I am in as much fault as you about writing and visiting; do not think my visit to Bury was delayed from resentment, etc. No such thing. It was partly that I was expecting to hear from you concerning the time, etc. (you had also thought of coming over for a sail on the Orwell) and partly because I had to go many times forward and backward between Geldestone. Over that house hangs a black cloud; and I see no symptom of its clearing away. Kerrich has got into the same state of mind that made his Father and Grandfather put the pistol to their heads. Perhaps to do this would be best; he is miserable himself. His wife and children are very unhappy; he is not at all fit to manage them, or his affairs: and yet not ill enough to have that charge taken from him. Eleanor does wonders in attending to him, her children, and all.

I left Boulge a fortnight ago on a little trip: have been for some days on the Devonshire coast: and am now staying with my sister.[1] I am going tomorrow to visit an old fellow-collegian who screamed to me out of the railway carriage—and I had not seen him for fifteen years—*Duncan* his name;[2] you may remember him at my rooms—a dry Saturnine humorous man. He lives in a little hole of a parsonage in Dorsetshire, and there I am going to see him. About the end of September I shall be travelling homeward; and shall call on you at Bury, as I hope. I am glad you have some literary jobs to do; which will amuse and repay you, I hope. I see that Cowell has stept into the Westminster Review[3] with an article on Persian Poetry. He did not tell me of this: but I nosed him in a stray Number that fell into my hands. His article is quite unaffected; he writes at present *without a style*; which is a good feature in a young writer, I think. Generally a man comes out dressed after Gibbon, or after Hume, or after Macaulay, etc. But Cowell seems only to wish to say what he knows; and has thought more about *knowing* than telling. He ought to do something in the world; for, as far as I see, his delicacy of discrimination is as great as his capacity for amassing—a rare combination.

Barton's portrait is a faithful one, but not, I think, a happy view of his face. Laurence made him sit *high*; so as to foreshorten the nose; a thing which few English faces will bear. I don't know about a lithograph; but perhaps it would be worth making one of so good, genial, and agreeable a man.

I am sorry Donaldson[4] fags his school so; it is a great mistake, I am sure. It is for *himself*, not for his boys, he does it, I doubt. So you are going to see little Brampton:[5] who will be full of important political disclosures.

Yours ever,
E.FG.

[1] Andalusia de Soyres at Bath.

[2] Francis Duncan, Rector at West Chelborough, near Evershot, Dorset.

[3] "Persian Poetry," *Westminster Review*, July, 1847.

[4] John William Donaldson (1811-61), headmaster of King Edward VI Grammar School at Bury St. Edmunds, 1841-55.

[5] T. Brampton Gurdon (1797-1881) of Grundisburgh Hall, near Woodbridge, and Letton Hall, Norfolk, a Suffolk magistrate and M.P. for West Suffolk, 1857-65. A note in *A FitzGerald Friendship* (p. 18) confuses Donne's prospective host with his son, W. Brampton Gurdon (1840-1910). Although the son could appropriately be identified as "little Brampton," it is unlikely that he could have been "full of important political disclosures" at the age of seven. The *Friendship* note also errs in assigning the dates 1865-74 to the younger man.

To Bernard Barton
(Fragment)

Gloucester
Aug^st 29/47

My dear Barton,

. . . After I wrote to you at Exeter, I went for three days to the Devonshire coast; and then to Lusia's home in Somersetshire. I never saw her look better or happier. DeSoyres pretty well; their little girl grown a pretty and strong child; their baby said to be very thriving. They live in a fine, fruitful, and picturesque country: green pastures, good arable, clothed with trees, bounded with hills that almost reach mountain dignity, and in sight of the Bristol Channel which is there all but Sea. I fancy the climate is moist, and I should think the trees are too many for health: but I was there too little time to quarrel with it on that score. After being there, I went to see a parson friend in Dorsetshire; a quaint, humorous man. Him I found in a most out-of-the-way parish in a fine open country; not so much wooded; chalk hills. This man used to wander about the fields at Cambridge with me when we both wore caps and gowns, and then we proposed and discussed many ambitious schemes and subjects. He is now a quiet, saturnine, parson with five children, taking a pipe to soothe him when they bother him with their noise or their misbehaviour: and I!—as the Bishop of London said, "By the grace of God I am what I am." In Dorsetshire I found the churches much occupied by Puseyite Parsons; new chancels built with altars, and painted windows that officiously displayed the Virgin Mary, etc. The people in those parts call that party "Pugicides,"[1] and receive their doctrine and doings peacefully. I am vext at these silly men who are dishing themselves and their church as fast as they can.

[1] A term derived from the name of the leader of the High Church faction, Edward Bouverie Pusey (1800-82). His followers were more commonly called "Puseyites."

To Frederick Tennyson

[Leamington][1]
[September 4, 1847]

My dear Frederic,

I believe I must attribute your letter to your having skipped to Leghorn, and so got animated by the sight of a new place. *I* also am an Arcadian: have been to Exeter—the coast of Devonshire—the Bristol Channel—and to visit a Parson in Dorsetshire. He wore cap and gown when I did at Cambridge—together did we roam the fields about Grantchester, discuss all things, thought ourselves fine fellows, and that one day we should make a noise in the world. He is now a poor Rector in one of the most out-of-the-way villages in England—has five children—fats and kills his pig—smokes his pipe—loves his home and cares not ever to be seen or heard of out of it. I was amused with his company; he much pleased to see me: we had not met face to face for fifteen years—and now both of us such very sedate unambitious people! Now I am verging homeward; taking Leamington and Bedford in my way.

You persist in not giving me your clear direction at Florence. It is only by chance that you give the name 'Villa Gondi' of the house you describe so temptingly to me. I should much like to visit you there; but I doubt shall never get up the steam for such an expedition. And now know that, since the last sentence was written, I have been to Cheltenham, and called at your Mother's; and seen her, and Matilda, and Horatio:[2] all well: Alfred is with the Lushingtons and is reported to be all the better for the water-cure. Cheltenham seemed to me a woeful place: I had never seen it before. I now write from Leamington; where I am come to visit my Mother for a few days. . . .

All the world has been, as I suppose you have read, crazy about Jenny Lind:[3] and they are now giving her £400 to sing at a Concert. What a frightful waste of money! I did not go to hear her: partly out of contradiction perhaps; and partly because I could not make out that she was a great singer, like my old Pasta. Now I will go and listen to any pretty singer whom I can get to hear easily and unexpensively: but I will not pay and squeeze much for any canary in the world. Perhaps Lind is a nightingale: but I want something more than that. Spedding's cool blood was moved to hire stalls several times at an advanced rate: the Lushingtons (your sister told me) were enraptured: and certainly people rushed up madly from Suffolk to hear her but once and then die. I rather doubted the value of this general appreciation. But one cause of my not hearing her was that I was not in London for more than a fortnight all the Spring: and she came out but at the close of my fortnight. . . .

. . . You are wrong, as usual, about Moore and Eastlake:[4] all the world say that Moore had much the best of the controversy, and Eastlake only remains cock of the walk because he is held up by authority. I do not pretend to judge which of the two is right in art: but I am sure that Moore argues most logically, and sets out upon finer principles; and if two shoemakers quarrelled about the making of a shoe, I should be disposed to side with him who argued best on the matter, though my eyes and other senses could not help me to a verdict. Moore takes his stand on high ground, and appeals to Titian, Michel Angelo, and Reynolds. Eastlake is always shifting about, and appealing to Sir Robert Peel, Etty, and the Picture-dealers. Now farewell. Write when you can to Boulge.

[1] This letter, begun before EFG left the West Country, was completed at Leamington. Cheltenham, which he mentions, would be on his route to Warwickshire.

[2] Mrs. Tennyson wrote to Frederick in December, "Thy friend Mr. Fitzgerald

call'd a short time since upon us, he is a nice friendly man, I like him very much" (*Letters to Frederick Tennyson*, p. 81).

[3] Jenny Lind had made her sensational London debut on May 4 at Her Majesty's Theater as Alice in Meyerbeer's *Robert le Diable*. "Her voice is astonishing," the *Illustrated London News* reported on May 8. ". . . the delight of hearing something so new and so natural has taken the most phlegmatic by storm." EFG proved to be more than phlegmatic. He did not hear her until the following May, "and—was disappointed in all ways!"

[4] During the closing weeks of 1846 and early in 1847, EFG's art-critic friend, Morris Moore, through letters to the *Times*, had engaged in a controversy with Charles Eastlake, then Keeper of the National Gallery. Moore's portion of the dispute, "The Abuses of the National Gallery," signed "Verax," charged Eastlake with bad judgment in purchasing pictures and with general mismanagement of the gallery. The criticism included claims that pictures had been mutilated in cleaning and that superior works had been removed to make room for inferior pictures. Moore's letters were published by Pickering in 1847.

To Bernard Barton

Leamington, Wednesday
[September 8, 1847]

My dear Barton,

Here I have been for near a week: tomorrow I go on my road to Bedford. In doing so, my face will be turned toward Suffolk:—which will be a comfort to me, as doubtless it will be to that county. Crabbe wrote me a letter—but I thought I perceived in it marks of being written against the grain: I don't mean, in anger—but as if he were not in a cue to write at all. The sentences followed one another drop by drop, I thought. Great part of his letter was taken up by a tirade against Pickwick: Pickwick was the Scape-goat on whom Crabbe vented his discontent. I must get home, and with a violent onslaught, shake the blue devils out of him.

My Father and Mother are pretty well. This place is really pleasant: the town lively without being full of showy; the country around green, with several points of interest within a few miles—Warwick Castle, Kenilworth, Stoneleigh, Stratford, etc. The "*Pugicides*" flourish about here too, I see—great dickeys![1] not seeing how they are running upon their own destruction. The Morning Post of yesterday tells of the Queen's residence in Scotland:[2] and says the eyes of all the Scotch are bent to see if she will have Divine Service performed by a Clergyman of the Established Church next Sunday. For it appears that, last Sunday, no such dignitary was at hand: and the service was read by some layman: when, says the Post, the most important part of the

Service was left out; or of no effect: namely, that pretty piece of stuff called "*the Absolution*" which (says the Post) can have no effect unless delivered by one on whom the Power of Heaven has come by Apostolical Succession! So sings the Post; no great authority indeed: but against that Post so many fine Ladies and Gentlemen rub themselves every morning over their breakfast. At Gloucester last Wednesday a gentleman got up into the pulpit, and told us he held the keys of St. Peter. Farewell. Direct to me at "Alderman Browne's, Bedford."

E.FG.

[1] Suffolk for donkey.

[2] At Ardverikie, a hunting lodge belonging to the Marquess of Abercorn on Loch Laggan, Inverness-shire, where the royal family spent a month from August 21 to September 17.

From Thomas Carlyle

Scotsbrig, Ecclefechan
14 Sept^{r}, 1847

Dear Fitzgerald,

Your Letter lay waiting me here, when I arrived, the other night: thanks for your remembrance of me, for your pleasant glimpses into life in the Southwest. I write a word today to satisfy you about Spedding; whom indeed I have not seen or directly communicated with, but of whom I heard lately from Marshall of Leeds,[1] his neighbor in the North Country, and a sure hand. Know then that Spedding has been unwell; even dangerously so, I believe; the disorder, dysentery (if I mistake not); but is now well again, or at least out of danger: this is the fact concerning Spedding;—which, among so many rumours, may be well worth a penny stamp to you.

As for myself I have been a pilgrim, tho' a lazy one, ever since you heard from me:[2] a visitor of Dovedale; of Buxton, with its bottomless tedium; of the Spar Caves, Tors, and the Devil's—(establishment) i' Peak: next a sojourner for some time on one of the hilltops of Yorkshire Airedale; then in Manchester for some days; and finally was flung down here, out of the Glasgow Coach and Carlisle rail, after midnight, on Thursday last; where I have rested since, the idlest of all men.

I will tell you many things about my Derbyshire Spar-Caves and etceteras, whenever I find you disposed over a pipe, and capable of such details. The Spar caves indeed are an indubitable bore: but Derbyshire in itself I found a really interesting country, and was well pleased to look upon it. Beautiful old grey villages, silent as churchyards; fresh green moon wild limestone cliffs and chasms;—and, above all things, a cleanly, diligent, welldoing population, in whom, as in a *living* Bank of England, one could trace the funded virtues of many generations of humble good men. I found the Grave of Richard Arkwright[3] (no monument, no name or date to him); I found, at Cromford, the earliest Cotton Mill in the world, the "Mother of all the Mills";[4] Richard's great-grandson has let it fall almost silent now. In the northern quarter of the Shire, I sought for James Brindley's baptismal register, and exact birthplace;[5] but could not yet find it: no man had ever heard of Brindley, his place knew him not, knew not that *it* had turned England upside down! In Manchester I saw—But not a word more, except the mere names of Ex-Quaker Bright the Member,[6] and Bamford the Radical;[7] that you may long to meet me the more!

How long I shall be here I know not: if you were still at Bedford as I came past, it would be a great temptation to me to pause. We shall see. Mrs. C. parted from me at Leeds a week ago; she is now home and safe: I went the other way, half an hour after. Railways are becoming my abomination!—Adieu; and love the Man of Ross[8] and me. Kind regards to Mr. Browne.

Yours very truly
T. Carlyle

[1] James Garth Marshall, wealthy cloth manufacturer of Headlingley Hall, Leeds, and Lake Coniston, who had married Stephen Spring Rice's sister Mary Alice. Marshall and his father, John, had been generous friends of Carlyle's.

[2] Carlyle and his wife had spent ten days in August in Derbyshire, chiefly at Matlock Bath. Buxton, to which he refers, is a watering-place; Devil's i' Peak, now called Peak Cavern, the largest of the many limestone caverns in the county.

[3] Richard Arkwright (1732-92), inventor of the spinning frame and, subsequently, wealthy mill owner. Carlyle at the time contemplated writing a biography of Arkwright (Espinasse, *Literary Recollections*, p. 147).

[4] The mill at Cromford was the second built by Arkwright.

[5] James Brindley (1716-72), pioneer builder of English canals, was born at Thornsett. Among the canals built by him were the Manchester and Liverpool and the Grand Trunk, from the Trent to the Mersey Rivers.

[6] Carlyle had met John Bright (1811-89), M.P., at the Rochdale home of Bright's brother Jacob. During the evening Carlyle and the reformer engaged in heated controversies on slavery, railways and education (Espinasse, *Literary Recollections*, p. 152).

[7] Samuel Bamford (1788-1892), English labor politician. He opposed violence but had run afoul of the law by addressing the protest meeting at Peterloo, Manchester, in 1819. His *Passages in the Life of a Radical* was published 1840-44.

[8] John Y. Kyrle (1637-1724), philanthropist of Ross, Herefordshire.

To Bernard Barton

Pmk., Bedford
September 20, 1847

My dear Barton,

I am just going off to a place near Kimbolton—to pay a visit—shall perhaps return here at the end of the week for a day or two—and then I really do hope to be put in train homeward. You can, if you please, yet direct to me at Alderman Browne's—I am pressed to stand as *proxy for an absent Godfather* in behalf of the child of a high-Church Divine living near here—as he is an old friend, I cannot well refuse him: so I must officiate. Whether I shall be arrayed for the occasion in an *alb*, or a mitre, I don't know. I have some wish to get a glimpse of Donne at Bury, in case I go home that way: but this is as yet uncertain.

I don't know whether I shall have time to make a sketch of Goldington: I don't know whether, if I had time, my hand yet remembers its cunning sufficiently to draw the perspective of roof and gable. Churchyard should be here for the purpose. You never mention him in your letters: yet I should be glad to hear that he is well, and also to know what he is about in the painting line. I have heard nothing from Moore: and conclude from this that he is gone abroad for a while. On the other hand, he may have sworn an eternal enmity against me, which is perhaps as probable as the other conclusion.[1]

Autumn is come in good earnest—howling winds and pelting rains, and leaves that are already turned yellow, some of them: and some whirled away from the trees before their time. One begins now to think of one's winter quarters. What book shall we read together of nights this winter?

Was not Carlyle's letter a good one? I want him to see yet more of the English *country*, and I think he would modify some of his views. Doubtless all these impressions of Derbyshire will come out in print ere long: I can see by his letter that his thoughts are settling towards some such consummation.

Farewell. Yours,
E.FG.

I am sorry for the Nortons: and that the Abbey is again to become empty.[2]

[1] Morris Moore, EFG asserted, contrived to antagonize most persons who tried to help him.

[2] The Abbey, an ancient residence adjacent to the parish church in the heart of Woodbridge.

To Thomas Carlyle

Alderman Browne's, Bedford
Pmk., September 20, 1847

Dear Carlyle,

I was very glad of your letter: especially as regards that part in it about the Derbyshire villages. In many other parts of England (not to mention my own Suffolk) you would find the same substantial goodness among the people, resulting (as you say) from the funded virtues of many good humble men gone by. I hope you will continue to teach us all, as you have done, to make some use and profit of all this: at least, not to let what good remains to die away under penury and neglect. I also hope you will have some mercy now, and in future, on the "Hebrew rags"[1] which are grown offensive to you; considering that it was these rags that really did bind together those virtues which have transmitted down to us all the good you noticed in Derbyshire. If the old creed was so commendably effective in the Generals and Counsellors of two hundred Years ago,[2] I think we may be well content to let it work still among the ploughmen and weavers of to-day; and even to suffer some absurdities in the Form, if the Spirit does well upon the whole. Even poor Exeter Hall[3] ought, I think, to be borne with; it is at least better than the wretched Oxford business. When I was in Dorsetshire some weeks ago, and saw chancels done up in sky-blue and gold, with niches, candles, an *Altar*, rails to keep off the profane laity, and the parson (like your Reverend Mr. Hitch)[4] *intoning* with his back to the people, I thought the Exeter Hall war-cry of "The Bible—the whole Bible—and nothing but the Bible" a good cry: I wanted Oliver and his dragoons to march in and put an end to it all. Yet our Established Parsons (when quiet and in their senses) make good country gentlemen, and magistrates; and I am glad to secure one man of means and education in each parish of England: the people can always resort to Wesley, Bunyan, and Baxter,[5] if they want stronger food than the old Liturgy, and the orthodox Discourse. I think you will not read what I have written: or be very bored with it. But it *is* written now.

I am going to-day into the neighbourhood of Kimbolton:[6] but shall be back here by the end of the week: and shall not leave Bedford till next Monday certainly. I may then go to Naseby for three days: but this depends. I would go and hunt up some of the Peterboro' churchmen for you; but that my enquiries would either be useless, or precipitate the burning of other records.[7] I hope your excursion will do you good. Thank you for your account of Spedding: I had written however to himself, and from himself ascertained that he was out of the worst. But Spedding's life is a very ticklish one.

Yours truly,
E. FitzGerald

[1] Once, when Carlyle called at Tennyson's London lodgings, the two crossed swords on the subject of immortality. "Eh! old Jewish rags: you must clear your mind of all that," Carlyle protested. "Why should we expect a hereafter? Your traveller comes to an inn, and he takes his bed, it's only for one night, he leaves next day, and another man takes his place and sleeps in the bed that he has vacated." "Your traveller," Tennyson responded, "comes to his inn, and lies down in his bed, and leaves the inn in the morning, and goes on his way rejoicing, with the sure and certain hope and belief that he is going somewhere, where he will sleep the next night." "You have him there," said EFG, who was present (Tennyson *Memoir*, II, 410).

The *Memoir* conveys the erroneous implication that the conversation took place "in the closing years" of Carlyle's life. The exchange reads remarkably like a portion of the conversation reported to Barton by EFG in the letter of May 5, 1846.

[2] Alluding to the Commonwealth under Cromwell.

[3] A large public hall in the Strand on the site now occupied by the Strand Palace Hotel. It was principally used for choral concerts, but missionary societies and other Evangelical organizations held annual meetings there each May.

[4] In January, 1644, Oliver Cromwell, as Governor of Ely, visited the cathedral and found the Rev. William Hitch "somewhat too scrupulous about obeying" an interdict by Parliament on ritualism. "Whereupon Oliver ordered him, 'Leave off your fooling and come down, Sir!' . . . which Mr. Hitch instantly gave ear to" (Carlyle's *Cromwell*, 1845, I, 193).

[5] The Reverend Richard Baxter (1615-91), writer and chaplain to Colonel Whalley's regiment, present at several engagements. He was imprisoned and fined by Judge Jeffrys on charge of libelling the Church in his *Paraphrase of the New Testament* (1685).

[6] To visit William Airy at Keysoe.

[7] As Squire of Yarmouth said he had done with his Cromwell papers.

To John Allen

Alderman Browne's, Bedford
October 1/47

My dear Allen,

I have just returned from Naseby: where I went to meet my Father and Mother. And now I want to spread wing homeward at once, but I know not if I shall not have to go up to London for some days next week—to stay with my Mother. This is at present uncertain: *tomorrow* I shall know; but I write to you *today*, because there is post to London, and you will be in town to get my letter. I want to know how your engagements stand;[1] when will be best for you to go and see me; what time you can give me: whether you must see Norwich on the way, etc. So I wish you would (if you could) give me a few lines by return of post just to say what light you have on the subject. I shall leave Bedford on Tuesday, I fancy.

I have been [on] a visit of some days to Airy at Keysoe—he and his are well. I warned him not to meddle too much with Church *decorations*: but he has a turn for such things. I see a strange account in the papers of some Anglican performances at Rampisham in Dorsetshire—a village near Duncan. He told me there were great preparations making for such an exhibition. I hope the Bishop will interfere. But what a pity the hierarchy do not meet, cleanse the ritual of such doubtful and obsolete forms and expressions as these Oxford apes make so much of.

Well, I will not give you more to read, when I want you to write me a few lines. So good bye.

Yours,
E.FG.

P.S. Do you know anything of Spedding? He was ill of dysentery six weeks ago: and got better. But I want to know if he is *quite well.*

[1] Allen's itinerary as inspector of schools. He did not visit EFG until December.

To Bernard Barton

Bedford
Octr 5/47

My dear Barton,

You will think I am dead, or disgusted with all sublunary things. But neither is the case. I have been retrograding into Northamptonshire; to meet my Father and Mother at Naseby. And, since that, have had a correspondence on foot with my Father concerning my accompanying my Mother to Paris! This, however, I believe will *not* take place; but not wholly certain yet.[1] You need not be surprised at all if you see me drop in upon you one evening at the latter end of this week;—for conveyances to Cambridge and Bury are so restricted and uncertain, that I know not if I shall not be obliged to give up my visits to those two places; and rush in one day's journey through London right to Woodbridge. I have delayed here so long, being pressed to do so for the pleasure of meeting with one of the members of the family, who has been coming home day after day for the last fortnight;—but who did *not* arrive till yesterday.

I have no news to tell you of any kind; nor are any hopeful epistolary ideas shooting in my head—which is sufficiently occupied with an ache of its own—For yesterday I went out to a large, hot, noisy, dinner, when I eat a wing of goose, with all its "*glory*" (which means, you know, the inside stuffing) and drank a heap of port, and smoked a great black cigar. Again, you see, I give you no direction, whereby a letter from you may reach me: but peradventure I may ring at your bell just when you would be about to sit down to write, supposing you had got a direction.

So farewell—I have got a note from Ellis Walford who has named me as one of a Committee for the National Schools of Debach, Dallinghoo, and Charsfield. But I must see what is to be done before I accept the honour.[2]

Yours ever,
E. FitzGerald

1 The problem was solved by Mr. FitzGerald's accompanying his wife.

2 There is no evidence that EFG accepted the appointment. All three villages are within a four-mile radius of Boulge. The Reverend Ellis Walford was Rector of St. Mary's, Dallinghoo.

To E. B. Cowell

Boulge
Friday [October 15, 1847]

My dear Cowell,

I am at last returned to my home—have been back a week. Whenever you have leisure or pleasure to come and see me, I shall be glad to entertain you. Or shall we go and see Donne at Bury? I promised him a visit, which I have not been very energetic to pay.

Some one said you were to be married this month, or the next![1] Is this so? If so it be, you have no leisure to go visiting, I suppose. But let me hear from you the truth of all this.

I am now going on with Homer, whom I was very negligent of in my travels. I am now in the sixteenth Book, where Patroclus turns the tide of battle away from the ships. The Trojans indeed are frightened enough at his appearance; one is surprized the Greeks themselves make no comment—that no: Τις εἴπεσκεν ἰδὼν ἐς πλησίον ἄλλον.[2] "Is this Achilles himself—or if not Achilles, surely it is a sign that he is relenting." The fighting within the Greek camp seems to me rather dull, and protracted; till Hector calls for fire to burn the ships, and Ajax stands on the stern of one, knocking down whoever comes with a torch. Do you remember that phrase, when Hector rushes on toward the ships, Zeus pushing him on behind χειρὶ μάλα μεγάλῃ.[3]

I am also going on now with Thucydides, getting to the close of the third book.

Such is my state of affairs, who am not going to be married. Let me hear of yours, who *are*. Let me hear at all events that you are better than when you last wrote to me. Get air and exercise!

Yours,
E. FitzGerald

[1] Cowell and Elizabeth Charlesworth were married eight days later, October 23. For an account of the friendship between EFG and the Cowells, see Biographical Profile on the Cowells or Terhune's *Life*, chap. X.

[2] "One would say looking at another man close by" (*Iliad*, 2.371).

[3] "With his very mighty hand."

To John Allen

Boulge, Woodbridge
Pmk., October 19, 1847

My dear Allen,

Your note (which I got this morning) gave me the most sincere glow of pleasure I have felt for a long time. I love the Bishop of Lichfield for having the sense and goodness to do what he has done;[1] for I am sure there is not one of his former acquaintances, nor in all the county of Salop, who deserves the office so much as yourself. I only hope one day to see you a Bishop: and then I shall be thoroughly reconciled to the Bench of Bishops, who are just at present falling a little into disrepute with me. I want them to stir themselves and the Clergy, prune away all the needless and foolish things yet standing in rubrics and rituals, (on which the silly Puseyites lay hold, and which should anyhow be expunged. I send you a note I had from Duncan last week, giving me an account of the re-opening of a Church which I saw re-decorating near him. Either the Bishop of Salisbury should (if his power allowed) have visited this Clergyman with something more than a reprimand; or he should stir matters till he *should* have power to do so. The "*Pugs*" in Duncan's letter means *Puseyites*; whom the poor people in Dorsetshire called "Pugycides"—"Rooke"[2] is the name of the Clergyman.

Though I shall be very glad indeed to see you here, yet I will not have you bother yourself to fulfil so small an engagement, now you have much to do and to think of. Many persons about here wished to see you; but if you will only stay one day, I am the more willing to let you off. You will, I am sure, understand my true motive in saying this.

If all be well, and all favorable, I shall certainly go and see you next year in Shropshire. To do that will be most agreeable to me. Farewell—and that you really may be a Bishop is the sincere wish of yours affectionately

E.FG.

[1] Bishop John Lonsdale had appointed Allen Archdeacon of Salop and Honorary Prebend of St. David's.

[2] John Frederick Rooke.

To W. B. Donne

Pmk., Woodbridge
November 5, 1847

My dear Donne,

I am not so exorbitant as Barton in demanding letters: I supposed you were busy to some better purpose. Indeed, *my* letter the less called for an answer, being of itself a sort of apology for not calling upon you in propriâ personâ. How do you stand engaged next week? I think I might contrive to run over to Bury for two days in it; but am not quite sure, as we expect my Father and the Kerrich party here very soon. Kerrich is somewhat better. Will you give me one line as to your liabilities and conveniences next week?

I do not think my brother knows Lord Calthorpe[1] any longer. Did not my Lord go crazy, and get into confinement? I think so.

Tell Miss Johnson I think she has a spite against me (probably arising from my accidentally calling her *Miss Donne* last year) and that she makes the worst of my sayings. Seriously, I would not have you suppose that I made any heavy charge on you behind your back, or said what I would not say before you. Surely, we have had many fights about "the Blimbers"[2] face to face. Besides words lightly spoken seem grave when reported; perhaps, only when *written*, as I see them in your letter.

As to Jenny Lind, I don't care what I say about her. I cannot endure that she should clutch more money on the strength of her good character than the Italian whores ever stand out for. At Norwich I hear she got £12,000[3] and gave back £200—something like Mrs. Blaize's Charity.[4] Of all Avarices the worst is that which apes Liberality, surely.

Barton is overworked in his Bank; they ought to be more considerate to the old man. Pray write him a letter out of kindness. I never see Geldart's[5] paper; but I know his prejudices might easily turn savage.

Farewell, ever yours,
E.FG.

[1] George Gough-Calthorpe (1787-1851), of Calthorpe, Norfolk. One of his homes was Ampton Hall, five miles north of Bury St. Edmunds.

[2] Dr. Blimber, the harsh schoolmaster, and his daughter in Dickens' *Dombey and Son*. EFG and Donne had evidently discussed discipline in English public schools and perhaps specifically the exacting regimen of Dr. Donaldson at Bury St. Edmunds, where Donne's sons were enrolled.

[3] EFG probably intended to write £1,200. The editors of *A FitzGerald Friendship* state (p. 20, n.2) that Miss Lind contributed £200 to Norwich charities in 1847 and £1,253 in 1849.

[4] Oliver Goldsmith's "Elegy on . . . Mrs. Mary Blaize" begins:

Good people all, with one accord,
  Lament for Madam Blaize,
Who never wanted a good word—
  From those who spoke her praise.

The needy seldom pass'd her door,
  And always found her kind;
She freely lent to all the poor,—
  Who left a pledge behind.

[5] Joseph Geldart, a Norfolk artist; friend of Samuel Laurence's.

To Lucy Barton

[December, 1847]

Dear Miss Barton,

I enclose a syllabus of the first six chapters of the 2nd [Book] of Samuel; which (as the 10th draws near) may save time.[1] I will not answer for my quotations being in good proportion; perhaps the particulars of Saul's Death need not be so full. But you can judge of this. At least I have not omitted any necessary particulars. I should think that to the end of the *5th* Chapter—the conquest over the Philistines—will be quite enough for one number.

Yours truly
E.FG.

[1] EFG was aiding Lucy Barton in preparing her MS, *Bible Stories for Children*, published in book form in 1849. His reference to the "10th" and a note on the MS in Lucy's hand, "Copied for December 1847" suggest that the stories originally appeared in some periodical.

To Bernard Barton

Holbrook, Monday
[December 13, 1847]

My dear Barton,

I should have written to you yesterday, to apologize to you for not making my appearance, with Allen, at your house on Saturday. But the truth was, we were obliged to come over here in my Father's Carriage, not by Coach: could not leave Boulge till a late hour and were obliged to come direct over here, to anticipate nightfall. I assure you that, though we have done very well here, it was my absolute wish to have had Allen at Boulge on the Sunday; and down at Woodbridge on Sunday Evening: but I could not properly manage this. Allen has today examined Wilkinson's schools, and is just gone off to London. He particularly begged me to remember him to you and to Miss Barton, both [of] whom he wished much to see again.

I hope to be home on Wednesday or Thursday.

Yours ever
E.FG.

From Alfred Tennyson

[Late December, 1847]

My dear Fitz,

Ain't I a beast for not answering you before? not that I am going to write now, only to tell you that I have seen Carlyle more than once, and that I have been sojourning at 42 Ebury for some twenty days or so, and that I am going to bolt as soon as ever I can, and that I would go to Italy if I could get anybody to go with me which I can't, and so I suppose I shan't go, which makes me hate myself and all the world; for the rest I have been be-dined usque ad nauseam. A pint of pale ale and a chop are things yearned after, not achievable except by way of lunch. However, this night I have sent an excuse to Mrs. Procter[1] and here I am alone, and wish you were with me. How are you getting on? Don't grow quite into glebe before I see you again.

My book is out[2] and I hate it, and so no doubt will you.

Never mind, you will like me none the worse, and now goodnight. I am knocked up and going to bed.

Ever yours,
A. Tennyson

[1] Wife of EFG's friend, Bryan Waller Procter, "Barry Cornwall."
[2] *The Princess*, published in November.

To John Allen

Boulge, Woodbridge
January 1/47 [1848][1]

My dear Allen,

Wilkinson sends me the enclosed for you: which I think you will be glad to receive. You have doubtless seen many good men in your wanderings: but I have seen no other Wilkinson. You know I am a sharp observer of people's faults: in twenty years I have never known Wilkinson do anything, or say anything, he believed to be wrong—I verily believe!

The same post which brings me his letter, brings me a note from A. Tennyson, who is in London: but wants to go to Italy: but cannot find a companion. I have bought his new poem; which I cannot read through: nor is my first impression concerning it altered.[2] I am really grieved that such a man, who should now be doing something like Dante and Milton, should have dwindled to such elaborate trifling as "the Princess." Justo Dei judicio damnatus est.[3] His idle, selfish, and unheroic way of life has wasted away the heroic poetical faculty, I doubt: I nevermore expect a great work from him.

The Hampden business[4] is too long to meddle with much. I wish Lord John had chosen a man whom no one could have found fault with—such as Baptist Noel.[5] But I am glad he will not be bullied by Exeter[6] and the wretched Oxfordites. Now is a good opportunity to purify the Church—which you will deny—perhaps. But, my dear Archdeacon, only do you discountenance all Puseyism. Kind regards to Mrs. Archdeacon; and believe me yours ever,

E.FG.

A good New Year to you all.

1 EFG thoughtlessly dated his letter "1847."

2 See letter to Cowell, May 8, 1847.

3 "It [the trifling] is damned in the rightful judgment of God."

4 Renn Dickson Hampden (1793-1868), Professor of Divinity at Oxford and a leader in the Broad Church Movement, had been appointed Bishop of Hereford by Lord John Russell, who had little sympathy for High Church doctrines. In spite of violent opposition from many bishops and other High Churchmen, Hampden was consecrated in March, 1848.

5 Baptist Wriothesley Noel (1798-1873), Evangelical minister of St. John's Chapel, Bedford Row, London. In 1848 he left the Church of England and the following year became minister of John Street Baptist Chapel.

6 Henry Phillpotts, Bishop of Exeter. See letter to Barton, Jan. 4, 1845, n.5.

To Bernard Barton

Geldestone, Beccles
Wednesday
[January 5, 1848]

Dear Barton,

You will be surprized to find me dating from this place. George Crabbe offered me a ride in his gig to Beccles; so I came hither to pay a long-promised visit.

But I write to you for a further purpose—I told *Causton*[1] that, if it were not convenient to return to Woodbridge by *Thursday* (tomorrow), I would play a hymn for him, if necessary, on the evening of that day. Now, Causton may have written to me to ask me to do so;

and I am out of the reach of doing what I engaged to do. Now I want Miss Barton to be so very kind as to cause enquiry to be made at Causton's house *whether he be returned*; and, if he be not back, whether a hymn is wanted tomorrow Evening, and, lastly, if it be wanted, I want her to fulfil my promise for me, and play the needful, as she has done before. She can easily suit the boys with one of the hymns played last Sunday: with "*Nottingham*" for instance—And also with one of the *Chaunts*, if that be also requisite.

I did not remember what I had engaged to do till this morning: nor do I hurry back to do it (if it is to be done) because I know she *can* do it as well for me; and I *think* she will. Let me hear of you, and of all this.

Yours,
E.FG.

[1] William Causton, organist and music teacher of Woodbridge. His name was misread "Camston" by F. R. Barton (*Some New Letters*, pp. 144, 145).

To Bernard Barton

Geldestone
Jan^{ry} 8, *[1848]*

Dear Barton,

Pray thank Miss Barton for so kindly undertaking the organ for me. I should not have left Boulge, had I remembered my promise before I set out. But it had not been clenched in my head by positive acceptance; on the contrary, the people at Causton's house told me he probably would be home on Wednesday. But all is well that ends well. I have no doubt Miss Barton got on well; and that her concluding *squawk* was not worse than my introductory one.

Sam of Oxford[1] deserves all ridicule; and I hope will get it. I wrote again to Wilkinson to advise him to get up an address of encouragement to Lord John.[2] For if my Lord is sincere in his professions, he ought to be thanked; if he is not, he ought to be made to see that it is worth his while to be sincere.

I have just construed a long speech in Thucydides, to the great trouble of my eyes: and I am now going to talk nonsense with the children. Write your autobiography if you will—but think twice before you publish it.

I enclose a cheque, which be kind enough to send; and *let me hear directly* if it is honoured.[3] In these times, this is not so certain.

I hope to be home by this day week.

Ever yours,
E.FG.

[1] Samuel Wilberforce (1805-73), Bishop of Oxford, signed the remonstrance of bishops opposing the appointment of Renn Dickson Hampden to the See of Hereford. He subsequently withdrew from the controversy.

[2] EFG became so concerned about the growth of the High Church that he eventually drew up his own petition. See Dec., 1850.

[3] Britain experienced a financial crisis during the autumn of 1847; and EFG's father, whose resources had long been taxed by the coal mine at Pendleton, was on the verge of bankruptcy.

To E. B. Cowell

Geldestone
Jan. 13/48

My dear Cowell,

Your letter found me scratching very angrily and impatiently at a passage in Thucydides; the 73rd. chapter of the Fourth Book; a most confused account of the motives which kept two armies from attacking each other—such a confusion of *αὐτοὶ, σφι[σιν], ὁποτέρων, ἐκείνων*, etc., as drove me mad; till at last I shut the book without any clear notion of those motives; and, in truth, not much caring to understand them; the upshot of the whole movement being clear. I am consoled by seeing that, in the notes to my Hobbes's[1] Translation, the judicious critic selects the latter part of this chapter as one of those passages which caused Dionysius of Halicarnassus to abuse Thucydides' style. I was very much pleased with the account of the siege of Pylos, and the blockade of the island Sphacteria a little way back.[2] On the whole, I jog on through Thucydides with a good heart; totally forgetting the details, but sufficiently instructed with the main history. Your Persian and Sanskrit extracts were, as usual, very grateful to me. That one about Thought and Speech I have read over more than twice, but do not yet understand. The word *Form* puzzles me; it is, I suppose, the opposite to the Platonic *form*; indeed so very unessential a notion, that it proceeds from *speech*, which itself is only the coarser evolution from Thought. It is a fault, too, to have Thought the Sea, and Speech a wave; which makes them of the same substance. Is Speech the motion of Thought? But you must explain this to me when we meet: which I hope will be soon. I shall return from this place to Boulge in a few days: and it will not be long, I dare say, before I go to Ipswich. I liked the Persian image of the caravan-fire in the desert greatly.

Have you seen Tennyson's new poem? I see the Spectator and Athenaeum[3] agree with me wholly about it: the criticism in the Athenaeum candid and true, I think. I would so gladly have persuaded Tennyson not to publish it; but I should have had all his friends about my ears if I had done so. And now they will say that the Public cannot understand an original thing at once, and at first, etc. It may be so; but I still rely sufficiently on my intuition to trust to it in this case. I despair now of Tennyson's doing anything great; and mourn over this grotesque abortion at the mezzo del cammino of his life when he should have been conceiving a poem like Dante's. But Milton's theory, that he that would write an Heroic poem must live heroically,[4] is negatively proved by Tennyson. I know nothing that would now restore him to his native and abdicated powers, but such an event as the invasion of England! That would shake him up from his inglorious pipe, petty digestive solicitudes, and make him burst the whole network of selfishness twined about him by so many years of self-indulgence and laziness.

I suppose you have seen Carlyle's thirty-five Cromwell letters in Fraser.[5] I see the Athenaeum is picking holes with them too; and I certainly had a misgiving that Squire of Yarmouth must have pieced out the *erosions* of "the vermin" by one or two hot-headed guesses of his own. But I am sure, both from the general matter of the letters, and from Squire's own bodily presence, that he did not forge them. Carlyle has made a bungle of the whole business; and is fairly twitted by the Athenaeum for talking so loud about his veneration for Cromwell, etc., and yet not stirring himself to travel a hundred miles to see and save such memorials as he talks of.

My best remembrances to your wife. And I am yours as ever

Edward FitzGerald

[1] Thomas Hobbes (1588-1679) had published a translation of Thucydides' *History of the Peloponnesian War* in 1628.

[2] Thucydides, *Peloponnesian War*, 1-41.

[3] *Athenaeum*, Jan. 1; *Spectator*, Jan. 8, 1848.

[4] Milton in his "Apology for Smectymnuus," as the work is popularly called. The passage reads, "And long it was not after, when I was confirm'd in this opinion, that he who would not be frustrate of his hope to write well hereafter in laudable things, ought himselfe to bee a true Poem, that is, a composition, and patterne of the best and honourablest things."

[5] See letter to Carlyle, June 29, 1847.

To Bernard Barton

Pmk., Beccles
January 13, 1848

My dear Barton,

I am rather surprized not to hear from you by this time. I sent you a letter last Saturday, enclosing a cheque on Coutts; of whose acceptance I wished to have the earliest tidings. Doubtless you have very good reason for not writing yet about that; but how comes your pen (usually so ready) to falter in its correspondence on other less worldly matters?

I desire to be home on Saturday: but am not quite sure I shall be able to get off; as there are *birthdays* in the wind: but I shall positively get away if I can. All have colds here—influenzas—I have hitherto escaped the contagion; but I fancy I feel "hot-and-dry-in-the-mouth-like"[1] today. Anyhow, will you give me a line by return of post, to say if you have any news for me—at least to say that you received my letter of last Saturday. I hope you are not *unwell.*

I have had a long letter from E. Cowell this morning; full of Persian and Sanscrit quotations. His wife has had the influenza, in common with all the world, but she is now getting well, he says. My Father and Mother both suffer from it in Paris; but the disease has not been so mortal there as in London, they say.

Today, the sun shines, and the air is warmer; and Spring seems taking a first peep at the world.

And now I must go out; and so goodbye for a little while.

Yours,
E.FG.

[1] A Suffolk phrase (F. R. Barton note).

To Bernard Barton

Geldestone
Pmk., January 18, 1848

My dear Barton,

You will accuse me of my usual uncertainty in being here now, when I should be at Boulge. The truth is, however, that a severe cold, or Influenza, which has been going through this house, and which I have been staving off some days came upon me with such violence on Sunday, that I gave up all thought of going yet. It is better to have this sort of illness where a *little* company is; I am so heavy in the head and eyes I can scarce read; so I get the children to read to me. Such are the joys of a Bachelor's life.

You will have, I believe, a note from my Father about paying me £100—For I wrote to him about the deficit at Coutt's instantly: and he does not wholly understand how it is; since he desired the Quarterly dividends to be paid to Coutts by the 10th of this month—But of all this when I see you. I shall be home before the end of the week, unless my cold be very obdurate: at present I am fit for nothing but to loll in a chair.

Yours ever,
E.FG.

I see they put my letter into the Ipswich Journal.[1]

[1] EFG's letter is undoubtedly one signed "Common Sense," published in the *Journal*, Jan. 15. Its subject is the appointment of Dr. Hampden as Bishop of Hareford.

To E. B. Cowell

Boulge, Wednesday
[January 25, 1848]

My dear Cowell,

I liked your paper on the Mesnaví[1] very much—both your criticism and your Mosaic legend. That I may not seem to give you careless and undistinguishing praise, I will tell you that I could not quite hook on the latter part of Moses to the former; did you leave out any necessary link of the chain in the hiatus you made? or is the inconsequence only in my brains? So much for the legend: and I must reprehend you for one tiny bit of Cockney about Memory's rosary at the end of your article[2]—which, but for that, I liked so much.

So judges Fitz-Dennis; who, you must know by this time, has the judgment of Molière's old woman, and the captiousness of Dennis.[3] Ten years ago I might have been vext to see you striding along in Sanscrit and Persian so fast—reading so much—remembering all—writing about it so well. But now I am glad to see any man do anything well; and I know that it is my vocation to stand and wait, and know within myself whether it *is* done well.

I have just finished, all but the last three chapters, the fourth Book of Thucydides; and it is now no task to me to go on. This fourth book is the most interesting I have read; containing all that blockade of Pylos; that first great thumping of the Athenians at Oropus, after which they for ever dreaded the Theban troops. And it came upon me "come stella in ciel," when, in the account of the taking of Amphipolis, Thucydides, ὃς ταῦτα ξυνέγραψεν,[4] comes with seven ships to the rescue! Fancy old Hallam[5] sticking to his gun at a Martello tower! This was the way to write well; and this was the way to make literature respectable. Oh, Alfred Tennyson, could you but have the luck to be put to such employment! No man would do it better; a more heroic figure to head the defenders of his country could not be.

Yours,
E.FG.

1 A collection of moral and ethical precepts by Persia's greatest Súfí poet, Jelál-eddín Rúmí (1207-73). Cowell's essay appeared in the *People's Journal*, vol. 4, 355-58.

2 Cowell concluded his article, "We will give our readers one more gem ere we conclude, and as it is so small, let each hang it on memory's rosary, and farewell!

This world is like a valley, and our actions are like *shouts*!
And the echo of the shout reverberates even to *ourselves*!"

3 John Dennis, the 18th-century critic. The "old woman" to whom EFG refers could be Madame Pernelle in Molière's *Tartuffe*.

4 "Who composed these things."

5 Henry Hallam, the historian.

To Samuel Laurence

Boulge, Woodbridge
[January 30, 1848]

My dear Laurence,

How are you—how are you getting on? A voice from the tombs thus addresses you; respect the dead, and answer. Barton is well; that is, I left him well on Friday; but he was just going off to attend a Quaker's funeral in the snow: whether he has survived that, I don't know. To-morrow is his Birth-day: and I am going (if he be alive) to help him to celebrate it. His portrait has been hung (under my directions) over the mantel-piece in his sitting room, with a broad margin of some red stuff behind it, to set it off. You may turn up your nose at all this; but let me tell you it is considered one of the happiest contrivances ever adopted in Woodbridge. Nineteen people out of twenty like the portrait much; the twentieth, you may be sure, is a man of no taste at all.

I hear you were for a long time in Cumberland. Did you paint a waterfall—or old Wordsworth—or Skiddaw, or any of the beauties? Did you see anything so inviting to the pencil as the river Deben? When are you coming to see us again? Churchyard relies on your coming; but then he is a very sanguine man, and, though a lawyer, wonderfully confident in the promises of men. How are all your family? You see I have asked you some questions; so you must answer them; and believe me yours truly,

E. FitzGerald

To John Allen

Boulge, Woodbridge
March 2/48

My dear Allen,

Pray let me hear from you: how you are: how you settle, etc. If an Archdeacon's duties are not very absorbing, you must spare time to tell me thus much. I have not left this place since you were here:[1] except to go to Geldestone; and I am not thinking of leaving home as yet. Every year I have less and less desire to go to London: and now you are not there I have one reason the less for going there. I want to settle myself in some town—for good—for life! A pleasant country town—a cathedral town perhaps! What sort of a place is Lichfield?[2]

I say nothing about French Revolutions,[3] which are too big for a little letter. I think we shall all be in a war before the year; I know not how else the French can keep peace at home but by quarrelling abroad. But "come what come may."

My old friend Major Moor died rather suddenly last Saturday:[4] and this next Saturday is to be buried in the Church to which he used to take me when I was a boy. He has not left a better man behind him.

I have not seen Groome since you were here: but am going over to him on Tuesday. I had a letter from poor Mazzinghi; and one also from Duncan, who says he will read your *Charge*, which he has not done for any Archdeacon. I hope you discountenance utterly the "dilgrout school"[5]—i.e., the Pusey. There is a capital quiz on the medieval gentlemen in Thackeray's Xmas book: "Our Street". What do you think of Lord John's [Russell] new Bishops?[6] I rejoice in them. I have bought Tennyson's Princess: which seems to me now just as bad as I thought it last year. But I believe the wits think highly of it.

Now give my very kindest remembrances to Mrs. Allen: let me hear that she and all your chicks are well: and believe me

Yours,
E.FG.

[1] The previous December.

[2] A cathedral town 38 miles southeast of Allen's living at Prees.

[3] A revolt in Paris, February 24, had forced Louis Philippe to abdicate.

[4] February 26.

[5] "Dilligrout," a thick soup.

[6] A reference to Lord John Russell's last two appointments in 1847—that of James Price Lee as the first Bishop of Manchester in October and of Renn Dickson Hampden to the See of Hereford in November. Both men were liberal in politics as well as in religion.

To E. B. Cowell

Boulge, Saturday
[March, 1848]

My dear Cowell,

How is it I have not heard from you these two months? Surely, I was the last who wrote. I was told you had influenza, or cold: but I suppose that is all over by this time. How goes on Sanscrit, Athenaeus, etc. I am reading the sixth Book of Thucydides—the Sicilian expedition—very interesting—indeed I like the old historian more and more and shall be sorry when I have done with him. Do you remember the fine account of the great armament setting off from the Piraeus for Sicily—B. 6, ch. 30, etc.? If not, read it now.

One day I mean to go and pay you another visit, perhaps soon. I heard from Miss Barton you were reading, and even liking, the Princess—is this so? I believe it is greatly admired in London coteries. I remain in the same mind about [it]. I am told the Author means to republish it, with a character of each speaker between each canto;[1] which will make the matter worse, I think; unless the speakers are all of the Tennyson family. For there is no indication of any change of speaker in the cantos themselves. What do you say to all this?

Can you tell me any passages in the Romans of the Augustan age, or rather before, telling of decline in the people's morals, hardihood, especially as regards the Youth of the country?[2]

Kind remembrances to Miladi, and I am yours ever,

E. FitzGerald

[1] *The Princess* consists of seven parts, each, supposedly, composed by a different narrator. The form explains Tennyson's subtitle, "A Medley." The proposal to add identifications of the speakers, if entertained, was not adopted.

[2] A query evidently prompted by EFG's labor on a passage in *Euphranor.*

To John Allen

Boulge, Friday
[March, 1848]

My dear Allen,

Thank you for your first and second letter: and for all the kind invitations therein conveyed, both yourself and Mrs. Allen. I do not think of moving your way as yet—not till summer. And, as things are, we cannot tell how we may all be by summer. I suppose you do not meddle much with politics: but you take a daily paper, you tell me.

I suppose by a "Minister Pool" in Lichfield, you mean a select coterie of Prebends, Canons, etc. These would never trouble me. I should much prefer the society of the Doctor, the Lawyer (if tolerably honest) and the singing men. I love a small Cathedral town; and the dignified respectability of the Church potentates is a part of the pleasure. I sometimes think of Salisbury: and have altogether long had an idea of *settling* at forty years old. Perhaps it will be at Woodbridge, after all!

You tell me you hope never to hear the names of Puseyite and Evangelical again: don't you also hope not to see the *thing* again? But indeed I do hope that men are coming to their senses on the matter.

I have just returned from Soham, where I saw Robert Groome and family well and hearty. And now, good bye; kind regards to all.

Ever yours,
E.FG.

To Bernard Barton

Geldestone, Saturday
[April 8, 1848]

My dear Barton,

Behold your Sunday letter! I have spent a very pleasant week here with my delightful nieces—so simple-minded, affectionate, and open to all innocent pleasure. Here I am like the Father of a delightful family, without the responsibilities attached. These girls are now all grown up, or growing up; *ladies* in the only true sense of the word: finding their luxury in going among the poor: and doing what good they can.

I wait here till *Tuesday*: and then, if Mrs. Faiers[1] be well enough to receive me, shall fly to her arms. And here you can perhaps do me a little service. As how? Why, I wrote yesterday to Vignati[2] to beg him to let me know if my *Matron* were well enough to receive me; but I hear today that Vignati is gone to London:—nay, talks of going to Italy! So, if you should happen to see Jones[3] tomorrow (Sunday) would you ask him whether he can give a bulletin of Mrs. F's recovery: and will you give me a line (also tomorrow) to convey his report?

We had indeed wondrous weather here for the first three days of my stay: but in this house one is independent of weather. Kerrich is pretty well: Eleanor so-so. This morning I read some of my old friend Sir Charles Grandison in bed—the old "Cedar Parlour."[4] It is a curious history of old manners: but we are greatly improved since. You see people are all agog as to what the Chartists are to do on Monday:[5] I think, nothing. Ireland gets worse and worse.

Farewell,
E.FG.

1 His housekeeper at the cottage.

2 His brother-in-law.

3 Richard Jones, Woodbridge physician.

4 *The History of Sir Charles Grandison*, by Samuel Richardson (1689-1761). "Cedar Parlour," a drawing room in which the characters exchange confidences.

5 EFG proved to be sage in his prediction. The Chartists proposed to present a new mammoth petition, demanding reforms, to Parliament April 10 and stated that 300,000 people would assemble on Kensington Common and march to the House of Commons. The throng fell far short of the estimated number; and, in the face of vigilant police measures taken by the government, the march was canceled.

To Bernard Barton

Cambridge, Sunday
[April 16, 1848]

My dear Barton,

You will not get a Sunday letter from me, but a Tuesday one, as I suppose. I got to Bury on Friday: found I could not get on to Cambridge that day: so abode at Donne's, who is well and bonny: came here early yesterday: my brother gone;[1] so here I wait till tomorrow, when I return to Bury, and stay with Donne till Thursday:—when he goes to London. And then I shall most likely return home: only I would be glad if, amid your business, you could give me a line to assure me from Jones' mouth whether my housekeeper be fairly well again. I do not wish to return till she be: and I will go on and pay my London visit rather than importune the old Lady—so pray let me know the plain truth: not hopes, or wishes. (N.B. This sarcasm is aimed at *Mrs. Gunn*, not at Mr. Barton) Donne is going to take me to see Sir Joshua's portrait of Lady Sarah Bunbury,[2] when I return to Bury. And now my paper is done, and I am yours ever,

E.FG.

[1] Probably John, whose arrivals and departures were unpredictable.

[2] Sir Henry Edward Bunbury (1778-1860), a friend of Donne's and owner of a choice picture gallery, lived at Barton Hall, near Bury St. Edmunds. The portrait, painted in 1763, is now in the Art Institute, Chicago. F. R. Barton misread the name "Banbury" and misdated the letter "April 17."

To E. B. Cowell

Boulge
April 24/48

Dear Cowell,

You will have guessed I was not at home when your letter came. I did not indeed get home, or receive your letter, till last Saturday night —far too late for your invitation, which, as I understood, was for *last* Monday.

I have been at Bury and Cambridge: and I hope you will go over with me to see Donne one day. Thanks for the Athenaeum which I have scarce had time to read, having been in a muddle ever since I got here.

Can it be your invitation was for *this Monday*? Your note was not dated, and I left home last Friday week. But anyhow I could not have gone: I must be here tomorrow.

Yours in haste
E.FG.

I am beginning Lucretius again.

To E. B. Cowell

[Boulge]
[c. May 1, 1848]

My dear Cowell,

I send you a translation of Paullus' speech,[1] which I hunted out two days ago. It is more for the benefit of your wife than of yourself: and yet a plain prose translation is better than what I send.

I tack on a free translation of a fine bit of Lucretius, which doubtless you know. Certainly, if ever book wanted a new and good Editor it is Lucretius: I am astonished at the diversity of guesses by divers annotators in the notes to my edition. What is the history of the MSS? They must be as corrupt as those of Aeschylus. Pray read the sad and grand lines from 569-580 of Book Two.[2]

I am going to London, I believe, for a day or two: but desire, and hope, to be back directly.

Yours,
E.FG.

How prosperously I have served the State,
And how in the Midsummer of Success
A double Thunderbolt from heav'n has struck
On mine own roof, Rome needs not to be told,
Who has so lately witness'd through her Streets,
Together, moving with unequal March,
My Triumph and the Funeral of my Sons.
Yet bear with me if in a few brief words,
And no invidious Spirit, I compare
With the full measure of the general Joy
My private Destitution. When the Fleet
Was all equipp'd, 'twas at the break of day
That I weigh'd anchor from Brundusium;
Before the day went down, with all my Ships
I made Corcyra; thence, upon the fifth,
To Delphi; where to the presiding God
A lustratory Sacrifice I made,
As for myself, so for the Fleet and Army.
Thence in five days I reach'd the Roman camp;
Took the command; re-organis'd the War;
And, for King Perseus would not forth to fight,
And for his camp's strength could not forth be forced,

I slipped between his Outposts by the woods
At Petra, thence I follow'd him, when he
Fight me must needs, I fought and routed him,
Into the all-constraining Arms of Rome
Reduced all Macedonia.
And this grave War that, growing year by year,
Four Consuls each to each made over worse
Than from his predecessor he took up,
In fifteen days victoriously I closed.
With that the Flood of Fortune, setting in
Roll'd wave on wave upon us. Macedon
Once fall'n, her States and Cities all gave in,
The royal Treasure dropt into my Hands;
And then the King himself, he and his Sons,
As by the finger of the Gods betray'd,
Trapp'd in the Temple they took refuge in.
And now began my over-swelling Fortune
To look suspicious in mine eyes. I fear'd
The dangerous Seas that were to carry back
The fruit of such a Conquest and the Host
Whose arms had reap'd it all. My fear was vain:
The Seas were laid, the Wind was fair, we touch'd
Our own Italian Earth once more. And then
When nothing seem'd to pray for, yet I pray'd;
That because Fortune, having reach'd her height,
Forthwith begins as fatal a decline,
Her fall might but involve myself alone,
And glance beside my Country. Be it so!
By my sole ruin may the jealous Gods
Absolve the Common-weal—by mine—by me,
Of whose triumphal Pomp the front and rear—
O scorn of human Glory—was begun
And closed with the dead bodies of my Sons.
Yes, I the Conqueror, and conquer'd Perseus,
Before you two notorious Monuments
Stand here of human Instability.
He that was late so absolute a King
Now, captive led before my Chariot, sees
His sons led with him captive—but alive;
While I, the Conqueror, scarce had turn'd my face
From one lost son's still smoking Funeral,

And from my Triumph to the Capitol
Return—return in time to catch the last
Sigh of the last that I might call my Son,
Last of so many Children that should bear
My name to Aftertime. For blind to Fate,
And over-affluent of Posterity,
The two surviving Scions of my Blood
I had engrafted in an alien Stock,
And now, beside himself, no one survives
Of the old House of Paullus.

1 The enclosures are missing, but EFG also sent a copy of the Paullus speech to F. H. Groome. The lines, which paraphrase an address by Lucius Aemilius Paullus to the people, in Livy's history of Rome (lib. xlv. c. 41), follow this letter. EFG subsequently revised the draft thoroughly to form the opening segment of his blank verse poem, "The Two Generals." See two Donne letters dated [Dec., 1873].

2 EFG refers to a passage in *De Rerum Natura*. The latter half reads in translation, ". . . now here now there the life-bringing elements of things get the mastery and are o'ermastered in turn: with the funeral wail blends the cry which babies raise when they enter the borders of light; and no night ever followed day nor morning night that heard not mingling with the sickly infant's cries, wailings, the attendants on death and black funeral" (H.A.J. Munro's translation, 4th ed., 1900, III, 41-42).

To Frederick Tennyson

Boulge
May 4, July 2, 1848

My dear Frederic,

When you talk of two idle men not taking the trouble to keep up a little intercourse by letters, you do not, in conscience, reflect upon me; who, you know, am very active in answering almost by return of post. It is some six months since you must have got my last letter, full of most instructive advice concerning my namesake;[1] of whom, and of which, you say nothing. How much has he borrowed of you? Is he now living on the top of your hospitable roof? Do you think him the most ill-used of men? I see great advertisements in the papers about your great Grimsby Railway. . . . Does it pay? does it pay all but you? who live only on the fine promises of the lawyers and directors engaged in it? You know England has had a famous winter of it for commercial troubles: my family has not escaped the agitation: I even now doubt if I must not give up my daily two-pennyworth of cream and take to milk: and give up my Spectator and Athenaeum. I don't trouble myself much about all this: for, unless the kingdom goes to pieces by national bankruptcy, I shall probably have enough to live on: and, luckily, every year I want less. What do you think of my not going up to London this year; to see exhibitions, to hear operas, and so on? Indeed I do not think I shall go: and I have no great desire to go. I hear of nothing new in any way worth going up for. I have never yet heard the famous Jenny Lind, whom all the world raves about. Spedding is especially mad about her, I understand: and, after that, is it not best for weaker vessels to keep out of her way? Night after night is that bald head seen in one particular position in the Opera house, in a stall; the miserable man has forgot Bacon and philosophy, and goes after strange women. There is no doubt this lady is a wonderful singer; but I will not go into hot crowds till another Pasta[2] comes; I have heard no one since her worth being crushed for. And to perform in one's head one of Handel's choruses is better than most of the Exeter Hall performances. I went to hear Mendelssohn's Elijah last spring: and found it wasn't at all worth the trouble. Though very good music it is not original: Haydn much better. I think the day of Oratorios is gone, like the day for painting Holy Families, etc. But we cannot get tired of what has been done in Oratorios more than we can get tired of Raffaelle. Mendelssohn is really original and beautiful in *romantic* music: witness his Midsummer Night's Dream, and Fingal's Cave.

I had a note from Alfred three months ago. He was then in London: but is now in Ireland, I think, adding to his new poem, the Princess. Have you seen it? I am considered a great heretic for abusing it; it seems to me a wretched waste of power at a time of life when a man ought to be doing his best; and I almost feel hopeless about Alfred now. I mean, about his doing what he was born to do. . . . On the other hand, Thackeray is progressing greatly in his line: he publishes a Novel in numbers—Vanity Fair—which began dull, I thought: but gets better every number, and has some very fine things indeed in it. He is become a great man I am told: goes to Holland House, and Devonshire House:[3] and for some reason or other, will not write a word to me.[4] But I am sure this is not because he is asked to Holland House. Dickens has fallen off in his last novel,[5] just completed; but there are wonderful things in it too. Do you ever get a glimpse of any of these things?

As to public affairs, they are so wonderful that one does not know where to begin. If England maintains her own this year, she must have the elements of long lasting in her. I think People begin to wish we had no more to do with Ireland: but the Whigs will never listen to a doctrine which was never heard of in Holland House. I am glad Italy is free:[6] and surely there is nothing for her now but a Republic. It is well to stand by old kings who have done well by us: but it is too late in the day to *begin* Royalty.

If anything could tempt me so far as Italy, it would certainly be your presence in Florence. But I boggle about going twenty miles, and *cui bono?* deadens me more and more.

July 2. All that precedes was written six weeks ago,[7] when I was obliged to go up to London on business. . . . I saw Alfred, and the rest of the sçavans. Thackeray is a great man: goes to Devonshire House, etc.: and *his* book (which is capital) is read by the Great: and will, I hope, do them good. I heard but little music: the glorious Acis and Galatea;[8] and the redoubtable Jenny Lind, for the first time. I was disappointed in her: but am told this is all my fault. As to naming her in the same Olympiad with great old Pasta, I am sure that is ridiculous. The Exhibition[9] is like most others you have seen; worse perhaps. There is an "Aaron" and a "John the Baptist" by Etty far worse than the Saracen's Head on Ludgate Hill. Moore is turned Picture-dealer: and that high Roman virtue in which he indulged is likely to suffer a Picture-dealer's change, I think. Carlyle writes in the Examiner about Ireland:[10] raves and foams, but has nothing to propose. Spedding prospers with Bacon. Alfred seemed to me in fair plight: much dining out: and his last Poem is well liked I believe. Morton is still at Lisbon, I believe also: but I have not written to him, nor heard from him. And now, my dear Frederic, I must shut up. Do not neglect to write to me sometimes. Alfred said you ought to be in England about your Grimsby Land.

[1] Edward Marlborough Fitzgerald, whose unsavory reputation was largely responsible for EFG's practice of substituting initials for his full signature. Their identities appear often to have been confused, much to EFG's vexation.

E. M. Fitzgerald left Cambridge without a degree about the time EFG entered the University. In 1846, deeply in debt and guilty of infidelity, he was estranged from his wife; Thackeray advised him to leave the country. He crossed Frederick Tennyson's path in Italy the following year. "By the bye," Frederick's mother warned him in December, "I have been told by undoubted authority that the Mr. Fitzgerald thou mentionest (if the same) is a very disreputable character. He is considered nothing better than a swindler! He cheats at Cards, borrows money and never pays again. . . . I hope he did not borrow money of thee as thou wilt never get it again" (*Letters to F. Tennyson*, p. 82). Thackeray wrote to EFG the following spring, "Your namesake they say has been stabbed in the *bas ventre* at Civita Vecchia. I am afraid he is recovering. The world does not contain a greater villain" (*Thackeray Letters and Papers*, II, 366. See also Thackeray's letter to E. M. Fitzgerald, April 30, 1846, II, 236-37). In *Letters from Edward*

FitzGerald to Bernard Quaritch, the man is identified as "a book-thief" (p. 40, n.a.). His name does not have a capital G.

[2] As a young man EFG had heard Pasta (1798-1865), the soprano, at the Italian Opera House in the Haymarket. His admiration for her singing and acting never waned. See letters to Pollock, June, [1872], and to F. Kemble, Dec. 6, 1880.

[3] Centers of the political and literary world of the time. Holland House was a rendezvous for Whig politicians, a fact to which EFG subsequently alludes.

[4] Within a few days EFG received a letter Thackeray had begun in March. In closing Thackeray wrote, "I am always yours, and like you almost as much as I did 20 years ago. God bless you my dear old fellow" (*Thackeray Letters and Papers*, II, 367).

[5] *Dombey and Son*.

[6] The victories of Italian revolutionists at this time proved to be only temporary. The old order was quickly restored.

[7] Actually eight weeks.

[8] Handel's opera, which EFG had praised highly to Frederick when he first saw it in 1842. See letter of Feb. 6, 1842.

[9] Of the Royal Academy.

[10] "Repeal of the Union," April 29; "Legislation for Ireland," May 13.

To Bernard Barton

London
Pmk., May 18, 1848

Dear Barton,

Will you kindly send me hither a Post Office order, or cheque (whichever is proper) for £5? I shall be home on Friday or Saturday: and so will beg of you a note by return of post.

All my friends are in London, I believe; but I have seen no one as yet except Spedding and Moore—not even Alfred the Great—who is up. I have also seen and heard the famous Jenny Lind:—whom we will talk over.

Yours,
E.FG.

To Bernard Barton

[London]
Pmk., May 20, 1848

My dear Barton,

Thank you very much for your letter, and its contents. I am not yet able to leave town: and have now just completed two very laborious letters on Trustee business, of which I want to see the upshot, ere I leave. You will soon know, perhaps, what I have been busied about here.[1] I have just time to write this scrap; which you will get for your Sunday breakfast. I saw Carlyle and Thackeray yesterday—both as usual.

Yours,
E.FG.

[1] Matters relating to his father's impending bankruptcy.

To E. B. Cowell

Boulge
Monday, June 5, [1848]

My dear Cowell,

I only returned home on Saturday night—when I found your letter. I was delayed in London on unpleasant business:[1] but managed to see most of my friends there. I saw Tennyson two or three times: he was in good case: correcting, I think, a fifth edition of his Poems. The Princess flourishes I believe. He is now gone from London, I believe: but I know not whither: he was doubting between Scotland, Italy, and the Isle of Sark.

Carlyle is in statu quo—*rather* sobered perhaps for a time by what is going on on the Continent,[2] which is something of his own Hercules vein[3] put into act, and cutting rather queer capers. Things seem to get worse and worse everywhere.

I am glad you liked the translations.[4] As to Lucretius, he never could become naturalized in England, I think, had he Tennyson for a translator; so dry is two-thirds of him. There are scarce two hundred lines in the first two books that one can call Poetry: and as Philosophy it is not considered good. As to what remains, I suppose I could translate a good part of it very fairly: but the *great bits*, which alone keep alive Lucretius to most men would require a great poet to render. I am not of the common opinion in only looking to these half dozen passages as all that is fine in Lucretius: I find whole pages of sad and grand thought and music, which make me like him more than any of the Latin poets.

If you ask me to translate, I can very conscientiously return the compliment in desiring you to keep to your intention of re-editing Lucretius. Never did linen want washing so much.

I hope to go with you to Bury before very long: just at present I must be here.

Yours,
E.FG.

[1] Bankruptcy matters, no doubt.

[2] The Paris revolt of February 24 had been followed in March by successful uprisings in Italy, Austria, and the German states.

[3] Carlyle's theory of the Hero or Great Man as the savior of society. Many interpreters distort Carlyle's views on the subject. His "Right is Might," for example, is read as "Might is Right."

[4] Enclosed in the letter of [c. May 1].

To John Allen

Boulge
June 5/48

My dear Allen,

I only returned from London last Saturday, when I found your note on my table. You must believe I love you well as ever though I do not return to see your face. I was there on very disagreeable business all the while: business I could easily tell you of: but which is long to write about, and, I am glad to say, not at all affecting you or yours.

I was lucky to see most of my friends while I was up: Spedding especially; always wisest and kindest of all. Tennyson is, I believe, gone: I saw but little of him, as he lived some way off me, and was much engaged in company. You must manage to see Thackeray: who immersed as he is in Marquisses and Dukes does not forget you. I hope you like his book:[1] I think that on the whole it must do good among the great people with whom it and he are at present the fashion.

I do not yet know about my summer excursion; my means are likely to be crippled, and so I must suit my movements to their pace. This, you know, does not much annoy me, who am very well content to sit on my bottom. I really talk of moving somewhere this winter; to Cambridge, Bury, Lowestoft, or—*Woodbridge*!

I should be glad to hear you and your family are all well. And now I must say good bye, for I am obliged to go in a hurry to Woodbridge. But I would not miss a post.

Yours ever,
E.FG.

Isabella and her husband still reside here[2]—the Wilkinsons are gone to Cheltenham for a fortnight. Both are pretty well.

[1] *Vanity Fair*, being published in monthly numbers.
[2] The Vignatis were living at Boulge Hall.

To W. B. Donne

[Boulge]
[Mid-June, 1848]

My dear Donne,

It is a long time since I have heard of you: even Barton, I think, has no news. I fancy you must be in the midst of Examinations, etc.[1]—for I think this is about the time. Let me have a line to say how you all prosper. Cowell and I talked of running over to Bury for a day: we talked of this six weeks ago. Since then, I have been to London—a visit of business—my poor Father's affairs all in the worst confusion, so that now he is obliged to give up his rents, etc. into Creditor's hands. I am so far mixed up in this, that I also am a Creditor to the amount of £10,000—as are all my brethren and sisters; out of the interest of which we live for the present. It remains to be seen how much we and others shall get of our money: in the meanwhile I keep on the windy side of care, and don't care half so much for all these matters as I should for my finger aching. To each his troubles—

Some one said you talked of coming into these parts in August: I expect to be in Bedfordshire some time then. But let us hear your plans, and come here if you can while all of us are here.

I saw most of the wise and good when I was in London—Spedding, who is both, I saw much of: to my great profit. I went with him to hear Lind: and was—disappointed in all ways! Here is another point on which Spedding sets me down as a one-eyed man—and so will you, I dare say. But I only heard her once; and I am told one must learn to like her. But all that is not worth while. I saw a little of Tennyson: Thackeray is grown a great man: I mean, a man of great company.

Yours,
E.FG.

[1] Donne at times aided Dr. Donaldson, headmaster of Bury Grammar School.

To E. B. Cowell

Boulge
Friday [June 30, 1848]

My dear Cowell,

Will you let me know what book you have belonging to the London Library—I mean, the *name* of it—that is all I want. We are required to send in a list of what books we have in hand this time of year. The book itself neither I nor the library want.

How do you all get on? If the coast be all clear, I will go over and see you very shortly: which I should like to do. I have been lately engaged in what vulgar mortals call *troubles*; my poor father's affairs getting, by the natural Milesian declination, to a state of Bankruptcy. I am one of his Creditors, poor man: and as I now subsist on the interest of what he owes me, shall (I suppose) suffer like the rest. But I can raise some money: and don't care a snap about what is gone. This sort of thing does not trouble me; but an aching finger does trouble me hugely. I am no great philosopher; but can bear those ills I have no mind to etccc. (This sentence growing into Milesian obscurity, I leave it—)

When I go to you I shall bring with me an old Blackwood with some little Essays on Homer by Herder.[1] Do you know them? There is nothing that is *now* new in them; but they are vivified with genius still. Don't you like this remark on the anxious Geographies and topographies made about Homer?

"Where *does* Troy lie?—where *did* it lie? where stood the Bed of Priam?—where those of his sons?—*Where they stand in Homer.*"

I left off Thucydides when I went to London and have only lazily taken him up since; but am just upon the close. When I reach that, I shall begin on the Hellenics of Xenophon. You said there was a doubt about the Eighth Book being Thucydides' own; Arnold says it must be—only perhaps left incomplete. One wonders that there is no more exact account of the gradual change from democracy to the oligarchy at Athens: one plumps suddenly upon it.

Yours,
E.FG.

[1] *Blackwood's Magazine*, Nov., 1837, "Herder's Homer a Favourite of Time," pp. 702-14; "Homer and the Epos," pp. 734-44.

To E. B. Cowell

Boulge
Tuesday [July 11, 1848]

Dear Cowell,

Tomorrow I go to Ipswich and you will find me at the Hockley's[1] when your day's work is over. I can then walk home with you; or (if there be no way of sending my carpet-bag) you must drive me. I enclose Donne's note.

Yours,
E.FG.

[1] Major Thomas Henry John Hockley, Indian army, retired, and his sister, Mary. See letter to Pollock, [Mid-June, 1842], n.7.

To E. B. Cowell

Boulge
August 15/48

My dear Cowell,

How are you and wife, and how goes on Rámáyana?[1] I have been shamefully idle since I saw you, scarce looking into any book worth looking into. I have not got far with Xenophon; whom yet I like better than you do. I do *not* find him dull: and some of his speeches seem to me good and to the purpose, as those of Theramenes and Critias (if that is the name) in the second Book. And how tragical and picturesque is that little glimpse of Alcibiades out of his strong tower at Lampsacus, coming forth for a moment, like an apparition, to warn the Greek generals of their mistaken tactics before the final Battle of Aegospotami.[2] This little episode takes hold of my imagination.

When I was at Mr. Biddell's of Playford a fortnight ago, he showed me some wheat produced from grains found in a mummy[3] belonging to Lord Bristol.[4] The wheat produced from these grains is not the common Ægyptian wheat, but the small Spanish, or Talavera, wheat. Biddell says there is some notice in Herodotus of Phoenician Merchants touching at Spain, and bringing wheat to Ægypt; and I mention this to provoke you to attack Herodotus—which indeed you may have done before this.

In default of any gleanings from great men, I will transcribe you a passage from a little one, who had at least the ambition of a great man, and writes well when he speaks of it. It is Sir Egerton Bridges.

"When I look back beyond the six years I have passed out of England, it seems a long and countless age, and the distance so great that I can scarcely see distinctly the point whence I set out. I can never seriously and assuredly persuade myself that I shall see my native country again—perhaps my bones may rest there—not, as Lord Byron's have done, covered with glory, and [intensely] wept over by an awe-struck and idolizing people; but silently, and without notice, landed beneath the frown of that beetling [and immortal] cliff pictured by Shakespeare, and born in humble obscurity a few short miles to the rustic church [of the wooded hill], which is separated but a few paces from the neglected chamber where the light of this world first beamed upon me."[5]

This sentence *grows* finely and clasps life and death at the end of it. There is nothing so true, unaffected, and fine, in all Landor. Poor Sir Egerton! his memoirs are sad and curious.

I see that the Memoirs, and hitherto unpublished remains, of Keats are just come out;[6] some very fine fragments I see in the Athenaeum. Also read if you can the final Memorials of C. Lamb.[7] Really his life was heroic and sublime—a living martyrdom—tempered by brandy-and-water, poor fellow; but let no one grudge him one defect amid trials supported in a way which few tee-total hermits and saints could equal.

I have translated some more Lucretius in a rough way—from the end of the third book. But it is not worth sending you; and indeed is not very Christian reading.

I believe I shall have to go to London almost directly about my Father's affairs;[8] but I hope to go over and see you again one of these days. I was much pleased with my visit to you. But I now decline all visits to the *genteel*; I do not say or do this out of contempt for them: but because of my growing unfitness for dress company—the usual upshot of solitude and bachelor-ship, they tell me. Be it so; I think the tendency in me is too strong to fight against; and Lucretius will assure me that it does not signify much whether I overcome it or no. Farewell. Kind regards to Lady.

Yours truly
E.FG.

[1] *The Rámáyana*, one of the two great Hindu epic poems, the second being the *Mahábhárata*. The *Rámáyana*, which deals with the war waged by Rama against the Giant Rávan, dates from about 300 B.C. "Indian Epic Poetry," published by

Cowell in the *Westminster Quarterly Review*, Oct., 1848, resulted from his study of the Sanskrit epics.

[2] *Hellenica*, II. 1. 25.

[3] "A grain of wheat, taken from an Egyptian mummy, having been sown this year in the garden of Mr. Cutbush, of Maidstone, has produced no less than 66 ears" (*Illustrated London News*, Aug. 28, 1847, p. 135). Mr. Biddell was Arthur Biddell, a gentleman farmer.

[4] Frederick William Hervey (1769-1859), fifth Earl of Bristol, of Ickworth Park, near Bury St. Edmunds.

[5] From *Recollections of Foreign Travel*, by Sir Samuel Egerton Brydges, 2 vols., 1825, Letter xxxv, II, 70-71. Sir Samuel lived chiefly at Geneva after 1818. See letter to F. Tennyson, July 26, 1841.

[6] *Life, Letters and Literary Remains of John Keats*, edited by FitzGerald's friend, Richard Monckton Milnes, 2 vols., 1848. Milnes was Keats's first editor.

[7] *Final Memorials of Charles Lamb*, by his friend Thomas Noon Talfourd (1795-1854), 2 vols., 1848.

[8] Mr. FitzGerald had filed a petition in bankruptcy August 5.

To E. B. Cowell

[Boulge Cottage]
[Late August, 1848]

My dear Cowell,

I am just going off to visit my brother at Southwold where I shall be for some days. As to next week, I am not certain; if I can I will go to you; and will let you know in good time what I can do. In the meantime, do not you forego any engagement while this with me stands uncertain. I do not know that I praised Xenophon's imagination in recording such things as Alcibiades at Lampsacus; all I meant to say was that the history was not dull which *does* record such facts, if it be for the imagination of others to quicken them. Is there imagination in Thucydides? Does he do more than tell plain fact? I do not remember that he does. As to Thucydides' *speeches*, my impression is they are rather over-rated; the greater part only Athenian Gammon and special pleading after all—excepting what the soldiers say. But then I only state the impression left on my mind after one reading, when the difficulty of getting at the sense may in some measure have wearied the mind too much to recognise its lustre. As to Sophocles, I will not give up my old Titan. Is there not an infusion of Xenophon in Sophocles, as compared to Aeschylus—a dilution? Sophocles is doubtless the better artist—the more complete; but are we to expect anything but glimpses and ruins of the divinest? Sophocles is a pure Greek temple; but Aeschylus is a rugged mountain, lashed by seas, and riven by thunderbolts—and which is the most wonderful, and appalling? Or if one will have Aeschylus too a work of man, I say he is like a Gothic Cathedral, which the Germans say did arise from the genius of man aspiring up to the immeasurable, and reaching after the infinite in complexity and gloom, according as Christianity elevated and widened men's minds. A dozen lines of Aeschylus have a more Almighty power on me than all Sophocles' plays; though I would perhaps rather save Sophocles, as the consummation of Greek art, than Aeschylus' twelve lines, if it came to a choice which must be lost. Besides, these Aeschyluses *trouble* us with their grandeur and gloom; but Sophocles is always soothing, complete, and satisfactory.

As to your Landor image of Hercules and Apollo—Apollo might have dished Hercules with his arrows, but I doubt if he would not be dished *by* Hercules in a stand-up fight with fists. Unless the weapons, and mode of fighting, be the same, (as they are with Aeschylus and Sophocles) the comparison is not a logical one. And do you in your heart believe that Apollo would beat Hercules—except perhaps by some little Greek artifices not admitted into fair pugilism?

Yours,
E.FG.

To Bernard Barton

London, Saturday
[September 9, 1848]

Dear Barton,

Your Sunday's breakfast!—here is my contribution: which must be a small one—as I have twenty places to go to.

I suppose you will have heard of our Creditors' meeting on Thursday: a room in the City filled with miserable, avaricious, hungry, angry, degraded, cunning, faces—amid them *Wilkinson*, like the one good man in a den of thieves—attorney Ward's sharp voice grinding disreputable reports and surmises—a drunken greengrocer clamouring for two years' pay, etc. Wilkinson told me afterward that he was on the point of getting up to open the meeting with prayer! a thought to fill the Eyes with tears.

Of the result, all I can say is that, so far so well. All depends on a meeting on the 4th October; which I shall help on as much as I can. I do so because I am convinced it is best for the Creditors, who are the *only* party I consider.

I am now going to Bedford to see about the raising of some money. But I shall soon be back in Suffolk; where I want to be to push on affairs. I believe Boulge furniture will be sold.

I have seen no one in London but Lawyers and Creditors and the one poor Debtor.

Farewell.

Yours,
E.FG.

To Bernard Barton

Bedford
August [September] 13/48[1]

My dear Barton,

I got your friendly letter last night—thank you for it. My Father has protection at least as far as all the debts contained in the Schedule are—more I know not.

I shall return to London before the end of this week, and shall then remain there, or run down to Boulge before the sale. I should not mind being there during the sale for my own part—but other people might be embarrassed by my presence.

As to my future residence, that also is yet uncertain. The diminution of wealth and reputation would make not the slightest difference to me; but I doubt about remaining in the centre of so many creditors, who must always look to me, *in some measure*, for help which I cannot, or will not, give. I have disposed of my own Bond to the best advantage I can for *three* creditors, who, I thought, most needed it; and I am determined to draw the line there. I shall do all I can to push my Father's petition through, *not* for his sake, poor man: but for that of his Creditors; who are the only party I feel very much pity for.

I wrote yesterday to Churchyard who perhaps will tell you some of my plans and doings—not much to tell of. I am now here consulting with my practical and mercantile friends concerning the raising of a small sum of money on my reversion; very little will content my wants—I should perhaps sell the whole reversion at once; but I wish to leave it to others who will, I hope, make better use of it than I myself shall, or any Annuity Office would, put it to.

Farewell for the present.

Yours ever,
E. FitzGerald.

[1] The letter is postmarked Bedford, Sept. 13.

To W. B. Donne

60 Lincoln's Inn Fields
Septr 20/48

My dear Donne,

You see where I date from; inhabiting Spedding's room while he is absent. For I have been obliged, and am still obliged, to be much in London to lend a hand to save a little out of the wreck of my Father's affairs. I have also to assist in the pleasing office of raising money for myself—the best offer I can at present hear of being that I must pay £3000 in order to enjoy £2000. In all this matter however I do not desire, nor need, sympathy—many are my defects—but solicitude for money and luxury is not among them: and as I and all my family shall have *enough*, independent of this smash, when my Mother dies, we should be base to fret ourselves now.

I have scarce seen Tennyson this year: have not the least idea where he is. Frederic T. was over here a fortnight ago: as usual giving me no information of his presence till it was too late. I believe we were in London together without knowing it. I have no doubt whatsoever that Alfred knew nothing at all of this eagle business:[1] only you know a man of genius does hit upon the right thing instinctively and prophetically. If the wedded eagle clasp were fitted for an ornament of dress for those days, as we somehow feel it was, so it was fitted for some allegory of Church or State. So the Cross is now worn—at balls as well as in Churches. I think your friend may cease his anxiety on this subject.

How long I shall be here I scarce know. All the goods and chattels at Boulge are going to be sold, I believe: including my Cottage furniture. And I know not if all these troubles will not drive me from that neighbourhood. I could remain very quietly there but for the solicitations of my Father's creditors whom I *cannot* satisfy, and whom my presence yet keeps in hope.

Farewell for the present.

Yours,
E.FG.

[1] In "Godiva" (1842) Tennyson wrote:

. . . and there
Unclasp'd the wedded eagles of her belt,
The grim Earl's gift. . . .
ll. 42-44

To E. B. Cowell
(Fragment)

[London]
Pmk., Sept. 22, 1848

. . . troubles: but I am sure you will hardly guess how little I do trouble myself about it. I am here in London entirely to push on matters for the good of the Creditors at large; and when I am about it, I will not fling away more money in raising supplies for myself than I am able. I shall delight in Philoctetes as much as ever when I meet you; and I make my apology to books in general, who, in spite of what I have often said of them, have certainly supplied me with better idols than love of wealth and splendour and gentility. Your Herodotus bits are delightful. I have rumbled through four books of Xenophon only: I grant it *is* growing dull; and I have not given it even my ordinary attention, because of these affairs of mine.

Farewell—kind remembrances to my Lady.

Ever yours,
E.FG.

To E. B. Cowell

Boulge, Wednesday
[September 27, 1848]

My dear Cowell,

I got here last Saturday; and find a good deal to do as yet. It is possible I may by able to get over to Ipswich, and to give you a look on Friday; but not certain. I will call at your mother's house in case I go: but do not you expect me to any inconvenience to yourself. I have still a good deal to arrange here; and on Monday shall have, I suppose, to return to London. I am quite uncertain as to my winter quarters; sometimes think of Cambridge, or Ipswich; if I could find a *cheap* as well as airy lodging. I have bought eight chairs, one bed, one table, and twelve towels, from the forfeited furniture of this deserted place.

Yours,
E.FG.

To Mrs. Cowell

Boulge Sunday
[October 1, 1848]

Dear Mrs. Cowell,

Thank you for all your kind solicitude. I have not been able to get away from here yet: must probably go to London almost directly: will steal a look at Bramford if I can on my way. You were good to ask your brother about me; and he is good to offer his assistance; but I believe I do not want for good and honest advisers. I will call upon him and thank him in London.

Barton and Miss B. go out tomorrow to the seaside for a week. He is not well. Cowell must nurse at home; the wet weather has been very cold-giving.

Yours very truly
E. FitzGerald

To Bernard Barton

[Boulge]
Pmk., October 3, 1848[1]

Dear Barton,

I enclose you an agreeable note from Spedding, which I have just received. It may amuse you. The sale of pictures is just over;[2] I have bought four—one more than I thought for. And now how to send them off to their owners is the difficulty. I have bought 1. Lely—2. Sigismunda—3. Cenci—and 4. that bad copy of Raffaelle. Mrs. Corrance[3] bought two vast affairs: the *Fytt*, and the Caravaggio.[4] I advised her to buy the last; and I should think Frederic will whip her for it. Churchyard bought you Mrs. Claypole for £5.[5]

Yours,
E.FG.

Churchyard does not write because I have told you the news.

[1] F. R. Barton misdated this letter October 2, 1842. The letter is addressed, "Hopton Rectory, near Old Yarmouth," where Barton was visiting.

[2] At Boulge Hall.

[3] Wife of Frederick Corrance, of Loudham Hall, four miles from Woodbridge.

[4] John Fyt, Flemish painter (1625-71). Michaelangelo da Caravaggio (1569-1609).

5 Probably a portrait of Oliver Cromwell's daughter, Elizabeth (1629-58), who married John Claypole, parliamentarian, in 1646.

Spedding's letter, enclosed with the preceding note:

Mirehouse
23 Sept. [1848][1]

My dear Fitz,

I am glad that you have found my rooms[2] habitable. I hope the paper is more successful than the last, which I have always thought the ugliest I ever saw. But my way is to leave the choice entirely to other people, and then whatever be the result, it is nothing to me. When I choose a thing myself, and it proves a failure, (which it generally does) I am unhappy as long as I look at it.

I daresay that in the intervals of your legal pursuits, you will see Laurence; (who, by the way, has not yet written to me to announce the production of the complete thing, though I understand that he has advanced as far [as] the Dutch perfection already, and is only waiting till he has turned out a Venetian specimen) and you will probably be passing some day within a few yards of Rodd, the bookseller. I observe by the paper that a portrait of Bacon (painter anonymous) was bought by Rodd at Stowe. I have some reason to believe that it is only another version of the portrait by Vansomer,[3] and none to expect that it has any value for me. Nevertheless I should like to know something about it.

I have been occupied for the last week in trying whether I could sail the boat with a kite. It was necessary first to make one; and I had forgotten how. When I had made him to look like such kites as I have seen fly, it was necessary to teach him that art, about which I must say he was extremely awkward. And when I had partly brought him into order, we had three calm days. However this morning I succeeded in making him fly beautifully. He was more like an eagle than a kite, you would have thought it was only the string that prevented him from flying up to the 12 o'clock sun: but you would have been mistaken: for when the string broke and he might go where he would, his aspiration suddenly collapsed and he fell absurdly through flickering gyres upon the upper branch of an oak. Having recovered him (not undamaged) from his perilous position, I took him to the boat and got him up again, and succeeded in steering quite across the lake without oars,—I then wore; and was on my way to the other shore with a side wind; when he unfortunately dislocated his left wing in a gust, and after flying lame for some time at last came down head foremost into the lake like a seagull at a fish. I brought him home like the prodigal, "lean, rent, and beggared with the strumpet wind." I think of making a bigger.

While you are making arrangements with your reversionaries, are you in need of any present supply? My banker is in easy circumstances, and I can lend you all that you are likely to want without any inconvenience.

Ever yours,
Jas. Spedding

[1] Text taken from F. R. Barton's *New Letters*, where the letter is misdated "1842."

[2] 60 Lincoln's Inn Fields.

[3] Paul Vansomer (1576-1621), portrait painter of Belgian birth who settled in England.

To Bernard Barton

19 Charlotte St.
Rathbone Place
Pmk., October 28, 1848

Dear Barton,

You see I am in old quarters: and thence indite you a few inane lines for your Sunday's breakfast. The thing that most weighs on my mind is the loss of the only good coat I had in the world: a blue one with gold buttons. I have missed it for some time: Mrs. Faiers knew not of it; I hoped to have found it here; but do not find it; and where I have left it I cannot tell. I shall not get a new one before Xmas, I believe: so my friends must suffer by the sight of the seedy old one. They are the only sufferers; what is it to me?

I find old Spedding up here; and tonight I rather intend to go to Chelsea, to consult the oracle there.[1] But this will depend. Laurence has gone down to Beccles for some days. Thackeray I have not heard of: but have shot off a line to apprize him of my being here.

Is it some *coffee* I am to get at Freshwater's, ask Miss Barton?—and what is the name of the Coffee?—Also, have you any other commissions?

I scarcely know how our affairs are going on—for my own private business I am negociating a rather successful annuity out of my Reversionary property. So my friends tell me; indeed, they are managing it for me—but all may drop to the ground.

Yours ever,
E.FG.

[1] Carlyle.

To Bernard Barton

[London]
Pmk., November 4, 1848

Dear Barton,

Instead of myself at your Breakfast table tomorrow, behold my letter. I hope to be down before the end of next week, however. I stop here chiefly to see *Frederic* Tennyson, who is just off again to Florence, where he will be absent another five years perhaps. He entreats me much to go with him: and I am foolish not to do so, for this winter. But I suppose it will end in my not going. Alfred is also here, having just emerged from the water-process at Malvern. He now drinks a bottle of wine a day, and smokes as before; a sure way to throw back in a week or two all the benefit (if benefit there were) which resulted from many weeks of privation and penance.

I can scarcely give you an accurate account of our proceedings at the meeting of Creditors on Wednesday. The proceedings that had taken four months to arrange were totally abandoned: and never begun. But with their mode of operation, and probable success, I am almost unacquainted. I shall yet meddle a little perhaps: and then have done with the business.

Thank you for your little view of Aldbro. Isabella is now located there; I saw the Signor[1] in London just before his departure hence to join her.

I went one evening to Carlyle's: he lectured on without intermission for three hours: was very eloquent, looked very handsome: and I was very glad to get away. He gave an account of a Quaker who had come to remonstrate with him concerning certain doctrines about Peace, etc.—"when" (said Carlyle) "I went on with a deluge of hot matter like what I have been pouring out to you, till I almost *calcined* my poor Quaker—Ah me!" Fancy *Frederic*[2] gradually dissolving under the fiery torrent.

Yours ever,
E.FG.

I ordered some coffee at the Place: they have not sent it yet.

[1] Vignati, his sister Isabella's husband.
[2] Evidently F. Tennyson accompanied EFG to Chelsea.

To Bernard Barton

[London]
Pmk., November 11, 1848

Dear Barton,

I am so late today, I have but time to write ten lines before post. The reason is, that A. Tennyson, having only two days ago set off with his brother to *Florence*, re-appeared in my rooms this day at noon, and has usurped my day till now that it is five o'clock. I have packed him off with a friend to dine; and have ten minutes to write to you, and another man.

I must be here till the middle of next week certainly: as I have my own money loans to settle: and lawyers at least are in no hurry. I have no news of other transactions.

I have bought you a *silver mug*, to drink porter out of—it will not hold enough to hurt you. And I have bought a plaster *statuette* of Dante for Miss Barton to put up over her bookshelf.

Yours in desperate haste,
E.FG.

To E. B. Cowell

19 Charlotte Street
Rathbone Place
[Late November, 1848]

My dear Cowell,

It is a long time since we have corresponded. The truth is, I have read so little of late—indeed, next to nothing—that I have no heart to address you who are always reading—who have probably read more since you last wrote to me than I shall read in the next ten years, should I live so long. Here is a letter, however; and let me have one from you to tell me how you and gude-wife are: and also what realms of gold you have discovered since I last heard of you.

I have been some time in London—chiefly on business; indeed it is a business that still promises to end and still will not end, that has detained me thus long. I shall have to go to Brighton[1] before I return home.

I have seen Carlyle but once; he was very grim, very eloquent; and altogether I have not been tempted there again. A. Tennyson is now residing in London, at 25 Mornington Place, Hampstead Road; a short walk from me. I particularize all this because, should you come to London, you can call upon him without any further introduction. I have often spoken about you to him, and he will be very glad to make your acquaintance. Can you not run up here for a day or two before I leave? I can give you a crib, and all board but dinner; but do not come without giving me notice: as I may have to be at Brighton at any time. Altogether, I hope to reach Boulge by the beginning of December.

If you come, we will go and see Carlyle, whom I must visit once before my return. Tennyson is emerged half-cured, or half-destroyed, from a water establishment: has gone to a new Doctor who gives him iron pills; and altogether this really great man thinks more about his bowels and nerves than about the Laureate wreath he was born to inherit. Not but he meditates new poems; and now the Princess is done, he turns to King Arthur—a worthy subject indeed—and has consulted some histories of him, and spent some time in visiting his traditionary haunts in Cornwall. But I believe the trumpet can wake Tennyson no longer to do *great* deeds; I may mistake and prove myself an owl; which I hope may be the case. But how are we to expect heroic poems from a valetudinary? I have told him he should fly from England and go among savages.

Well, you see I have not forgot to talk confidently, in proportion as I grow more ignorant perhaps.

Yours ever,
E.FG.

[1] To visit his mother.

To E. B. Cowell

19 Charlotte St.
Rathbone Place
Pmk., November 29, 1848

My dear Cowell,

I live in such a state of uncertainty, awaiting the pleasure of lawyers and others, that I am scarce able to answer for a lucid interval. Yesterday, a brother[1] came suddenly over from Ireland, and stopped my Brighton journey; and I am not quite sure now when it will take place. However, do you make your own arrangements for next week; perhaps *rather later* than Tuesday will be more apt to find me disengaged. I shall try to get to Brighton the end of this week: and to be back about Monday or Tuesday. But I cannot be sure if I am to go till Friday.

I saw Carlyle two days ago: and he is so gloomy and destructive (I mean as regards men in general, not me) that I got quite impatient; and really know not if I can stand another visit without telling him so. But on this we will confabulate. I write now in infinite hurry: and am yours ever

E.FG.

[1] Peter.

To Bernard Barton

[London]
Pmk., December 2, 1848

My dear Barton,

I was just on the point of forgetting to send you your weekly dole, in the hurry of starting off to visit my Mother at Brighton. I am just going off: my brother Peter bearing me company. He has been staying with me this last week. And who should walk into my rooms on Thursday night but George Crabbe—to whom I have also given bed and board (such as it was) till today: when he returns to his parish duties. I have enjoyed his visit much; and, odd to say, felt a twinge at his going away. Last night we were at Thackeray's, who gave us all good things—good company included.

I shall be at Brighton till Wednesday: then return here, when I *hope* to find my law matters forward toward completion. Edward Cowell proposes to be in London about the same time, when I am to shew him two literary lions, in the persons of A. Tennyson, and Carlyle—the latter of whom is more rabid than ever.

I had a nice note from Job Smith[1] this morning: he reports all well at Boulge, both in family and parish. I suppose Miss Barton's Dante has got to his new home by this time: has been resuscitated from his coffin, and promoted to another and a better locality. This puts me in mind of Meller;[2] who puts me in mind of the transitoriness of earthly things—rail carriage among them—and I must be off with Peter—so farewell.

Ever yours,
E.FG.

[1] Tenant farmer on the Boulge estate.
[2] Thomas W. Meller, Rector at St. Mary's Church, Woodbridge.

To E. B. Cowell

19 Ch. St.
R.P.
Monday night [December 11, 1848]

My dear Cowell,

I am expecting a man from Bedford tonight on business: who, if he comes, will keep me engaged also tomorrow morning. I shall certainly have to go to a Lawyer's in Red Lion Square toward noon tomorrow; and so you see I really can not answer for myself. If I can get to Finsbury Square I will: but do not *you* keep in for me; for you I shall see in the evening. I wrote to Carlyle: shall hear from him tomorrow, and if he be not at home, we will go to a wiser man—Spedding. Look in for me here at *five o'clock* at latest.

E.FG.

To E. B. Cowell

[Boulge]
[c. December 23, 1848]

Dear Cowell,

I do not see why I should not go to you on Wednesday next: so let that stand agreed on, unless Fate interposes with either of us. If I went to Bury, I should probably remain a day or two there: but we will talk of that.

I also have finished Thucydides—today: having been a year and a half reading what has taken you but two months or so. I will bring you my third Volume of Arnold, where are elaborate maps of the Sicilian campaign. The Hindu Drama I meant to speak [about] is one translated in an old Blackwood: I think the name is "The Toy-cart"[1]—I can bring it to you if you like.

Tell Mrs. C. my Father has been, and I believe is, very ill. My old parson Reynolds is just dead:[2] he and I sat in an arbour in his garden the day before he was seized with the final apoplexy.

Farewell.[3]

Yours,
E.FG.

[1] "Mrichchakati, or The Toy-Cart," *Blackwood's Edinburgh Magazine*, Jan., 1834, pp. 122-50. Literally translated, the title means "little clay cart." The play was thought by Cowell to be the earliest Hindu drama, a conjecture questioned by subsequent scholars.

[2] The Rev. Osborne Shribb Reynolds, Rector of Boulge, died December 23, 1848.

[3] Someone, probably Cowell, has used the blank portion at the end of the letter for an exercise in Greek. The script is not EFG's.

To W. B. Donne

Boulge
Decr 27, [1848]

My dear Donne,

You have sent me two or three kind messages through Barton. I hear you come into Suffolk the middle of January. My movements are as yet uncertain; the lawyers may call me back to London very suddenly: but should I be here at the time of your advent, you must really contrive to come here—to this Cottage—for a day or two. I have yet beds, tables, and chairs for two. I think Gurdon[1] is also looking out for you.

I only returned home a few days ago—to spend Christmas with Barton: whose turkey I accordingly partook of. He seems only pretty well: is altered during the last year; less spirits, less strength: but quite amiable still.

I saw many of my friends in London—Carlyle and Tennyson among them—but most and best of all, Spedding. I have stolen his noble book[2] away from him—noble, in spite (I believe, but am not sure) of some *adikology* in the second volume: some special pleadings for his idol—amica Veritas, sed magis, etc. But I suppose you will think this the intolerance of a week stomach.

I also went to plays and Concerts which I could scarce afford: but I thought I would have a Carnival before entering on a year of reductions. I have been trying to hurry on, and bully, Lawyers: have done a very little good with much trouble; and cannot manage to fret much though I am told there is great cause for fretting.

Farewell for the present: come and see me if we be near Woodbridge at the same time: remember me to all who do remember me; and believe me yours as ever,

E.FG.

[1] Brampton Gurdon, of Grundisburgh, near Woodbridge.

[2] *Evenings with a Reviewer, or Macaulay and Bacon*, a two-volume dialogue in which Spedding thoroughly anatomizes Macaulay's essay on Bacon to expose its errors of fact and judgment. Spedding printed his work privately in 1848; a trade edition was published in 1881.

To John Allen
(Fragment)

[London]
[December, 1848][1]

. . . and I despair of his ever doing what he was born to do. "He that would write an heroic poem must make his life an heroic poem," said Milton.[2] "The Princess" threw down all my hopes. However, I see a good deal of Alfred, who lives not far off me: and he is still the same noble and droll fellow he used to be. A lithograph has been made from Laurence's portrait of him; *my* portrait:[3] and six copies are given to me. I reserve one for you; how can I send it to you?

Laurence has for months been studying the Venetian secret of colour in company with Geldart; and at last they have discovered it, they say. I have seen some of Laurence's portraits done on his new system; they seem to me to be really much better up to a certain point of progress: but I think he is apt, by a bad choice of colours, to spoil the effect which an improved system of laying on the colours should ensure. But he has only lately begun on his new system, of which he is quite confident; and perhaps all will come right by and by.

I have seen Thackeray three or four times. He is just the same. All the world admires Vanity Fair; and the Author is courted by Dukes and Duchesses, and wits of both sexes. I like Pendennis[4] much; and Alfred said he thought "it was quite delicious—it seemed to him so *mature*," he said. You can imagine Alfred saying this over one's fire, spreading his great hand out.

I wrote to your brother William last week to recommend to his kindly notice a young Royal Engineer who was going down to Pembroke, to the Docks, knowing nobody. And I met *Tom* in the street the other day: he was quite hearty, and kind. Your brother Joshua has kindly consented to become a Trustee for my Father's property; and is, and will be, of the greatest use in the matter.

Here is a long letter! As I do not go to you, I have at least written largely to you. My kind regards and thanks to Mrs. Allen; remembrances to the clan Gertrude; and I am yours ever

E. FitzGerald

P.S. As all the world turns Author, so have I; in the shape of the piece of Music[5] which I send to you. (N.B. This is, as you see, printed —but not *published*, ahem!) I did not think of sending it when I began to write: but it will amuse you to have it. Besides, the words are really fine; and the music is not inappropriate, I think. You may give it, if you like, to the organist of Lichfield Cathedral, to make his men and boys shout it in a stately solid English way. You may also do what you like with it.

Yours truly
The Composer!

[1] Included in part by Aldis Wright among letters of Feb., 1849, *Letters and Literary Remains*, I, 279-80.

[2] Paraphrasing a passage in Milton's *Apology against a Pamphlet . . . against Smectymnuus*. EFG refers to A. Tennyson.

[3] See letter to Laurence, May, 1844, n.7.

[4] Thackeray's *Pendennis* began appearing in numbers, November, 1848.

[5] Approximate dates of composition can be assigned to only two or three of EFG's musical compositions.

To E. B. Cowell

Boulge
Sunday [January 21, 1849]

My dear Cowell,

I have brought down with me more than my complement of books already; and so cannot reasonably send for more just now. I dare say I shall soon have to go to London again, when I will ask for your book. Are you sure it is in the London Library?

I have been down here a month, except a trip to London last

Wednesday: and I hope to be quiet for a time. By the bye I must go into Norfolk, I believe, before long.

I should like to see Nottidge's Memoir and Correspondence,[1] which I suppose you have; and which I will get you to lend me one day.

There was an interesting article in the Quarterly about Layard's Nimroud researches—accounts of the remains of Ægyptian palaces built over the sunken remains of Assyrian ones.[2]

Yours in haste
E.FG.

[1] *J. T. Nottidge: Selections from his Correspondence*, with a memoir by Charles Bridges, 1849. For Nottidge, see letter to Cowell, Jan. 13, 1847, n.2.

[2] The article was a review of A. H. Layard's *Nineveh and its Remains*, 2 vols., 1848, published in the *Quarterly Review*, Dec., 1848, pp. 106-53. Layard did not find the remains of an Egyptian palace at Nimroud, as EFG reports. Above the ruins of a Ninevite palace, the reviewer states, were uncovered graves containing ornaments which were Egyptian in "character and form."

To W. B. Donne

Boulge
Jan^{ry} 21/49

My dear Donne,

I doubt you will have left Bury, before this letter reaches you; but I hope it will follow you, and that you will give me a line from Hampshire, where I am told you are bound.

W. Browne is in need of a woman of mature age who will take care of his little children—a sort of nursery governess—to teach them at least to have decent manners, to read, to spell, etc., but not *accomplishments*. It has struck me your *Mrs. Frost*[1] would be just the thing. Will you let me know: first, What her qualifications are? 2. whether she be willing and able to undertake this place. I do not know if W. B. have yet heard of any one. I always liked the looks, the voice, and the presence, of Mrs. Frost: and I think her *age* is a good one for this purpose, all things considered. Please give me a line as soon as you can: and make needful enquiries.

I *was* obliged to be in town on Wednesday last, to be badgered by a lawyer in the Court of Bankruptcy.[2] But I got back the same day: and should have been glad to see you here.[3] But it appears that Captain Brooke's house was not in fine trim enough.

Barton seems to me ill: labours with great difficulty of breath:[4] and

I think the Doctor suspects disease in the heart. Certainly B. B. is greatly altered in strength, appetite, spirits, and personal favour this last winter. Sic transit—

I manage to keep on the windy side of care. Crabbe has lost his youngest son of consumption: but I am going tonight to console him with an account of Mr. Layard's Assyrians,[5] which will make [him] snap his fingers at Moses.

Ever yours,
E.FG.

[1] Formerly employed as a nurse by the Donnes (*FitzGerald Friendship*, p. 26, n.1).

[2] Mr. FitzGerald had filed a petition in bankruptcy on August 5, 1848, listing debts and liabilities totaling almost £200,000. He was declared bankrupt December 20, but litigation continued for three years. His eight children were creditors for £10,000 each, and on January 17, 1849, EFG had established proof of debt.

[3] Donne had expected to spend three days with F. C. Brooke at Ufford, beginning January 15, and had accepted EFG's invitation of December 27 to spend a day or two at Boulge Cottage.

[4] Although Barton died within a month, his afflictions failed to quench his humor. Five days before his death he spoke of suffering from shortness of breath in a letter to Crabbe of Bredfield. "But," he concluded, "if the hairs of one's head are numbered; so, by a parity of reasoning, are the puffs of one's bellows" (British Museum Add 36756).

[5] Alluding to the review mentioned in the preceding letter.

To Samuel Laurence
(Fragment)

Boulge, Woodbridge
Feb^r^ 9/49

My dear Laurence,

Roe promised me six copies of his Tennyson.[1] Do you know anything of them? Why I ask is, that, in case they should be at your house, I may have an opportunity of having them brought down here one day. And I have promised them nearly all to people hereabout.

Barton is out of health; some affection of the heart, I think, that will never leave him, never let him be what he was when you saw him. He is forced to be very abstemious . . . but he bears his illness quite as a man; and looks very demurely to the necessary end of all life. Churchyard is pretty well; has had a bad cough for three months. I suppose we are all growing older: though I have been well this winter, and was unwell all last. I forget if you saw Crabbe (I mean the Father) when you were down here.

You may tell Mr. Hullah, if you like, that in spite of his contempt for my music, I was very much pleased with a duett of his I chanced to see—"O that we two were maying"[2]—and which I bought and have forced two ladies here to take pains to learn. They would sing nicely if they had voices and were taught.

[1] A lithograph of the portrait of Tennyson Laurence had painted for EFG in the early years of their friendship.

[2] By John Pyke Hullah (1812-84), composer, but best known as a teacher of choral music and conductor of mammoth choruses in concerts at Exeter Hall. The duet was one of his most popular compositions.

To E. B. Cowell

[Woodbridge]
[c. March 1, 1849]

Dear Cowell,

All I have to say about B. B.'s funeral I have sent to the Ipswich Journal[1]—very little—with twenty lines of verse added. You know how little I think of my verses. I never wrote more than twenty good ones in my life. These are not worth twopence—but they came into my head, and so I have treated B. B. as he treated so many others. What solemnity there was at the grave was lost when we got into the Meeting: when three or four very dull but good people spoke in a way that would have been ludicrous but that one saw they were in earnest. At the grave, Mr. Shewell[2] said some few appropriate words—but he began to *sing* when once he was in the Chapel.

I am not sure but I must now stop here a week more to look over some of Barton's papers. It appears it will be a comfort to Miss B. to do so. Farewell: let me hear any good news of your wife and yourself.

Yours ever,
E.FG.

[1] Published March 3, 1849; reprinted in *Literary Remains*, VII, 419-20. The closing lines read:

Thou, that didst so often twine
  For other urns the funeral song,
  One who has known and lov'd thee long,
  Would, ere he mingles with the throng,
Just hang this little wreath on thine.

Farewell, thou spirit kind and true;
Old Friend, for evermore Adieu!

[2] John Shewell, prominent Quaker of Ipswich.

To W. B. Donne

Boulge, Woodbridge
March 9, 1849

My dear Donne,

Our good friend Barton has died leaving very little worldly goods behind him; and we do not yet know what Miss B. will have or what else she is to do with herself.

I (who was to have gone to Norfolk a fortnight ago) have waited here, looking over his papers, letters, etc., more because it amused her, poor thing, to turn over all these things with one so intimate with her father, than for any good that can come of it. There are letters from C. Lloyd, Mitford,[1] Southey, etc: but no great shakes; and B. B.'s life would scarce make a thread to hang these on, even if they were available in other respects. I want to ask you about a volume of *Selections* from B. B.'s poems; which I propose for two reasons; first that Miss B. desires to see such a monument to her father: and secondly *I* think it might be made the means of bringing in some pounds into her pocket, a matter she does not think of. . . .[2]

Out of the nine volumes B. B. published, I am sure one might be got of agreeable poetry, better than sermons at all events.

I should not meddle with this to be sure but that I wish to do a service to Miss B.

Now I want you to think of this and give me your advice about it. . . .

Pray let me hear from you as soon as you can give any advice on all this.

Yours ever
E. FitzGerald

[1] Charles Lloyd (1775-1839), poet and friend of Coleridge and Lamb. John Mitford (1781-1859), editor of *The Gentleman's Magazine*, Rector of Benhall, Suffolk.

[2] *Selections from the Poems and Letters of Bernard Barton* was published by subscription in September. The title page credits Lucy Barton with being the editor; but the book was prepared by EFG, who also wrote the introductory memoir. See letter to Crabbe of Bredfield, Nov. 9, 1849, n.4.

To W. B. Donne

[Woodbridge]
[c. March 15, 1849]

My dear Donne,

Thanks for your letter. As far as I can see nothing of B. B.'s would have a general interest except a Small Selection of his Poems: and *a short Memoir*, with a few letters, by way of specimen of the Man. From what I have seen of his letters, I cannot imagine there is any more in them than ease and good humour: of which a little is enough for the world at large.

I have now looked over *all* his Volumes with some care; and have selected what will fill about 200 pages of print—as I suppose—really all the best part out of *nine volumes*! Some of the poems I take entire—some half—some only a few stanzas, and these dovetailed together—with a change of a word, or even of a line here and there, to give them logic and fluency. It is wonderful when you come to look close into most of these poems to see the elements of repetition, indistinctness, etc. which go to make them diffuse and weary. I am sure I have distilled many pretty little poems out of long dull ones which the world has discarded. I do not pretend to be a poet: but I have faculty enough to mend some of B. B.'s dropped stitches, though I really could not make any whole poem so good as many of his. As a matter of *Art*, I have no doubt whatsoever I am right: whether I am right in *morals* to use a dead man so I am not so certain. Tell me candidly what you think of this. I only desire to do a good little job for his memory, and make a presentable book for Miss B.'s profit.

You say Selections *are Extracts*: and as such are permissible even from Copyrights. But are Selections of *whole pieces extracts*? Was it ruled in Southey v. Grimshawe[1] that *whole* letters might be taken without penalty?

We have had "May you like It" Tayler[2] here lately—a man versed in books and booksellers. He approves of all that has been done—advises Subscription—and a London Publisher. Whom do you recommend for one?

I must go over one day and show you something of our doings. I do nothing without Miss B.'s approbation.

Yours,
E.FG.

I find that Tayler and Miss B. rather desire *more* letters.

P.S. We think *300* pages including letters, etc. (perhaps fifty letters of B. B.'s). There are also some of Southey's—C. Lloyd's.[3] What ought these 300 pages to *cost* per volume, for subscribers?

[1] A suit over copyright to portions of Cowper's correspondence. Southey and the Rev. T. S. Grimshawe had published editions of Cowper's works contemporaneously.

[2] The Rev. Charles B. Tayler, Rector of Otley. His *May You Like It* (1822), a collection of stories, went through many editions between 1822 and 1863.

[3] Hannay misread Lloyd's as "Lloft's" and in his footnote conjectured "Capell Lofft," charging EFG with a spelling error. *FitzGerald Friendship*, p. 29, n.5.

To W. B. Donne
(Fragment)

Geldestone, Beccles
April 4/49

My dear Donne,

I have had all your packets of B. B.'s letters, and of Mr. Tayler's kind note of information. We all seem to incline to *one* Volume; but to get in all we have got, the printing must be closer than in the specimen Tayler sends down. I am to speak to *Childs*, the Bungay printer, on this subject.

I have tried what I can to make Miss B. undertake the whole editorial responsibility: a thing she is well fitted for, and which the world will expect her to do. She will *perhaps* yield about the general Editorship: but has so strong a dislike to writing any Memoir of her father, that I have agreed to do so much. It will take but few pages. But with poems and letters and all I should say the Book would consist of *400* pages—*and no room lost*, though with no need for a crowded type. This however will be hereafter considered by Mr. Childs.

I send you a draught for a Prospectus. This would be a perfectly easy thing to do, if it were not (as I think it is) necessary to forewarn subscribers that some *alterations* are made in the poems: else people might reasonably accuse us of giving them for their money what they never bargained for. Miss B. says that what I have written will make them suspect more has been altered than *has been* altered; and others advise no mention of alterations at all. Do you read, mark, and *suggest*. I write it out *at the worst*; as if *I* were editing; if Miss B. will put her name to it, you will see much may be spared: as of course *she* need make no excuse for altering her Father's poems; it will be concluded by all she

[Remainder of letter missing]

To John Allen

Geldestone, Beccles
April 25, '49

My dear Allen,

Whose fault it is that we communicate so little I scarcely know. Perhaps you think mine, who was dilatory perhaps in not going to see you last year. But indeed I had plenty to think of, plenty to do, last year: and little money for excursions. I am not much better off this year: but the first long jaunt I make shall assuredly be to see you; if you like it. I heard from Spedding your wife had not been well—and was going, I think he said, to pass the winter away from home. Is this so? You should write and tell me of such things as affect you so nearly. I have had nothing to tell but things of the same sort as I had to deal with last year—family troubles, etc.—sales of houses and property—Bankruptcy meetings. Tomorrow is another Bankruptcy meeting—I do not go to it. I did what I could to keep things *from* a Bankruptcy, because I was sure it would be best for the Creditors to adopt other measures—but they have done it; and now they must manage it for themselves. I have consulted your brother several times. Even now he is considering how you and I are to authenticate my Sister Lusia's Bond for £10,000 on my Father.

I left London close upon Christmas; and have been since then at Boulge—till the last three weeks when I have been here. My old friend Barton died in February: I am now helping to get up a volume of Selections from his poems and Letters for the benefit of his Daughter, who is left with scarce anything I doubt. If you will let me hear of you, I will send you prospectuses when all is ready: you may get subscribers though you need not subscribe—having a large family. I will *give* you a copy if you will put down your name. The volume will be just an agreeable one—to subscribe will be an essential service to Miss B. who always behaved nobly to her father—you might really do some good in this way. I suppose that about ten shillings will be the price—not more.

I have had three weeks' pleasure with the good children here. They are nearly all girls, and are quite pure in heart, loving, simple, childish, and sensible. They have grown up much as I wished them: finding most of their employment in doing good among the poor. Kerrich is just as ever—an insane man,[1] now in good spirits—in half a year he will be in bad. His wife has almost lost her health, and *almost* (but *not*) her reason in living with him, and attending him—she suffers from an hysterical affection of the head—always. My Father and Mother are separated—both living in London. John has had a bilious fever that has almost cleared his head of the little good sense he ever had—and so we go on. You will laugh at all this—and then think me very flippant. But it is all true: and I will not worry at what I can't help. You see I am the same as ever at all events. Well, write me a letter; and let us hear something more of each other in future. Farewell my dear Archdeacon.

Ever yours,
E. FitzGerald

I shall be home at Boulge the end of next week.

[1] Not to be read literally.

To E. B. Cowell

Bury St. Edmunds
May 14/49

My dear Cowell,

I enclose you some *prospects*—pray get subscribers wherever you can. The only way is to ask everybody.

I have now been away from home for six weeks—tomorrow I return. I shall be in Ipswich, I believe, at about half past one: and I should be glad to catch a glimpse of you. It is, I know, market-day, and you will be busy till the afternoon; but do give me a call when you can at the Hockley's.

Yours ever
E.FG.

P.S. I can give you, or leave you, some prospects tomorrow.

To R. M. Milnes

[c. May 15, 1849]

Dear Milnes,

My old friend Bernard Barton is dead—as perhaps you know: and has left a daughter very slenderly provided for, I doubt. She always behaved very nobly to him: only caring for his comfort, without looking to her own future. And now he dying, and his pension, and Clerk's salary dying with him, she is left with scarce anything.

Her friends have therefore persuaded her to make a selection of his letters and poems—and to publish them by subscription. And as you are very open to any fair claims of this kind, I beg of you to help us as well as you can. Miss B. (as I have told you) deserves support: and the book will be a fairly agreeable one. I shall be obliged to you if you will forward this letter and a prospectus to Lord Northampton,[1] who was kind to my old friend—and will, I think, do a service to his daughter. And if you get other subscribers among your many acquaintance[s] I shall be really obliged to you.

I write from my friend Donne's at Bury St. Edmunds, but am just going homeward to

Boulge Cottage
Woodbridge

if you should have occasion to write me.

And now you must pardon my troubling you: and believe me yours truly

Edw[d] FitzGerald.

[1] S.J.A. Compton (1790-1851), second Marquis, who took ten copies; Milnes took two.

To E. B. Cowell

Boulge
Friday [May 25, 1849]

Dear Cowell,

I hope to go to you sometime next week—will that do? But when I come, do not think it necessary to take me out to Elmsett[1] or elsewhere. If it falls in our way, well; otherwise I would rather be quietly at home, and have a general dislike to a set visit.

I cannot doubt that Aristotle is a great man; but surely your friend must err in calling *his* Ethics the Pagan Bible. Surely the Phaedo, the Crito, and other dialogues of Plato, are more that. One day I mean to read the Nicomachean Ethics. I cannot say I see much in the sentence you send me; though your word διαλάμπει[2] sounds fine and cuts a figure in the sentence as you write it. Surely it is no wonderful thing to say—"Good fortune makes a man happier—bad fortune makes even the best man less happy, though goodness will shine through all adversity etc." I perceive too even in this one sentence that fatal thing in nearly all moral essays—the ὅμως[3]—that is the exception that is sure to come to any general rule laid down. "It is good to be brave—but, on the other hand, it is not good to be rash, etccc." And on this very balance of the virtues (as they are called) I think you told me A's Ethics were based. Then it is all about nothing: except that like other metaphysical essays it teaches you to think etc. But the result to Virtue, or Morals, is just nothing.

Now, when Plato tells me to choose the best form of Religion abroad, and on that to embark, and so sail over these perilous waves of Time and mortal Life, he tells me something available. Doubtless he has his balderdash—in reams—but then the poetical element comes to gild even that. Has A. anything so fine as the sentence I allude to?

I know people say this Aves is Aristophanes' best play. I do not yet think so—but one day I may perhaps.

Yours ever,
E.FG.

[1] Near Ipswich. Maria Charlesworth, Elizabeth's sister, a minor novelist, lived there.

[2] "Shine through."

[3] "Nevertheless."

To E. B. Cowell

Boulge
June 3/49

My dear Cowell,

I am obliged to go to London tomorrow—and must postpone my visit to Bramford till I have been there. I hope not to be there more than a week: most disagreeable is London to me at this time of year when the country is most divine—

See what is coming in the distance dim—
A golden galley all in silken trim:
Three rows of oars are lightening moment-whiles
Into the verdurous bosom of those isles;
Towards the shade, under the castle wall
It comes in silence—now 'tis hidden all.
The Clarion sounds; and from a postern gate
An echo of sweet music doth create
A fear in the poor herdsman who doth bring
His beasts to trouble the enchanted spring;
He tells of the sweet music and the spot
To all his friends, and they believe him not.

The sacrifice goes on—the pontiff knife
Gleams in the sun, the milkwhite heifer lows;
The pipes go shrilly, the libation flows;
A white sail shows above the green-head cliff
Moves round the point, and throws her anchor stiff:
The mariners join hymn with those on land.[1]

[1] The two passages are from lines by Keats on "unconnected subjects," prompted by a dream, sent in a letter to J. H. Reynolds, March 25, 1818, and first published by Milnes in his *Life and Letters of Keats.* The longer excerpt was suggested by Claude Lorrain's *Enchanted Castle.* Milnes misread Claude as "Leland," an error corrected by Buxton Forman in his edition of Keats.

To E. B. Cowell

19 Charlotte St.
Rathbone Place
Monday [June 11, 1849]

My dear Cowell,

I propose returning to Suffolk on Wednesday. Shall I go to you "en passant"—on Wednesday evening—or afternoon—or have you lost all hope of my veracity in word and deed? Give me a line by return of post.

Yours,
E.FG.

To Frederick Tennyson

Boulge, Woodbridge
June 19, 1849

My dear old Frederic,

I often think of you: often wish to write to you—often intend to do so—determine to do so—but perhaps should not do so for a long time, but that this sheet of thin paper happens to come under my fingers this 19th of June 1849. You must not believe however that it is only chance that puts me up to this exertion; I really should have written before but that the reports we read of Italian and Florentine troubles[1] put me in doubt first whether you are still at Florence to receive my letter: and secondly whether, if you be there, it would ever reach your hands. But I will brace myself up even to that great act of Friendship, to write a long letter with all probability of its miscarrying. Only look here; if it ever does reach you, you must really write to me directly: to let me know how you and yours are, for I am sincerely anxious to know this. I saw great reports in the paper too some months back of Prince Albert going to open Great Grimsby Docks.[2] Were not such Docks to be made on your land? and were you not to be a rich man if they were made? And have you easily consented to forgo being paid in money, and to accept in lieu thereof a certain quantity of wholly valueless shares in said Docks, which will lead you into expense, instead of enriching you? This is what I suppose will be the case. For though you have a microscopic eye for human character, you are to be diddled by any knave, or set of knaves, as you well know.

Of my own affairs I have nothing agreeable to tell. . . . When I met you in London, I was raising money for myself on my reversionary property: and so I am still: and of course the lawyers continue to do so in the most expensive way; a slow torture of the purse. But do not suppose I want money: I get it, at a good price: nor do I fret myself about the price: there will be quite enough (if public securities hold) for my life under any dispensation the lawyers can inflict. As I grow older I want less. I have not bought a book or a picture this year: have not been to a concert, opera, or play: and, what is more, I don't care to go. Not but if I meet you in London again I shall break out into shilling concerts, etc., and shall be glad of the opportunity.

After you left London, I remained there nearly to the end of December; saw a good deal of Alfred, etc. Since then I have been down here except a fortnight's stay in London, from which I have just returned. I heard Alfred had been seen flying through town to the Lushingtons: but I did not see him. He is said to be still busy about that accursed Princess. By the by, beg, borrow, steal, or buy Keats' Letters and Poems; most wonderful bits of Poems, written off-hand at a sitting, most of them: I only wonder that they do not make a noise in the world. By the by again, it is quite necessary *your* poems should be printed; which Moxon, I am sure, would do gladly. Except this book of Keats, we have had *no* poetry lately, I believe; luckily, the ——, ——, ——,[3] etc., are getting older and past the age of conceiving—*wind.* Send your poems over to Alfred to sort and arrange for you: he will do it: and you and he are the only men alive whose poems I want to see in print. By the by, thirdly and lastly, and in total contradiction to the last sentence, I am now helping to edit some letters and poems of—Bernard Barton! Yes: the poor fellow died suddenly of heart disease; leaving his daughter, a noble woman, almost unprovided for: and we are getting up this volume by subscription. If you were in England *you* must subscribe: but as you are not, you need only give us a share in the Great Grimsby Dock instead.

Now there are some more things I could tell you, but you see where my pen has honestly got to in the paper. I remember you did not desire to hear about my garden, which is now gorgeous with large red poppies, and lilac irises—satisfactory colouring: and the trees murmur a continuous soft *chorus to the solo which my soul discourses within.* If that be not Poetry, I should like to know what is? and with it I may as well conclude. I think I shall send this letter to your family at Cheltenham to be forwarded to you;—they may possibly have later intelligence of you than I have. Pray write to me if you get this; indeed you *must*; and never come to England without letting me know of it.

1 Florence had been torn by revolution and counterrevolution all spring. The city had been declared a republic in February; but in April the Grand Duke, Leopold II, was invited to return. He accepted, but at his request Austrian troops also returned and Florence again fell under Austrian domination.

2 Prince Albert laid the cornerstone for the docks April 18. See letter of June 12, 1845, n.8, on Frederick's property at Great Grimsby.

3 These and the other deletions in the letter appear in *Letters and Literary Remains*, from which the text is taken. The manuscript is missing.

From Thomas Carlyle

Chelsea, 22 june, 1849

Dear Fitzgerald,

On Thursday next I am going off for Ireland; intending to have a stroll for three or four weeks there,—my patriotic feelings and my state of health bodily and mental, suggesting such an expedition to me. *Quod faustum sit.*[1] I do not well know my course yet; but think generally of crossing and thwarting the whole Island (perhaps going round by the Coast Towns mainly); so that I may carry off some real view of that unfortunate province of God's Creation, such as my own eyes and observation shall authentically yield: Duffy, Traitor Duffy,[2] who, apart from the repeal frenzy which indeed he has now abandoned, is a really excellent fellow,—will probably escort me thro' part of my course; at least initiate me into the modes of Irish travel; after whom there is a certain English Forster,[3] a young Devonshire-Yorkshire Man, "Transitive-Quaker" and extensive man of business at Bradford, an excellent cheery friendly character too, who will perhaps carry me into Munster. I think of bathing once or twice at Kilkie, and of looking in for half a day upon Gurdon and Lord G. Hill:—in short, all is yet *in nubibus*, and a most manageable matter: except that I *am* to sail from the Tower Wharf for Dublin by steam on Thursday morning first, and that is a matter that can only be managed by such rules as are its own. Meanwhile I am picking up all manner of notices of *notabilia*, a few introductions to desirable men included; these will constitute so many lucent-points in the dark labyrinth of Ireland, and serve to indicate routes for me when once in Dublin. It is partly with that view too that I now send you this advertisement.

If you were a sufficiently adventurous fellow, and would appear with your knapsack on board the Dublin Steamer on Thursday, and undertake to bear me company by sea and land—that would really be a handsome and hopeful thing; that would be the right thing! And I do believe good would come of it; and it might easily be made to answer very well. But failing that—you see what it is I want. If you remember anywhere in Ireland a man whom you think it would in real truth be mutually profitable that I should see in passing, give me a Note to him, and I will at least try to deliver it. Failing men, or along with men, give me note of things worth seeing,—such as rise *first* in your mind; for those probably will be the truest;—and indeed it is not worth while, either as to men or things intended here, that you should be at the cost of any study or bother: such hints as occur to you, dashed off in half an hour, will fully satisfy me; and if there should be no "man" mentioned at all, perhaps that would be no damage,—for it is very uncertain whether, even with letters in my pocket, I shall be able to muster "faith and hope" enough to make many new acquaintances in the Sister Island, or penetrate into private houses there. Aubrey de Vere (of the Limerick Monteagle clan) has undertaken to present me to "*Six* really good landlords," of whom I can remember only a Sir Charles Coote, and the Gurdon Lord above mentioned. A[y] Sterling and Commissioner Twisleton[4] give me notes for some Dublin people; Duffy, I calculate, has the best access to Priests, etc. (which clan I naturally want to look at); I am asking myself whether any of the big *English Irish* (Fitzwilliam, etc., to whom I might procure access on application) who perhaps have intelligent "Agents" on their Estates, capable of enlightening me, might be worth disturbing with that view? And to such length hitherto, and no farther, has the adventure proceeded; and there I leave it with you, to try what threads out of your skein will suit into the tissue of it;—to beg your blessing on the business at any rate. If you would go with me indeed—But you will not! Remember however that Thursday is the day, and that time is getting valuable.

I have nearly got the *Cromwell* hustled off my shoulders, tho' the Printers are yet far behind with it; hardly more than half done, I think. The *Squire Papers* go as a kind of outlying baggage into a corner of one of the Volumes, where a gap of room was at any rate ready for them; they and certain Committee Lists, etc., which you will get in a separate shape so soon as they are printed. I am already sick of that business; and often ask impatiently, *Quando sit finis?*[5]

We are much interested in Mazzini[6] and Roman matters during these weeks. It is beautiful and even solemn to me to reflect on poor Mazzini (one of the purest and highest souls now in this world, but filled with democratic and other nonsense in the head of him); and how the Eternal Destinies take note of what real good is in a man, and do at last bring him to the place where he can to right profit expend the same! It is Mazzini's . . . religious, enthusiastic spirit that I believe to be now principally animating Rome to this resolute resistance: a *protest* against the "wretched old Chimera of a Pope," which is fast becoming impatient, and is already impressive to all the world. Honour to the poor noble Mazzini; and joy to him if he ever leave his life there, —as he will be right willing to do, I believe, if there be a call for it among other things.

London offers no point of news to me that is in the least worth transmitting by pen and ink. Flunkyism, Fashionablism; idle talk, idle thought, and still idler action fill up as heretofore the (intrinsically scandalous) course of Man's life in this place. "Quam diu, Domine!"[7]

[Signature cut off]

[1] "May it be successful."

[2] See letter from Carlyle, Sept. 22, 1846, n.2.

[3] William Edward Forster (1818-86), later Chief Secretary for Ireland.

[4] Anthony Sterling, brother of John whose biography Carlyle published two years later. Edward Turner Twisleton (1809-74), politician.

[5] "When may the end be?"

[6] Giuseppe Mazzini (1805-72), Italian patriot.

[7] "How long, O Lord!"

To E. B. Cowell

Boulge
June 23/49

Dear Cowell,

I have civil notes from Captain Brooke and Donaldson:[1] both which I enclose. You can now decide whether you like to come over here on Monday, while Brooke is out, or wait till he returns etc. Do as you like.

My head sometimes runs on that grand grotesque Spanish Play:[2] fit to be acted in the Alhambra. I shall read Calderón one day.

I also enclose a letter just received from Carlyle, as it may interest your party. I do not want any of these back. Yours, with best remembrances to the two Ladies,

E.FG.

Beg, borrow, steal, buy, Keats.

[1] F. C. Brooke of Ufford and Dr. Donaldson of Bury School.

[2] Cowell evidently had translated a play of Calderón's for EFG during the latter's recent visit to Bramford. This was the seed which produced EFG's translations of Calderón's plays.

To Thomas Carlyle

[June, last week, 1849]

Dear Carlyle,

I will send a note to my Kildare relatives to apprize them of your probable approach.[1] Their address is

Mrs. Purcell
Halverstown
Kilcullen

in County Kildare, about thirty English miles from Dublin: and going through some of the best cultivated part of Ireland.

You do not love the picturesque for picturesque's sake—But go into Wicklow so far as the "Seven Churches" by the side of their lake in Glendalough[2]—spend a summer's evening there.

Poor dear old Ireland: certainly some native blood stirs within me at the recollection of some of these places.

I would have written to you by return of post if I had got your letter yesterday: but I am out for four days. Pray write when you have a mind. I can read travels though I do none.

You should get letters to the *Duke of Leinster*, who is, I am told, a very good sort of man in all ways. And doubtless you could easily make his acquaintance. He lives close to Maynooth.

There is a Jesuit school not far from Halverstown—I forget the name—which perhaps you would like to see.

Thank you for your name for my poor old friend's Book—for his daughter's sake.

And now "bon voyage!"

Yours truly
E.FG.

[1] While planning a tour of Ireland for the summer, Carlyle had asked EFG for introductions to his Irish relatives. Mrs. Purcell, whose address follows, was Monica, widow of EFG's uncle Peter. Carlyle recounts his visits to members of the FitzGerald family in *Reminiscences of My Irish Journey*, published by J. A. Froude in 1882.

[2] A deep ravine in the Wicklow Hills some 20 miles from Dublin, noted for its scenic beauty and monastic ruins known as the Seven Churches.

From Thomas Carlyle

Halverstown, Kilcullen
10 july, 1849

Dear Fitzgerald,

I enclose for you, by way of symbol, a twig of heath plucked yesterday among the ruins of Glendalough; whither your Brother[1] honourably escorted me, where we had a day full of interesting adventures, a day which I find I shall very long remember. No more striking object, full of ragged tragical pathos, ever offered itself to my contemplation than those old black ruins and the crowds of famishing beggars that hovered round us all the time we were there. Thanks for your mention of Glendalough; I had meditated the thing before, but perhaps might have omitted it had not your suggestion come to second me.

All Ireland seems as if it flung its arms open to receive me; in Dublin I really was like to be done to death by the civilities of men,—all sorts of men from the King or vice-King upon the throne to the theology Professor of Maynooth:[2] surely a *social* race of men, for one thing! Your Kinsfolk here have welcomed me as if I had been their own Brother; and have done, and are doing, the sacred rites in a way to touch the heart of the Pilgrim who, for the time, has no home of his own. Long life to them; and, as the people yesterday said, "St Kevin's be their bed!"[3]

This afternoon (it is now close on breakfast, in a room you well know, one of the nicest in Ireland, looking out on the "big stone" I have heard of your sitting on while reading), I set off (after the Curragh,[4] etc.) for Kilkenny, and thence to Waterford, Cork and the barbarous regions of the West. Pray for me,—and pray for those! The potatoes, numerous beyond former years, are all in luxuriant flower, and everybody looks at them for the last two weeks especially, as at the horn of Doom,—for countless multitudes will again die starved, if the potatoe still fail. Good Heavens! In spite of my indignation, I have almost lost the heart to continue my old prayer on that point, That the potatoe might *continue* dead.[5] Breakfast bell! Adieu, dear F. —Your Letter waited me at Dublin, and you perceive it is all right.

Yours ever truly
T. Carlyle

[1] Peter.

[2] The Royal Catholic College of Maynooth, the principal Roman Catholic seminary in Ireland, had been the cause of violent dissension in Britain in 1845. A bill

introduced by Peel to provide funds to support the college was passed by Parliament after prolonged and bitter controversy.

[3] St. Kevin, a hermit, founder of the settlement at the Seven Churches in the sixth century.

[4] The Curragh, "a sea of beautiful green land," Carlyle wrote; almost 5,000 acres of grazing land (crown lands) and site of the Curragh race course.

[5] In 1846, the second year of the potato famine, Parliament had passed a law which required landowners to pay a portion of the relief costś. The bill impressed Carlyle as the most important ever passed for Ireland. It marked "the beginning, I do hope, of a new time for that wretched Land:" he wrote to a brother, "I almost *rejoiced* at the black Potato fields, which had brought it about . . . since the loss of them was leading us a little towards justice" (*New Letters of Thomas Carlyle*, II, 25).

To E. B. Cowell

Pmk., Woodbridge, July 16, 1849

Dear Cowell,

Since you gave 2.6 for a Voss in which this song of Lyons was not, I send you the song and translation now.[1] I copy it from a book in poor Miss Barton's house, while she gets ready her books and pictures for a sale. Farewell.

E.FG.

[1] Probably a poem by Johann Heinrich Voss (1751-1826), German poet and translator. Cowell wrote to a friend in December, "I am going to send you in this letter a German song by Voss, which FitzGerald and Tennyson delight in, as being one of the most perfectly Greek things modern days have seen" (Cowell biography, p. 56).

To E. B. Cowell

Boulge
August 1/49

My dear Cowell,

I have sometimes thought (and I dare say said) that some of Barton's little pieces had something of the artless elegance of some of the Greek Epigrams. You have an Anthology, and you know its contents well—can you help me to any illustrations of my doctrine? At all events I should be glad to borrow your Anthology, unless you can help me to a remembrance of one or two cases in point from it. For I speak from confused recollection, not from distinct data of comparison.

Give me a line as to this. I will go over one day to see you, an you will: look at the Anthology: and bring back my *Spedding*[1] which I want.

Yours,
E.FG.

[1] *Evenings with a Reviewer.*

To John Allen

Boulge, Woodbridge
Aug. 15/49

My dear old Allen,

I want to know whether your Father-in-law, Mr. Higgins, did not tell me at Kentish Town that he desired to subscribe to B.B.'s book? *If* he did (I do not wish you to ask him if he did not) I want his exact address. Also, your brother Joshua told me to put down his own name, and that of another Allen—a Lady I think. *His* name and address I know well—but *hers*? Do you know of her? I can of course write to Joshua, if you do not know: but I take the opportunity of asking the question of you, that I may not only hear about that but other things. I want to know how your wife is. Pray tell me—as also about your family, and yourself, how you all are.

I have been here since I saw you in London—correcting proof of this little Book. For Miss B. is so bothered and bewildered she has scarce time or thought to bestow on it. She has been selling all her furniture by auction, poor thing: and is going to take a situation as Governess—at Mrs. Hudson Gurney's,[1] I believe. Is it not noble of her to insist on paying all her Father's debts? The Book will almost clear her of them! How glad I am we ever thought of it. I believe that 1100 copies are subscribed for. I suppose it will be out in a month. I have just despatched a Memoir to the Printer—a job I detested more than I can tell you. For it really is an awful job to speak of a man dead, to attribute qualities and motives to him, etc! A thing which none but men of the *greatest intuition* are capable of doing, I think—or women—and what I should not have done had not Miss B. so asked me to dilate more on the subject. And as I have written nothing but what she has seen and approved, I cannot help it. All the religious people here think I only describe B.B. as a *good fellow*, without understanding his better qualities—Vae mihi! if ever I meddle with such a job again.

Apart from this, the book will really be a very pleasant one; and you ought to like all the letters, and some of the poems—"I am satis."

I have no thought of going anywhere except to see my Mother at Richmond when clear of the Book. You don't know how much I should like to go and see you—next summer—perhaps—but I never look forward to a next summer.

Farewell my dear old fellow—my kind regards to *Mrs.* I saw you had got into the Record[2] again. How did they answer you?—about Maurice, I mean. I am sorry to write so badly: but my hand has the fidgets.

Yours ever and aye
E.FG.

[1] The Gurneys, of Keswick Hall, Norfolk, members of a family of wealthy Norwich bankers with whom Lucy Barton made her home for the next seven years. Hudson Gurney had served six terms in Parliament. Many of the Gurneys were Quakers, but biographers have erred in identifying Hudson Gurney with that faith.

[2] The *Record*, an ecclesiastical weekly newspaper. Allen was a zealous contributor of letters to the press. One friend wrote of him:

For much he reckoned, fancy fed,
On wide-spread circulation,
Whereby corrections might be spread
Thro' every land and nation.
(Grier's *John Allen*, p. 60)

Allen and F. D. Maurice, to whom EFG refers, had been colleagues at King's College, London. For Maurice, see letter to Allen, Nov. 18, 1842, n.5.

To George Crabbe of Merton

Terrace House, Richmond
October 22/49

My dear George,

Warren's analysis of my MS.[1] is rather wonderful to me. Though not wholly correct (as I think, and as I will expound to you one day) it seems to me yet as exact as most of my friends who know me best could draw out from their personal knowledge. Some of his guesses (though partly right) hit upon traits of character I should conceive quite out of all possibility of solution from mere handwriting. I can understand that a man should guess at one's temperament, whether lively or slow; at one's habit of thought, whether diffuse or logical; at one's Will, whether strong and direct or feeble and timid. But whether one distrusts men, and yet trusts friends? Half of this is true, at all events. Then I cannot conceive how a man should see in handwriting such *an accident* as whether one knew much of Books or men; and in this point it is very doubtful if Warren is right. But, take it all in all, his analysis puzzles me much. I have sent it to old Jem Spedding the Wise. You shall have it again.

If my Mother should remain at this place you must one day come and see her and it with me. She would be very glad to receive you. Richmond and all its environs are very beautiful, and very interesting; haunted by the memory of Princes, Wits, and Beauties.

Today my Mother's four old black horses are sold at Tattersall's.[2] Two of them should have been shot instead. She is going to job a pair. Greathurst[3] seemed to think that one of these horses would suit you; but the best of them he thought would be too big for you, and the others I would not meddle with. I have told him all your adventures with your Cob.

Here, and hereabout, I shall be for another fortnight at least; and always glad to hear from Bredfield. Give my kind remembrances to all and believe me yours ever

E.FG.

N.B. Can Mr. Warren be our *discarded Butler*!

[1] This is the second occasion on which EFG was fascinated by analysis of character from handwriting. For the first, see letter to Pollock, [May 1-3, 1842], n.2.

[2] Famous auctioneers of horses, then located in Grosvenor Place; headquarters, also, of "sporting and betting men." Bets placed at Tattersall's established odds throughout Britain.

[3] Mrs. FitzGerald's coachman.

To W. B. Donne

Terrace House, Richmond
Novr 2/49

My dear Donne,

Your letter found me here, where I came a fortnight ago to visit my Mother. I have had much to thank you for about this Book: and you yet continue your kind exertions in its behalf. I shall read your Paper with pleasure. As to the Edinburgh, it is almost too great an exaltation to be dreamed of: you must decide on all that for yourself:[1] but do not bore yourself, or employ upon me room you want to fill with other matter.

As to my Memoir, you over-rate it and me; but you and old Spedding (I have long known) will monster the nothings of your friends. Don't complain of the much you have written: nor desire me to write: it is easy enough to write an agreeable account of an agreeable man one has known so long. You have had to do with Emperors, etc., whom you never knew—dead 2000 years ago. You have given much useful information about them: when you get to your Norfolk Worthies, you shall be pleasant, picturesque, and humorous, and write as if you were talking as you often talk to me.[2]

My dear old Crabbe has published a volume on God,[3] etc.—he has sent it to me—has he to you? I am more vext than I can tell you about it; for I am sure he will be disappointed in all ways. It seems to me a sad mistake—the dotage of logic—terms misapplied, inconsequent arguments, etc. Crabbe had not the advantage of good logical training, and he scarce knows how the world has got on of late. He, you see, wrote a very delightful Biography of his Father; then he should have stopped.

I have been once to the play at half price, and saw two stupid farces acted by the Keeleys, Buckstone,[4] etc. I am sure the farces were at least as dull as I was. Why won't you, or can't you, come up to London while I am hereabout, and go with me to see Macbeth[5]—and Carlyle! The latter I have once seen; he was very mild to me, who do not antagonize with him: he only *smouldered* about Ireland; but I am told he blazes up generally. I thought what he said of it true.

Thompson is still very ill at Cambridge—unable to do tutorial duties. S. Rice goes to see him tomorrow; and I shall go and visit him ere long, I hope. Thackeray has been dangerously ill of a bilious fever; I found him just able to creep upstairs, but beginning (he told me) to eat enormously. He is now at Brighton.

Kind remembrances to all. Again take my thanks for all your kind offices—and

believe me ever yours,
E.FG.

1 Evidently Donne had offered to write a review of the Barton volume for the *Edinburgh Review*.

2 When Donne wrote his reviews and histories, he forgot "the fun in him," EFG said, so that his style was "of the Quaker-coat cut." The "Norfolk Worthies" mentioned was a collection of biographical essays which Donne began but never completed.

[3] *An Outline of a System of Natural Theology* published in 1840. EFG seems to have read the work without noting the date of publication. His previous ignorance of the book and the tardy presentation may be explained by reluctance on Crabbe's part to submit the treatise to a friend who persistently questioned his theological doctrines as EFG was wont to do. (See letter to Crabbe, Nov. 9.) The biography subsequently referred to was written for the 1834 edition of the poet Crabbe's works.

[4] Robert Keeley (1793-1869); his wife, Mary Ann (Goward) (1805?-99); and John Buckstone (1802-79), all comedians.

[5] Macready was appearing in Shakespeare's principal tragedies at the Haymarket Theater. *Macbeth* was given the following Wednesday, November 7.

To E. B. Cowell

Terrace House
Richmond, Surrey
Nov. 4, 49

My dear Cowell,

Have you finished the second volume of Spedding? Let me know, please; for I want to send it elsewhere—when you have done.

I left Boulge more than a fortnight ago, to visit my Mother here. A beautiful place this is; but I do not much like the air, which seems to me encumbered with the moisture arising from the wide-watered and wooded valley below. I have been but little in London—spent one evening with Carlyle, who seems pretty well. He smoulders about Ireland; at least, he smouldered to me; but I am told that he blazes at a breath of opposition, which I did not venture. Indeed, I agreed with all he said to me on the subject—of Tennyson I heard nothing.

What are you reading? Give me a few lines on this and any other subject that comes to hand. Anyhow let me hear about Spedding's book: and speedily. I believe I shall leave this place at the end of the week.

Yours,
E.FG.

To George Crabbe of Bredfield[1]

Terrace House
Richmond, Surrey
November 9, 1849

My dear Crabbe,

I had yesterday begun a letter to you on the subject of your book.[2] In the middle of it your letter came and soon after I was obliged to go to London, so I will not resume my half-finished letter but begin afresh.

You know that I have very little taste for metaphysics or argument. I never read even Paley's "natural Theology," only two of the Bridgewater treatises. Butler's "Analogy" is almost the only book that has ever proved to me a point of the kind you handle, and how little comparatively does he attempt to prove! You will not allow that I have very little talent for this sort of argument, which, however, I know very well; and, indeed, the total want of taste for it almost necessarily argues the deficiency of some power for it. One could scarce have strong argumentative talent without desiring to exert it.

Well, notwithstanding all this, I have read your book carefully. I agree in many of your conclusions. I will not say that I fully trace all the steps of the argument that leads to them. And in saying this I do not assert that what fault there may be is not mine. I have told you alone, and have told you always, how little genius I have for such controversy. I can very sincerely say that I shall be very glad if your book convinces hundreds of thousands—you have set a noble object before you. I like much the last chapter—the con[clusion where you have] done with the argument and sum up the whole. It is written in clear, hearty English.

What I say will little content you; for you despise all praise but for the one object you deem all-important. But I will honestly say that I would rather read your very beautiful biography of your father than all the theologies that you or the Bridgewater folks have written or may write. Now, don't be offended at this. I have been told that you resent any praise of your biography; I suppose because it contains some ejaculatory theology not proved. Be it so; that cannot affect the other many merits of the book; its manly affection, openheartedness, genial love of man and nature, unaffected narrative, etc. Why, here are people praising my little scrap of a narrative of B.B. Is not your book worth

10,000 of it? Yes, as superior as your father was a better poet than B.B.

Dear old B.B.! Had he been alive, would he not have wholly agreed with me in preferring your biography to your polemic? Yes, and you would not have been angry with him; do not be angry with me, his elegant biographer.

N.B. When I talk of you being angry, mind, I do not hint at your being angry because of my undervaluing your talent, but at my undervaluing argument, and especially theological argument, altogether. You get vexed with me for being so indifferent to what is so all-interesting to you. But now remember you have known this of me for some years. God send we have had all our quarrels out on that score. I have told you over and over again to make up your mind to a trifler like me, and I hope you have resigned yourself to it.

If you loves me as I loves you
No theology shall cut our loves in two.

I hope, therefore, to have a civil letter from you, and a reception of no common elegance when I ring at the door of Bredfield parsonage again.

I leave this place on Monday; shall be some days in London, and then go to Bedford to transact money matters. I shall also visit a sick friend at Cambridge.[3] I suppose it will be another month at least before I get home. I send a paper in which Donne inscribes my praise; George wanted to see it. There is a better article in the Spectator,[4] more of B.B.'s letters which I would much rather my good friends would quote than "monster my nothings." I do not know the Spectator man, so he is more just.

Yours, with kind regards to all

E.FG.

[1] A copy of this letter, clipped from an unidentified periodical, was furnished by the late Miss Madeleine de Soyres, EFG's grandniece. The MS has not been found. The portion of the copy enclosed in brackets was made illegible by a fold in the paper.

[2] *An Outline of a System of Natural Theology.*

[3] W. H. Thompson.

[4] In the *Spectator* the reviewer stated, "The memoir is one of the best things of the kind we have seen, both as regards judgment and execution. The poet and the man are thoroughly appreciated, and, what is rare when the biographer is a friend, are rated at their true value—the good qualities each perceived, the failings not overlooked but touched gently" (*Spectator*, Nov. 3, 1849, pp. 1042-43).

To E. B. Cowell

Terrace House
Richmond, Surrey
Novr 9/49

My dear Cowell,

If you were not able to write all you had to say in one letter, you must do so in another. What excuse have you? I was glad to hear from you again, and accepted gratefully the sweet little Greek Epigram.

Have you got the Poems of Oliver de Basselin, the old Norman Anacreon, and Vaudeville-ist?[1] I have been reading some of his songs in Dibdin's Tour—capital songs. Somehow I think the Vaudeville songs are the most amiable part of the French character. I always did think so; and I retain no impression of France and the French so agreeable as the remembrance of the groups collected round an organ under the trees in the Boulevards on some sunny evening, joining chorus with the organ from some little books of songs they had bought from the organ man. I remember one called "Le bon Prêtre"[2] they sang—couplets of advice to his parishioners telling them to go to Church on Sunday mornings, to dance under the oak in the Evenings, "Et le bon Dieu vous bénira"—so ended each couplet. This was the last:

Loin des cendres de sa mère
    Chez vous un pauvre exilé
Dévorait sa peine amère,
    Dieu vers lui l'a rappelé;
Qu'importe si sa prière
    De la vôtre différa?
Priez pour lui—c'étoit votre frère,
    Et le bon Dieu vous bénira—

Chorus the two last lines. I cannot now write this couplet without an "attendrissement" toward that foolish, vain, unprincipled, people.

I cannot go to Bramford yet: next week I shall be going to Bedford; and it will be a month, I dare say, before I find my way back to Suffolk again. When I do, you shall see me directly.

Kind remembrances to the Wife.

Yours ever
E.FG.

[1] French poet (c. 1400-c. 1450) from Val-de-Vire in Normandy, whose drinking songs became famous under the name of Vaux-de-Vire, later corrupted into

"vaudeville," a light popular song, commonly satirical or topical. EFG usually adds "de" to Basselin's name.

[2] EFG normally refers to this as "Le Bon Pasteur." He copied the song into one of his commonplace books, to which, in his letters, he gave the title, "Half Hours with the Worst Authors." The book, now in Trinity College Library, bears the title, "Half Hours with Obscure Authors."

To George Crabbe of Bredfield (Fragment)

Novr 20, [1849]

. . . perhaps:—direct to me
at Joseph Browne's
Caldwell St.
Bedford

Tuesday: Nov^{r}: 20. Lo! I *am* at Bedford—at the address as above—with this vile new pen to write with. And what a letter to send to a Clergyman—all piecemeal and blotty—it may reach him on that very day of his tithe-dinner!

As to the "great Scotchman," I spent an evening with him in London: and told him exactly your experiences of his writings; how you detested his German jargon, but how his Burns and Johnson made you laugh and cry alternately. He declared he will go one day to Boulge (provided Mrs. Corrance[1] be not at Loudham) to see us all;—but (to tell you the truth) I don't much want him. He is too laborious a Guest. I agree with you in all your admiration of him; you must read his *Past and Present* when I get home.

Now I must wind up. Write to me and tell George to write—

ever yours
E.FG.

[1] Wife of Frederick Corrance, of Loudham Hall, near Woodbridge.

To Frederick Tennyson

Bedford
Decr 7/49

My dear old Frederic,

Your note came to me to-day. I ought to have written to you long ago: and indeed did half do a letter before the summer was half over:

which letter I mislaid. I shall be delighted indeed to have your photograph: insufficient as a photograph is. You are one of the few men whose portraits I would give a penny to have: and one day when you are in England we must get it done by Laurence; half at your expense and half at mine, I think. I wish you had sent over to me some of your poems which you told me you were printing at Florence:[1] and often I wish I was at Florence to give you some of my self-satisfied advice on what you should select. For though I do not pretend to write Poetry you know I have a high notion of my judgment in it.

Well, I was at Boulge all the summer: came up thence five weeks ago: stayed three weeks with my Mother at Richmond; a week in London: and now am come here to try and finish a money bargain with some lawyers which you heard me beginning a year ago. They utterly failed in any part of the transaction except bringing me in a large bill for service unperformed. However, we are now upon another tack: and I believe I am about to borrow £8,000 on literally iniquitous terms. My Father's affairs get worse and worse, I fancy: lawyers swallowing up the little that Creditors ought to have. But I have given up bothering myself about a thing I can do no good in.

In a week I go to London, where I hope to see Alfred. Oddly enough, I had a note from him this very day on which I receive yours; he has, he tells me, taken chambers in Lincoln's Inn Fields. Moxon told me he was about to publish another edition of his Princess, with interludes added between the parts:[2] and also that he was about to print, but (I think) not to publish, those Elegiacs on Hallam.[3] I saw poor old Thackeray in London; getting very slowly better of a bilious fever that had almost killed him. Some one told me he was gone or going to the Water Doctor at Malvern. People in general thought Pendennis got dull as it got on; and I confess I thought so too: he would do well to take the opportunity of his illness to discontinue it altogether. He told me last June he himself was tired of it: must not his readers naturally tire too? Do you see Dickens' David Copperfield?[4] It is very good, I think: more carefully written than his later works. But the melodramatic parts, as usual, bad. Carlyle says he is a showman whom one gives a shilling to once a month to see his raree-show, and then sends him about his business.

I have been obliged to turn Author on the very smallest scale. My old friend Bernard Barton chose to die the early part of this year, leaving his daughter worse off than pennyless. We have made a Book out of his Letters and Poems, and published it by Subscription for her benefit and I have been obliged to contribute a little dapper Memoir, as well as to select bits of Letters, bits of Poems, etc. All that was wanted is accomplished: many people subscribed. Some of B.B.'s letters are pleasant, I think, and when you come to England I will give you this little book of incredibly small value.

I have heard no music but two concerts at Jullien's[5] a fortnight ago—very dull, I thought: no beautiful new Waltzes and Polkas, which I love. It is a strange thing to go to the Casinos and see the coarse whores and apprentices in bespattered morning dresses, pea-jackets, and bonnets, twirl round clumsily and indecently to the divine airs played in the Gallery—"the music yearning like a God in pain"[6] indeed. I should like to hear some of your Florentine Concerts; and I do wish you to believe that I do constantly wish myself with you: that, if I ever went anywhere, I would assuredly go to visit the Villa Gondi. I wish you to believe this, which I know to be true, though I am probably further than ever from accomplishing my desire. Farewell: I shall hope to find out your Consul and your portrait in London: though you do not give me very good directions where I am to find them. And I will let you know soon whether I have found the portrait, and how I like it.

Ever yours
E.FG.

[1] Frederick's volume, privately printed, did not appear until 1853.

[2] To the third edition of *The Princess*, published in 1850, Tennyson added a number of lyrics, five of which were placed at the end of cantos. Among the additions are two of the poet's most popular songs, "Sweet and Low" and "The splendour falls on castle walls," commonly known as "The Bugle Song."

[3] A private printing of *In Memoriam* distributed to friends in May, a month before the trade edition was published.

[4] Published in monthly numbers, 1849-50.

[5] See letter to F. Tennyson, [Sept. 25, 1845], n.2.

[6] Keats's "The Eve of St. Agnes."

To John Allen

Bedford
Dec. 13/49

My dear old Allen,

Thanks for your letter. I was indeed about to write to you to account for my non-appearance at Prees. The fact is, I have been for a whole year confiding in a Bedford Lawyer raising me an Annuity on my Reversionary interest at rather more favorable terms than one can ordinarily get at. This has ended only in his bringing me in a long bill for doing nothing: and I am now obliged to set to work on another tack. I employed this lawyer at W. Browne's recommendation: and I am told by every one the man has done his best: only his Client who was to advance the money withdrew, and I (by the Laws of such transactions, it appears) pay the cost of his deficiency. I have been here three weeks: have now begun another negociation which I hope to conclude early in next year. Enough of this: only it will explain why I have not gone to you. As it is, I shall defer my visit to you till next year: when I hope all these things will be settled. I am going to pass Xmas with my Mother: and then go to Boulge: and the leaves may be on the trees before I set off for Prees (nearly verse this, I see)—but, *if I live*, and you and yours live and be well, I will assuredly go to you sometime next year, and make up by a long stay for all former unfulfilled intentions. This I hereby promise to do—witness my hand and seal.

E.FG.

I am glad you like the Book. You are partly right as to what I say about the Poems. For though I really do think some of the Poems very pretty, yet I think they belong to a class which the world no longer wants. Notwithstanding this, one is sure the world will not be the worse for them: they are a kind of elder Nursery rhymes; pleasing to younger people of good affections.

The letters, some of them, I like very much: but I had some curiosity to know how others would like them. Pray bid all who *pay*, pay to Jones of Woodbridge:[1] inasmuch as the Publishers take five per cent from all subscriptions received by them.

I see the Case of Exeter and Gorham is going on:[2] and I cannot but be interested in it. I believe several Clergymen I know of would secede at once if the Council decide in favor of the Bishop—Wilkinson among the number: and they say that many of the High Church Party would join Rome if Gorham got the day. I thought that the leading article in the Times yesterday spoke rather "piano" of a cause concerning which it has been accustomed to speak high: but I don't know.

I believe I shall meet the De Soyres at Richmond at Xmas; my Mother writes me word that they go to her, infantry and all—for a month. Quis potest superare dolor fraudesque Jobai.[3]

Farewell, my dear old Allen; give my best regards to the Wife—don't abjure me as a perjured knave for not going to you: very truly I say it, I should *much like* to be with you now.

Yours ever
E.FG.

[1] Richard Jones, the physician, and his wife were close friends of Lucy Barton.
[2] The Reverend George Gorham had been appointed to a living in Dorsetshire; but the Bishop of Exeter, Henry Phillpotts, had refused to install him on grounds that Gorham did not believe in baptismal regeneration. The Bishop was supported by the Court of Arches; but an appeal to the Privy Council resulted in a reversal in Gorham's favor in March, 1850. "All the high-flyers and Puseyites will be angry and provoked," Charles Fulke Greville recorded (*The Greville Diary*, P. W. Wilson, ed., 2 vols., 1927, II, 303). The interference of a secular court in ecclesiastical litigation did, in fact, stimulate defection to Rome.
[3] "What grief and deceptions of Job can prevail."

To E. B. Cowell

Terrace House
Richmond, Surrey
Decr 26/49

My dear Cowell,

What is become of the fine letter you promised me two months ago? At all events, let me hear that you and the Wife are well. I have but ten minutes to write in: but I write, because it comes into my head to write to you. Not but that I often think of you, and of pleasant Bramford, which I hope to see ere long.

I have been for five weeks away at Bedford—with lawyers. I am now come to spend Xmas week here: and know not yet if I must return to Bedford for a while, or get back to my own domain in Suffolk. I have seen no one you care to know about. A happy Xmas and New Year to you and yours

E.FG.

To W. B. Donne

19 Charlotte St.
FitzRoy Square, London
[January 17, 1850]

Dear Donne,

It is long since I have heard from you. I meant to write to you about Vipan[1] whose death I saw announced in a newspaper: but I have put it off till today. I conclude it was *your* Vipan.

After I left Richmond, whence I last wrote to you, I went to Bedford, where I was for five weeks: then returned to spend Christmas at

Richmond: and now dawdle here hoping to get some accursed Lawyers to raise me some money on what remains of my Reversion. This they *can* do, and *will* do, in time: but, as usual find it their interest to delay as much as possible.

I found A. Tennyson in chambers at Lincoln's Inn: and recreated myself with a sight of his fine old mug, and got out of him all his dear old stories, and many new ones. He is republishing his Poems—the Princess with songs interposed. I cannot say I thought them like the old vintage of his earlier days, though perhaps better than other people's. But, even to you, such opinions appear blasphemies. A.T. is now gone on a visit into Leicestershire: and I miss him greatly. Carlyle I have not seen, but I read an excellent bit of his in the Examiner, about Ireland.[2] Thackeray is well again, except not quite strong yet. Spedding is not yet returned: and I doubt will not return before I have left London.

I have been but to one play: to see the Hypocrite,[3] and Tom Taylor's burlesque at the Strand Theatre. It was dreadfully cold in the pit: and I thought dull: Farren almost unintelligible: Mrs. Glover good in a disagreeable part. Diogenes has very good Aristophanic hits in it, as perhaps you know: but its action was rather slow, I thought: and I was so cold I could not sit it half through.

Can't you come up here? I believe I shall be here a week more, and can give you a bed, and all that belongs to the *tea-table*, morning and evening. At all events, give me a line.

They are going to reprint B.B's. book: Miss B. (as I advised her) keeping out of all risk. I believe it is now in course of printing.

Best remembrances to your party.

Ever yours,
E.FG.

P.S. Friday: I find I must go to Bedford tomorrow: for a week at least. Write me a line at W.B's.

[1] David Vipan died December 10, 1849. See letter to Donne, Sept. 27, 1833, n.5.

[2] "Trees of Liberty," from "Mr. Bramble's unpublished 'Arboretum Hibernicum,'" contributed by Carlyle to *The Nation* (Dublin), edited by his friend, Gavan Duffy, and published in December, 1849. Reprinted in part in the *Examiner*, Jan. 12, 1850, as Carlyle's "Advice on Ireland." "Many Irishmen talk of dying, etc., for Ireland," Carlyle wrote, ". . . Before 'dying' for your country, think, my friends, in how many quiet strenuous ways you might beneficially live for it" (Duffy, *Conversations with Carlyle*, p. 147).

[3] Given on January 11, author unknown. William Farren played the part of Dr. Cantwell; Mrs. Glover, of Old Lady Lambert. Taylor's *Diogenes and his Lantern*; or, *The Hue and Cry after Honesty* concluded the program.

To W. B. Donne

Boulge
Sat: Feb^r 16/50

My dear Donne,

I got your papers safe, and have read what I suppose are your articles in them with great pleasure. I think that this writing in a *paper* is more salutary for you than writing in a grandiose *Review*: you are not put on your good behaviour so much, and can bring out the humour and anecdote which you possess so much of. I do not say then an elaborate Review for the Edinburgh may not be a better thing than one of these Weekly News articles: but you will write better reviews for the Edinburgh: yes, and better books of your own—because of the activity and ease that these less exacting and punctilious Papers have gained for you.

I found an article that I wanted—*not* yours—beside the pleasure of reading yours. I shall lend the papers to Crabbe; and then return them safe, I hope, to you. Can you send me the paper regularly to look at? If you can conveniently, I shall be glad.

Yours,
E.FG.

To John Allen

Boulge
March 4/50[1]

My dear Allen,

I assure you (as I think I assured you before) it is not want of will that has kept me from Prees during the past year. On the contrary, I reserve my visit till I can pay you a *good one*, and, I hope, clear of the bother that has more or less stuck to me lately. I do not think to go to you yet: nay, I am not sure if it will not be Autumn, or even the beginning of Winter, before I go: but go I assuredly shall this year if we all live and are well.

I have now been home about three weeks, and, as you say, one sees indications of lovely spring about. I have read but very little of late—indeed my eyes have not been in superfine order. I caught a glimpse of the second Volume of Southey's Life and Letters[2]—interesting enough. I have also bought Emerson's "Representative Men," a shilling book of Bohn's: with very good scattered thoughts in it: but scarcely leaving any large impression with one, or establishing a theory. So at least it has seemed to me: but I have not read very carefully. I have also bought a little posthumous Volume of Eb[enezer] Elliott:[3] which is sure to have fine things in it.

I believe I love poetry almost as much as ever: but then I have been suffered to doze all these years in the enjoyment of old childish habits and sympathies, without being called on to more active and serious duties of life. I have not put away childish things, though a man. But, at the same time, this visionary inactivity is better than the mischievous activity of so many I see about me—not better than the useful and virtuous activity of a few others: John Allen among the number. Wilkinson is fairly well: and asks about you. He wants a curate at Holbrook: can you recommend such a one as might [satisfy] a man so fastidious in those respects as he is?

I was in London two months ago: but did not see much of men we both know—Thackeray once only, I believe: he is got well. Pendennis is very stupid, I think—Dickens' book I like.[4]

And now I am going to get some potatoes and what else my old woman can give me: and then must go to Woodbridge. I rejoice that the Wife is better: my best remembrances to her and all.

Ever yours,
E.FG.

1 Misdated by Aldis Wright March 9.

2 Edited by his son, Charles Cuthbert Southey, and published in six volumes, 1849-50.

3 Ebenezer Elliott (1781-1849), "the corn-law rhymer," who had died December 1.

4 Both published serially, *Pendennis* in 1848-50, *David Copperfield* in 1849-50.

To Frederick Tennyson
(Fragment)

[Bramford]
Direct to Boulge, Woodbridge
March 7/50

My dear old Frederic,

. . . I saw Alfred in London—pretty well, I thought. He has written songs to be stuck between the cantos of the Princess, none of them of the old champagne flavour, as I think. But I am in a minority about the Princess, I believe. If you print any poems, I especially desire you will transmit them to me. I wish I was with you to consider about these: for though I cannot write poems, you know I consider that I have the old woman's faculty of judging of them: yes, much better than much cleverer and wiser men; I pretend to no Genius, but to Taste: which, according to my aphorism, is the feminine of Genius. . . .[1]

. . . Please to answer me directly. I constantly think of you: and, as I have often sincerely told you, with a kind of love which I feel towards but two or three friends. Are you coming to England? How goes on Grimsby! Doesn't the state of Europe sicken you? Above all, let me have any poems you print: you are now the only man I expect verse from; such gloomy grand stuff as you write. Thackeray, to be sure, can write good ballads, half serious. His Pendennis is very stupid, I think: Dickens' Copperfield on the whole, very good. He always lights one up somehow. There is a new volume of posthumous poems by Ebenezer Elliott: with fine things in it. I don't find myself growing old about Poetry; on the contrary. I wish I could take twenty years off Alfred's shoulders, and set him up in his youthful glory: . . . He is the same magnanimous, kindly, delightful fellow as ever; uttering by far the finest prose sayings of any one.

[1] EFG later included in *Polonius*, Entry XXXIII, "Taste is the feminine of genius."

To E. B. Cowell

Pmk., Woodbridge
March 12, 1850

Dear Cowell,

I return you Petrarch for Laberius. It seems to me the last sentence but one of Petrarch's Latin prose wants new pointing: but I point it as I find it. I must ask Brooke about it: it will be a job for him. I suppose you know the sonnet I attach to the Latin: a lovely one, I think. But I do not think you care for these love affairs: and I can only care for what is past whether in time or hope; which makes me spoonily like spooney Petrarch.

My going to Bramford can scarce please you so much as it does me. I hope soon to be there again. Yours with all due remembrances to the Lady—

E.FG.

Memorabilia quadam de Laura manua propria Francisci Petrarca scripta in quodam codice Virgilis in Papiensi Bibliotheca reperto

Laura propriis virtutibus illustris & meis longum celebrata carminibus primum oculis meis apparuit sub primum adolescentiae meae tempus Anno Domini 1327. die 6. Aprilis in Ecclesia S. Clarae Auinioni hora matutina. & in eadem ciuitate, eodem mense Aprilis eodem die sexto, eadem hora matutina. Anno autem Domini 1348, ab hac luce lux illa subtracta, cum ego forte Veronae essem, heu fati mei nescius. Rumor autem infelix per literas Ludouici mei me Parmae reperit Anno eodem mense Maio die XVIII. mane. Corpus illud castissimum, ac pulcerrimum in locum Fratrum Minorum repositum ipso die mortis ad Vesperam: animam vero eius, ut de Africano ait Seneca, in Caelum, unde erat, redysse mihi persuadeo. Haec autem ad acerbam rei memoriam amara quadam dulcedine scribere visum est, hoc potissimum loco, qui saepe sub oculis meis rediit, ut cogitem, nihil esse debere, quod amplius mihi placeat in hac vita, & effracto majori laqueo tempus esse de Babylone fugiendi, crebra horum inspectione, ac fugacissimae aetatis aestimatione commouear, quod praeuia Dei gratia facile erit praeteriti temporis curas superuacaneas, spes inanes, & inspectatos exitus acriter & viriliter cogitanti.[1]

Gli occhi di ch'io parlai sí caldamente,
E le braccia, e le mani, e i piedi, e 'l viso,
Che m'avean sí da me stesso diviso,
E fatto singular da l' altra gente;

Le crespe chiome d' òr puro lucente,
E 'l lampeggiar de l' angelico riso
Che solean fare in terra un paradiso,
Poca polvere son, che nulla sente.

Et io pur vivo; onde mi doglio e sdegno,
Rimaso senza 'l lume ch' amai tanto,
In gran fortuna, e 'n disarmato legno.

Or sia qui fine al mio amoroso canto:
Secca è la vena de l' usato ingegno,
E la cetera mia rivolta in pianto.[2]

[1] Translated, Petrarch's note on the death of Laura, recorded in his copy of Virgil, reads:

Laura, who was distinguished by her own virtues, and widely celebrated by my songs, first appeared to my eyes in my early manhood, in the year of our

Lord 1327, upon the sixth day of April, at the first hour, in the church of Santa Clara at Avignon; in the same city, in the same month of April, on the same sixth day, at the same first hour, in the year 1348, that light was taken from our day, while I was by chance at Verona, ignorant, alas! of my fate. The unhappy news reached me at Parma, in a letter from my friend Ludovico, on the morning of the nineteenth of May, of the same year. Her chaste and lovely form was laid in the church of the Franciscans, on the evening of the day upon which she died. I am persuaded that her soul returned, as Seneca says of Scipio Africanus, to the heaven whence it came. I have experienced a certain satisfaction in writing this bitter record of a cruel event, especially in this place where it will often come under my eye, for so I may be led to reflect that life can afford me no farther pleasures; and, the most serious of my temptations being removed, I may be admonished by the frequent study of these lines, and by the thought of my vanishing years, that it is high time to flee from Babylon. This, with God's grace, will be easy, as I frankly and manfully consider the needless anxieties of the past, with its empty hopes and unforeseen issue (J. H. Robinson and H. W. Rolfe, *Petrarch*, 1909, pp. 88-89).

[2] Petrarch Sonnet No. CCXCII.

To E. B. Cowell

Boulge, Wednesday
April 9/50[1]

Dear Cowell,

Will you bring with you, or send, to your Ipswich home,[2] a brown-paper roll I left in my bedroom at Bramford? Tomorrow I am going to Holbrook: and will call at your home: I shall return either Saturday or Monday.

When I left you you had cold and face-ache; I shall hope to see, or hear of you, better. If Mrs. Charlesworth be with you, give her my best remembrances: as also to the Lady of Bramford.

Yours ever
E.FG.

[1] Wednesday was the 10th. The postmark reads April 10.
[2] The home of Cowell's mother.

To Frederick Tennyson

Portland Coffee House, London
April 17/50

My dear Frederic,

You tell me to write soon: and this letter is *begun*, at least, on the day yours reaches me. This is partly owing to my having to wait an hour here in the Coffee room of the Portland Hotel; whither your letter has been forwarded to me from Boulge. I am come up for one week—once more to haggle with Lawyers—once more to try and settle my own affairs as well as those of others for a time. When I went yesterday to see a Lawyer on whom much depends, of course he was only yesterday taken ill with rheumatism for the first time in his life, and nursing himself, away from office, at his elegant suburban retreat principally acquired by dishonest six-and-eight-pences. And you too are in all this mess with your vile Railways; which, I declare, vexes me as much as my own uncertainties. I was vext last year to hear you say you had meddled at all with your brother's money. Do get rid of the accursed shares, at any present loss, rather than reserve them for additional knaveries to be practised upon you.

I don't think of drowning myself yet: and what I wrote to you was a sort of safety escape for my poor flame when sitting in the clean cheerful little parlour of that delightful grey-haired quadragenerial, as you call her.[1] The fact is it is not the loss of her alone that makes me hate myself for a fool, but other contingencies which may flourish into worse,[2] and might make me prefer the pond. Vain hope! It is only idle and well-to-do people who kill themselves; it is ennui that is hopeless: *great* pain of mind and body "still, still, on hope relies":[3] the very old, the very wretched, the most incurably diseased never put themselves to rest. It really gives me pain to hear you or any one else call me a philosopher, or any good thing of the sort. I am none—never was—and, if I pretended to be so, was a hypocrite. Some things—as wealth, rank, respectability—I don't care a straw about; but no one can resent the toothache more, nor fifty other little ills beside that flesh is heir to. But let us leave all this.

I am come to London; but I do not go to Operas or Plays: and have scarce time (and, it must be said, scarce inclination) to hunt up many friends. Dear old Alfred is out of town; Spedding is my sheet-anchor, the truly wise and fine fellow: I am going to his rooms this very evening: and there I believe Thackeray, Venables, etc., are to be. I hope not a large assembly: for I get shyer and shyer even of those I knew. Thackeray is in such a great world that I am afraid of him; he gets tired of me: and we are content to regard each other at a distance. You, Alfred, Spedding, and Allen, are the only men I ever care to see again. If ever I leave this country I will go and see you at Florence or elsewhere; but my plans are at present unsettled. I have refused to be Godfather to all who have ever asked me; but I declare it will give me sincere pleasure to officiate for your Child. I got your photograph at last: it is a *beastly thing*: not a bit like: why did you not send your Poems, which *are* like you; and reflect your dear old face well? As you know I admire your poems—the only poems by a living writer I do admire, except Alfred's, you should not hesitate. I can have no doubt whatever they ought to be published in England: I believe Moxon would publish them: and I believe you would make some money by them. But don't send them to Alfred to revise or select: only for this reason, that you would both of you be a little annoyed by gossip about how much share each of you had in them. Your poems can want no other hand than your own to meddle with them, except in respect of the choice of them to make a volume which would please generally: a little of the vulgar faculty of popular tact is all that needs to be added to you, as I think. You will know I do not say this presumptuously: since I think the power of writing one fine line transcends all the "Able-Editor" ability in the ably-edited Universe.

Do you see Carlyle's "Latter Day Pamphlets"?[4] They make the world laugh, and his friends rather sorry for him. But that is because people will still look for practical measures from him: one must be content with him as a great satirist who can make us feel when we are wrong though he cannot set us right. There is a bottom of truth in Carlyle's wildest rhapsodies. I have no news to tell you of books or music, for I scarce see or hear any. And moreover I must be up, and leave the mahogany coffee-room table on which I write so badly: and be off to Lincoln's Inn. God bless you, my dear fellow. I ask a man of business here in the room about Grimsby: he says, "Well, all these railways are troublesome; but the Grimsby one is one of the best: railway property must look up a little: and so will Grimsby."

Ever yours,
E.FG.

[1] Elizabeth Cowell.

[2] His ambiguous promise to Barton which resulted in his unhappy marriage to Lucy Barton.

[3]
The wretch condemn'd with life to part,
Still, still on hope relies;
Goldsmith's "Captivity Song"

[4] An impeachment of British political institutions and denunciation of *ad hoc* remedies for social ills. Four of the essays had been published between February 1 and April 15: "The Present Time," "Model Prisons," "Downing Street," and "The New Downing Street." The eighth and last appeared in August. EFG's statement on the "Pamphlets" is a brilliant capsule critique of Carlyle's role as writer and reformer.

To James Spedding

Boulge, Woodbridge
May 7/50

My dear old Spedding,

Whenever Alfred returns to London, tell him to be sure to send me a copy of those Elegiac poems he is printing.[1] He promised he would let me have them. Now, he might give me *two* copies: one for myself, and one for the Cowells who will greatly prize it. I am obliged to trouble *you* with this because I can't be sure when that Kraken[2] will rise up into Lincoln's Inn Fields, etc. Please to do me this favour.

I have a delightful remembrance of the last day I spent with you in London—a very Platonic day,[3] I call it: that walk through London Streets, the pictures—meeting Laurence on his way to Richmond—then Carlyle—then our steam voyage, that man playing on his glasses—our dinner—and then that fellow on his two horses at Astley's.[4]

Yours ever:
E.FG.

[1] *In Memoriam*, published by Edward Moxon June 1.
[2] Tennyson had published a poem, "The Kraken," in 1830.
[3] See letter to F. Tennyson, Aug. 15, 1850.
[4] Astley's Amphitheatre, Westminster Bridge Road, where equestrian spectacles and melodramas were produced.

To E. B. Cowell

Boulge, Friday
[May 10, 1850]

My dear Cowell,

I have been away from home the last three weeks—chiefly in London, on business. I managed to catch sight of Tennyson, Spedding, and Carlyle, however; but have nothing new to report of any one of them.

May 1850

I am just looking into Brooke's copy of Petrarch's Letters—"looking," and little more. For the book though in clear type is written in contracted Latin: and what I have decyphered is scarce worth the trouble: commonplaces about death, fortune etc. from Cicero, Virgil, Seneca etc. "O scelus infandum! O patria infelix etc!" There are doubtless good things: but I dare say my cursory glance will scarce show them to me. I have however an account of a dream for you, which you are sure to like.

Buy Oliver Basselin's Vaux-de-vire when you see them cheap. They are delightful. I will write you out one. I always say the most amiable part of the French character is their "chanson" and Vaudevilles.[1]

What news have you of Mrs. Charlesworth etc. I mean to give you a look soon. Ah! it is nearly a whole year since I paid you a pleasant summer visit!

Yours,
E.FG.

I saw some lines of a letter of Abelard[2]—like drops of blood!

[FitzGerald copied off Olivier Basselin's "La Probité et Joie" at the end of the letter, omitting the final stanza.]

On plante des pommiers ès bords
Des cimetieres, près des morts,
Pour nous remettre en la memoire
Que ceux dont là gisent les corps
Ont aimé comme nous à boire.

Si donc de nos predecesseurs
Il nous faut ensuivre les moeurs,
Ne souffrons que la soif nous tue:
Beuvons des pommiers les liqueurs
Ou bien de la plante tortue.

Pommiers croissans ès environs
Des tombeaux des bons biberons
Qui ont aimé vostre beuvrage,
Puissions-nous, tandis que vivrons,
Vous voir chargez de bon fruitage!

[1] See letter to Cowell, Nov. 9, 1849, n.1.

[2] Abélard, or Pierre Abailard (1079-1142), who held a chair at Notre Dame and was nominated canon, became more celebrated for his love affair with Heloise than for his great influence on the course of Medieval thought. Their tragic affair and secret marriage resulted in the famous correspondence to which EFG refers.

To John Allen

Boulge
May 29/50

My dear old Allen,

You must believe me wholly when I assure you it is *not* indolence which keeps me from going to see you. I have every desire to pay you a visit: but I am reserving my visit until it will really be of some service, as well as of much pleasure, to myself. For a time you must be content to believe this, as I trust you will: you will one day perhaps see, if not reason for it, at least such reason as a FitzGerald thinks good. I am yet undecided in some of my plans: I will only say that yours is the first place I shall ever go to; as well because it is the longest engagement, as also, I sincerely assure you, the one I most wish to carry out. I was in London about three weeks ago—wholly upon business—and this time I really managed to get a little done—a little regarding myself which is, as far as it goes, satisfactory. My Father's affairs still stick in the Lawyers' hands; we are told there is to be some upshot in October.

In London I saw Spedding, Tennyson, Laurence, and Carlyle—and that was all. O yes—I one day met Maurice[1] in the street, who asked me to breakfast with him; which I did, and was pleased; but I could not understand his theology. With so much genius and sense, yet he seems to me a hopelessly ineffective man in that way. I must say his Novel is the only thing of his I can read.

Moore has bought a Raffaelle, as he says, for £67, for which he wants £300 or so. It is an early picture, and I believe I could see a great deal to admire: Spedding says Apollo might have painted it. But I fancy a *print* of it would give one nearly all of it that was most valuable. But I believe that I gradually brutify, and grow dead to the recondite beauties which require scholarship and experience to discern. Do you see Carlyle's last Pamphlets?—there seems to me a bottom of Truth in them: but not in

[Lower half of p. 3 has been cut away. Apparently FitzGerald discusses Carlyle's Pamphlets, for p. 4 reads:]

proportion to so much surface of rabies and froth.

I have just been to our little Church: I am just going out to walk in the fields. Farewell, my dear Allen. I rejoice your wife is better: give her my kindest remembrances: and make her believe in my willingness to go to Prees. Love to all the Children.

Yours ever affectionately,
E.FG.

[1] Frederick Denison Maurice. EFG's difficulty in understanding Maurice was shared by many. Donne, after reading Maurice's *Kingdom of Christ*, wrote, "Much of so much as I understand of it is admirable, some things I scratch my head at, and at some shake it altogether" (*Donne and Friends*, p. 48). The novel to which EFG refers is *Eustace Conway.*

To E. B. Cowell

[Monk Soham][1]
Pmk., June 1, 1850

My dear Cowell,

If you go to Oxford, proffer the enclosed to him it is addressed to—a very modest and sensible scholar, I am told: though a fellow and tutor of Balliol. He may perhaps be able to introduce you to *Müller*[2] who is now editing the Vedas.

I told R. Groome here of your visit to Oxford: and he proposed the letter to his friend. You must know Groome some day when you return; in the meanwhile present this.

Yours,
E.FG.

[1] Written at the home of EFG's friend, Robert Hindes Groome, Rector of Monk Soham.

[2] Friedrich Max Müller (1823-1900), Oxford Orientalist who became a friend of Cowell's. His edition of the Sanskrit classic *Rigveda* (1849-73), was commissioned by the East India Company.

To E. B. Cowell

Boulge
July 19/50

My dear Cowell,

Shall I go over to you about the middle of next week? That lies well open to me; but do not let that force your convenience.

Yours ever,
E.FG.

August 1850

Inscription on the Fountain of the Fauxbourg St. Germain, Paris—

Urnam Nympha gerens dominam properabat in Urbem;
Hic stetit, et largas laeta profudit aquas.[1]
Santeuil

1 "A nymph bearing an urn was hastening into the imperial city;
She stopped here, and joyfully poured forth abundant waters."

Piganiol de la Force states that these two lines were engraved in golden letters on a marble tablet, but that in the collection of Santeul's poems, the inscription has four lines:

Urnam Nympha gerens dominam properabat in Urbem;
Dum tamen hic celsas suspicit illa domos
Fervere tot populos, questam credidit Urbem,
Constitit et largas laeta profudit aquas.

(*Description de Paris, de Versailles, de Marly* . . . , Paris, 1742, p. 90).

Jean-Baptiste de Santeul, sometimes spelled Santeuil (1603-97), one of the regular canons of St. Victor at Paris, was distinguished as a writer of Latin poetry.

To E. B. Cowell

Boulge
August 1/50

My dear Cowell,

I have this note from Spedding, returning me your bit of Calderón. Spedding's letter can be read aloud, except the part enclosed in Brackets, which only refers to A. Tennyson's (whose signature is A) curiosity in pains, and love of a new Doctor. You see Spedding tells me nothing of his movements: yet he must be at Bury tomorrow:[1] and I am going to Soham today till Saturday. I shall write him a note before I go to say how things are.

I transcribe a little bit of Goethe's Autobiography which I saw when waiting for the Coach on Monday. It is all I have [se]en.[2] He describes Lake Garda in his Italian Travel as very fine and goes on, "Volkmann teaches me that this lake was formerly called 'Benacus,' and quotes from Virgil . . .

Fluctibus et fremitu resonans, Benace, marino.

"This is the first Latin verse, the subject of which ever stood visibly before me, and now, in the present moment, when the wind is blowing stronger and stronger, and the lake casts loftier billows against the little harbour, it is just as true as it was hundreds of years ago. Much, indeed, has changed, but the wind still roars about the lake, the aspect of which gains even greater glory from a line of Virgil's."[3]

E.FG.

P.S. I have written a line to Spedding to say how glad you would be to see him: and asking if he would not meet me at Bramford on Monday. I will let you know directly I hear.

[1] To speak at the Tercentenary Celebration of the King Edward VI Grammar School at Bury St. Edmunds, August 2.

[2] Page torn.

[3] EFG quotes from a letter headed "Torbole, 12th September" in *The Autobiography of Goethe*, translated by A.J.W. Morrison (2 vols. 1849, II, 257). He quotes Morrison correctly; however, in Virgil's *Georgics* (II, 160) the line is

Fluctibus et fremitu assurgens, Benace, marino?

As a guidebook for his travels in Italy, Goethe used Johann Jakob Volkmann's *Historisch-kritische Nachrichten von Italien* (1770-71).

To E. B. Cowell

Boulge, Saturday
[August 3, 1850]

My dear Cowell,

You see Spedding talks of going to you on Tuesday—a bad day for you: but one must make the best of it.

I shall perhaps go over to you on Monday.

Yours,
E.FG.

P.S. I *will* go to you on Monday: and so I tell Spedding: if he can go to you that Evening, why *well.* He requires *no* entertainment of any kind—more than Socrates would.

To E. B. Cowell

[Boulge]
[August 8, 1850]

Dear Cowell,

Don't come on Monday, unless you get to Woodbridge at 8 o'clock A.M. in time to join a boating party down the river. Which indeed would do you great good. Why should you not? Do if you can. But if you don't like boating, or don't like it so early, don't come over that day; but later. Let me hear of you. Perhaps I shall be able to drive over to Ipswich one day and carry you back.

Also be so kind to enquire once more what houses are to be let furnished in or near Ipswich—respectable houses for a gentleman, his wife, and child etc. Rent not above £70 a year or so. Some there are on the W[h]itton Road. Please bear this in mind.

The Sappho morsel is delightful; enough to make one desire to sit with folded hands all one's life time, mumbling it as Hindoos do some sacred verse. The Juvenal I well remember noting, as you do, for its Cheapside truth.

Farewell.
E.FG.

To E. B. Cowell

Boulge, Monday
[August 12, 1850]

Dear Cowell,

I shall expect you on Wednesday: and can give you a good bed at the Hall. If Wednesday be very bad, come Thursday.

Would you mind the *she Crabbes*[1] coming to tea, for two hours or so? They [are][2] quite homely, good, people: but I ask this for *their* sakes, not yours. Give me a line as to this. I know you dislike it, "prima facie"—and I would not ask them without telling you.

E.FG.

P.S. There being bed etc. why should not you stay *over* Thursday? We could go a little excursion.

P.S. I rather expect to be in Ipswich tomorrow: if so, shall give you a look in St. Clement's.[3] If *not*, let me have a line by return of post. And also (if I do not get to Ipswich) please to buy for me, and bring with you, as good a tongue as Ipswich can afford (taking Wife's and Mother's advice as to the shop etc.) N.B. This tongue is not for *you*: so pray do not scruple to buy it for me. I expect a man here at the end of the week who is to eat it: and I must have it.

[1] Daughters of George Crabbe of Bredfield.

[2] Page torn.

[3] The Cowell home in St. Clement's Street.

To Frederick Tennyson

Boulge, Woodbridge
August 15/50

My dear Frederic,

Let me hear something of you. The last I heard was three months and more ago, when you announced I was a Godfather. I replied instantly. Since all this, Alfred has got married.[1] Spedding has seen him and his wife at Keswick: and speaks very highly of her. May all turn out well! Alfred has also published his Elegiacs on A. Hallam:[2] these sell greatly: and will, I fear, raise a host of Elegiac scribblers.

Since I wrote to you, I have been down here, leading a life of my usual vacuity. My garden shows Autumn: asters about to flower: chrysanthemums beginning to assert their places in the beds. The corn cutting all round. I have paid no visits except where the Lady of my old Love resides.[3] A week ago Spedding came down into Suffolk: and we all met: very delightfully. I propose being here till October, and then must, I believe, pay John Allen a visit in Shropshire. Sometimes I turn my thoughts to paying you a visit in Florence this winter: but I doubt that would end in nothing. Yet I have several reasons for going: yourself not the least, pray believe.

I have begun to nibble at Spanish: at their old Ballads: which are fine things—like *our*, or rather the North Country, old Ballads. I have also bounced through a play of Calderón[4] with the help of a friend—a very fine play of its kind. This Spanish literature is alone of its kind in Europe, I fancy: with some *Arabian* blood in it. It was at one time overrated perhaps: I think lately it has undergone the natural reaction of undervaluing. But I am not a fit judge perhaps: and after all shall never make much study of it.

I was in London only for ten days this Spring: and those ten days not in the thick of the season. So I am more than usually deficient in any news. The most pleasurable remembrance I had of my stay in town was the last day I spent there—having a long ramble in the streets with Spedding, looking at Books and Pictures: then a walk with him and Carlyle across the Park to Chelsea, where we dropped that Latter Day Prophet at his house; then getting upon a steamer, smoked down to Westminster: dined at a chop-house by the Bridge: and then went to Astley's: old Spedding being quite as wise about the Horsemanship as about Bacon and Shakespeare. We parted at midnight in Covent Garden: and this whole pleasant day has left a taste on my palate like one of Plato's lighter, easier, and more picturesque dialogues.

When I speak of the Latter Day Prophet, I conclude you have read, or heard of, Carlyle's Pamphlets so designed. People are tired of them and of him: he only foams, snaps, and howls, and [makes] no progress, people say: this is almost true: and yet there is vital good in all he has written. Spedding, beside his Bacon labours, which go on with the quietude and certainty of the Solar System, contributes short and delightful bits to the Gentlemen's Magazine: which has now turned over a new leaf, and is really the best Magazine we have. No pert Criticism; but laborious and unaffected information.

Merivale is married![5] to a daughter of *George* Frere's, a lawyer in London. I have not heard of M. since this fatal event: but I stayed two days with him in his Essex parsonage just before it. He is grown very fat—a regular Johnian hog—an Archdeacon, if ever there were one—and tries to screw himself down to village teaching, etc. He does all he can, I dare say: but what use is an historical Fellow of a College in a Country parish? It is all against the grain with him—and with his people.

You see Daddy Wordsworth is dead,[6] and there is a huge subscription going on for his monument in Westminster Abbey. I believe he deserves one; but I am against stuffing Westminster Abbey with any one's statue till a hundred years or so have proved whether Posterity is as warm about a Man's Merits as we are. What a vast monument is erected to Cider Phillips—to Gay![7]—the last of whom *I* love, but yet would not interfere with the perfect Gothic of the Abbey to stick up his ugly bust in it.

I went to one Opera in London—*Zora*[8]—Rossini's own *re*-version of his Moise. I stayed about an hour and came away. It was good music, well sung, well acted, but the house was hot! To this complexion do we come at last.

Thackeray goes on with Pendennis: which people think very clever, of course, but rather dull. It is nothing but about selfish London people. Dickens's novel is much like his others. I should be sorry not to read it, and not to like it.

Pray let me hear from you soon. How do Grimsby railways get on? Give my love to my Godchild. Why don't you send me your Poems? You really ought to do that. Damn the Daguerreotype.[9]

Ever yours
E.FG.

[1] Tennyson had married Emily Sellwood, June 13. The couple visited Spedding at Mirehouse en route to Coniston, Cumberland, where they spent part of their honeymoon.

[2] *In Memoriam*, published in June.

[3] Elizabeth Cowell.

[4] *El Mágico Prodigioso*, which he read with Cowell.

[5] Charles Merivale married Judith Frere, sister of his friend John and niece of William Frere, former Master of Downing. See Biographical Profile.

[6] Wordsworth had died April 23.

[7] John Philips (1676-1709), poet, whose principal work was *Cyder*, an essay in blank verse on the production and virtues of cider. John Gay (1685-1732); *Beggar's Opera*, 1728. There is a monument to Philips in the Poet's Corner, Westminster Abbey, and Gay is buried there.

[8] One of many names of Rossini's *Mosè in Egitto.* EFG saw it April 20 at the Royal Italian Opera, Covent Garden.

[9] See letter to F. Tennyson, April 17.

To E. B. Cowell

[Boulge]
[August 22, 1850]

Dear Cowell,

I have a note from your wife suddenly calling on me to decide about your house;[1] a thing I can scarce do on the sudden: and hoped not to have been put to till Michaelmas should light up some particulars for me. All this is no reason why you should not make sure of letting your house when you can: do so therefore, and let things take their chance with me. I am obliged to you for having thus delayed clenching the nail in order to give me notice: I hope the delay will not do you any mischief.

I might say much about my future: but this is not the time—nor the occasion. Do you let your furniture with the house? or sell it? I shall really want some of that: and would buy some *very plain*, and pretty cheap.

I have copied out the dream of Petrarch for you.[2] It really is delightful. I have since looked at another letter rather good: but I see nothing like this. Really some one should edit a small volume of P's letters: some two dozen.

I answer your Lady's letter to *you*, because she desired me to do so. She knows that I thank her for all her good offices, and good wishes too.

Yours,
E.FG.

[1] Cowell planned to leave the Bramford cottage to take up residence at Oxford early in 1851.

[2] A dream of the death of Giacomo Colonnas, Bishop of Lombez, his earliest friend and patron (Giusseppe Fracassetti, *Epistolae de Rebus Familiaribus et Variae*, 3 vols. Florence, 1859-63, Book V, letter 7).

Mrs. Cowell reported to a friend in September, 1850, that her husband was "having the hottest correspondence just now in Latin with E.F.G." The two letters which follow are the only survivors of FitzGerald's portion of the exchange. He was undaunted by lapses in knowledge of grammar and diction when he composed them, as he was, also, a quarter of a century later when he engaged sporadically in a correspondence in French with Crabbe of Merton.

To E. B. Cowell

Holbrook Vodensdies (!)
[September 25, 1850]

Cowelle noster,

Hodie in hanc paroeciam perveni, visurus Wilkinsonos. Transivi sane per Ipswich, non tamen domum tuam urbanam et Clementinam adii: tam matutine enim iter feci, ut te non de lectulo illo dilecto expergisse credidi. Tui tamen non oblitus sum. Istum enim libellum, Cardani Vitam, quem tu valde desiderasti, et ego tibi diu promisi, apud *Chorum* pro te reliqui: ille se cum te persaepe versari profitetur—homo justus est, theologus, in officiis solicitus: illi ergo libellum confidenter tradidi.

Credo me cras rediturum in Suffolciam Altam; si non cras, certe "die post cras" (?) Tum, sive cras fuerit, seu die postcras, domum tuam Clementinam petam. Tu autem non te a libris et uxore tua divellas ut me indignum recipias: sed fore ut placet omnino.

Perpaucos libros legi, *since* apud me tu, et uxor tua, commorastis—et quos legi a te pendeantur. Paucos versus Heroicos quas non sane contemptu haberes—alia autem vetera Musae Anglicanae fragmenta, ab Egertono Brydges collecta, et ejusmodi vanitates, quae tu ab altitudine illa Sanscritiana vix fugienti oculo agnoscere voluisses.

Hockleium Majorem in viis vidi: qui se tecum Persicos apparatus struere nunciavit.

Vale
E.FG.

Translation

Holbrook Wednesday (!)
[September 25, 1850]

Our Cowell,

I arrived in this parish today to see the Wilkinsons. I passed through Ipswich, however I did not go to your urban Clementine home,[1] for I traveled so early in the morning that I did not think that you had risen from your beloved bed. However I did not forget you. For I left with the *Chorus*[2] that booklet, The Life of Cardan,[3] which you so much desired, and which I long have promised you: he claims that he very often tarries with you—he is an upright man, a theologian, zealous in his duties: to him therefore I entrusted the booklet with confidence.

I trust that I will return to High Suffolk tomorrow; if not tomorrow, surely day after tomorrow. Then, if it is tomorrow, or day after tomorrow, I will seek your Clementine home. You, however, would not tear yourself from your books and your wife to receive unworthy me: but [I hope] that it will be altogether satisfactory.

I have read very few books since you and your wife visited at my house, and those I did read would be [lightly] esteemed by you—a few Heroic verses, which to be sure you would not hold in contempt—moreover other old fragments of English poetry collected by Egerton Brydges, and trifles of this sort, which you from that lofty height of Sanskrit would scarcely wish to scan with flitting eye.

I saw Major Hockley on the road, who announced that he was with you preparing Persian splendor.

Farewell
E.FG.

[1] The home of Cowell's family in St. Clement's Street.

[2] EFG's nickname for James Read, bookseller of Ipswich. Cowell wrote that "FitzGerald used to compare him to the Greek chorus from his occasionally bringing in moral observations."

[3] Girolamo Cardan (1501-76), Italian mathematician, physician, and astrologer.

To Mr. and Mrs. E. B. Cowell

[Holbrook]
September 29, 1850

Amici mi,

Ni fallor, in illis Latinis (et elegantissimis) epistolis quas tibi novissime scripsi, et quas in tuis archivis sine dubis servas, dixi me, in reditu meo ad Boulge, ad tuas Clementinas foras pulsare. Tu autem in epistolis tuis quas hodie accepi, scribis te in Bramfordia me expectare. Illic ego autem non possum transire: equum enim meum, seu equulum (Anglice, poney) ad Boulge hodie pervenire necesse est: nec ausim tam pusillum equum, (satis adhuc fatigatum meo pondere in vehiculo gig deposito) tam longe a via distrahere.

Secundum promissum meum, Clementinam tuam domum visam: si tu non illic fueris, has epistolas pro te relinquam. Spero autem me cito te visurum.

Vale. . . . Valete!
E.FG.

Translation

[Holbrook]
September 29, 1850

My Friends,

Unless I am mistaken, in those Latin letters (very elegant ones) which I wrote to you very recently, and which you doubtless are keeping in your archives, I said that I, on my return to Boulge, would knock on your Clementine doors. You, however, write that you are expecting me in Bramford. However, I cannot go there; for my horse, or rather, pony must come to Boulge today; I would not dare to drag my poor little horse (already quite tired by my weight put in the gig) so far from the road.

According to my promise, I will visit your Clementine home: if you are not there, I will leave these letters for you. I hope, however, to see you soon.

Farewell. . . . Farewell
E.FG.

To E. B. Cowell

Boulge
Septr 29/50

Dear Cowell,

On Wednesday *Hines*[1] (not Robert) Groome, comes over here to meet Crabbe and one or two more. He dropt a hint of wishing to see you: you may be sure *I* should be glad to see you too. And hereby I give you notice: but I do *not* press you, for your own sake—for no doubt Hines is rather a bore with his Welsh: though a good-natured, worthy, man in the main. You will understand me when I write thus to you: I do not wish you to come unless you like it: nor to put you to any trouble to frame an excuse.

I shall perhaps be over in Ipswich next week: and then will give you a look. You know it would gratify me if you and wife, or you alone, would come over here as before, any day.

Yours in haste
E.FG.

[1] John Hindes Groome, Rector of Earl Soham, elder brother of EFG's friend, Robert Hindes Groome.

To W. B. Donne

Boulge, Friday
[October 4, 1850]

My dear Donne,

I have been some while intending to send you a few lines—to report my continued existence—to thank you for the Papers, which I and my dear old Crabbe read and mark—and to tell you I was much pleased with Laurence's sketch of you, which he exhibited to me in a transitory way some weeks ago. Has he been to Bury again? To Sir H. Bunbury's?[1]

I am packing up my mind by degrees to move away from here on a round of visits: and will give you a look at Bury if you like it. I am really frightened that it is a whole year since I have seen you: and we but two hours asunder! I *know* it is not want of will on my part: though you may wonder what other want detains me; but you will believe me when I say it is *not* want of will. You are too busy to come here: where indeed is nothing to come for. I wished for Charles[2] last Monday: for people came to shoot the three brace of pheasants inhabiting these woods—had I remembered the first of October, I would have let him know. Otherwise, I am afraid to invite the young, whom I cannot entertain.

H. Groome came over and dined with me on Wednesday: and Crabbe came to meet him: but the latter had no hearty smoker to keep him in countenance, and was not quite comfortable. H. Groome improves: his poetical and etymological ambitions begin to pale away before years that bring the philosophic mind, and before a rising family.

I like your Articles on Pepys much. How go on the Norfolk worthies? I see by your Review that you are now ripe to write them at your ease: which means (in a work of that kind) successfully.

I find it is later by the Clock than I had thought for: and I must put on my hat and be out. I am just blowing away (I hope) the remains of a bad cold.

Farewell: Love to all.

Yours ever,
E.FG.

Don't trouble yourself to answer these letters.

P.S. You have done *quite right* about the subscription—one can rely on you to do the Gentlemanly, and yet prudent thing for one.

[1] Sir Henry Bunbury of Barton Hall, near Bury St. Edmunds.

[2] Donne's eldest son.

To E. B. Cowell

Boulge, Monday
[October 28, 1850]

My dear Cowell,

I talk of going over to you on Thursday: if that suit: on Saturday I shall propose to go to Donne at Bury: I have not seen him for more than a year.

It was no trouble at all to write out the Calderon.

Yours,
E.FG.

To Mrs. Cowell

Boulge, Wednesday
[October 30, 1850]

Dear Mrs. Cowell,

Since you have written me a letter for your husband, you shall also read one that would otherwise have been addressed to him. To say that tomorrow (Thursday) I really start for Ipswich—where I expect to be at the Mulberry Tree Inn, Woodbridge Road, at about one o'clock. And what I want to know is if *Strepsiades*, or any one else who commands your gig, can carry my carpet bag to Bramford some time in the afternoon. Or will Cowell himself be going? I shall *walk* with pleasure; after paying a visit to M[ary] Hockley.

It now strikes me that you will yourselves be going to St. Peter's Church: and I may disarrange plans. So heed me not: for I can quite easily take a *toothbrush* in my pocket: and the bag may follow next day. I will however call at St. Clement's to hear tidings of you: for if you *be* coming to St. Peter's, I had best wait for you, and so walk back with you at night.

Yours truly,
E.FG.

To John Allen

Boulge, Woodbridge
Novr 2/50

My dear Allen,

I suppose you have wholly given me up. But I have not given you up: and am prepared to go and see you this winter if you like it, and all be convenient to you. But you must entirely go by your own convenience. It is a long time since I have heard of you: much of sickness or of worldly trouble may have visited you since you last wrote to me. Let me hear, at all events, from you how all fares with you. I shall shortly be moving from here to London: where I shall be for about a fortnight: then ready to go to you or to Lusia at Bath, to whom I have promised a visit. But all this can be put off (you know I love to put off) at your pleasure.

I hear a Dividend on my Father's debts is to be declared this November. And I fancy that *you and I* must receive whatever falls to Lusia's share—at least, so far as £10,000 are concerned—keep it in our Trust, doling out to her the small interest that will accrue from the small dividend Capital. But this, I believe, will not be ill for them: for the interest being so small, my Mother will be obliged to continue the allowance she now makes them: and the Capital will subsist meanwhile, and not be dissipated.

I hate to talk of these affairs, having talked so much, and to so little purpose. And I now find I have in some instances not acted wisely—though with no such want of wisdom as will ever cause me to blush for it.

I write now in a hurry: but I thought best to send you a line: on the two topics before mentioned. If I go to you ere long I will talk out much more than I could write; if not, I will write to you some of it.

My best regards to all.

Yours ever:
E.FG.

Urged by his wife, who was convinced that her husband possessed "the universality of genius," Cowell, after a prolonged struggle to overcome a lack of confidence in himself, had decided to matriculate at Oxford on November 14 and to go into residence the following term. FitzGerald learned of the decision with misgivings. The intellectual stimulus his friend provided gave zest and direction to his own wide but random reading. Moreover, he cherished the companionship of both the Cowells and the domesticity of their simple Bramford home. At first, it appears, he did not oppose the plan; but six days before Cowell was to matriculate, he wrote the following letter.

To E. B. Cowell

W. Donne's
Bury St. Edmunds
[November 8, 1850]

My dear Cowell,

I was telling Donne yesterday (as your wife desired me to do) of your projected move to Oxford: and he was so much struck by the news as to speak to me seriously on the subject. He thinks it a *false* move: that you will be for a time leaving Oriental studies which are, and should be, your strong point (since Greek and Latin everyone does) without any prospect [of] getting eventually such an Oriental Professorship by that sacrifice as you aim at. For such Professorships, he says, are given, *not to merit*, but by interest and party prejudice. You object Wilson:[1] but Wilson, says Donne, came *from India* trumpeted thence as an Oriental Scholar, and then only got the Professorship by a tooth and nail contest. If you were a dining-out plausible man, you had more chance: but you are not. It is true you must live somewhere

—and why not at Oxford? But the mischief would be in having to dabble in Greek and Latin verses etc., losing time which might be given to your final study of the East. Donne says that it would be far better to apply to Sanscrit etc., and then try for a Professorship at one of the *London* Colleges: where Professors *are* chosen by merit, and an University degree is not insisted on.

I really have thought it best to tell you this: because Donne is a sagacious accurate man who has seen much of these things: and sincerely desires your well-doing. I almost wish you could come and have a *talk* with him: which you could do any day. I shall be here till the end of the week, at least: but Donne will be glad (for I have asked him) to see you now or afterward. Why not come over by an early train, and go back in the evening? If you *have* given up the Counting house, you must (as I said before) live *somewhere*; and may as well at Oxford perhaps as elsewhere: except that it is assuredly dearer than so many other places. But I would not undertake the harness of College discipline (which also brings its extra expenses) unless that harness sat so lightly, and consumed so little of my time, that I could prosecute my other and proper Studies along with it, and *more* than it.

Yours,
E.FG.

[1] Horace Hayman Wilson (1786-1860), Professor of Sanskrit at Oxford.

In despair, Mrs. Cowell wrote immediately to George Kitchin, a school friend of her husband who had only recently completed a brilliant career at the University.

. . . And now for my story of trouble, all through my own wretched fault! Edward has always told me not to talk of his going to Oxford, but the time drew so near, and it seemed so certain, that I asked him if I might send word by E.F.G. to Mr. Donne, who, being a great scholar, I thought would rejoice in it, feeling a kind interest for Edward. Par malheur *he has taken up very strongly and impressed E.F.G. with it, the idea that all is done and given at Oxford by favour, etc., all Edward could hope for, and that he had far better try for something (of all* nonsense *to talk!) in the wretched Scotch or London Universities. This is never to be thought of. . . . But the mischief of it is that to prove their point they so* distort *College life, in the dreadfully long letters E.F.G. is rousing up his languid energies to send us, that Edward, who was just beginning, to my heartfelt thankfulness, to* rise *to the occasion, and really feel the fitness of his*

tastes and energies for the career before him, is now almost wholly turned back again, and ready to set off for Bury, as they want him to do, to talk with Mr. Donne,—and if he does that, I fear, but for God's help, the mischief will be done!*—and that* I *should have done it! whose hope and dream has been his Oxford career! . . . But we must act, not weep . . . E.F.G. may write again, or very probably return here in a day or two. I wrote to try and stop his writing, or using such influence, but* quite *in vain; it only brought on fresh arguments (Cowell biography, pp. 90-91).*

To Mrs. Cowell
(Fragment)

[Bury St. Edmunds]
[November 10, 1850]

. . . [Donne] takes great interest in Cowell: and says he is sure that if he were to go on with his Oriental Studies, he would command a Professorship in one of the London, or one of the Scotch Universities. If he were to edit, or translate, some Oriental Book, it would make his name known, and establish his credit in that way, better than any degree at Oxford; the study for which degree will prevent any such prosecution of Oriental Study. Meanwhile, he might be going on with Reviews etc., bringing something into pocket, and helpful towards study itself, and reputation. Donne says he believes the Edinburgh would be glad of some Articles on Oriental Literature: and he would be glad to help your husband to an introduction in that quarter.

I think now, as when I first wrote, that Cowell would do well to come over here and talk with Donne on the subject. If Donne be a reasonable man, as he is, he will admit any good arguments for Oxford; and if those arguments be sound they need not fear the touch of reason and experience.

Yours truly
E.FG.

The day Mrs. Cowell received the preceding letter, she wrote again to Kitchin:

. . . E.F.G. and Mr. Donne are now daily expecting to hear from or see Edward at Bury, and pressing his going over there to argue *the* point *with them, and I have been* just *able, day by day . . . to persuade*

him not *to go or write. . . . Edward asks if I have fairly represented E.F.G. and Mr. Donne to you,—perhaps not . . . they only meant kindly . . . and are both really men of the highest principle, as far as* man *can be, who doubts if Scripture be altogether the highest guide, —and also men of fine taste and real scholarship (Cowell biography, pp. 91-92).*

To W. B. Donne

Boulge, Saturday
[November 16, 1850]

My dear Donne,

I wished to have written to you from Cambridge: and to have told you yesterday: how much pleased I was with my stay among you. I am really grateful to you for your constant kindness to me.

I told Charles to tell you about Thompson; who is not well, though it may be that he is suffering from the *cure* just yet. He is no doubt much better than he was, judging by the accounts he gave me of his former sufferings.

I want to know the name of those steel pens which I tried at yours, and found good. Just write the name: and no more. You have plenty to do: with the School and all to attend to. It seems to me Donaldson[1] may take hold of this accident to leave the School: if so, why should not *you* get it? You are the man for it: and you have now all interest towards it.

Yours,
E.FG.

[1] J. W. Donaldson, headmaster of Bury St. Edmunds Grammar School.

To E. B. Cowell

Boulge, Friday
Novr 22/50

My dear Cowell,

I had begun to suppose your Wife had forbid you to write to me, for fear of my bad communications corrupting your good designs. You both so far misunderstood me that I had no desire to *stop* your Oxford plans for good and all, but only to advise you to consult so capable a man as Donne before you decided. When you write to me that you are not persuaded you have made a false move, I can say in return "neither am I persuaded you have." I only wished you to hear the advice of one sensible and experienced man: you may have heard as good advice to a contrary effect from others which quite justifies your decision.

I enclose you the scene from Calderón—though too late for your Review,[1] it will amuse you.

I have myself all reason to dissuade you from leaving Suffolk. You and your wife are about the only people I go out to see: and I shall certainly miss you both more than I could miss any one else. With whom shall I change a word on Aeschylus now—from whom shall I learn anything about Persian Spoons? But every day I get more dogged in expecting less and less of Life.

I have been to Cambridge as well as Bury, and became an Undergraduate once more. I came back last Saturday: and, happing on that famous scribble of "Phidippus"[2] in my desk, I seized it, and during the week past have licked [it] into a sort of shape—so as I would like to show it you: though there is much in it you would disapprove. I know very well the utmost value of it—very small—but also it does not cost much labour.

I rather think of going to Bungay on Monday: and perhaps shall look in at Bramford going or returning. We must have one more prose together before you go hence and be no more seen.

Yours, and the indignant Wife's, ever

E.FG.

[1] From *El Mágico Prodigioso.* Cowell published an article on "Spanish Literature" in the *Westminster Review* the following January.

[2] "Phidippus," published in January as *Euphranor.*

To E. B. Cowell

Pmk., Woodbridge, Dec. 11, 1850

My dear Cowell,

I cannot tell if you be home at Bramford yet: if you be, give me a line to say so. I am perpetually going off into Shropshire—and yet would give you a look before I do so. And yet why?—only to see you two there whom I shall never see there again!—for before I get home from Shropshire you will be at Oxford.

I am foolish enough to be printing Phidippus—a little thing I *know* to be full of error, both in point of narrative and argument; and very unlikely to sell. I might have bettered it with pains; but there it was—nearly done, after its kind—and so I finished it after its kind in a few days and sent it to Childs.[1] You shall have a copy, to be sure: and if you honestly think it deserving, or, *in the main* useful (which is all *I* think it may be) you shall give me a quotable word of praise in the Westminster:[2] not in a whole Review, but incidentally or in a note: such as may be quoted in an advertisement. I should be well content if it paid its expenses, at the same time doing no harm—whether likely to do harm or not is a question, however, as I know. Your wife would hate it. Anyhow please to say nothing of me as the Author—neither of you—either now or hereafter.

Yours ever
E.FG.

[1] Childs and Son, printers of Bungay.
[2] Cowell reviewed *Euphranor* in the *Westminster Review*, April, 1851.

From Thomas Carlyle

Chelsea, 17 dec^{r}, 1850

Dear Fitzgerald,

Thanks for your friendly human Letter; which gave us much entertainment in the reading (at breakfast-time the other day), and is still pleasant to think of. One gets so many *in*human Letters, ovine, bovine, porcine, etc., etc.: I wish you would write a little oftener; when the beneficient Daimon suggests, fail not to lend ear to him.

We are looking forward to a pleasant evening or two when you get to Town:—a melancholy errand, indeed; but, as you see, there is good in all things! By no means fail us. Any evening, almost *any* evening or day. I quit my pretended studies here daily between 2 and 3 o'clock, and go out to walk in idleness,—if that hour happen to suit you. At 5 there is some kind of dinner of herbs; fit for the dyspeptic constitution; suitable potluck for an abstemious philosopher that happens to be passing; tea is at 7, and there burns a fire upstairs for narcotic nicotian problems. We are hardly ever out; nor, alas, are my employments almost ever of a kind which it is *not* proper to interrupt!

I left these parts in the very end of July, and fled into S. Wales, by Bath and Bristol; one of the most thoroughly down-broken mortals;

seeking rest in this world, and knowing beforehand that there was none, most likely, to be found. A writing man, with his liver all gone to wrack, is a terrible fellow in these epics of the world! Sir Lytton Bulwer would really do well to build some *diversorium*, *hospitium*, or the like Establishment,[1] with an old dumb cleanly woman in it, and no *Cocks* within earshot,[2] for poor creatures in that situation, that they might repose there for a week or two on occasion. But he won't; no one will. —I fled out of Wales, after 3 weeks or more, dumb, opening not my mouth; fared along, under variations of horrors, to my mother's house in Annandale, and then flung myself down,—sorry only that I could not lie down in silence forever. Such a business is the Viewing of *Latter-Day Pamphlets*[3] in a heart otherwise given to acidity. I went no farther than the Border; did nothing while there but saunter over the Moors, or lie idle by the side of brooks: in about a month I had again to move; came over to Cumberland, saw Tennyson, the Speddings,[4] and numerous to me insignificant or even impertinent "Pikes" of Langdale, Pikes and Fells and Becks of this and that;—and in a day or two more, got packed into the Express Train, and after about 10 hours of screaming clangour, and chaotic raging *Dissonance* which I think might fit the Devil for dinner-music (if he was in want of such a thing),—was shot out at Euston Square, and so ended the Northern part of my tour. We were in Hampshire[5] three weeks more: and at the end of all, I could not say that I was in the least better; but now after two months of almost continual silence and isolation, I do begin to feel sometimes a little more composed. *Ay de mi*! But it is pusillanimous to lament; so I will say no more; but hope the gods will give me again some bit of work to do: it is really all the amends one can get of this perverse world,—which at any rate is so rapidly taking itself away, and making us *rid* of its perversities and shortcomings!

Mrs. Alfred is a very nice creature, cheerful, good-mannered, intelligent, sincere-looking: Alfred and she, I since hear, are in these parts, "looking for houses", but I have seen nothing of them since. James Spedding was as much the philosopher as ever, and as fond of tobacco: Tom[6] I found labouring under some misgivings as to certain *Pamphlets*, and still obstinately disposed to hope that the world w[d] mend *itself*; otherwise well and happy. Adieu dear F.; come and let us denounce "the Papal Aggression"[7] together.

Yours ever

T.

[1] Sir Edward Bulwer Lytton in 1845 had praised hydropathy in *The Confessions of a Water Patient*.

[2] The "demon fowls" kept by Carlyle's next-door neighbor. Thanks to their zeal in disrupting Carlyle's slumbers, the cocks have become famous.

[3] See letter to F. Tennyson, April 17, n.4.

[4] Carlyle had spent three days with the Speddings at Mirehouse the end of September. He then visited James Marshall at Coniston while the Tennysons, on their honeymoon, were also guests.

[5] Visiting Lord and Lady Ashburton.

[6] Spedding's oldest brother, a favorite friend of Carlyle.

[7] On September 29, Pope Pius IX had issued a papal brief establishing a diocesan hierarchy in Britain, with Cardinal Nicholas Wiseman as Archbishop. The "Papal Aggression" was bitterly resented and "No Popery" became a slogan. The Pope's action increased EFG's mistrust of Puseyism in the Established Church. See his "Petition to Lord John Russell," which follows.

To the Right Honourable Lord John Russell[1]

[Late 1850]

My Lord,

We, the undersigned, being deeply attached to the Protestant Faith, have seen with sorrow the Pope's recent creation of a Roman Hierarchy in England.[2]

But, in tracing this act to its cause, we are compelled to admit,—1st. —That this advance of the Pope's results less from any unusual aggression on his part, than from some unusual invitation from ourselves; so many Ministers of the Church of England (encouraged by some Bishops) having been so long and so loudly proclaiming the essential Unity of the Church of England with that of Rome; practising some of Rome's vain Ceremonies; advocating some of her most dangerous Doctrines, such as Auricular Confession; the Power of Regeneration, Sanctification, and Absolution, residing in the Priest; and, finally, by going themselves, and drawing many of their people, over to the Church to which they had striven to liken their own.

But—(2ndly)—these persons have in many instances sheltered themselves from effectual reprehension under certain words in the Liturgy and Rubric of the Church of England, which seem to authorize such doctrines and practices; words which wiser men had long looked on as dead-letter remnants of the Popish ritual from which that of England was drawn,—words whose mischievous tendency when quickened into life is sufficiently testified in the events we are deploring.

The evil being thus traced home to the Liturgy of the Church of England, we venture to suggest to your Lordship, that here the cure of the evil ought to begin; such words in the Liturgy or Rubric as have given countenance to these errors being removed, so as to prevent any like danger for the future from foolish or designing men. For, of all Churches, it seems proper that one which is established by *Law* in a Country, and its support made in some measure compulsory on a whole people, ought to be as pure as human wisdom can make it—certainly not by some words so easily removed give countenance to the worst errors, and draw foreign interference upon us.

And this seems the proper time to effect this, and any other Reform in the Church which may seem good; the feeling of the Country being so manifestly aroused against the intrusion of the Pope, or any practices at home that lead to it.

And believing, as we do, that the security of a Religion lies in its own purity, and in the sincerity of the People professing it, not in any legislative enactments against other Religions; we hope that no restrictions which the milder policy of late years has removed from the Roman Catholics will be reimposed upon them, at least until some more injurious effects follow this measure of the Pope's than the mere assumption of empty Titles.

And, considering besides that, while exclaiming against the Pope's invasion of her Hierarchic Titles, Protestant England has appropriated not only the Titles, but the Revenues, of Papal Ireland; we further beg to suggest to your Lordship if such Honours and Revenues may not be more equitably distributed,[3] according to the claims of the Irish people; either by returning them in part to their original owners, or so disposing them in Protestant hands as better to secure the advance of a purer Faith.

[1] Text taken from *Some New Letters of Edward FitzGerald*, pp. 148-50. The "draft" from which the editor, Captain F. R. Barton, transcribed the petition has not been found. There is no evidence that EFG sent his appeal to the Prime Minister.

[2] See preceding letter, n.7.

[3] A proposal Lord John Russell had made to the Commons as early as 1834.

To E. B. Cowell

Lawford
Friday night [December 20, 1850]

Dear Cowell,

I find we are *expected* rather to leave this place[1] tomorrow: and (if my sheets are not sent to the wash at Bramford) I may perhaps run on to press them once again tomorrow night: once more sleep under a roof that is really dear to me.

E.FG.

P.S. I believe Phidippus was left at Bramford Station.

[1] Charles Merivale's rectory at Lawford, Essex, where EFG and W. H. Thompson were guests.

To E. B. Cowell

Boulge
[December 31, 1850]

My dear Cowell,

I really believe I should not send you the enclosed[1] out of *Vanity*—for in my heart I believe Spedding's praise unconsciously overcharg'd partly from his usual devotion to his friends, and partly from the nature of the Dialogue from which blows a gale of old Recollections bestowing a momentary bliss, and a sympathy with the Author—*not* momentary—sure to last as long as dear old Spedding's heart beats! I send his note because you will like to see it: and because I was going to notify you that Pickering publishes—and I suppose the Book will be out next week. If you can give me an honest lift, you will do so.

As I lie awake of nights I think of the empty shell of Bramford!

E.FG.

New Year's Day?—no—the last of 1850. May the next Year—bring you back to Bramford! I may as well enclose a note from Carlyle.[2] Send both back.

[1] A note from Spedding that has disappeared. Spedding obviously had read *Euphranor* in MS.
[2] Probably the letter of December 17.

To Frederick Tennyson[1]

[Boulge]
Decr 31/50

My dear old Frederic,

If you knew how glad I am to hear from you, you would write to me oftener. You see I make a quick return whenever I get an epistle from you. I should indeed have begun to indite before, but I had not a scrap of serviceable paper in the house: and I am only this minute returned from a wet walk to Woodbridge bringing home the sheet on which I am now writing, along with the rest of a half-quire, which may be filled to you, if we both live. I now count the number of sheets: there are nine. I do not think we average more than three letters a year each. Shall both of us, or either, live three years more, beginning with the year that opens to-morrow? I somehow believe *not:* which I say not as a doleful thing (indeed you may look at it as a very ludicrous one). Well, we shall see. I am all for the short and merry life. Last night I began the sixth Book of Lucretius in bed. You laugh grimly again? I have not looked into it for more than a year, and I took it up by mistake for one of Swift's dirty volumes; and, having got into bed with it, did not care to get out to change it.

The delightful lady . . . is going to leave this neighbourhood and carry her young Husband to Oxford, there to get him some Oriental Professorship one day. He is a delightful fellow, and, *I* say, will, if he live, be the best Scholar in England. Not that I think Oxford will be so helpful to his studies as his counting house at Ipswich was. However, being married he cannot at all events become Fellow, and, as so many do, dissolve all the promise of Scholarship in Sloth, Gluttony, and sham Dignity. I shall miss them both more than I can say, and must take to Lucretius! to comfort me. I have entirely given up the *Genteel* Society here about; and scarce ever go anywhere but to the neighbouring Parson,[2] with whom I discuss Paley's Theology, and the Gorham Question.[3] I am going to him to-night, by the help of a Lantern, in order to light out the Old Year with a Cigar. For he is a great Smoker, and a very fine fellow in all ways.

I have not seen any one you know since I last wrote; nor heard from any one: except dear old Spedding, who really came down and spent two days with us, me and that Scholar and his Wife in their Village,[4] in their delightful little house, in their pleasant fields by the River side. Old Spedding was delicious there; always leaving a mark, I say, in all places one has been at with him, a sort of Platonic perfume. For has he not all the beauty of the Platonic Socrates, with some personal Beauty to boot? He explained to us one day about the laws of reflection in water: and I said then one never could look at the willow whose branches furnished the text without thinking of him. How beastly this reads! As if he gave us a lecture! But you know the man, how quietly it all came out; only because I petulantly denied his plain assertion. For I really often cross him only to draw him out; and vain as I may be, he is one of those that I am well content to make shine at my own expense.

Don't suppose that this or any other ideal day with him effaces my days with you. Indeed, my dear Frederic, you also mark many times and many places in which I have been with you. Gravesend and its ἀνήριθμοι[5] shrimps cannot be forgotten. You say I shall never go to see you at Florence. I have said to you before and I now repeat it, that if ever I go abroad it shall be to see you and my Godchild.[6] I really cannot say if I should not have gone this winter (as I hinted in my last) in case you had answered my letter. But I really did not know if you had not left Florence; and a fortnight ago I thought to myself I would write to Horatio at Cheltenham and ask him for news of you. As to Alfred, I have heard of his marriage, etc., from Spedding, who also saw and was much pleased with her indeed. But you know Alfred himself never writes,[7] nor indeed cares a halfpenny about one, though he is very well satisfied to see one when one falls in his way. You will think I have a spite against him for some neglect, when I say this, and say besides that I cannot care for his In Memoriam. Not so, if I know myself: I always thought the same of him, and was just as well satisfied with it as now. His poem I never did greatly affect: nor can I learn to do so: it is full of finest things, but it is monotonous, and has that air of being evolved by a Poetical Machine of the highest order. So it seems to be with him now, at least to me, the Impetus, the Lyrical oestrus, is gone. . . . It is the cursed inactivity (very pleasant to me who am no Hero) of this 19th century which has spoiled Alfred, I mean spoiled him for the great work he ought now to be entering upon; the lovely and noble things he has done must remain. It is dangerous work this prophesying about great Men. . . . I beg you very much to send me your poems, the very first opportunity; as I want them very much. Nobody doubts that you ought to make a volume for Moxon. Send your poems to Spedding to advise on. No doubt Alfred would be best adviser of all: but then people would be stupid, and say that he had done all that was good in the Book—(wait till I take my tea, which has been lying on the table these ten minutes)—Now, animated by some very inferior Souchong from the village shop, I continue my letter, having reflected during my repast that I have seen two College men you remember since I last wrote, Thompson and Merivale. The former is just recovering of the water cure, looking blue: the latter, Merivale, is just recovering from—Marriage!—which he undertook this Midsummer, with a light-haired daughter of George Frere's. Merivale lives just on the borders of Suffolk: and a week before his marriage he invited me to meet F. Pollock and his wife at the Rectory. There we spent two easy days, and I heard no more of Merivale till three weeks ago when he asked me to meet Thompson just before Christmas. . . . Have you seen Merivale's History of Rome, beginning with the Empire? Two portly volumes are out, and are approved of by Scholars, I believe. I have not read them, not having money to buy, nor any friend to lend.

I hear little music but what I make myself, or help to make with my Parson's son and daughter. We, with not a voice among us, go through Handel's Coronation Anthems! Laughable it may seem; yet it is not quite so; the things are so well-defined, simple, and grand, that the faintest outline of them tells; my admiration of the old Giant grows and grows: his is the Music for a Great, Active, People. Sometimes too, I go over to a place elegantly called *Bungay*, where a Printer lives who drills the young folks of a manufactory there to sing in Chorus once a week. . . . They sing some of the English Madrigals, some of Purcell, and some of Handel, in a way to satisfy me, who don't want perfection, and who believe that the *grandest* things do not depend on delicate finish. If you were here now, we would go over and hear the Harmonious Blacksmith sung in Chorus, with words, of course. It almost made me cry when I heard the divine Air rolled into vocal harmony from the four corners of a large Hall. One can scarce comprehend the Beauty of the English Madrigals till one hears them done (though coarsely) in this way and on a large scale: the play of the parts as they alternate from the different quarters of the room.

I have taken another half sheet to finish my letter upon: so as my calculation of how far this half-quire is to spread over Time is defeated. Let us write oftener, and longer, and we shall not tempt the Fates by inchoating too long a hope of letter-paper. I have written enough for to-night: I am now going to sit down and play one of Handel's Overtures as well as I can—Semele, perhaps, a very grand one—then, lighting my lantern, trudge through the mud to Parson Crabbe's. Before I take my pen again to finish this letter the New Year will have dawned—on some of us. "Thou fool! this night thy soul may be required of thee!" Very well: while it is in this Body I will wish my dear old F.T. a happy New Year. And now to drum out the Old with Handel. Good Night.

New Year's Day, 1851. A happy new Year to you! I sat up with my Parson till the Old Year was past, drinking punch and smoking Cigars, for which I endure some headache this morning. Not that we took *much*; but a very little punch disagrees with me. Only I would not disappoint my old friend's convivial expectations. He is one of those happy men who has the "boy's heart throbbing and trembling" under the snows of sixty-five.

On reading, or rather trying to read, the foregoing letter, I have determined that this half-quire of paper shall not see my life out at all events. For of all the beastly stuff I ever knew it is the worst. It shall forthwith go to the Privy: and I only hope it may not deceive my fingers there as it does here. I doubt if you can read half what I write. But it shall go. Pray write soon.

E.FG.

P.S. Don's abuse the "Powers that be"[8] in letter. Believe that I cordially agree with all you think of them: and so say no more. You may get evil bother else; which is as well let alone, when no good follows from it.

[1] Only the portion of this letter added by EFG on New Year's Day, 1851, has survived in MS. The two paragraphs at the end were deleted by Wright.

[2] Crabbe of Bredfield.

[3] See letter to Allen, Dec. 13, 1849, n.2.

[4] Spedding went to Bramford, August 6, after speaking at the tercentenary celebration at Bury St. Edmund's School.

[5] "Countless."

[6] See letter to F. Tennyson, April 17, 1850.

[7] John Forster complained when Tennyson failed to inform him of the marriage. Tennyson responded, "I told nobody not even her who had most right to be told, my own mother. She was not angry, why should you be?" (C. Tennyson, *Tennyson*, p. 244).

[8] A reference, probably, to a coterie of Alfred Tennyson's friends. Spedding among them, who praised each of the poet's publications enthusiastically but not objectively. Lavish praise of *In Memoriam* very likely prompted EFG's warning.

Index